Introducing the NEW TESTAMENT

Its Literature and Theology

Introducing the

WILLIAM B. EERDMANS PUBLISHING COMPANY

NEW TESTAMENT

Its Literature and Theology

Paul J. Achtemeier

Joel B. Green

Marianne Meye Thompson

GRAND RAPIDS, MICHIGAN / CAMBRIDGE, U.K.

Published 2001 by

Wm. B. Eerdmans Publishing Company

2140 Oak Industrial Drive N.E., Grand Rapids, Michigan 49505 /

P.O. Box 163, Cambridge CB3 9PU U.K.

www.eerdmans.com

Printed in the United States of America

20 19 18 17 16 15 14   14 13 12 11 10 9 8

Library of Congress Cataloging-in-Publication Data

Achtemeier, Paul J.

      The New Testament: its literature and theology / Paul J. Achtemeier,

  Joel B. Green & Marianne Meye Thompson.

         p. cm.

   Includes bibliographical references.

   ISBN 978-0-8028-3717-2 (alk. paper)

      1. Bible. N.T. — Introductions. I. Green, Joel B., 1956-   II. Thompson, Marianne Meye

  III. Title.

BS2330.3 A34 2001

225.6′1 — dc21

                                   2001019359

Contents

Maps

Abbreviations

Adv. Haer.	Irenaeus, *Adversus Haereses*
Ant.	Josephus, *Antiquities of the Jews*
Ap.	Josephus, *Contra Apionem*
2 Bar	*2 Baruch*
Ben.	Seneca, *De Beneficiis*
1 Clem.	*1 Clement*
1 En	*1 Enoch*
Ep.	Pliny, *Epistulae*
Hist. Eccl.	Eusebius, *Historia Ecclesiastica*
JETS	*Journal of the Evangelical Theological Society*
Hist. Eccl.	Eusebius, *Historia Ecclesiastica*
Haer.	Irenaeus, *Contra Haereses*
J.W.	Josephus, *Wars of the Jews*
KJV	King James Version
LCL	Loeb Classical Library
LXX	Septuagint
NIV	New International Version
NRSV	New Revised Standard Version
NT	New Testament
OT	Old Testament
par.	and the parallel passages
Pss. Sol.	*Psalms of Solomon*
RSV	Revised Standard Version
Spec. Leg.	Philo, *De Specialibus Legibus*
Vermes	Geza Vermes, *The Complete Dead Sea Scrolls in English* (New York: Penguin, 1997)

1. *What Is the New Testament?*

The New Testament (NT) is a collection of twenty-seven separate documents that, together with the Old Testament (OT), has exercised such significant influence in the history of the world that its impact would be difficult to measure and hard to exaggerate. Undoubtedly, the NT remains the focus of studied attention and continues to inspire because of its recognition as Scripture in the Christian church. Together with the books of the OT, these documents are regarded by the various Christian communions around the world as the decisive witness to Jesus Christ and hence as normative for shaping Christian belief and practice. Fundamental to the nature of the Christian Bible is its division into these two parts — "old" and "new," "first" and "second." The "oldness" of the OT and the "newness" of the NT derive from the respective relationships of these two collections to the figure of Jesus, who is the unifying center of Scripture for Christians. In relation to Jesus, the OT precedes and anticipates, the NT follows and proclaims. "Testament" — from Latin *testamentum,* itself a translation of Greek *diathēkē* — names and interprets these collections of books in relation to the covenanting God — the one "covenant" ("old") taking its character from Mount Sinai, the other ("new" or "renewed") inaugurated by Jesus. The most distinctive characteristic of the NT documents is surely their function as Scripture within the Christian church. Can more be said to answer the question, What is the New Testament?

Written by about a dozen different authors, these documents were not originally intended to be part of a collection known as "The New Testament." During the years in which these narratives and letters were being written, neither "Old Testament" nor "New Testament" was used to refer to a collection of documents. In fact, our earliest evidence for the use of these designations comes from the second century CE. Prior to that time, what we refer to as the "Old Testament" was called by a variety of names, such as "the Scriptures" or "the Law and the Prophets."

1

Each of the documents now gathered together under the rubric "New Testament" was originally written to stand on its own. The Gospel writers, sometimes called Evangelists, could scarcely have imagined that their work would be included in a collection of four Gospels ("the Fourfold Gospel"), let alone in an amalgamation of Pauline epistles and other letters and documents. Paul certainly hoped that at least some of his letters addressed to specific churches would be read in other churches as well (see 2 Cor 1:1-2; Col 4:16), but he could hardly have supposed that so many of his letters would be read by each of his churches, let alone by Christians around the world after two millennia. Even if it serves this purpose admirably, the book of Revelation was not written as a kind of "capstone" for the NT, let alone the climactic work of what would come to be the Bible of the Christian church. Such historical intentions notwithstanding, for centuries the Christian church has cherished and read these twenty-seven books under the heading "New Testament," with

Codex Vaticanus (fourth century), open to the end of Luke's Gospel and the beginning of John's

the conviction that they properly fit together under just that designation. The story of how these somewhat disparate materials, each with its own historical and literary integrity, came to be gathered into a collection is properly considered under the history of the canon — a story to which we return in chapter 25. For now it is enough to ask what sort of collection we have in the NT. What is the NT?

The question is important because the answer to it will go a long way toward shaping how we read and study the NT. Moreover, it can be answered in a number of different ways depending on one's point of view, convictions about the NT, and general awareness of its character and historical origins. Viewed in historical perspective, the NT can be considered as a series of documents of the early Christian movement that emerged in the first century CE in the area surrounding the Mediterranean. The NT can also be classified according to the variety of forms, or genres, contained within it. And it can be approached with special attention to its concern for faith and belief. A look at each of these angles of approaching the NT will not only illumine for us its character, but also suggest appropriate ways of reading that do it justice. Just as one has different expectations of, and hence different approaches to, various specimens of modern writing, such as a historical account, work of fiction, newspaper editorial, personal letter, or business memo, so one will bring different expectations in reading to the documents of NT depending on how one regards them.

1.1. THE LITERARY ANGLE

We can consider the NT first by simply examining its contents. It consists of four Gospels, a historical narrative, twenty-one letters (or documents that more or less have features characteristic of letters), and one apocalypse. Of these twenty-seven documents, nine (the Gospels, Acts, Hebrews, and the Epistles of John) come to us anonymously. When we read documents like the four Gospels or 3 John, we naturally assume that the headings or titles we see in our New Testaments accurately reflect the authorship of those works. They may, but it is important to remember that these books were originally "published" (that is, made available for copying by hand) with no names attached. Current authorial headings such as "The Gospel according to Matthew" or "The Third Letter of John" reflect early Christian traditions. Matthew or Mark did not "sign" their biographies of Jesus. Bylines were not used, with the result that in some instances, on the basis of evidence both within and outside those books, scholars continue to debate the attribution of these books to their traditional authors.

The other twenty-one documents include designations of the author or authors. Among them are Paul and his coauthors Sosthenes, Silvanus, and Timothy; James; Peter; Jude; and John. Some of the letters also designate their intended readers, which include the churches of the cities of Rome, Corinth, Colossae, Thessalonica, and Philippi; the Roman provinces of Pontus, Galatia, Cappadocia, Asia, and Bithynia; and various individuals, including Timothy, Titus, Philemon, Apphia, and Archippus. Other so-called letters, like Hebrews or James, provide few clues regarding their intended destinations. Similarly, narratives contained in the NT, the Gospels and Acts, express no particular addressee and were probably written for a wider, less geographically identified, Christian readership. So far as we can tell, all these documents seem to have been composed during the period stretching from the middle to the very end of the first century CE. Among their many functions, they serve to narrate, exhort, correct, edify, interpret, guide, and encourage. Hence, one way to describe the NT is as a collection of documents in diverse forms written by a number of different individuals both named and unnamed to an assortment of churches and individuals living in different areas or with few or no hints as to their addressees, and for a variety of reasons. From this vantage point, the NT materials comprise a mélange that defies easy categorization or attempts to describe commonality.

Dating the New Testament

Many of the NT books are notoriously difficult to date, since they provide few or no references to external persons or events. A general sense of the flow of literature:

ca. 6-4 BCE	Birth of Jesus
30 (or 33) CE	Death and Resurrection of Jesus
50s–early 60s	Letters of Paul
late 60s–mid 90s	Gospels and Acts
90s	Letters of John and Revelation

That the NT is this sort of collection reminds us that each of its "books" must be approached on its own terms. In a sense, the NT is like an anthology containing a number of different kinds of literature, each of which must be read and studied in light of the characteristics of that particular form. It is important when reading the NT, then, to be aware of the diverse forms of literature found within it. Sheerly from the literary aspect, Revelation is a different sort of book than either Philippians or Acts, and neither of these is exactly like Matthew or Hebrews. Ignoring the literary differences and distinctives of each document will inevitably lead to misreading them. The differences can be easily observed by any modern reader, who will find that a few pages of Revelation are rather different from a few pages of James. Similarly, Jesus' parables differ markedly from Paul's carefully reasoned theological arguments in Romans. The long historical narrative comprising the book of Acts is not the same sort of literature as Paul's short letter to Philemon.

Writers like Paul or Luke choose a particular literary form or forms as they write, drawing on forms already present in their cultural contexts. Forms, or genres, reflect ways of representing reality within particular cultures. "Letters," for example, are vital in historical contexts wherein persons need to be present to communicate a message but cannot be: a letter overcomes geographical distance while maintaining relative chronological proximity, thus serving as a kind of stand-in for its writer or writers. Paul wrote letters for this reason, just as John Wesley, in the eighteenth century, would frame extensive theological treatises in the form of lengthy correspondence. The ease of travel and the availability of the Internet have in our own day relegated letter-writing almost entirely to a distant memory, a lost art. This reminds us that, in NT study, even literary sensitivities require historical imagination.

The choice of a particular genre, then, establishes a kind of "covenant" on the part of the writer, a covenant that is shared when readers (or hearers) recognize the genre of work before them. Writers agree to follow certain protocols in their writing, and readers and hearers agree to these same protocols as they interpret. Of course, sometimes writers will depart from normal protocols to catch their audiences unaware or to drive home in a particularly poignant way the message they hope to communicate. This common practice only underscores the importance of our awareness as readers of the NT of the genre choices available to writers in Roman antiquity.

The literary character of the NT thus demands that we pay attention to ancient forms of literature that might help us to account for the shape of the documents in the NT. This need not mean that any single document of the NT can be completely accounted for by knowing its literary genealogy. Nevertheless, our recognition that ancient historians had certain standards for writing history that are not universally shared by our contemporaries aids greatly our reading of the Gospels and Acts. Similarly, if we are aware that in the ancient world there existed a genre of writing that shared many features with the book of Revelation, then we can gain valuable clues to reading Revelation with the sensitivities of its first, and first-century, readers — and we can find encouragement in the good probability that its first readers found it far less baffling than many generations of readers since! In the chapters that follow, we will return again and again to discuss the main genres of literature found in the NT, as well as a number of other important literary features of these documents.

Because the NT is first a collection of *written documents,* we need to attend closely to their character and characteristics as literature, or written works. This includes a primary concern with genre and form, but other interpretive issues as well. As we learn to take seriously such elements of writing as the use of symbolism and imagery and other literary devices, different literary styles, the use of rhetorical conventions, and the structure of any work in the NT, our understanding of its message will be enlarged and our appreciation for these documents on their own terms will be deepened.

1.2. THE HISTORICAL ANGLE

Already to acknowledge the importance of "genre recognition" in NT study is to underscore the historical character of these documents. They come from other times and places and assume customs, cultures, history, and experiences that are not our own. No document in the NT was first written for a twenty-first century reader. None was written in English. None was written after nearly twenty centuries of the spread of the Christian church throughout the world. Instead, written in Greek, for people of the first century, as the church arose in its native Palestinian soil and began to spread throughout the Roman Empire, these documents minimally require translation, not to mention explanation and interpretation, to be understood by contemporary readers. Those who can read Koine Greek, the original language of the NT, and are students of the ancient Mediterranean world, have access to the NT in a way that other readers do not. Indeed, those who have themselves been reared in contemporary agrarian-based cultures may have more direct access to the pages of the NT, and especially the Gospels, than most people reared in our urban centers. To understand Jesus' proclamation of the kingdom of God, Paul's concern for eating meat offered to idols in 1 Corinthians, Paul's speech to the Athenian philosophers in Acts, or Revelation's tirade against the presumptuous dominance of the Roman Empire, one needs to know something about ancient religious, philosophical, and social movements and contexts mentioned in the NT. Hence, one implication of studying the NT with the recognition of its historical character is that we must pay close attention to its historical features and allusions, the history *within* the text — languages, geography, customs, and so on.

There is also a history *behind* the text — the historical movements, circumstances, and events that gave rise to and shaped the documents as we now have them. Most of the letters in the NT, for example, are *occasional* in nature. That is to say, they are written for specific readers, such as Philemon or Timothy, specific congregations or groups of congregations in a single city, such as Corinth or Rome, or churches throughout a wider geographical region, such as Asia Minor or Galatia. Often the documents treat very specific situations and deal with very specific problems. To some extent, our understanding of the contents of these letters depends on or is at least enhanced by our ability to reconstruct the situations for which they written. And our ability to understand the issues dealt with often depends in large degree on our knowledge of the ancient world in which the early Christians lived.

In a more general sense that applies to the Gospels and Acts, to Revelation, and to the NT epistles equally, the meaning of any act of communication is related to its historical situation. This is because only a small portion of the meaning of any utterance is represented by the actual words used, whether spoken or written. For example, if one of the NT documents *most noted for its occasional character,* Philemon, had fallen into the wrong hands — say, a Gentile shopkeeper in Pessinus who had no exposure either to Judaism or this Jewish sect we know as the Christian movement — what would he make of it? The opening of Philemon reads, "Paul, a prisoner of Christ Jesus, and Timothy our brother. To Philemon our dear friend and coworker, to Apphia our sister, to Archippus our fellow soldier, and to the church in your house." The questions are numerous: Who is Paul? Who is "Christ Jesus"? Why has Paul been imprisoned by this Christ Jesus? For whom are Paul and Archippus mercenaries ("fellow soldier")? What is the nature of the "assembly" (= "church"); does it have military (revolutionary?) intentions? And so on. When Paul and Timothy penned this letter, they had no need to spell out all these matters; they could presume a significant degree of shared knowledge, a common pool of presuppositions. Remembering that the NT materials derive from a different time and place brings with it the corollary that we who read the NT today have different sets of assumptions, and that part of our task as interpreters is to familiarize ourselves as much as possible with the social conventions and other elements of shared knowledge that are not spelled out explicitly in the pages of the NT.

There are other ways of considering the NT as a set of historical documents too. Thus, one might focus not only on the history *in* the text or the history *behind* the text, but also on these documents as part of a larger historical movement of the birth of early Christianity. For the historian whose interest lies primarily in ancient religions, the NT provides evidence of the origin of the early Christian movement. From the pages of the NT we learn of disagreements among early Christians over matters of both belief and practice. Mark, for example, reports that Jesus declared all foods clean, but this comment is lacking in the Gospel of Matthew; indeed, Matthew's Gospel seems not to dismiss the dietary regulations of the OT so readily. We see these conflicts continuing in the NT, as the churches in Acts and later the churches of Paul in Galatia and elsewhere struggled with the relationship of the law of Moses to the Christian faith, particularly with respect to food laws and circumcision and the like. Here Christians seem not to have been of one mind. No document of the NT actually provides a historical narrative of these conflicts, discussion of what the differences were, and how, if at all, they were resolved. Instead, we see documents that reflect brief moments in these debates, some that engage in polemics on either side of it. In other words, we have the sediment of the early Christian movement, rather than a first order account of it. Historians of early Christianity sometimes read the NT to gain a sense of what really went on in the early church.

The NT is not, however, the only evidence historians have for this task. Other documents were written by early Christians, many of which are available still today though they are not included in the NT. Some of these books were written toward the end of the first century, such as *1 Clement,* written by the bishop of Rome to the Corinthian churches, or in the early second century, such as the various epistles of Ignatius, bishop of Antioch in Syria, written about 110. Still other documents dating from this same period include the *Didache* (i.e., "The Teaching of the Twelve Apostles"), the *Epistle of Diognetus,* the *Shepherd of Hermas,* the *Epistle of Barnabas,* and others. Some of these were used by Christians for several centuries as important works of Christian authors to be read alongside the NT as useful for instruction in matters of belief and conduct. Reading the NT within the context of other early Christian documents reminds us that the NT is not the only account of early Christianity, nor the only documents written by early Christians.

Again, the NT bears witness to the rise and spread, beliefs and practices, of the early Christian church — but not to all the branches of the early Christian church. There is little, for example, in the NT that helps us to trace the movement of the church to places such as Egypt, where we know that the early Christian movement flourished in the first several centuries. To call the NT a source for the origins of early Christianity is certainly correct. But much early Christian history is not covered in its pages.

In short, to speak of the NT from the historical angle entails a variety of ways of studying or approaching the NT. All the tools historians use — the study of ancient languages and cultures, the sifting of ancient documents for historical data, the attempt to track down allusions to persons, places, customs, or beliefs perhaps not known to us, and more — can be used to help us understand the NT. Even for those who cannot become experts in one or all of these areas, awareness of the historical dimension of the documents of the NT often makes the NT come alive. Some efforts to reconstruct early Christian history are notoriously more speculative, and sometimes even hostile to the orthodox tradition of Christianity. These efforts have led some Christians to regard the whole enterprise of historical investigation as suspect or dangerous. The mere fact that historical study of the NT has sometimes been done badly is no reason to abandon it. Rather, this fact argues for a more careful and diligent historical approach to the NT. The truth is, historical study is simply necessary, given the character and origin of these documents.

1.3. THE NEW TESTAMENT AS THE CHURCH'S SCRIPTURE

The very character of the NT demands that we pay attention to its literary and historical features. But most people who read the NT do so not because they find it interesting as literature or history. They read it because they share the conviction that this collection of documents, together with the OT, comprise the Scriptures of the church, its normative witness to the work of God in the world through Jesus Christ. As Scripture, the NT thus has a unique place in the life of the church and of individual believers. As Scripture, the NT shapes faith and conduct, corporately and individually, and so nourishes life with God. Each of these observations can be developed a bit further.

Although many people who pick up the NT today find it bound together with the OT, the assumption that this should be so is not necessarily and certainly not universally a foregone conclusion. Jewish persons, who regard what Christians call the "Old Testament" as Scripture, the Bible, do not accept the authority or witness of the NT. In fact, many of the claims made regarding the role of the law, of Jesus, and of the nature of God's people are to Jewish believers theologically offensive, if not blasphemous. For their part, not all Christians have readily accepted the OT as part of their authoritative Scripture. Already in the early centuries of the church, voices were raised in opposition to retaining the OT as a normative source for the life of the church. According to those voices, the NT should not be added to but should replace the OT. Marcion, a second-century Christian, deemed the OT to be so inferior that he rejected it altogether. But the mainstream Christian church did not follow suit, with the result that today when Christians speak of "the Bible," they rarely stop to think that the writing and collection of the books of the Bible in the present form in which Christians cherish it actually occurred over many centuries. That the church, at least in its Protestant form, would end up with sixty-six books in the "Old" and "New" Testaments was scarcely self-evident in the first century.

That the Old and New Testaments should be held together reveals significant convictions about what the NT is and how it should be read. It cannot be read apart from the recognition that it continues the narrative found throughout the pages of the OT, the narrative of God's mercy in calling out and sustaining a people who are to live in obedience to him and to be a servant of divine mercy to all the nations of the world. Authors of books of the NT often allude to, cite, and expound passages from the OT. They use the language of prophecy, promise, and fulfillment, reminding their readers that the NT cannot be read apart from the OT. The NT authors view themselves as interpreting the texts of the OT, and doing so in light of the conviction that what God has done through Jesus Christ for the salvation of all the world was anticipated by the work of God in and through the people of Israel, the primary witness to which can be read in the pages of the OT.

In fact, when the early Christian movement is located historically in the first century, it becomes obvious that its leadership was involved in a kind of "battle for the Bible." The church's self-understanding that it is continuous with the ancient people of God had to be worked out in a context where others within Judaism were reading those same texts from the Scriptures of Israel and hearing in them a message that stood in opposition to Christian readings. Early Christian interpretation of Israel's Scriptures, then, was oriented toward finding avenues of continuity with ancient Israel and thus with the purposes of God.

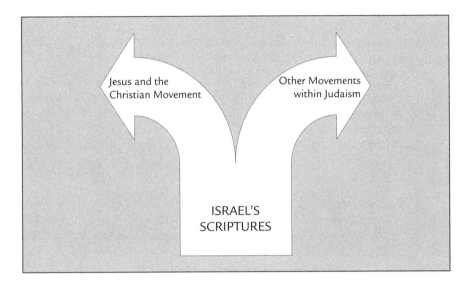

Jesus and the Christian Movement

Other Movements within Judaism

ISRAEL'S SCRIPTURES

This historical understanding is the foundation for a key theological affirmation — namely, that the gospel proclaimed in the NT cannot be grasped apart from an understanding of the God who raised Jesus from the dead, and this God is the one who revealed himself in many and various ways within ancient Israel. The OT thus does more than provide key interpretive concepts for NT writers and readers. The OT thus provides far more than "background material," as though for NT readers it was on a par with the Dead Sea Scrolls or the *Testaments of the Twelve Patriarchs*. The OT is thus more than a preface to the good news of Jesus Christ. It is the revelatory narrative of God's dealings with Israel, of the story of God's saving purpose, which reaches its completion in the advent of Jesus. It is in this sense that the OT prepares the way of the Lord and the NT proclaims that the Word became flesh and dwelt among us.

This brings us to a crucial point about the nature of the NT. While it assumes, records, and discusses certain historical events surrounding the life, death, and resurrection of Jesus of Nazareth, it interprets those events. This is already evident in the simple observation that the NT authors regularly link their writings together with the writings of the OT. The authors of the NT documents are not dispassionate observers of events, but are writing rather as those who have a vested interest in bringing their readers to see and understand and embrace Jesus in certain ways. To understand Jesus in those ways, one needs to read the NT through the lens of the OT, not least because Jesus himself read and quoted these books as Scripture and interpreted his own ministry and work in light of it. The church continues this pattern in presenting Jesus as the climactic manifestation of God's love and covenant faithfulness first demonstrated to Israel. To read the NT on its own terms, then, is to read it in concert with the OT. The narrative woven implicitly and explicitly throughout the NT must be understood as beginning not with

𝔓46, a papyrus manuscript from about 200 CE, here showing parts of Romans 15 and 16

the birth of Jesus but long before the days of Jesus, with God's creation of the world and call of Israel.

The documents of the NT are documents written "from faith for faith." Not only are they written by individuals who believe, and believe passionately, in the truth to which they bear witness, but they also hope to persuade their readers to join in sharing their convictions about the significance of Jesus and orienting their lives to serve faithfully the God of Jesus Christ. While historical and literary studies can greatly illumine the NT, the primary importance of the NT lies neither in the historical information it provides nor in its literary and stylistic artistry but rather in its function within the church as Scripture, as those writings that uniquely and ultimately guide, nourish, and shape our faith and life with God. No other documents, whether contemporaneous with the NT itself or from any other era of church history, can take the place of the witness of the NT. This is what it means to read the NT as Scripture.

In the end, no methods of study correspond precisely to the conviction that the NT, together with the OT, comprises the Scriptures of the Christian church. No particular way of reading, studying history, learning Greek, or acquiring knowledge of ancient geography, customs, and culture is specific to reading the NT as Scripture. Rather, precisely because these documents come to us as historical works, they require the sort of study that all historical documents do. Because they are literary documents, they demand the sort of study appropriate to literature, including study of their original languages, attention to imagery, and awareness of their purpose and context. To treat them with anything less than the most thorough and diligent study would be to treat them disrespectfully.

But because the NT is also the church's Scripture, there are certain dispositions and sensitivities that ought to accompany the reading of these texts as Scripture. These include sensitivities to the way Christians throughout the ages have heard and read the Scriptures, both with respect to their content as well as to the ways in which they have functioned to shape the life of the church together, as well as the lives of individual Christians, before God. Of course, our appreciation of the history of NT interpretation must account for the reality that the story of the ways in which Christians have read Scripture is not unrelievedly positive. The Scriptures have been used to support all manner of injustice, including cruel dictatorships, abuse of women, the institution of slavery, and persecution of Jews. To know something of the misinterpretation and misuse of Scripture can serve as a warning to the ways in which our own presuppositions and prejudices can so cloud our vision that interpretations bear no good fruit. And it is precisely because of the human tendency toward self-justification that the Scriptures ought to be read in the community of the faithful, as well as in the solitude of private reflection and study.

To acknowledge the NT as the Scripture of the church provides a fruitful prejudice for reading and hearing the NT. The church has regularly assumed that the NT is about human life before God and that its texts offer both descriptions of, and prescriptions for, that way of life. To attend to this dimension of these texts is to hear them on their own terms. To come openhanded to these texts, ready to be challenged and formed by them and thus to assume what the church at its best has assumed about the NT, will foster, rather than preclude, meaningful engagement with the NT.

FOR FURTHER READING

Paul J. Achtemeier, *Inspiration and Authority: Nature and Function of Christian Scripture* (Peabody: Hendrickson, 1999)

Joel B. Green, ed., *Hearing the New Testament: Strategies for Interpretation* (Grand Rapids: Eerdmans, 1995)

Joel B. Green and Max Turner, eds., *Between Two Horizons: Spanning New Testament Studies and Systematic Theology* (Grand Rapids: Eerdmans, 2000)

John Goldingay, *Models for Scripture* (Grand Rapids: Eerdmans, 1994)

Mark Allan Powell, ed., *The New Testament Today* (Louisville: Westminster/John Knox, 1999)

2. The World of the New Testament

The New Testament is in Greek. The ease with which we accept this fact masks two important realities. First, with such an array of modern translations in English, the NT is readily accessible to us — so much so that we perhaps too easily assume that its words, familiar to us in translation, also carry commonplace meaning from our world. Reading the NT today in English, it is easy to imagine that people in the ancient Mediterranean world experienced life much as we do.

Second, when we recall that the NT is written in Greek we are reminded of the impressive gains made by Alexander the Great and the cultural forces he initiated in the fourth century BCE. By the time of Jesus and Paul, Luke and John, the world of the NT had been the setting of almost four hundred years of *cultural influence from the Greeks*. The very language in which the NT was written provides evidence of the reach of the massive cultural transformations that shaped the NT period.

In more recent decades, Rome had come to occupy a significant place on the landscape of the NT world. Rome, with its institutions and agents, infiltrated the larger Mediterranean world, and the NT books were written well after the arrival of *Roman political dominion* in Palestine and far beyond. As a renewal movement within Judaism, moreover, the early Christian movement was drawn out of and itself drank deeply from the well of the *formative traditions and life of Israel*. This is perhaps seen most fully in the use of the Scriptures of Israel as a crucial ingredient in religious and ethical discourse, in the shared belief in Yahweh, the one God, and in the presence and influence of Jewish forms of worship in the pages of the NT. Underlying and pervading the writings of the NT, then, is the convergence of these three great rivers of tradition: Israel, Greece, and Rome.

How those traditions should be understood with respect to their influence on the life and thought of the early Christian movement is not and cannot be a matter of dispassionate reporting, however. In our study of the book of Revelation, for example, we might encounter two fundamentally opposed perspectives on Rome. On the one hand, one might understand Rome — the city, the empire, and all that came to represent Roman civilization — as an agent of world peace, midwife of economic stability, supplier of jobs, builder of highways and aqueducts, merchant of the seas. One might even refer to Domitian, emperor of Rome during the time when Revelation was written, as "lord and god" (Suetonius, *Domitian* 13). On the other, Rome could be understood as a blasphemous power whose every move was calculated to frustrate the purpose of God and to compromise the faith of God's people. Not as the savior of the world, but as "a habitation of demons and haunt for every unclean spirit" — this is how Rome is characterized by John's Revelation (18:2). *Pax Romana* (Roman peace), then, is only one way to characterize the spirit of the NT world. Peace is important to this era, but it is also selective. Peace for whom? At what price? At whose expense?

Among the twenty-seven books that comprise the NT, Revelation is not alone in providing this tale of two cities. Nor is Rome the only prominent fixture on the horizon of the NT world to be viewed in such an ambivalent way. This underscores at once the importance of our understanding the broader world in which the NT books were written. It also highlights the importance of recognizing how those various writers perceived and addressed that world.

In other words, in order to grapple with the message of NT texts, we need an understanding of the world in which that message took shape and found meaning for our ancestors in the faith as they grappled with the concrete implications of the gospel. Because our world is not simply a recapitulation of theirs, we need to achieve as full a description of that world as possible. After all, all language is embedded in culture. In order to gain a hearing in their first-century world, NT writers had to work with the pre-understandings, values, thought patterns, and language of their world. This is not to say, however, that the NT writers were so trapped in their worlds that they could not point beyond them. In order to proclaim and define their message *as good news,* those writers had to move beyond what was already normal in their world in order to challenge it and, indeed, to portray an alternative world, the world purposed by God and manifest in Christ.

The invitation to read the NT is in part a summons to enter into its sometimes familiar, sometimes strange world. Learning to listen to its message from within that world is a lifelong process of becoming sensitive to the everyday realities largely taken for granted by people of those first-century communities of faith. We can begin this process by adopting an interpretive framework that highlights, first, *environmental conditions* (the big picture of the general cultural, political, and economic contours of the period) and, second, *institutional contexts* (fundamental patterns of behavior supported in that world, together with the organizations that propagate those patterns).[1] First, however, it will be helpful to draw a crucial distinction regarding the several ways we may understand the phrase, "the world of the New Testament."

2.1. THE MANY WORLDS OF THE NEW TESTAMENT

Every description of a "world" is from a particular perspective. It is true that we might all count the same number of trees in a given area, but their significance depends on who is doing the counting. If a farmer, those trees may be looked upon with disdain, an obstacle to enhanced productivity. Children may have visions of ropes and tires draped from those limbs as makeshift swings. Zoologists, lumber companies, and environmentalists will each have their own competing viewpoints. As a matter of course, we render the world in relation to ourselves.

What is more, we tend to assume that our rendering of the world is "the way the world is" in itself, or even the way God made the world. Not surprisingly, then, we also tend to assume that others — local and far removed, past and present — share (or should share!) our understanding of reality. For this reason, our efforts at locating the NT in its own world require that we suspend some of our judgments about the nature of the world. We must do so in order to listen to sometimes alien voices and perspectives. This is a world where Jesus can be said to walk on water and raise the dead, where speaking in tongues can serve missionary ends, where the institution of slavery was largely taken for granted, where the measure of one's wealth was not as important as the measure of one's status, where the extended family was the basic social and economic unit, and where all of life was lived in varying degrees under the shadow of the empire. An important prerequisite for those of us who want to understand the writings of the NT will be to place our judgments regarding the values and institutions of its world in abeyance. Increasing our awareness of the taken-for-granted realities of those who inhabited the world of the NT will help us to understand better the message of the NT. Reading the NT is, in part, an exercise in intercultural communication.

What do we mean by the "world of the NT"? This phrase can have several nuances. First, we may refer to *the social-historical realities of the first-century Mediterranean world* in which the events to which the NT refers took place and in which the writings themselves took shape.

This initial focus on the "real world" brings to the surface an immediate problem. The NT writings derive from the first-century Mediterranean world, but

---

1. The method employed here is adapted from Robert Wuthnow, *Communities of Discourse: Ideology and Social Structure in the Reformation, the Enlightenment, and European Socialism* (Cambridge: Harvard, 1989) esp. 1-12.

even this was no monolithic society. When one speaks of the world of the NT, then, one must differentiate between, say, the world of Palestine and the world of Achaia (the southern portion of Greece). Each had its own history, its own ethnic mix, its own view of everyday life, and, among the followers of Jesus, its own distractions and temptations. And even within Palestine such distinctions must be drawn: the whole land of Israel versus the holy city of Jerusalem, rural Palestine versus urban, Galilee versus Samaria, and so on. Although from a sociological vantage point some generalizations are not only possible but also necessary, our readings of the NT will benefit from our sensitivity to the varieties experienced by people in this real world.

We have access to this world not only via the writings of the NT, but also through other sources. One thinks of the Jewish historian Josephus (37–*ca.* 100 CE). Born in the years immediately following Jesus' death, Josephus wrote in part to represent Jewish culture and religion to a Roman audience. Portions of his multivolume *Jewish Antiquities* and most of his account of *The Jewish War* help to fill in the sociohistorical picture of first-century Palestine. Of course, like any historian, ancient or modern, Josephus worked with his own biases — for example, his concern to portray to his fellow Jews Roman conduct *vis-à-vis* the Jewish people in the best light. Apart from Josephus other writings are of significance: the books of

The Qumran caves

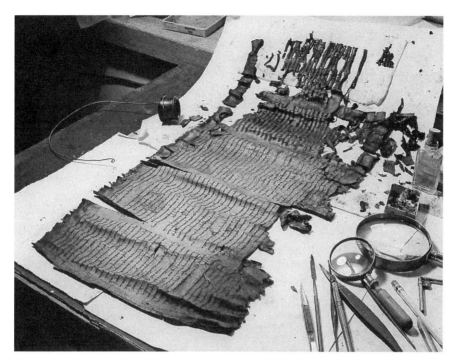

A Qumran scroll — the Genesis Apocryphon from Cave 4 *(Israel Museum)*

the Alexandrian Jew Philo, a contemporary of Paul, for example; the Dead Sea Scrolls along with other writings of Palestinian Judaism, which provide valuable insight into the diversity of the Jewish people; papyri and inscriptions, together with other evidence of an archaeological nature; and, of course, the historical, biographical, entertaining, and philosophical writings of the larger Greco-Roman world.

None of these source materials is complete or objective. Nor can we expect the various writings of the NT to represent exhaustively the many and diverse ingredients of the real world of the first-century Roman Empire. These materials are partial, both in the sense of being incomplete and in the sense of arising out of particular commitments. Hence, there is, second, *the world as the NT materials actualize it* — that is, the world as portrayed by each writer. Given limited space, with what ingredients of the real world did each writer choose to interact? The world as represented by a NT writer will overlap with but is not identical to the real world, since authors shape their messages by emphasizing what they regard as having particular importance. Luke and John emphasize the presence and significance of Samaria and Samaritans, but Matthew and Mark are silent on these. In literary terms, this second sense of world is sometimes referred to as the "narrative world" of the author; it is the world at the level of the discourse as this is represented by the author.

Third, "the world of the NT" signifies *the world of hope.* This is the world to which a NT writer points, the vision of a new era, the new world that is breaking into the old. An Evangelist like Mark is not content to present the world "as it really is," but purposefully shapes his writing in such a way that some of its facets are undermined, others legitimated. So, although it is helpful to know as much as we can about the world of Mark (in the first sense), it is just as critical if not even more so to see how that world fares in his hands.

If we are concerned with the world of Mark, then, we must attend to how his narrative represents and challenges the world of the first-century Mediterranean. Consequently, we will be interested above all in reading the Second Gospel on its own terms, albeit against the backdrop of what we otherwise know about the first-century world. The text is thus given a chance, as it were, to speak back to, as well as within, its own world.

A further dilemma must be faced. Given that all portraits of the world are partial, with what commitments do we proceed in this presentation? In the last century of NT study, this question has focused repeatedly on whether it is best to read the early Christian movement against a Hellenistic or Jewish backdrop. It has become increasingly clear, at least in studies of Jesus and the early Christian movement, that this is a false dichotomy. Long before the time of Jesus, the threads of the Judaism into which Jesus was born and out of which the Christian movement grew had been woven together with the threads of Hellenism. Although this growing realization highlights the problem of proceeding with too narrow an emphasis on one tradition or the other, still our dilemma remains in a revised form. To what degree had Hellenism and Judaism been intertwined in this or that location? To what degree does a particular NT document draw on and perpetuate Hellenistic (and not Jewish) concerns? Do we read the NT materials through the lens provided by Judaism; and if so, how strong a Hellenistic filter can be assumed? As it is, this question can be worked out only on a case-by-case basis, since the answer for the Letter to the Hebrews will not be the same as that for the Acts of the Apostles.

Hence, background issues will surface throughout the chapters that follow. Nevertheless, we should acknowledge that in what follows we will examine the world of the NT from a perspective within Jewish history. Among the several reasons for this decision the most important include, first, the birth of the Jesus movement preeminently as a Jewish renewal movement that only later came to separate from Judaism; second, the pervasiveness throughout the NT writings of the struggle with the place of Gentiles within the people of God — a concern that would arise only from an insider's (i.e., Jewish) point of view; and, third, the unparalleled importance of the OT in its use as a both explicit and implicit subtext for theological and ethical discourse in the NT.

2.2. ENVIRONMENTAL CONDITIONS

In exploring the social world in which the NT writings took shape, we will draw a general distinction between environmental conditions and institutional contexts. The former refers to the big picture of the NT world, the general cultural, political, and economic contours of the NT period.

2.2.1. Hellenism

Shaping the cultural map of the NT world in a far-reaching way were the cultural innovations and upheavals in the Near East following in the wake of the military successes of Alexander the Great (356-323 BCE). Earlier in the fourth century BCE, the Macedonians (located on the northern periphery of the Greek world) had not only made their bid to achieve recognition as Greeks, but under Philip II, Alexander's father, had extended Macedonian rule to the Greek city-states to the south and the Balkans to the east. Under Alexander, a vast expanse — including Asia Minor, Phoenicia, Palestine, Egypt, and Babylonia — was added to the empire. By the time of his death, he had opened up the Near East to the migration of Greek language and cultural expressions. Parochial societies with closely kept boundaries thus began to be shaped into a more cosmopolitan and interrelated culture. Separated by different ethnic origins and cultural histories, these peoples were nevertheless joined by increasing cultural intercourse, symbolized above all by the spread of Attic Greek as the *lingua franca.* "Hellenism" thus refers to the spread and embrace of the Greek language, but also to the way of life, business, education, and ethos mediated through the spread and use of that language.

The significance for the NT of the cultural machinery set in motion by Hellenism is, in one sense, immediately obvious. Though its documents originated from various sites throughout the Mediterranean world, they are all in Greek. Their authors were all more or less at home in the Greek language and wrote to audiences that could read Greek or at least understand spoken Greek. Jesus and his Galilean disciples would have been able to communicate in Greek, even if their first and more common language of daily discourse was Aramaic.

The NT evidences additional Hellenistic influence of an obvious nature. Most of its citations of the Jewish Scriptures are from the Greek translation, the Septuagint (abbreviated LXX), rather than from the Hebrew text. The forms of the NT writings are also indebted to the traditions of writing known in wider Hellenistic circles. Note, for example, the close relationship between Greco-Roman biography and historiography and the Gospels and Acts, or the epistolary style of the Pauline writings. In his form of argumentation, too, Paul has been influenced — whether directly or indirectly — by the conventions of ancient rhetoric.

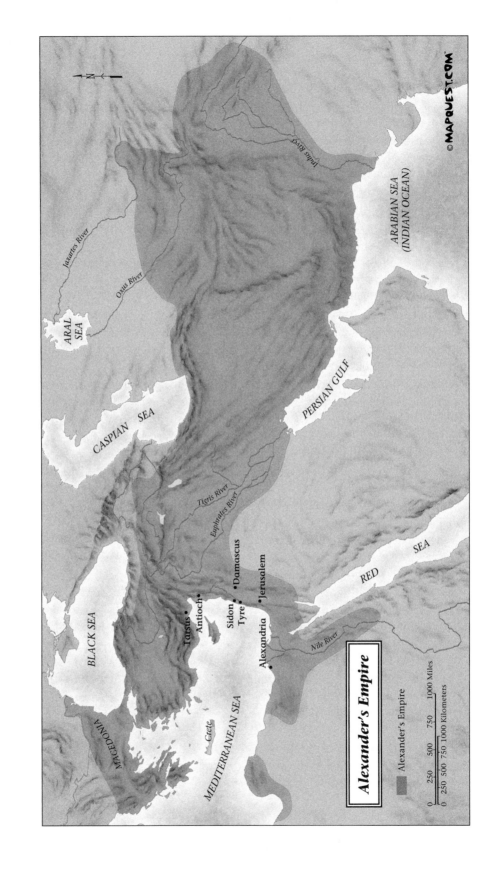

Alexander's Empire

Alexander's Empire

In another sense, the influence of Hellenism on the NT is less transparent. To a significant degree, the diversity within the Judaism of Jesus' day was a corollary of the range of Jewish responses to the challenges of Hellenism. To take two extremes, Philo was willing to dress the law of Moses in Hellenistic clothing, but the Jewish community at Qumran stripped itself as fully as possible from such alien vestiges. Growing out of Judaism, initially as a renewal movement within Judaism, the Jesus movement was located at the intersection of potentially opposing challenges represented by Hellenistic and Jewish lifestyles. As the literature of this movement, the NT embodies the ongoing struggle with issues of faithfulness to God in a Hellenistic world.

Because of his early death, Alexander the Great was able to do little more than set in motion the wheels of progress toward the Hellenization of the Mediterranean world. Soon after his success in the Near East, he was dead and his empire was divided among his generals. In a military and political tug-of-war, Judea was first ruled along with Egypt by the Ptolemies, then by the Seleucids to the north. Throughout this period, until the early second century BCE, the Jewish people largely acquiesced to their foreign overlords; after all, the hand of foreign rule was not heavy during this period, and the Jewish people enjoyed relative freedom, not least in things religious. At the same time, however, the tentacles of Hellenism were reaching slowly, almost imperceptibly into the Jewish mainstream.

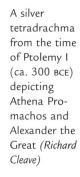

A silver tetradrachma from the time of Ptolemy I (ca. 300 BCE) depicting Athena Promachos and Alexander the Great *(Richard Cleave)*

In 168-167 BCE, the Seleucid king Antiochus IV (Epiphanes) moved forcibly to make the Jewish people Hellenists. Even if he seems to have had support from some among the Jewish leadership, his agenda for Hellenistic inculturation far exceeded the openness of most of the Jewish population. He profaned the temple by erecting an altar to Zeus. And he compelled the Jewish people to violate the law of Moses and to transgress their ancestral faith. Jewish resistance to this forced inculturation gave rise to legends of faithful heroism, including some

A Tale of Faithful Heroism
from the Period of Antiochus IV

Eleazar, one of the scribes in high position, a man now advanced in age and of noble presence, was being forced to open his mouth to eat swine's flesh. But he, welcoming death with honor rather than life with pollution, went up to the rack of his own accord, spitting out the flesh, as all ought to go who have the courage to refuse things that it is not right to taste, even for the natural love of life. Those who were in charge of that unlawful sacrifice took the man aside because of their long acquaintance with him, and privately urged him to bring meat of his own providing, proper for him to use, and to pretend that he was eating the flesh of the sacrificial meal that had been commanded by the king, so that by doing this he might be saved from death, and be treated kindly on account of his old friendship with them. But making a high resolve, worthy of his years and the dignity of his old age and the gray hairs that he had reached with distinction and his excellent life even from childhood, and moreover according to the holy God-given law, he declared himself quickly, telling them to send him to Hades. "Such pretense is not worthy of our time of life," he said, "for many of the young might suppose that Eleazar in his ninetieth year had gone over to an alien religion, and through my pretense, for the sake of living a brief moment longer, they would be led astray because of me, while I defile and disgrace my old age. Even if for the present I would avoid the punishment of mortals, yet whether I live or die I shall not escape the hands of the Almighty. Therefore, by bravely giving up my life now, I will show myself worthy of my old age and leave to the young a noble example of how to die a good death willingly and nobly for the revered and holy laws." When he had said this, he went at once to the rack. Those who a little before had acted toward him with goodwill now changed to ill will, because the words he had uttered were in their opinion sheer madness. When he was about to die under the blows, he groaned aloud and said: "It is clear to the Lord in his holy knowledge that, though I might have been saved from death, I am enduring terrible sufferings in my body under this beating, but in my soul I am glad to suffer these things because I fear him." So in this way he died, leaving in his death an example of nobility and a memorial of courage, not only to the young but to the great body of his nation. (2 Maccabees 6:18-31, NRSV)

mentioned in Heb 11:32-38. As the king worked to remove the peculiarities of Judaism (food laws, Sabbath keeping, etc.), a longstanding policy of religious tolerance came to an end. Jewish groups rebelled against Antiochus and established a short-lived interval of self-rule under Hasmonean leadership. Even self-rule proved to be unsatisfying, however, since the character of Hasmonean rule did not so much reflect the original impetus toward religious liberty as an emerging desire for political independence and dynastic power. The resulting instability set the stage for the invasion of Judea by Rome in the mid-first century BCE.

Some Important Dates

336-323 BCE	Palestine Conquered/Ruled by Alexander the Great
175	Onset of Rule of Palestine under Antiochus IV (Epiphanes)
167-164	The Maccabean Revolt
150-100	Essene Community Founded at Qumran
37-4	Palestine under Herod the Great
ca. 6-4	Birth of Jesus
26-36 CE	Pilate Governs Judea
30 (or 33?)	Death of Jesus
ca. 33-35	Paul's Experience on the Damascus Road
66-70	Jewish War

The extent of Hellenism in Palestine and its influence on Jews scattered throughout the ancient Mediterranean world remains a matter of speculation. Two points are clear, however. First, the degree of Hellenistic influence depends in large part on location. Urban areas encountered more traffic and thus experienced more cultural exchange. It is clear that some urban Jews, because they followed intellectual hunger or sought acceptance and honor in the changing world or for other reasons, embraced these cultural innovations quite deliberately. Elsewhere, though, especially in more remote, rural areas, evidence of the reach of Hellenism was less pronounced and certainly less welcomed. Second, and at the same time, it must be recognized that we are dealing here with a continuum from more to less Hellenistic encroachment. Refusal to adapt to the changing world, at least minimally, was not an option. Even this way of putting things may require further nuance, however. The question may not be how thoroughly the Jewish people were Hellenized but rather how strongly they — as a whole or in different localities — resisted the intrusion of Hellenism.

2.2.2. The Roman Empire

Of the emperor Augustus (63 BCE–14 CE), the Roman historian Tacitus (born *ca.* 56 CE) wrote,

> He organized the state, not by instituting a monarchy or a dictatorship, but by creating the title of First Citizen. The empire had been fenced by the ocean or distant rivers. The legions, the provinces, the fleets, the whole administration, had been centralized. There had been law for the Roman citizen, respect for the allied communities; and the capital itself had been embellished with remarkable splendor. (*Annales* 1.9, LCL)

With such words Tacitus drew attention to the general accolades enjoyed by the emperor following his success in the civil wars that had ravaged the Roman republic. The words of the historian are temperate, however, when compared with the acclaim elsewhere. Adopted as the son of Julius Caesar, Octavian took for himself the name Augustus ("venerable, revered") following his military and political triumphs. The Myrian inscription refers to him as "Divine Augustus Caesar, son of a god, imperator of land and sea, the benefactor and savior of the whole world . . . ," and similar sentiments are not hard to find in this period. This marriage of political accomplishment and divine benefaction was integral to the larger Roman world, even though the notion of the emperor's divinity was more loosely held in the west of the empire than in the east. This provided an implicit legitimization of the extension of Roman power and the Roman system of governance throughout the empire.

The world of the NT is of course the world of Rome, an empire that would eventually comprise the lands bordering the Mediterranean, from the coasts to far into the interior, as well as into Europe as far north as the southern tip of Scotland and into Germany. The stretch of the empire was fortunate for Roman Italy, incapable of feeding its own population of some two million, half of whom lived in the environs of the capital itself. Rome enjoyed a parasitic relationship with its provinces, and Tacitus's affirmation of the "remarkable splendor" of the capital stands uneasily alongside his assertion of Roman "respect for the allied communities." The primary aims of the imperial government were, first, the maintenance of Roman peace within its borders and the occasional extension or protection of those borders and, second, the maintenance of a system whereby food and revenues from taxes made their way to the center of the Roman world, Rome itself.

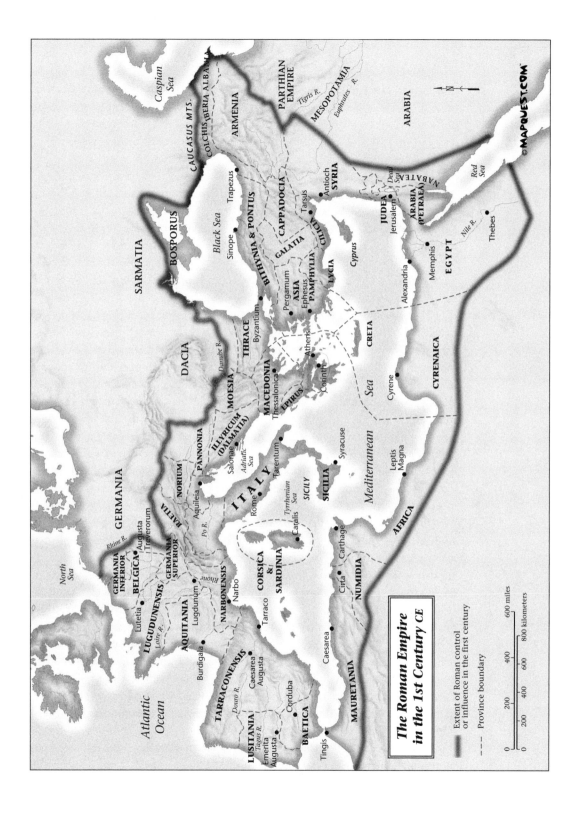

The Roman Empire
in the 1st Century CE

Extent of Roman control
or influence in the first century

Province boundary

0   200   400   600 miles

0   200   400   600   800 kilometers

Military maneuvers and the trade and taxation on which the empire was dependent required efficient means of transportation and communication. One finds literary and archaeological evidence of Roman merchant ships, for travel on both inland waterways, including Roman canals, and the Mediterranean. The larger of these would have served the grain supply; presumably this is the sort of ship boarded at the Lycian port of Myra by Paul and his military escort according to Acts 27:6, Myra being an important stopping point for grain shipments from Egypt. Although Rome's control of the water routes made such travel relatively safe, the weather presented its own peril, particularly in the winter months. Roman rule also supported an extensive network of roads — useful for trade and the military, but also for easier communication. With no "postal service" in place, letters would be placed in the hands of travelers — and better roads meant there were more travelers. These advances in transportation would have been a boon for the early Christian movement.

The Roman system throughout the rule of Augustus and, indeed, throughout most of the first century CE, supported little bureaucracy. Military installations were spread throughout the empire but, except in troubled areas (like Galilee and Judea), direct Roman intrusion into daily affairs was minimal. For the maintenance of law and order Rome depended largely on the administrative function of cities — some of which it founded, others of which were already present — which were largely self-governing.

Nor did the various forms of Roman taxation result in increased layers of bureaucracy. This was due in part to the fact that taxes were collected primarily for wages and military expenses, not to provide what we might today call social services. Although Rome had a visible and direct presence in the conquered provinces through its military, it was present to collect taxes indirectly. Tribute — in two forms, a percentage of land production and an assessment (probably) for each adult male — was collected annually by cities, in Palestine by Jewish councils, acting as agents of the state. Tolls on the movement of goods from one urban area to another were collected at tollbooths in each town or city by the "toll collectors" known to us in the Gospels. These were persons to whom the business of collecting duty had been contracted by the empire. They represented the primary form of entrepreneurial, private enterprise of the Roman world and served as the front line of a system little regulated and open to gross abuse throughout the first century. Roman Italy was itself exempted from taxes, except in unusual cases where immediate and increased revenues were needed to fund a military operation. Outside Italy, the urban wealthy were also capable of avoiding taxation, with the consequence that the burden for financing the empire fell above all on the mass of the population that lived at or near the subsistence level.

What was the tax burden? Accurate figures are notoriously difficult to determine; our sources are not only ambiguous but also leave unclear how long certain

Prominent Roads and Ship Routes of the Eastern Roman Empire

— Prominent Roads
--- Ship Routes

A floor mosaic from Ostia depicting Roman ships *(Ostia Museum)*

tax rates were enforced. Estimates fix Roman tribute, in both of its forms, at approximately sixteen percent of gross income annually. However, the aggregate tribute for an area was fixed in advance of the farming year, with the result that, in cases of agricultural disaster, the overall tax burden was not thereby diminished. Jewish farmers were also expected to pay tithes and taxes to support the temple system in Jerusalem, conservatively estimated as adding an additional fifteen to twenty percent to the overall tax burden. Tolls on trade transported from town to town would be calculated and collected separately. Other taxes were levied, too: an inheritance tax, a tax on the manumission of slaves, and so on.

If the Roman government was not active in the provision of social services, how did municipalities meet their collective needs? The emperor himself modeled what was expected of the wealthy elite in every locale — namely, generous benefaction. Rather than pay taxes, the wealthy contributed time and money in the service of the cities and towns. This form of benefaction was not managed centrally, in which case wealth might have been distributed where needed most. Instead, gifts were made at the whim of givers. What is more, though private involvement of this kind was required by deficiencies in the city treasury, it was to the advantage of the wealthy that the city's finances be kept in a weakened condition. Private benefaction was the primary means by which the wealthy were recognized as those

most deserving of public office and prestige in the community, so only the wealthy could enjoy the honor and advancement reserved for those who gave so "generously."

A Roman aqueduct leading to Caesarea on the coast of Palestine

2.2.3. Jewish Identity

The onset of the series of changes among the Jewish people that set the stage for understanding the Judaism of the Roman period can be conveniently dated from 586 BCE. The fall of Jerusalem, the destruction of the temple, the end of the Davidic monarchy, and the exile of Israel's leading families under Babylonian King Nebuchadnezzar profoundly shaped what would emerge in the centuries after the Exile as Judaism. Of course, the Israel of Persian, Hellenistic, Hasmonean, and Roman times was deeply rooted in the Yahwism known to us through Israel's Scriptures, but it can also be distinguished by the fresh emphases required for a people living under foreign domination. In this case, these fresh emphases can be understood as characteristic marks of family resemblance, since one of the primary features of first-century Judaism was its diversity of expression. All Israel sought faithful responses to the cultural upheavals around them, but some Jews opposed the forms of response adopted by others. Hence, in spite of their common cause, some Jews found themselves aligned against other Jews.

The changes that resulted from the loss of land and political autonomy in the Babylonian invasion shaped Israel in decisive ways — so much so that Josephus observes that those returning from Babylonia should be called "Jews" rather than "Israelites" (*Ant.* 11.5.7 §173). Judaism, of course, saw itself as the continuation of preexilic Israelite religion or Yahwism, and shared with it the fundamental belief in one God, Yahweh, who created the world, chose Israel (the Jews) to be his people, delivered them from Egypt, and entered into a covenantal relationship with them. Moreover, even if they were ruled by foreign kings, Jews nonetheless maintained their sense of identity with the land of Israel and of the holiness of Jerusalem and its temple. On the other hand, with the Exile came the demolition of the ancient tribal structure of Israelite society. Jews that did return to the land did so as clans, and many Jews did not return but were dispersed throughout Babylonia and, in time, the entire Mediterranean world. Thus Judaism took on more a religious and less a national identity. Although the center point of this religion remained the temple — now the Second Temple, with restoration work and extensive renovations dating from the late sixth century BCE well into the first century CE — this was supplemented on a local level by the synagogues, whose activities supported the fresh emphasis on prayer and ongoing study of the Scriptures.

2.2.3.1. Diverse Voices within Judaism

In the centuries before the birth of Jesus and the beginning of the Christian movement, it became clear that, in spite of foreign rule, the Jewish people would not be

---

Josephus on the Pharisees

The Pharisees simplify their standard of living, making no concession to luxury. They follow the guidance of that which their doctrine has selected and transmitted as good, attaching the chief importance to the observance of those commandments which it has seen fit to dictate to them. They show respect and deference to their elders, nor do they rashly presume to contradict their proposals. Though they postulate that everything is brought about by fate [i.e., providence], still they do not deprive the human will of the pursuit of what is in human power. . . . They believe that souls have power to survive death and that there are rewards and punishments . . . : eternal imprisonment is the lot of evil souls, while the good souls receive an easy passage into the next life. Because of these views they are . . . extremely influential among the townsfolk. . . . (Josephus, *Ant.* 18.1.3 §§12-15)

simply assimilated into the dominant culture around them. Full adaptation was not an option; instead, they would follow the law of Moses. The rejection of a merger into wider cultural currents raised the important question, How might the Jews remain faithful as God's people while under alien rule? After all, following the Mosaic law assumed some level of distinction between Jew and Gentile. Related to this was another issue, that of Jewish leadership. This was in part a question of who would be authorized to represent to the Jews God's just ways for constituting faithful life. In the early years of the postexilic era, scribes emerged in this role, but scribal dominance in religious discourse was soon challenged by priestly voices. In fact, the revolt against Antiochus Epiphanes was led by rural priests who were to become rulers of the new independent Jewish nation.

Josephus on the Sadducees

The Sadducees hold that the soul perishes along with the body. They own no observance of any sort apart from the [written] laws. . . . There are but few to whom this doctrine has been made known, but these are persons of the highest standing. . . . (Josephus, *Ant.* 18.1.4 §16-17)

Another alternative voice materialized during this era, however. This was the voice of apocalypticism, a sociohistorical movement whose primary spokespersons were seers and mystics. Often living far from the thresholds of power in this much-conflicted era, such groups placed little hope in the possibility of reform and instead anticipated a new order of reality that would soon overthrow and replace the present world. Among these people and in their literature developed sometimes wide-ranging speculation regarding the spiritual world. The failure of Israel's primary institutions, the prominence of evil, and the suffering of the righteous — such desperate times called for transcendent answers: resurrection as God's vindication of the faithful not from but through death, developed hierarchies of angels engaged in battle against God's foes, and so on.

Albeit in adapted form, apocalyptic themes (e.g., final judgment and resurrection) are present throughout the NT. More immediately obvious in its pages, and especially in the Gospels and Acts, are evidences of the diversity within Judaism that grew out of the sociohistorical exigencies we have outlined. Josephus refers to four parties within Judaism — the Pharisees, the Sadducees, the Essenes, and the "Fourth Philosophy." Reference to these groups begins to suggest how in

---

Josephus on the Essenes

The doctrine of the Essenes is wont to leave everything in the hands of God. They regard the soul as immortal and believe that they ought to strive especially to draw near to righteousness. They send votive offerings to the temple, but perform their sacrifices employing a different ritual of purification. . . . They hold their possessions in common, and the wealthy receives no more enjoyment from property than the one who possesses nothing. . . . (Josephus, *Ant.* 18.1.5 §§18-22)

---

divergent ways Judaism addressed the questions of faithfulness to God and religio-political leadership in the Second Temple period.

Who were the Pharisees? Some were priests, but most were not. They accorded privilege to the Torah and regarded the ancestral traditions of interpretation as also binding. The latter resulted in an emphasis on the laws of purity — normally focused on priests and the activity of the temple but now also transferred to everyday life. And this led to a heightened emphasis on the table and table fellowship, what one ate and with whom. In fact, the Pharisees are often presented in the Gospels as concerned to monitor Jesus' behavior at table, for example, or on the Sabbath. Their struggles with Jesus typically revolved around faithful interpretation (and embodiment) of the law. Although Pharisees would not necessarily have enjoyed high status because of their economic or professional location in the larger world, as persons concerned with the interpretation and appropriation of the Scriptures they would have been influential in their own communities. This is especially true when it is remembered that Pharisees often lived in the villages and towns of Israel, away from the immediate influence of the urban elite, whose interpretations would have struck sometimes quite different chords. It is not easy to determine the typically Pharisaic stance toward Hellenism and the Roman Empire. This fact alone may be telling, however, for it suggests a certain ambivalence and lack of consensus toward these larger realities. Apparently, many Pharisees believed that everyday holiness before God was possible without addressing critically the status quo of Roman rule.

While Pharisees were located throughout the villages and cities of Israel, Sadducees were found in Jerusalem. They included the leading priests (the "chief priests" in the Gospels) and others of the urban elite for whom faithfulness to God was signaled above all by faithful maintenance of the temple cult. Consequently, cooperation with Rome was for them an acceptable compromise, for it ensured the ongoing, relatively independent functioning of the temple apparatus.

An opposite perspective is represented by the Essenes, for whom separation from Gentiles, Gentile influence, and even those Jews who trafficked with Gentiles was axiomatic. Their emphasis on purity led them to separate themselves into their own communities, whether within cities and towns or in isolated sites in the wilderness (e.g., Qumran). These sectarians held an apocalyptic form of eschatology, viewing themselves as the faithful, the "sons of light," who would join God in the final battle against the "sons of darkness."

The "Fourth Philosophy," as Josephus calls it, were largely Pharisaic in their beliefs, though with one important proviso — their "passion for freedom since they take God as their only leader and master" (*Ant.* 18.1.6 §23). How its members demonstrated their passion for freedom is not developed by Josephus, and it would be a mistake to identify the Fourth Philosophy too readily with the Zealots, revolutionaries who would appear in the 60s CE. No doubt there were various ways of expressing dissent in regard to Israel's enemies. Those of the Fourth Philosophy may have found their precursors in those faithful Jews who resisted the compromise of their faith in the face of their foes by giving up their lives in innocent suffering.

In any case, the groups Josephus mentions hardly tell the whole story of Second Temple Judaism. Most Jewish people belonged to no identifiable group at all, and the Gospels usually portray "the common people" as prospective believers in Jesus. At the turn of the era, numerous messianic movements and revolutionary prophets vied for attention and sought a following among the people. We should situate John and Jesus among those movements. Both men must have seemed to the Romans and to the Jewish people like one more in the line of those who proclaimed a message of renewal and sought a following. The presence of revolutionaries and renewal movements is itself a barometer of the level of unrest arising from the ongoing social pressures of Hellenistic influence and the constant economic and military reminders of Roman rule, as well as popular dissatisfaction with official Jewish responses to these alien intrusions.

Josephus on "the Fourth Philosophy"

As for the fourth of the philosophies, . . . this school agrees in all other respects with the opinions of the Pharisees, except that they have a passion for liberty that is almost unconquerable, since they are convinced that God alone is their leader and master. They think little of submitting to death in unusual forms and permitting vengeance to fall on kin and friends if only they may avoid calling any person master. (Josephus, *Ant.* 18.1.6 §§23-25)

2.2.3.2. Common Judaism

Thus far we have emphasized the diversity of Jewish responses to the realities of the Second Temple period. Can one speak of a "common Judaism" — that is, of a unity within this diversity? Archaeological discoveries in the twentieth century, together with increased familiarity with the extant literature of Second Temple Judaism, have underscored the many expressions of that Judaism. At the same time, it is possible by painting with broad strokes to portray those elements of faith and behavior that would have characterized most Jews during this period.

The foundation on which Second Temple Judaism was built accounts not only for the unity but also the diversity of Judaism in this period. The "Judaisms" of which some scholars have come to speak shared a common heritage, but each "Judaism" interpreted this heritage along divergent lines. Those central components of faith that bound them together, when set within the context of invasive Hellenism and Roman political dominion, would become the focal points of discord.

What were these shared elements? First and foremost, Jews of the Greco-Roman world clung to the fundamental conviction contained in the *Shema'*: "Hear O Israel: The Lord our God, the Lord is one" (Deut 6:4). Recitation of the *Shema'* was required twice daily (Deut 6:7), and Josephus remarks that the recognition of the one God is common to all the Hebrew people (*Ant.* 5.1.27 §112). Such a confession stood in contrast to the Hellenistic approach to religious diversity as well as to the early Roman position, which were characterized by the very syncretism rejected in Judaism. Although Rome ceased to be so accommodating in its religious pluralism during the period of the empire, its new distaste for syncretism did not lead it to discard its basic polytheism. Hence, throughout the Hellenistic and Roman periods, the Jews were extraordinary in the wider world for their exclusive monotheism. Some Jews could portray other figures as Yahweh's divine attendants or write of Yahweh's self-expression in personal ways (e.g., "Word/Logos" or "Wisdom"), but this need not have marked a substantive departure from Jewish monotheism.

Second, Judaism was grounded in the belief that Israel was God's people at God's own behest; they were the people chosen by God, and he had initiated a special covenant relationship with them. Of course, this conviction of divine election is deeply rooted in Israel's collective memory — in the divine promise to Abraham and in God's mighty acts of deliverance and leadership in the story of the Exodus. Israel was to be a "holy nation," and this required careful negotiation of the practical terms of Hellenistic reform and Roman presence.

Third, and as a corollary to these first two, God's people responded to God's gracious initiative in terms set forth in the Torah, God's law. Not only did Torah relate the story of God's election of Israel, it also set forth how that relationship would be regulated. The early ascendancy of the scribal office in Jewish life following the Exile is testimony to the importance given to understanding and articulating the meaning of Torah among God's people. Later, priests would share in this function in local communities, and the reading of Torah became a cornerstone of piety for the Jew. The development and propagation of the synagogue as a house of prayer and scriptural exposition, too, suggest the central importance of Torah for Israel's self-understanding in the Greco-Roman world.

Jewish self-identity as the people of God, together with its covenantal ties to the Torah, came to focus in three practices that were generally shared across the lines of Jewish diversity. We have already mentioned the first in relationship to Pharisaic behavior — namely, consideration of food laws and table companions. The Book of Daniel, for example, narrates how Daniel was able to maintain Jewish identity while living under alien domination by concentrating on dietary concerns (Daniel 1). In the persecutions related to the reign of Antiochus IV, refusal to eat unclean food symbolized faithfulness to the covenant (e.g., 1 Macc 1:62-63). Diodorus Siculus observed that the Jews in the mid-first century BCE did not fellowship at the table with any other nation. In addition, remaining faithful to their heritage as God's people, the Jews practiced circumcision (Gen 17:9-14) and observed the Sabbath (Exod 20:8-11). These practices were characteristic of Jews across party lines and helped to mark the boundaries separating those who lived by Torah from those who were "without the law" or "outside the law" *(anomos)*.

A fourth common element in Second Temple Judaism was the primacy of the temple itself. It is true that the Essenes (at least those at Qumran) withdrew from the temple, but this seems to be because they regarded the priesthood as hopelessly corrupt. Hence, they regarded themselves as the temple of God and looked forward to the rebuilding of the eschatological temple. It is also true that other temples had been constructed by Jewish communities, especially in Egypt, but these seem also to have resulted from criticism of the priesthood in Jerusalem by groups committed to the rival high-priestly dynasty of the Zadokites. Writing in the first century CE, though, Philo could argue that Israel's *one* temple unified Israel under *one* God (*Spec. Leg.* 1.12 §67). In this way, the ideology of the temple served to bind together Jewish monotheism and exclusivity.

2.2.4. The Peasant and Urban Life

A further way of taking account of the people of the world of the NT is to recall the general opposition of urban and rural life. In the Gospels, one thinks immediately, for example, of the presence of the Pharisees in the villages and towns of Galilee. There the Pharisees appear to wield considerable power, an impression that can skew our overall picture of first-century Judaism so that we might wrongly assume that Pharisees were significant power brokers throughout the Jewish world. The Sadducees, on the other hand, appear to work in concert with the leading priests against Jesus from a distance until Jesus reaches the environs of Jerusalem. The antagonism between Jesus and the Pharisees portrayed in the Gospels is thus in large part a result of not only their competing interpretation of Scripture but also the physical location of Jesus' ministry where Pharisees had carved out their primary spheres of influence.

Similarly, one can draw a broad distinction between urban and rural locations with respect to Hellenism. Village life is basically conservative, therefore biased against adopting Greek language and Greek ways. It is interesting, then, that Jesus' ministry — according to the Synoptic Gospels, primarily oriented toward village and peasant life — is never said to have embraced the Hellenistic cities of Tiberias and Sepphoris, in spite of their relative proximity. The city, on the other hand, is often seen as the locus of change, where new ideas could win a hearing and take hold. Worthy of note in this regard is the success of the Pauline mission in urban areas. Also meriting reflection is the process and rapidity with which the Christian message, first planted on rural, Palestinian soil, was transplanted and indeed blossomed in the cities of the larger empire.

2.2.4.1. The Life of the Peasant

Peasant societies typically evidence a general (though not absolute) polarity between the city — locus of power, wealth, and privilege — and the village or countryside. In a negative way, this polarity is implicitly embodied in a statement by Paul, where he records dangers in the city, wilderness, and sea (2 Cor 11:26). Dividing the world of his experience in this way, he leaves no room for interaction with the rural populace, village dwellers; outside the city there is only "wilderness." Paul thus presents himself as a man at home in the city. Peasants had their own biases, of course. Persons who lived outside the village were by definition not only outsiders but enemies. For this reason, urban leaders often dealt with peasants indirectly, through brokers of various kinds. The majority of the population of Palestine lived in villages and small towns, where they worked the land and fostered the central values of loyalty and kinship.

An old proverb portrays peasants as people standing permanently up to their necks in water, so that any disturbance in the water would be sufficient to cause drowning. This is not to say that peasants lived in constant worry or anger about their lot in life, but it is to point out the tenuousness of life at the subsistence level. Each year the harvest must be sufficient to produce enough seed for the following year's planting, for the household to eat and/or trade for other necessities like salt, and for the omnipresent and unrelenting claims of outsiders (like the Jewish temple and the empire). In addition, each household faced certain ceremonial or social obligations — wedding feasts, for example. Under these circumstances, even the partial failure of a crop might result in a loss of standing in the community, loss of relative independence as a family unit of production, or even loss of life through starvation. The notion of planning, for a peasant, would focus on the relative stability of one year's planting and harvest cycle followed by the next, not on the possibility of events in the more distant future. Against such a background, Jesus' feeding of the thousands, the question of his disciples' behavior in gleaning a field, his seed parables, and the like would have pointed meaning.

2.2.4.2. Urban Elite and Urban Life

Hellenistic-Roman cities are virtually absent in the Gospels, whose primary settings include villages and small towns, like Capernaum, which had a population of about 1700-2500. In Galilee, Tiberias and Sepphoris qualify as Hellenistic-Roman cities, and their populations can be estimated at 24,000 each. These urban centers would have stood as centers of consumption, with their needs leading to a form of agricultural industry quite unlike the family farms known to the peasantry. Beyond the industries necessary to provide food for their inhabitants (granaries, mills, olive presses, and the like), these cities spawned other markets as they served as centers of small businesses (e.g., pottery) and interregional commerce. Such cities were self-governing, each with its own council.

The city that looms the largest in the Gospels is, of course, Jerusalem, site of the Jewish Council or Sanhedrin, as well as of the holy temple. This made Jerusalem the center of the world of the Jewish people, its importance rooted in the intertwining of social, economic, political, and religious threads. In fact, geographically Jerusalem had little to commend its importance; it was not strategically located on a river or port, had no natural east-west passage for trade through the mountains, and had little in the way of natural defenses against invasion. Nor was it situated in an agriculturally rich area so that it could be easily supported. Hence, its importance was narrowly focused: within its walls was the abode of God, the sacred temple. The city survived and prospered on the revenues attracted by the temple.

The cities of the empire were normally located strategically on natural roadways and near water sources. They were centers of consumption but also of redistribution, their streets and marketplaces crowded with traders, peddlers, and the hubbub of barter. Under Hellenistic influence, many cities had a main street, with colonnades and a covered walkway, from the city gate to a public square. There one might find large public buildings — temples and the palace of the local leader. This public square or agora served as the marketplace and center of public discourse, whether for business and social intercourse or for formal and informal public meetings. Major cities had their own gymnasia, institutions for the education of the children of those elite able to pay the required fees. This provided a chief form of socialization and inculturation in Hellenistic-Roman life. Higher education focused above all on training in rhetoric, the art and techniques of persuasion in public life.

Peasant life might be defined by its relationship to the working of the land. By comparison, the elite, the aristocracy of the city, distanced itself from physical labor. The development of character, of virtue, the exercise of self-sufficiency, and the pursuit of a satisfying life of leisure depended on freedom from manual work. The elite were thus at liberty to engage in civic leadership and public service. Not all wealth was equal, then. Wealth that brought with it high status was "old money" — that is, money tied to the ownership of real capital and gained through inheritance, not through work. Not all city dwellers were of the elite, of course. The agora and small workshops teemed with persons of a variety of professions — leather workers, grocers of various kinds, bakers, and the like. Rather than passing down their wealth from generation to generation, these people trained their children to take on the family business.

In addition to the central role of the family (see below), clubs were prevalent in the Roman cities. These were voluntary associations occasioned by any of a number of needs — religious identity and practices, business or trade, provision for the burial of club members, and so on. Cities, too, were the locus of religion, and various forms of public worship were central to the lives of urbanites. After all, religion was embedded in the political structure of Rome, with leaders often doing double duty as political authorities and priests of the state religion. The rule of the day provided for multiple forms of religious expression, with the state giving sanction to a range of official gods. Among these, the most distinctive would have been the imperial cult itself. Particularly in the East, under Augustus the cult of Rome *(Roma)* was easily transformed into a cult of *Roma* and the emperor, or simply replaced by the cult of the emperor. In this way official religion served to convey official ideology, focusing the loyalty of the provinces on the person of the emperor himself.

2.2.5. Conclusion

As promised, in this section we have been able to paint the picture of the NT world with broad strokes. We have focused thus far on *environmental conditions,* a macro-picture of the general cultural, political, and economic contours of the period. We have seen the degree to which the shape of that world had been determined by the massive, sweeping influence, first of Hellenism in the period following Alexander's conquest and then by the domination of the Roman Empire throughout the Mediterranean basin. As a renewal movement within Judaism,

Christianity took root in the midst of these upheavals, but its shape was also profoundly determined by Jewish commitments that could not simply be swept away by these cultural forces. The possibility of faithfulness to Yahweh and to the law of Moses within the context of these formative historical realities helped to determine the many faces of Judaism in the first century. Consequently, this helped to determine the contours of the Christian movement, which grew out of Second Temple Judaism.

2.3. INSTITUTIONAL CONTEXTS

Having filled in the mural of the larger social-historical context of the NT period, we are now in a position to adjust our lens somewhat more narrowly. In this section we turn to an examination of important *institutional contexts* — that is, the fundamental patterns of behavior characteristic of the world of the NT, together with the organizations that propagated those patterns. By "institutions" we refer to patterns of expected behavior reinforced by social sanctions as well as to those organizational situations in which those behaviors and the discourse surrounding them found embodiment and propagation.[2]

In proposing to deal with "institutions," we should recognize an immediate hurdle. Many people reared in the West are unaccustomed to accounting for the role of institutions in human life and behavior. An almost obligatory antagonism exists between our love affair with individualism and any suitable accounting for the role of institutions in our lives. "We think in the first place that the problem is probably with the individual; if not, then with the organization. This pattern of thinking hides from us the power of institutions and their great possibilities for good and for evil."[3] This pattern of thinking also keeps us from reflecting fully on how God's intervention in the world might condemn or redeem social behavior patterns and their organizational forms — an issue of great consequence in our understanding of the message of the NT.

A second obstacle is our contemporary tendency to segregate life into discrete categories — the economic from the religious, the religious from the political, etc. Hence, we must remind ourselves that we are concerned with the world of the NT, and not our own. We are concerned with the social construction of the world of that time and place, and not with how we might understand the way the world works. How might Jews or Romans have constructed their understanding of the world in which they lived? Recent work, especially in the sociology of knowl-

---

2. Cf. Wuthnow, *Communities of Discourse,* 5-17; Robert N. Bellah, et al., *The Good Society* (New York: Knopf, 1991) 10-11.

3. Bellah, et al., *Good Society,* 11.

edge but also more broadly in cultural anthropology, has underscored the degree to which a people's experience of the world is socially determined, communicated, and conserved. Institutions such as the Roman Empire or the Jewish leadership in Jerusalem are not only built on and belong to that socially constructed understanding of the world, but also actively work to perpetuate that understanding or worldview. Institutions at the center of this "world" come to believe and, indeed, to foster the idea that the way things "are" is the way they are supposed to be, the way they were created to be. God (or the gods) made them this way. Things as they are are divinely legitimated. Political violations are by definition religious, then, just as religious transgressions are political. They upset the moral order, they disturb the proper and regular distribution of power, and they operate according to an alternative and competing understanding of "the world."

What are the fundamental patterns of behavior sanctioned in the world of the NT? What are the organizations that propagate those patterns? An introduction to the issues raised in these questions, with reference to the world of Roman antiquity, will provide a helpful stage for reflecting on how these institutions fare at the hands of the characters and writers of the NT materials.

2.3.1. Power and Sources of Legitimization

In order to illustrate the nexus between the religious and the political, the religious and the economic, the religious and the social, it will be helpful, first, to consider the question of legitimization in the world of the NT. Legitimization is the means by which the possession and exercise of power or the existence of superior status or privilege is justified or sanctioned in a society. It also refers to the boundaries within which power may be appropriately exercised. On what basis are people exercising authority or claiming a position of honor? How does one measure whether particular actions are legitimate? Here we will discuss briefly two examples, both drawn from Judaism and both having significance in the Christian struggle with self-identity *vis-à-vis* Judaism.

2.3.1.1. The Temple: Holiness and Purity

Within Judaism, holiness (as an attribute of God) and purity (without which one could not draw close to God) were interrelated and found their special focus in the Jerusalem temple. This symbolism of the temple and its function in society-at-large is formalized in a rabbinic text that describes degrees of holiness as concentric circles around the Holy of Holies: the land of Israel is more holy than other lands, the walled cities of Israel holier still, the city of Jerusalem holier still, the temple mount holier still, the rampart holier still, the Court of Women holier still,

the Court of the Israelites holier still, the Court of the Priests holier still, the area between the porch and altar holier still, the sanctuary holier still, and the Holy of Holies holiest of all (Mishnah *Kelim* 1.6-9). This emphasis on relative holiness was correlated with considerations of relative purity (or ritual cleanness) and, thus, relative status before God. Lepers, for example, were forbidden to enter the walls of a city (Lev 13:46); hence, walled cities were more holy than the outlying areas. As the abode of God, as the link between the human and the divine, and as inviolable territory, the temple provided the center point around which human life was to be oriented. With its system of restricted spaces, the temple brought together the concepts of holiness and relative purity. Gentiles were to be separated from Jews, then, and Jewish women from Jewish men, Jewish priests from non-priests, and the high priest from other priests. In this way, the temple functioned as the center of the Jewish understanding of the world. It served as the center of the social world, defining what would count as appropriate social interaction.[4]

The architecture of the temple thus provided the visible grounds for social inequality distinguishing different levels of competence (fundamentally by virtue

Herod's temple in the model of first-century Jerusalem at the Holy Land Hotel in Jerusalem (*Joel Green*)

4. This idea of "culture center" has been borrowed from Clifford Geertz, "Centers, Kings, and Charism: Reflections on the Symbolics of Power," in *Local Knowledge: Further Essays in Interpretive Anthropology* (New York: Basic, 1983) 121-46 (122-24).

The Western Wall ("Wailing Wall") in Jerusalem

of birthright!) to come close to the Holy of Holies, God's dwelling place. The centrality of the temple had as its direct corollary the presumed legitimate power of the High Priest and the leading priestly families; they enjoyed the divine sanction that came from access to the court of priests and the temple itself. To priests more broadly belonged the almost exclusive right to perform sacrifices on behalf of the people, to distinguish clean and unclean, and to handle what was set apart to divine service. In the world of the NT, then, a criticism raised against the priesthood was a criticism of the temple, and a criticism of the temple was a criticism of God.

Given the temple's preeminence, what would it mean for Jesus to speak against the temple? How could the Christian movement claim to represent God's purpose if it did not take with utmost seriousness the authority emanating from God's house? In compromising conventional understandings of pure and impure, clean and unclean, did not those early followers of Jesus compromise the temple and call into serious question the divine underpinnings of the world it served? Such questions were not abstractions for Jesus' disciples in the era between Jesus' crucifixion and the destruction of the temple in 70 CE. With the temple standing, the sacrificial system operative, and the priesthood active, how would Jesus' followers comport themselves with regard to the temple? On what authority would they dissolve the social barriers — between Jew and Gentile, but also between priest and lay, male and female — authorized by the temple itself?

2.3.1.2. The Scriptures

The Scriptures were crucial for the self-identity of the Jewish people and for establishing the coordinates of their covenant relationship with Yahweh. Scripture also played a constitutive role in ongoing ethical discourse within Judaism, even if the widely assumed authority of Scripture must be counterbalanced with the diversity of ways in which scriptural texts were employed in such discourse. Pharisees, for example, tended to be more imaginative in their exegesis, Sadducees much less so. Jesus often found himself at odds with his Jewish contemporaries — not on the authority of particular texts but on their interpretation. Similarly, scriptural exegesis in the NT writings, while often recognizably Jewish in form and style, nonetheless often departs from contemporary Jewish interpretation because of Christian preunderstandings related to the relationship of Jesus and/or the church to

---

The Problem of the "Old Testament"

References to the "Old Testament" or even to the "Scriptures of Israel" employ a shorthand that clouds a series of complex issues related to historical ambiguities. First, before there was a "New Testament," there could not yet be an "Old Testament," strictly speaking. If "Old Testament" is an anachronism, however, it is one hardly overcome in historical discussion by reference to the "Hebrew Bible" or the "Hebrew Scriptures." On the one hand, even if a set of Scriptures had been fixed in a *de facto* sense by the first century CE, as seems likely, this does not mean that a canon of Scripture had been formally established by this time. Of course, NT writings sometimes refer to OT books and texts as "Scripture" *(graphē)*, and this suggests that the authority of Scripture was operative even when the parameters of the OT canon had not been established. On the other hand, the use of the expression "Hebrew Bible" in discussions of the early Christian use of the OT founders on the reality that, more often than not, the NT writings employ a Greek translation of the OT (the Septuagint [LXX]), available already from the third and second centuries BCE onward.

Which Bible?

THE HEBREW BIBLE	THE SEPTUAGINT	THE OLD TESTAMENT
Torah	**Law and History**	**The Pentateuch**
Genesis	Genesis	Genesis
Exodus	Exodus	Exodus
Leviticus	Leviticus	Leviticus
Numbers	Numbers	Numbers
Deuteronomy	Deuteronomy	Deuteronomy
	Joshua	
Former Prophets	Judges	**Historical Books**
Joshua	Ruth	Joshua
Judges	1 Kingdoms (1 Samuel)	Judges
Samuel	2 Kingdoms (2 Samuel)	Ruth
Kings	3 Kingdoms (1 Kings)	1 Samuel
	4 Kingdoms (2 Kings)	2 Samuel
Latter Prophets	1 Chronicles	1 Kings
Isaiah	2 Chronicles	2 Kings
Jeremiah	1 Esdras	1 Chronicles
Ezekiel	2 Esdras (Ezra-Nehemiah)	2 Chronicles
The Twelve:	Esther	Ezra
Hosea	Judith	Nehemiah
Joel	Tobit	Esther
Amos	1 Maccabees	
Obadiah	2 Maccabees	**Poetry and Wisdom Books**
Jonah	3 Maccabees	Job
Micah	4 Maccabees	Psalms
Nahum		Proverbs
Habakkuk	**Poetry and Prophets**	Ecclesiastes
Zephaniah	Psalms	Song of Solomon
Haggai	Odes	
Zechariah	Proverbs	**Major Prophets**
Malachi	Ecclesiastes	Isaiah
	Song of Solomon	Jeremiah
Writings	Job	Lamentations
Psalms	Wisdom (of Solomon)	Ezekiel
Job	(Wisdom of) Sirach	Daniel
Proverbs	(Ecclesiasticus)	
Ruth	Psalms of Solomon	**Minor Prophets**
Song of Solomon	Hosea	Hosea
Ecclesiastes	Amos	Joel
Lamentations	Micah	Amos
Esther	Joel	Obadiah
Daniel	Obadiah	Jonah
Ezra-Nehemiah	Jonah	Micah
Chronicles	Nahum	Nahum
	Habakkuk	Habakkuk
	Zephaniah	Zephaniah
	Haggai	Haggai
	Zechariah	Zechariah
	Malachi	Malachi
	Isaiah	
	Jeremiah	
	Baruch	
	Lamentations	
	Epistle of Jeremiah	
	Ezekiel	
	Susannah	
	Daniel	
	Bel and the Dragon	

Israel's ongoing story. The prominent role of the Scriptures in discussion of community identity and ethical formation underscores its legitimating function, even if competing interpretive vantage points meant that different parties might employ the same scriptural texts and images in contradictory ways.

The presence of God in the temple and the purpose of God behind the Scriptures thus became powerful bases for justifying the authority of certain persons (e.g., the High Priest) and the superior status of some persons over others (e.g., Jew versus Gentile). Other sources of legitimization were operative, however, and these were likewise deeply rooted in the collective subconscious of people as they lived out their lives. These shared values are often best brought to the surface in an exploration of particular shared patterns of behavior. In the Mediterranean basin, these would include the central commitment to loyalty and kinship, the relationship between kinship and economic exchange, the web of relationships accorded privilege by the politics of patron-client relations, and the cardinal value of status honor.

2.3.2. (Fictive) Kinship

"Kinship" refers to family relations and alliances; "fictive kinship" broadens this focus somewhat, embracing also those persons who are treated as though they were kin. The first-century world highlighted the role of the community over the role of the individual in a way captured well by the African proverb, "We are, therefore I am." Whereas today someone introducing himself or herself might refer to individual accomplishment, persons in the world of Jesus and Paul might refer instead to their genealogy, their village, their community of reference. Their identities were embedded in their communities, their kin-groups.

The family was the basic social unit of the empire, though by "family" is meant "extended family" or "household" *(domus)*. The *domus* included husband, wife, children, slaves, and others living in the house, and this enlarged sense of family had significant repercussions for the expansive authority wielded by the father *(paterfamilias,* the oldest living male ascendant) and for the transmission of wealth and status. The authority of the Roman father was legendary in the Greco-Roman world. At the birth of his children (whether the child was born to his wife or a slave woman did not matter), he was able to determine whether it would be raised within his household or be given up for adoption, sold, or exposed. His legal authority over the child's life and death continued as long as he lived, and to this should be added his rights to scourge the child, pawn the child, allow or refuse the child's marriage or divorce, maintain the child's property as his own, or sell the child into slavery. Happily, a review of the father's *legal* rights is not necessarily a measure of actual practices. In fact, with the onset of the empire this gruesome picture was mollified as fatherly authority began to be grounded more in affection and devotion rather than cruelty. Nevertheless, tales of physical (including sexual) cruelty are not difficult to locate in the Roman world.

The image of the household was not limited to the extended family. Rome itself was imagined as one household with Caesar as the father of all. This portrait surfaced in the ongoing characterization of the emperor as the sire of his people, their benefactor and savior.

In a father-oriented society like this one, children, like slaves, were among the weakest, most vulnerable among the population. They had little implicit value as human beings, a reality that is perhaps related to the high likelihood that they would not survive into adulthood. Even if women procured their place in the household by bearing children, especially sons, the children themselves were of low status.

Given these realities it may be surprising to find Jesus and NT writers referring to God as father and encouraging the welcoming of children. This is an excellent illustration of how the world in which the NT was written need not be taken for granted within its pages, but might also be qualified, even overturned. An Evangelist like Mark, for example, can undercut authoritarian, father-like practices within the community of believers (e.g., 3:31-34; 9:33-37; 10:13-45), while at the same time portraying God (Abba, Father) as Jesus' intimate and as the one who acts with patience and mercy to bring salvation.

From the classical period images of friendship had been idealized to such a degree that authentic friendship was possible only among social equals who were themselves of sufficient wealth to devote themselves fully to the pursuit of virtue and service. Friendships in this form were to be characterized by mutuality and equality, like-mindedness and mutual affection. More usual in the Greco-Roman world were relationships of a much less idealistic sort, involving intricate webs of obligation. In practice, almost without exception, claims of equality among friends were a charade. As Pliny remarked, someone might have many friends — superior friends, equal friends, lesser friends, and clients — and the cataloging of one's friends into these categories was a function of the relative quantity of their social and economic resources (*Ep.* 7.3.2).

Hence, social nearness and distance — one's social relationships, whether among those who shared blood or who were friends — was symbolized especially in the forms of economic exchange into which people would enter.

2.3.3. Reciprocity and Patronal Piety

The ethics of reciprocity is therefore central to our understanding of social relations in the world of the NT. Two systems of economic exchange are especially characteristic of agrarian life. The first is generalized reciprocity — that is, a transaction characteristic of those who share close kinship ties, whereby the exchange is essentially one-sided, altruistic, the giving of a gift without explicit stipulations for any reciprocation in kind. The second is balanced reciprocity — the direct exchange of goods of approximately equal value within a relatively narrow period of time.[5]

Here, it is important to observe the central role allotted kinship relations, evaluations of social distance and nearness, in everyday life. People in Roman antiquity exhibit a marked concern for determining the boundaries of "our group" and stipulating the nature of appropriate interaction with those outside the group. And how one person behaved toward another economically was a function and symbol of the perceived social relationship between the two. The economic sharing — whether missionary support, almsgiving, or the sharing of community goods — mentioned by various NT voices thus assumes a Christian movement that saw itself as an expanded (fictive) kin-group.

In addition to these two systems of reciprocity, we may refer to the patronage system characteristic of the Mediterranean world — a system of relationships grounded in inequality between the two principals. A patron is one who has resources that are needed by a client. In return, a client can give expressions of loyalty and honor that are useful for the patron.

After the final victory of Octavian in the civil wars, Rome was unified not only under one emperor but also by a political order based on the ethic of patronage. Octavian took for himself the name Augustus, but also other titles. He was *princeps* — that is, *the* patron of the Roman people. He thus conceptualized the empire as a household indebted to him as its head.

Augustus assumed for himself the role of benefactor, a role that during this period was pervasive throughout the empire. Slaves were indebted to their masters, the *paterfamilias* (i.e., the patriarch of an extended family). Sons were under the rule of their fathers. Clients were bound to their patrons, and often had clients of their own. Patrons shared clients. And so on. Seneca observed that the exchange of favor and services in the Roman world bound together human society (*Ben.* 1.4.2). The resulting web of overlapping obligation spread throughout the empire, ultimately with everyone indebted to the emperor as benefactor — either as a result of his direct patronage as emperor or indirectly through networks of obligation that found their way back to him.

But even the emperor was a client of a sort, for the hierarchy of patronal relations extended beyond the sphere of humans to include the gods. The gods had shown favor to Rome, and especially to the *princeps,* the patron, the emperor. Although he was not always regarded as divine, he was certainly the recipient of divine patronage and served as the special envoy of the gods. Thus, the reciprocity of

---

5. For these concepts, and especially the relation of kinship distance to reciprocity variation, see Marshall Sahlins, *Stone Age Economics* (London/New York: Routledge, 1972) 185-230.

patronal relations obligated slaves to masters, sons to fathers, the elite to the emperor, and the emperor, together with all of Rome, to the gods.

In this way, the political order, the binding ethic of patronage, was rooted in the divine. The ethic of obligation found its legitimization in the gods themselves. It was sacred.

2.3.4. Status Honor

Finally, the world of the NT is one in which social status and social stratification are vital considerations. This is not to say that people in Roman antiquity were especially concerned with economic class — for example, as a function of one's relative income or standard of living, or as related to one's relationship to the means of production (as in Marxism). Such matters of industrial and post-industrial society have little meaning in the ancient world. Rather, the social world was defined around power and privilege (see Figure 2.1),[6] and is measured by a complex of phenomena — religious purity, family heritage, land ownership (for nonpriests), vocation, ethnicity, gender, education, and age.

This does not mean that wealth is not a factor in understanding social relations in Roman antiquity. It is, but wealth is not itself the instrument of exchange for securing or advancing one's social position. Wealth was useful if it brought higher status, but it could do so only if it were accompanied by other desirable qualifications. Thus, for example, landed (inherited) wealth was of greater significance than earned wealth, hence the importance of family heritage. Along similar lines, a Jewish priest had high status in his community because he was a priest (assuming he did nothing to jeopardize this standing), an accident of birth, as it were.

The status of Romans was based on the social estimation of their relative honor, the perception of those around them regarding their prestige. One source of honor is *ascription*, a focus on which would suggest that social status is a property of the external world. In this case, honor is ascribed to a person through no merit of his or her own, but is imputed on the basis of one's family heritage, gender, or other inherited attributes (e.g., physical deformities). A second source of honor was *performance*, whereby honor might be gained by means of one's actions — education, marrying well, or other conformity to socially prescribed behaviors. According to texts like Lev 21:16-24 it is evident that priestly communities accorded privilege to ascription, not performance; one was a priest because one was born into a priestly family, but any of a number of inherited physical maladies could lead one to be excluded from the priesthood. According to the NT, the

---

6. Gerhard Lenski, *Power and Privilege: A Theory of Social Stratification* (2nd ed.; Chapel Hill: University of North Carolina, 1984) 284.

Christian community was to throw open the doors previously closed to those excluded because of low ascribed status. Membership in this new community was not related to factors outside one's control; instead, one could surmount such liabilities voluntarily by reorienting one's life around the lordship of Jesus.

2.4. CONCLUSION

All language is culturally embedded, and the language of NT texts provides no exception to this axiom. The writing of a letter like Paul's to the Galatians, for example, assumes shared knowledge often of an unspoken sort. The sociohistorical realities that shape a people's grasp of the world are often assumed in a discourse. Hence, it behooves the contemporary student of the NT writings to develop as much as possible "insider knowledge" of the taken-for-granted world of the NT.

Specific NT texts often draw on a level of background information not available in a brief introductory chapter of this kind. Hence, in the chapters that follow, more specific and detailed information will be mentioned when necessary. Here we have been able to work on a larger canvas, tracing the historical sweep of the cultural traditions and commitments that coalesce in the NT era. In this way, we have been able to underscore repeatedly the level of tension operative in this world, as well as the degree to which people of this world found their identity in their kinship groups and saw and experienced life as an integrated whole. Clearly, for many people living in the English-speaking world today, our cultural experience is not that of the NT world. If we are to appreciate how the message of Jesus and his followers was "good news," we must develop eyes and ears sensitive to the cultural sensibilities of their world.

FOR FURTHER READING

For historical data, the best single source for the world of the NT is Everett Ferguson, *Backgrounds of Early Christianity* (2nd ed., Grand Rapids: Eerdmans, 1993). Individual essays on a range of topics related to the world of the NT are available in standard reference works, such as the following:

David Noel Freedman, ed., *The Anchor Bible Dictionary,* 5 vols. (New York: Doubleday, 1992)

Joel B. Green and Scot McKnight, eds., *Dictionary of Jesus and the Gospels* (Downers Grove: InterVarsity, 1992)

Gerald F. Hawthorne, et al., eds., *Dictionary of Paul and His Letters* (Downers Grove: InterVarsity, 1993)

Ralph P. Martin and Peter H. Davids, eds., *Dictionary of the Later New Testament and Its Developments* (Downers Grove: InterVarsity, 1997)

3. The Nature of the Gospels

Though written later than many of the other NT writings, the four Gospels share a place of prominence in the NT order of books. Located at the beginning of the NT, they point to the centrality of their subject matter, the good news of Jesus Christ, for the biblical witness. Together they propose via the story of Jesus an essential and seamless continuity between the story of Israel and the story of the church. The story of Israel is thus positioned to point toward Jesus, the story of the church to see him as the fountainhead of its character and life. This, of course, is a theological affirmation about the nature of the Gospels, but it is one that has had enormous historical consequences. This is evident not least in discussion over the last two centuries concerning the nature of the Gospels, since interest in the study of Jesus has both assumed and perpetuated certain ways of thinking about their character. Because of the apparent difference in its subject matter, the nature of the Acts of the Apostles has typically been treated as a separate issue. As we will see, however, as a historical narrative Acts shares many affinities with the Gospels and the question of its nature cannot be separated from the issue of theirs (see chapter 7 below).

3.1. JESUS AND THE GOSPELS: MILESTONES

Turning to the first page of the NT raises immediately the question, What is a Gospel? This is because the first four books of the NT claim in their headings to be "Gospels." Even if those titles are not original to these documents but were added decades later as a way of describing how they were to be understood, the issue of the primary attributes of these writings remains.

Palestine in the 1st Century CE

Extent of Herod's kingdom
- Herodian fortress city
○ Decapolis city (time of Herod)
• Other city

Sidon

ABILENE
Abila
ITUREA
Abana R.
Damascus
SYRIA
Mt. Hermon
Pharpar R.
Leontes R.
Caesarea Philippi
Tyre

PHOENICIA
TRACHONITIS
Raphana
L. Huleh
Hazor
R. Jarmok
GALILEE
Chorazin
Capernaum
Bethsaida
GAULANITI
TETRARCHY
OF PHILIP
Ptolemais (Acco)
Gennesaret
Sea of Galilee
Gergesa
Mt. Carmel
Cana
Magdala
Hippos
R.
BATANEA
Sepphoris
Tiberias
Yarmuk R.
AURANITIS
Kishon R.
Nazareth
Mt. Tabor
Gadara
Abila
Mediterranean Sea
Nain

Dor
Megiddo
Caesarea (Strato's Tower)
Scythopolis
Pella
Dion

SAMARIA
DECAPOLIS
Sebaste (Samaria)
Salim?
Gerasa
Mt. Ebal
Jordan R.
Amathus
Mt. Gerizim
Sychar
Jabbok R.
Me-Jurkon
Antipatris (Aphek)
Alexandrium
Joppa
PEREA
Philadelphia (Amman)
(SEMI-INDEPENDENT MUNICIPALITY)

Jamnia
Cyprus
Jericho
Esbus (Heshbon)
Azotus (Ashdod)
Emmaus
Mt. Olivet
Bethany
Jerusalem
Bethany beyond Jordan
Medeba
Bethlehem
Hyrcania
Ashkelon
JUDEA
Herodium
Machaerus
Hebron
Gaza
Adora
Dead Sea
Arnon R.
Raphia
IDUMEA
Masada
Beer-sheba
Arad
NABATEA
Malatha
Besor Br.

Zered Br.

N

0   10   20   30 Miles
0   10   20   30 Kilometers

©MAPQUEST.COM

3.1.1. The (First) Quest of the Historical Jesus

Until the mid-twentieth century, the study of the Gospels, especially those of Mark, Matthew, and Luke, was tied to the study of the historical Jesus. Even though these two areas of exploration have by and large been separated, the questions of history and historicity raised in life-of-Jesus studies continue to influence how the Gospels are read. Hence, it will be useful to provide a brief sketch of the primary contours of the quest of the historical Jesus.

The Quest of the Historical Jesus, now typically referred to as the "First Quest," encompassed the period from the late eighteenth century to the turn of the twentieth. Although the roots of such study can be traced further into the bedrock of the rise of rationalism, the onset of the quest of the historical Jesus is usually dated to the posthumous publication of an essay by H. S. Reimarus (1694-1768), entitled "On the Intention of Jesus and His Disciples," in 1778. Here was the first in a long series of attempts to salvage a historically plausible picture of Jesus from a collection of writings, the NT Gospels, whose supernaturalism, it was alleged, could never be accepted by rational people.

Though not the originator of the Quest, one of its prominent figures was David Friedrich Strauss (1808-74); his "life of Jesus" helpfully indicates how the study of Jesus has assumed and perpetuated certain views regarding the nature of the Gospels. Strauss's primary concern was to repudiate both the belief in the supernatural held by orthodox Christians and the attempts by rationalist scholars to retrieve through reason the historical core of the supernatural events recorded in the Gospels. In Strauss's view, neither approach to the Gospels accounted for their essentially mythic, legendary content. He accepted as historical the basic outline of Jesus' life as the Gospels have it, then argued that this historical skeleton had been fleshed out by the creative imagination of the early church. The church's agenda, he averred, was to show that Jesus was the fulfillment of prophecy, and the church was not opposed to fashioning accounts so as to make clear this connection. If, for example, speculation had it that the Messiah would be a worker of miracles, then the early church would find means for portraying him in this way, irrespective of the availability of corroborative historical data. Hence, for Strauss, the Gospel portrait of Jesus the miracle-worker was the outcome of creative piety, not a vestige of historical reality.

How does one decide what in the Gospels is historical? Strauss asserted, first, that "when the narration is irreconcilable with the known and universal laws which govern the course of events," then such an account is not historical. By "known and universal laws," Strauss would have had reference to Isaac Newton's (1642-1727) laws of motion; these constituted the prevailing scientific view of the world until Newtonian mechanics was undermined in the twentieth century by Albert Einstein. According to Strauss:

The traditional location of Jesus' birth: a cave beneath the Church of the Nativity in Bethlehem. The tradition that Jesus was born in a cave dates back to the second century.

Now according to these laws, agreeing with all just philosophical conceptions and all credible experience, the absolute cause never disturbs the chain of secondary causes by single arbitrary acts of interposition, but rather manifests itself in the production of the aggregate of finite causalities, and of their reciprocal action. When therefore we meet with an account of certain phenomena or events of which it is either expressly stated or implied that they were produced immediately by God himself . . . , or by human beings possessed of supernatural powers . . . , such an account is *in so far* to be considered as not historical.

Consequently for Strauss, accounts of the miraculous or the prophetic and other records of "the intermingling of the spiritual world with the human," being "irreconcilable with all just conceptions," could only be the stuff of inauthentic record. To this first criterion Strauss added the axiom that when one account contradicts another — say, on the question of whether Jesus began his ministry prior to John's imprisonment — one of the two is unhistorical.[1]

The response to Strauss's reading of the Gospels was immediate and, in some cases, quite vitriolic. Nevertheless, his approach is representative of this First

1. David Friedrich Strauss, *The Life of Jesus Critically Examined*, ed. Peter C. Hodgson, tr. George Eliot (Life of Jesus Series; Philadelphia: Fortress, 1972 [1835-36]) 88.

Quest. Like the works of Reimarus and others before and after him, Strauss's work expresses two of the key characteristics of the Quest — namely, an unassailable confidence in reason and a consequent commitment to divorcing religion (or theology) from history. Indeed, what is particularly important about this example from Strauss is the way in which "history" functioned in his analysis. Enlightenment thinking held that all knowledge is historically grounded; as a corollary, the meaning of the Gospel texts was tied to the history to which those texts point — that is, to the life of Jesus understood within his own historical context. Such claims notwithstanding, it is clear that Strauss submitted traditions about Jesus to Strauss's own history, his own understanding of what could and could not have taken place. The portrait of Jesus he presents is thus a Jesus who would not upset the sensibilities of those eighteenth- and nineteenth-century skeptics for whom the world allowed no place for the supernatural.

An important study written near the close of the First Quest illustrates further the choices facing students of Jesus and the Gospels a century ago. This is William Wrede's *The Messianic Secret*, first published in 1901.[2] Though the Gospel of John had figured prominently in the early days of the Quest, in the nineteenth century it had been dismissed as a theological rather than historical account of Jesus. In its place had surfaced the Gospel of Mark — almost universally hailed as the earliest and therefore most historical of the four Gospels. Against this near-consensus, Wrede insisted that Mark was no objective chronicler of history but rather the theologian responsible for broadcasting the idea of the "messianic secret" in the Second Gospel. Why does Jesus urge people not to speak of his messiahship to others? This, according to Wrede, is Mark's way of smoothing over the fact that, during his lifetime, Jesus neither claimed to be the Messiah nor was recognized as the Messiah. Wrede proposed that Mark wove into his Gospel the notion that Jesus secretly revealed his messiahship to his closest followers, who would then make his identity clear to others following his departure. The messiahship of Jesus was thus for Wrede not precisely a Markan invention, since the messianic idea was apparently already present in the tradition, but it was propagated by Mark and, to this degree, the Gospel of Mark belongs properly to the history of doctrine; Mark provides no real view of the historical life of Jesus. After Wrede, many thought that Mark and the other Gospels might provide windows into the beliefs of the early church but could never be employed as source material for recovering the life of Jesus.

What of the promise of rationalism in the study of Jesus? Did it produce the sort of historical certainty proffered by people of the Enlightenment? In surveys of the First Quest of the Historical Jesus, it has become common to observe how

---

2. William Wrede, *The Messianic Secret* (Library of Theological Translations; Cambridge: Clarke, 1971).

Science and the Gospels

Studies of the historical Jesus and assessments of the historicity of the Gospels have been guided in part by common assumptions about the scientific nature of the world. The quest of the historical Jesus has taken place in the context of Sir Isaac Newton's (d. 1727) laws of motion, also known as Newtonian mechanics:

- First Law: "every body perseveres in its state of rest, or of uniform motion in a right [i.e., straight] line, unless it is compelled to change that state . . ." — that is, mass possesses inertia, the tendency to resist any change in its state of motion;
- Second Law: whenever an immobile object is set into motion, or a moving body changes its velocity, a force is responsible; and
- Third Law: for every action there is an opposite and equal reaction.

Theologically, Newtonian mechanics is well suited to a closed universe and has given the impression that the universe is a machine (even if Newton himself regarded his career as a lifelong quest for God). In study of the historical Jesus, Newton's laws of nature have led to the axiom that every natural effect must have a natural cause, so that the miraculous is ruled out from the beginning.

Already in the 1950s, scholars began to explore the effects of the new science on theological understanding. Quantum theory and chaos theory (popularized in movies like *Jurassic Park* or the television series *Star Trek: The Next Generation*) have become potential sources of openness in physical processes. Each in its own way allows for natural unpredictabilities and urges that they be interpreted as signals of an underlying openness in the universe itself. These new horizons in science fund the proposal of divine agency within the cosmos.

"the historical Jesus" had become a convenient mirror for reflecting one's own commitments, as scholars projected their own concerns onto the historical figure of Jesus. In 1906 Albert Schweitzer narrated the history of life-of-Jesus research from the 1770s to 1901 and reached this conclusion. Surprisingly, this awareness of the inherent subjectivity of historical Jesus study did not keep Schweitzer from providing his own portrait of Jesus of Nazareth. In fact, he used the form of a survey of other lives of Jesus as a foil by which to set up his own as the only credible choice.[3]

3.1.2. The New Quest

In the years following Schweitzer, lives of Jesus continued to proliferate, but serious study of the subject had departed from the mainstream of NT study. Some refer to this as the period of No Quest, since it was marked above all by the influential position of Rudolf Bultmann. He taught that it was both impossible and (thankfully) unnecessary to know anything about the life of Jesus of Nazareth, apart from the mere fact (the "that") that he lived. Authentic faith can never rest on historical research, he insisted, for then it would no longer be faith. What is needed instead is an encounter with the Christ of Christian proclamation. This period, which extended into the mid-twentieth century, did not provide any significant alternative understanding of the nature of the Gospels. Even if some scholars like T. W. Manson and Vincent Taylor in Great Britain were strong voices against the skepticism of Bultmann and his substantial following, the basic dichotomy left by the First Quest remained: history *or* theology in the Gospels.

Bultmann's own students were responsible for breathing fresh life into serious historical study of Jesus. Ernst Käsemann, for example, insisted against his former teacher that the early church had indeed been interested in the life of Jesus, or else would not have produced narratives of that life. Others, too, became obsessed with the question of continuity between the man from Nazareth who proclaimed the kingdom and the Christ proclaimed by the early church. Such interests fueled the New Quest, or Second Quest, of the historical Jesus.

At the turn of the twentieth century, Ernst Troeltsch had stepped forward to articulate a disciplined form of historical inquiry. He proposed three principles, and these became axiomatic in the New Quest. First, he insisted on the principle of doubt — that is, that all statements of an historical nature are open to doubt and require corroborative evidence if they are to be accepted. The second was the principle of analogy — that courses of events in the ancient world followed the same internal logic as events in the modern world. Hence, if we do not see adult males walking on water today, then by analogy we would conclude that the Gospel record of Jesus walking on water cannot be regarded as a historical reminiscence. Third, Troeltsch (following the physical laws devised by Isaac Newton) posited the principle of correlation, by which he understood that every event in the natural world is the result of (i.e., most be correlated with) a natural cause. In this manner,

---

3. Albert Schweitzer, *The Quest of the Historical Jesus: A Critical Study of Its Progress from Reimarus to Wrede* (London: SCM, 1954).

the possibility of a miracle was ruled out of court as a presupposition in historical inquiry.

Along with these principles, participants in the New Quest employed a series of criteria honed to demonstrate for each of the sayings or actions attributed to Jesus in the Gospels either authenticity or inauthenticity. Clearly, the fundamental understanding of the Gospels did not shift with the Second Quest. Rather, practitioners continued to speak in terms of peeling back the layers of theological interpretation in the Gospels in order to recover the historical kernel of those accounts. Armed with ever more precise instruments for engaging in such cutting and slicing, scholars in the Second Quest continued to think of history and theology in opposition.

Chief among the criteria employed in the New Quest were multiple attestation and dissimilarity. The first calls to mind images of the courtroom, with witness after witness called to the stand to report on an event. In study of Jesus, a tradition was regarded as (more likely to be) authentic if testimony to it came from multiple independent sources. In one of its most prominent uses, this criterion depends on prior decisions about the nature of the sources used by the Evangelists and about the literary interrelationships shared by their writings (see below). Thus, for example, if a single saying attributed to Jesus could be traced back to more than one more source, this saying, it may be presumed, is more likely to have originated with Jesus. An additional sense in which the criterion of multiple attestation is employed has to do not with *sources* but with *forms.* In this case, if an idea is expressed in multiple forms — whether a saying of Jesus, a parable, a miracle account, or an exemplary story — there is a strong presumption in favor of the attribution of that idea to Jesus. The fundamental historicity of Jesus' instruction on "service," for example, might be supported with reference to the saying in Mark 10:45 ("The Son of man came not to be served, but to serve. . . ."), his parabolic teaching in Luke 12:35-38 (when the master returns from the wedding banquet, he will have the faithful servants sit at the table and serve them), and the footwashing scene in John 13:1-17.

The criterion of dissimilarity gives a bias in favor of authenticity to those traditions about Jesus that are incongruent with Jewish tradition and with the early church. To put it more crassly, according to this criterion the authentic Jesus emerges at those points where he is neither influenced by the Judaism of his world nor influential among his disciples.

Not surprisingly, the Second Quest made almost nothing of Jesus the Jew, nor did it have much to say about the continuity between Jesus and the church or between the historical Jesus and the church's Lord. What is surprising, perhaps, is that, in spite of its precision instruments and related claims of objectivity, in spite of the minimalist portraits of Jesus it produced, the New Quest also proved incapable of spawning a single portrait of the historical Jesus on which all could agree.

Its most notable legacy was its skepticism about our potential for knowing anything about Jesus of Nazareth, not the historical certainty regarding him that it had sought.

The New Quest, which dates roughly from the 1950s to the end of the twentieth century, corresponds both chronologically and conceptually with other transformations in Gospels research. In a way roughly congruent with the notion that the historical Jesus is largely lost to us, study of the Gospels in the early twentieth century was concerned especially with the origin and development of traditions about Jesus. The Gospels were not reservoirs of raw data for the construction of a biography of Jesus, but neither were they coherent narratives endowed with consistent theological perspectives. They were thought of as collages — vignettes pasted together against a background. Following World War II, however, the Gospel writers came to be viewed as more than scissors-and-paste artists, as theologians in their own right. Study of the Gospels, in turn, began to focus on how the Gospel writers had amended and deployed their sources in order to ascertain the nature of their thinking and historical setting. This form of criticism ("redaction criticism," on account of its portrait of the Evangelists as "redactors," that is, as editors of their sources) signaled a shift from the use of the Gospels as windows into the life of Jesus to their use as windows into the life of selected Christian communities in the late 60s CE and beyond.

3.1.3. The Third Quest

Beginning already in the late 1970s and continuing into the present is a Third Quest of the historical Jesus. What immediately distinguishes this one from its predecessors is its transformed (or, at least, transforming) notion of history. Politics, religious experience, economics, etc. — these were sundered from one another in the West during the modern period, but are now increasingly seen as integrated aspects of social existence. Similarly, the reporting of historical events and the writing of historical narratives are increasingly seen as an interpretive, even theological, enterprise. To use the previous analogy, whereas the New Quest sought to peel back the layers of theology to recover the historical core of the Gospel accounts, in the Third Quest it is increasingly granted that no layer is devoid of either history or theology.

Innovations of this sort have led to two related developments. First, the Gospels can be studied each on its own terms as coherent narratives providing a theologically shaped narrative of the career of Jesus. Second, it is held that historical study of Jesus should never see itself as providing *the* single unbiased record of Jesus of Nazareth; rather, such study will always result in more-or-less satisfactory accounts possessing both interpretive and historical force.

Practitioners of the Third Quest have tended to resist the hard-and-fast lines drawn and defended in earlier study of Jesus. As a Jew, Jesus must be seen within the diversity of Jewish beliefs and practices in the Second Temple period. As a teacher with disciples, Jesus must be seen as exercising a formative influence on the community that gathered around him and continued after his crucifixion. As a Galilean, Jesus must have worked within (and against) the cultural realities of everyday experience, and his message must be correlated more intimately with the social, economic, political, and religious realities of his world. From a practical standpoint, these considerations have given rise to the primacy of one question in the Third Quest: Why was Jesus crucified? Any interpretation of Jesus' career and claims that does not lead to his execution on a Roman cross and make socio-historical and theological sense of it cannot be taken seriously, according to the Third Quest.

3.1.4. Conclusion

We can thus see how closely related study of the historical Jesus and attitudes about the nature of the Gospels have been. What remains to be observed, though, is how often those beliefs about the Gospels have been assumed rather than explored. Before the eighteenth century, the simple historicity of the Gospels had indeed been questioned, but scholars largely took for granted the plausibility of their numerous attempts to harmonize those narratives into a single record of the life of Jesus. The outline and basic substance, though only rarely the supernatural content, of one or another Gospel was typically assumed to provide a historical basis for constructing a biography of Jesus in the original Quest. Such optimism was shattered, first, when it became apparent that modern biographers of Jesus had to provide their own interpretive frameworks for the events they recounted — and even further when it became clear that the Gospel writers had done the same. Even if one granted the historicity of individual events in the Gospels (and on these opinions were divided), the narrative framework of the Gospels (including transitional material, summaries, and even the overall "plot" of the individual Gospels) could not be granted this status. And so on the story goes. Recognition of both the importance of these considerations and their status as assumptions led finally to the studied exploration of the question, What is a "Gospel"?

3.2. WHAT IS A "GOSPEL"?

The answer to this apparently simple query is actually quite elusive. For most readers of the NT, a Gospel is a book that narrates the career of Jesus, focusing especially on the nature of his public ministry, his suffering and death, and the empty tomb. Because of our familiarity with this usage, we may be surprised to discover that it was not always so — and that, in fact, there is no reason to imagine that the writers of the Gospels, or Evangelists, saw themselves as creating a new kind of narrative called a "Gospel." It was Justin (d. 165 CE), writing in his *First Apology*, who referred to these documents as "the memoirs of the apostles, which are called Gospels" (66.3).

The term itself, "gospel," is obviously important in early Christianity. For Paul "gospel" or "good news" served as a weighty term for the salvific message of Jesus Christ, and he uses the term in its noun or verb forms more than seventy times. Mark uses it too, and his usage helps to suggest its significance in the early church. Mark 1:1 — "The beginning of the gospel of Jesus Christ, Son of God . . ." — is often translated and regarded as a title either for the Second Gospel or for its

The beginning of the Gospel of Mark and a portrayal of Mark writing in a fifteenth-century Greek manuscript codex *(University of Michigan Library)*

opening. This popular rendering results from a problem in punctuation, however, since the following words, "just as," intimate the closest possible connection between these opening phrases. We may translate as follows:

> The beginning of the gospel of Jesus Christ, the Son of God, as it is written in the prophet Isaiah:
>
> > "See, I am sending my messenger
> >   ahead of you, who will
> >   prepare your way;
> > the voice of one crying out
> >   in the wilderness:
> >   'Prepare the way of the Lord,
> >   make his paths straight.'"   (Mark 1:1-3)

Accordingly, "the beginning of the gospel" is not for Mark the beginning of his book, as though he were referring to it as a "Gospel." This would be a usage for which there would have been almost no precedent. Instead, Mark insists at the outset that, in order to understand the significance of the advent of Jesus Christ, Son of God, one must look first in Isaiah. Not coincidentally, Isaiah uses the term "to proclaim the gospel" or "the gospel that is proclaimed" repeatedly in a profoundly theological sense with reference to the eschatological coming of God and God's dominion. Thus, the messenger of Isaiah 40, the one "crying out in the wilderness," is charged to proclaim, "Your God has come!" (v. 9). Similarly, in Isa 52:7 "bringing the gospel" is set in apposition with "proclaiming peace and salvation" and announcing, "Your God reigns!" By grounding his presentation of the career of Jesus in Isaiah, then, Mark is performing an interpretive move of vast proportions; he signals that the Isaianic hope has come to fruition in the ministry of Jesus. "To believe the gospel" is for Mark to embrace this interpretation of Jesus and reorient one's life accordingly (Mark 1:14-15).

Mark, then, did not refer to his book as a "Gospel," and the other Evangelists are no more helpful in this regard. Matthew identifies his writing as a "book" (Matt 1:1), Luke describes his as a "narrative" (Luke 1:1), and John employs no such label.

All of this is to say that the term "gospel" is not self-interpreting as a reference to a "book" or "document." At the same time, prior usage of this word with reference to the act and content of Christian proclamation suggests that the documents to which we now refer as "Gospels" were seen as the proclamation of Jesus in written form. It is certainly significant, then, that early Christian usage referred to the first four books of the New Testament simply with the titles, "According to Mark," etc. According to this reckoning, there existed only one "gospel," though it might represented in four ways.

In the larger Roman world, "gospel" refers above all to the announcement of good news, such as victory in battle or the birth of a child. Interestingly, the birthday of the emperor Augustus is known to have been regarded as the beginning of good news for the whole world — a fact that would not have been lost on those who expressed their allegiance to Jesus, and not Caesar, as Lord.

What, then, is a "Gospel"? One helpful way of addressing this question is to imagine a librarian in an ancient center of learning like Alexandria. Given a copy of one of these early Christian documents, where would he shelve it? Speaking generally, he would have been faced with three choices. As a narrative text (rather than, say, a philosophical treatise or poetry) within the first-century world of books and readers, the available options would have been historiography and biography, which take as their respective focus events that happened and people who lived, and novel, which possesses no necessary historical referent. Most now see the Gospels as conforming most closely to the genre of biography.

Plutarch on "Biography"

Plutarch (45-125 CE) wrote fifty biographies of prominent Greek and Roman men, and in the first chapter of his *Alexander* he reflected on his approach:

> In writing for this book the life of Alexander the king . . . I have before me such an abundance of materials that I shall make no other preface but to beg my readers not to complain of me if I do not relate all of his celebrated exploits or even any one in full detail, but in most instances abridge the story. I am writing not histories but lives, and a man's most conspicuous achievements do not always reveal best his strength or his weakness. Often a trifling incident, a word or a jest, shows more of his character than the battles where he slays thousands, his grandest mustering of armies, and his sieges of cities. Therefore as portrait painters work to get their likenesses from the face and the look of the eyes, in which the character appears, and pay little attention to other parts of the body, so I must be allowed to dwell especially on things that express the souls of these men, and through them portray their lives, leaving it to others to describe their mighty deeds and battles.

But attempts to characterize the Gospels as biographies of Jesus require important caveats. First, the designation "biography" is better suited to Matthew, Mark, and John than Luke since the Third Gospel is actually the first of a two-volume narrative comprising Luke and Acts — or, as it is often labeled, Luke-Acts. As will become clear in chapter 7, Luke-Acts is best understood as an example of historiography rather than biography. The difference implied by this distinction is not extreme, since biography as a genre grew out of the practice of historiography as particular persons, rather than "the great deeds of men," became the focus of study and writing. Early on, biographies, like historiography, proceeded along roughly chronological lines; with time, however, these "lives" were arranged topically.

Second, it is not enough to analyze the character of the Gospels by comparing them simply with contemporary Greco-Roman literature. This is because of the self-consciously Jewish orientation of these works. Even if no OT books have the form of the Gospels, parts of some of those books, such as the Abraham-cycle or the Elijah-accounts, are suggestive precursors. A complete accounting for the character of the Gospels cannot overlook the important influence of OT and subsequent Jewish historiography, not least in their shared undertaking to represent the outworking of the divine will in historical narratives.

Third, we would be mistaken to imagine that, by "biography," we should understand this form of literature, or genre, as analogous to contemporary expressions of the genre. Psychological motivations, childhood influences, physical appearance, date of birth — these and other data figure prominently in our expectations of contemporary biography but have little or no role to play in the Greco-Roman world. In antiquity a biography related the significance of a famous person's career, rarely focusing on his childhood but often including reference to the way he died (for how a person died was regarded as a measure of his character). Moreover, "famous" persons acquired their fame not through their individuality or idiosyncratic behavior. The modern, Western conception of individuality has little place in Roman antiquity, where the identity and importance of persons were determined in relation to their groups of reference. Thus, an individual might be represented in a biography because he exemplified the qualities valued by society. One of the reasons for regarding the NT Gospels as having been written primarily for Christian communities rather than as evangelistic tools for non-Christians is the degree to which they assume that their readers have begun already to adopt the unconventional values proclaimed and lived by Jesus.

Finally, it is worth remembering that, as narratives, the Gospels are especially well suited to including a host of other literary forms, including parables, birth stories, genealogies, farewell discourses, sermons, and many others. This fact is important for understanding the growth of the Gospel-tradition leading up to the weaving of these narratives. It is also important since each of these other literary forms invites particular approaches to reading and interpretation (see below).

If our Alexandrian librarian were to place, say, the Gospel of Matthew among other examples of ancient biography, what might this entail for those who found it on the shelf? What expectations might they bring to it? Several points come to mind: (1) an unveiling of Jesus' public life along chronological and/or topical lines (2) indicating by what standards and how Jesus was to be accorded the status of one deserving biographical treatment; (3) a commitment on the part of the author to holding in abeyance the temptation for wholesale creation of events; (4) an overall interpretive aim guiding the framing of events into sequences of cause and effect; and (5) a presentation of Jesus that, to some significant degree, presents him and his behavior as exemplary for readers.

3.3. THE GOSPEL TRADITION

None of the Gospels is a signed document, and this bespeaks their traditional nature. Indeed, the very concept of "authorship," denoting individual responsibility for a literary product, largely taken for granted in modern society, is problematic when projected into ancient societies. Although it is possible to speak of an "author" with primary responsibility for the final form of the Gospel narratives, it must also be remembered that the materials woven into that narrative predate those narratives. Assuming that Jesus' crucifixion can be dated into the early 30s CE, some thirty-five to seventy years would have passed before the final composition of the NT Gospels; hence, one of the questions that has occupied students of Jesus and the Gospels is how best to account for those intervening years.

3.3.1. Oral Transmission

The events to which the Gospels witness date for the most part to the late 20s or early 30s, though the birth and infancy material in Matthew 1–2 and Luke 1–2 belongs mostly in the period of approximately 6-4 BCE. Given Jesus' status as a teacher, his popularity as an itinerant prophet, and his investment in a circle of disciples, it is certain that during his public career (1) his sayings and especially his deeds were the stuff of ordinary rumor transmission and (2) his teaching would have been subject to reminiscence and recitation by those who shared closest in his work. The latter reflects the well-documented practice of Jewish pedagogy at several levels, while the former belongs to the essence of village life. We who have been reared in literate societies have learned to depend on notes and books and computers for the preservation and maintenance of our memories, so it is difficult for us to appreciate modes of transmission in oral cultures. Nevertheless, these are two modes of oral transmission that are well documented in Jewish and Christian sources of the period (as well as in oral cultures more generally).

A further form is just as certain to have played an important role in the preservation and handing on of Jesus-material. This is the informal but controlled transmission of Jesus' sayings and deeds within the communities that formed around or on the basis of his ministry. Some believers would have passed on the tradition in the context of worship. For example, it is likely that accounts of Jesus' death and its interpretation in light of the OT Scriptures took form in the context of worship and, especially, the practice of the community meal in which Jesus' words and deeds at the Last Supper were remembered (see 1 Cor 11:23-26). The formation of communities would also have provided the arena for transmittal of Jesus-material — whether in the form of baptismal practices or for the purpose of general instruction, on the analogy of Jewish pedagogical practices or in order to prescribe appropriate behavior within the community. That is, accounts of Jesus' sayings and deeds would have been used to develop and propagate the identity of the community and to maintain its boundaries. These contexts need not have had the formality of the gymnasium or school, but those authorized by age or experience in the community would have carried the responsibility of ensuring the accuracy of the recitation and thus the stability of the tradition.[4]

How the oral tradition coalesced to the point of inclusion in the NT Gospels and continued to develop even after the writing of the Gospels will always be a matter of speculation. What is certain is that there existed in both Jewish and wider Greco-Roman societies the means for accurate transmission of oral materials, even if we can only hypothesize about when, by whom, and how closely these protocols were followed in the case of the Jesus-tradition. Given the conventional association of pools of tradition with key figures in a movement, however, it is probable that certain traditions converged around such figures as Peter, James the brother of Jesus, Mary Magdalene, and others. No doubt, much of the material associated with these figures would have overlapped, while others contributed to the uniqueness of their circles. Such traditions and collections of traditions, then, would have been shaped by and given shape to the beliefs and practices regarded as normative in those circles. Undoubtedly, some Jesus-materials would have increased in importance in the context of competing views of faithfulness to Jesus' message of the kingdom. In this way, formative Christianity would have mirrored somewhat the unity and diversity of the Second Temple Judaism of which it was a part — a unity and diversity that is now reflected among the NT Gospels.

4. See the discussion in Kenneth E. Bailey, "Information Controlled Oral Tradition and the Synoptic Gospels," *Themelios* 20 (1995) 4-11.

3.3.2. Sources and the Synoptic Gospels

In its preface, the Third Gospel makes reference to the presence of other "narratives" of "the events that have been fulfilled among us" (Luke 1:1-4). Luke thus provides a clear witness to the existence of other written accounts, but otherwise provides no hints as to their content. Scholars today differ markedly regarding the nature of the sources available to the Evangelists — for example, with some positing one or more written "sayings sources," some urging the view that an account or accounts of Jesus' suffering and death took written form already in the 30s or 40s, and others arguing that none of these had achieved *written* form prior to the writing of the first Gospel.

Examination of the Gospels themselves, however, makes it clear that common sources were employed by two or more of the Evangelists, and that the first three Gospels share some sort of literary relationship. Matthew, Mark, and Luke share a high degree of similarity of content. (Their commonality has given rise to their being labeled "Synoptic" Gospels, having a "common view.") The Gospel of Mark has less than thirty verses unique to it, so that more than 95 percent of the Second Gospel appears also in Matthew or Luke or both. This fact alone suggests that Mark either knew and used the First and Third Gospels as sources in an attempt to combine them, or that Matthew and Luke each made use of Mark.

Additionally, these Gospels

Luke 16:9-21 in Bodmer Papyrus XIV (𝔓75), ca. 175-225 CE *(Bodmer Library, Geneva)*

share a common structure, following a common chronological order. Most important, though, is the startling similarity in vocabulary and literary style in those many sections where the Synoptic Gospels coincide in content. Why is this remarkable? (1) Even though Jesus spoke primarily in Aramaic and reports of his deeds and teaching would have circulated originally in Aramaic, the Synoptic Gospels register a high degree of verbal similarity in Greek. (2) Unlike English, where word order is closely monitored, in Greek the order of words is quite free and irregular. Yet, commonality extends not only to word choice but to word sequence, repeatedly. (3) The possibility that three authors, writing at different times and in geographically diverse settings around the Roman Empire, would use the same language in the same order in account after account is minute. Evidence of this sort has led to the conclusion that the Synoptic Gospels share a literary relationship.

The possibilities for Synoptic relationships are several, but three scenarios are championed today. (1) Mark wrote the earliest Gospel, which was then used independently by both Matthew and Luke; both Matthew and Luke had access to a further Sayings Source, called "Q" (from the German word for "source": *Quelle*), as well as to additional materials, whether oral or written. This is the Two-Document Hypothesis. Those who prefer to think of Matthew's third source as a written one sometimes abbreviate it as "M"; similarly, Luke's third source can be referred to as "L." Accordingly, the Two-Document Hypothesis is expanded to become the Four-Document Hypothesis.

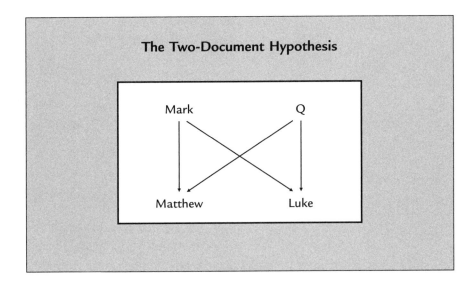

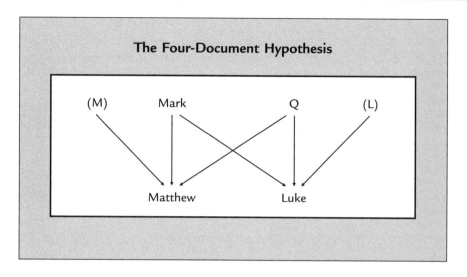

(2) In recent years, the nature and existence of Q has received a great deal of attention. Some have gone so far as to refer to Q as an extant source — presumably a hyperbole chosen to urge the certainty of the existence of a saying source shared by Matthew and Luke. Among the most ardent supporters of the existence of Q are some scholars who believe they have discerned layers of tradition in Q itself. Accordingly, they speak of a series of recensions of the sayings source, and attribute each version to a particular community of Jesus' followers. Not everyone is convinced, however. Many accept the theory that Mark was written first (a view referred to as "Markan Priority"), but either deny altogether the existence of Q or

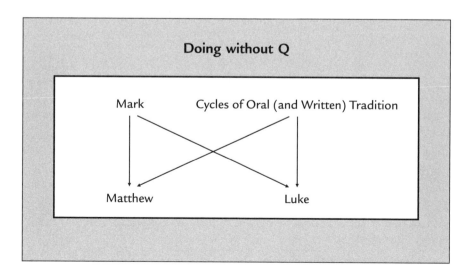

continue to speak of Q only as a collection of Jesus' sayings without insisting that this collection was written or that it had achieved anything resembling a fixed form. These first two theories of Synoptic relationships are closely related and together have attracted the support of the vast majority of scholars.

(3) For centuries it was understood that the Gospel of Matthew, which appears first in the NT, must also have been the first Gospel to be written. Mark, then, used Matthew and Luke used Mark. More recently, a number of scholars have embraced the view that Matthew was the first Gospel, that Matthew was used by Luke, and that Mark employed both Matthew and Luke as sources. This view is usually referred to as the Griesbach Hypothesis, due to its advocacy by J. J. Griesbach in the eighteenth century.

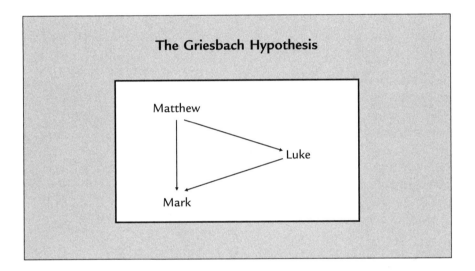

This view has not won widespread support due to a number of weaknesses — especially (a) the difficulty in imagining that Mark would have used the First and Third Gospels but would have neglected to include in his book reference to Jesus' birth and infancy, to Jesus' post-resurrection appearances, and to much of his teaching (the Beatitudes, for instance); and (b) the lack of evidence in earliest Christianity of a perceived need for a document like Mark, the sole purpose of which, under this hypothesis, is to alleviate the tension between the Gospels of Matthew and Luke. Indeed, the fact that the NT in its canonical form has not one but four Gospels is evidence enough that placing these documents side-by-side, in spite of or perhaps even because of their differences, did not constitute an insurmountable obstacle.

The discussion surrounding the existence of Q is more difficult to assess. The

most pressing evidence in its favor is the number of close verbal agreements between Matthew and Luke that are not shared with Mark. These might be explained
by the possibility that Luke used Matthew (the notion that Matthew used Luke has
rarely been proposed). But Luke's treatment of Matthew could then only be described as implausible. What has happened to the major teaching sections in the
First Gospel, for example? What is more, one finds little evidence that Luke has
amended the Gospel of Mark in ways that Matthew has done — suggesting that
Luke used this material as it came to him from Mark and not as it would have been
mediated by Matthew. According to the data available to us from the First and
Third Gospels, the Q-tradition would have consisted of at least 230 verses —
mostly sayings of Jesus devoid of marks of setting or context — but whether this
tradition comprised a secure, written document remains a matter of speculation.

During most of the twentieth century the study of the Gospels proceeded on
the basis of one or another of these hypotheses regarding the relationships among
the Synoptics. Such work has become increasingly problematic because of growing unease with all of these scenarios. The search for simple lines of transmission
has given way in some circles to a recognition of the possibility of more and more
complex veins of tradition, with oral and written materials circulating side-by-
side and interacting in now untraceable ways. Although these developments in the
conversation have not undermined the basic assumption that Mark was the
earliest Gospel to be written, they have opened the door to wider circles of influence as accounts of Jesus' actions and teaching were put to use in the formation of
communities seeking, sometimes in debate with each other, to be faithful to their
Lord.

3.3.3. The Gospel of John and the Synoptics

Although the question of the relationship between the Fourth Gospel and the Synoptics will resurface in chapter 7, a brief comment is relevant now. The differences
between the Gospels of Matthew, Mark, and Luke on the one hand and John on
the other have attracted attention for centuries. According to the church historian
Eusebius, Clement of Alexandria remarked early on that, whereas the historical
data had already been provided, John set out to compose a "spiritual Gospel"
(*Hist. Eccl.* 4.14.7). Of course, in general outline the Gospel of John bears some
similarity to the Synoptics, but only in the most general sense: Jesus' public career
precedes his suffering and death, and so on. Closer scrutiny reveals, for example,
that material located toward the end of Jesus' career in the Synoptics, especially as
this pertains to Jesus' work in Jerusalem, has in several cases been moved forward
and scattered throughout the Fourth Gospel. Again, the parables of Jesus in the
Synoptics and the tradition of Jesus' proverbs have been replaced in John by

lengthy and well-developed sermons. In the end, the degree of overlap between the Gospel of John and the other NT Gospels is less than ten percent.

In the last two centuries, observations of this sort have led almost all students of the Gospels to posit Johannine independence from the Synoptic Gospels. Those few points where there is significant overlap, such as the accounts of the anointing of Jesus prior to his passion, are typically explained with reference to common sources rather than to John's use of the Synoptic Gospels (and Mark in particular) as sources. If one allows for the continuing influence of oral and written tradition following the writing of the first Gospels, this is a plausible theory. Others have begun to proffer a mediating view, suggesting that it is unthinkable that the Fourth Evangelist, writing near the end of the first century, would have been unaware of his predecessors. According to this line of thinking, John knew the other Gospels but, being motivated by different interests, did not employ them *as sources*.

3.3.4. Conclusion

Our agenda in this survey has been not so much to reach certainty on Gospel relationships as to suggest how the NT Gospels came to be. Much of what we might want to know about sources and traditions and literary interrelationships is unknowable, at least with certainty, so that the best we can do is to produce and examine theories about them. Even in the absence of certitude on such details, however, we can move forward on the basis of some conclusions. Most importantly, we can with good reason imagine the development of lines of tradition grounded first in events in the life of Jesus, then shaped and recited in oral and written reminiscence before they were recorded in the Gospels. It is true that each stage of the transmission process was capable of adding interpretive nuance to these accounts, but this is only to admit what we have already seen — namely, that history is always understood in relation to communities of record. It is also clear that the Evangelists were themselves links in the ongoing chain of transmission, so that their accomplishments in narrating the story of Jesus must be viewed within the context of those communities of Jesus' followers for whom those accounts were significant.

3.4. LITERARY FORMS IN THE GOSPELS

The importance of our discussion of the genre of the Gospels has rested largely on the implications of the recognition of genre for interacting with and interpreting a text. One will naturally employ different reading protocols when confronted with a theological treatise and an allegorical novel. Genres develop over time, coming to represent conventional and repeatable patterns of discourse that assist communication among people in particular sociohistorical settings. In the case of the Gospels, we can recognize both how they participate in ways of writing conventional in their day — in the case of Matthew, Mark, and John, biography, while in the case of Luke-Acts, historiography — and, at the same time, take advantage of the flexibility inherent in all genres or literary forms in order to bring content and form into concord. That is, the *content* of the Gospels, their focus on Jesus of Nazareth and his message, helped to shape their *form,* to bring more into the foreground the basis of their story in the history and Scriptures of Israel.

One of the special geniuses of narrative is that individual narratives are capable of playing host to many other forms of discourse. When approaching a narrative text, then, one is interested initially in the question, What sort of narrative is this? But then the reader must give attention also to this narrative's constitutive subgenres or literary forms. These, too, invite particular expectations and reading protocols; each contributes to the overall interpretation of the narrative at the same time that the meaning of each is constrained in part by its location within the larger narrative. Within the Gospels, numerous subgenres might be named — for example, genealogy, symposium, type-scene, farewell discourse, passion narrative, summary, and parable. This is only a partial list, but these are representative. (The particular challenge of the speeches in Acts will be discussed in chapter 9.)

3.4.1. The Genealogy

Both Matthew and Luke include genealogies of Jesus in their Gospels (Matt 1:1-17; Luke 3:23-28), and the importance of ancestry is marked in other, less formal ways (e.g., Luke 1:5, 27). At its most abstract, a genealogy is a record of relationships of descent. In reality, though, genealogies serve important social roles since they provide the basis for membership in particular groups of kin. For this reason, in Israel's history, in the Greco-Roman world, and in many contemporary cultures genealogies are not marked by strict biological accuracy, but serve instead to structure history, to mediate status and power, and so on. In some cases, certain ancestors or groups of ancestors can simply be dropped from genealogical lists, or records can be adjusted to reflect better the needs of a contemporary social and kinship structure. Readers of genealogical records, then, typically must navigate between the actual and the ideal in the structures of ancestral relationships.

In the Gospel of Matthew, for example, the opening genealogy purposefully fashions the history of Israel into sets of fourteen and draws special attention to Jesus' royal, Davidic lineage. Surprisingly, five women are included in his record — surprising since women would not ordinarily have been included and all the more since the intrusion of these names into the genealogy rehearses aspects of Israel's past that some might think should best be forgotten. Some are noted in Israel's history for their promiscuity and others as non-Israelites, so it is obvious that they were not added to enhance Jesus' stature. Rather, their inclusion helps to communicate something about the nature of the good news of Jesus' coming.

Genealogies often move from the eldest to the most recently born. Luke's moves in the opposite direction, from Jesus back to "Adam, son of God." The key to making sense of the purpose of Luke's ancestral list lies not so much in the patterns and numbers, as in Matthew's Gospel, as in the surrounding emphasis on Jesus' identity. In the infancy narrative Jesus was announced as "Son of God" (Luke 1:32, 35), a role he embraces already at age twelve in the temple (2:49). At Jesus' baptism, God himself identifies Jesus as his Son (3:21-22), and this is followed immediately by Jesus' genealogy. Not coincidentally, Luke introduces his ancestral record by observing that Jesus was thought to be what he was not — namely, the son of Joseph. Afterwards, Jesus is led by the Spirit into the wilderness where the devil tests him with regard to the nature of his sonship (4:1-13). Luke's agenda to have his audience recognize that Jesus' status as Son of God is thus paramount, and the literary form of "genealogy" is employed to this end.

Elsewhere, too, in the Gospels and in Paul, concern with ancestral heritage can play a similar role of providing indications of status and kinship (e.g., Luke 1:5; Phil 3:5).

3.4.2. The Symposium

Especially in the Third Gospel the literary portrait of the Greco-Roman symposium has been woven into the narrative of Jesus' career. In contemporary practice and literature, the symposium was the second course of a banquet, a drinking-and-talking party. Typically, symposia were characterized by a common cast of characters: the host, usually noted for his wealth and/or wisdom, the chief guest, notable for his wit and wisdom, and others, who might participate to varying degrees in the discussion. Symposia also possessed a typical structure, moving from the identification of the guests, to an action or event that determines the topic or introduces the topic of the day, to the discourse itself. The symposium was also characterized by an etiquette suited to it. As with meals in general, those on the invitation list consisted of persons (typically men) whose presence would preserve and enhance the status of the host. In addition, guests were placed around the outside of a U-shaped table, reclining at the table in positions that marked their relative status. Such a public representation of status was not to be the subject of conversation, however, since the symposium was marked by its role as a friend-making meal, where table talk was to nurture good relations, not divisiveness.

Read against this literary-cultural backdrop, several of Luke's accounts come

Plutarch on "Table Talk"

Plutarch (45-125 CE) is famous for his almost eighty essays on moral philosophy and religion, including "How to Distinguish a Flatterer from a Friend" and "Advice to Married Couples." Here he notes the importance of what happens around the table:

My brother Timon, upon an occasion when he was host to a considerable number of guests, bade them each as they entered take whatever place they wished and there recline, for among those who had been invited were foreigners as well as citizens, friends as well as kinsmen, and in a word, all sorts of people.

Now when many guests were already assembled, a foreigner came . . . and when he had run his eyes round the guests who had settled in their places, he refused to enter, but withdrew and was on his way out when a number of the guests ran to fetch him back, but he said that he saw no place left worthy of him.

[Plutarch's father observed] If he had arranged the placing of his guests at the beginning, as I told him to do, we would not be under suspicion of disorderliness and liable to public audit under the rule of a man skillful "in marshaling horses and shield-bearing men."

Thus it is ridiculous for our cooks and waiters to be greatly concerned about what they shall bring in first, or what second or middle or last — also, by Zeus, for some place to be found and arrangement made for perfume and crowns and a harp-girl, if there is a girl — yet for those invited to this entertainment to be fed at places selected haphazardly and by chance, which give neither to age nor to rank nor to any other distinction the position that suits it, one which does honor to the outstanding man, leaves the next best at ease, and exercises the judgment and sense of propriety of the host. [Plutarch responds:] . . . but if we humble some of them and exalt others, we shall rekindle their hostility and set it aflame again through ambitious rivalry. (*Moralia* ["On Table Talk"] 1.2 §§1-5, LCL)

into sharper interpretive focus — pointing most notably to Jesus' open practices at the table, indicating his willingness to share the table with persons of low status, even women (see Luke 5:27-32; 7:36-50), his unconventional discourse to his table companions, urging them not to concern themselves with status-seeking and positions of honor (14:1-24), and the outrageous behavior of his followers, who argue over greatness at the table (22:24-27).

3.4.3. The Type-Scene

Type-scenes are episodes that occur at critical moments in a character's life that are comprised of an established pattern of motifs. In the Gospels, type-scenes are often in evidence in the way the Evangelists make use of OT patterns, though a Gospel writer is also capable of forming his own repeated scenes. The birth narratives in the First and Third Gospels are interesting in this respect, since the attentive reader easily picks up reverberations from earlier stories in the recounting of Jesus' birth. The elements — announcement of birth, name of child, future of the child — appear in Gen 16:7-13; 17:1-21; 18:1-15; Judg 13:3-20; Matt 1:20-21; Luke 1:11-20, 26-37; 2:9-12. Similarly, one finds in the Gospels scenes of commission that borrow from OT precedents (see Judg 6:14; Jer 1:7-10), the familiar man-meets-woman-at-the-well type-scene (see John 4:1-42), and so on. In the Third Gospel, Luke establishes and repeats a pattern concerning Jesus' practices at the table that lead one to interpret one scene in light of the other (see Luke 5:27-32; 15; 19:1-10).

Once they are recognized, type-scenes are important in two related ways. First, they establish expectations on the part of the reader, helping her to anticipate what might come next. Thus, when we hear that Elizabeth and Zechariah are old and childless, we may immediately wonder if they, like Sarah and Abraham, will be the recipients of divine benefaction in the form of a miraculous pregnancy. On the other hand, patterns can be employed precisely in order to subvert expectations. Sometimes a writer will provide telltale reminiscences of a type-scene in order to surprise the reader with a sudden, unexpected turn in the account.

3.4.4. The Farewell Discourse

The farewell discourse is a literary form known in the OT and in both Jewish and Greco-Roman literature. In the OT, farewell discourses are attributed to Jacob (Genesis 48–49), Moses (Deuteronomy 31–34), Joshua (Joshua 23–24), and others. Generally, the elements of the farewell discourse include the following: reference to approaching death, gathering of one's kin or followers, review of one's life, exhortation, predictions, and warnings, and blessing and final prayer. In NT narratives, farewell discourses are discernible in Luke 22, John 13–17, and Acts 20:17-38. Their purpose is always to instruct those who remain behind, but, in doing so, the farewell discourse can also take on the form of a defense of the one saying farewell. In such cases, though, even this serves to underscore the fundamental values and practices that the ongoing community should embrace. The particular significance of the farewell discourse lies most pointedly in the fact that it reports the honored person's *last words,* allowing the sum of that person's message to be capsulated into one teaching moment of special gravity.

3.4.5. The Passion Narrative

Each of the Gospels devotes significant sections of its narrative to an account of Jesus' suffering and death (Matthew 26–27, Mark 14–15, Luke 22–23, John 12–19). In doing so, they obviously bring into the foreground the centrality of Jesus' death for the narration of God's intervention in history to bring good news, and they do so by drawing on what would have been a well-worn literary form. This is the "story of the vindication of the innocent sufferer" found in the OT and in subsequent Jewish literature. Set against a legal or royal setting, the chief characters in these accounts are recognized for their outstanding qualities; their lives are endangered, often through malicious scheming; even though they are innocent, they suffer persecution; and, finally, they are vindicated. Examples of this literary form include the accounts of Joseph in Genesis 37–42 and the book of Daniel. Early on in representations of this form, rescue and vindication came prior to death, but in the literature of the Maccabean period rescue and vindication might be postponed to come after, and through, death (see 2 Maccabees 7 and Wisdom 1–2, 4).

These narratives participate in a large and probing literature in Israel and Judaism having to do with the suffering of the righteous. This depository of texts included the psalms of the suffering righteous (see especially Psalm 22) and the song of the Servant of Yahweh in Isa 52:13–53:12, a text that combines the twin motifs of vindication of the innocent and effective death on behalf of others. The passion narratives of the Gospels have their roots deeply intertwined with these and other Scriptures, which contributes depth of significance and interpretation within the redemptive plan of God to the shameful, horrific death of Jesus on a Roman cross.

3.4.6. The Summary

Though the "summary" has an important role in the Gospels, it is not so much a subgenre or literary form as it is a literary device. "Summary" is one of the many ways of marking time in a narrative. Sometimes, when the narrator wants to slow down the process of reading and draw special attention to a scene, more detail will appear in the narrative, more time indicators, more words, more background, more color, and the like. But with the summary the narrator uses far less narrative space to relate the passing of time and occurrence of events. The Evangelists employ summaries often to provide transitions from one scene to the next and to provide important background information (e.g., Mark 1:45). What is crucial for readers of the Gospels and Acts, though, is the way "summary" serves to emphasize what is "typical" in the narrative (e.g., Luke 8:1-3; Acts 2:42-47). One can generally assume that practices mentioned in narrative summaries have the force of habits; though mentioned only once or twice, they actually sketch what is characteristic and pervasive.

3.4.7. The Parable

In spite of decades of serious study, the nature of parables continues to elude the grasp of students of Jesus and the Gospels. In part, this is because of the desire on the part of interpreters to lasso into a single definition what actually appears in the Gospels as a multifaceted phenomenon. In part, it is also due to our distance from the world of Jesus' parables, so that their substance easily escapes us. We often think of parables as short example stories. Although this is one possible meaning, the term "parable" might just as easily be used in the Gospels with reference to a proverb or axiom, a brief comparison, a simile, a lesson drawn from everyday life, or metaphorical language in general. Often key to the definition of "parable" is the notion of "parabolic" — that is, employing what is known in order to provide insight into what is not known. In the end, though, this is not a very helpful way to think about "parable" because of the inherently metaphorical nature of all language; referring to the metaphorical role of parable tells us little that is unique to parable. It is true in the case of Jesus' teaching, though, that we may have a difficult time moving with the parable from "what is known" to "what is unknown" because what the parable presumes is no longer so well "known." Unfortunately, our unfamiliarity with some or many of the sociohistorical referents of parables has led sometimes to a desire to make sense of all parabolic teaching as though they were best appreciated as allegories referring to God, Jesus, and humanity. Here is one of those arenas where greater familiarity with the first-century world of Jesus and the Gospels can be particularly beneficial.

As a *literary form,* "parable" is nevertheless capable of greater definition. *Generally,* a parable is an imaginative story — possessing a beginning, a middle, and an end — developed from the stuff of everyday life and related for its pedagogical value. Parables *may* point beyond themselves, evoking the larger story of God-human relations, or they *may* depend for their message simply on people applying the lessons of everyday life to the life of discipleship. Luke in particular rehearses parables of Jesus where the audience is best served simply by hearing the story: You know how it is in the world out there, Jesus says; why have you not learned to apply what you know to life before God (e.g., Luke 16:1-9)? *Sometimes,* the parable communicates by introducing into the narration a surprising twist, the introduction of the unexpected or the relating of the unconventional in order to provoke the audience to reflect more deeply on the story's meaning — and on the nature of all reality. Such parables often embody and sponsor an alternative vision of the world and of life before God. *Often* parables are not oriented toward passing on cognitive lessons as much as toward effecting responses. They are not words of comfort. "The parables make a backdoor assault on the familiar worlds in which people live with God, with a lightning speed that the evasive heart of the listener is hard put to match."[5]

3.4.8. Conclusion

Parables, passion narratives, and the rest — these are only a selection of the literary forms embraced by the Gospel narratives. To these others might have been added — miracle stories, hymns, call narratives, and pronouncement stories, for example. Ongoing interaction with the Gospels will build one's sensitivities to these subgenres, as well as develop one's ability to interpret them.

In reading the Gospels and Acts, however, it is also important to remember that these forms are contained within the larger narrative, which constrains how they are to be interpreted. Or, to be more precise, these smaller literary forms help to give meaning to the narrative even as the whole narrative helps to determine the significance of these parts. A parable, for example, might provide an interpretive commentary on all or part of the Gospel in which it is located, or even serve to push the plot of the Gospel forward.

3.5. READING NEW TESTAMENT NARRATIVES

As Luke has it, the Gospels and Acts narrate "the events that have been fulfilled among us" (see Luke 1:1-4). Of course, as we have seen, the Gospels are more focused on a *person* than *events on the world stage*. Nevertheless, these documents are thus seen to have as their intent a particular form of "representation." This is the recounting of the impact of Jesus' career, not the representation of "what really happened" but of events-in-their-significance, in relation to Jesus' followers. An analogy from the visual arts may be helpful, even if it is limited. How might Jesus be portrayed? A photograph might be taken, providing a relatively objective snap-

---

5. John Goldingay, *Models for the Interpretation of Scripture* (Grand Rapids: Eerdmans, 1995) 80.

shot of an actual moment in the life of Jesus. Or an abstract painting might be produced, providing us with perhaps only the vaguest impression of Jesus. Alternatively, an artist might paint a portrait of Jesus — a medium allowing for selectivity, nuance, and interpretive attention to detail, but nonetheless a portrait of Jesus.[6] Any photographer will recognize the limitations of this analogy, since many interpretive choices mark the photographer's art. Nevertheless, this comparison points helpfully to the nature of the Gospels as selective documents, selective in the choices of both what to include and how to combine that material into coherent narratives.

When people narrate the career of Jesus and the life of the early church, they are manifestly engaged in significance-making, with the result that those involved in the quest of the historical Jesus have generally had one agenda, students of the Gospels another. Students of the Gospels are not interested primarily in reading behind the Gospel texts in order to take the measure of the raw materials employed by the Evangelists. Recognizing the biographical and historiographical character of the Gospels and Acts establishes certain readerly expectations and an agenda for study. Influence from the OT and later Jewish literature on the Gospels raises the question, How has history been shaped in this framing of theological commitments in the form of a narrative? Influence from Greco-Roman biography and historiography raises questions about the Gospels' focus on this person, Jesus, and his exploits: How has Jesus been portrayed? How do these scenes work together? What do they show and tell about his character and identity? What do they show and tell about the character of those who would follow him in faithful discipleship? Our recognition of Greco-Roman influence on the Gospels and Acts might provoke our interest in how these narratives portray the overarching purpose being served in the narrative. What are the roots of this narrative presentation? To what end is it directed?

"Historical knowledge," then, is not the same thing as "what actually happened." Historical knowledge borrows from the past environmental situations, events, and persons, and gives significance to the past. Hence, "history" in the sense of historical knowledge is both less and more than "the past." This is because (1) no historical account is capable of recovering the totality of any past event, since the content of those events is virtually limitless, (2) the past consists of events and situations, while history locates those events and situations in an account that tells a story about what happened, (3) historical narratives must choose from the available data base provided by the past, and those choices are always guided by a sense of what is important, and (4) because historians know the future of the past, as it were, they must shape their accounts in order to take into account

6. Robert A. Guelich, "The Gospels: Portraits of Jesus and His Ministry," *JETS* 24 (1982) 117-25.

where the past has led. Within Christian communities, the Gospels are thus recognized as authorized interpretations of the significance of the situations and events related to the life of Jesus.

For example, it is difficult to imagine that a Roman historian writing in the mid-40s CE would ever have mentioned the death of Jesus. What role would this event have served in his historical narrative, after all? This question is especially potent when it is remembered that Roman historians were generally concerned to extol the virtues of eternal Rome. If our imaginary Roman historian were to mention Jesus' death at all, it would have been as a mere illustration of troubled Roman-Jewish relations during this period. If the Gospel writers not only mention this death but actually make it central to and climactic in their narratives and if historians in later centuries spoke in profoundly theological terms of Jesus' execution, this is because these other writers regarded this event as something more than a footnote in the annals of the Roman Empire. For them Jesus' crucifixion had the status of an epoch-making event. To put it differently, our Roman historian and the Evangelist Matthew might have used a similar pool of events, situations, and characters to narrate history, but they were concerned with different plots, with different views of what was significant.

If we wish to take seriously the narrative presentation of the Gospels and Acts, then first we must take seriously the total shape of these writings as narrative in their final form — complete wholes, internally coherent and interactive. In studying the Gospels and Acts as narratives, we are interested in establishing links between the narrative text and the values, institutions, and practices of which the wider culture consists, but priority goes to the analysis of the literary artistry of a narrative text, to its capacity to define an internally coherent world, and its power to persuade readers to embrace its understanding of reality.

Analysis of NT narratives features two interrelated assumptions about the way narratives work. The first has to do with the distinction drawn between "story" and "narrative." We may tend to use these terms interchangeably in ordinary discourse, but they are quite distinct. "Story" refers to the *content* of narration, while "narrative" refers to its particular *expression;* story refers to the "what," narrative to the "how." This distinction assumes that the elements of a story, a set of events, might be told in any number of ways, but that each of these ways would differ in meaning from the others. We are interested in how those events are arranged and expressed in a given narrative, with reference to the order of events and causal relationships among events. As Aristotle observed, "narratives" are characterized by temporal sequence and an orientation toward the realization of an objective or the resolution of a dilemma — that is, they possess a beginning, a middle, and an end. The NT Gospels might be regarded as case studies for representing the difference between story and narrative, since in two, three, and sometimes all four of these books the same events appear, but they are recounted within narrative sequences that provide these same events with different significances.

The second assumption concerns our access to the author and readers of the Gospel narratives. New Testament narratives are anonymous, and almost everything we know about their authors (e.g., their skill in Greek, their predilection for urban life, or whatever) comes to us via a close reading of these narratives themselves. This, of course, gives us access not so much to the "real authors," but to the authors as they are known to us from the texts — that is, the "model authors."

Similarly, we have no direct access to the actual first readers of the Gospels and Acts. We know nothing in particular of their needs or concerns, nor anything about how they might have heard these narrative texts. What we do have access to is the sort of reader that the text seems to presume — that is, the model reader. From the information provided by the text itself, we can extrapolate the sort of reader imagined by the narrative and even follow the narrative to see how it seems to be calling forth responses on the part of this model reader. From this interpretive vantage point, the goal of reading is for the real reader, as it were, to become the model reader — that is, to enter into a kind of interpretive dance whereby one is able to deal interpretively with the text in a way that corresponds to how the author has dealt with it generatively. This, in fact, becomes a test for validity in narrative interpretation: Does the text itself provide the basis for anticipating that the reader should respond in this way?

This does not mean that the Gospels contain within themselves all that is needed for their interpretation. Taking the narrative texts seriously *as narratives* is important, but it is also crucial that we remember that "what is written" always assumes a great deal that is not written. Authors always assume on the part of their readers certain kinds of knowledge, so that gaps in the narrative text often signal points at which the author presumes that she and her audience share common presuppositions. Since the Gospels were written not to one church or one community, but to a wide-ranging audience made up mostly of Christian believers in Roman antiquity, many of those shared assumptions will relate to normal cultural conventions, many others will relate to a common heritage grounded in the Scriptures of Israel, and perhaps still others will relate to various levels of rudimentary knowledge concerning the story of Jesus (see Luke 1:4). Hence, "reading the Gospels as narrative" is always related to developing sensitivities to the world these narratives presume.

The practice of narrative reading also calls for attention to a number of elements within the narrative that contribute to its overall dynamic — six of which we can mention and briefly develop here. (1) Chief among these is the establishment early on in the narrative of a fundamental *aim,* the potential achievement and/or frustration of which creates tension within the narrative and drives the narrative forward. Concentration on the identification and attainment of this aim on the part of the reader draws attention to two aspects of the Gospels and Acts that are often lost in other forms of reading — namely, the degree to which NT narratives are about God and the achievement of God's aim, and the urgency with which the reader is confronted to align himself or herself for (or against) this aim. In this reckoning, for example, the Gospel of Luke and the book of Acts are not so much about Jesus and his witnesses as they are about the ancient purpose of God now coming to fruition. Emphasizing the issue of narrative aim also brings into the foreground the motif of conflict as characters and institutions within the narrative arrange themselves over against the aim of God and those who serve him.

(2) Additionally, narrative analysis concentrates on the *sequence of events* as they are arranged within the text. The importance of order is highlighted by the fact that, when reading narrative texts, readers encounter and judge the significance of each event in the light of the events that have preceded it. Narratives typically work not only with a pronounced sense of teleology, with events rushing toward an aim, but also with attention to causal relations; prior events are understood in some sense to set the stage and provide the basis for later ones.

(3) The progression of events is also related to issues of *timing*. Sometimes the Evangelist will pass over scenes quickly, providing summaries that indicate what is typical and expected. At other points, the crucifixion scene for example, the writer will slow down the narrative pace, providing time indicators and a wealth of detail in order to prompt the reader to linger over an event. At still others, the Evangelist will recount a series of similar events or sayings, or even call attention to an event repeatedly, either in prospect or retrospect; in these and other ways, significance is allocated through the use of the narrative devices of frequency and duration.

(4) The identification and formation of *characters* within the narrative are also crucial to narrative analysis, and the Evangelists draw on a substantial repertoire to indicate the nature of the persons they introduce: brief character references, access to inner thoughts, reports of characteristic activity, and the like.

(5) Also of consequence is the *point of view* from which statements are made. Because of the esteem with which God is held in the Gospels and Acts, messages that represent the divine point of view — whether they be from angels or the Scriptures or God's own voice — become the benchmarks of valid interpretation within the narrative. Moreover, because the narrators of the Gospels and Acts so fully align themselves with God's point of view, their assessments are to be taken at face value. This is not true of everyone within the narrative, however, since Jesus' opponents, the wicked within parables, and sometimes even Jesus' disciples themselves are depicted as unreliable.

(6) We are also concerned with *presuppositions* — including, first, the initial assumptions a narrative makes about its audience and, following this, the building up of presuppositions within the narrative itself. For example, it is notable that the

Gospel of Mark opens with an assertion that it never attempts to prove, namely that Jesus is the Messiah and Son of God. Apparently, the Second Evangelist can assume that his audience will embrace this characterization of Jesus, even if the narrative he then relates is decidedly oriented toward shaping in what sense his audience might understand the nature of Jesus' messiahship and divine sonship. This illustration also draws attention to how a narrative is able to provide new definitions for old concepts and thus to build for its audience a new lexicon of meaning as fresh information is provided about assumed values and conventions. Thus, the Second Evangelist may not devote his narrative to proving that Jesus is the Messiah, Son of God, but he does go to great lengths to shape how his audience might come to understand the content of that inaugural affirmation.

Within the Gospels and Acts, one of the expectations that come most to the fore is that audiences will already have become intimate with the Scriptures of Israel. Through direct citation of Old Testament texts, or allusions, or even sometimes faint echoes, Israel's Scriptures provide added texture to the significance of these narrative texts.

3.6. EPILOGUE: THE GOSPELS AND ACTS AS SCRIPTURE

One of the important roles of narrative in the NT canon is to serve as a counterbalance to what might appear to be its overwhelmingly didactic table of contents. Of the twenty-seven NT books, five are narrative texts, one is an apocalypse, and the remainder consists of letters and treatises of various kinds.

These particular narratives have a historiographical intent, bearing witness to historical events and persons at the heart of the gospel and its propagation. At the same time they bear witness to what can never be domesticated by the scrutiny of historians, the larger aim served by these people and events. In an ultimate sense, these NT narratives are about God — God's purpose, God's intervention, God's graciousness, and God's achievements. Although they have both ethical content and ethical ramifications, more fundamentally these narratives promote a particular vision and stimulate a particular imagination. They are not first about what we must be or do, but about a transformed view of God. They illustrate the dispositions and behaviors entailed by faith, but only as corollaries to a changed perspective, without which neither codes nor examples of behavior will be of much use. These narratives are thus concerned with the exposition of God, and their power as Scripture rests above all in their capacity to evoke in their audiences new ways of listening and seeing.

FOR FURTHER READING

James L. Bailey and Lyle D. Vander Broek, *Literary Forms in the New Testament: A Handbook* (Louisville: Westminster/John Knox, 1992)

Richard J. Bauckham, ed., *The Gospels for All Christians* (Grand Rapids: Eerdmans, 1998)

William R. Farmer, *The Gospel of Jesus: The Pastoral Relevance of the Synoptic Problem* (Louisville: Westminster/John Knox, 1994)

Joel B. Green, Scot McKnight, and I. Howard Marshall, *Dictionary of Jesus and the Gospels* (Downers Grove: InterVarsity, 1991)

Martin Hengel, *The Four Gospels and the One Gospel of Jesus Christ: An Investigation of the Collection and Origin of the Canonical Gospels* (Harrisburg: Trinity Press International, 2000)

David Lowenthal, *The Past Is a Foreign Country* (Cambridge: Cambridge University Press, 1985)

4. The Gospel according to Matthew

One of the pressing issues for the community that gathered around Jesus and persisted beyond his death was continuity. This is no simple question, but comes to us in two related forms: (1) What is the relationship between the earthly life of Jesus and the continuing commitments and existence of the church that seeks to order itself after him in discipleship? (2) What is the relation of the earthly life and ministry of Jesus to the activity of God and faith of Israel prior to Jesus' birth?

The first book in the NT does not circumvent these central questions, but begins to address them forthrightly, and immediately in its opening chapters. For this reason, the Gospel of Matthew, often called the First Gospel because of its location in the NT, functions as an effective bridge within the Christian canon of Scripture — from the OT to the NT. Readers of the Gospel of Matthew find here a portrayal of Jesus with deep roots in the OT together with branches that clearly embrace the church that grew out of Jesus' own ministry to restore Israel.

This means, on the one hand, that Matthew has explored the vital relationship between Jesus' life and the history and hope of God's historic engagement with Israel. By locating the beginning of his biography of Jesus (1) in the identification of Jesus in relation to David and Abraham (1:1), (2) in his rehearsal of Jesus' ancestral heritage as a Jew (1:2-17), and (3) in the affirmation of Jesus' status as the Jewish Messiah and Son of God (chs. 1–2), Matthew avers that the events of Jesus' career cannot be understood adequately apart from the grand story of God's interactions with and promises to Israel.

On the other hand, throughout the last two millennia, the Gospel of Matthew has justifiably been esteemed as "the Gospel of the church." Matthew is the only NT Gospel that employs the word *ekklēsia* ("church" — 16:18; 18:17), and one finds in the pages of this Gospel heightened concerns with church discipline, liturgical practices, and mission (e.g., 6:9-13; 18; 26:26-28; 28:16-20). Thus the Evangelist has brought traditions about Jesus to bear on the needs of the still youthful Christian community struggling with important issues of power and authority, identity and witness, and, so, of internal behavior and relations. Insisting on the church's genesis in the mission and message of Jesus and its continuity with historic Israel, Matthew works to aid his readers as they endeavor to find their way as a new religious movement in the Mediterranean world of the first century.

These and related data from the Gospel of Matthew speak to the fundamental coherence between Israel and the church via the biography of Jesus. At perhaps the most obvious level, continuity is guaranteed by the episodes of the gathering and teaching of disciples and the narration of the resurrection and appearances of Jesus in Matthew. These intimate the renewal of Israel and the coherence from Jesus to the community of his disciples with regard to authority, mission, and message. At a perhaps more profound level, historical and theological harmony is accomplished by means of a literary-theological innovation that is often more implicit than developed in the Gospel. This is the merging of the times or "eras" — that is, the blending of the time of Jesus with that of the church, as though they were coterminous. The earthly Jesus is none other than the exalted One whose ongoing presence invites worship and faithful mission. The disciples are Jesus' first followers, of course, but Matthew's narrative also invites future generations of disciples to identify themselves with these first followers — so that their failures and successes become warnings and examples. This does not mean that the Matthew has presented the life of Jesus as more ancient novel than biography, as though he read his own concerns and those of his audience into the situations and people of Jesus' life and ministry. He has not, like some medieval painting, presented Jesus in garments or actions so anachronistic as to render him unrecognizable or irrelevant to first-century Galilee and Judea. Rather, Matthew manifests in his Gospel the task of the Evangelist: to demonstrate, by telling the story of Jesus, the ongoing claim on God's people and, indeed, on all humanity of the pivotal work of God in Jesus Christ.

To insist that the Gospel of Matthew is concerned especially with continuity and coherence, however, does not mean that the transition from Judaism to Jesus and the church is an easy or smooth one. The genealogy with which the Gospel opens may identify Jesus as the Messiah, and the ensuing narrative of Jesus' birth may depict him as the culmination of Israel's history and hopes, but these opening chapters also contain unexpected and unsettling notes. The inclusion of women in a genealogy is not completely without precedent, but the presence in Jesus' ancestral list of such controversial women in Israel's history as Tamar, Rahab, Ruth, and Bathsheba can hardly be said to work in his favor, if Matthew's primary point is to establish for Jesus and the church a winsome continuity with Israel of old. Moreover, in ch. 2, although a choir of voices — including Gentile magi, Herod the

Great, Jewish chief priests and scribes, and Hebrew prophets — together vocalize the identity of Jesus as the one born to be "King of the Jews," only the Gentile magi respond to this news with celebration and worship. Herod "and all Jerusalem with him" (2:1-3) exhibit distress at the news of the Messiah's birth, and the Jewish leaders and inhabitants of Jerusalem apparently join Herod in seeking the life of this potential rival to kingly power (2:20: "those who were seeking the child's life"). In this way, the Evangelist locates Jerusalem not simply at the center of the Jewish world, a status it occupied historically, but even more importantly as the capital of opposition to Jesus. Later in the narrative, when Jesus himself journeys finally to Jerusalem, we are not surprised to see him encounter the fate that was laid out for him first at the time of his birth: rejection and death.

The Gospel of Matthew is thus not only a narrative of continuity with the people of God but also of conflict. And herein lies a pressing issue for readers of this Gospel: How are we to construe Matthew's understanding of the relationship between Jesus and Judaism, and, thus, between his followers (the church) and Judaism? Such striking emphasis is given the motif of hostility in this Gospel that some scholars in the late twentieth century simply dismissed Matthew as anti-Jewish. This is a simplistic and one-sided reading of Matthew. It fails to account for the Gospel's unmitigated concern with the nature of authentic life before God and thus the genuine character of God's people, and it fails to take seriously the variegated representation of Jesus' position *vis-à-vis* the history, law, people, and traditions of the Jews. What, then, is Matthew's agenda in his presentation of the Jewish people and Jewish institutions? Such questions must occupy us later in this chapter, following a discussion of Matthew's presentation of the life of Jesus.

4.1. THE PLAN OF THE GOSPEL OF MATTHEW

Matthew has left his readers no shortage of structural features by which to help make sense of his emphases. In fact, he has left so many that it has been difficult to sketch his overall narrative plan with much certainty.

It is important, first, to take seriously this narrative's status as a Greco-Roman biography. "Genres," it will be recalled, refer to the category or form of literature to which a document belongs; they constitute more or less formal and implicit "contracts" between authors and their audiences, launching certain expectations for interpreting particular texts (see pp. 5-6 above). Since Matthew's Gospel is a kind of ancient biography, we may anticipate a primary focus on Jesus' career and death and a pronounced emphasis on the embodiment within the narrative of esteemed values. Given the Jewish orientation of the Gospel of Matthew, we may also expect abundant evidence of the outworking of the divine will in historical narrative, in ways reminiscent of such biographically oriented scriptural materials

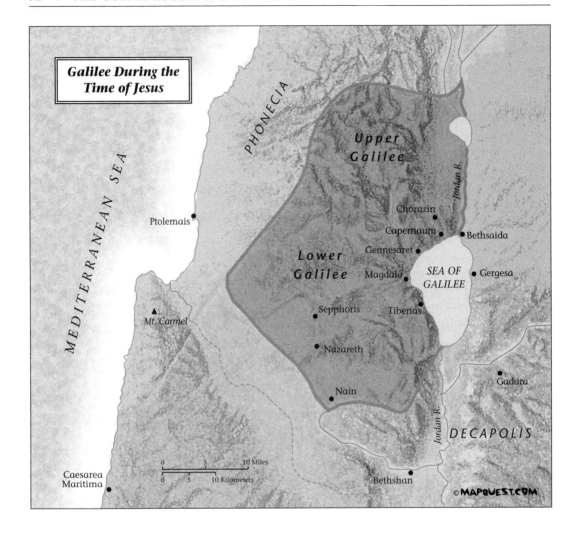

Galilee During the Time of Jesus

as those associated with Moses, Abraham, or Elijah. Recognition of the biographical genre of the Gospel of Matthew raises a cluster of additional expectations, including:

- a focus on Jesus' public life, organized either chronologically or topically (or both),
- indications concerning how and why Jesus would have been regarded as one who deserved biographical treatment,
- a commitment on the part of the author to hold in abeyance the temptation for wholesale creation of events,

- an overall interpretive aim indicating the cause-and-effect relations among the events that make up the narrative, and
- a presentation of Jesus and his behavior as exemplary for the Gospel's audience.

Such expectations as these are pivotal for our reading of the Gospel of Matthew, but are hardly peculiar to Matthew's narrative. The same might be said of the Gospels of Mark and John and, to a lesser degree, the Gospel of Luke (which, together with the Book of Acts, belongs to the related genre of historiography). What more can be said of the plan of Matthew's Gospel?

Because we are reading a narrative with a main character or primary protagonist, Jesus, much can be learned about the emphases of the Gospel of Matthew by attending to Jesus' first and last words in the Gospel. A protagonist's first words often help to set the agenda for the work as a whole, while "last words" are often not only final but climactic in function. Jesus' first words in Matthew respond to John the Baptist's attempt to prevent Jesus' baptism. Jesus declares, "Let it be so now, for it is proper for us in this way to fulfill all righteousness" (3:15). This utterance — which contains two terms, *plēroō* ("fulfill") and *dikaiosynē* ("righteousness"), that are crucial to the ensuing narrative — serves a programmatic role for the Evangelist. Even before the onset of his public ministry, Jesus manifests, first, his capacity to discern "what is right" and, second, his commitment to obeying it. In this narrative location, "what is right" can refer to nothing less than the will of God. The phrase "the will of God" does not refer superficially to rules and regulations, as though Jesus might announce at this early juncture of his career his commitment to embrace God's ordinances in such a limited sense. Rather, Jesus announces at his baptism *both* his grasp of the ancient and ongoing intention of God *and* his resolve to live out that intention. He thus situates himself firmly and centrally within the narrative of God's will as its climax. The divine voice at Jesus' baptism ("This is my Son, the beloved, in whom I am well pleased," 3:17) affirms Jesus' understanding of the necessity of his baptism using words borrowed from Ps 2:7 and Isa 42:1, correlating this event with the consummation of the hopes embedded in the Scriptures of Israel. Jesus actualizes the hopes of Israel as one who grasps and conforms to the will of God, and in doing so exemplifies the commitments and behavior expected of his true followers.

The final words of Jesus are spoken to his disciples on a Galilean mountain:

"All authority in heaven and on earth has been given to me. Go therefore and make disciples of all nations, baptizing them in the name of the Father and of the Son and of the Holy Spirit, and teaching them to obey everything that I have commanded you. And remember, I am with you always, to the end of the age." (28:18-20)

This paragraph is both retrospective and prospective — calling to mind "everything that I have commanded you" at the same time that it outlines the church's missionary and disciple-making agenda. The continuity between Jesus and his disciples with respect to message, mission, and authority is undergirded and highlighted by the promise of Jesus' ongoing presence within the community of his faithful disciples.

Within the plan of the Gospel of Matthew, Jesus' final words play yet another role, for they complete an *inclusio* (i.e., they help to frame the whole Gospel) around the notion of the ongoing, redemptive presence of God. In the Gospel's opening account, an angel of the Lord directs Joseph to name Mary's son "Jesus," "for he will save his people from their sins" — this in fulfillment of Isaiah's prophecy, "'They shall name him Emmanuel,' which means, 'God is with us'" (Matt 1:22-23). The connection between this scene and Jesus' closing promise, "I am with you always, to the end of the age," can hardly be accidental. Together with a similar promise in 18:20 ("Wherever two or three are gathered in my name, I am there with them"), these declarations ground a central motif of Matthew's Gospel: In Jesus, the Messiah and Son of God, God is present to provide redemption for his people. In addition, the progression of these three affirmations clarifies the identity of "his people," the ones for whom Jesus' advent spells salvation. "His people" are comprised of the church, those who gather in allegiance and submission to him and who carry out the mission that takes its direction and authority from Jesus himself. The form of Jesus' closing words, "to the end of the age," allows Matthew's own audience to read themselves into the community of discipleship and salvation among whom and for whom Jesus is redemptively present.

What of other structural features within the Matthean Gospel that help to shape its interpretation? Students of Matthew have long been impressed with the clustering of the teachings of Jesus into five lengthy discourses, each of which concludes with "When Jesus had finished these words. . . ." These discourses are intertwined with lengthy sections of narrative, with the result that some have imagined the story of Jesus in Matthew as having been presented in five books:

1. an introductory narrative (3:1–4:25) followed by Jesus' teaching on the higher righteousness of the new community (chs. 5–7; see 7:28),
2. an introductory narrative (8:1–9:35) followed by Jesus' teaching on the mission of the new community (ch. 10; see 11:1),
3. an introductory narrative (11:2–12:50) followed by Jesus' teaching in parables (ch. 13; see 13:53),
4. an introductory narrative (13:54–17:21) followed by Jesus' teaching about forgiveness and church discipline (ch. 18; see 19:1), and, finally,
5. an introductory narrative (19:2–22:46) followed by Jesus' teaching on the judgment to come (chs. 24–25; see 26:1).

According to this framework, the main thrust of the Gospel is the nature of the church, with Jesus portrayed primarily in the garb of a teacher. Some interpreters have gone so far as to imagine that Matthew thus portrays Jesus as the New Moses presenting a New Torah. However, the alternation between narrative and discourse is not nearly so clean as this outline suggests, and in fact discourse material is well represented in material identified as narrative. More importantly, this way of thinking about the plan of the Gospel makes little room for the birth, death, and resurrection narratives of Jesus in Matthew; they simply do not fit the pattern! As a result, it is probably better to see the fivefold repetition of the formulaic phrase, "When Jesus had finished these words . . . ," as transitional in function, helping to move the narrative forward. Together, these five lengthy discourses do not constitute a "new law," then, but they do depict Jesus as authoritative teacher.

Yet another formula, "From that time on Jesus began . . . ," appears in 4:17 and 16:21, points in the narrative where a new phase of Jesus' ministry is initiated, allowing the Evangelist to sum up ahead of time the material that will follow. This allows for a threefold partitioning of the Gospel, in this case oriented much more centrally around christological affirmations. Thus,

1:1–4:16 presents the preparation of Jesus the Messiah, Son of God,
4:17–16:20 sets forward the proclamation of Jesus the Messiah to Israel, and
16:21–28:20 narrates the death and resurrection of Jesus the Messiah, Son of God.

Like biographies as they developed in the imperial period of Roman history, so Matthew seems thus to organize the ministry of Jesus topically.

Still other textual markers within the Matthean narrative might be championed as keys to understanding Matthew's narrative plan. More likely is that all the structural features we have described, and others besides, serve primarily to move the narrative along toward its climax in Jesus' death, resurrection, and postresurrection appearances. What is incontrovertible about Matthew's plan is the gathering of Jesus' teaching into discourses, each with its own thematic focus, and together accentuating the picture of Jesus as authoritative teacher. The importance of this narrative feature is highlighted in Jesus' closing words in 28:18-20, which place a premium on the substance of Jesus' teaching. Equally transparent is the biographical character of Matthew's Gospel — that is, its primary focus on the *bios* or life of Jesus, with the result that we cannot escape its fundamental aim to promote a particular vision of Jesus' person and work. Jesus is and remains at center stage throughout the Gospel.

In discerning the movement of the Gospel it is also important to recall the importance of conflict for narrative in general, and especially for Matthew's account of Jesus. Finally, as might be expected of a biography, the narrative portions of the Gospel of Matthew follow a general chronological sequence, from birth to baptism, Galilean ministry, journey to Jerusalem, passion, resurrection, and postresurrection appearances. Woven into this chronological progress are the lengthy sections of Jesus' teaching.

In what follows, then, we will make room for various structural features, but will allow neither of the previously mentioned formulas to determine our understanding of the progression of the narrative. Instead, priority will be given to the twists and turns the Matthean account takes in relation to the support and/or hostility Jesus receives, to the import of the placement of the major blocks of Jesus' teaching within the narrative, and to the thematic (or topical) character of this "biography" of Jesus.

4.2. THE NARRATIVE OF MATTHEW

Preparation for the Ministry of Jesus the Messiah, Son of God
    (1:1–4:22)
Jesus proclaims the good news and heals the sick (4:23–9:34)
    Introduction (4:23-25)
    Jesus' first discourse (5:1-7:29)
    Jesus' powerful ministry (8:1-9:34)
The emergence of the church in Israel (9:35–16:20)
    Jesus' second discourse — on mission (9:35–10:42)
    Growing hostility toward Jesus (11:1–12:50)
    Jesus' third discourse — in parables (13:1-53)
    Violence and confession intensify (13:54–16:20)
Christology, discipleship, and the life of the church (16:21–20:34)
The ministry of Jesus the Messiah in Jerusalem (21:1–25:46)
    The question of Jesus' identity and authority (21:1–22:46)
    Jesus criticizes his opponents (23:1-39)
    Jesus admonishes his disciples concerning readiness (24:1–25:46)
The death and resurrection of Jesus the Messiah, Son of God
    (26:1–28:20)

4.2.1. Preparation for the Ministry of Jesus the Messiah, Son of God (1:1–4:22)

Matthew opens his narrative of the public ministry of Jesus with an extended introduction, the primary focus of which is christological. That is, Matthew recounts the ancestry and birth of Jesus, followed by the preparation for Jesus' ministry through baptism and temptation, in order to clarify the nature of Jesus' person and mission and to set the stage for their subsequent development in the ensuing narrative.

The Gospel's opening line functions as a superscription for Matthew's portrayal of Jesus. Although many English translations render *genesis* in 1:1 as "the genealogy" (of Jesus Christ), it can be translated as "the book of origins." Read in this way, the parallel in Gen 2:4; 5:1 is suggestive of something more auspicious. Just as "the book of origins" in Genesis refers to divine creation, so here it points to the consummation of God's plan in the advent of Jesus. This ensures that we read the genealogy of Jesus as something more than a means of introducing yet one more person into the family tree. As the very first verse declares, Jesus is the Messiah, son of David and son of Abraham; soon, he will be introduced as the Son of God as well (see Matt 1:18-25; 2:15; 3:13-17; 4:1-11).

Genealogies typically function to establish someone's status. The association of Jesus with David and Abraham in Matthew's superscription is developed immediately in the genealogy and birth narrative to illuminate both the nature of Jesus' messiahship and the wide reach of the salvation proffered in his coming. He is Messiah in the lineage of David, his coming marks the fulfillment of Israel's hopes and God's promises across the generations of God's people, and the redemption he brings embraces Gentile as well as Jew.

Though the angel announces to Joseph that Jesus "will save his people from their sins" and the birth narrative is so Jewish in orientation that one might expect that "his people" will include only the Jews, there are many signs to the contrary in these opening verses. Abraham, it will be recalled, was to be the father of *many nations*. The introduction of Bathsheba as "the wife of Uriah" in the genealogy (1:6) brings to mind her marriage to a foreigner, Uriah the Hittite, with the result that she joins Tamar, Rahab, and Ruth (1:3, 5) as Gentile women among Jesus' ancestry. Three magi "from the East," Gentiles all, recognize in the stars testimony to the birth of the king of the Jews, and they come to pay him homage. From 3:13 on, Matthew seems to underscore Jesus' orientation to Galilee; Jesus comes from Galilee to be baptized by John (3:13), returns to Galilee to proclaim the kingdom (4:12-17), and in Galilee calls his first followers (4:18-22). But this is "Galilee of the Gentiles" (4:15). In all these ways, the Evangelist signals the universalistic impulses of his narrative.

Matthew nevertheless portrays Jesus as one possessing impressive credentials among the people of Israel. Jesus appears in the birth narrative, and subsequently, in the guise of Moses. Like Moses, Jesus is threatened by a ruler and narrowly escapes, returns from exile on divine instructions, and so on. Each step of his birth and infancy is grounded in the fulfillment of Scripture (1:22-23; 2:15, 17-18, 23; cf. 2:5-6; 4:14-16). These inscribe the beginnings of Jesus' life in the history of Israel and in scriptural words of promise, and they signal for Matthew's audience that this Jesus is none other than the one to whom the Scriptures pointed. He is the one through whom the history and legacy of Israel will continue.

Another Portrayal of a Messiah

In its description of the messianic figure who will come from the tribe of Levi, *Testament of Levi* 18:4-8 has uncanny parallels to the accounts of Jesus' baptism in Matt 3:13-17; Mark 1:9-11. The *Testament of Levi* is not easy to date because it underwent lengthy editorial development (second century BCE–second century CE). It may have been influenced by the Gospel of Mark, but it nonetheless represents traditional Jewish perspectives.

This one will shine forth like the sun in the earth;
    he shall take away all darkness from under heaven,
    and there shall be peace in all the earth.
The heavens shall greatly rejoice in his days
    and the earth shall be glad;
    the clouds filled with joy
And the knowledge of the Lord will be poured out on the earth
        like the water of the seas.
    And the angels of glory of the Lord's presence will be
        made glad by him.
The heavens will be opened,
    and from the temple of glory sanctification will come upon him,
    with a fatherly voice, as from Abraham to Isaac.
And the glory of the Most High shall burst upon him.
    And the spirit of understanding and sanctification shall rest
        upon him [in the water].
For he shall give the majesty of the Lord to those who are his sons
        in truth forever.
    And there shall be no successor for him from generation
        to generation forever. *(OTP)*

Matthew not only presents Jesus as son of David, son of Abraham, and the New Moses, but also stresses that he is the Son of God. Employing the words of Hos 11:1, Matthew identifies Jesus as God's Son and thus as the embodiment of true, obedient Israel (Matt 2:15). We are prepared for this reading by the angelic announcement that Jesus was conceived by the Holy Spirit and born to a virgin; it is pressed further with the identification of Jesus as "my Son" by the heavenly voice in 3:17, then confirmed by Jesus' unequivocal obedience and loyalty to God in the face of diabolic temptation (4:1-11).

Such positive notes regarding Jesus' identity and God's salvific embrace of the Gentile world stand in stark contrast to Matthew's more negative portrayal of the Jewish reception of Jesus in these opening chapters. Clearly, the Jews read the signs and the Scriptures differently. Herod finds in Jesus' birth the threat of rivalry, and the people of Jerusalem join their king — himself only half-Jewish — in his fear and malice (see 2:3, 20). Interestingly, the elite among the Jews, chief priests and scribes of the people, apparently do not recognize what the "wise men from the East" have seen: evidence of the birth of a Jewish Messiah. Jesus associates himself with the ministry of John the Baptist, and together Jesus and John "fulfill all righteousness" (3:15). This, however, is the very John whose vision of reform has propelled him into the wilderness where, apart from the temple, he stands over against the Pharisees and Sadducees, proclaims repentance, and invites baptism and confession of sin. John, moreover, speaks of the coming one who will judge between wheat and chaff (3:11-12). Thus established in the opening sections of Matthew's Gospel is a motif that will add to the suspense and tragedy of the narrative, the motif of hostility.

4.2.2. Jesus Proclaims the Good News and Heals the Sick (4:23–9:34)

Matthew 4:23 marks the beginning of the second main section of the Gospel. This verse finds a close parallel in 9:35, for both speak of Jesus' itinerancy and his "teaching in their synagogues, proclaiming the good news of the kingdom, and curing every disease and every sickness." The first use of this formula highlights Jesus' growing fame, however, and thus prepares for reports of Jesus' teaching (chs. 5–7) and powerful deeds (chs. 8–9). The second comes after accounts of Jesus' ministry of preaching and healing and thus stresses the need for assistance in the "harvest." Not surprisingly, then, the next section of the Gospel contains a discourse (ch. 10) with Jesus' instructions to his disciples regarding their involvement in mission. This parallelism underscores again the continuity between Jesus and his disciples alluded to earlier.

4.2.2.1. Introduction (4:23-25)

Matthew summarizes the nature of Jesus' ministry throughout Galilee with three verbs — teach, preach, and heal. The content of Jesus ministry, given here as "the good news of the kingdom," was communicated already in the same way at the close of the previous section: "Repent, for the kingdom of heaven is at the door!" (4:17). The same words were spoken by John the Baptist in 3:2. This ties the ministries of John and Jesus into God's overarching salvific intervention, which Matthew envisions as a complex of events that have been set in motion but await final consummation. For John and Jesus, the nearness of the kingdom is the basis for human response: repentance. In the case of Jesus the kingdom's advance is marked by ministries of proclamation and healing; both of these aspects of Jesus' kingdom-ministry will be sketched in Matthew 5–9. Matthew's audience will thus gain a clearer view of the nature of repentance and authentic life before God, in addition to a series of windows into how the advance of the kingdom spells good news for those who live beyond the pale of respectable society.

4.2.2.2. Jesus' First Discourse (5:1–7:29)

A hill in Galilee, the traditional site of the Sermon on the Mount *(Phoenix Data Systems, Neal and Joel Bierling)*

Jesus' first discourse, known almost universally as the Sermon on the Mount, is separated from its narrative context both by its content (teaching) and by an important structural feature: in 5:1 Jesus ascends the mountain, and in 8:1 he descends. This marks the beginning and end of the sermon and reminds us of Matthew's interest in painting Jesus as the New Moses, deliverer and teacher of God's people. This does not mean that the Sermon on the Mount can be read apart from

the surrounding narrative material, however. Jesus' *words* here cannot be separated from the subsequent record of his *deeds,* nor can the sometimes maverick quality of his teaching in chs. 5–7 be segregated from the presentation of Jesus' authoritative status in chs. 1–4. As the narrative develops it will become increasingly transparent that Jesus "practices what he preaches" — that is, he embodies his own instruction — and that he insists that his followers do the same with regard to the will of God. Moreover, the salvation Jesus promises and the behavior he demands in this discourse are grounded in his sovereignty as the New Moses, the Messiah and Son of God.

Jesus' first discourse has as its immediate audience the disciples, including at the very least those whom he has called in 4:18-22: Simon Peter, Andrew, James, and John. As Matthew presents it, there is another audience, the crowds; their identity is presently nondescript, but their presence makes it clear that Jesus' words lay a claim on persons far beyond the narrow gathering of the disciples. What is more, by narrating Jesus' address as he does, Matthew allows Jesus to speak beyond the narrative; the "you" to whom Jesus repeatedly addresses his words reaches even Matthew's own audience and lays a claim on their lives. Just as Moses' words in Deuteronomy speak to generations after the escape from Egypt, so Jesus speaks to future generations of his followers. Accordingly, all — the small group of Jesus' disciples mentioned in Matt 5:1, the crowds, and those who read Matthew's Gospel — are confronted with the same offer of divine blessing, demand for piety and ethical comportment, and threat of judgment as these are sketched within the Sermon.

Matthew 5–7 consists of three sections — a prologue (5:3-16), the body of the discourse (5:17–7:12), and the conclusion (7:13-29). The prologue, which contains Jesus' Beatitudes, is a précis of Jesus' dual vision. First, he highlights the abundance of God's blessing, though, surprisingly, he names as the recipients of those blessings an unusual cast of characters: the poor in spirit, those who mourn, the hungry, and so on. Second, he anticipates the mission of the church (see 28:18-20), employing the metaphors of salt and light to underscore the grave importance of the witness of the church's own life for its outward-looking mission.

The main body of Jesus' sermon is framed with references to the law and prophets (5:17; 7:12) and is quite naturally concerned with the incarnation of the will of God in the lives of God's people. Here Jesus holds in tension his commitment to the persistent authority of Torah and his own status as the legitimate interpreter of God's will. His teaching, therefore, does not constitute an annulment of the Torah as much as it insists that God's will in Scripture must be understood as "living Torah," in need always of interpretation in new contexts. In this conviction Jesus was not unique among Jews in the Second Temple period, for many (especially among the Essenes and Pharisees) worked to articulate the ancient law for fresh situations. Startling, rather, is Matthew's presentation of Jesus as the "only teacher" (see 23:8), who grounds his teaching in his own authority (see 7:29). Jesus "fulfills" Torah, and so his teaching and commandments are definitive for the people of God.

Summarizing the Law

According to a tradition dating to the early first century CE, a Gentile approached Rabbi Hillel, desiring to become a Jewish proselyte, but only on the condition that he could be taught all of Torah while standing on one foot. Hillel replied,

> What is hateful to you, do not to your neighbor. That is the whole Torah, while the rest is commentary; go and learn. (Babylonian Talmud, *Shabbath* 30b)

Other traditions had their own formulations of "The Golden Rule." For example, the ancient Greek historian Herodotus (fifth century BCE) wrote, "I will not myself do that which I consider to be blameworthy in my neighbor," and Confucius said, "Do not do to others what you would not want others to do to you." When compared to these, Jesus' statement is remarkable for being in positive rather than negative terms: "Do to others as you would have them do to you" (Matt 7:12).

This perspective is underscored in the strongest possible way by the Sermon's conclusion (7:13-29). No claim to vital association with the Lord can be made apart from obedience to Jesus' instruction. In Matthew's case, then, "righteousness" is not a gift from God (as though he were interested in how one might be "made right with God"); instead, for Matthew, one must show that one is right with God by behaving righteously. Even if persons speak of Jesus as "Lord," even if they claim a personal relationship with him, even if they manifest in their lives such charismatic gifts as prophecy or the capacity to exorcise demons — none of these can substitute for "doing the will of my Father in heaven" (7:21). And "doing the will of my Father in heaven" is nothing less or more than "hearing these words of mine," that is, of Jesus, "and acting on them" (7:24).

The first great sermon in the Matthean narrative, delivered in the second person, is difficult to read in a removed, dispassionate way, as though Jesus were speaking only to persons gathered around him on the hillside. Jesus' repeated reference to "you" invites those who read this Gospel to consider how fully they should read themselves into the narrative. Are we, readers of Matthew's Gospel, persons who assert ourselves within the community of God's people? Do we claim for ourselves high status on the basis of piety and Spirit-endowed capacities? Those of Matthew's audience who answer such questions in the affirmative can scarcely escape Jesus' chastisement for their lack of obedience to the will of God. Such persons have come to mirror in their lives the dispositions of the Pharisees and Jewish leaders, and so, having failed to possess a righteousness that surpasses that of the scribes and Pharisees, have no place in God's kingdom (5:20). This is not to say that Matthew sets himself against expressions of piety or charismatic expression, but rather that these must emanate from a life of obedience to God. The Sermon on the Mount spells out the form and substance of such a life.

4.2.2.3. *Jesus' Powerful Ministry (8:1–9:34)*

Matthew 4:23 proposed a dual emphasis in Jesus' kingdom-ministry: proclamation and healing. Having completed the first discourse, his first sustained proclamation of the kingdom, Jesus now turns to the healing of the sick. This is graphic testimony to the openness of this Evangelist to the sort of powerful, charismatic phenomenon mentioned in 7:15-23, but Matthew's staging of this section of the Gospel prioritizes his interests. Miraculous deeds and those who perform them are not on that basis self-legitimating. As the Pharisees themselves will observe, the capacity for powerful deeds can be traced to quite disparate origins, including the diabolic (9:34). The association of Jesus' Sermon on the Mount with these reports of healing and powerful deeds, first, forbids that we separate the content and authority of Jesus' teaching from that of his healing ministry and, second, reminds us of the holistic and robust character of the salvation Jesus conveys. The audience for both forms of ministry activity remains the same, and both are viewed as manifestations of the in-breaking kingdom of God. In this section, the spotlight falls primarily on Jesus, while in the next section, beginning with 9:35, the narrative lens will enlarge to include the mission of the disciples.

Perhaps the most critical point of this section of Matthew's Gospel is simply the potency of Jesus' ministry. Miraculous events seem to be lined up, one after the other, with little connection between them or progression among them. Even if read in this way, what is said of Jesus' ministry is significant. Repeatedly, Matthew depicts him as one who makes available the presence and power of God's dominion to those dwelling on the periphery of Jewish society in Galilee — a leper, the slave of a Gentile army officer, an old woman, the demon-possessed, a paralytic, a collector of tolls, a young girl, and the blind. Typically, these accounts function at two levels simultaneously. On the surface, Matthew recounts the restoration to physical health of those who are diseased. Such a casual reading masks ancient views of health and healing, however, for it assumes modern, Western notions of medicine and biology. In a culture like that of ancient Palestine, where the whole of life was understood in a more integrated way, chronicles of restoration to physical health such as those Matthew narrates also recount the restoration to status within one's family and community, the faith-full reordering of life around God, and the driving back of demonic forces. Thus, for example, cleansing a leper allows him new access to God and to the community of God's people (8:1-4; see Leviticus 13–14), healing a paralytic is tantamount to forgiving his sins (Matt 9:2-8), extending the grace of God to toll collectors and sinners illustrates the work of a physician (9:9-13), and, as throughout the biblical tradition, recovery of sight serves too as a metaphor for the insight of faith (9:27-31).

If the powerful deeds of Jesus are the main focus of this narrative section, however, they are integrated into a more encompassing theme having to do with how people respond to Jesus' ministry. This is most transparent at the close of this section, in 9:33-34, where the crowds take an overwhelmingly positive view but the Pharisees respond negatively. (See also the responses in 8:10, 27; 9:3, 8, 11.) In amazement, the crowds gush, "Never has anything like this been seen in Israel!" In an attempt to belittle Jesus and to counter his influence among the people, the Pharisees relegate his ministry to the realm of the demonic. The way the narrative holds in tandem these conflicting responses to Jesus illuminates Matthew's agenda in the whole of chs. 8–9. Why is one of the first episodes of healing one that involves Jesus' interaction with a Gentile (8:5-13)? This portends the end of Matthew's Gospel, of course, with its focus on mission to "the nations" (28:20). In addition, in its own narrative context it serves also to indicate the means by which Gentiles might be embraced as God's people — namely, through active faith. The "many [who] will come" from the far reaches of the earth to share in the kingdom banquet are those with faith who act on it, while "the heirs of the kingdom [who] will be thrown into the outer darkness" are those who fail to do so (8:11-12).

4.2.3. The Emergence of the Church in Israel (9:35–16:20)

Matthew's report of Jesus' missionary instructions to his disciples is in many ways closely tied to earlier material, for it shows how the mission of Jesus is to be recapitulated among his disciples. In fact, chs. 10 and 11 initiate an important transition within the narrative, bringing the disciples — and with them, the church — more and more onto center stage. According to Matthew, this is not accidental, but proceeds on the basis of intensifying hostility toward Jesus on the part of official Judaism. More and more, the disciples are said to form a coherent unit, until fi-

nally Jesus actually introduces the word "church" into the lexicon of this Gospel
(16:18).

4.2.3.1. Jesus' Second Discourse — On Mission (9:35–10:42)

As we have seen, Matt 9:35 repeats the earlier summary of Jesus' ministry in 4:23.
As with many instances of repetition, this one is marked by similarity as well as
difference. On the one hand, the way these parallel summary statements bracket
chs. 5–9 suggests that we are to think of these chapters as containing what was typical in the ministry of Jesus: throughout the course of his work, he proclaimed the
gospel in word and deed in just this way. On the other, this second summary goes
on to highlight Jesus' recognition of the need for leadership for the people (9:36-
37). And this leads into Matthew's account of Jesus' instructions for the mission of
the disciples.

What is surprising about this new section of the Gospel is that, though Jesus
summons, empowers, and sends his disciples (10:1, 5), they never seem to go anywhere. At the close of this training session, the narrative is occupied with Jesus'
teaching and preaching and does not follow the disciples' ministry (Matt 11:1).
This may be no more than a gap in the narrative, with Matthew's audience left to
imagine the missionary activity of the disciples in much the same way that they
are to imagine the calling of *twelve* disciples. Matthew, after all, has narrated the
calling of only *five* (see 10:1; 4:18-22; 9:9). The lack of a report of the mission of
the disciples in this narrative context may serve another purpose, however; standing as they do apart from such a mission, his words of instruction take on an almost timeless quality, as though the narrator were seeking to shape the missionary
life of his own audiences in this account. In this case, it is remarkable that Jesus' instructions emphasize identification with himself, with his person and the form of
his ministry. Like Jesus, the disciples/church will:

- have authority to exorcise demons and to heal (cf. 4:23; 9:34; 10:1, 8);
- proclaim the nearness of the kingdom (cf. 3:2; 4:17, 23; 9:35; 10:7);
- raise the dead and cleanse lepers (cf. 8:1-4; 9:18-26; 10:8); and
- experience inhospitality and rejection (cf. 5:39-42; 8:19-20; 9:34; 10:11-15,
  16-23).

This concentration on identification with the Messiah may be remarkable, but it is
not surprising — as Jesus teaches, "A disciple is not above his teacher, nor a slave
above his master; it is enough for the disciple to be like his teacher, and the slave
like his master. If they have called the master of the house Beelzebul, how much
more will they malign those of his household!" (Matt 10:24-25).

One might entertain the possibility that Matthew has communicated mixed messages in his presentation of Jesus' instruction. Twice in this discourse, Jesus limits the mission to the house of Israel (10:5-6, 23). At the same time, there is plenty of evidence that Jesus is in the process of constructing a new "household," a family whose ties run deeper than ancestry and blood, whose fundamental identity is found in embracing the obedience, behavior, and fate of Jesus as its own. This paradox reflects the early experience of Jesus and his followers within the Gospel narrative, as well as that of those disciples outside the narrative — that is, Matthew's audience: having begun within Israel, they increasingly find themselves in tension with Israel so that they are forced to ferret out their identity as God's people with reference to values and sources other than family lineage.

4.2.3.2. *Growing Hostility toward Jesus (11:1–12:50)*

Nestled between the second and third of Jesus' extended discourses is this section in which Matthew depicts the increasing opposition Jesus encounters in his itinerancy. At their meeting at the Jordan River, John the Baptist recognized Jesus as "the one who is more powerful" (3:11-14), but now the baptizer seems disenchanted with Jesus. "Shall we look for another?" he asks (11:3). John's question provides the impetus for a rehearsal of Jesus' remarkable deeds, and also of Jesus' endorsement of John. But these serve to contrast Jesus' assessment of John and summary of his own career with the rejection both have experienced by "this generation." John played a pivotal role in the advent of God's work of salvation, yet he was opposed and thrown into jail (4:12). God himself has revealed to Jesus his divine sonship (11:25-27), but this perspective has not been widely embraced — even by those cities who have experienced more than their share of God's powerful deeds at the hands of Jesus.

John may have been disenchanted with respect to Jesus' messianic identity, but his perplexity pales in the face of the opposition Jesus encounters from the Pharisees and synagogue leadership. "The crowds," who up until this point have responded positively toward Jesus and have served in the narrative primarily as potential disciples — even they are likened to stubborn, unfaithful Israel in Moses' day; like their predecessors, they will receive the judgment that falls on "this [evil] generation" (11:16; 12:45; cf., e.g., Exod 32:9). Clearly, Jesus is not the Messiah, Son of David, whom they have anticipated. The open invitation to follow Jesus persists still (Matt 11:28-30), but the lines continue to be carefully drawn. Those who belong to the family of God, Jesus says, are those who do "the will of my Father in heaven" (12:50). Jesus draws on Israel's Scriptures to show that his messianic task would be to include the Gentiles in this new family (Matt 12:18-21, with reference to Isa 42:1-4).

4.2.3.3. Jesus' Third Discourse — In Parables (13:1-53)

Jesus' response to opposition in Matt 12:15 was to make his exit, a move to which he will repeatedly turn in the face of hostility (see 14:13; 15:21; 16:4). Against the horizons of growing estrangement with Israel in chs. 11–12, faced with building obstinacy, Jesus turns away from the crowds to his disciples (13:1-2, 36). The crowds are able to hear the first of Jesus' teaching in parables; what separates the crowds and the disciples, then, is not "hearing" but "hearing and understanding." As Jesus explains with reference to the parable of the seeds, the good soil is "the one who hears the word and understands it, who indeed bears fruit and yields . . ." (13:23; see 13:51).

Throughout this section on parables, Jesus maintains a tension between ethics and eschatology. Judgment will come, but in the meantime church and world consist of good and bad, wheat and weeds. Disciples are to take the measure of their own faithfulness using the calculus of the future fulfillment of the kingdom; this requires a greater orientation toward faithful response to Jesus (hearing, understanding, and performing the will of God) than toward ensuring the purity of the church in the present. Jesus' perspective also underscores the inevitability of his own missionary experience — as well as that of his followers. Experiences of hostility and rejection are simply aspects of present life for those who live faithfully among "this evil generation." In the midst of opposition and charlatanism, God remains at work, and participation in that work — that is, embracing God's kingdom — is worth any price.

Jesus' teaching regarding selling all in order to purchase the field or pearl (13:44-45) may have had additional importance for Matthew's readers. In Matthew's account of Jesus' missionary instructions (10:8-10), there is a marked interest in what one takes and acquires on the missionary journey. Paul struggled with itinerant missionaries who peddled the word of God for profit (2 Cor 2:17), and it may be that Matthew is similarly concerned with disciples of Jesus who have in this way lost the radical edge of their discipleship, whose expectations extend beyond the provision of basic sustenance. Seen within these interpretive parameters, these parables sound a clear note regarding the inestimable value of the kingdom, worthy of possession at any cost, that would likewise call Jesus' followers to robust, self-denying discipleship (see Matt 10:37-39).

4.2.3.4. Violence and Confession Intensify (13:54–16:20)

Jesus' parabolic teaching in ch. 13 is bracketed by episodes with a parallel theme — namely, the identity of Jesus' family. In the first, Jesus' mother and brother wish to speak to Jesus, a request that wins Jesus' remark that "whoever does the will of my Father in heaven is my brother and sister and mother" (12:50). Afterward, Jesus returns to his hometown, where he is dismissed by those who fail to understand the nature of his filial relationship with God and, thus, the character of his true family (13:55-56). As this new section of the Gospel gets underway, then, Matthew's own audience is bombarded with the necessity of reviewing their own assessments of Jesus and their own status *vis-à-vis* his family.

Matthew continues his depiction of the ever-widening chasm between those who reject Jesus and those who follow him in faith. First, he reports the execution of John the Baptist, an account that has chilling implications for Jesus (14:1-12). Herod, hoping to gain influence with his subjects, has had John beheaded, and now he has taken an interest in Jesus. Will Jesus experience a similar fate? An answer to this question is delayed by Jesus' well-timed departure (14:13). Not long afterward, Pharisees and legal experts from Jerusalem locate Jesus and interrogate him concerning the traditions of the elders (15:1-20). Again, a sinister note is sounded, for Jerusalem was introduced early on as a city set against Jesus (2:1-20); and again, Jesus makes his exit (15:21). Finally, he is accosted by Pharisees and Sadducees demanding a sign, some form of proof that Jesus' person and ministry are sanctioned by God. This, according to Jesus, proves their incapacity to understand at all what God is doing in history, and he withdraws yet again (16:1-4). Such animosity represents only one of two strands of this narrative section.

The other is spun of threads evidencing Jesus' compassion, his distribution of God's blessings, and the recognition of his status as Savior and Son of God. His compassion extends to the people of Israel, as one might anticipate (14:14; 15:32); in addition, even a Canaanite woman seeks his mercy and, on account of her startling faith, receives it (15:21-28). This is a reminder that Matthew is, in part, interested in showing how the age-old barrier between Jew and Gentile might be surmounted. This woman recognizes Jesus for who he is, Son of David; addresses him as Lord, thus signaling her submission and loyalty to him as the benefactor of God's saving power; and persists in her hope for help. Peter, drowning in the lake, cried out, "Lord, save me!" She too begs, "Lord, help me!" All of this Jesus recognizes as faith — indeed, as great faith — and so this Canaanite woman becomes, like the centurion in 8:5-13, a model of how Gentiles might be included among the people of God.

The climactic recognition of Jesus comes soon after. The question of Jesus' identity has been broached before: "What sort of person is this?" (8:27). "Are you the one who is to come, or shall we look for another?" (11:3). "Can this be the Son of David?" (12:23). And so on. Now Jesus himself raises the issue, and receives from Peter a confession of such profundity that it could only have come from God: "You are the Messiah, the Son of the living God!" (16:16). The contrast with the representatives of Judaism could not be more stark, for they have consistently and entirely failed to perceive or adopt God's perspective and disclosure regarding Jesus. The growing rift between the synagogue and Jesus' followers now culminates in the founding of a new people, known for the first time in the Gospel of Matthew as "the church."

4.2.4. Christology, Discipleship, and the Life of the Church (16:21–20:34)

Clearly in this instance, Matthew's "from that time on . . ." points to a monumental shift in the development of the narrative. In this section, Jesus' opponents, the Pharisees and Jewish leadership, are pushed almost completely offstage. This is ironic, since it is precisely because of their opposition to Jesus that he now focuses so intently on the community life of his followers.

Permeating this section, too, is Jesus' disclosure of his fate to his followers. Matthew's audience has been aware of the malicious forces aligned against Jesus since ch. 2, when Herod sought to execute Jesus as a newborn. Subsequent news of a plot to kill Jesus (12:14) and the report of John's decapitation on Herod's order (14:1-12) have further served to anticipate Jesus' demise at the hand of his opponents. Functioning almost as a heading for the present section is Jesus' first prediction of his suffering and death, and this one is soon followed by others (16:21; 17:22-23; 20:17-18). As Matthew presents it, news of Jesus' impending death and his submission to it spills over into lessons regarding the character of discipleship and, then, the life of the church. This is evident first in 16:21-28, where a sketch of the cost of discipleship is appended to Jesus' revelation concerning his passion and execution.

The correlation of Jesus' fate as God's Messiah with the life of the church pervades this entire narrative section in more organic ways as well. Matthew 16:21–20:34 comprises three subsections — with the first and third (16:21–17:27; 19:1–20:34) sharing common interests that help to determine the substance and interpretation of the second (18:1-35). The first, 16:21–17:27, draws a line between Jesus and the disciples on the basis of their competing visions of suffering and glory. Jesus' self-understanding and his experience of transfiguration (17:1-8) intimate that the experience of suffering and rejection among humans is not inconsistent with being clothed in divine honor. Suffering in this instance is neither a surprise to God nor an indication that Jesus has somehow been excluded from divine favor; to the contrary, as the Son of Man Jesus "must," of divine necessity, "go to Jerusalem and undergo great suffering" (16:21). Will the disciples adopt analogous commitments and practices?

Speaking for the disciples, Peter sets forth a point of view on these matters that is startling in its contrast with Jesus'. Jesus has disclosed to his disciples that, according to the plan of God, he must suffer and die. Peter construes the plan of God so differently that he meets Jesus' announcement with the strongest of denials: "God forbid it!" How could Jesus be the Messiah, Son of the living God (16:16)

Money in the Gospels

Talent		an amount of silver worth 6000 drachmae	Matt 18:24; 25:14-30
Mina		an amount of silver worth 100 drachmas	
Stater		a Greek silver coin worth about 4 drachmas	Matt 17:27
Shekel		a Judean coin worth about 4 drachmas	The temple tax (Matt 17:27) was a half-shekel (approximately one didrachmon) for each Jewish man.
Didrachmon		a Greek silver coin worth 2 drachmas	
Drachma			Luke 15:8
Denarius		Greek and Roman silver coins each about the value of a day-laborer's wage	Matt 18:28; 20:1-16; 22:19 par.; Mark 6:37; 14:5; Luke 7:41; 10:35
As or Assarion		a Roman bronze coin worth about $1/16$ drachma	Matt 10:29 par. Luke 12:6
Quadrans		a Roman bronze coin worth $1/4$ assarion	Matt 5:26; the worth of the widow's two coins in Mark 12:42
Lepton		a Greek bronze coin worth $1/8$ assarion	Luke 12:59; the widow's two coins in Mark 12:42 par. Luke 21:2

and suffer so shamefully, so heinously? It is no surprise, then, that Peter fails to understand the significance of Jesus' transfiguration (17:4-5) and that the disciples fail to implement the power of God on behalf of a demonized boy (17:14-21). They respond to Jesus' second prediction of his suffering not with insight and discernment, but with distress (17:22-23).

The disciples' lack of insight in this first subsection is underscored again in the third, 19:1–20:34, where their dispositions and behavior provide the occasion for censure. The warning to the disciples centers in the ambiguity of Jesus' parable of the vineyard workers in 20:1-16. In this story, groups of workers are employed for different lengths of time during the day, but all are paid the same. This leads those who worked longest to grumble and complain, alleging that they have been treated unjustly even though they received everything that was promised. Is this parable told against the Jews — who, then, would object to the situation in which their priority would be overlooked as the blessings of God were distributed also to Gentiles? This is a possible reading, but a second reading garners support from the Matthean narrative. In this case, those Christian disciples with claims to status in the community — whether on account of their age in the faith, association with the earliest Jesus-movement, possession of special gifts, or whatever — are represented by those workers who complain that God's blessings were distributed with-

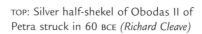

out reference to such human-oriented values or status markers. These two readings are not mutually exclusive; indeed, it would be consistent with Matthew's overall program to employ a critique of the Jewish people in order to point a critical fin-

TOP: Silver half-shekel of Obodas II of Petra struck in 60 BCE *(Richard Cleave)*

CENTER: Silver denarius of Emperor Vespasian celebrating the victory over Judea in the 70s CE *(Richard Cleave)*

BOTTOM: Bronze lepta of Antiochus VII struck in Jerusalem in 131 BCE *(Richard Cleave)*

ger at those in the church whose lives reflect more the character of Jesus' enemies than that of Jesus himself.

Could this really be a problem within the church? Note the surrounding material in Matthew's narrative: Jesus disciples' belittle children as unworthy of Jesus' attention, failing to understand that the kingdom of God belongs to just such persons who, in the Roman Empire, occupied the lowest possible rungs of society's ladder of status (19:13-15). The disciples are astounded at Jesus' words regarding the impossibility of a rich man entering God's kingdom, thus implicating themselves in the conventional but grossly mistaken notion that the wealthy (necessarily) have their riches and status on account of divine blessing (19:16-25). And controversy breaks out among the disciples after a mother requests seats of status in the kingdom for her two sons, with the result that Jesus must compress his message concerning status and honor into the clearest possible terms (20:20-28). It is no coincidence that this last episode is followed immediately by another involving two men; though blind, they recognize Jesus' identity as Lord and Son of David, and their eyes are opened (20:29-34). Within Matthew's narrative, their healing functions as a parable of the disciples' need also of having their eyes opened.

Located between these two subsections is a third, 18:1-35, which constitutes Jesus' fourth discourse in the Gospel of Matthew. Here Jesus takes up the character of the church's inner life, but the force of his instruction is not altogether plain as he moves back and forth between two poles. On the one hand, Jesus outlines for the community a concern with purity and tight internal cohesion; at this point, his concern with boundaries seems almost sectarian. On the other, he admonishes his followers to adopt the manner of his own comportment, putting aside their own freedoms on behalf of the welfare of others, and he speaks as though the reservoir of forgiveness and grace could never be depleted. On the one hand, procedures are sketched for excommunicating the recalcitrant (18:15-17); on the other, the most severe punishment is reserved for those who do not forgive their brothers and sisters (18:21-35).

Between these two poles is a community struggling with its identity and, so, with its boundaries, with the nature of its relations toward outsiders as well as the character of its internal bonds. Of great consequence is the staging of this discourse. It is true that Jesus spells out a process for church discipline that has as its end the exclusion of a former member, but it is also true that, before this, Jesus highlights the importance of humility, warns the community not to present a stumbling block to its weaker members, but to care and search for the lost. After the instructions on church discipline, moreover, Jesus speaks of the reach of forgiveness in the most effusive terms. The integrity of the community is important, but even this concern must be set within the larger context of the expansiveness of grace.

4.2.5. The Ministry of Jesus the Messiah in Jerusalem (21:1–25:46)

The beginning of ch. 21 marks a momentous, foreboding shift in the Matthean narrative. The city of Jerusalem was first introduced in 2:3-4 for its hostility to the news of Jesus' birth, and in 15:1 it is a group of Pharisees and scribes from Jerusalem who become embroiled with Jesus in controversy. Thus far in the narrative, since 4:23, the center of Jesus' ministry has been the region of Galilee (see 17:22), apparently out of harm's way. With ch. 21, though, Jesus comes near Jerusalem, enters the city, and teaches in the temple before moving across the valley from Jerusalem to instruct his disciples at the Mount of Olives. Dramatic tension is raised all the more by Jesus' recent announcements that it will be in Jerusalem that he will fulfill the divine will in his suffering and death (16:21; 20:17-18).

4.2.5.1. The Question of Jesus' Identity and Authority (21:1–22:46)

Matthew has staged Jesus' entry into Jerusalem in such a way that it raises profoundly the question of Jesus' status, his identity and the source of his authority. The manner of his entry (with a donkey and a colt — cf. Zech 9:9), the exclamation of the crowds, the witness of the Scriptures, Jesus' action in the temple, even the cursing of the fig tree — each of these in its own way brings to the surface the query voiced by the temple leadership, "By what authority are you doing these things, and who gave you this authority?" (Matt 21:23). This is a crucial moment within the Matthean narrative, for herein lies the chief point of controversy for Jesus and the Jewish people. Does he speak on God's behalf? Indeed, how could he speak on God's behalf, this one who causes trouble in the temple and propounds a message that stands contrary to God's will as this has been represented by the traditions of the elders and by the Jewish elite in Jerusalem? Although Jesus ostensibly refuses to identify the authority by which he teaches (21:27), the parables he relates and the exchanges in which he engages through the end of ch. 22 nonetheless address the issue of his authority indirectly. He identifies himself as God's Son. And he goes further, (1) denouncing the Pharisees, chief priests, Sadducees, and scribes for their failure to understand and embody the will of God and (2) anticipating the wrenching of the kingdom of God from the Jewish people to be given to a new people who will produce the fruit of the kingdom (see 21:43; 22:8-14).

4.2.5.2. Jesus Criticizes His Opponents (23:1-39)

Matthew 23 comprises a single, lengthy tirade against the scribes and Pharisees; at least, so it would appear. From a rhetorical viewpoint, it is of interest that Jesus begins to castigate the Pharisees and scribes in the third person: "the scribes and Pharisees . . . they . . . they. . . ." In 23:8, however, he changes to the second person "you," even though his audience consists of only "the crowds and his disciples" (23:1). His censorious address may be directed most immediately within the narrative against the scribes and Pharisees, but this speech can work for Matthew only because Jesus' invective can be aimed against the church as well. Apparently, the line between the blameworthy behavior of the scribes and Pharisees on the one hand, and that of the church on the other is all too thin. It will not do to demonize the Pharisees and scribes and thus miss the value of this woeful chapter as a word spoken to indict, warn, and instruct those who wish to follow Jesus.

Jesus' speech can be divided into three main parts. The first, 23:1-12, draws on a variety of images rooted in first-century Palestinian culture related to claims of advanced status. For the sort of jockeying around relative rank and position pictured here, Jesus substitutes the primacy of mutuality ("you are all siblings," 23:8), humility, and service ("the greatest among you will be your servant," 23:11). The second section contains a series of seven woes, each growing out of the allegation of hypocrisy. The nature of this charge may escape the contemporary reader accustomed to equating "hypocrisy" with play-acting, deceit, or insincerity. Even if this term could have embraced such ideas in the Greek world, Matthew's Gospel is more likely influenced by the concept of "hypocrisy" as this is developed in the LXX; there, the word is often used for behavior grounded in a misconstrual of the divine will. Therefore, Jesus does not castigate the scribes and Pharisees for their insincerity, but for their failure to interpret rightly the will of God. That discerning and conveying the will of God featured centrally in the vocation of Pharisees and scribes renders these charges all the more damning. Finally (23:32-39), Jesus turns to the consequences of the charges he has brought against the Pharisees and scribes, which is divine judgment and, specifically, the destruction of Jerusalem.

4.2.5.3. *Jesus Admonishes His Disciples concerning Readiness (24:1–25:46)*

Jesus' lament over Jerusalem provides an easy transition into his fifth and final extended discourse. That a new segment of the narrative has begun is marked by the change of scene from the temple courts to the Mount of Olives and by an even further narrowing of Jesus' audience. During the whole of his instruction in chs. 24–25, Jesus speaks only to his disciples.

The content of his teaching is determined by the two parts of the question his disciples pose to him in 24:3. After his pronouncement of the impending fall of the temple, the disciples ask him, "Tell us, when will this be, and what will be the sign of your coming and of the end of the age?" In 24:4-35, Jesus takes up the question concerning the "sign," and in the remainder of the address he deals with the question "When?" For those disciples interested in measured certainty on either question, his responses are disappointing. This is because he discusses not "the sign" but a host of signs that, together, mark the coming of the end. What is more, the signs he describes are lacking the sort of specificity for which one might hope, if one is interested in calendar-watching. Borrowing from an arsenal of stock apocalyptic images of the coming of the end, Jesus rehearses the troubles and deceptions that will accompany the consummation of God's plan. Within his discussion, these images are less useful for satisfying curiosity and energizing speculation and more helpful as a warning to prepare oneself for the difficulties ahead and to maintain readiness.

Nor is Jesus forthcoming on the question, "When will this be?" In fact, he specifically denies that this can be known by anyone other than God (24:36). This could have marked the termination of the discourse, but it does not. Rather, for Jesus the incapacity to know the divine timetable pushes to the surface the necessity of preparedness. He thus addresses his disciples directly and in parables to counsel constant readiness. The nature of the preparedness needed takes on a peculiarly Matthean twist, one that becomes transparent in the great vision with which Jesus closes his address (25:31-46). At the end-time throne scene, when sheep and goats are segregated, there is basically one standard of judgment. It is not whether one claims faith or possesses status as a leader in the community of God's people, or one's prophetic or other charismatic abilities. In a way fully consonant with the close of the Sermon on the Mount (especially 7:21-27), Jesus proposes that the standard of judgment will be whether persons have exhibited in their lives, especially with respect to the least, the lost, and the left out, obedience to the will of God.

4.2.6. The Death and Resurrection of Jesus the Messiah, Son of God (26:1–28:20)

In the closing scenes of Matthew's Gospel the various threads of his narrative reach their resolution. Most obviously, Matthew's story of conflict reaches its high point in the narrative of Jesus' passion and death, though it continues beyond his death.

At the outset, the chief priests and elders conspire against Jesus, cutting a deal with one of the disciples, Judas, in order to accomplish their objective. Here and throughout the passion narrative, the Jewish elite are noteworthy for their deceit and malice. When they finally have Jesus in their grasp, for example, they immediately seek "false evidence against Jesus so that they might put him to death" (26:59). Their malevolence is such that it even spills over onto the Jewish populace present in Jerusalem. Early on, the people served as a buffer between Jesus and the Jerusalem leadership (26:5), but in the end they, too, call for Jesus to be executed and take on themselves the guilt of his death (27:15-26). Opposition to Jesus may find its climax in his shameful, apparently impotent presence on a Roman cross and his final breath, but Jesus' death does not spell the end of hostilities. As if to account for the ongoing repudiation of Jesus' message and movement following his death, Matthew goes on to narrate the duplicity of the chief priests and elders in fabricating and perpetuating a lie to explain away his empty tomb (28:11-15).

In some ways, the deceit of the Jewish leadership in Jerusalem is encapsulated in the figure of Jesus' betrayer. He is scorned in the narrative for his apparent avarice. Twice he addresses Jesus, and in both instances the honorific title, "Rabbi," falls sweetly from his lips. For Matthew, though, "Rabbi" has only negative connotations. It is the language of Jesus' enemies. By employing it, Judas shows that, though he has been one of Jesus' disciples, he has no insight into Jesus' identity.

Judas, of course, is not the only disciple mentioned in these closing chapters of the Gospel. Indeed, if Matthew draws together the cords of hostility in this narrative, he also concerns himself with the story of Jesus' disciples. On one level the role of the disciples is overshadowed by other, apparently minor characters, including a woman who anoints Jesus at Bethany (26:6-13), a centurion who acknowledges Jesus' sonship (27:54), Joseph of Arimathea, who buries Jesus (27:57-60), and above all the women who have followed Jesus from Galilee and continue faithfully with him (27:55-56, 61; 28:1). The cause of Jesus' other disciples is not thereby lost, but it must be reclaimed as the disciples are restored and empowered for mission (26:31-32; 28:9-20).

The comportment of the Jews *vis-à-vis* Jesus contrasts sharply with witnesses to his innocence (Judas in 27:3-4, Pilate's wife in 27:19, and Pilate in 27:23-24), but even more so with Matthew's presentation of Jesus' authoritative status as Son of God. Jesus speaks first in the passion account and maintains the initiative throughout, as though he sets in motion the events that lead to his death. True, he is derided on the cross by those who find in his crucifixion unimpeachable evidence against his status as Son of God (27:38-44), but this is because they have understood so little of God's agenda. To the contrary, that Jesus willingly undergoes suffering and death proves his identity as God's Son. This is demonstrated in his prayer in Gethsemane (26:36-46). At his arrest he acknowledges his ability to call for massive angelic assistance (26:53). But more important than his personal safety is the divine will: the Scriptures must be fulfilled (26:24, 26-29, 54, 56). Matthew's passion narrative serves, then, to demonstrate Jesus' true identity as the obedient Son of God who goes to his death to accomplish God's salvific will.

Jesus' resurrection from the dead is crucial to Matthew's narrative in large part for the same reason: in this epoch-making event, God provides for Jesus the ultimate vindication. The resurrection proves that Jesus' death was in accordance with the divine will, that Jesus does bear divine authority, that he is the decisive interpreter of Torah, and, so, that his teaching represents God's will. For this reason, it is crucial for Matthew to affirm the resurrection as a historical event — and for the Jewish leadership to deny it. Matthew provides an airtight apologetic for the empty tomb in 27:62-66: the tomb is secured by Roman soldiers.

The Death of the Righteous Man (Wisdom 2:12-20)

According to the Wisdom of Solomon, a Jewish text from the late first century BCE or the early first century CE, the voice of the ungodly is heard in words that parallel material in Matthew 27:

Let us lie in wait for the righteous man, because he is inconvenient to us and opposes our actions; he reproaches us for sins against the law, and accuses us of sins against our training. He professes to have knowledge of God, and calls himself a [son] of the Lord. He became to us a reproof of our thoughts; the very sight of him is a burden to us, because his manner of life is unlike that of others, and his ways are strange. We are considered by him as something base, and he avoids our ways as unclean; he calls the last end of the righteous happy, and boasts that God is his father. Let us see if his words are true, and let us test what will happen at the end of his life; for if the righteous man is God's [son], he will help him, and will deliver him from the hand of his adversaries. Let us test him with insult and torture, so that we may find out how gentle he is, and make trial of his forbearance. Let us condemn him to a shameful death, for, according to what he says, he will be protected. (NRSV)

The resurrection of Jesus is important for another reason too. As a consequence of the resurrection, the mission begun with Jesus' advent continues in the mission of the disciples, who may therefore continue to experience the presence of Jesus with them always.

4.3. THE GOSPEL OF MATTHEW, THE JEWS, AND THE CHURCH

Why is the question of Matthew and the Jews important? At one level, it may be enough simply to say that his Gospel is permeated by material related to this issue. Indeed, it is not much of an exaggeration to say that every passage in the Gospel can be read against the interpretive backdrop of "the problem of the Jews." Of course, the stakes in this discussion are raised somewhat by the diversity of ways in which Jewish people and institutions are portrayed within the Gospel. How can we read the Gospel of Matthew while giving full weight to all sides of the evidence? For Matthew's first readers, as well as for all subsequent readers, however, the question of Matthew and the Jews has even greater significance than this. Because of the way the Evangelist frames this issue, it has immediate relevance to his readers. A close reading of the Gospel reveals that Matthew does not lambaste the scribes and Pharisees because he is angry at those historical groups. There was undoubtedly hostility between Jesus and these representatives of Judaism; after all, Jesus' concern with faithful appropriation of the Scriptures would have had the immediate effect of positioning him in dialogue with others concerned with proper interpretation of Torah. Even among the scribes and Pharisees, debate of this sort could be heated, so it is no surprise that these groups engage with Jesus in ways that suggest how high the stakes have been raised. Matthew's narration is motivated by something more than antiquarian interest, however. His narrative representation of history is also concerned with the ongoing relevance of the antagonism between Jesus and the scribes and Pharisees for the Christian movement. That is, by exposing Jesus' distress with Jewish leaders of the synagogue and temple, Matthew is similarly unmasking the problematic character of leadership in subsequent Christian communities. There is in Matthew's narration a not-so-subtle irony, for the denunciation of those Jews in authority is nothing less than an invective against those disciples of Jesus whose dispositions and behavior are calibrated along similar lines.

It is possible to state the issue with more nuance and greater accuracy by probing Matthew's basic concern with *identity*. Who are the people of God? For Matthew, this question must be resolved on two fronts simultaneously: with reference to *internal cohesion* and with reference to *relations with outsiders*. By resolving the dilemma of the dispositions and practices appropriate to those within the community of God's people, Matthew at the same time draws a line that rejects the problematic dispositions and practices of outsiders and especially their influence on the community of God's people. To put it bluntly, Jesus' followers have developed commitments and are implicated in behaviors that are all too reminiscent of these Pharisees and scribes, and one of the primary ways Matthew addresses this situation is to paint with sharp lines and brazen colors those scenes in which Jesus castigates the Pharisees and Jewish leaders for behaving in precisely those ways.

Of course, it is true that the Gospel of Matthew has long been regarded as the most Jewish of the NT Gospels. According to this tradition of interpretation, the idea that Matthew is working to draw a distinction between his own Christian communities and the Jews would be erroneous. In fact, some interpreters have even found in Matthew's Gospel an attempt to win the Jewish people over to faith in Messiah Jesus. The Evangelist obviously takes as authoritative and determinative in the course of history the Scriptures of Israel; indeed, he records Jesus' declaration, "Do not think that I have come to rescind the law or the prophets . . . , for truly I tell you, until heaven and earth pass away, not one letter, not one stroke of a letter, will pass from the law until all is accomplished" (5:17-18). The Evangelist employs Semitic terms — for example, *raka* (5:22), *mamōnas* (6:24), and *korbanas* (27:6) — without translation or explanation, and refers without commentary to such Jewish conventions as handwashing at meals (15:2), phylacteries (23:5), and restrictions on Sabbath travel (24:20). In these and a myriad other ways, we gain a window into the Jewishness of this Gospel and recognize the extent to which the form of Christian discipleship it fosters coheres with the faith of Israel. This is not the whole story, however.

Matthew's narrative gives us plenty of reasons for imagining that the Evangelist has been influenced in his writing by the church's struggle at various stages of transition from self-identity and existence as one among other forms of Judaism to a self-identity and existence as a new people. There were Pharisees and there were Christians — both of whom belonged, with others, under the large umbrella of first-century Judaism, but now Christians are hammering out an identity separate from Judaism. Even though churches have begun to receive Gentiles into their numbers, they continue to see themselves primarily in Jewish terms and in continuity with historic Israel; at the same time, hostility with Jewish people outside the Christian community remains fresh and rivalry between "church" and "synagogue" is an ongoing and pressing concern. Thus, for example, Matthew normally presents Jewish groups and leaders in a negative light. This is nowhere more true than in ch. 23, with its unrelenting tirade against the Pharisees and scribes. Not surprisingly, then, the synagogue — a house for study and instruction in Torah — is not a welcome place for Jesus and his disciples. Associated with scribes and Pharisees, the synagogue belongs to "them"; it is "their" or "your" synagogue(s) (e.g., 4:23; 10:17; 13:54; 23:6, 34). And "their" scribes can be distinguished from Christian scribes (7:29; 13:52; 23:34). If Jesus and his followers can never be "home" in the synagogue, the same cannot be said of the "church," which, founded by Jesus, seems already to have replaced the "synagogue" for this new people. People enter discipleship and, thus, the church through its own rite of entrance and liturgical formula, baptism "in the name of the Father and of the Son and of the Holy Spirit" (28:19). Within the church, there remains a firm commitment to Torah, but the authoritative words of Jesus have preeminence (e.g., 5:17-19; 7:24-27; 28:20). Even more jarring in its implications is the constellation of sayings in which the transfer of God's kingdom to a new people, which includes Gentiles, is portended: "Therefore I tell you, the kingdom of God will be taken away from you and given to a people that produces the fruits of the kingdom" (21:43; see also, e.g., 8:5-13).

But the Gentile world is no safe haven either. Jesus explicitly warns his disciples that "all the nations" *(panta ta ethnē)* will hate them, and he urges the disciples in their missionary endeavors to anticipate resistance and maltreatment at the hands of Gentiles as well as Jews (24:9; 10:17-18). Matthew's transparent commitment to the Gentile mission (28:16-20) cannot be allowed to overshadow his critical position *vis-à-vis* Gentiles in the Sermon on the Mount and elsewhere (5:47; 6:7, 32; 18:17). This suggests that he has a certain ambivalence to the larger world outside the community of the faithful, so that the church must find its identity, at least in part, *in contrast to (or over against) society at large.* This need helps to explain Matthew's invective against Jewish people and institutions as well as his less strident depictions of Gentile resistance to Jesus' followers.

Neither is the Christian community itself a safe haven, pure and simple. If the kingdom of God has been taken away from the Jewish people it is because they have failed to produce the fruits of the kingdom. What if this new "people" fails likewise to produce the fruits of the kingdom? Israel failed because of its resistance to God's salvific initiative in the coming of Jesus. What will be the fate of this new "people" if it does not respond faithfully? The invitation to discipleship is a gift, to be sure, but it is wrapped in the demand for faithful response. And, apparently, Matthew remains concerned with the habits that have possessed Christian "insiders" — people who have begun to recapitulate in their lives the very attitudes and behaviors against which Jesus railed. They may acknowledge Jesus with appropriate language, even manifest in their lives the power of prophecy and exorcism, but they are "false prophets in sheep's clothing," "doers of unrighteousness" (7:15-23). The problem of the Jewish leaders was their failure to embrace and embody the will of God, yielding in their lives the fruit of righteousness. Matthew employs the same standards of character and behavior in his own discourse situation. As Jesus declares in the Sermon on the Mount, "unless your righteousness exceeds that of the scribes and Pharisees, you will never enter the kingdom of heaven" (5:20), and "Not everyone who says to me, 'Lord, Lord,' will enter the kingdom of heaven, but only the one who does the will of my Father in heaven" (7:21).

Who is responsible for the narration of the Gospel of Matthew? The first and last word that must be spoken in an attempt to address this question is that we do not and cannot know, at least not with any certainty. Like the other Gospels, this one was written without the ancient equivalent of a byline. According to one old tradition, it was written by Matthew the apostle, who sought to produce a Gospel that reflected Jewish style (Eusebius, *Hist. Eccl.* 3.39.16); this identification is supported by the title given the Gospel, "According to Matthew," in the second century. Others have found in Matt 13:52 — "And he said to them, 'Therefore every scribe who has been trained for the kingdom of heaven is like the master of a household who brings out of his treasure what is new and what is old'" — the author's reference to himself. In this case, "Matthew" would not be the toll collector/disciple (9:9; 10:3), but a Christian scribe. For those who read the Gospel of Matthew, a decision between these two possibilities or the presence of still others is not crucial. In part, this is because we know nothing of the author of this Gospel apart from what we can glean from the Gospel itself — for example, that Matthew is Jewish, in dialogue with first-century Jewish thought and practices, and adept in his handling of Israel's Scriptures. That the Gospel credited to Matthew is anonymous is itself of significance, since it underscores the point that more important than our identification of the person who wrote the book is our engagement with the one about whom it was written.

FOR FURTHER READING

Craig L. Blomberg, *Matthew* (New American Commentary 22; Nashville: Broadman, 1992)

W. D. Davies and Dale C. Allison, Jr., *Matthew*, 3 vols. (International Critical Commentary; Edinburgh: Clark, 1988-97)

Donald A. Hagner, *Matthew*, 2 vols. (Word Biblical Commentary 33; Dallas: Word, 1993/95)

Craig S. Keener, *A Commentary on the Gospel of Matthew* (Grand Rapids: Eerdmans, 1999)

Ulrich Luz, *The Theology of the Gospel of Matthew* (Cambridge: Cambridge University Press, 1995)

Mark Allan Powell, *God with Us: A Pastoral Theology of Matthew's Gospel* (Minneapolis: Fortress, 1995)

Graham N. Stanton, *A Gospel for a New People: Studies in Matthew* (Edinburgh: Clark, 1992)

5. *The Gospel according to Mark*

5.1. NARRATING THE STORY OF JESUS

Although the Gospel according to Mark appears second in the NT canon and is therefore sometimes called the Second Gospel, it is usually regarded as the first of the NT Gospels to have been written. For this reason, students of the Gospels have sometimes turned to it as not only the earliest but also the most historical of the narratives of Jesus' ministry.

To some, Mark the Evangelist has appeared as little more than a chronicler, having put the story of Jesus' career in written form for the sake of posterity. This view has been helped along by the ancient tradition stating that Mark served as Peter's interpreter, writing down accurately, though not in order, Jesus' sayings and deeds as related by Peter (Eusebius, *Hist. Eccl.* 3.39.15). Later, we will assess the importance of this tradition for the identification of the author of this Gospel. Here it is necessary to dispel any notion of Mark as having exercised nothing more than the chronicler's craft. Mark himself wraps his presentation of Jesus in the robe of christological significance already in the opening line of the Gospel: "the beginning of the gospel of Jesus Christ, the Son of God, as it was written in the prophet Isaiah . . ." (Mark 1:1). It is immediately clear that Mark's is no dispassionate, objective reporting of the life of Jesus. Rather, his narrative is transparently concerned with Jesus' identity, and with the meaning of his person and work against a backdrop provided by the story of Israel and, especially, the proclamation of the prophet Isaiah.

Also in his introductory section, Mark takes a further step, revealing something about Jesus even more profound than this opening line might on its own suggest. The message Jesus proclaims is nothing less than "the good news of God"

(1:14), and this indicates that the story of Jesus is at a more significant level the story of God's activity. Mark's Gospel is thus concerned with God's intervention in history to bring to fruition the promises of Scripture and to inaugurate God's reign and rule, his kingdom. In an ultimate sense, then, the Gospel of Mark is about God.

This observation intimates something important about Mark's Gospel — namely, that Mark's primary objective, and the primary basis of the authority of his narrative, rests in its capacity to speak on behalf of God. Historical events do not generally contain within themselves their own interpretation. This is true even of those events whose central character is Jesus of Nazareth. Mark's narrative is a presentation of Jesus' public career, to be sure, but it is one oriented toward providing a divine perspective on that career.

Like the other Evangelists, Mark must be seen as a communicator, drawing on and representing the traditional materials concerning Jesus to his audience in a way that will address the realities of their lives. In doing so, he wants ultimately to say something about God and the nature of God's project in history. And in order to do this, he weaves a narrative whose primary focus falls on Jesus' identity and ministry and the nature of discipleship, set within the horizons of the Scriptures on the one hand and fierce hostility on the other.

If Mark was the first Evangelist, then why did he choose to communicate in the form of a narrative? Other forms of response to community struggles had already been pioneered — Paul's letters, for example. What realities led to Mark's decision to sketch the public life of Jesus in the form of a biographical narrative? We might be helped by refocusing the question: What do narratives do well? Several answers are possible. First, they encourage in their audiences a sense of affinity, or identification, with their central character or characters. This is certainly true of the Gospel according to Mark, which invites its audience to identify with Jesus and, in a different way, to puzzle over the role of the disciples. Second, narratives are capable of indicating the rich interrelations among the many forces that help to shape human experiences in concrete situations. This is also true of Mark, who has woven together numerous forces — some mundane and personal, others cosmic and institutional — that together shape the lives of persons within the narrative as well as the outcome of the story. This phenomenon is perhaps most transparent in 14:21, where Jesus observes, "For the Son of man goes as it has been written of him, but woe to the one by whom the Son of man is betrayed!" Here Jesus grounds his passion in the Scriptures at the same time that he insists on the culpability of his betrayer. Third, narratives work to draw their audiences into their worlds so as to undergird shared values or to challenge the imaginations and views of their audiences, as well as their thoughts and practices. How the Gospel of Mark accomplishes this task becomes evident as we see how it has grappled with the identity of Jesus.

5.2. JESUS, THE DISCIPLES, AND THE AUTHORITIES IN MARK

Readers or hearers of the Gospel may perhaps be forgiven for imagining that, in writing his narrative, Mark struggled with how to present two, apparently conflicting, images of Jesus. In fact, the juxtaposition of these two images helps to determine the overall shape of the Gospel in a way that has resisted attempts to sketch an outline of its narrative. The Gospel communicates less through a structured outline than as a musical score that has woven together a leading melody and its countermelody. When the Gospel is viewed as a whole, most noticeable is its concern to portray the ministry of Jesus as a relentless progression of events leading to the crucifixion of the Messiah. Fully one-third of the Gospel is given over to the events of Jesus' last days, marked by repeated prophecies of his coming suffering and death and a detailed and picturesque presentation of his passion. More than this, one encounters, already in the earlier chapters, intimations, implicit and explicit, of swelling malice against Jesus. As early as 2:18-20, Jesus anticipates his sudden, unexpected departure, and by 3:1-6 antagonism has progressed to the point that Mark can record, "The Pharisees went out and immediately conspired with the Herodians against him, how to destroy him." Perhaps this is not surprising, since Mark had already noted the arrest of John, who spoke on God's behalf, and would go on to relate John's execution under Herod (1:14; 6:14-29). Clearly, from Mark's vantage point, the ministry of Jesus cannot be understood apart from the cross, which casts its shadow back across the whole Gospel.

This is not the whole story, however. At the same time that it follows the Messiah's journey to Golgotha, the Markan narrative is punctuated again and again with evidence of Jesus the popular miracle worker, powerful healer, and authoritative teacher. He casts out demons, astounds his own followers by walking on the Sea of Galilee, feeds the thousands, heals the blind and lame, and confounds those who listen to him by the nature of his teaching. Especially in the first half of the Gospel, the Evangelist often seems more interested in presenting Jesus in this way than in recounting the details of his healing ministry or the content of his proclamation. Using the narrative device of summary, he often prefers to *tell* his audience about Jesus the powerful teacher rather than show them, and to record the overwhelmingly positive and pervasive support Jesus attracted from the general populace. Even so, evidence of Jesus' powerful ministry abounds, so that we are left with the impression that Jesus is the authoritative teacher who manifests the power of God, the herald of God's rule in whose ministry the power of God has been made available.

Mark's audience is left to wonder: powerful teacher and rejected Messiah — how can Jesus be both? The key to Mark's narrative is to take it as a narrative, and this narrative both affirms that these two presumably competing portrayals are true *and* insists that Jesus' true identity cannot be grasped apart from the correlation of these two portrayals. Jesus not only demonstrates power but also experiences rejection, suffering, and death. Indeed, Jesus' activity as authoritative teacher and agent of miraculous power is the immediate cause of the hostility directed against him. He forgives sins by healing a paralytic, so that he is charged with blasphemy (2:1-12). He breaks the boundaries of conventional piety — eating with toll collectors and sinners, refraining from teaching his followers to fast and failing to keep the Sabbath — and on this basis is censured by the Pharisees monitoring his behavior (2:13-28). He heals on the Sabbath, and this serves as the impetus for the first recorded organized conspiracy against him (3:1-6). And so on. Even those who admit his power attribute it to the devil (3:22), while others request a sign in order to test him (8:11).

The integration of these two images of Jesus is demonstrated in another way as well. At the Gospel's center point in ch. 8, Jesus asks his disciples, "Who do you say that I am?" (8:29). Taking account of the Markan narrative from its beginning to this point, we might agree with Peter in his profession of Jesus as the Messiah of God, and mean by it that Jesus is the long-awaited deliverer, the one through whom the power of God had come to visible expression. If Jesus the authoritative, power-working teacher constitutes the melody of Mark 1–8, however, the countermelody consists of those numerous anticipations of Jesus' passion to which we have already called attention. Mark's portrait in these first chapters is not as univocal as it might at first appear, then. Similarly, once Jesus attempts to qualify Peter's understanding of his identity by drawing together into one whole the profession of messiahship with the plain prediction of the rejection and suffering he would experience (8:31-33), suffering and death enter the conversation regularly (especially 9:31; 10:31-34). But this does not signal the end of the miraculous in Mark's narrative. Even these prophecies are indicative of Jesus' status as God's agent, supernatural portents accompany the crucifixion (see 15:38), and Mark's Gospel closes with an account of the empty tomb (16:1-8). Even in the latter half of the Gospel, melody is matched with countermelody.

For Mark, these two portraits of Jesus — powerful wonder worker and suffering servant — are not contradictory, nor does one correct or exclude the other. Rather, together they disclose one fully integrated portrait of Jesus and his mission. *Jesus goes to the cross as the worker of powerful deeds and authoritative teacher.* These merge together in order to signify the full nature of his redemptive mission. "The Son of man came not to be served but to serve, and to give his life a ransom for many" (10:45).

Swirling around the fundamental issue of Jesus' identity are two motifs, conflict and discipleship. It is not only at the pivotal point of the Gospel, in 8:27-29, that the question of Jesus' identity comes to the fore. Following Jesus' first episode of authoritative teaching, the crowds inquire of one another, "What is this?" (1:27). Demonic spirits have no need to ask such questions, for they perceive his identity already: "I know who you are, the Holy One of God!" (1:24; see 1:34; 5:7). Jesus silences these voices, not because their words are wrong but because they represent empty affirmations from beings who have positioned themselves over against Jesus' ministry. Others ask, "Where did this man get all of this? What is this wisdom that has been given to him?" (6:2). "By what authority are you doing these things?" (11:28). "Are you the Messiah, the Son of the Blessed One?" (14:61). The narrator, Mark, is clear about Jesus' identity, however. Jesus is the Messiah and Son of God (1:1), an affirmation that finds confirmation in the divine voice at Jesus' baptism and transfiguration (1:11; 9:7).

The disciples do not understand. They may hold the mystery of the kingdom, they may be witnesses of Jesus' powerful deeds, and they may have heard his predictions of rejection and death, but they have not been able to put these pieces together. Hence, they are stunned by Jesus' mastery of the storm and sea: "Who is this, then, that even the wind and waves obey him?" (4:41). Is he a ghost (6:49)? Failing to understand the identity of Jesus and the nature of his message, they reject plain talk about his suffering (8:32), puzzle over his expectation of vindication (9:10), and repeatedly fail to comport themselves as befits those who follow a Messiah who resists the status quo on issues of honor and shame and even presents himself as a servant (see 9:33-41; 10:35-45).

The Markan story of the disciples, then, is repeatedly one of disappointment, with the disciples not only lacking in understanding but, often enough, actually standing in opposition to Jesus and his teaching. Instances of the motif of conflict branch out beyond the circle of Jesus' followers, though, to include diabolic forces and, especially, the Pharisees and the Jewish and Roman authorities in Jerusalem. Particularly in Galilee, the Pharisees, together with supporters of Herod, are cast consistently in the role of Jesus' opponents. The Pharisees monitor his behavior and question his teaching and ministry practices. They plot against him and seek to entrap him (see 2:1–3:6; 12:13). In the passion account, their role is taken over by the chief priests, scribes, and elders, who form a kind of triumvirate responsible for orchestrating Jesus' final demise. Pilate participates in these affairs to do the crowds a favor, according to Mark, who thus underscores again the inexorable animosity of the Jewish elite in Jerusalem.

For Mark, the final confrontation between Jesus and his opponents is grounded in his attitude toward the temple. When Jesus is brought before the Sanhedrin, they bring forward false witnesses, certifying, "We have heard him say, 'I will destroy this temple made with hands, and in three days I will build another not made with hands'" (14:58). While on the cross, Jesus is scorned with these words: "Aha! You who would destroy the temple and rebuild it in three days, save yourself, and come down from the cross!" (15:29-30). Finally, as Jesus breathes his last, Mark notes as the consequence of his death that "the veil of the temple was torn in two, from top to bottom" (15:38). This material concerned with the temple

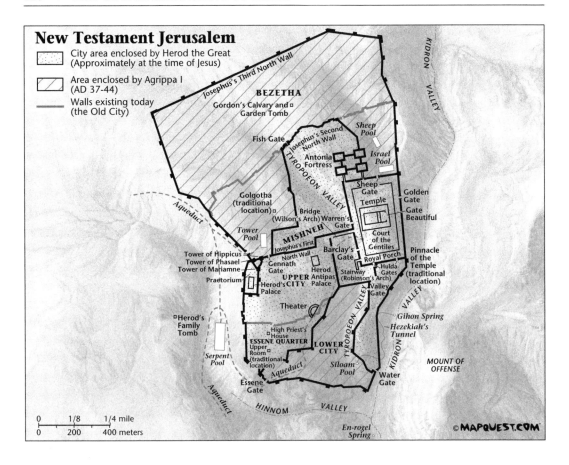

in Jesus' passion is anticipated earlier in the narrative. First, Mark interweaves the account of Jesus' cursing the fig tree with his action in the temple, as though to communicate that Jesus intended not simply to cleanse the temple but to curse it (11:15-21). The time of the temple had passed, for it had lost its fruitfulness. Second, when Jesus teaches his disciples about faith that can move mountains, his statement, "If you say to this mountain, 'Be taken up and thrown into the sea . . .'" (11:23), can refer only to the mountain on which the temple was built. Finally, in Mark 13, Jesus portends the coming destruction of the temple as a historical event in keeping with God's eschatological purpose.

Mark's interest in the identity of Jesus is thus not a speculative affair, as though he were concerned merely with passing on a correct understanding of the Messiah. Instead, Mark's narrative braids together these two strands, christology and discipleship, in order to show that how one understands the first will influence one's understanding of the second (and vice versa). Against this backdrop, the motif of conflict serves a number of important roles in addition to adding suspense to the narrative. For example, that the Jewish elite actually side with the devil and his minions in opposing Jesus' mission signals how far the institution of the temple and its supporters have departed from their service in God's redemptive purpose. Moreover, Mark uses the motif of conflict to show that even Jesus' followers are capable of misunderstanding and therefore opposing Jesus. Finally, Mark demonstrates that conflict is only to be expected when one identifies, as Jesus has, with God's redemptive purpose, for this means adopting a form of life out of step with "this adulterous and sinful generation" (8:38).

5.3. MARK'S DRAMATIC NARRATIVE

Our earlier adoption of the image of the musical score for making sense of this Gospel does not prevent us from thinking in more general terms about the structure of the Gospel. In fact, the number of proposed outlines of this narrative almost equals the number of its interpreters! Most agree that the episode in Caesarea Philippi in 8:27–9:1 marks the pivot point of the Gospel, but beyond this viewpoints proliferate rapidly. In what follows, we will use broad categories in order to probe the unfolding of the Gospel's drama in four parts.

Introduction: Jesus is Messiah, Son of God (1:1-15)
Jesus, bearer of the kingdom of God (1:16–8:26)
    Jesus' authority and responses to it (1:16–3:12)
    Jesus' disciples (3:13–6:6)
    The training of the disciples (6:7–8:26)
The road to Golgotha (8:27–15:41)
    The journey to Jerusalem (8:27–10:52)
    Jesus in the temple (11:1–13:37)
    Toward the cross (14:1–15:41)
Epilogue: he is risen! (16:1-8)

5.3.1. Introduction: Jesus Is Messiah, Son of God (1:1-15)

The boundaries of Mark's prologue are set by matching references to "gospel" (*euangelion*) in vv. 1 and 14-15:

The traditional location of Jesus' baptism by John: Yardenit, on the Jordan River just south of the Sea of Galilee *(Phoenix Data Systems, Neal and Joel Bierling)*

The beginning of the gospel of Jesus Christ, the Son of God, as it was written in the prophet Isaiah (1:1);

Jesus came to Galilee proclaiming the gospel of God (1:14);

Repent and believe the gospel (1:15).

In this way, Mark announces that the significance of Jesus is rooted in these two titles, "Messiah" and "Son of God," and in the message of Isaiah. What must not be overlooked is that though the Evangelist provides this perspective for his audience, it is not available to characters in the narrative other than Jesus. That is, Mark provides the primary interpretive point of view for understanding Jesus, but he does so for his readers and auditors, not for the disciples, the Pharisees, and others who enter the Gospel only with the beginning of the story proper in 1:16.

In other ways, too, Mark reads the importance of Jesus within the contours of Isaianic prophecy. Note the following parallels:

- The coming of John (compare 1:4-8 with Isaiah 40)
- The baptism of Jesus (compare 1:9-11 with Isa 42:1; 61:1)
- Jesus in the wilderness (compare 1:12-13 with Isaiah 40 and 65)
- Jesus' proclamation of the gospel of God (compare 1:14-15 with Isa 40:9; 52:7; 61:1-2)

Mark thus signals the most profound connection between the promise of God's salvation in Isaiah and the gospel or good news of Jesus Christ. And he demonstrates in his record of Jesus' baptism that his understanding of Jesus is harmonious with the divine perspective: "You are my Son, the Beloved" (1:11). Jesus is God's agent of salvation who heralds the presence of God's dominion — but this is "insider information" to which characters within the narrative have no immediate access.

Mark 1:14-15 provides a programmatic summary of the message of Jesus: "The long-awaited time has been fulfilled; the kingdom of God has drawn near. Repent and believe the gospel!" Because of their location at the beginning of his narrative, and because of their status as a précis of his proclamation, these verses are key to Mark's presentation of Jesus. On the one hand, Jesus' message is directed backward, so that it embraces the hopes of Israel for divine intervention in history to bring peace and justice. On the other hand, this announcement points to the present breaking-in of this new reality in which God is king. Jesus' mission is thus intimately related to the inauguration of God's kingdom, and the accounts of teaching, healing, table fellowship, and calling and sending of the Twelve and even the lengthy description of Jesus' suffering and death must be understood in this light. What is more, according to Mark's synopsis of Jesus' proclamation, the new era initiated by Jesus' ministry has clear and present implications for life before God. People are to respond in light of this message, believing that God has come and embracing this new reality with their whole lives. As is typical of OT accounts of salvation, so here the activity of God is prevenient: People are to respond *because* the ancient project of God has been initiated in Jesus' ministry — and not *in order that* God's work might be established.

5.3.2. Jesus, Bearer of the Kingdom of God (1:16–8:26)

Mark uses this first major section of the narrative to flesh out the summary of his presentation of Jesus' identity and message in the Gospel's introduction. From the closing verses of Mark's prologue we have evidence of Jesus' status as the bearer of the divine kingdom. Now Jesus demonstrates what shape God's dominion will take, and he does so through ministries of teaching and miracle-working. Indeed, the first eight chapters of the Gospel contain fifteen miracle stories, together with five editorial summaries concerned in part with Jesus' healing activity and exorcisms. In the Markan perspective, teaching and healing are not so much separate activities as they are indications of the same reality. Through his presentation of Jesus' ministry, Mark goes so far as to suggest that miracle-working has a pedagogical role — teaching people about the nature of God's gracious intervention in the world and thus about the character of Jesus. The lessons of Jesus' ministry do not come easily, however, but give rise rather to conflict and misunderstanding.

If the success of Jesus' ministry were evaluated on the basis of public opinion polls, we would have to conclude that his work in Galilee was triumphant. Repeatedly, Mark asserts the pervasiveness of the positive response to his ministry: "the whole city gathered around the door," "a great multitude from Galilee followed him," "they came in great numbers from Judea, Jerusalem, Idumea, beyond the Jordan, and the region around Tyre and Sidon," "people at once recognized him and rushed about that whole region," and so on (1:32-34; 3:7-11; 6:53-56). Mark 3:8 is particularly compelling, since it describes the positive response to Jesus garnered from the populace of the whole area of Jewish settlement in the Holy Land. Such a response is hardly puzzling, though, given the character of Jesus' ministry in this section of the Gospel.

Everywhere, Jesus' status as a conqueror of evil comes to expression. He overcomes diabolic spirits and enables his followers to do the same (1:23-27; 5:1-20; 6:7; 7:24-30). Against his detractors, Jesus insists that his success in controlling demonic activity is due not to his collusion with Satan, but to his having entered into and plundered the house of the strong man, that is, the devil himself (3:27). The so-called nature miracles in chs. 4 and 6 are likewise evidence of Jesus' power over evil. When we recall that "the sea" was symbolic in Jewish antiquity of chaos and evil (cf. Pss 65:7; 89:9; 106:9; Rev 21:1), Jesus' calming of the storm and walking on the sea (4:35-41; 6:47-52) must be understood as much more than his mastery over the forces of nature. He is acting as God acts, manifesting his authority over evil powers. Indeed, during the storm, Jesus *rebukes* the wind and *silences* the sea just as he has *rebuked* and *silenced* demons in 1:25; 3:11-12.

Jesus' popularity is also explained by his demonstrations of power by healing. He cures a fever, cleanses a leper, enables a paralytic to walk, heals a man with a withered hand, and more. No wonder, then, that the crowds were "astounded be-

yond measure, saying, 'He has done everything well; he even makes the deaf to hear and the mute to speak'" (7:37). Moreover, he feeds the thousands — first with five loaves and two fish (6:33-44), then with seven loaves and a few small fish (8:1-10). Mark thus underscores Jesus' compassion for the people as well as his capacity to provide for them as shepherds provide for the sheep under their care.

Interestingly, these feeding episodes point beyond themselves to a further, important motif in this section of the Gospel. This is the crossing of purity lines, suggested in two different ways by these two accounts. On the one hand, it is worth remembering simply that mealtimes provided the center point of Jewish practices related to the concepts of clean and unclean. Meals were for nourishment, and this is clearly their importance in the instances of food provision Mark recounts. But meals were also highly significant social occasions, in which social boundaries and rankings were operative. What one ate and with whom — these tightly intertwined issues were at the heart of what it meant to observe the law and thus to be faithful to God. In this context, the episodes of feeding the masses are of interest for their complete lack of concern with such questions. Food was shared without regard for the normal concerns that governed the partaking and sharing of food. It is no wonder, then, that in 7:1-23 Jesus can declare all foods clean. Though his statement comes in a different setting, it nonetheless relates centrally to his meal practices with toll collectors and sinners (2:13-17) and his behavior regarding food in the open field. Such distinctions belong to the old age and are no longer relevant in light of the inbreaking kingdom of God. On the other hand, it should not escape our attention that the first feeding mira-

A mid-fifth century pavement mosaic in a church at et-Tagbah on the Sea of Galilee, the traditional location of Jesus' multiplication of loaves and fishes

Apollonius of Tyana: Exorcist and Holy Man

A first-century-CE wandering ascetic, Apollonius is remembered as a teacher and holy man who performed exorcisms and miracles. The following account, from Philostratus's *Life of Apollonius of Tyana* 4.20 (third century CE), is often compared to Mark 5:1-20:

Now while he was discussing the question of libations, there chanced to be present in his audience a young dandy who bore so evil a reputation for licentiousness, that his conduct had long been the subject of coarse street-corner songs. His home was Corcyra, and he traced his pedigree to Alcinous the Phaeacian who entertained Odysseus. Apollonius then was talking about libations, and was urging them not to drink out of a particular cup, but to reserve it for the gods, without ever touching it or drinking out of it. But when he also urged them to have handles on the cup, and to pour the libation over the handle, because that is the part of the cup at which men are least likely to drink, the youth burst into loud and coarse laughter, and quite drowned his voice. Then Apollonius looked up at him and said, "It is not yourself that perpetrates this insult, but the demon, who drives you on without your knowing it." And in fact the youth was, without knowing it, possessed by a devil; for he would laugh at things that no one else laughed at, and then he would fall to weeping for no reason at all, and he would talk and sing to himself. Now most people thought that it was the boisterous humor of youth which led him into such excesses; but he was really the mouthpiece of a devil, though it only seemed a drunken frolic in which on that occasion he was indulging. Now when Apollonius gazed on him, the ghost in him began to utter cries of fear and rage, such as one hears from people who are being branded or racked; and the ghost swore that he would leave the young man alone and never take possession of any man again. But Apollonius addressed him with anger, as a master might a shifty, rascally, and shameless slave and so on, and he ordered him to quit the young man and show by a visible sign that he had done so. "I will throw down yonder statue," said the devil, and pointed to one of the images which were in the king's portico, for there it was that the scene took place. But when the statue began by moving gently, and then fell down, it would defy anyone to describe the hubbub which arose thereat and the way they clapped their hands with wonder. But the young man rubbed his eyes as he had just woke up, and he looked towards the rays of the sun, and assumed a modest aspect, as all had their attention concentrated on him; for he no longer showed himself licentious, nor did he stare madly about, but he had returned to his own self, as thoroughly as if he had been treated with drugs; and he gave up his dainty dress and summery garments and the rest of his sybaritic way of life, and he fell in love with the austerity of philosophers, and donned their cloak, and stripping off his old self modeled his life in the future upon that of Apollonius. (LCL)

cle takes place among Jewish people while the second is set within Gentile environs. Again, it is as though Mark were attempting to insist in this way that the kingdom of God brought near in the ministry of Jesus was devoid of even this distinction.

Mark 1:16–8:26 can be further divided into subsections that each begin with an episode concerned with disciples. *1:16–3:12* focuses on Jesus' authority and the varied responses it attracts, emphasizing above all the growing hostility his ministry attracts from the Pharisees and supporters of Herod. *3:13–6:6* introduces a key distinction among Jesus' varied audiences: Some are on the "inside" and thus receive special instruction, while others are on the "outside." What is remarkable, though, is the degree to which this motif is weighted with irony — with the consequence that those who might be expected to be "on the inside" repeatedly fail in this respect. *6:7–8:26* is concerned mainly with the training of the disciples. Though Jesus remains the central figure, Mark repeatedly observes that the disciples are with Jesus; it is here, too, that the disciples participate firsthand in Jesus' ministry after he has empowered them and sent them out. All three subsections begin with an emphasis on disciples and discipleship — the first recounting the call of the first disciples and their instantaneous obedience and willingness to identify completely with Jesus (1:16-20), the second narrating the choice of the inner group of disciples, the Twelve, to be with him and to be sent out by him (3:13-19), and the last describing Jesus' sending of the Twelve to engage in ministries of proclamation, exorcism, and healing (6:7-13).

Built into the very structure of this section of the Gospel of Mark, then, is the importance of discipleship to the Markan project. If Mark is concerned with the identity of Jesus and the character of his mission, he is equally concerned with the implications of Jesus' mission for the shape of discipleship. Unfortunately, throughout this section of the Gospel, the disciples rarely present themselves in any fashion that would invite emulation. To the contrary, they show themselves to be as concerned with issues of status and boundary-drawing as those who have not banded together with Jesus. By the end of this major section of the Gospel, the relationship between Jesus and his followers has deteriorated significantly. For this reason, the closing account of Jesus' healing a blind man takes on parabolic significance within the Gospel. Touched by Jesus, this blind man is able to see somewhat, but he mistakes human beings for walking trees. He requires further intervention on Jesus' part, just as the disciples will require more if they will be able to see clearly the nature of God's activity in the ministry of Jesus.

5.3.3. The Road to Golgotha (8:27–15:41)

The Markan narrative takes a decisive, though not altogether unexpected turn with the unmistakable, obvious teaching of Jesus to his disciples regarding his im-

The Messiah in *Psalms of Solomon* 17

Written in the first century BCE, the *Psalms of Solomon* contain one of the most straightforward descriptions of the Messiah in pre-Christian, Second Temple Judaism. After sketching both the divine promise to David regarding his everlasting dynasty and the judgment that befell Israel, the text continues with hope in "God our Savior" (17:3):

> See, Lord, and raise up for them their king,
>> the son of David, to rule over your servant Israel
>> in the time known to you, O God.
> Undergird him with strength to destroy the unrighteous rulers,
>> to purge Jerusalem from gentiles who trample her to destruction;
>> in wisdom and in righteousness to drive out the sinners from
>>> the inheritance;
> to smash the arrogance of sinners like a potter's jar;
> to shatter all their substance with an iron rod;
> to destroy the unlawful nations with the word of his mouth.
> At his warning the nations will flee from his presence;
>> and he will condemn sinners by the thoughts of their hearts.
> He will gather a holy people
>> whom he will lead in righteousness;
> and he will judge the tribes of the people
>> that have been made holy by the Lord their God.
>
> And he will have gentile nations serving him under his yoke,
>> and he will glorify the Lord in (a place) prominent (above)
>>> the whole earth.
> And he will purge Jerusalem
>> (and make it) holy as it was even from the beginning,
> (for) nations to come from the ends of the earth to see his glory,
>> to bring as gifts her children who had been driven out,
> and to see the glory of the Lord with which God has glorified her.
> And he will be a righteous king over them, taught by God.
> There will be no unrighteousness among them in his days,
>> for all shall be holy,
>> for their king shall be the Lord Messiah.
>
> (17:21-32)

pending demise. The death of Jesus was anticipated earlier, but now it breaks out onto the scene, rarely departing center stage as the story moves toward its finale. Interestingly, as Mark relates it, even this plain talk about the death of God's Messiah is charged with meaning for would-be followers of Jesus, since discipleship is organically related to christology. This connection is perhaps most clear in three ways.

First, when the question of Jesus' identity comes finally to a head, Peter, speaking for the whole band of Jesus' disciples, professes Jesus as the Christ. This is followed by a dialogue between Jesus and Peter, the nature of which portends their incompatible understandings of Jesus' divine destiny. Presumably having reflected on the portrait of Jesus as the powerful worker of miracles and bearer of the kingdom that has been so much of his experience since he attached himself to Jesus (in 1:16-20), Peter finds no room in his understanding of Jesus for motifs of suffering and death. He rebukes Jesus, but thus proves only that he is thinking like a mere human, without any access to the divine perspective. Jesus' reply builds a bridge from the fate of Jesus, Messiah and suffering Son of Man, to the way of discipleship. In doing so, he emphasizes the importance of the reconstruction of a new identity, based on one's association with Jesus rather than the relationships and emblems of status valued conventionally. One must also "take up the cross," living as though one were, like Jesus, condemned to death, carrying the cross-arm to the place of crucifixion (8:27-38).

Second, not long afterward, James and John attempt to reserve places of honor at the table of the glorious kingdom of God. Their request belies their fallacious understanding of the identity of this man they have come to follow, and of the character of the kingdom he proclaims. They want to associate themselves with the honor that befits the Messiah. Apparently, they have heard nothing of his teaching about his imminent shameful death. Jesus replies first by instructing them in the ways of discipleship: "Whoever wishes to become great among you must be your servant"; then he comes to the high point of his argument and, indeed, of the whole Gospel's perspective on his death: "The Son of Man came not to be served but to serve, and to give his life a ransom for many." Jesus thus presents his own obedience to the mission given him by God and his own orientation to others as exemplary for those who would embrace the kingdom of God. He also indicates the depth of meaning that his death would carry; for Mark, the cross is not only exemplary for life among the people of God but is also the means by which persons might be included among the covenant people (10:32-45).

Third, the correlation between the Messiah and community of disciples is developed in the parallel between Jesus' suffering in Mark 14–15 and the anticipated suffering of the community, related in Mark 13. Jesus' teaching shows clearly that the suffering of the church in history is intimately related to the birth pangs of the coming of God's dominion. The church will participate in the woes through which the new era of peace and justice breaks into the world — woes that have already begun in the passion of Jesus.

At least two pertinent observations flow from these parallels. First, it is clear that the new era prophesied by Jesus has already been inaugurated in Jesus' own ministry. His suffering and death are not a contradiction of God's plan, but actually serve to bring that plan to completion. What is more, the suffering of Jesus' disciples must never be regarded as a contradiction of their status as disciples or dismissed as irrelevant to the divine purpose. The difficult times faced by Jesus' disciples must now also be interpreted within the framework of the woes accompanying the birth of the kingdom. Again, then, we see that Mark has melded these two, christology and discipleship, into a single narrative thread.

Already it is clear that this second major section of the Gospel brings to the foreground the motif of Jesus' suffering and death. This is accented by repeated references to the journey to Jerusalem, identified as the place of Jesus' death. The centrality of the cross is marked by two related emphases. On the one hand, Mark is at pains to ensure that his audience faces the reality that Jesus goes to his death on account of his divine mission. Thus, Jesus repeatedly refers to his upcoming passion under the heading of "the divine must" *(dei):* "The Son of man must suffer many things . . ." (8:31; 9:31; 10:32-34). Moreover, the mural of Jesus' death is painted with hues borrowed from OT promise. These include such specific texts as Zech 13:7 (cited in Mark 14:27) as well as the interpretive traditions associated with the Suffering Righteous One and the Suffering Servant. However, more than these, Mark seems to be concerned with the more simple, yet more profound, notion that the cross of Christ brings to consummation the will of God revealed in the Scriptures — all of them.

On the other hand, Jesus' death is portrayed as the only possible destiny of one who has identified so radically with the divine will. And so the final chapters of Mark's Gospel are taken up with tracing the crescendo of hostility that Jesus has attracted, particularly on his arrival in Jerusalem. Using language reminiscent of descriptions of rebellious Israel during the days of the exodus, Jesus identifies his own generation as a wicked generation (8:38). Set against the ways of God, they can hardly choose another path than to set themselves also against God's Anointed One.

The narrative of Mark 8:27–15:41 proceeds in three discrete sections. The first, *8:27–10:52,* highlights the motif of the journey to Jerusalem, with the language of traveling along "the way" repeated in 8:27; 9:33, 34; 10:1, 17, 32, 46, 52. This language is reminiscent of the reference to "the way of the Lord" in 1:1-3, and this invites our reflection on the journey of Israel from Egypt to the land of promise. The journey Mark portrays is, first, the journey of Jesus as he moves toward the goal set before him by God. It is also the journey of disciples, though, since it is along the way that Jesus instructs them. Interestingly, this section is bordered at

Parallels between Mark 13 and Mark 14–15

Jesus predicts the destruction of the temple (13:2).	Witnesses accuse Jesus of threatening to destroy the temple; at his death, the temple veil is split in two (14:58; 15:38).
The disciples are to watch (13:5, 9, 23, 33, 35, 37).	At Gethsemane, the disciples fail to watch (14:34, 37-38).
Jesus predicts that the disciples will be delivered over to religious and political authorities (13:9-13).	Jesus is delivered up to Jewish and Roman authorities (14:10, 11, 18, 21, 41, 42; 15:1, 10, 15).
Jesus predicts that the disciples will be betrayed by those with whom they share family-like relations (13:12-13).	Jesus is betrayed by one of the Twelve, an intimate, one with whom he has shared table fellowship (14:10, 20, 43)
Jesus observes that no one knows the hour (13:22, 33).	At Gethsemane, Jesus proclaims that the hour has come (14:32-42).
Jesus predicts that "in those days" "the sun will be darkened" (13:24).	At Jesus' crucifixion, "darkness came over the whole land" (15:33).
Jesus predicts that the Son of Man will be seen coming in clouds with great power (13:26).	At his hearing before the Jewish council, Jesus affirms the coming of the Son of Man seated at the right hand of the Power and coming with the clouds of heaven (14:62).
In 13:35, Jesus says, "Therefore, keep awake — for you do not know when the master will come, in the evening, at midnight, at cockcrow, or at dawn."	Throughout 14:17–15:1, these same time designations — evening, midnight, and early morning — are used.
Jesus describes the actions of the master of the house: he comes and finds you sleeping (13:36).	At Gethsemane, Jesus came and found the disciples sleeping (14:37-38).

the beginning and end by accounts of the healing of blind persons. Before the beginning of the journey, the blind man from Bethsaida is healed; it is from him, though, that we learn of the need for a second touch if genuine (in)sight is to be achieved. At the end of this section, Bartimaeus both receives his sight and joins

Crucifixion

In the Roman world, there was apparently no set procedure to be followed for executing someone by crucifixion. For example, in his eyewitness account of the Roman siege of Jerusalem, Josephus observes how hundreds of Jewish prisoners were "scourged and subjected to torture of every description . . . , and then crucified opposite the city walls." In the hope that the morbid sight would induce the Jews to surrender the city, Titus, the Roman commander, gave his soldiers leave to continue the crucifixions as they pleased. "The soldiers out of rage and hatred amused themselves by nailing their prisoners in different positions . . ." (*J.W.* 5.11.1 §§449-51).

Accounts are not always clear whether crucifixion was an act of execution or impalement — that is, whether it took place before or after the victim's death. Victims might be tied to the cross or nailed, and crossbeams were not always used. Where a common practice can be discerned, it included: flogging the condemned, the victim carrying the crossbeam to the place of execution, fixing the victim to the cross with arms extended, and raising the cross. Death came through shock, or though the process of asphyxiation as the muscles used in breathing suffered fatigue. The corpse was typically left on the cross as carrion for the birds or to rot.

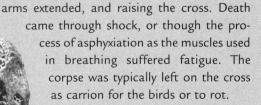

The heel bones of Jehohanan ben Hagalgol, a man crucified at Jerusalem by Roman authorities during the first century CE. The single nail through both feet is still attached. *(Erich Lessing/Art Resource, NY)*

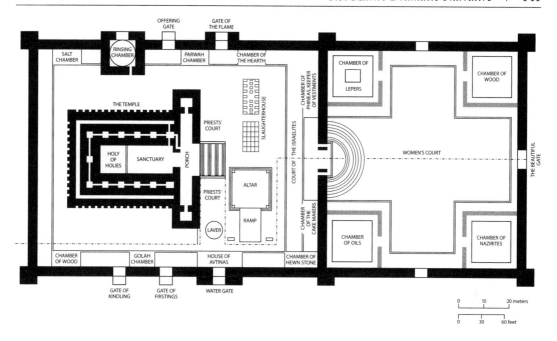

Jesus "on the way." The disciples, too, require a second touch if they are to lose their fuzziness of perception and receive eye-opening perceptiveness into Jesus' identity and the nature of discipleship.

11:1–13:37 is no longer set "on the way"; rather, we find Jesus in and around the Jerusalem temple. Here the hostility against him reaches a new level as the Jerusalem elite react to the provocation of his teaching and actions in and against the temple. *14:1–15:41* serves in many ways as the climax of the Gospel of Mark, since it is to this series of events that the Gospel has been oriented. Like a litany, one hears again and again references to Jesus as Messiah and king set in proximity to his death. How could the Messiah suffer on the cross? The sixfold use of the term "king" with reference to Jesus (15:2, 9, 12, 18, 26, 32), combined with the threefold mockery of Jesus on the cross (15:29-32), signals the irony of the crucifixion scene. Jesus, condemned as a pretender to the throne, does indeed have royal status, but it is the sort of majesty that befits one who has proclaimed a kingdom that accords privilege to the "least among you" — the least, the lost, and the left out. Not surprisingly, then, it is the "little people" of Mark's narrative who exercise insight into Jesus' true station and mission — a woman who proleptically anoints Jesus' body for burial and thus shows that she understands the nature of his mission far more than his most intimate followers do (14:3-9), Simon of Cyrene, who "takes up his cross" (15:21; cf. 8:34), and women who remain at the cross after the disciples have fled (15:40-41). These belong to the company of others in the Gospel according to Mark

The plan of Herod's Temple (adapted from *Encyclopedia Judaica*)

— a Gentile demoniac (5:19-20), an unclean woman (5:25-34), and a Syrophoenician woman (7:24-30), for example — whose roles are relatively minor, yet who have flashes of insight that mark them as Jesus' true family.

5.3.4. Epilogue: He Is Risen! (16:1-8)

The Gospel according to Mark almost certainly ended with 16:8. Because this ending seemed so unsatisfying to later scribes, especially in light of the robust resurrection-and-appearance stories in the other NT Gospels, various attempts were made to provide a more suitable finale for the story of Jesus. In fact, however abrupt it may be, closing the Gospel with v. 8 provides a powerful way to end this Gospel — or, rather, to leave this story open-ended in a provocative way. In 15:42-47, Mark presents Joseph of Arimathea as a representative of the best of Judaism, motivated by Mosaic Law to undertake final arrangements for Jesus (see Deut 21:22-23). The manner of Jesus' burial by Joseph is akin to that of a criminal, though that is rectified by Mary Magdalene, Mary mother of James, and Salome when they anoint Jesus' body. This sequence of events provides the occasion for the encounter of these women with the angel at the tomb. The angel's primary role is that of an interpreter — to remind the women, and Mark's readers, of Jesus' earlier words (see 14:27-28).

If Jesus' crucifixion represents the climax of the Gospel of Mark, the scene at the empty tomb serves as its denouement. Mark brings together two important motifs. The first is the motif of the trustworthiness of Jesus as a prophet. If all other aspects of his prophetic utterances have come to fruition, then is it not reasonable to assume that his predictions of his own resurrection, and his return, would also take place? The second is the motif of failure of the disciples. Throughout Mark's Gospel, Jesus' followers have repeatedly fallen short in their comprehension of Jesus' identity and mission and in their own practices as disciples. Now, at the end of the Gospel, these three women typify the response of the disciples as they react in fear and refuse to speak to anyone. On the one hand, Mark's audience knows that, in the end, the women did speak of their encounter, since he has recorded it. Initial failure is no guarantee of ultimate failure, and the narrative strategy Mark employs portends the eventual faithfulness of the disciples, who have thus far made such a poor showing. On the other hand, these final verses speak more directly to Mark's audience, inviting them, as it were, to complete the story he has begun. Mark thus lures his audience into self-reflection, to mull over the implications of this narrative for present-day discipleship. Will they respond in fear and silence like these disciples? Or will they embrace with confidence and boldness the gospel of Jesus Christ, Son of God, orient their lives around the new reality of the inbreaking kingdom of God, and invite others to do the same?

The Ending of Mark

Given the evidence currently available, Mark 16:8 offers the most probable ending of the Gospel of Mark: "They went out and fled from the tomb, for they were trembling and astonished. They said nothing to anyone, for they were afraid." Already in the early centuries after the publication of the Gospel of Mark, however, this ending proved unsatisfactory. Its abruptness undoubtedly contributed to feelings of dissatisfaction, and the location of the Gospel of Mark alongside the Gospels of Matthew, Luke, and John pressed this issue even further. This is because Mark alone thus failed to provide witness to the appearances of the Risen Lord. Among the attempts to address this void are the shorter and longer endings provided in most of the recent English translations of the Gospel of Mark, typically separated from the end of the Gospel by appropriate headings and explanations. Of course, the evidence cannot prove decisively that the Gospel ended with v 8, but both the external evidence drawn from the extant manuscript tradition and the internal evidence based on Markan style and language are decisive in rejecting the authenticity of the other endings proposed by the manuscript tradition.

If the women "said nothing to anyone, for they were afraid," how do we know the Gospel story? Most contemporary readers of Mark make sense of this strange ending by observing that the Gospel anticipates the resolution of its crises outside of the narrative itself. The regathering of the disciples and their faithful witness to Jesus' person and mission (see 14:28; 16:7) are promised and fulfilled. In the same way, Jesus' promise of the Spirit's presence in the midst of persecution (13:9-13) and, indeed, the promise of his own glorious return (13:24-27; 14:62) are also to be trusted.

5.4. THE SETTING AND PURPOSE OF MARK'S GOSPEL

To speak definitively of the origin of Mark's Gospel, it would be helpful to have complete and reliable information about such introductory matters as the identity of the Evangelist and his audience and when and where he wrote it. But we know nothing certain on any of these issues.

Like the other NT Gospels, this one is anonymous. The author makes no self-reference within the narrative by which we might identify him, nor has he "signed" his account. The title, "The Gospel according to Mark," was added only decades after the Gospel's completion. This anonymity may be the result of a deliberate decision on the part of the author — who thus directed attention away from his own creative contribution and toward the subject of his work, the coming of God in Jesus of Nazareth. It might signal as well the degree to which the material woven into the Gospel narrative, and perhaps even the basic framework of the Gospel itself, was traditional by the time it was recounted in this fashion. Alternatively, it might be that the author simply assumed that his audience knew who he was. These choices are not mutually exclusive, of course. At the same time, we should remind ourselves in the case of this last possibility that "authorship" was not so closely guarded a practice in antiquity as it has become in the last two or three centuries, especially in the West. Even if we should probably assign the completion of the Gospel of Mark in its final form to one person, this would preclude neither the heavy influence of tradition nor the role of the author's own worshiping community in the unfolding of the narrative.

According to the earliest available tradition, this Gospel was written by "Mark," the interpreter of Peter — so Eusebius quotes Papias, who himself credits "the Elder" as the source of this information (Eusebius, *Hist. Eccl.* 3.39.15). This tradition, which probably dates back to the opening decade (or decades) of the second century CE, is picked up and echoed in the latter part of that century by Irenaeus and Clement of Alexandria, for example. What do we learn from this information? In a serendipitous way, it points to the nature of Mark's creative contribution, since "the Elder" reports that Peter passed on to his interpreter only "anecdotes" while Mark has provided a full-blown narrative. This encourages the view that Mark's innovation consisted above all in the choice of episodes to recount and in the way he has woven them together to signal causality and purpose, rather than in the wholesale creation of episodes apart from the tradition available to them. There is no reason to reject out of hand the association of this Gospel with Peter, even if the picture painted by Eusebius must be regarded as overly simplistic. Mark, after all, is not providing a record of events for the sake of posterity, as though the written page was needed to replace oral tradition. Rather, he is presenting a narrative whose character is rhetorical, in the sense of having a persuasive intent. But who is this "Mark"? *Markus* was one of the most common names in the Roman world, so, again, we owe it to popular tradition that the "Mark" who came to be associated with the production of this Gospel is none other than the "John Mark" of Acts 12:12, 25; 13:13; 15:37-39; Phlm 24; Col 4:10; 2 Tim 4:11; 1 Pet 5:13 — and thus a sometime companion of both Paul and Peter.

In the end, however, little is gained by identifying the author of Mark's Gospel as "Mark," even if this person was in fact "John Mark." This is because we know next to nothing about this Mark *except what we can glean from the Gospel itself.* In the terminology of literary study, the "author" of the Gospel of Mark to whom we have most direct access, then, is the "implied author," that is, the implicit image of the author that shines in and through the narrative text itself. The author of Mark, for example, would thus clearly be one who could work in common Greek, and who possessed intimacy with the OT, particularly in its Greek version, and especially the Psalms, Isaiah, and Zechariah. The Evangelist seems to have a developed understanding of Judaism and Jewish practices, even if he writes to an audience that repeatedly needs to have both explained (e.g., 7:3-4; 12:18).

Nor can we speak with certainty about the date of the Gospel of Mark. Early tradition urges a date after Peter's death in Rome, which is usually assumed to have been in 64 or 65 CE (Irenaeus, *Haer.* 3.1.1; see the anti-Marcionite prologue). For further evidence, scholars often turn to the text of Mark itself. Mark 13:14, with its instructions "to flee to the hills" at the destruction of Jerusalem, makes little sense in light of the historical realities of the Roman siege on Jerusalem. The Roman army had completely surrounded the city with a seamless blockade, making such an attempt at escape inadvisable and probably impossible. Similarly, that the "abomination of desolation" is not more directly related to the pillaging of the temple by Titus, the Roman commander, suggests that Mark 13 was written before the fall of Jerusalem in 70 CE. Consequently, many date the completion of the Gospel of Mark to the later 60s, during the Jewish War but before the destruction of Jerusalem.

Even this range of dates is helpful for grasping the purpose of Mark's Gospel since it portends a climate of heightened tension. What sort of audience does the narrative imply? We can assume a predominately Christian audience — that is, an audience that would accept in at least some sense that Jesus is "Messiah, son of God," since Mark begins his Gospel by presupposing this belief (1:1). Such an audience would have shared something of the author's own familiarity with the OT, or at least we may presume that the author believed they would be capable of hearing his scriptural citations, allusions, and echoes. In addition, we may presume that Mark's audience had some familiarity with (or expectation of) persecution. The courtroom scene in 8:34-38 intimates the existence of situations in which disciples might be called upon to disavow their association with Jesus. According to 13:9, legal interrogations by both Roman and Jewish authorities are the lot of Jesus' followers. In addition, in 10:28-30 there is the surprising addition of a reference to "persecutions" in the list of "gifts" received by those who give up everything to follow Jesus. We may also refer to the warning concerning trouble and persecution in 4:17, as well as to the stark promise of 13:13: "You will be hated by all on account of my name." Even if the exact nature of this persecution escapes us (local or widespread? methodical or random? official or informal?), affliction and unrest seem to characterize the experience of Mark's audience. Indeed, the progression of Jesus' instruction in ch. 13 makes good sense within the difficult historical circumstances of the late 60s, circumstances that would have fueled doubts and temptations of various kinds. Such experiences of duress would perhaps only naturally have raised questions about the nature of Jesus' "victory," the character of his power, and the shape of the kingdom he proclaimed.

Some might have found in these exigencies the impetus for a retreat into end-time speculation. Others might have heard the rebel call to take up arms and to join the cause against Rome. Still others might have been tempted to leave their faith in disillusionment. Jesus advises an alternative route: "The end is still to come. . . . This is but the beginning of the birth pangs" (13:7-8). Such trials provide the arena for alertness and watchfulness (13:5, 9, 23, 33, 37). These events furnish opportunities for discerning the presence of the kingdom of God (ch. 4) and for extending the mission to all nations (13:10). The measure of Jesus' ministry embraced powerful acts of healing and authoritative teaching, to be sure, but also service on behalf of others as well as death.

One can go further. Perhaps the Markan narrative envisages persons who have already failed in the context of duress. Mark's readers and hearers may have been struggling with present, concrete expressions of discipleship failure. This would help to make sense of the striking emphasis Mark places on the failure of Jesus' inner circle of followers within the narrative. Such people would undoubtedly hear the Markan Gospel as good news. On the one hand, the failure (and anticipated restoration) of Jesus' own disciples would have softened the blow of parallel instances of failure in later Christian communities. Failure need not be the most resounding or final word. On the other, the Gospel of Mark would allow its readers and hearers to locate the perplexity and pain of persecution against a wider interpretive horizon. Suffering, according to Mark's narrative, is not a denial of one's status before God or among the people of God. Jesus, as a part of his divine mission, journeys to Jerusalem with the full knowledge that entering Jerusalem can lead only to his shameful death.

Of course, neither does Mark attempt to glorify suffering, or urge that duress is the indisputable trademark of the faithful disciple of Jesus. Clearly, he envisions the possible death of disciples on account of their faithfulness in identifying with Jesus. But the fundamental issue for Mark is not one's capacity or willingness to embrace suffering and death; he is no sadist, and he does not present Jesus as a masochist. Jesus' central commitment is to fulfilling God's purpose for him, to serving the will of God foretold in the Scriptures. In doing so, he becomes the object of controversy and hostility. So, too, must Jesus' disciples reckon with the cost of living a life so radically oriented toward God in a "sinful generation" (8:38).

FOR FURTHER READING

Christopher Bryan, *A Preface to Mark: Notes on the Gospel in Its Literary and Cultural Settings* (Oxford: Oxford University Press, 1993)

Robert A. Guelich, *Mark 1-8:26* (Word Biblical Commentary 34A; Dallas: Word, 1989)

Robert H. Gundry, *Mark: A Commentary on His Apology for the Cross* (Grand Rapids: Eerdmans, 1993)

Larry W. Hurtado, *Mark* (New International Biblical Commentary; Peabody: Hendrickson, 1989)

Joel Marcus, *Mark* (Anchor Bible; New York: Doubleday, 2000-)

W. R. Telford, *The Theology of the Gospel of Mark* (Cambridge: Cambridge University Press, 1999)

6. The Gospel according to Luke

The Gospel of Luke, often referred to as the Third Gospel because of its position in the NT, contains some of the most influential and best remembered of all of the parables, including the prodigal son and the good Samaritan. When compared to the other NT Gospels, though, Luke is most noted for its narrative of the birth of Jesus (chs. 1–2), the lengthy "travel account" that comprises the central section of the Gospel (9:51–19:48), and its unrelenting interest in the marginalized and dispossessed. Additionally, as a comparison of the prefaces to both books suggests, Luke's Gospel and the Acts of the Apostles are closely related to each other (Luke 1:1-4; Acts 1:1-2). Luke is the only Evangelist who regarded the story of Jesus as somehow incomplete without its continuation in the life of the community and mission of Jesus' followers.

Luke's message is fundamentally oriented around the theme of salvation — its derivation, scope, and embodiment. Within the conflicted world of the first-century Mediterranean, views of the divine purpose like that sponsored in Luke-Acts — views that run roughshod over important social conventions related to one's honor and status in the community and one's religious identity — would naturally have been the source of controversy and uncertainty. This is especially true of Luke-Acts, since here we have a narrative whose aim is to present the timeline of the history of God's people so that it must pass through (and not bypass) Jesus and his disciples. Against this backdrop, the purpose of Luke-Acts would have been to strengthen the Christian movement in the face of opposition by ensuring them in their interpretation and experience of the redemptive purpose and faithfulness of God and by calling them to continued fidelity and witness in their service of the kingdom of God. Hence, the focus of Luke-Acts is ecclesiological. It is concerned with the history and practices that define the community of God's people, and with the invitation to participate in God's redemptive project.

Not surprisingly, then, the Gospel of Luke is centered on God. Even if God makes few direct appearances in the Gospel, the design that governs the progression of the narrative is God's. He is known as "God my Savior" (1:47), and he reveals his purpose in a variety of ways — through the Scriptures, through heavenly messengers, through the Holy Spirit, through his own voice, and through the divine choreography of events. The Evangelist uses a constellation of terms to express God's design — "purpose," "it is necessary," "to determine," and others. Especially in the central section of the Gospel (9:51–19:48) Jesus attempts to transform the view of God held by his followers, so that they might recognize God as their Father, whose desire is to embrace them with his gracious beneficence (e.g., 11:1-13; 12:32).

God's will is accomplished through the Spirit-anointed ministry of Jesus (3:21-22; 4:18-19) and will be continued in Acts by means of the Spirit-empowered witness of Jesus' followers (24:44-49). Fundamental to this mission is the appropriate interpretation of Scripture, and this interpretation is Spirit-enabled, a matter of revelation. Indeed, Jesus' disciples are repeatedly castigated for their failure to understand the purposes of God, until Jesus "opens their minds to understand the Scriptures" (24:49). In Acts, they are able to serve as Spirit-empowered interpreters who discern correctly how to read the Scriptures as expressions of God's ancient purpose.

Luke's emphasis on the divine purpose serves his ecclesiological and hermeneutical interests. As the Christian community struggles with its own identity, the coherence between God's aim and the ministry of Jesus becomes crucial. In fact, it is not too much to say that Luke's narrative both expresses and is itself engaged in a battle of interpretation. Who understands God's purpose? Who interprets the Scriptures faithfully? For Luke, the advent of Jesus is deeply rooted in the ancient covenant with Abraham and the promise of a Messiah in the lineage of David, and his mission is fully consonant with God's promises and intent. This is demonstrated ultimately by the divine vindication pronounced over him in his resurrection and ascension.

If God's aim drives the Lukan narrative forward, the main character in Luke's first volume is Jesus. Compared with people within the narrative (whether disciples, Pharisees, or others), Luke's own audience is fortunate in its awareness, from the very beginning, of Jesus' identity and role in God's plan. Jesus is portrayed as a prophet, but more than a prophet: He is the long-awaited Davidic Messiah, Son of God, who fulfills his career as a regal prophet for whom death, while necessary, is not the last word. For Jesus' disciples, then, the struggle is not so much to discern *who* Jesus is, but how he can be the Messiah *and* undergo humiliation and death. Their own views of God and the world remain conventional throughout most of the Gospel, with the result that they are unable to correlate Jesus' status as God's Messiah with the prospect and experience of his heinous suffering.

Early on, Jesus is identified as Savior (2:11), and this is the role he fulfills in numerous ways. Among the most visible are his miracles of healing and exorcism, together with the nature of his table fellowship. Both embody the truth of the inbreaking kingdom of God, demonstrating how Jesus reads the progression of time backward, so to speak: The future is breaking into the present, so it is the future realization of God's purpose that must determine one's commitments and practices today. Jesus heals those who, on account of their maladies, live on the margins of their communities. His table companions are not carefully chosen to maintain and broadcast his status in the wider world; rather, he eats with toll collectors and sinners (e.g., 15:1-2). In all these ways, Jesus communicates the presence of divine salvation for those who dwell on the peripheries of acceptable society. This is congruent with his inaugural proclamation:

> "The Spirit of the Lord is upon me!
> He has anointed me!
> He has sent me to proclaim good news to outcasts!" (4:18)

These ministry practices are also consistent with Jesus' teaching, which occupies major sections of the Gospel of Luke, especially in the lengthy narrative of Jesus' journey to Jerusalem. What is often striking about Jesus' instruction is its orientation toward a reconstructed vision of God and the sort of world order that might reflect this vision of God. Jesus, the Son of God, is God's representative; his life is characterized by obedience to God, and he interprets for others God's nature and plan and the contours of appropriate response to God's graciousness (e.g., 9:35). Will they listen?

The call to discipleship in Luke is fundamentally an invitation for people to align themselves with Jesus' mission and thus with God's purpose. This means that the focus for inclusion in the community of God's people is removed from issues of inherited status, and a premium is placed on those whose lives reflect God's own dispositions. Genuine "children of Abraham" produce "fruits in keeping with repentance"; they "hear and obey the word," especially in expressing openhanded mercy to those in need. Jesus calls people to live as he lives, in contrast to the competitive forms of life typical of the larger Roman world. Do good to those who hate you. Extend hospitality to those who cannot return the favor. Give without expectation of return. These are the behaviors that grow out of service in the kingdom of God. They are possible only for those whose convictions and commitments have been transformed by the goodness of God. Within the Gospel, the primary competitor for this focus is wealth — not so much money itself, but the rule of money, expressed in the drive for social praise and in forms of life divorced from the least and the lost.

The Lukan narrative is concerned throughout with salvation not as a merely spiritual or primarily future matter, but as a matter that embraces life in the present. Salvation signals the restoration of the integrity of human life and the commissioning of the community of God's people to put God's grace into practice among themselves and toward every-widening circles of outsiders.

6.1. THE CHARACTER OF LUKE'S GOSPEL (AND ACTS)

It is the historical relationship between Luke and Acts that helps us to understand the nature of Luke's narrative and theological enterprise. Although the Gospels of Matthew, Mark, and John all share close kinship with the Greco-Roman biographical genre, the connection of Luke to Acts suggests that the category of a *bios* or "life" is not entirely appropriate. This is because, although the Gospel of Luke seems especially centered on Jesus, the book of Acts cannot be squeezed into that form. In fact, in the opening of his Gospel, Luke locates his work alongside other "narratives," and the chief prototypes of "narrative" in antiquity were the historical accounts written by Herodotus and Thucydides. Moreover, Luke notes in his preface that his concern is not with a "person" or persons, but with events, and this again encourages a reading of his work in the context of historiography.

The opening of Luke's Gospel (1:1-4) is thus reminiscent of historical narratives, but there is a great deal more evidence that points toward the identification of Luke and Acts together as historiography. Genealogical records (see 3:23-38), meals as scenes for instruction (e.g., 5:27-39; 14:1-24; 22:14-38), travel narratives (9:51–19:48), speeches, and dramatic episodes such as Jesus' rejection at Nazareth (4:16-30) — these are the stuff of historiography.

Forms of literature are not naive containers, but are important at an interpretive level, and this is certainly true of the identification of Luke and Acts with historiography. Most immediately, it suggests something about the purpose of Luke's writing.

If Luke-Acts belongs to the genre of historiography, this does not mean that Luke is concerned primarily to represent to his audience "what actually happened." Historical writing in general has a broader set of purposes than recording events in the form of a chronicle. With historiography, four interrelated benefits of the past are put forward: validation, continuity, identity, and pedagogy. In Roman antiquity age was a powerful criterion for legitimating beliefs and practices, even peoples. This bias, together with the longstanding Jewish interest in the revelatory significance of historical events, emphasizes the importance of historical knowledge within first-century Judaism. When Josephus set out to legitimate Judaism and the Jewish people in the Roman world, he did so by narrating *The Antiquities of the Jews*. "We are very old" was an important consideration in self-presentation. According to some Hellenistic Jewish historians, Judaism was a force to be reckoned with in part because of Abraham — a man of noble birth and piety, to whom Phoenician astrology, Chaldean science, and even the discovery of the alphabet could be traced. Within the Gospel of Luke, Jesus himself asserts that "the old is good," and in doing so denounces his opponents as peddlers of "new wine," in contrast to the ancient purpose of God, which is being actualized in his ministry. "After drinking old wine," he says, "no one desires new" (5:39). Similarly, in the Acts of the Apostles, Luke follows the practice of Hellenistic writers of history in narrating the reenactment of significant events to show that the story of the early church has been written into the story of Jesus, the story of Jesus into the story of Israel, and all three into the story of God's ancient purpose for his people. The result is a continuous, almost seamless story of the articulation and realization of God's plan.

As historiography, then, Luke's narrative draws a continuous line from the Scriptures of Israel into the birth, life, death, and resurrection of Jesus, and from Jesus into the fledgling community of Christian believers. By this means, Luke gives the Christian community continuity with Israel of old, identity with God's purpose, and validation as God's people. Luke thus teaches his audience who they are and how they are to live out the substance of their faith in discipleship.

How is this continuity expressed? In the narrative of Jesus' birth (1:5–2:52), for example, the birth of Jesus is wrapped dramatically in the cloth of Israel's hopes and woven with the threads of scriptural idiom through the Songs of Mary, Zechariah, and Simeon. Undoubtedly, God's promises to Abraham are being actualized in the conception and birth of Jesus, and God's promises to David regarding the everlasting throne are coming to fruition in the conception and birth of Jesus. These conclusions are inescapable because they are presented by reliable spokespersons — the angel Gabriel as well as women and men whose piety is irreproachable and who speak under the inspiration of the Holy Spirit — and because they are deeply rooted in the Scriptures of Israel. Already at its beginning, then, the Lukan narrative is inscribed into the past story of God's promises to Israel and his activity on behalf of his people.

Throughout the Gospel, similarly, Jesus is portrayed in garb that identifies him with Israel's heroes — especially Moses, but also the prophets Elijah and Elisha. What is more, he articulates his own sense of divine mission in words borrowed from the prophet Isaiah (Luke 4:16-30). In the same way, Jesus' witnesses are portrayed in Acts in ways that tie their identities and ministries into his. Like Jesus, Peter, Paul, and others work "signs and wonders." Like Jesus, they heal the sick and proclaim the good news. Luke's account of the death of Stephen includes powerful reminders of the death of Jesus, including Stephen's final utterances,

"Lord Jesus, receive my spirit," and "Lord, do not hold this sin against them" (Acts 7:59-60; cf. Luke 23:34, 46). Throughout Acts, the mission is directed by Jesus, who pours out the Holy Spirit on those who believe. Luke is thus concerned to demonstrate that the story of the early church is of the same fabric as the story of Jesus, and both are nothing less than the continuation of the story of Israel and the realization of God's redemptive will.

The importance of Luke's achievement is heightened when it is placed within the context of Judaism in the Roman period. Given the diversity of Jewish communities at the time, it is self-evident that the one story of Israel was capable of spawning many narratives — that is, many ways to represent the continuation of that story. Within this cultural and religious diversity, Luke stakes an ambitious and provocative claim — namely, that God's promises come to fruition *here,* God's purpose for Israel is realized *here,* in the advent of Jesus and the missionary church. In order to make this claim, Luke's narrative must be concerned with far more than recounting selected events; he must demonstrate their significance and interpret them against the horizons of Israel's past, Israel's Scriptures, and Israel's hopes.

6.2. THE UNITY OF LUKE-ACTS

Our discussion of the message and character of the Gospel of Luke has proceeded thus far on the assumption that Luke and Acts in some sense comprise a unity. We may understand this "unity" in several ways. First, especially on the basis of the prefaces (Luke 1:1-4; Acts 1:1-2), practically everyone agrees that the Gospel of Luke and the Acts of the Apostles were written by the same person. These two books share *authorial unity,* therefore, making the writings of this author the single largest contribution to the NT (28% of the whole). But who is the author? Like the other NT narratives, Luke and Acts are unsigned documents and come to us anonymously. The oldest Greek manuscript of the Gospel of Luke (Papyrus Bodmer XIV, known as 𝔭75), dating from *ca.* 200 CE, uses the title, "Gospel according to Luke." This, together with other witnesses from the second century, indicates how quickly the name was attached to these books in the tradition.

"Luke" appears three times in the NT (Col 4:14; Phlm 24; 2 Tim 4:11), with reference to a companion of Paul who is thus traditionally identified as the author of Luke and Acts. Assuming that these texts refer to the same person, they suggest a person of considerable stature in the Christian mission, a missionary colleague (and not an assistant) of Paul, who was either a Gentile or at least a non-Jewish Semite. Colossians refers to him as "beloved physician," and this indicates that Luke was not one of the quacks known to take advantage of a naive public but was in fact respected for his knowledge and skill in the healing profession. The portrait of Luke as a sometime companion of Paul, though neither a constant travel part- ner nor a disciple of Paul, is congruent with the evidence of Acts 16:10-17; 20:5– 21:18; 27-28; these are the "we-passages," in which the narrator presents himself as a participant in segments of the Pauline mission. There is little reason to reject the traditional identification of Luke as the author of these two books, though in the end, because we know next to nothing about him, this identification helps us little in our reading and interpretation of either the Gospel or the Acts.

Discussion of the issue of authorship raises also the question of audience: To whom was Luke writing? Luke dedicated his work to Theophilus (Luke 1:3), and this has led some to assume that Theophilus either was Luke's audience or that he was representative of the audience Luke hoped to reach. In Roman antiquity, how- ever, "patron" and "audience" cannot be equated. Without printing presses and a well-developed book market, "publishing" occurred when an author allowed his book to be copied and circulated by others. The business of patrons, then, was to introduce a book to their network of friends so that the book might gain a wider hearing. The quest for the historical Theophilus, then, is a blind alley in the search for Luke's audience.

In fact, study of Luke has failed to achieve anything approaching a consensus regarding the identity of a particular audience (i.e., a certain community, or per- sons located in a particular city or region of the Roman Empire) for the Gospel and Acts. Most assume that these books were written primarily for Christians (i.e., they have an ecclesiological focus more than an evangelistic one) throughout the empire.

One can speak of the unity of Luke and Acts in terms other than authorship. For example, one can think also of *narrative unity* and *theological unity*. Since Aris- totle, "narrative" has been understood primarily in terms of temporal sequence and aim. Simply stated, a narrative must have a beginning, a middle, and an end, with the progression from one narrative stage to the next guided by a particular objective or end. In the case of Luke and Acts, narrative aim is expressed in (1) the orientation of the opening chapters of the Gospel around the dawning of salvation and (2) the opposition that the agents of this salvation, John the Baptist and Jesus, encounter. Conflict, then, pushes the narrative forward, as we read further to dis- cover how (or whether!) God's aim to bring salvation in all its fullness will be real- ized in the midst of hostility and competing aims. Indeed, the narrative plots the alignment of its characters — John, Jesus, and their parents; people like Simeon, Anna, the disciples, and other faithful women; the crowds, the Pharisees, and the Jewish elite in Jerusalem; and others — either *with* God's purpose of bringing sal- vation or *against* it. The narrative unity of Luke and Acts is grounded in the reality that Luke presents key expectations or needs early in the Gospel, including the res- toration of Israel and the embrace of the Gentiles in the community of God's peo- ple, which are not actualized in the Gospel but must wait until the book of Acts.

This perspective also accounts for the interesting portrayal of the disciples in the Gospel. Mostly, they are simply "with" Jesus; never are they assigned their own defining portfolio in the service of the kingdom of God. One must wait until the opening of Acts for the disciples to come into their own, so to speak, and to understand and embrace their particular contributions to the mission of God.

If Luke and Acts share this unity, why are they separated into two volumes? This question must be answered at two levels. From a material perspective, it was simply impossible to present these two books in one volume. Luke's Gospel, with about 19,400 words, and Acts, with about 18,400, each require a papyrus roll of some 35 feet, which was the maximum length. It is therefore interesting that these two volumes share a notable symmetry not only in relative size but also in the span of years covered (about 30 years) and in that, just as the account of Jesus' suffering and death comprises some 25% of the Gospel, so Paul's arrest and trials account for some 25% of Acts. Theologically, the ascension of Jesus, narrated both at the end of the Gospel and the beginning of Acts, serves as the narrative hinge and, together with Jesus' resurrection, the theological focal point of the narrative.

Of course, Luke and Acts are not unified in the canon, but are separated by the Gospel of John. Given the forces drawing Luke and Acts together, to be read as a single narrative, the forces that divided them into separated canonical "addresses" in the New Testament must have been powerful indeed. It seems likely that those forces came from two directions at once. First, given the similarity of the Gospel of Luke to the Gospels of Matthew and Mark, this Gospel was pulled into a relationship with these other two, and we now know all three as "Synoptic Gospels" on account of their "common view." Second, as a bridge from Gospel to Letters and from Jesus to Paul, Acts was pulled to a position after the Fourfold Gospel. From this *canonical* perspective, then, the Gospel of Luke is located in an interpretive relationship with the other Gospels, which together proclaim the one gospel of Jesus Christ.

6.3. THE NARRATIVE OF THE GOSPEL OF LUKE

Although some of the details might be debated, the broad strokes of the development of Luke's narrative of Jesus' mission are clear: a birth narrative is followed by Jesus' mission in Galilee, which is followed by his long, meandering journey from Galilee to Jerusalem, which in turn is followed by accounts of his teaching, death, and resurrection in Jerusalem. Geography thus plays a pivotal role in the shaping of the Gospel of Luke.

Prologue (1:1-4)
The birth and childhood of Jesus (1:5–2:52)
Preparation for the ministry of Jesus (3:1–4:13)
The ministry of Jesus in Galilee (4:14–9:50)
   The gospel proclaimed in synagogues (4:14-44)
   Mission and controversy (5:1–6:11)
   Jesus teaches his disciples and the crowds (6:12-49)
   Healing and teaching (7:1-50)
   Broader ministry (8:1-56)
   Jesus' identity and the nature of discipleship (9:1-50)
On the Way to Jerusalem (9:51–19:48)
   Teaching on discipleship and the kingdom (9:51–10:42)
   Teaching on prayer (11:1-13)
   Escalating hostility (11:14-54)
   Teaching on vigilance (12:1–13:9)
   Who will participate in the kingdom of God? (13:10–17:10)
   Responses to the kingdom (17:11–19:27)
   Jesus arrives in Jerusalem (19:28-48)
Teaching in the temple (20:1–21:38)
Jesus' suffering and death (22:1–23:56)
Jesus' exaltation (24:1-53)

6.3.1. The Prologue (1:1-4)

According to ancient handbooks, the preface of an oral speech ought to prepare the audience to be well disposed toward the oration, attentive and ready for instruction. Much the same might be said of a preface such as the one Luke has provided to his narrative. His preface is a clear attempt to locate the work within Greco-Roman literature and is reminiscent of what we find in other examples of historical writing. Luke casts himself as one of "us," a member of the larger community of persons whose lives have been shaped by the events he will recount; he is an interested party, a member of "the people of the Way." He calls special attention to the extent of his research and inquiry, to the order of the narrative, and to the character of his narrative as proclamation. Luke is no mere chronicler of events; rather, he is set on persuading his audience that his interpretation of recent events is reliable.

Luke's Prologues in Comparison with Those of Josephus

Luke 1:1-4; Acts 1:1-2

Josephus, *Ap.* 1.1. §§1-3; 2.1 §§1-2

Since many have undertaken to set down an orderly account of the events that have been fulfilled among us, just as they were handed down to us by those who from the beginning were eyewitnesses and ministers of the word, I too decided, after investigating everything carefully from the beginning, to write an orderly account for you, most excellent Theophilus, so that you might know the truth concerning the things about which you have been informed.

In my history of our *Antiquities,* most excellent Epaphroditus, I have, I think, made sufficiently clear to anyone who may peruse that work the extreme antiquity of our Jewish race, the purity of the original stock, and the manner in which it established itself in the country which we occupy today. . . . Since, however, I observe that a considerable number of persons . . . discredit the statements in my history concerning our antiquity . . . , I consider it my duty to devote a brief treatise to all these points; in order at once to convict our detractors of malignity and deliberate falsehood, to correct the ignorance of others, and to instruct all who desire to know the truth concerning the antiquity of our race.

*   *   *

*   *   *

The first book I wrote, Theophilus, concerned everything Jesus did and taught from the beginning until the day he was taken up into heaven, after he had commissioned the apostles whom he had chosen through the Holy Spirit.

In the first volume of this work, my most esteemed Epaphroditus, I demonstrated the antiquity of our race. . . . I shall now proceed. . . . (LCL)

6.3.2. The Birth and Childhood of Jesus (1:5–2:52)

With 1:5, Luke actually begins his narrative, and the transition from prologue to narrative is arresting. The prologue is written in relatively refined Greek, while the birth narrative has a "biblical" feel, suggesting continuity from the LXX to the beginning of the Gospel. We abruptly depart from a more elite cultural milieu, signified by Greek preface-writing, and enter into the small-town

The ruins of a third- and fourth-century synagogue in Capernaum *(Werner Braun, Consulate General of Israel in New York)*

struggles of a little-known priest and his wife and a peasant girl from Galilee. The atmosphere is permeated by the piety of Second Temple Judaism and Jewish hopes for divine intervention. The juxtaposition of these two worlds speaks to the universal significance of the events Luke will narrate. Here Luke will celebrate the pouring out of God's love for Israel and, indeed, for all humanity. God's promises are coming to fruition, and the birth narrative is a virtual festival of salvation.

Two features help to structure the narrative and give it meaning. The first is the movement from divine promise to evidence of fulfillment to responses of praise (see the table below). Viewing the birth narrative from this perspective highlights both how integral promise and fulfillment are to the beginnings of this Gospel and the essential place of these songs in the fabric of chs. 1–2. In fact, the Songs of Mary, Zechariah, and Simeon all function similarly — to stop the progression of events momentarily so that Spirit-inspired interpretations of these momentous events might be heard clearly. A sense of the miraculous intervention of God pervades the whole narrative. It is clear that God is taking the initiative to bring his redemptive purpose to fruition, and this is cause for celebration and praise.

Character	Promise	Evidence of Fulfillment	Response of Praise
Zechariah	His wife would bear a son.	John is born.	Song of Zechariah
Mary	She would conceive a son.	Unborn John bears witness to Jesus in the womb; Elizabeth blesses Mary.	Song of Mary
Simeon	He would see the Messiah.	He encounters Jesus in the temple.	Song of Simeon

The second feature is the point-by-point parallelism between John and Jesus that embraces the whole of these two chapters (see below). The way in which these two stories, that of John and that of Jesus, are thus interwoven indicates that these two births and these two sons belong to the one story of God's salvation. Both births constitute "good news" (1:19; 2:10). This is not to say that John and Jesus are equals, however. For example, Luke spends almost twice as much space recounting the birth and childhood of Jesus. Again, John is "prophet of God Most High," while Jesus is "Son of the Most High" (1:32, 76). John is central to the unveiling of the new era of salvation, but his role is one of preparing for Jesus.

John	Event	Jesus
1:5-7	The Introduction of Parents	1:26-27
1:8-23	The Annunciation of Birth	1:28-38
1:24-25	The Mother's Response	1:39-56
1:57-58	The Birth	2:1-20
1:59-66	Circumcision and Naming	2:21-24
1:67-79	Prophetic Response	2:25-39
1:80	The Growth of the Child	2:40-52

The birth narrative also focuses our attention on Jesus' identity, a concern that will continue in the Gospel, especially in its opening chapters. Above all else, Jesus is the Son of God. This is how Gabriel presents him to his mother in anticipation of Jesus' birth (1:32-35), interpreting his sonship in terms borrowed from images of the Davidic Messiah. It is portentous, then, that he is conceived as "the Holy Spirit comes upon" Mary, and "the power of the Most High overshadows her," so that God himself is responsible for Jesus' conception (1:35). Moreover, the birth account closes with Jesus affirming as a youth that his father is none other than the God of the temple: "Did you not know that I must be in *my Father's house?*" (2:49).

6.3.3. The Preparation for the Ministry of Jesus (3:1–4:13)

Just as the birth narrative moves back and forth in its focus on John and Jesus, so in this second section of the Gospel we anticipate the onset of Jesus' ministry by learning first of John's. John enters the scene as a prophet, and the presentation of his mission by Luke holds two concerns in dynamic tension: John (1) provokes a crisis and directs popular hopes to the coming of a messianic deliverer and (2) attracts hostility, leading inevitably to his imprisonment. 3:1-20 presents John's public career in relation to the religio-political elite of his day and against the backdrop of Isaiah's message of the universal reach of God's salvation. His "good news" centers on a repentance-baptism, by which he calls on the Israelites to realign themselves with God's purpose and to demonstrate their allegiance to God through daily conduct in keeping with God's own concerns with justice and compassion. The new epoch has begun already with John's ministry, with its promise of blessing and woe, and of division, and this sets the stage for the appearance of God's agent of salvation, Jesus, the Son of God.

Central to Jesus' preparation for ministry is his identity as Son of God and experience of the Spirit; these two are inseparable and provide the primary focus for the scene of Jesus' baptism (3:21-22). Jesus is Son of God in consequence of his extraordinary conception. This is confirmed by God at Jesus' baptism, then developed further in the genealogy in 3:23-38. In 3:23 Luke admits that people would think that Jesus was Joseph's son, whereas the genealogical record indicates that Jesus is actually God's Son. This clash over Jesus' identity helps to shape the narrative as it unfolds, as people repeatedly act on the basis of an erroneous understanding of who Jesus is and therefore misconstrue the significance of his presence among them.

First, however, Jesus' sonship becomes the basis for his encounter with the devil in the wilderness. "If you are the Son of God," the devil says, admitting that Jesus is in fact God's Son (the translation, "*Since* you are the Son of God" would be appropriate), but debating with Jesus on the significance of that designation. Jesus, "full of the Holy Spirit," defines his identity in terms of Israel's experience in the wilderness (Deuteronomy 6–8) and thus in terms of his fundamental allegiance and obedience to God. Israel was tested in the wilderness, and so is Jesus. Israel failed the test, but Jesus does not. The devil wants to distract him from God's claims so as to redirect Jesus' mission toward his own ends. The reality of a second, and competing, purpose is established here: Will Jesus align himself with God's will and thus embrace fully his identity and role as Son of God? Will his life reflect the character and commitments of God? Or will Jesus adopt this diabolic aim and pervert his identity and role, making of himself a son of the devil? Empowered by the Spirit, full of the Spirit, led by the Spirit, Jesus proves his fidelity in the midst of the diabolic onslaught and thus his readiness to engage in ministry publicly as God's Son.

6.3.4. The Ministry of Jesus in Galilee (4:14–9:50)

After the first two sections of the Gospel, we have a keen sense of *what* we might expect of God's gracious visitation, but thus far the narrative has been less forthcoming on *how* God's purpose will be achieved. Luke 4:14–9:50, centered in the region of Galilee, articulates the pattern of ministry by which God's aim is to be realized. First, it presents a definitive understanding of the outworking of Jesus' sonship and empowerment by means of a publicly proclaimed missionary program (4:16-30). Following this is a litany of episodes of teaching and healing that demonstrate the character of that program in concrete terms. The call of the disciples in 5:1-11 does not yet signal the involvement of others in Jesus' ministry, but it does portend the key role of the gathering of the people of God in Jesus' work. Jesus' message occasions discipleship, but also attracts hostility. Clearly, Jesus' itinerant ministry of proclamation and miraculous activity provokes a crisis leading to a division within Israel.

Jesus proclaims the good news in Galilean synagogues in 4:14-44, establishing the nature of his identity and mission as God's Son. Often regarded as programmatic for the whole of Jesus' ministry, his sermon in Nazareth in 4:16-30 is his first public address. Indeed, although, as 4:16 reads, it was Jesus' custom to read the Scriptures and to teach in the synagogue on the Sabbath, this is the only occasion on which Luke records the content of that teaching; this suggests that Jesus' message in 4:16-30 sets the tone and establishes the horizons of his preaching in other synagogues on Sabbath days. Drawing on Isa 61:1-2/58:6, Jesus interprets his ministry as the fulfillment of the eschatological Jubilee (see Leviticus 25), a dramatic cipher for the age of salvation, marked above all by the ministry of "release." This "release" is illustrated immediately in accounts of healing and exorcism

(4:31-44). Throughout the Gospel we see Luke develop this concept and experience of "release" in three ways: (1) release from diabolic power, so that people are healed (e.g., 13:10-17; cf. Acts 10:38), (2) release from the debilitating cycle of debt by which those of higher status and greater means control the lives of those without power and privilege (e.g., 6:27-36; cf. the Jubilee legislation in Leviticus 25),

The End Time in 11Q13

A document found at Qumran, Cave 11, and known as 11QMelchizedek or 11Q13, borrows from Isa 61:1 and Leviticus 25 to proclaim the nature of the end time, the eschatological jubilee. This text follows a line of interpretation similar to that found in Luke 4:16-30 — though, in this case, the heavenly deliverer is Melchizedek and the motif of judgment is far more prominent.

> . . . And concerning that which He said, In [this] year of Jubilee [each of you shall return to his property; and likewise, And this is the manner of release:] every creditor shall release that which he has lent [to his neighbor. He shall not exact it of his neighbor and his brother], for God's release [has been proclaimed]. [And it will be proclaimed at] the end of days concerning the captives as [he said, To proclaim liberty to the captives. Its interpretation is that he] will assign them to the Sons of Heaven and to the inheritance of Melchizedek; f[or He will cast] their [lot] amid the po[rtions of Melchize]dek, who will return them there and will proclaim to them liberty, forgiving them [the wrongdoings] of all their iniquities.
>
> And this thing will [occur] in the first week of the Jubilee that follows the nine Jubilees. And the Day of Atonement is the e[nd of the] tenth [Ju]bilee, when all the Sons of [Light] and the men of the lot of Mel[chi]zedek will be atoned for. [And] a statute concerns them [to prov]ide them with their rewards. For this is the moment of the Year of Grace for Melchizedek. [And h]e will, by his strength, judge the holy ones of God, executing judgement as it is written concerning him in the Songs of David. . . . And Melchizedek will avenge the vengeance of the judgements of God. . . . This is the day of [Peace/Salvation] concerning which [God] spoke [through Isa]iah the prophet. . . . (English translation from Vermes, 500-501.)

and (3) "release" or "forgiveness" of sins (e.g., 7:47-49). The particular recipients of this good news are "the poor" — defined throughout the Gospel by a variety of criteria: economic standing in the community, family heritage, religious purity, health, vocation, and so on. "The poor" are those whose existence is eked out on the margins of society, so that even a wealthy man like Zacchaeus can be the recipient of good news, since as a toll collector his social standing is that of an outcast, a sinner (19:1-10).

Luke 5:1–6:11 follows hard on the heels of Jesus' announcement of the divine necessity of his engaging in an itinerant ministry (4:43-44) by recounting just such a mission. Jesus begins this segment of his ministry by calling disciples (5:1-11), who then fade into the background. In the Gospel narrative their primary vocation is to learn and to exemplify appropriate response to Jesus and his message (cf. 5:11, 28). Though Jesus pronounces that "from now on you will be catching people" (5:10), they will engage in such activity only rarely until the opening of the Acts of the Apostles.

In the calling of the disciples, Jesus demonstrates the sort of people with whom he is willing to associate. Peter is a self-professed "sinner"; others throughout this section are known similarly. In fact, a variety of maladies is intertwined with a condition of sinfulness, so that Peter's status prepares for the larger emphasis in this section on sin, sinners, and forgiveness of sins (5:8, 13-14, 20-24, 30-32; 6:2, 7, 9). While Jesus orients his concern toward these outsiders and thus makes of them objects of God's grace, those who are religious view Jesus with suspicion, even hostility (5:21, 30, 33; 6:2, 7, 11). As Jesus retorts, "I have come to call not the righteous but sinners to repentance" (5:32).

The disciples do reappear in the next subsection, 6:12-49, where Jesus undertakes to set before them the substance of his message. Again, discipleship is presented primarily in terms of preparation: Jesus names apostles (6:12-16), but provides them with no particular portfolio. With 6:17, he defines in constructive terms the new conditions of faith and life within the community being gathered around him. Here are the dispositions and practices that characterize and flow naturally from this new people. Remarkably, what Jesus sketches is nothing less than a frontal assault on the beliefs and actions taken for granted by the Pharisees and scribes of the previous section. Those who discriminate in their choice of table companions, those who do not fast on appropriate days, those who withhold the grace of healing on the Sabbath, those who question the offer of forgiveness — such persons will find little with which to identify in Jesus' sermon. Indeed, Jesus' message is one of reversal. Following God must be characterized by mercy (6:36), by inclusion of those people who formerly were not to be tolerated and restoration of them to the community of God's people. The depth to which Jesus is willing to go is suggested by his use of the term "hypocrite" in 6:42. Although in general usage today "hypocrite" refers to those who say one thing but do another, in the LXX "hypocrite" described someone whose behaviors were not determined by God (cf. Job 34:30; 36:13; 2 Macc 6:21-25; 4 Macc 6:15-23). The use of the same term in the Roman theater for "someone acting a part" is also apropos. Jesus' final plea not only to hear but also to do (6:46-49) strikes a chord that will recur in the Gospel and that emphasizes here the importance of living out in one's life the character of what Jesus says in this extended sermon.

Immediately, Luke recounts episodes where the message of Jesus in ch. 6 is on full display in people's lives (7:1-50). What is surprising, though, is the identity of those through whom this occurs. That Jesus' ministry, which occupies center stage in this narrative unit, is characterized by compassion is no surprise (see especially 7:11-17), but it is startling to see a Gentile centurion embodying the message of Jesus by denying his worthiness and thus his authority to order Jesus into his home. It is startling to hear Jesus say of a Gentile army officer, "Not even in Israel have I found such faith" (7:9). And it is astonishing to find a woman known in the city as a sinner serve as an exemplar of authentic hospitality, a paragon of appropriate response to the gift of salvation manifest in Jesus' ministry (7:36-50). The nature of Jesus' ministry and the people it attracts are apparently so stunning that they raise questions for John the Baptist about whether Jesus is indeed the Messiah. John has prophesied messianic judgment, but where is it? John's question typifies the ease with which people throughout the Gospel, failing to appreciate fully the nature of God and thus his agent of salvation, attempt to draft Jesus to their own ends or misconstrue what he is (or ought to be) about.

The little summary Luke provides in 8:1-3 introduces the major motifs that occupy the next subsection of the Gospel, 8:1-56. First is the status of Jesus as the one who broadcasts the word of God and brings salvation. The second is the active presence of diabolic activity and influence, which Jesus confronts and overcomes in his ministry. Finally, the gathering of followers is highlighted, underscoring the importance of authentic response to Jesus' message. All three motifs are woven into Jesus' teaching, though the emphasis falls especially on the need for genuine hearing, demonstrated in the fecundity of faithful obedience (8:8, 10, 12, 13, 14, 15, 18, 21). The devil works against authentic hearing (8:12), and the diabolic is on further display as Jesus and his followers attempt to cross the Sea of Galilee (in Jesus' "rebuke" of the wind — cf. the metaphorical identification of the powers of nature with the demonic in the OT) and in Jesus' encounter with the Gerasene demoniac. The superior power of Jesus is thus dramatized.

The final unit of the Galilean ministry of Jesus brings together the issue of Jesus' identity with the question of the nature of discipleship (9:1-50). Questions about Jesus' identity (e.g., 4:22, 36; 5:21; 7:16, 19-20, 39, 49; 8:25) now reach their acme in Herod's questions (9:7-9) and in the pronouncements of Peter (9:18-20) and God (9:28-36). The disciples are active in a way that is unique in the Gospel thus far (9:1-6), but heightened activity provides no accurate measure of their awareness of who Jesus is. They question his ability to provide for the crowds (9:12-17) and fail miserably to grasp the correlation of advanced status before God and humiliation among people (9:21-27, 35, 37-50). Indeed, as though contemplating the significant degree to which the disciples' beliefs and commitments have *not* been transformed thus far, Luke concludes that the meaning of Jesus' destiny "was concealed from them" (9:45).

6.3.5. On the Way to Jerusalem (9:51–19:48)

With 9:51, Luke begins a fresh section of the Gospel. Previously, he has worked to establish the nature of Jesus' messianic mission, peppering his account with illustrations of Jesus' ministry of "release." This is no longer the case, for Luke has no more need to establish the contours of Jesus' identity and mission. The concerns of this new section are represented by its character as a journey. A reflection of Israel's exodus journey, the journey Jesus takes with his followers is especially concerned with their formation as disciples. He teaches them more centrally about the character of God as the gracious Father who is ready to bestow the blessings of salvation in all its fullness to all people. Additionally, this is a journey with a destination, Jerusalem, interpreted especially as the place of divine destiny, the locus of hostility toward Jesus. Hence, the journey is characterized not only by the formation of disciples (and the standing invitation for others to associate themselves with God's purpose as this is embodied in and proclaimed by Jesus), but also by a growing hostility that reaches its acme in Jerusalem itself. Tragically, the disciples themselves are not immune to ideas and practices that stand in opposition to Jesus' message. Repeatedly, in fact, they are implicated in dispositions alien to the kingdom of God, and, by the end of the journey narrative, they seem almost to have disappeared from view, so fully have they failed to identify themselves with Jesus.

With the departure of Jesus and his followers for Jerusalem, Jesus makes it clear that "following" him is related to joining him in the journey and in proclaiming the kingdom of God (9:51–10:42). Disciples must hear and do the word. The stark demands of discipleship (9:51-62) are followed by the sending out of the seventy-two — a high point in the life of the disciples, who not only enjoy success in their ministry but also receive from Jesus rare insight into his person and mission (10:1-20). Although this is not the first occasion, it is perhaps the most direct; here we see that, for Luke, the prayers of Jesus are accompanied by divine revelation concerning him (cf., e.g., 3:21-22; 9:18, 28, 29). The episodes Luke recounts in this subsection also develop the importance of "welcoming" Jesus, his messengers, and his message — that is, of showing hospitality and care. Whether the would-be disciples do so is not stated (9:57-62), nor is it clear whether the Jewish lawyer responds positively to the parable in which Jesus presents a compassionate, hospitable Samaritan (10:25-37). The brief episode in 10:38-42 provides in the person of Mary a portrait of how to welcome Jesus, as well as in Martha a portrait of one whose behavior is not illustrative of one who extends the sort of welcome in which the authentic hearing of discipleship is integral.

In 11:1-13, Jesus turns a request for instruction in prayer into a lesson on the Fatherhood of God — on God's character, but also on fidelity as dependence on God and imitation of his graciousness. This concern will resurface in 12:1–13:9, but the intervening material is taken up with escalating hostility and attempts at censure (11:14-54). The juxtaposition of these accounts drives home Luke's portrayal of how mistaken the scribes and Pharisees are with regard to their portraits of God and, consequently, of faithful life in God's service. Hostility presses the urgency of a decision regarding Jesus. However, as Jesus' instruction on vigilance in the face of crisis clarifies (12:1–13:9), a decision *for* Jesus may well introduce one to the sort of persecution and testing that seems now to surround Jesus. Indeed, Jesus admonishes his followers to beware of the Pharisees' hypocrisy precisely because the values they serve are not exclusive to Pharisees; those who follow Jesus are not so different from those who oppose Jesus, at least not yet.

From 13:10–17:10 on the Gospel is fundamentally concerned with the question, Who will participate in the kingdom of God? Jesus' answers revolve around the related motifs of table fellowship, celebration with a shared meal, and the extension of hospitality. 15:1-2 makes it clear that Jesus is in the dock for his table habits. By summarizing the charges against Jesus in this way, Luke borrows from one of his most pervasive frames, that of meals. In addition to their obvious importance in the provision of food, meals serve significant social functions. In 13:22-31, presence at the end-time meal means participation in the kingdom of God. In 14:1-24, meals establish "in-group" boundaries and embody values pertaining to status and purity. In these texts, the table is an expression of kinship and dining manifests concerns for honor and acceptance. Jesus has a habit of flaunting these social and religious protocols, repeatedly eating with the "wrong" people — wrong, that is, as defined by the usual standards (e.g., 5:20-32; 7:34, 36-50; 14:1-6, 13, 21, 23; 19:1-10). Meals foster existing bonds of community, but in Luke's portrayal Jesus uses table fellowship to establish new, unexpected bonds.

Given the social and religious importance of meals, it is not surprising that Jesus attracts hostility for his table practices. Nor is it surprising, given the flow of the Gospel of Luke thus far, that the Pharisees and scribes are the sources of that hostility. Though Luke can speak more positively of the Pharisees, when they appear with the scribes they function as antagonistic monitors of Jesus' behavior. In this capacity, they repeatedly conclude that he has neglected God's law and consistently oppose his ministry. On the one hand, then, Jesus' disregard for the usual conventions regarding table companions helps to construct a people who, like the

The prodigal
and the pigs as
depicted by
Albrecht Dürer
(British Museum)

toll collectors and sinners of 15:1-2, hear and heed his message. "Let anyone who has ears to hear listen," Jesus has just proclaimed (14:35), and immediately these social outcasts are presented as those who "listen to him" (15:1). On the other hand, this new community of Jesus' followers raises by its very existence an unflattering and threatening voice against the attitudes and practices embraced by Jesus' adversaries.

Jesus has much to answer for, and the parables of Luke 15 are cast as his defense of the character of his entire ministry. Jesus highlights the disposition of his ministry as the necessary complement to God's character. The positive response of toll collectors and sinners as they gather around Jesus constitutes a restoration of the lost that results in heavenly joy and calls for earthly celebration, including feasting. In welcoming such social and religious outcasts to the table, Jesus is only giving expression to the expansive grace of God. What is more, as Jesus' teaching in ch. 16 urges, wealth is always to be used to extend hospitality to those in need; those who use wealth in this way are not behaving in any extraordinary way (17:1-10), but are simply following Moses and the prophets (16:29).

Luke 17:11–19:27 functions as a kind of "thematic summary" for the journey narrative, drawing together key motifs in Jesus' instruction and providing a heightened need for response to his message. In a real sense, the journey up to this point has been more an "idea" than an actuality, with Luke more interested in the journey motif than in Jesus and his entourage making real progress toward Jerusalem. Now, however, the pace of the journey is quickened and Luke provides clear markers showing Jesus passing between Samaria and Galilee, approaching Jericho, and, finally, entering Jerusalem. As Jerusalem looms closer on the horizon, Jesus takes care to interpret the significance of his arrival. Contrary to some expectations, the eschatological consummation of the kingdom of God is not tied to his entry into Jerusalem. Instead, prior to the End, the Son of Man must suffer many things (17:26; 18:31-33); indeed, Jerusalem is to be the site of his passion and death. Of course, Jesus' death is not to be the last word, and he articulates not only his resurrection but also his return with royal authority. The interlude between these last two events presents the need for faithfulness (see 18:8). Importantly, as they draw near to Jerusalem, the disciples do not comport themselves as models of fidelity. Such models are provided by a surprising list of persons: a Samaritan leper who recognizes in Jesus' ministry the beneficence of God (17:11-17), a widow who exemplifies God's chosen ones (18:1-8), a toll collector who humbles himself (18:9-14), little children (18:15-17), and a toll collector and sinner (19:1-10). Throughout this segment of the Gospel, the direct correlation between faithfulness and proper identification of Jesus is paramount.

With 19:28-48, Jesus arrives in Jerusalem. This momentous occasion is marked above all by Jesus' entry into Jerusalem and attempt to reclaim the temple for its purpose in God's plan. This means wresting it away from the temple leadership, who use it to camouflage their own injustices (cf. Jer 7:1-15). The excitement generated by Jesus' entry into the Holy City notwithstanding, Jesus knows already the inhospitable reception he will receive, and so he pronounces prophetic judgment on the temple and city for its failure to recognize that, in his coming to its walls, God himself has drawn near with his graciousness.

6.3.6. Teaching in the Jerusalem Temple (20:1–21:38)

Jesus' prophetic action in the temple (19:45-48) was an attempt to prepare the temple for his ministry in its precincts. His teaching engenders immediate and pervasive opposition, with conflict revolving around the question, Who has legitimate authority? The stakes are high. Even if those whom Luke mentions in this narrative unit might differ among themselves, all — chief priests, scribes, elders, Sadducees, and the Jerusalem wealthy — draw their legitimation from their relationship to the temple; hence, all are threatened by the appearance and teaching of Jesus. What is at stake is how God will be represented to the people of Israel — and, if God, then also faithfulness to God. Jesus has one view, the Jerusalem elite another. Who will sway the crowds? "The people" thus play a key role. They provide a buffer between Jesus and his opponents, so that Jesus does not go prematurely to his death; and their presence as Jesus' audience raises the question whether Jesus will succeed in persuading Israel to embrace a portrait of God and God's purpose that runs counter to that proffered by the temple authorities. In the end, Jesus undercuts the authority of those who use the Scripture and the temple system to tyrannize and oppress the weak of society (20:45–21:4) and forecasts the calamity and destruction that will come as the old order gives way to the new (21:5-38).

6.3.7. The Suffering and Death of Jesus (22:1–23:56)

The twin motifs of conflict and the fulfillment of God's purpose reach their high point in this narrative unit, which, then, is inexorably linked to the first twenty-one chapters of the Gospel. Jesus is aligned with the divine aim, and with him as his supporters are his disciples and "the people" who have listened to his message and received from his ministry. On the other side are the Jerusalem elite, who are aligned with the rule of darkness, with the devil (cf. 22:53). If the Jewish leadership in Jerusalem are to have their way with Jesus, they must succeed in winning the crowd over to their side — which they do, if only for a moment. The people join the chief priests and leaders of the people in crying out for Jesus' crucifixion, but almost immediately respond in sorrow and contrition (23:48). Even the intimacy of the band of disciples is breached, as Satan enters into Judas and Judas sides with the Jewish leadership against Jesus (22:3-6, 47-48). The Jewish leadership must also gain the partnership of the Roman leadership, Pilate in particular, and, in spite of his repeated protestations regarding Jesus' innocence, Pilate hands him over to their will (23:23-24).

The great irony of the conflict that climaxes in this narrative section lies in the juxtaposition of these two aims: the will of God and the will of Satan. Those who oppose Jesus believe that they are serving God, yet unwittingly serve a diabolic purpose. And, given their grasp of the will of God, they do the only thing that could be done. After all, Jesus had repeatedly departed from the demands of Torah, according to their perspective, and engaged in teaching and activity in the temple that could only be labeled perverse, again from their perspective. Indeed, they present Jesus to Pilate as a false prophet, using words reminiscent of the legislation in Deuteronomy 13, and, faithful to that OT text, they call for the death penalty (see Luke 23:1-5). For his part, Jesus goes to his death in the same manner that has characterized his life — namely, in obedience to the will of his Father (cf. 22:39-46). His was the death of a prophet, but more so the death of the regal prophet, the Royal Messiah, the Righteous One who suffers unjustly, the Servant of Yahweh.

6.3.8. The Exaltation of Jesus (24:1-53)

Luke's account of Jesus' resurrection appearances are startling in their initial portrayal of Jesus' followers. The empty tomb leads first to perplexity (24:4) and amazement (24:12); the testimony of the women who have seen the empty tomb and encountered the angels is met with cynicism and disbelief (24:11); the disciples on the road to Emmaus are clueless regarding the significance of Jesus' death, astounded by reports of the empty tomb, and unable even to recognize that their traveling companion is the risen Lord (24:13-22). Disbelief and astonishment continue even in the presence of the risen Jesus (24:41). It is as if the disciples simply lack the interpretive categories for rendering recent events in a meaningful way. Indeed, the cross and empty tomb are not self-interpreting but require elucidation, and this requires the depth of insight available only to those who have had their minds opened to understand the Scriptures (24:45). Jesus' passion is not a contradiction of his status and mission, but their fulfillment. He is the rejected prophet, the suffering Messiah, who, according to the Scriptures (when understood correctly), actualizes God's purpose. In the same way, Jesus' resurrection and ascension are grounded in the Scriptures; they demonstrate the validity, from God's perspective, of the manner of Jesus' life and the substance of his message. Again, the proclamation of repentance and forgiveness of sins to all nations — that is, the mission of Jesus' followers who will serve as his witnesses in the book of Acts — are written in the law of Moses, the psalms, and the prophets (24:45-47).

Luke 24 thus brings closure to the Gospel of Luke, but also anticipates more, including above all the mission to all nations, but also, and intricately related, the baptism with the Holy Spirit. Jesus' ascension, reported at the close of Luke as well as in the opening of Acts, is both the midpoint of Luke's narrative and the guarantee of the coming realization of salvation in all its fullness to all people.

6.4. "HE HAS LIFTED UP THE LOWLY"

This line, borrowed from the Song of Mary in Luke 1:46-55, helps to focus two important issues. The first concerns faith and wealth, and Luke's presentation of Jesus' mission among the marginal, while the second has to do with the place of Israel in God's plan according to the Gospel of Luke.

6.4.1. Faith and Wealth

Prominent among the several motifs serving the larger theme in Luke of advancing the purpose of God is the issue of discipleship and possessions. Jesus addresses the relation of these subjects relentlessly.

Was Jesus himself economically disadvantaged? Sentimental pictures have been painted of his lowly beginnings in a stable, as though he were homeless, but Luke more likely envisages a peasant home in which family and animals slept in one enclosed space, with the animals — and, in the overcrowded conditions of the census Luke portrays in Luke 2, Mary, Joseph, and the newborn Jesus — located on a lower level. More to the point is the sacrifice offered by Jesus' parents in 2:24: "a pair of turtledoves or two young pigeons," the prescribed offering for the poor (Lev 12:8). Later, Jesus is said to depend on the support of others (8:1-3). On the way to Jerusalem, Jesus says of himself that he has no place to lay his head (9:58), perhaps with reference to his lack of a home, but more clearly a warning concerning the rejection to be expected of those who follow in his footsteps.

Jesus' dependence on the benefaction of others (8:3) rules out any picture in Luke of an ascetic Jesus who rejects outright the use of wealth. To this may be added the refrain of his participation in dinner parties sufficiently ample that he could be characterized by others as a glutton and a drunkard (7:34; cf., e.g., 7:36; 11:37; 14:1-24; 19:1-27). In fact, throughout the Gospel Jesus interacts with both peasants and the wealthy; all need God's good news.

If wealth is not evil in and of itself, why does Jesus regard it as dangerous? What lies behind his warning that no one can serve both Mammon and God (16:13)? Why is it hard for those with wealth to enter the kingdom of God (18:24)? Why must would-be disciples give up everything (14:33)? Clearly for Luke, wealth presents itself as a temptation to prestige and security apart from God and for this reason is suspect (e.g., 12:13-21, 33-34). Two aspects of ancient Mediterranean life help us to grapple more deeply with the problems Luke addresses.

First, economic sharing was embedded in social relations. To share with someone without expectation of return was to treat them as kin, as family. Conversely, to refuse to share with others was tantamount to relating to them as though they were outside one's community. Hence, in 18:18-23, when the rich ruler refused to sell what he had and give the proceeds to the poor, he was making not only an economic decision but a social one as well. In choosing to preserve his own wealth he distanced himself from those in need — an action that is outside the bounds of discipleship in a Gospel where God has declared his salvific purpose to be realized in raising up the lowly and filling the hungry with good things (1:52-53).

In such a context, "almsgiving" cannot be understood according to modern lexicons as "charity" or "missionary giving." Rather, giving to the poor signified friendship with the poor. For this reason, the Pharisees and scribes are soundly reprimanded for not sharing and for acts of greed and wickedness (11:39-41; 20:46-47). For the same reason, the rich man, whose distance from the beggar Lazarus was maintained by the gate of his estate, finds himself following death in Hades (16:19-32).

Second, in insisting that giving take place in a context where one has no expectation of return, Jesus strikes at the root of one of the most prevalent models of friendship in antiquity, the patron-client relationship. In this environment, a potential patron possessed some commodity required by a client. In exchange, the client would provide appropriate expressions of honor and loyalty to the patron. The point is that, having received patronage, the client now existed in a state of obligation, of debt. The possibilities for exploitation and the exercise of controlling, coercive power are high. Jesus sets himself and his message over against this way of life, contrasting the behaviors that characterize everyday life in his world with behaviors that grow out of service in the kingdom of God. In the Sermon on the Plain (6:27-36), Jesus challenges his listeners to be God's people, who refuse the coercive, control-dominated system of relationships characteristic of the wider world but instead give freely, without expectation of return.

This message is well summarized in the petition in Luke's version of the Lord's Prayer, "And forgive us our sins, for we ourselves forgive everyone indebted to us" (11:4). In this case, "debt" must be understood within the framework of patronal friendships. Consequently, Jesus is urging his followers to forgive debts — that is, to treat one another as kin, giving freely, not holding over one another obligations for praise and esteem.

Luke's material on the rich and poor, then, is woven into a larger fabric than talk of money and treasure might at first suggest. Wealth is intricately spun together with issues of status, power, and social privilege. For this reason it cannot remain long outside the purview of the gospel. Entry into the way of discipleship raises immediately the question of possessions, with Luke calling for forms of distribution in which the needy are cared for and the wealthy give without expectation of return.

6.4.2. Israel and Luke

Finally, the question remains, Are not the Jewish people the lowly to whom Mary's Song refers? Are they not the focus of God's gracious visitation to bring salvation?

What is the place of Israel in God's salvation according to Luke? This is not an easy question to address, precisely because of the diversity of evidence within the Gospel. The scribes (also known as "lawyers" and "teachers of the law") are consistently portrayed in negative terms, for example. They question and test Jesus, complain about him, look for a way to accuse and execute him, and participate in his execution (cf. 5:17, 21, 30; 6:7, 9, 22; 10:25; 15:2; 19:47; 20:19; 22:2, 66; 23:10). Likewise, the Jewish synagogue is not a welcome place for Jesus and his message, especially as the narrative unfolds. Jerusalem and especially the Jerusalem-based priesthood are portrayed in negative terms, set against the purpose of God as this is articulated in Jesus' ministry.

On the other hand, Torah is never abrogated, even if it must always be interpreted in line with God's ancient purpose. Faithful obedience to the law is depicted positively, as are various acts of Jewish piety, including prayer, worship, fasting, and expectant waiting. Of course, the Scriptures of Israel themselves are crucial to the narrative Luke weaves, and repeatedly we learn that Jesus' message is continuous with the story of God and God's people in the Old Testament.

How does one move beyond this ambiguity? Crucial in this respect is Jesus' concern that his disciples not fall into hypocrisy — that is, that they not become like Pharisees and scribes who do not understand God's purpose and therefore whose commitments and behavior do not reflect God's character. Put sharply, the temple, the priesthood, and even the Scriptures of Israel must always be understood in ways congruent with God's purpose. Failure to grasp God's plan renders persons and institutions capable only of working at cross-purposes with God. Apart from this, they can give only the impression of piety and faithfulness. The religion of Israel — its institutions, its customs, its practices — is to be embraced fully when understood genuinely in relation to the redemptive purpose of God. But in order to be understood thus, Israel's religion must cohere with the purpose of God as this is articulated by God's own authorized agent of interpretation and salvation, God's Son, Jesus of Nazareth.

FOR FURTHER READING

Darrell L. Bock, *Luke*, 2 vols. (Baker Exegetical Commentary on the New Testament; Grand Rapids: Baker, 1994/96)

Henry J. Cadbury, *The Making of Luke-Acts* (2nd ed., with a new introduction by Paul N. Anderson, Peabody: Hendrickson, 1999)

Joel B. Green, *The Gospel of Luke* (New International Commentary on the New Testament; Grand Rapids: Eerdmans, 1997)

———, *The Theology of the Gospel of Luke* (Cambridge: Cambridge University Press, 1995)

Luke Timothy Johnson, *Luke* (Sacra Pagina; Collegeville: Liturgical, 1991)

7. The Gospel according to John

7.1. IN THE BEGINNING

However we assess the purposes and genre of the NT Gospels, they are clearly accounts of the life, work, death, and resurrection of Jesus. As we have seen, each Evangelist introduces his Gospel and subject in a way particularly appropriate to that Gospel's portrait of Jesus. Matthew introduces Jesus with a genealogy, tracing Jesus' family line back through two key figures in Israel's history, David and Abraham (Matt 1:1). After designating Jesus as "the Messiah, the Son of God" (Mark 1:1), Mark recounts the ministry of John the Baptist, who announced the coming of the one "mightier than I" and baptized him in the Jordan River in the Judean wilderness. And Luke promises his readers that he will write an account of all the things having to do with Jesus, beginning with the accounts of the birth of the forerunner of Jesus, John the Baptist, and of Jesus himself. These three Gospels anchor their narratives of Jesus' life firmly in the events and circumstances surrounding the beginning of Jesus' public ministry, his family, and his place in Israel's history.

The Gospel of John is also an account of the life, work, death, and resurrection of Jesus. But it opens with neither a reference to Jesus' genealogy nor an account of his birth. Rather, John opens with the words "in the beginning," the exact phrase with which the book of Genesis opens in the Greek OT (LXX; *en archē*). As is well known, the verse in Genesis ends with the assertion, "God created the heavens and the earth" (Gen 1:1). A reader of John who was familiar with the LXX would hear echoes of the Genesis account of God's creation of the world and would reasonably expect that John intended some connection to it. And such a reader would not be disappointed. John follows "in the beginning" with the declaration "was the Word." To emphasize the point that the Word was in the beginning, John adds "the Word was with God" (1:1) and rephrases the affirmation in the next verse: "This Word was in the beginning with God" (1:2). When God created the world "in the beginning," the Word already was. In fact, John continues, God created all things "*through* the Word" (1:3). This is John's commentary on the creation account of Genesis 1. It is hard to imagine what more could be said to underscore the dignity and mystery of this Word than is said in these affirmations. And yet John does say more. He asserts that not only was this Word "in the beginning" with God, as the agent of the world's creation, but that the Word "was God." The Word participates in the very life and being of God.

A few verses later there is a second set of affirmations regarding the Word: "And the Word became flesh, and dwelled among us, full of grace and truth" (John 1:14). The Word who was in the beginning with God, the Word through whom the world was made, the Word who was God, "became flesh." That Word took on the reality of existence as a human being who bore the name Jesus. With this affirmation, the reader is moved out of the primeval time of creation into the life of a particular human being and a concrete historical setting. That setting begins to be identified when a few verses later Jesus is called "the Messiah" (1:17), announced by a prophet named John (1:6, 15), and is compared to Moses, who gave the law (1:17). All these factors locate the Gospel within the world of first-century Judaism. Indeed, such a setting has already been adumbrated by the allusion to the opening words of Genesis, the Scriptures of the people of Israel.

These twin affirmations — that the Word was in the beginning with God and was God, and that the Word became flesh — express the identity of the one who is the subject of the Gospel. To be sure, the Gospel provides an account of Jesus' ministry, death, and resurrection. This is an account of the life of a human being of flesh and blood. But to grasp the significance of Jesus and his ministry, one must see him with the stereoscopic vision provided by these two affirmations. On the one hand, as a real human being, he lived and worked in a specific time and place. That time and place is Israel in the first century. Thus one must grasp the identity of Jesus as the Messiah of Israel and understand how he relates to figures such as John the Baptist and Moses, the great prophet of Israel, and to the law given through Moses, which the Jewish people of Jesus' day sought diligently to obey.

But, on the other hand, while understanding Jesus in the symbols and categories of Judaism is essential, that is not enough for a full comprehension of who he is. Jesus' identity can only be grasped fully as the one who is the Word made flesh, a Word who "was in the beginning with God." More than any other Gospel, John makes it clear that Jesus of Nazareth cannot be fully understood through the sort of account that a biography or chronicle of his life and work might offer. Rather, his story has to be read within the context of the cosmic drama of what God is doing through and in him. Readers who come to the Gospel expecting to find an account of the life, work, death, and resurrection of Jesus will find it. But they will also find that account shot through with the conviction that in Jesus the Word of God was made flesh. That one sentence, with its twin affirmations, serves as the lens through which Jesus' significance may be discerned.

7.2. JESUS, CONFLICT, AND CONFESSION

Having spelled out Jesus' identity, the Gospel shifts from explicit affirmations about him to a narrative which recounts words and deeds that manifest Jesus' identity as the Messiah who came from God. But these affirmations do not go unchallenged. In fact, the Gospel contains numerous episodes of discourse and debate in which the subject is Jesus' own identity. The Samaritan woman whom Jesus meets at a well reckons that he is a prophet, asks whether he is the Messiah, and invites her fellow townspeople to come meet Jesus, and they eventually profess Jesus to be "the Savior of the world" (ch. 4). After the feeding of the 5,000, Jesus talks at length about himself using the metaphor "bread of life." This discourse eventually leads many of his followers to desert him, although Peter and the disciples reaffirm their commitment to him as the one who has "the words of life" (ch. 6). A bitter dispute with "some Jews who had believed in him" (8:31) leads to Jesus' enigmatic assertion, "Before Abraham was, I am" (8:58).

In each of these episodes, the people whom Jesus encounters move either toward faith in him, recognizing and professing who he is, or away from faith in him, by misunderstanding and rejecting him and his claims. Although he is the Word of God incarnate, when he speaks many either do not understand or do not believe. Jesus' person and teaching clearly divide his audiences. More often than not, Jesus himself forces the issue by his bold claims to speak God's word on God's behalf and by God's authority. "My teaching is not mine but his who sent me" (7:16; 8:26; 12:49-50). Ultimately, the response to Jesus of each person in the Gospel is a response to the one who sent Jesus, to God. And belief and unbelief seem to be the only two possible options.

So strongly does the Gospel reject the possibility that anyone could remain on neutral ground with respect to Jesus and, ultimately, to God that it paints the contrast between the two potential responses to Jesus in the starkest possible terms. Faith in Jesus comes from "above," from God; it leads to life, light, truth, love, joy, peace, and knowledge of God; it results in the gift of eternal life (3:16, 21). By contrast, unbelief leads to death, darkness, error, and evil; it leads to judgment and ultimately to condemnation (3:19-20); it brands one as belonging not to God and the realm that is above, but to the world, the realm that is "below," and even to the devil (8:44-47).

In addition to Jesus' teaching and debates, the Gospel also contains accounts of Jesus' amazing deeds: he changes water to wine, feeds five thousand people, heals the sick, paralyzed, and blind, and raises the dead. Separately and together, these deeds reveal his identity as the one who brings life to the world, whether as abundant provision of food for the body or the spirit, healing, or restoration of life to the dead. But even the miracles of Jesus do not lead directly to belief. Those who see them sometimes fail to comprehend their significance (6:27-35), argue about the appropriateness of how and when Jesus has chosen to heal (5:16; 7:23; 9:16), or react by plotting to put him to death (11:47-53). While no one in the Gospel denies that Jesus does amazing deeds, less often do they come to grasp exactly that these deeds bear witness to him as one who has come from the very presence of God. In fact, witnesses to Jesus' miracles frequently state exactly the opposite view. The Pharisees' response to Jesus' healing of the blind man, coupled with the Evangelist's comment, summarizes it well: "Some of the Pharisees said, 'This man is not from God, for he does not observe the sabbath.' But others said, 'How can a man who is a sinner perform such signs?' And they were divided" (9:16).

Although the Gospel claims that Jesus makes God known (1:18), its episodes do not recount a series of triumphant and dazzling displays of divine glory, but rather the encounters of Jesus with a succession of different individuals who sometimes cannot see in Jesus anything more than a teacher whose brash claims belie his ordinary origins. "Is this not Jesus, the son of Joseph, whose mother and father we know?" (6:42). "How is it that this man has learning when he has never studied?" (7:15). "We know where this man comes from" (7:27). "We know that God has spoken to Moses, but as for this man, we do not know where he come from" (9:29). "It is not for a good work that we stone you but for blasphemy; because you, being a man, make yourself God" (10:33). What they will not or cannot accept is the assessment of Jesus given to the reader in the opening words of the Gospel. So much do Jesus' contemporaries oppose him that they seek to put him to death. In condemning Jesus to death, they have shut their ears to the Word of God and closed their eyes to the glory of God.

Cast in those terms, the Gospel appears to narrate a grim story of revelation gone awry. But, as already stated, the response to Jesus is mixed, and although rejection and hostility frequently characterize the reaction to Jesus, there are also individuals who believe in and follow him. Jesus calls disciples, elicits faith from them (2:11) and from a man whose child he heals (4:48-54), brings a Samaritan woman to confess him as Messiah and a whole town to honor him as Savior of the world (ch. 4), leads a former beggar to worship him as Lord (ch. 9), and finally leads Thomas to acknowledge him as his Lord and God (20:28). The opposing responses of belief and unbelief illustrate graphically the words of the prologue: "He came to what was his own, and his own people did not accept him. But to all who received him, who believed in his name, he gave power to become children of God, who were born, not of blood or of the will of the flesh or of the will of man, but of

God" (1:11-13). That is the underlying story embodied in each episode of the narrative as well as in the narrative as a whole. People either receive and believe in Jesus, or they reject him in unbelief. In his summary of the Gospel's purpose, the Evangelist notes that what is true for the people in the Gospel is true for its readers as well: "Now Jesus did many other signs in the presence of his disciples that are not written in this book. But these have been written so that *you may believe* that Jesus is the Messiah, the Son of God, and that *through believing you may have life in his name*" (20:30-31).

7.3. JOHN'S NARRATIVE

Prologue (1:1-18)
The book of signs (1:19–12:50)
  Confession of Jesus (1:19–4:54)
  Rising hostility (5:1–12:36)
  Summary (12:37-50)
The Passion (13:1–21:23)
  Jesus' last meal and instructions to his disciples (chs. 13–17)
  Arrest, trial, and crucifixion (chs. 18–19)
  Resurrection (20:1–21:23)
Postscript (21:24-25)

The Gospel itself is divided into two main parts bracketed by a prologue (1:1-18) and a brief postscript (21:24-25). The first main part, 1:19–12:50, recounts some of the signs that Jesus did openly or in public, his controversies with Jewish leaders, and the various sermons and dialogues in which he lays out his claims for himself and his work. In this portion of the Gospel, often designated the "Book of Signs," Jesus speaks of himself as the one who gives the gift of life from God, and performs signs that manifest his life-giving capacities. While Jesus does elicit positive responses, calling and making disciples, this part of the Gospel nevertheless closes with a summary that underscores the negative response to him (12:37-40), renews the invitation to believe in him (12:44-48), and repeats the claim that Jesus speaks the words of God (12:50).

The first part of the Gospel can be further divided into two major parts. *Chapters 1–4* contain scenes in which Jesus makes disciples and is acknowledged by them and others with a wide variety of epithets, including "King of Israel"

(1:49), "Son of God" (1:34, 49), "Messiah" (1:41), and "Savior of the world" (4:42). While some individuals, such as Nicodemus, fail to understand Jesus and grasp his message, the pervasive tone of these chapters is positive. Failure to comprehend Jesus comes closer to benign misunderstanding than overt hostility. To be sure, already in these chapters Jesus' death is foreshadowed (2:17-22), but the hour of his death lies still far in the future.

But in *chapters 5–12,* the second part of the "Book of Signs," the tone changes markedly. Sharp and bitter disputes between Jesus and his audience arise as Jesus' claims become more difficult for his audience to believe. Benign misunderstanding gives way to dangerous misperceptions of Jesus' purposes (6:14-15), doubt and grumbling (6:41-42, 52), debates about his identity (7:26-27, 40-44, 47-52; 9:16-17; 10:22-33), hostile disputes with Jewish authorities (8:52-58), desertion by former disciples (6:66), and, ultimately, the intention to seek Jesus' death (5:18; 7:1, 19, 25; 8:40; 11:47-53). While these chapters narrate a rising tide of negative reaction and hostility, that tide is matched by confession of Jesus as well. The blind man who had been healed acknowledges Jesus to be a prophet (9:16) and the Son of man with the confession, "Lord, I believe" (9:36-38). Martha, the sister of Lazarus, confesses Jesus as "the Christ, the Son of God" (11:27). Both opposition and acknowledgment crest at the raising of Lazarus from the dead.

The rising crescendo of hostility leads directly to that part of the Gospel which recounts Jesus' death. The second half of the Gospel, the so-called "Book of the Passion" or "Book of Glory" (13:1–21:23), turns to the events of Jesus' final days. This part can be subdivided into three parts which move back and forth between Jesus' encounters with his disciples and with the authorities. *Chapters 13–17* recount Jesus' last meal with his disciples, his lengthy instructions to them about what they are to expect and how they are to conduct themselves in his absence, and his prayer on their behalf. *Chapters 18–19* tell of Jesus' arrest and subsequent trial before Jewish and Roman authorities, and his crucifixion. Only two disciples, Peter and the anonymous "disciple whom Jesus had loved," play a significant role in these chapters. Peter's denial of Jesus contrasts with the persistent faithfulness of the other disciple, who alone is found at the foot of the cross as Jesus dies. Finally, *chapters 20–21:23* focus again on Jesus and the disciples. Even as they had once recognized Jesus and followed him, so now again the challenge comes to recognize and follow the risen Lord.

These two major parts of the Gospel are bracketed by a prologue (1:1-18), which introduces the main actors in the Gospel as well as foreshadowing the action that unfolds in it, and a postscript (21:24-25), a brief editorial comment noting that the Gospel contains only a few of the many stories that could be told about Jesus. This remark reminds the reader not only of the selectivity that the author has exercised but also that Jesus cannot be confined to the pages of any one book, even a Gospel. Such an admission is fully in keeping with the prologue's presentation of Jesus as the incarnation of one who existed before the world was ever created.

7.3.1. Prologue: "In the beginning was the Word" (1:1-18)

As already noted, the opening verses of the Gospel introduce its protagonist with the twin affirmations embodied in the assertion that "the Word was made flesh." Jesus of Nazareth was the man the Word became. But the prologue has yet more to

---

Wisdom Speaks

This speech of Wisdom from Sirach 24:3-12 has suggested to many scholars that John has adapted some of these motifs into the "Wisdom christology" in his prologue:

> I came from the mouth of the Most High,
>   and covered the earth like a mist.
> I dwelled in high places,
>   and my throne was in a pillar of cloud.
> I alone have made the circuit of the vault of heaven
>   and have walked in the depths of the abyss.
> In the waves of the sea, in the whole earth,
>   and in every people and nation I have a possession.
> Among all these I sought a resting place;
>   I sought in whose territory I might lodge.
> Then the Creator of all things gave me a commandment,
>   and the one who created me assigned a place for my tent.
> He said, "Make your dwelling in Jacob,
>   and in Israel receive your inheritance."
> From eternity, in the beginning, he created me,
>   and for eternity I shall not cease to exist.
> In the holy tabernacle I ministered before him,
>   and so I was established in Zion.
> In the beloved city likewise he gave me a resting place,
>   and in Jerusalem was my dominion.
> So I took root in an honored people,
>   in the portion of the Lord, who is their inheritance.

---

say about how to understand the Word made flesh. It describes the Word with images and terms from Jewish Wisdom speculation found in the OT, particularly Proverbs 8, and in the OT Apocrypha in Sirach and the Wisdom of Solomon. In Prov 8:22-31, Wisdom is said to have existed in the beginning, prior to the creation of the world, to have been God's agent in creation, to have brought life and light to those who accept it, and to have been rejected by human beings. According to Sirach 24:8, Wisdom came forth from the mouth of the Most High, from a dwelling place in heaven, and was commanded by the Creator to dwell in Israel, where it "took root," growing up into a tree whose branches were "branches of glory and grace" (John 1:14; 15:1-11). Sirach also equates Wisdom with the law given through Moses, which makes people full of understanding (24:26, 28) by giving them instruction or enlightenment (chs. 27 and 32). By contrast, in John the fullness of grace and truth (1:14, 16) is said to have been revealed through the Son, the true light of the world (vv. 4, 5, 9), and not through the law (v. 17). Jesus takes on the functions and role of Wisdom, dwelling with the people of God, giving them instruction, and revealing God's glory and grace to them.

Beginning with the use of the wisdom motif, the prologue is full of imagery having to do with revelation, instruction, guidance, seeing, and understanding. Like both wisdom and the word of the Lord, Jesus is compared to a light shining in darkness (1:5; 7-9; see Ps 119:105). His "glory," a typical OT expression for the visible manifestation of deity, could be seen (1:14). He made God known (1:18). John the Baptist, who makes a cameo appearance in the prologue, illumines the way to the true light (1:6-8). From beginning to end, these eighteen verses stress that Jesus' role as the Word who "became flesh" was to reveal God, to shine as a light on the path to God, to give instruction of truth analogous to the Mosaic law (1:17). Those who see by this light are given power "to become children of God" (1:12), a description that echoes OT descriptions of Israel (Deut 32:18; Ps 82:6; Hos 11:1). To become a child of God is to become part of the people of God.

The total effect of portraying Jesus in comparison with wisdom, Moses, and the law and of describing the result of faith in terms of the creation of "the children of God" is to suggest that the Gospel must be read as part of God's dealings with Israel. The theological point the Evangelist makes about Jesus' significance and role can be comprehended only in light of the narrative of God's calling and redemption of Israel. Jesus must be understood within the context of the ongoing narrative of God's creation and sustenance of a people who belong to God.

In the prologue, then, the reader is introduced to the Word, whose work and significance can be discerned only with reference to God's cosmic work of creation and historical work of the creation of a people. At the outset, the Evangelist provides the reader with his own perspective on Jesus' identity. Clearly, this whole densely woven tapestry of conviction is not available to the characters in the Gos-

> ### The Logos
>
> The Alexandrian Jewish apologist, Philo, has a "logos theology" with strik-
> ing parallels to that found in the Gospel of John. In the following quota-
> tion, "the One" and the "Self-existent" refer to the one true God; the Logos
> makes that God known.
>
> > The first of all is he who is elder than the One, the Monad, and the
> > Beginning. Next is the Logos of the Self-existent, the seminal essence
> > of all beings. And from the divine Logos, as from a fountain, the two
> > powers are separated. The creative power, by virtue of which the Cre-
> > ator established and ordered all things, is named "God" *(theos),* and
> > the kingly power by virtue of which the Creator rules that which has
> > come into being is named "Lord" (*kyrios*). (*Quaestiones in Exodus* 25.22)

pel, for they do not encounter Jesus with a copy of the Gospel in hand. But the
prologue alerts its readers to the confession to which the Evangelist ultimately
hopes that the Gospel will lead them (20:30-31). It thus grants them a privileged
position from which to read the Gospel.

7.3.2. "He manifested his glory" (1:19–12:50)

At 1:19 the Gospel shifts from explicit affirmations about Jesus to a narrative of his
words, deeds, and encounters with others, which illustrate both the positive and
negative responses mentioned in the prologue. This section opens with an account
of the ministry of the Baptist, whose sole purpose in the Gospel is to bear witness
to Jesus. Whereas in the Synoptic Gospels the Baptist calls people to repentance, in
the Gospel of John he bears witness to Jesus, thus calling people to faith. Speaking
in the language of the prophet Isaiah (John 1:23; Isa 40:3), John denies that he is
the Messiah (1:20), Elijah (1:21), or a prophet like Moses (1:21), and he promises
one coming after him who is the Lamb (1:29, 36) and Son of God (1:34). The Gospel has left behind the primeval realm of creation and eternity and has moved to
the Jordan River to present the story of Jesus of Nazareth, one who "became flesh,
and lived among us." John bears witness to him.

Indeed, the question of *Jesus' identity* remains central throughout the first
part of the Gospel. In the first chapter alone, Jesus is called Lamb of God (v. 29),

Son of God (v. 34), Rabbi (v. 38), Messiah (v. 41), King of Israel (v. 49), and Son of man (v. 51). This roll call of designations for Jesus could almost be included in the author's prologue, except that they are found on the lips of various characters in the Gospel, including John (the Baptist), the future disciples Andrew and Simon, Philip, and Nathanael, who also serve as witnesses to Jesus. Discipleship thus clearly involves recognizing and confessing Jesus in these terms, which, as already noted, are at home in first-century Judaism, and bearing witness to him as the one who rightfully deserves these various epithets. Elsewhere in the Gospel, other terms at home in the same milieu are suggested for Jesus as well. He is thought to be the Prophet (4:19; 6:14; 7:40), compared with Moses (1:17, 45; 3:14; 5:45-46; 6:32; 7:19-23; 9:28-29), deemed greater than Abraham (8:52-58) and Jacob (4:12), and addressed as Lord (9:38; 13:36; 14:5).

Throughout the Gospel the question of the adequacy of these various designations for Jesus looms large. The first such designation is introduced early, when in the prologue Jesus is named as the Messiah (1:17). Later, the Evangelist sums up his purpose in writing by stating his hope that his Gospel will lead people to believe in Jesus as "the Messiah, the Son of God" (20:31). The Baptist, whose chief role in the Gospel is that of bearing testimony to Jesus, denies that he is the Messiah, pointing instead to Jesus' messianic mission (1:20; 3:28). Jesus' disciples acclaim him as Messiah (1:41), both Samaritans (4:29-30) and Jews (7:25-31, 40-43, 52; 12:34) discuss his messiahship, and the confession of Jesus as Messiah is met with expulsion from the synagogue (9:22; cf. 12:42; 16:2).

But in spite of the obvious importance of the designation, Jesus evades crowds who want to make him king (6:14-15) and refuses to answer when asked whether he is the Messiah (10:24). Clearly a redefinition of "Messiah" weaves its way through the Gospel. Jesus is hailed as "king of Israel" (1:49), but the significance of that epithet is later explained in terms of Jesus' ruling a kingdom given to him by God rather than by human acclamation or force (18:33-37; cf. 6:14-15). Pilate quizzes him at length about his kingship and goads both Jesus and the Jews with the claims that he is a king (19:3, 14-16, 21-22). But Jesus warns Pilate that all power is given by God and that Jesus exercises his kingship by God's authority, not by Roman decree. The placard on the cross reads "King of the Jews" in Hebrew, Greek, and Latin, ironically announcing a messianic rule extending far beyond the walls of Jerusalem. Jesus' "messiahship" is not limited to rule over a restored kingdom of Israel, nor does it aim to establish the political sovereignty of Israel over other nations. Instead, the Gospel's purpose is to bring all its readers to understand Jesus as the Messiah (20:31), God's chosen agent for gathering together a people who will live obediently before God.

In many ways, this understanding of "Messiah" shades over into the role of prophet. At other places in the Gospel, Jesus is acclaimed as a prophet or, more specifically, as "the Prophet." While various prophets had been sent to Israel, some

The Messianic Age

A description of the messianic age from a Jewish document of about 100 CE:

> The earth will also yield fruits ten thousandfold. And on one vine will be a thousand branches, and one branch will produce a thousand clusters, and one cluster will produce a thousand grapes, and one grape will produce a cor of wine. And those who are hungry will enjoy themselves and they will, moreover, see marvels every day. . . . And it will happen at that time that the treasury of manna will come down again from on high, and they will eat of it in those years because these are they who will have arrived at the consummation of time. (*2 Baruch* 29:5-8, *OTP*)

Jews and groups of Jews expected that a final prophet would appear in the end times, thus fulfilling the promise of Moses to the people in Deut 18:15, "The LORD your God will raise up for you a prophet like me." The expectation of a "prophet like Moses" was known among the Samaritans (cf. John 4:19) and the community at Qumran, as various documents found among the Dead Sea Scrolls attest (4QTest 5–8). In keeping with the prophetic role, such a figure is more of a teacher of God's will than a royal figure. Just as the Baptist is asked whether he is the Messiah, so also is he asked whether he is the Prophet (1:21, 25). He denies that he is, because, as is clear elsewhere in the Gospel, the title is deemed fitting for Jesus. Following the feeding of the five thousand, the people exclaim, "Surely this is the Prophet who is coming into the world!" (6:14). Later they debate whether Jesus is "the Prophet" (7:40) or the Messiah (7:41).

And yet while both "Prophet" and "Messiah" capture some aspect of Jesus' mission, neither fully or adequately portrays him. In ch. 4, the Samaritan woman's tentative suggestions that Jesus is both prophet and Messiah are clearly surpassed by the confession that he is the "Savior of the world" (4:42). And whereas the blind man initially declares Jesus to be a prophet, he comes to the recognition of Jesus as the Son of man and as Lord (9:38). The very structure of these episodes shows the inadequacy of titles such as Messiah and Prophet, for each episode moves from acceptable but not fully adequate confessions of Jesus to confessions that come closer to encapsulating the shape of Jesus' work and the mystery of his identity. To understand Jesus on the Gospel's terms, one must also come to see that while Jesus speaks on behalf of God as a prophet and bears God's own sovereign authority as

Messiah, neither title captures the most essential elements of his identity. A fuller understanding of him must be sought along another path.

As already hinted, some of the mystery of Jesus' identity can be garnered from recognition of him as the Word made flesh. But Jesus does not speak of himself in these terms. He does, however, speak of himself as Son of man (1:51; 3:13-14; 9:35), an obvious allusion to the enigmatic figure who appears with "the Ancient of Days" in Daniel's visions of the heavenly court (Daniel 7). The first reference in the Gospel to this mysterious Son of man compares him to Jacob's vision of a ladder spanning earth and heaven (1:51; Gen 28:12). The open heaven and the angelic ladder are images of revelation. Even as the angels journeyed between heaven and earth on that ladder, so heaven and earth are joined by the Son of man. When the heavens are opened in revelation, the Son of man appears (John 1:51; 6:27, 53, 62), to exercise judgment and give life (5:27; 3:15; 6:53). Just as he descended, so he will return (3:13-14; 6:62; 12:34). People find Jesus' references to this Son of man baffling. When Jesus asks the healed blind man whether he believes in the Son of man, he asks, "Who is he?" (9:35). Later the crowds ask Jesus a similar question, "How can you say that the Son of man must be lifted up? Who is this Son of man?" (12:34). Thus while people attempt to understand Jesus in terms of various labels or titles, they cannot understand him on his own terms, as the Son of man, the one who came down from heaven.

The description of Jesus as the Son of man who came down from heaven takes us back to words of the prologue, with its declarations that the Word who was in the beginning with God became flesh. Some of the most distinctly and characteristic Johannine material, the so-called "I am" sayings of Jesus, need to be understood against the background of the prologue and in the context of the confession of Jesus as the Son of man who has come down from heaven. Speaking along the lines of the prologue, Jesus presents himself in a series of memorable affirmations, "I am the bread of life" (6:35); "I am the light of the world" (8:12; 9:5); "I am the gate for the sheep" (10:7); "I am the good shepherd" (10:11); "I am the resurrection and the life" (11:25); "I am the way, the truth, and the life" (14:6); and "I am the true vine, and my Father is the vinegrower" (15:1). In each of these affirmations Jesus speaks of himself as one who brings that revelation from God which grants life, understanding, and knowledge of God. He is the light and the way that lead to God's truth; he is bread from God which nourishes life, a vine that God tends and from which one can draw sustenance; he is the gate through which one can pass to eternal life; he is the shepherd who will give his life to save the sheep. Jesus brings life from God by illuminating the way that leads to the truth of God. The language of illumination, instruction, and revelation, already introduced in the prologue with its emphasis on themes from the wisdom literature, is repeatedly echoed throughout the Gospel in the teaching and sayings of Jesus.

Not only does Jesus use the language of illumination and revelation, but he also speaks in tones reminiscent of God's speech to the people of Israel, as recorded in the book of Isaiah, to underscore his role as an agent of God's self-revelation. "I, I am the LORD, and besides me there is no savior"; "I am God, and also henceforth I am He"; "I am the LORD, your Holy One, the Creator of Israel, your King" (Isa 43:11, 13, 15). Jesus speaks the same majestic language of self-revelation when he announces "I am the light of the world" (John 8:12; 9:5), "I am the resurrection and the life" (11:25), and "I am the way, the truth, and the life" (14:6). With these assertions, Jesus identifies himself as the agent of God's salvation. At other places, "I am" stands on its own in a formula that itself may echo the name of God, "I am who I am," revealed to Moses in the burning bush (Exod 3:14). For example, in John 8:24 Jesus says, "You will die in your sins unless you believe that I am" (8:24; or that "I am he"); "When you have lifted up the Son of man, then you will know that 'I am'" (8:28); and "Before Abraham was, I am" (8:58). Through these provocative "I am" sayings, both in their absolute form and with predicates referring to his lifegiving role, Jesus speaks in the majestic revelatory language used by God, thus linking his work and person in the most intimate relationship with God and God's work.

The Good Shepherd *(Alinari/Art Resource, NY)*

The designation of God and Jesus as Father and Son further describes the character of this relationship. John uses the term "Father" for God over 120 times, always in relation to Jesus the Son. Jesus is called Son, and the Greek word *huios* differs from the word used of believers as "children" *(tekna)* of God. Clearly the relationship between Jesus and God is unique, so much so that Jesus' reference to God as Father leads his opponents to charge him with "making himself equal with God," claiming privileges and status properly belonging to God alone. When Jesus heals a man on the Sabbath (John 5), he claims that God has given him authority to work on the Sabbath, to give life, and to raise the dead. These three privileges belonged only to God. Jesus' claim that he rightfully exercises these prerogatives because God has authorized him to do so is not lost on his hearers, who hear in his words an impious claim to equality with God. Jesus' attempt to defend himself by arguing that he only does what God commands him to do, in obedience to God, merely exacerbates the problem, pointing as it does to Jesus' claim to intimate and exclusive knowledge of God and God's will.

Even as various designations from Judaism and the OT serve to identify Jesus, so various feasts of the Jewish calendar, including Passover, Tabernacles, and Dedication (Hanukkah), remind the reader that it is the Jewish, rather than Roman, calendar whose dates are significant for understanding the Gospel and interpreting Jesus' significance. Similarly, different Jewish practices, rituals, hopes, and expectations become the backdrop against which Jesus must be interpreted and understood. The first two public acts of Jesus' ministry make this point. At a wedding

Giotti di Bondone, The Marriage at Cana, a fresco from ca. 1305 (Edgar Boevé)

Jesus transforms the water set aside for the Jewish rites of purification into the wine symbolic of the presence of the messianic age (2:1-11; cf. Amos 9:13-14; Hos 14:7; Jer 31:12). The extravagant provision of wine at the wedding may allude to traditions that in the messianic age the yield of the vineyards would be enormous and spectacular (*1 En* 10:19; *2 Bar* 29:5; Irenaeus, *Adv. Haer.* 5.33.3). Jesus now offers the purification of the messianic age, a cleansing already promised under the rubric "baptism with the Spirit" spoken of by John. Those who understood Jesus' sign in this way "saw his glory" (2:11) and believed in him. The next episode, the cleansing of the temple, also presents Jesus against the backdrop of Jewish institutions by foreshadowing the way in which the resurrected person of Jesus, and not the temple, will become the focal point of God's presence on earth. It is there that God's glory will dwell. Once Solomon the king built a magnificent temple for God, but now Jesus the messianic king becomes the temple of God.

Since so much of the Gospel focuses on the question of Jesus' identity and how he is to be understood, it is not surprising that it also develops the themes of *recognition and response to Jesus.* Some seem genuinely puzzled by Jesus. For example, Nicodemus comes to Jesus with a hunch that Jesus is a "teacher come from God" (3:2). His superficially innocent comment initiates a dialogue characterized by misunderstanding of Jesus' words. Such dialogues are a staple feature of John. Jesus speaks, his words are misunderstood, and no revelation or instruction takes place. Those he speaks to remain uncomprehending, failing to understand what he says. Nicodemus, for example, misunderstands Jesus' charge to be "born again" (3:3), wondering incredulously how a person could enter the womb to be born "a second time" (3:4). But Jesus actually intends a rebirth that is "from above," initiated by God's own Spirit (3:5-8). In order to grasp what is going on in this dialogue, one must know that the Greek word *anōthen* can be translated either "again" or "from above." Jesus tells Nicodemus that he must be born "from above," by the power of the Spirit of God, but Nicodemus hears Jesus say that he must be born "again." Nicodemus's inability to grasp Jesus' words betrays his failure to recognize that Jesus himself comes *from above* and so can speak authoritatively with respect to the birth from above. Nicodemus's misunderstanding shows that he needs the very new birth of which Jesus speaks.

Other misunderstandings follow in the Gospel. The Samaritan woman assumes that Jesus' offer of living water will save her long and dusty trips to the well (4:15), whereas he is actually promising the refreshing cleansing water of the Holy Spirit (7:37-39). The crowds to whom Jesus promises "the bread of God that comes down from heaven and gives life to the world" think that he is speaking of bread that will satisfy their physical cravings and hunger (6:33-34). He is, in fact, speaking of his own role as the lifegiving bread of God (6:35). Jesus corrects each miscomprehension, thus graphically illustrating the point that those who misunderstand must be "taught by God" in order to "hear and learn"

Cleansing Water

In the following two passages from the OT book of Ezekiel and from the Dead Sea Scrolls, cleansing is used as an image for renewal through the Spirit (see John 3:5).

I will sanctify my great name, which has been profaned among the nations and which you have profaned among them. The nations will know that I am the LORD, says the Lord GOD, when I display my holiness before their eyes through you. I will take you from the nations, gather you from all the countries, and bring you into your own land. I will sprinkle clean water on you, and you will be clean from all your uncleannesses, and I will cleanse you from all your idols. I will give you a new heart and put a new spirit in you; and I will remove from your body the heart of stone and give you a heart of flesh. (Ezek 36:23-26)

God will refine all human deeds with his truth and will purify for himself the configuration of humankind, ripping out all spirit of injustice from the innermost part of human flesh and cleansing humankind from every irreverent deed with the spirit of holiness. He will sprinkle over them the spirit of truth like lustral water [in order to cleanse them] from all the abhorrences of deceit and from the defilement of the unclean spirit. In this way the upright will understand knowledge of the Most High, and the wisdom of the sons of heaven will teach those of perfect behavior. For they are those who have been selected by God for an everlasting covenant. (1QS 4:20-22)

what Jesus has to say (6:45). Unless they are taught by God, born from above, illumined by the Light, and instructed by the Word who comes from above, they will remain ignorant and uncomprehending, repeatedly failing to understand the words of Jesus, and so unable to come to faith in him. By reading the Gospel from beginning to end, the reader has the benefit not only of Jesus' explanatory words each time, but also of the cumulative effect of the various correctives he offers. Thus with each subsequent misunderstanding, the reader learns that to understand Jesus one must recognize him as the one who comes from God. To understand Jesus, one must be "taught by God." The reader learns from the doubts, failures to understand, anger, and unbelief of the characters in the story.

Readers are to allow the Gospel to be the vehicle by which they are "taught by God."

Just as people misconstrue Jesus' words, so also do they misinterpret his signs. John is the only Evangelist to use the term "signs" *(sēmeia)* rather than wonders *(terata)*, mighty deeds *(dynameis)*, marvels *(thaumasia)*, or strange things *(paradoxa)*, terms found in the Synoptic Gospels, for Jesus' miracles. Jesus' miraculous deeds are "signs" in that they point to a reality beyond themselves. If taken only as miraculous deeds of power, as ends in themselves, they are misunderstood. But when understood as manifestations of Jesus' identity as the one who works by God's authority, then they are properly understood. They always point beyond themselves to the unity of Jesus' work with the Father. And grasped in this way, they lead to faith and so to life. When Jesus heals the son of a royal official, the man and all his household come to faith (4:48-53). The blind man understands that Jesus is not a sinner who has violated the law, but rather a prophet, the Son of man, one who has come from God and is called "Lord" (9:35-38). Martha will soon come to see the full revelation of Jesus' glory as he raises her brother to life, a work which will seal her own acknowledgment of his claim to be resurrection and life (11:25-27). And so the signs lead to faith not in a wonder-worker of powerful deeds, but rather in Jesus as the revelation of God's glory and the one who bestows life.

But signs can easily be misunderstood, and particularly so when they are taken simply as miraculous displays of power or as ends in themselves. When Jesus feeds the five thousand at Passover, an act that recalls the exodus from Egypt at the time of the original Passover and God's giving of the manna to provide for the people of Israel (John 6), people clamor for a continual supply of bread. They understand that Jesus has done a miraculous deed and gladly ask for more of "this bread" (6:34). Jesus corrects their misunderstanding by saying, "*I* am the bread of life" (6:35). Once again, Jesus' word, here in the form of a revelatory "I am" statement, is needed to show people the path of understanding, the path of truth that leads to God. Without Jesus' words to guide and correct them, they continue to see his miracles as ends in themselves. What they have failed to see is that the deed is a sign, a pointer to the reality of the surpassing provision that he offers. Indeed, he offers himself to them, as "the bread of life," a self-sacrificing offering that will make his life accessible to all the world through his death (6:51-58). This is a long way from the supply of bread the people have in mind, and the gap between their understanding and what Jesus actually offers only highlights how far they are from recognizing and responding to Jesus.

The expectation that God's revelation should be clear and understandable is dashed on the rock of rejection of the Word made flesh. People do not understand Jesus as the "Word made flesh" precisely because the glory of the Word is veiled in the flesh. The flesh of the Word prohibits recognition of the Word made flesh. Indeed, that foundational statement of the Gospel — the Word was made flesh — makes misunderstanding of Jesus inevitable. For just the fact that the Word became flesh means that, without God-given insight into the mystery of Jesus' person, Jesus will always and only be misunderstood. Instead of marching through the Gospel with triumphant displays of glory and popular acclamation, Jesus' course attracts increasing opposition. No longer is the Word made flesh simply misunderstood: there is outright opposition.

The Word Made Flesh

One of the most influential twentieth-century commentators on the Gospel of John wrote this of John 1:14:

. . . the Word became flesh. It is in his sheer humanity that he is the Revealer. True, his own also see his *doxa* [glory] (v. 14b); indeed if it were not to be seen, there would be no grounds for speaking of revelation. But this is the paradox which runs through the whole gospel: the *doxa* is not to be seen *alongside* the *sarx* [flesh], nor *through* the *sarx* as through a window; it is to be seen in the *sarx* and nowhere else. If one wishes to see the *doxa*, then it is on the *sarx* that he must concentrate his attention, without allowing himself to fall a victim to appearances. The revelation is present in a peculiar *hiddenness*. (Rudolf Bultmann, *The Gospel of John*, p. 63)

The conflict becomes ever sharper throughout the "Book of Signs," leading finally to the account of the raising of Lazarus (John 11). Here, ironically, Jesus' self-revelation will lead to his own death on the cross, for, following the raising of Lazarus, the Sanhedrin doubts whether it can appease the Romans and control the crowds should such deeds continue. The price for peace with Rome will be the death of Jesus. The statement of Caiaphas, the High Priest, is an ironic prophecy. He tells his fellow council members, "You do not understand that it is better for you to have one man die for the people than to have the whole nation destroyed" (11:50). Little do the authorities know that even Jesus' death cannot save their nation from destruction. And yet there is a truth to his words, although he does not know it. He does not understand that Jesus' death, the death of "one man for the people," ultimately serves to save all the children of God now scattered among the nations (10:16; 11:51-52; 12:24). Jesus does "die for the people," but not at all in the way in which Caiaphas intends.

Caiaphas's unwitting prophecy is a classic example of *Johannine irony.* Such ironic statements, in which characters in the narrative unknowingly speak truths far beyond their comprehension, are characteristic of the Gospel. Nicodemus's assertion that Jesus "comes from God" is partially correct, for while Nicodemus thinks of a prophet or teacher commissioned by God, the Gospel has already shown that Jesus "comes from God" in speaking of the enfleshment of the Word (3:2, 13; 1:14). The invalid at the pool of Bethesda complains that "no human being" has been able to assist him, thus ironically speaking the truth that only God can help him (5:6). The Jewish authorities discount acknowledgment of Jesus as a prophet who speaks the words of God, because "we do not know where he comes from" (9:29), ironically betraying their lack of recognition of Jesus' divine origins. And when the Pharisees badger the healed beggar with "Who did it?" assuming that the answer will be found in naming the culprit who healed the man, the reader can supply the answers necessary: not only did Jesus do it, but God did this deed through Jesus.

If one reads these affirmations and questions through the lens of the prologue, one can see that in every case an understanding of Jesus' divine identity and origins answers questions, clears away misunderstanding, and demands a reformulation of the declarations. Through the use of irony, the Gospel emphasizes the necessity of God-given insight to see and understand Jesus' mission and identity. Only those who have ears and eyes that are "taught by God" (6:45) can hear and see the one who has come from God. Ultimately the failure to understand Jesus is due not to lack of information or misjudgment but to the inadequacy of human effort and categories to grasp the Word of God.

Yet even though the lack of understanding boils up into ever-increasing hostility and conflict throughout the Gospel, coming to its climax in the decision of the Sanhedrin to seek Jesus' death (11:45-52), the response to Jesus throughout the Gospel is not unrelievedly negative. Some people do voice their faith in Jesus. Jesus calls disciples, who believe in him (2:11), and they later refuse to abandon him even when others grow disenchanted and leave (6:66-71). The Samaritan woman wonders whether he could be the Messiah (4:29), while her neighbors make the sweeping confession that Jesus is the Savior of the world (4:42). An official at Capernaum, along with all his household, believes in Jesus (4:53), as does the blind man who is healed, and Martha, the sister of Lazarus. Noticeably missing are those who hold positions of authority within Judaism. They in fact mock certain common folk who believe (7:48) and in some cases expel from the synagogue anyone who confesses Jesus as Messiah (9:22). But their efforts to prevent belief in him prove futile, and in the end the authorities say to each other, "You see, you can do nothing. Look, the world has gone after him!" (12:19). Even as the prologue foreshadowed the rejection of Jesus by his own contemporaries, so, too, it promised that the darkness cannot overcome the light shining in the darkness (1:5) and that "all who received him, who believed in his name," became "children of God" (1:12-13). Their story is also narrated in the Gospel.

The Gospel also highlights the *antithetical consequences of belief and unbelief.* It allows no neutral territory: the consequences of faith and unbelief are described in the opposing categories of life and death, salvation and condemnation, judgment and acquittal. Indeed, judgment is one of the dominant themes of the Gospel. It presents its witnesses for Jesus, who offer their testimony about him: John the Baptist (1:6-8, 15, 19, 32-34; 3:26), Jesus' disciples (19:35), other persons (4:39; 12:17), the works or deeds of Jesus (5:36; 10:25), the Scriptures (5:39), Moses (5:46-47), the Paraclete (15:26), and God (5:36; 8:18). On the basis of the witnesses called, every person must pass judgment on Jesus. Each one becomes a judge in a court of law, adjudicating the truthfulness of the testimony borne by the witnesses. But the irony is that in assuming the role of judge and in passing judgment on Jesus, people indirectly pass judgment on themselves. If they deny that Jesus comes from God and makes God known, they reveal their alignment with "the world" rather than with God. While "world" can connote the physical creation and the arena in which human life is lived, most typically it refers to human life lived without regard to God, which, in this Gospel, means life lived without faith in Jesus. The responses of belief and unbelief thus reveal whether a person stands in light or darkness, in the realm of life or the realm of death. More than once the Gospel denies that Jesus has come to condemn the world to death. Rather, his express purpose is to bring God's life to the world. Those who do not believe pass the sentence of death on themselves. The tragic irony of the Gospel is that those who seek Jesus' death unwittingly reject the life that he has offered.

7.3.3. "His disciples believed in him" (13:1–21:23)

Jesus' death and the events leading up to it are narrated in the accounts of the so-called "Book of Glory" or "Book of the Passion," which is divided into three subsections: (1) *chapters 13–17,* a last meal with instructions to and prayer for the disciples; (2) *chapters 18–19,* Jesus' trial and crucifixion; and (3) *chapters 20–21:23,* the resurrection appearances of Jesus. These chapters show again the three themes of the revelation of Jesus' identity and the challenge to recognize him, the contrasting responses of belief and unbelief, and the judgment that falls on those who do not believe.

While "Book of Glory" might strike some as a misnomer for that part of the Gospel which focuses on Jesus' death, yet the Gospel of John speaks of the hour of Jesus' death as the hour of his glorification, the beginning of Jesus' return to the

Father and to the glory he had before the world was made. Rather than spell defeat for Jesus and his cause, the cross actually becomes the means through which Jesus returns to God and to the glory that rightfully belongs to him.

But the cross gives shape to Jesus' glory. Before his arrest and crucifixion, he eats a last meal with his disciples. At this meal, he prefigures his death through the act of washing the disciples' feet. By performing for his disciples an act that disciples sometimes performed for their teachers, Jesus provides a model of humility and self-giving love that the disciples are to emulate (13:11-17; 15:13). Also at this last meal Jesus gives his disciples lengthy instructions in the so-called "Farewell Discourses." The genre of the farewell discourse, a speech delivered in the face of imminent death or departure, is known from ancient Jewish literature. In it the speaker makes known his deepest desires and concerns for those he leaves behind. Accordingly, in this Gospel's Farewell Discourses we find Jesus concerned first for the community that he leaves behind, for the quality and character of their life together, and for the witness they bear to him in the world.

The life of the community is to be characterized, above all, by response to his commands, a response that is lived out in mutual love. The disciples' love not only shows their faithfulness to him, but also reflects the unity of the Father and Son and the unity that the disciples will have with Jesus even after his departure. They are to cling as closely to Jesus as branches do to a vine for sustenance (15:1-11). In this way, they will be sustained after Jesus' departure. But the disciples will find that Jesus' model also directs them along less desirable pathways. While they are to love as Jesus has loved, they will also suffer as Jesus suffered, experiencing the same sort of hostility and rejection that he has experienced. As they bear witness to Jesus, the response to them will mirror the world's response to Jesus.

Because the pathway of discipleship follows an uncertain course, Jesus also promises the Paraclete, the Holy Spirit (14:26) or the "Spirit of Truth" (14:16; 15:26; 16:13), whose distinctive ministry is to testify to Jesus (15:26) and to glorify him (16:14). The Paraclete assumes the role of teacher (16:13), guiding the disciples to recognize the truth. From the scenes recorded in these chapters, it is clear that the disciples will need such a teacher and guide, for they still struggle to recognize Jesus and are still in need of teaching about who he is and what he offers. Their request that he reveal God to them betrays how little they have actually understood him to be the one who makes God known (14:6-8). And even in these last hours Jesus continues to make himself known to them, speaking of himself as "the way, the truth, and the life" (14:8) and "the vine" in which the disciples will find life (15:1-11). At his death and with his departure, his instruction of and revelation to the disciples have not come to an end, but continue beyond the temporal limits of his historical ministry. In this regard, the Paraclete plays a central role. By serving as a witness to Jesus, the Paraclete reveals the sin of unbelief and hence the guilt of those who do not believe. The Paraclete thus functions indirectly as judge

(16:8-11; cf. 14:17; 15:18-26). The Farewell Discourses thus reiterate the themes of revelation, response, and judgment that run throughout the Gospel.

The narratives of Jesus' trial highlight the theme of judgment. As the climactic act of Jesus' mission and self-revelation, the cross serves as the instrument of judgment on those who have not believed (12:31), particularly on those who have sent him to the cross. This conflict is most vividly illustrated in the dialogue between Pilate and Jesus regarding Jesus' identity and Pilate's authority. Pilate taunts Jesus with the question, "Do you refuse to speak to me? Do you not know that I have power to release you, and power to crucify you?" (19:10). Jesus counters Pilate's claim to have the final sovereignty over his life: "You would have no power over me unless it had been given you from above; therefore the one who handed me over to you is guilty of a greater sin." But Jesus undercut Pilate's claim to hold Jesus' life in his hands already in the declaration, "No one takes my life from me, but I lay it down of my own accord. I have power to lay it down, and I have power to take it up again. I have received this command from my Father" (10:18). Pilate's powerlessness is illustrated by his role in the drama of the passion. In passing judgment on Jesus, Pilate unknowingly passes judgment on himself. By accepting Pilate's judgment, Jesus willingly and knowingly becomes the agent of God's life for the world.

Jesus' ministry comes to its climactic moment on the cross. In John alone, Jesus' words from the cross "It is finished!" signal the completion of his work of salvation. Jesus returns to God and to the glory that was his with God prior to the creation of the world (17:5). His death on the cross becomes the final act of revelation of his identity, calling again for recognition of his divine origin and mission and his unity with God. Jesus' death in no way undercuts the Gospel's claims that Jesus always does the will of God. Indeed, the resurrection attests that Jesus has been raised by God, affirming the truth of his earlier claim that "just as the Father has life in himself, so he has granted the Son also to have life in himself" (5:26). Jesus' resurrection is the final testimony to who he is and what he brings to humankind.

Accordingly the Gospel's resurrection appearances take the form of recognition scenes. Jesus' appearance to his disciples challenges them to recognize him as the living and life-giving Lord and to respond with faith. Mary, the first to see the risen Lord, initially mistakes him for the gardener. Only when he calls her by name, "Mary!" (20:16), does she recognize and respond to him. This scene graphically illustrates the parable that the good shepherd "calls his sheep by name" (10:3-5). Even in the resurrection appearances Jesus must take the initiative to reveal himself, to make himself known, to call the believer to himself. Without his guiding word, the disciples are unable to respond. In an appearance to the eleven, Jesus called Thomas to be "believing" rather than "unbelieving" (20:27). The options of response to Jesus after the resurrection are the same as earlier: belief and unbelief.

Indeed, Thomas becomes a model for all who are invited to believe without having seen Jesus.

In the final resurrection appearance, Jesus appears to his disciples while they are fishing in Galilee. While the others do not recognize him, the unnamed "disciple whom Jesus loved" does so with the confession, "It is the Lord!" (21:7). Even after his resurrection, Jesus is not easily recognized, and the disciples must learn to recognize Jesus all over again. And having recognized who he is, they are called to follow him. Jesus addresses Peter with the command "Follow me!" echoing the command given to Philip (1:43) in the opening chapter of the Gospel. The promise then was that those who followed Jesus would see "heaven opened and the angels of God ascending and descending upon the Son of man" (1:51). Following Jesus leads to a recognition of his glory. But though they have seen that glory, they have not yet fully understood who he is. Even at the end of the Gospel, the disciples are called to follow continually, so that they may recognize ever more fully who Jesus is.

7.3.4. Postscript: 21:24-25

There is little left to say at this point, if the Gospel has accomplished its goal of leading its readers to recognize and acknowledge Jesus as the Messiah, the Son of God, and to follow him on the path of discipleship. And yet, the Gospel suggests, so much more could be said. While, on the one hand, the editorial remark suggests the plethora of traditions about Jesus' life and words that were available, on the other hand it points to the one who, despite all attempts to understand, explain, and categorize him, always remains greater than the sum of the parts. Not all the books in the world, not even the Gospels, fully capture the identity of the Word made flesh.

7.4. JOHN AND THE OTHER GOSPELS

John's narrative of the life, death, and resurrection of Jesus has obvious similarities with the other Gospels. In all the Gospels, Jesus' public ministry begins with the baptizing ministry of John at the river Jordan. Throughout the course of his ministry, Jesus teaches the crowds, gathers twelve disciples around him, heals people of various ailments, has intense debates with various adversaries, particularly Pharisees, is eventually arrested, tried, crucified, and buried, and is subsequently reported to have appeared alive to his disciples. Other similarities could be noted, too. There is a feeding miracle, followed by a confession of Jesus by Simon Peter on behalf of the twelve, in each Gospel. The question of Jesus' identity, and particularly whether he will be Israel's Messiah, figures prominently. Sabbath healings create controversy about Jesus' authority and his relationship to the law. Jesus is betrayed to the authorities by Judas. Women, including those without public honor, have key roles to play, and they are the first to see the risen Jesus.

But there are numerous differences between John and the Synoptic Gospels. In the Synoptic Gospels, Jesus' teaching covers a broad spectrum of topics, including almsgiving, prayer, anger, marriage, divorce, paying taxes, forgiveness, retaliation, anxiety, love, wealth, mission, and so on. But in John, Jesus addresses none of these topics. Rather, Jesus' discourses focus on his own identity, function, and role, and particularly on his identity as the Son who is sent by the Father, a term that appears only a few times in the Synoptic Gospels but plays a central role in John. In the Synoptic Gospels, Jesus speaks in parables, aphorisms, and metaphors. But none of Jesus' best-known parables, such as the sower, the prodigal son, the good Samaritan, and the judgment of the sheep and the goats, is found in John. Rather, the Gospel contains long discourses and a series of statements beginning "I am . . . ," none of which is found in the Synoptics. As summarized in Mark 1:15, Jesus' message concerned the kingdom of God and the repentance necessary in light of its coming. But "kingdom of God" occurs only twice in John (3:3, 5), and the typical call to people is not to repent or to enter, welcome, or receive the kingdom, but to believe in Jesus.

According to the Synoptic Gospels, Jesus did "mighty works" (Greek *dynameis*) and exorcised demons. But John records no demon exorcisms and calls Jesus' miracles "signs," a term never used for the miracles in the Synoptics, where, in fact, Jesus explicitly refuses to give a sign. In the Synoptic Gospels, there are various responses to the miracles, including awe, wonder, fear, praise of God, and thanksgiving. But John typically divides response to the miracles into two categories, belief and unbelief, in keeping with the view that miracles reveal who Jesus is and so call for response to him. Moreover, the only miracle contained in all four Gospels is the feeding of the 5,000. All the other miracles narrated in John are found only in that Gospel. This includes such accounts as the changing of water to wine and the raising of Lazarus.

The order of events differs between John and the Synoptic Gospels. In the Synoptics, Jesus' ministry is centered in Galilee, and with the exception of the account of Jesus' visit to the temple in Jerusalem at the age of twelve in the Gospel of Luke, he goes to Jerusalem only at the end of his life. At this visit to Jerusalem Jesus cleanses the temple, and this event seems to precipitate his arrest. But in John, Jesus is in and out of Jerusalem from the beginning to the end of his ministry. The temple cleansing occurs not in conjunction with Jesus' work in Jerusalem directly before his death, but at the outset of his public ministry during an early trip to Jerusalem. The event that induces the authorities to seek his death is not his provocative action in the temple but the raising of Lazarus from the dead. But this climactic Johannine miracle does not occur in the other Gospels.

Finally, we note a substantial difference in vocabulary between John and the other Gospels. Most of the vocabulary central to John, including "life," "light" and "darkness," "witness," "truth," "world," "abide," and "Father" and "Son," can be found in the other Gospels, but none of these terms becomes a central feature in them of Jesus' teaching or descriptive of what Jesus brings or offers. To put the sharpest point on it, what is most characteristic of the Gospel of John is lacking in the Synoptics, and what is most typical of the Synoptics cannot be found in John.

How one should account for these differences has long been discussed. The early church fathers advanced various theories, and the attempt has not been abandoned today. An early Christian writer, Clement of Alexandria (*ca.* 150-220), asserted that while the Synoptic Gospels recounted the "physical" (or "bodily") facts, John wrote a "spiritual Gospel" (cited by Eusebius, *Hist. Eccl.* 6.14.7). In other words, John wrote a different kind of Gospel, one that endeavored to interpret the meaning of the ministry of Jesus as reported in the other Gospels through the lens of a spiritual interpretation. Origen (*ca.* 250), another theologian and biblical scholar, wrote of the difficulty of reconciling the differences of chronology and detail between John and the Synoptics, concluding, "I conceive it to be impossible for those who admit nothing more than the history in their interpretation to show that these discrepant statements are in harmony with each other" (*Commentary* 10.15). Origen thought that the way to account for and reconcile the differences was to approach them through different methods. The truth of the accounts in John was not to be found in their "outward and material letter," in the harmony of historical details, but in their spiritual or inner meaning.

Before the twentieth century, many interpreters would have adopted a view something like that of Clement, that John was written to offer a "spiritual" interpretation of the other Gospels. Others have suggested that John intends to supplement or even replace the accounts of Matthew, Mark, and Luke. John may have found one of the other Gospels lacking in some way, or simply wished to expand on, supplement, and interpret the significance of Jesus' life on his own terms. The similarities between John and the Synoptics can be accounted for by John's use of the other Gospels, while the differences have been variously attributed to the Evangelist's personality, intimate relationship to Jesus, access to different sources, or different historical setting or purpose. All these views assume that John was written with an eye on the other Gospels, and that John should be explained primarily with reference to them.

In the twentieth century a number of scholars have become convinced that John's traditions came to him through channels other than the written canonical Gospels. There is simply not enough overlap in the actual content of the material to argue convincingly that John drew his narrative of Jesus' deeds from one of the other Gospels. The differences in content, vocabulary, and emphases are too marked. In the account of the feeding of the 5,000, for example, the verbal overlap between Matthew and Mark in their narratives is about 65%, but between John and Mark only about 5%. Hence, the conjecture arose that while John probably drew on both written and oral sources for the basic material of his Gospel, he does not seem to have drawn on any of the Synoptics as a primary source. Of course, that the Evangelist knew of the other Gospels or assumed his readers would be familiar with one of them cannot be ruled out. But it is clear that John does not use Mark as a basic source document in the way that Matthew does. The shape of John's supposed sources remains a matter of conjecture. Numerous hypotheses have been suggested, and elaborate reconstructions of what John's sources must have looked like have been offered. Still, no source has ever been found, and all such theories remain speculative. Although a fuller knowledge of the source of John's material might help us to understand more of the historical origins of this unique Gospel, such knowledge would never fully explain it.

7.5. THE SETTING AND PURPOSE OF THE GOSPEL

A statement toward the end of the Gospel summarizes the Gospel's purpose: "Now Jesus did many other signs in the presence of the disciples that are not written in this book; but these are written that you may believe that Jesus is the Christ, the Son of God, and that believing you may life in his name" (20:30-31). The implicit contrast is between those who were witnesses to Jesus' doing of signs and the readers of the Gospel, who are not witnesses. They do not have access to the historical ministry of Jesus, but they do have the Gospel. The reader is invited, as were Jesus' disciples, to "come and see" who Jesus is, and so to come to faith in him (20:30-31). In other words, the Gospel has been written for those who, because they lived in later times or other places, were not witnesses to Jesus' ministry and the signs that he did. Though disciples at second hand, their faith and discipleship are not second class.

In the last several decades, further evidence from within the Gospel has been taken as suggestive of the historical origin of the Gospel. In the account of the man who is healed from blindness (ch. 9), certain persons are threatened with expulsion from the synagogue for acknowledging Jesus to be the Messiah (9:22), a threat of which Jesus speaks in his parting words to the disciples (12:42; 16:2). The problematic confession and punishment obviously point to a setting within Judaism and hint at a rift between Jews who confessed Jesus as Messiah and Jews who did not.

This brings us to one of the thorniest interpretative issues in John, the meaning and significance of the term "the Jews," which is used about seventy times in the Gospel of John, but fewer than twenty times in all the Synoptic Gospels together. At its simplest, the issue raised by this frequent use of "the Jews" is the

Separating Jesus from His People

During World War II, the Nazis under Hitler launched a program to exterminate all Jews and Judaism from Europe, resulting in the death of millions of Jews in the concentration camps. The movement was aided by virulently anti-Jewish theology, as the following quotations, from both government and church officials, graphically demonstrate:

"Our people need a new encounter with Christ without a detour through Judaism." (p. 144)

"Into the oven with the part of the Bible that glorifies the Jews [*sc.* the OT], so eternal flames will consume that which threatens our people." (p. 152)

"A 'murderer,' a 'liar,' a 'father of lies.' It is impossible to reject Jehovah and his Old Testament in sharper terms!" (p. 156)

"Because Christ was the 'opponent' of the Jews, it is impossible that he himself could have been of Jewish blood and spirit. . . . Jesus cannot, therefore, have been a Jew.'" (p. 156)

"Christ was no Jew. Christ himself was the greatest hater of Jews." (p. 156)

"Each Word of Jesus was directed against the Jew and hit him like the crack of a whip. No one recognized the nature of Judaism more clearly nor fought it more single-mindedly than precisely Jesus the Savior." (p. 160)

In 1936, Bishop Weidemann published an anti-Jewish translation of the Gospel of John, claiming that "true Christianity" was anti-Jewish, and that anti-Jewish religion was "the ultimate source of power for the National Socialist [Nazi] worldview. His translation endeavored to remove any elements that smacked of "Jewishness" and to emphasize "anti-Judaism." At John 1:29, in order to remove references to Jewish conceptions of sin and sacrifice, Weidemann translated "Behold the Lamb of God who takes away the sins of the world" as "Behold the chosen one of God, who through his sacrifice brings blessing to the world." (pp. 161-62)

Another translation sanctioned by and for the German Christian movement expunged references to the OT in the Gospels, and freed it from "Jewish-Christian accretions" as well as all the words "wrongly attributed to Jesus." These words included Jesus' prayer from the cross in Luke 23:34, "Father, forgive them, for they know not what they do." (p. 163; all quotations taken from Doris L. Bergen, *Twisted Cross: The German Christian Movement in the Third Reich* [Chapel Hill: University of North Carolina Press, 1996])

meaning and referent of the term: what does it mean and to whom does it refer? Although "Jews" clearly seems to refer to an ethnic and religious group distinguishable from all those who are not "Jews," what complicates the question is the use of "Jews" to distinguish some persons from others who are unmistakably Jewish as well. For example, the disciples of John the Baptist are reported as having a discussion with "a Jew" (3:25), but John's disciples were certainly also Jews. In ch. 9, the parents of the healed man are afraid of being expelled from the synagogue by "the Jews" (9:22; cf. 7:13) — but were they themselves not Jews, they would have no fear of such expulsion! And "the Jews" debate Jesus' teaching (6:52), are astonished by his words (7:15), and try to stone him (10:31). The overwhelming impression from the surface of the text is that "the Jews" is used to distance the antagonists of Jesus from Jesus and his followers and to refer to the former in an almost exclusively negative way.

Some have argued that these antagonists are primarily Judeans, and that "the Jews" is to be understood as Judeans as opposed to Galileans. Others have argued that John uses the term to refer exclusively to the Jewish authorities. Neither suggestion accounts for every instance of the use of "the Jews" in John. Clearly the language used in the Gospel betrays an antagonism between those who believed in Jesus and those who did not, both tracing their origins to the Jewish people. It is, in other words, a familial dispute, much like that between the Essenes and other Jewish factions in the first century. In this dispute, each side is struggling to define itself with respect to the other, and, ultimately, each defines itself not alongside but over against the other. Through the Gospel we have a reflection of these disputes.

The intensity of the polemic may be a reaction to Jewish measures, and particularly to expulsion from the synagogue (9:22; 12:42; 16:2), on the part of those who had become believers in Jesus, who could no longer be simply called "Jews." John's particularly sharp polemic against the Jews reflects this situation, describing it in the categories of the dualism alluded to earlier, which denies the possibility of neutral ground and describes the consequences of unbelief in terms of death and darkness. But the Johannine polemic also reflects the literary practices of the day, which allowed polemical arguments to use tactics such as name-calling, caricature, and hyperbole. Unfortunately, John's polemical style, coupled with the almost unremittingly negative characterization of "the Jews," has allowed John to be used as a basis for persecution of Jewish people throughout the centuries. Such a reading patently and deliberately misconstrues the purpose of John, whose aim is not to disparage Jews but to call for faith in the Jesus as the Messiah and King of Israel. The rhetoric used for this purpose strikes modern ears as harsh and vindictive, but for the Gospel of John the stakes are clearly high, and the Gospel is written in part to reiterate just what is at stake in believing in Jesus.

Because the Gospel expressly notes that it is written so that its readers may "believe," it has often been viewed as an evangelistic document, designed to make converts, perhaps from Diaspora Judaism. Others, however, suggest that the Gospel was written to encourage believers to persevere in their faith and not to desert Jesus when the situation becomes difficult (6:60-71) or, worse, to betray him like Judas. They are, instead, to join with Peter in his confession, "Lord, to whom can we go? You have the words of eternal life" (6:68). Although finding themselves ostracized from previous family ties and their religious and social networks, they are exhorted to continue to put their faith in Christ, for, in the words of Jesus, "If they persecuted me, they will persecute you" (15:20). As part of its hortatory function, the Gospel endeavors to clarify the relationship of Jesus to Judaism by showing his superiority to the patriarchs of the Jewish faith (4:12; 6:32; 8:53-58), the fulfillment through his work of the realities celebrated in Jewish feasts and religious institutions (2:1-11, 19-22; 6:32-41; 7:37-39), and the relationship between the law and Moses on the one hand and Jesus Christ on the other (1:17; 5:39-40, 45-47; 7:19-23). The consistency and intensity of this line of argument suggest that the Evangelist is trying to make a persuasive case for coming to faith in Jesus by using the symbols and realities of Judaism, which lodge Jesus firmly in his world.

When the Gospel was written has proved to be a difficult question. While many scholars suggest that the intense hostility between "messianic" and "non-messianic" Jews arose only after the destruction of Jerusalem and the temple in AD 70, other portions of the NT and early Christian literature do testify to strained and hostile relationships between Christians and Jews at an earlier date, beginning with the confrontation between Stephen and certain Jews in Jerusalem (Acts 6–8).

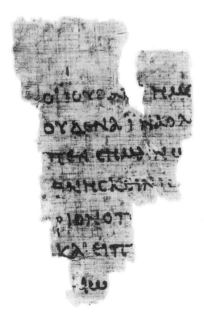
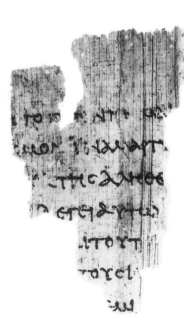

The earliest New Testament manuscript, 𝔓52 from about 125 CE, containing parts of John 18 *(Rylands Museum)*

Moreover, the conflicts reflected in John are by no means unique to a particular area or period in the first century, so it is difficult to pinpoint the Gospel's origin with accuracy. The sorts of disputes between messianic and nonmessianic Jews reflected in John can be found in other documents of the NT as well, including, for example, the Gospel of Matthew.

It was once fashionable to push the date of John into the second century. But such attempts have been rendered impossible by the discovery of a manuscript of the Gospel, Rylands Papyrus 457 (p52), an Egyptian codex fragment dated by scholars in the early second century that contains a few verses of John 18. This find suggests that John cannot have been published later than the end of the first century or the very early part of the second, but still does not help us to settle the date with greater precision. Various hypotheses have been advanced, fixing the date of writing or publication anywhere between AD 65 and 100. Most likely a date toward the end of that time period is to be preferred, and a conjecture of a date between AD 90 and 100 would square with the views adopted in the early church.

The traditional place of publication of the Gospel is Ephesus, but cities such as Alexandria in Egypt and Syrian Antioch have also been suggested. All these cities have in common a significant Jewish population and a location outside Palestine. Such a pluralistic location might help to account for the various streams of influence that are often detected in John, in which the currents of the OT, Judaism, and Hellenistic religions often seem to swirl together. Indeed, the conceptual background of the Gospel has been one of the most discussed issues in Johannine studies. For while the Gospel unquestionably reflects the symbols, rituals, and convictions of its Jewish heritage, at the same time the imagery through which it recounts the story of Jesus would be at home in many religious movements of the ancient world, including Judaism markedly influenced by Hellenism, such as is found in the works of the Alexandrian Jewish writer Philo.

The Gospel's basic images of life, death, light, darkness, bread, water, nurture, healing, birth, cleansing, and growth are found together not only in the Gospel of John but also in Judaism and other ancient religions and philosophies. In previous generations John was derogatorily labeled "the acute Hellenization" of the Gospel, a radical and thorough recasting of the Gospel into Greek terms and images fundamentally at odds with the native soil of Judaism. John's dualistic worldview, which contrasts Spirit and flesh, above and below, and eternal and natural realities, was judged to manifest a worldview that had more in common with philosophical movements of Greek thought, such as Platonism, than with Judaism.

One of the chief reasons for reconsidering such judgments has been the discovery, beginning in 1947, of various manuscripts known as the Dead Sea Scrolls, in caves near the northwestern shore of the Dead Sea. These scrolls exhibit a dualism between spirit and flesh, truth and error, and light and darkness in categories similar enough to John's to provide a plausible conceptual background for the

Gospel. These finds sparked renewed interest in the possibility of locating the Gospel of John within the orbit of Palestinian Judaism. To many interpreters, it no longer seemed necessary to appeal to Hellenistic religions as providing the formative influences on John's Gospel. Still, if one were to adopt the thesis that the traditions found in John's Gospel had their origins in Palestinian Judaism, that would not eliminate the possibility that it was written and published in another place where other influences had an impact on the final shape of the Gospel. Furthermore, few scholars today think that neat lines can be drawn between "Judaism" and "Hellenism" in such a way that necessitate placing the Gospel of John in either one camp or the other. The very language of the Gospel indicates that it was written for Greek-speaking persons, whether Jews or non-Jews. That John has adapted imagery and categories that would resonate with his readers to tell the story of Jesus is testimony to his genius.

In spite of all the insights gained through historical and literary analysis of John, it remains a matter of conjecture how John came to tell the story of Jesus as it does. Much ink has been spilled over the question of John's reliance on oral and literary traditions, the Gospel's historical and social setting and context, and its interpretative agenda. While archaeological finds and careful study have opened up certain avenues for interpretation, and closed off others, the various hypotheses advanced to account for the shape of the Gospel of John remain just that — hypotheses. In the end, the origins of the Gospel of John remain as elusive as Jesus himself is to characters in the story.

FOR FURTHER READING

George R. Beasley-Murray, *John* (2d ed., Nashville: Nelson, 1999)

Raymond E. Brown, *The Gospel according to John,* 2 vols. (New York: Doubleday, 1966, 1970)

Rudolf Bultmann, *The Gospel of John: A Commentary* (Philadelphia: Westminster, 1971)

R. Alan Culpepper and C. Clifton Black, eds., *Exploring the Gospel of John* (Louisville: Westminster John Knox, 1996)

Craig R. Koester, *Symbolism in the Fourth Gospel* (Minneapolis: Fortress, 1995)

Herman Ridderbos, *The Gospel of John: A Theological Commentary* (Grand Rapids: Eerdmans, 1997)

Rudolf Schnackenburg, *The Gospel according to St. John,* 3 vols. (New York: Herder, 1968-82)

D. Moody Smith, *The Theology of the Gospel of John* (Cambridge: Cambridge University Press, 1995)

Marianne Meye Thompson, *The God of the Gospel of John* (Grand Rapids: Eerdmans, 2001)

8. Jesus of Nazareth

8.1. THE QUEST OF THE HISTORICAL JESUS

The canonical Gospels of the NT present four portraits of Jesus, each painted with different pigments, in a different style, and from a particular perspective. Quite clearly the subject of the portraits is the same, but no two portraits are identical. A recognition of the differences among the Gospels has fueled intense interest in getting behind each portrait to discover the subject himself. In the field of NT studies, the attempts to use the Gospels and other traditions about Jesus to reconstruct a picture of their subject, Jesus of Nazareth, is known as "the quest of the historical Jesus" (see chapter 3).

Much ink has been spilled over the validity of the enterprise and the appropriate methods for undertaking it. The debate over the validity of the quest in no way calls into question the historicity of Jesus himself. Ancient sources, Christian, pagan, and Jewish, testify to his existence. Rather, the recognition that each Evangelist chooses to give us Jesus from a particular perspective has led scholars to doubt the wisdom, as well as the possibility, of searching for a Jesus "behind" the Gospels themselves. The Jesus recovered in this way would never be identical with the Jesus portrayed by any one Gospel. Instead, that Jesus would always be the product of historical reconstruction and of the best judgments of historians. In a sense, the reconstructed portrait of Jesus amounts to a fifth portrait of Jesus alongside the other four. And it is these four Gospels that, of all the possible choices, have found a place in the church's Scripture, and are thus its normative witness to Jesus of Nazareth.

Still, much insight can be gained into the mission and message of Jesus when they are set in their historical contexts. For example, while the Gospels present Jesus as teaching often about the kingdom of God, no Gospel actually includes an explanation of what "kingdom of God" might have denoted or connoted to a first-century Jewish audience. As historians place Jesus' teaching about the kingdom into the sociohistorical context of first-century Judaism, the contours of Jesus' own proclamation of the kingdom emerge from the shadows and become more sharply defined. Or, again, various prophetic figures and renewal movements referred to in Josephus's writings show how Jesus might have been interpreted and understood and what might have led to resistance and opposition to Jesus. Many aspects of his life and message gain texture and depth when they are seen in historical context. Even if the portrait of Jesus resulting from historical study can never have the same authority as the canonical portraits for the proclamation and witness of the church, and even if historians can only speak of their results in terms of probabilities, nevertheless, we can repeatedly illumine Jesus' mission and message by placing them in the cultural context of first-century Judaism. Those portraits that have been most compelling have at the same time been able to locate Jesus most convincingly within his first-century context.

In order to suggest how one might proceed to sketch a portrait of the historical Jesus from the Gospels, the following guidelines may be briefly set out.

(1) The Gospels of the NT are our primary and most important source for what we know about Jesus. Passing references in Jewish and pagan literature do not add substantially to our knowledge about Jesus. The *Gospel of Thomas*, which is sometimes claimed to supply additional information or an alternative and equally valid historical portrait of Jesus, is of secondary value as a historical source because of its date, its dependence on the Synoptic tradition, and its obviously Gnostic interpretation of Jesus.

(2) The primary historical context for understanding Jesus is first-century Palestinian Judaism. Jesus' actions and words and responses to him must be explained from within this context. We will especially need to know well the context of Jesus' native faith and home when we speak of his distinctiveness, that is, when we claim that his activity differs from, challenges, or runs counter to the common wisdom of his day.

(3) While Jesus' actions and words should be interpreted from within their context in first-century Judaism, they must also be interpreted in such a way as to explain credibly the rise of the early church. This is not to claim that there are no theological developments within the early Christian community, but only that one expects to find discernible lines of continuity from Jesus to the church.

(4) Any reconstruction of Jesus' life must endeavor to account for what is surely the most certain thing about him: he was crucified by the Romans. The significance of crucifixion itself, as well as the fact that he died at the hands of the Roman government, provides a critical vantage point for understanding the content and implications of Jesus' teaching and actions.

(5) Similarly, a historical reconstruction of Jesus will be deemed the more credible the more it can explain. To sketch a historical portrait of Jesus entails more than merely explaining various parts of his ministry, such as his miracles or proclamation of the kingdom of God, in their historical contexts. Rather, a historical reconstruction tries to account for the significance and relationship of the various elements of Jesus' life and ministry to each other.

(6) Finally, the whole is greater than the sum of its parts. Study of the historical Jesus has gotten bogged down in recent years over the issues of determining the authenticity of particular traditions in the Gospels. But those studies that have been most interesting and fruitful in recent years have not followed the approach of deciding the authenticity of every bit of material first. Rather, they have sought to advance an encompassing hypothesis about Jesus' mission and message which has endeavored to do justice to the Gospels' portraits of Jesus. Put another way, while in the past the goal of studies of the historical Jesus seems to have been to pare the Gospels down to the bare minimum, in more recent efforts the goal of studies about Jesus seems to have been to try to demonstrate how much we can know with a fair degree of confidence. Thus recent studies of Jesus have not been content with offering a rough sketch of the subject, but have tried to fill in the textures, shadows, and richness of detail and color to yield a powerful and evocative portrait of Jesus of Nazareth.

8.2. THE BEGINNING OF JESUS' PUBLIC MINISTRY

8.2.1. The Ministry of John the Baptist

According to all the Gospels, Jesus' public ministry began with his baptism by John at the Jordan (Matt 3:13-17; Mark 1:9-11; Luke 3:21-22; John 1:29-34; Acts 1:22; 10:37). Since the Gospels report almost nothing of Jesus' activities prior to this time — except his birth and a family pilgrimage to Jerusalem (Luke 2:41-52) — one cannot reconstruct Jesus' early years, his childhood, development, education, and so on. The numerous so-called apocryphal gospels, which were not included in the NT canon, include numerous fanciful tales about Jesus as a boy. In those gospels, Jesus exhibits magical and miraculous powers that have but distant parallels in the NT Gospels. Among other feats, he turns clay pigeons into live birds, lengthens a board that Joseph mistakenly cut too short, carries water for Mary in a piece of cloth, curses — thus putting to death! — playmates who annoy him, and refuses to learn his lessons from various teachers. The NT Gospels do not indulge in such speculation but begin their accounts of Jesus' ministry and teaching subsequent to his baptism by John. Yet the very fact that Jesus emerges on the public scene only with the ministry of John suggests that we may learn something

Josephus on John the Baptist

But to some of the Jews the destruction of Herod's army seemed to be divine vengeance, and certainly a just vengeance, for his treatment of John, surnamed the Baptist. For Herod had put him to death, though he was a good man and had exhorted the Jews to lead righteous lives, to practice justice towards their fellows and piety towards God, and so doing to join in baptism. In his view this was a necessary preliminary if baptism was to be acceptable to God. (*Ant.* 18.116-18)

of the contours of Jesus' ministry by examining the Gospel accounts of the Baptist's proclamation and activity.

John carried out his activity "in the wilderness" (Matt 3:1; Mark 1:4; Luke 3:2-3), a locale laden with symbolic significance in the Scriptures as pointing to a time of God's direct provision and guidance (Deut 8:2; Ps 78:13-16; Isa 32:15-17; Jer 2:2-3; Hos 2:14-16). John's choice of "the wilderness" may echo the prophetic call to "return to the wilderness," that is, to recover Israel's dependence on God's provision and care and to await God's deliverance. Indeed, other prophetic figures and reform movements of the first century saw the wilderness in such a light. Josephus comments on various Jewish nationalists who promised deliverance, sometimes urging the people to withdraw to the desert and wait for God to deliver Israel from Roman rule (*Ant.* 20.8.10 §§185-88; *J.W.* 2.254-65). One figure, Theudas, claimed that he would part the Jordan River (*Ant.* 20.5.1. §§97-98; Acts 5:36). Josephus describes his own teacher, Bannus, as dwelling "in the wilderness," living an ascetic lifestyle, and practicing frequent washing (*Life* 2 §11). The covenant community at Qumran, at the southern tip of the Dead Sea in the Judean wilderness, interpreted its role in terms of Isa 40:3, "In the wilderness prepare the way of the LORD" (1QS 8.12-16; 9.19-20). In short, the wilderness served as the symbol of hope for God's deliverance, and John called all Israel to repent in preparation for God's promised salvation.

Such willingness to devote oneself anew to God in anticipation of God's act of salvation and judgment was to be sealed in the act of baptism (see *Ant.* 18.116-19). It is difficult to locate precisely the background for John's baptism. The Levitical code of the OT required washing at various times to purify both men and women, in order to "keep the people of Israel separate from their uncleanness, lest they die in their uncleanness by defiling my tabernacle that is in their midst." Archaeological excavations have uncovered ritual baths at the temple and in private homes in Jerusalem and Sepphoris dating to the Roman period, pointing to the practice of ritual washing. The community at Qumran practiced repeated and regular washing to remove impurity as part of its communal life. John's call for a symbolic washing has parallels in its first-century context while at the same time carrying the distinctive note of repentance to allow one to stand in the face of the coming day of God's judgment. Not all Israel, however, was expected to respond to the call to repentance. Those who did would be gathered as wheat is gathered into a granary and would participate in the fulfillment of the prophetic hope for the renewal and restoration of God's people.

John spoke of a "stronger one" who would be the agent through whom the Holy Spirit, promised by the OT prophets for a future time of renewal, would be given (Ezek 37:1-10; Joel 2:28-29; Isa 61:1-3; 1QS 4.20-26). Later on John would send his disciples to ask Jesus whether he was truly that "stronger one" (Matt 11:2-3; Luke 7:18-19), to which Jesus responded with an allusion to passages in Isaiah that promise deliverance (Isa 35:5-6; 61:1).

8.2.2. The Baptism of Jesus

Jesus went out into the wilderness to be baptized by John. The fact that we know almost nothing of Jesus' life prior to his baptism by John suggests that John's baptismal ministry inaugurated Jesus' own public work. In their present form, the Gospel accounts present interpreted summaries of Jesus' identity as the Spirit-endowed Son of God. Through the ministry of the Baptist, Jesus responded to and received confirmation of God's call to him to undertake his own ministry of proclamation of God's kingdom.

The importance of John's ministry for understanding Jesus, and for understanding Jesus' own understanding of his own mission, is suggested by various passages throughout the Gospels in which Jesus aligns himself with John. Both are agents of God's call to Israel, both call for repentance, and, although their methods and styles differ, both are ultimately discounted or rejected by their contemporaries (Matt 11:16-19; Luke 7:31-35). Jesus, like John before him, saw Israel standing at the crossroads. Yet Jesus did not remain in the wilderness to undertake his work. Instead, he preached, healed, and taught primarily in the villages and towns of Galilee, with occasional excursions to neighboring regions and towns; he spoke of God's coming salvation, and he warned of the consequences of failing to heed his call.

Like John, who called Israel to repent and live as the people of God, so too Jesus urged Israel to orient its life fully and completely around the one whom they confessed daily in the words of Scripture: "Hear, O Israel: The Lord is our God, the Lord alone. You shall love the Lord your God with all your heart, with all your

Elimo Philipp Njau,
The Baptism
(Society for the
Propagation of the
Gospel, London)

soul, and with all your might" (Deut 6:4-5). Jesus later called this the greatest commandment in the law (Matt 22:36-37; Mark 12:29; cf. Luke 10:26-28). He challenged his disciples more than once with similar sharply formulated commands, calling for wholehearted devotion to God and reorientation to God's will and priorities: "But strive first for the kingdom of God and his righteousness" (Matt 6:33; Luke 12:31). "No one can serve two masters; for a slave will either hate the one and love the other or be devoted to the one and despise the other. You cannot serve God and wealth" (Matt 6:24; Luke 16:13). "The kingdom of heaven is like treasure hidden in a field that someone found and hid; then in his joy he goes and sells all that he has and buys that field" (Matt 13:44). These and other sayings of Jesus illustrate the radical reorientation of one's life to God to which Jesus called people. In such exhortation, one hears echoes of the preaching of John the Baptist. But it is in Jesus' proclamation of the kingdom of God and the way in which he speaks of his own role in bringing God's promise of salvation to Israel that his role and purpose differ from that of John.

El Greco,
*Baptism
of Christ
(Alinari/Art
Resource, NY)*

8.3. THE KINGDOM OF GOD

Frequently, statements summarizing Jesus' ministry and teaching in the Gospels combine his preaching and healing ministry under the rubric of "the kingdom of God." The Gospel of Mark states that Jesus came into Galilee with this message: "The time is fulfilled, the kingdom of God is at hand; repent, and believe the gospel" (Mark 1:15). Elsewhere Jesus moved from one village to the next with the assertion, "I must preach the good news of the kingdom of God to the other cities also; for I was sent for this purpose" (Luke 4:43; Mark 1:38). Parables sometimes begin with the introductory phrase, "The kingdom of God is like. . . ." In other places, Jesus claims to know who may enter the kingdom, and on what terms one may do so. That the kingdom of God formed the heart of Jesus' proclamation and provided the framework in which he understood his mission is virtually certain.

The phrase regularly translated into English as "kingdom of God" is Greek *basileia tou theou*. Matthew, however, more often has the Greek *basileia tōn*

Duccio di Buoninsegna, *The Calling of the Apostles Peter and Andrew* (early fourteenth-century) *(National Gallery of Art, Washington, D.C.—Samuel H. Kress Collection)*

ouranōn, generally rendered "kingdom of heaven," which reflects the Jewish practice of using circumlocutions for the name of God. In the first century, a variety of such euphemisms were available, including "the Name," "the Most High," "the Blessed One," "the Holy One," "Heaven," and many others. Thus "kingdom of heaven" is simply another way of saying "God's kingdom," as a glance at parallel Gospel passages will confirm (cf. Mark 4:11 and Luke 8:10 with Matt 13:11; Mark 10:23 and Luke 18:24 with Matt 19:23).

Behind the phrase "kingdom of God" lies the Aramaic *malkut shemayim* or *malkuta di elaha*. It is often argued that the Aramaic original lays the accent on God's activity of reigning, in keeping with the OT emphasis on God as king and sovereign of all the nations of the world. Modern English translations have attempted to capture the nuance of the original Aramaic with translations such as "reign" or "rule." Yet God's active rule cannot be separated from a particular place or people. Without a people, a king has sovereignty or dominion only in theory. Passages from the Psalms that speak of God's rule over Israel envision God's sovereignty or kingship with respect to a particular people. Elsewhere, God's rule is expected to be manifested on Mount Zion and to affect directly not only Israel but the nations of the world as well. Thus a long-standing debate about whether "kingdom of God" refers to the "rule" of God or the "realm" over which God rules constructs a false dichotomy. Clearly, both "reign" and "realm" are included in the understanding of God's kingdom. "Kingdom of God" covers that area or locale — be it heaven, the world, Israel, or Jerusalem — where God actively rules and that people — whether the nations of the world or the people of Israel — over whom God has sovereignty. The English word "dominion" aptly captures these two aspects of the phrase "kingdom of God." While in OT and Jewish literature the realm need not be coterminous with a particular nation or with any set of political or ethnic boundaries, God's dominion clearly becomes realized in time and place. Similarly, Jesus speaks of the kingdom both in temporal and spatial terms. But, as we shall see, he defines "kingdom of God" in part by redefining its temporal and spatial coordinates. To see how he gives shape to the "kingdom of God," we need first to discover the coordinates along which "kingdom of God" could have been plotted in the first century.

8.3.1. Kingdom in the Old Testament and Second Temple Judaism

Although the phrase "kingdom of God" does not occur in the OT, the root idea that God "rules" is thematic in a number of Psalms. A variety of expressions such as "his kingdom" (Ps 103:19), "your kingdom" (145:11, 12, 13), and "my kingdom" (1 Chron 17:14; cf. Obad 21, "kingship belongs to YHWH") all point to Yahweh's rightful claim to sovereignty. Specifically, God rules in Israel, calls for its allegiance, and protects and delivers it. Thus there is a particular and focused manifestation of God's rule in Israel, which joins together God's faithful protection and calls for Israel's obedience. But certain OT passages also affirm God's rule beyond Israel. Declarations such as "Thou art God, thou alone, of all the kingdoms of the earth" (2 Kgs 19:15) or "The LORD has established his throne in the heavens, and his kingdom rules over all" (Ps 103:19) limit the scope of God's rule neither to Israel nor to the present time.

Future manifestations of God's sovereignty are both expected and promised, especially among the writings of the exilic prophets. Deutero-Isaiah, for example, envisions God's forgiveness and deliverance of the people out of their exilic captivity, restoring them to the holy land distinguished by a rebuilt Jerusalem (Isa 43:1-8, 15; 44:6; 45:18-25; 52:7). God's messenger proclaims the good news of salvation that God reigns (52:7). Jeremiah prophesied the return of the scattered people from their exile and the gathering together of the twelve tribes, marked by a renewal of their covenant relationship with Yahweh (31:33). After the return from exile in Babylon, hopes for a regathering and renewal of Israel were not abandoned but continued to be used to express the hope for God's salvation (Isa 59:9-21; Zech 14:9, 16-19; Dan 2:44; 7:13-18; Tobit 13; Sir 36:1-17; 48:10; *Pss. Sol.* 8:28-34; 11:2-3; 17–18). In spite of the return to the land, and the rebuilding of Jerusalem and the temple, there lingered the hope that God would gather Israel together, with a restored Jerusalem and temple. "Restoration eschatology" shows the continuing power of Israel's hopes for a concrete realization of God's deliverance of Israel.

Such expectations come to expression in the book of Daniel, especially with the visions of successive kingdoms recorded in Daniel 7, which plays an important role in Jesus' interpretation of the kingdom and his role in it. The four exotic beasts of Daniel's visions (7:3-8) terrorize the earth for a set period, until their powers are taken away (7:12). Their powers are then given not to a fifth beast but rather to "one like a son of man," that is, a human being. This figure comes to "the Ancient of Days" and receives "dominion and glory and kingdom, that all peoples, nations, and languages should serve him; his dominion is an everlasting dominion, which shall not pass away, and his kingdom one that shall not be destroyed" (7:14). While the beasts represent four earthly powers or kingdoms along with their respective kings (Babylon, the Medes, the Persians, and the Greeks), the human figure, the "one like a son of man," represents "the people of the saints of the Most High" (7:27). The result of God's saving activity thus has a concrete social and political shape as Israel's various tribulations come to an end and its sovereignty is reestablished by God.

There are other views of God's kingdom and how God will establish it. Yet, in spite of the differences, certain factors pervade all expectations of the kingdom of God and serve as the coordinates along which variations of those hopes can be plotted. First, while biblical and Jewish literature everywhere assumes the sovereignty of God over the created world, the hope for a future and unmistakable manifestation of that reign persists. Thus the tension between the present reality of God's sovereignty and hope for the future visible manifestation of that sovereignty will be resolved as God's sovereignty over Israel as well as the nations of the earth must and will become manifest in a decisive way.

The second common element follows naturally from the first. Not only will God's kingly rule be established, but that rule will effect justice and righteousness because it is the rule of the one who is just and righteous. Hence, third, God's rule comes with salvation for those regarded as righteous and judgment for those known as wicked. Fourth, God's rule is expected to have specific, concrete, and visible consequences for Israel. Its defining institutions, such as the Mosaic covenant, with the Torah and its commands to purity and separation from all that is unclean, become renewed and even intensified.

And, finally, visions and hopes for the future carry with them implications for the present ordering of Israel's life. Where, for example, the future is defined as the renewal of the covenant, Israel's present life is to be structured in such a way that the contours of that covenant are embodied in its corporate life. The boundaries determining the future shape of the kingdom of God provide the guiding norms for Israel in the present. So, if the kingdom is limited to Israel in the future, it becomes important to know who or what constitutes "Israel." Those who are not to be found in the Israel of the future likewise have no real part in the Israel of the present. Those who stand outside the boundaries of the sphere of Israel are those who are judged, and those who are vindicated as righteous are those who have faithfully lived out what it means to be the people of God. Jesus' teaching about the kingdom of God repeatedly defines the shape of the kingdom of God by taking up exactly these hopes and expectations for the future realization of God's rule of righteousness, but by reshaping the nature of God's promised deliverance, as well as those who qualified as the "righteous" and "wicked."

8.3.2. Jesus and the Kingdom of God

The phrase "*kingdom* of God" echoes OT traditions and language about God's sovereignty, past, present, and future. Yet Jesus does not simply take over one set of expectations from either the OT or any particular strand of Judaism. Rather, using the language of the OT and drawing on its hopes, he creatively forges his own vision of how God's sovereignty has been manifested in the present and can be expected to be manifested in the future.

His message contained within it the tension between the present and future manifestations of God's rule found throughout the pages of the OT. His *proclama-*

tion about the kingdom moved back and forward between these two poles. Sometimes he spoke of the shape of the future kingdom, with its promised blessing and vindication of the righteous, judgment of the wicked, and restoration and renewal of God's people. At other times, he spoke of the present reality of the kingdom, the conduct appropriate to it, the blessings experienced by those in it, and the judgment due to those who reject it. But while Jesus' proclamation *about* the kingdom moves back and forth between these two poles, his *vision of* the kingdom cannot be ascertained simply by adding up the number of "future" statements and "present" statements, as though the reality of the kingdom were an equation to be solved or these elements needed somehow to be maintained in a balanced tension. Jesus spoke of the presence of God's dominion, while at the same time assuming its future manifestation in a reign of righteousness, with the vindication of the righteous, because his vision of the kingdom reflects that story implicit in the OT and Jewish literature. And while that story assumed that God rules in the present, it also pressed towards the climactic and glorious manifestation of that rule at a future time. Jesus took up that story and the tension inherent in it, but he made one substantial and significant change, which altered the entire schema: he saw the present not as moving inevitably towards a promised goal, but rather spoke of that future climax moving backward toward the present. In a word, his vision of the kingdom was thoroughly eschatological, anticipating a decisive and climactic manifestation of God's sovereignty. Precisely because of his anticipation of that decisive climax of God's rule, he saw the future shape of the kingdom as determinative for the way in which he carried out his ministry and the life to which he summoned his disciples and others.

The Gospels contain passages in which Jesus speaks of the kingdom as a future reality that is entered either after one's death or after the resurrection of the righteous. So, for example, entering the kingdom of God is contrasted with "being thrown into hell" (Mark 9:47), thus referring to a reality one enters after death. Jesus taught his disciples to pray, "your kingdom come," implying that it is not currently present or that, even if it is present in some ways, it lies yet in the future in other ways. He promised his disciples that they would judge the twelve tribes of Israel (Luke 22:29; Matt 19:28). Other passages contain Jesus' promise of inheriting eternal life (Matt 19:29; Mark 10:29; Luke 18:29-30). A future judgment that will divide the righteous from the wicked is pictured in the parable of the sheep and the goats (Matt 25:31-46). The righteous "inherit the kingdom" and receive "eternal life," while the wicked are sent into fire and punishment. This basic framework of expectation of future resurrection, judgment, and blessing or punishment is consistent with hopes and expectations known to us from Jewish literature of the time. It also fits with the conception of the kingdom of God as the righteous rule of God which entails the judgment on all unrighteousness.

Jesus, however, did more than claim that the righteous will be vindicated and

The *Gospel of Thomas*

The *Gospel of Thomas,* a Gnostic document probably dating to the second century, consists largely of sayings attributed to Jesus. While some resemble sayings in the canonical Gospels, others are quite different:

His disciples questioned him and said to him, "Do you want us to fast? How shall we pray? Shall we give alms? What diet shall we observe?" Jesus said, "Do not tell lies, and do not do what you hate, for all things are plain in the sight of heaven. For nothing hidden will not become manifest, and nothing covered will remain without being uncovered." (*Gospel of Thomas* 6; cf. Mark 4:22; Matt 6:2, 5, 16)

Jesus said to his disciples, "Compare me to someone and tell me whom I am like."

Simon Peter said to him, "You are like a righteous angel."

Matthew said to him, "You are like a wise philosopher."

Thomas said to him, "Master, my mouth is wholly incapable of saying whom you are like."

Jesus said, "I am not your master. Because you have drunk, you have become intoxicated from the bubbling spring which I have measured out." (*Gospel of Thomas* 13; cf. Mark 8:27-31)

The disciples said to Jesus, "Tell us what the kingdom of heaven is like."

He said to them, "It is like a mustard seed. It is the smallest of all seeds. But when it falls on tilled soil, it produces a great plant and becomes a shelter for birds of the sky." (*Gospel of Thomas* 20)

Jesus said to them, "When you make the two one, and when you make the inside like the outside and the outside like the inside, and the above like the below, and when you make the male and the female one and the same, so that the male not be male nor the female female; when you fashion eyes in place of an eye, and a hand in place of a hand, and a foot in place of a foot, and a likeness in place of a likeness; then you will enter the kingdom." (*Gospel of Thomas* 22)

the wicked punished. He also claimed to know who the truly righteous are, and his conceptions differed drastically from the common expectations of the day that the righteous were those within Israel who guarded Israel's holiness by carefully observing those laws that marked Israel as the distinctive people of God. But true defilement, according to Jesus, came from inside, not outside (Mark 7:15-20). In a parable about a toll collector and a Pharisee, it is the toll collector, a collaborator with Rome, who manifests the sort of righteousness that God desires, namely the righteousness of humility. The Pharisee, on the other hand, is able to point to his virtuous living — in contrast to the toll collector! — and his practices of tithing and fasting, but lacks genuine humility before God (Luke 18:9-14). But that a toll collector, who not only collected tolls for Rome but in so doing had likely hurt many of his own Jewish neighbors, should be regarded as righteous before God, rather than the Pharisee, whose guilt arose from his zealous devotion, offended Jesus' hearers (see Mark 2:15; Matt 11:19; Luke 15:1-2; 19:7). Other parables present God as one who seems to indulge sin (the prodigal son, Luke 15:11-32), who rewards the overlooked and rejected rather than the faithful and devoted (Matt 20:1-16), and who prefers to seek one lost person rather than tend flocks of the faithful (Luke 15:1-10). Jesus himself explained his mission as the mission of such a God, one who does not think it important to protect his honor against the possible slanders of those who mistake his grace for indulgence. As Jesus put it, "I came not to call the righteous, but sinners, to repentance" (Luke 5:32; Mark 2:17; Matt 9:13).

Jesus pronounced judgment on those within Israel, and particularly those in positions of leadership and power, rather than on Israel's Gentile overlords or the pagan nations around Israel. What kept Israel from genuinely living as the people of God was an internal, not external, problem, which could not be solved by eliminating the Romans. Judgment began with the household of God. Like the prophets of old, Jesus proclaimed that God's people had a particular obligation to live in accord with God's will, reflecting the very character of God. None of Jesus' contemporaries would have disagreed with this in principle. But Jesus, again like the prophets of old, emphasized that the moral requirements of the law — justice, mercy, and faith — were the heart of God's will for Israel and were to be the norms governing its life as a people of God. The parable of the "good Samaritan" drives home the point that to show mercy and compassion is to do the will of God (Luke 10:29-37). Matthew twice reports that Jesus quoted Hos 6:6, "I desire mercy, and not sacrifice," to show the primacy of mercy and justice over ritual purity (Matt 9:13; 12:7). In a scathing denunciation of the "scribes and Pharisees," Jesus upbraids them for "tithing mint, dill, and cumin and neglecting the weightier matters of the law, justice, mercy, and faith" (Matt 23:23). The OT command "be holy as I am holy" becomes in the Gospels "be merciful as I am merciful" (Luke 6:36).

Jesus thus took his stance with the prophets of the OT. In doing so, he rejected a program of purity for Israel, fleshed out in different ways by the covenant community of Qumran and the Pharisees. Whereas for these movements devotion to God and the law was understood to require careful observance of purity laws, Jesus taught that Israel's hope and God's will lay in quite another direction. The standards were high: in Matthew Jesus speaks of a "righteousness that exceeds that of the scribes and Pharisees" (Matt 5:20) and commands his followers to "be perfect, as your heavenly Father is perfect" (5:48). Yet that righteousness is defined throughout the Gospels in terms of meekness (Matt 5:3, 5), humility (Matt 7:1-5; Mark 9:35-37; 10:32-45), mercy (Matt 5:7; 18:23-35), forgiveness (Matt 5:23-25), generosity (Matt 6:2-4; Luke 11:41; 12:33-34), and purity of heart (Matt 5:8; 12:32-37; Mark 7:15-23). When asked what the greatest commandment in the law was, Jesus answered in terms of the twofold commandment to love God and one's neighbor (Matt 22:36-39). In short, while Jesus interpreted and proclaimed the will of God to his people, he did so as a prophetic interpreter of the Scriptures of Israel.

Jesus pictured the kingdom of God as a great feast, in which Abraham, Isaac, and Jacob, Israel's patriarchs, would eat together with Jesus and a great host coming from east and west (Matt 8:11 par.). At the Last Supper he spoke of drinking wine with his disciples in the kingdom of God (Mark 14:25 par.) and of eating and drinking at table with his disciples (Luke 22:29-30). Thus the coming kingdom of God was to be pictured primarily in terms of the fellowship of the faithful with each other and with Jesus. But such a hope was not merely relegated to the future. Rather, Jesus' table fellowship with his disciples and with others served as an enacted parable of the kingdom of God. More than once in the Gospels Jesus is accused of eating with toll collectors and sinners and of being a glutton and a drinker. He told some of his most famous parables, including the parable of the prodigal son, to portray the kingdom of God as God extending mercy to the poor, the outcast, and the ritually unclean, all people who were regarded by those carefully observant of the law as "beyond the pale." The kingdom belongs to those who, as sinners, respond to Jesus' call; it belongs to those typically regarded as of low social status, including women and children; it belongs to those who do not constitute the core of "Israel" and who would not have qualified for service in its priestly offices, such as lepers, cripples, and Samaritans.

These portraits of the kingdom of God, oriented as they are in Jesus' ministry to those far from the center of power and privilege in Jerusalem, could hardly have been regarded as anything other than a challenge to the status quo of the Jewish elite. Nothing less than the authority to represent God and God's will was at stake. It is hardly surprising, then, that Jesus would be regarded by the Jerusalem leadership as troublesome, even threatening.

The Gospels attribute to Jesus the use of various passages from Isaiah to picture the character of the kingdom and of the work of its messenger as liberating, redeeming, and healing (Luke 4:17-19; Matt 11:4-6). But Jesus did not describe Israel's deliverance as liberation from the rule of the Gentiles or the restoration of its political sovereignty and of the Davidic monarchy. So far as the Gospels report Jesus' teaching, he consistently avoided OT passages containing any reference to domination or power over others. In the one OT citation in the Gospels that does use royal language of Jesus, he is presented as a king who comes "humble and mounted on a donkey" (Matt 21:4-5).

When set in historical context, where it was often assumed that God's rule implies the vindication of Israel in the form of its supremacy over other nations, the absence of any such promise to Israel in the Gospels is striking. The pattern of passages Jesus uses of himself, as well as those he avoids, lies at the very center of his redefinition and proclamation of the kingdom of God. And yet it cannot be overlooked that Jesus used language that, in his cultural context, would have had clearly political — and even dangerous — implications. To speak of Israel's hopes for the realization of God's sovereign rule would have surely raised questions about the relationship of God's sovereignty, and of Israel, to the sovereignty of Caesar and Rome. The incident in which Jesus is asked about paying tribute to Caesar (Mark 12:13-17; Matt 22:15-22; Luke 20:20-26) shows that the relationship of Israel to Rome was a lively topic in Jesus' day.

Jesus spoke of the kingdom of God as God's gift to his "little flock" (Luke 12:32). But while Jesus spoke of deliverance, salvation, and blessing for those deemed the least likely candidates to receive it, he also announced judgment to those who refused to hear the call to repent, whether those of status and power or those who simply maintained a different vision of Israel's hope for the future and role in the present. As pointed out above, a common feature of hopes for the realization of God's rule of righteousness was that Israel's fortunes would change and its sovereignty would be restored. Many passages of Jewish literature assume the elimination from Israel of all impure elements, including the Gentiles. But the elimination or expulsion of the Gentiles from Israel or the kingdom of God does not find a place in the Gospels. While some passages do indeed limit Jesus' ministry to those within Israel (Matt 15:24), Jesus nowhere speaks of a kingdom from which the Gentiles are excluded: quite the contrary. Gentiles sometimes exemplify precisely the kind of faith and humility Jesus sought (Matt 15:28; 8:10).

Yet Jesus himself did not undertake an intentional mission to the Gentiles. Each of the Gospels, in its own way, indicates that a mission to the Gentiles and the fulfillment of God's promises to the Gentiles through Israel lay beyond the temporal and spatial bounds of Jesus' ministry (Matt 28:18-20; Mark 7:19; 15:39; Luke 24:47-49 and Acts 1:8; John 12:32). But Jesus' silence on the issue of the expulsion of the Gentiles from the kingdom and as the likely candidates for God's judgment provided a drastically different vision of the kingdom, which later paved the way for the church's own mission to the Gentiles. Paul's statement that "the kingdom of God is not food and drink but righteousness and peace and joy in the Holy

Spirit" (Rom 14:17) stands in continuity with Jesus' vision of the kingdom in terms other than Israel's political sovereignty. Apparently Jesus did not think that the limits of the kingdom of God were coterminous with the limits of a political kingdom of Israel. But that in itself is a political statement, for it undercut the hope that Israel's deliverance would come in the form of the restoration of its monarchy and independence, and it put another vision of the kingdom in its place. The kingdom of God was not to come as the result of radical change of the power structures or social orders of the world, but such changes followed as its effects or consequences.

Jesus took up and modified the hope for God's deliverance of Israel by reshaping the image of the kingdom into an image of service rather than domination. The "Son of man" as its head and representative figure, himself committed to "serve and not to be served and to give his life a ransom for many" in turn called his followers to serve and not to seek positions of power and domination (Mark 10:35-45). Thus Jesus stood on its head the vision of Dan 7:14, which promised to the son of man "dominion and glory and kingship, that all peoples, nations, and languages should serve him." The kingdom that Jesus announced came not to be served, but to serve.

Rather than proclaiming a visible kingdom that supplants other earthly realms, Jesus spoke of a kingdom discerned with the eyes of faith. Thus the kingdom could be compared to a seed growing secretly (Mark 4:26-29). While the farmer sleeps, the seed grows and produces a crop. Again, the kingdom of God is like yeast mixed into flour and water, causing a small lump to become a large mass of dough (Matt 13:33). It is like a tiny mustard seed that becomes a mature tree (Mark 4:30-32). And it may be pictured on analogy with a sower who, in spite of the vicissitudes of farming, will reap a harvest (Mark 4:1-8). These parables present a hidden kingdom, whose presence can be discerned only with the eyes of faith. Jesus himself said that the kingdom was not a reality whose coming could be predicted by certain signs, nor could one locate it in a certain place, for it was not that sort of reality (Luke 17:20-23). As a reality discerned by faith, it is nevertheless not simply a "spiritual" reality, as though it had no implications for how Israel was to live together, either corporately or individually. Jesus' proclamation not only contains affirmations and promises about the nature of the kingdom, but also many specific injunctions with respect to the sort of conduct appropriate to those who live in obedience to God's rule.

Jesus' proclamation about the kingdom was resolutely *theocentric*. Nowhere did Jesus use the phrase "the kingdom of Israel," and rarely did he speak of "my kingdom" (Luke 22:30). The kingdom belongs to God and comes from God. In this sense, it is a "transcendent" reality, for it belongs to the one who is transcendent, and it is not the result of human effort or the product of internal change. Jesus proclaimed that God's redemption of Israel was coming to its climactic phase in the renewal of the covenant relationship between God and his people. That reign of righteousness, which would be perfectly manifested in the future, was already discernible to eyes of faith in the present world order.

Out of the conviction that God's decisive work of salvation on Israel's behalf was indeed begun, Jesus called Israel to a radical reorientation of its priorities and loyalties. In short, Jesus called God's people to turn to God and to fall in step with the work of God. When formulated in these terms, Jesus' call emerges in all its offensiveness. For the implication of calling Israel to turn to God was that its present patterns of living and pursuit of righteousness were primarily oriented not towards God, but rather toward other realities — be they riches, earthly contentment, self-seeking, or status. The terse summary of Jesus' preaching found in Mark 1:15, "The time is fulfilled, and the kingdom of God has come near; repent, and believe the good news," underscores Jesus' proclamation of God's decisive work of salvation and the need to repent, or to get in step with the times and reorient one's life to God as made known through the kingdom announced by Jesus and to follow as his disciple in the way he taught.

8.4. THE MIRACLES OF JESUS

When the centrality of Jesus' proclamation of the dominion of God to his mission is taken seriously, the nature of his miraculous activity is thrown into sharp relief. What the Gospels record of him — his exorcisms, healings, and other deeds — are nothing less than enacted parables of the kingdom. They indicate the nature of the kingdom-power at work in Jesus' ministry and portend the sort of people for whom God's salvific purpose was coming to expression.

8.4.1. Initial Observations: Vocabulary, Definitions, Classification

In the Synoptic Gospels the word used most often for the miracles of Jesus is *dynameis,* frequently translated "mighty deeds." But one also finds *ergon* ("work"), *teras* ("wonder, portent"), *thaumasia* ("marvel, wonderful thing"), *paradoxa* ("strange things"), and *sēmeion* ("sign"), terms also used by pagans to characterize extraordinary happenings.

It is of course well known that more skepticism attaches to the miracles of the NT than to many other features. Applying Ernst Troeltsch's "principle of analogy," which states that we can study the past precisely because it is like the present, many scholars used their lack of experience of miraculous deeds as a yardstick to measure the possibility of miracles in the first century. Since miracles were not part of their experience, they assumed that such events could not have been part of experience in another time and place. Miracle stories were interpreted as myths or pious inventions. Form critics, who analyzed similarities between the accounts of miracles in the Gospels and those in non-Christian religions, concluded that the Gospel accounts were formulated on analogy with these pagan accounts rather than on the basis of actual events. Thomas Jefferson published an expurgated version of the NT in which he eliminated all unacceptable "supernatural" features, changing the Gospel message into a call to morality and rationality.

There is also the problem raised by the difficulty of defining a miracle. One of the most commonly accepted definitions today — that a miracle is God's *intervention* in historical events contrary to the "laws of nature" — would have sounded foreign to ancient ears. That definition implies that God is characteristically absent from the regular ordering of the universe, and that somehow the universe "runs on its own." But the demarcation between "natural" and "supernatural" was less sharply drawn for most first-century people, who more readily saw events in the world as the product not just of causes that could be explained scientifically or naturally, but as the result of the work of unseen spirits, good and bad.

And yet it should also be pointed out that assumptions about mythology, history, and the laws of nature have all undergone significant change in the last decades, so that quite a few books about Jesus, from across the theological spectrum, do argue or assume that Jesus accomplished miraculous cures. Whether or not one wishes to label some of these as "exorcisms" depends to a certain extent on how one assesses the existence of the spirit world and such entities as demons. Sometimes the exorcisms are subsumed under healing miracles, with the implicit assumption that they are psychosomatic cures rather than expulsions of spirit beings. At the point of other miracles, such as the walking on water, stilling a storm, or changing water to wine, many more scholars feel compelled to issue negative verdicts, or perhaps simply to withhold judgment as to the possibility of their occurrence. Whatever one thinks of the possibility of Jesus having done miracles, the entire miracle tradition of the Gospel does not stand or fall together.

8.4.2. Miracles in the Cultural Context of Jesus' Day

How Jesus' contemporaries would have regarded his healing ministry can be illumined by setting it in its historical context. According to the Jewish historian Josephus, Jesus was "a doer of startling deeds" (*Ant.* 18.3.3 §63). Josephus here probably speaks for other first-century Jews who believed Jesus did amazing deeds, but not that these deeds implied that Jesus was the Messiah or that one should believe in him because of what he had done.

There are stories of unusual or miraculous deeds or events in both the Jewish and non-Jewish Greco-Roman world. Greco-Roman religions incorporated such practices as interpreting dreams, determining likely events and recommending courses of action through astrology, predicting and foretelling the future through a variety of means, including reading the entrails of animals, and a variety of other practices that today might be labeled magic or superstition. There are documents, called the "Magical Papyri," that contain spells and charms for effecting cures, exorcisms, and curses. The spells often include exotic recipes (e.g., a falcon drowned in the milk of a black cow, mixed with honey), ritual actions, and the utterance of long series of unintelligible or foreign words, including the names of various deities.

In the non-Jewish world typically healings occurred at various shrines. There are accounts of healing of deafness, paralysis, and lameness. It has been suggested, for example, that the pool named in John 5, at which Jesus encountered a paralyzed or lame man, was actually a pagan shrine of healing. The Roman historian Tacitus reports how, after consulting with physicians, Vespasian used saliva to heal a blind man (*Histories* 4.81), and Suetonius reports the same incidents (*Vespasian* 7 §§2-3). Another ancient figure to whom miraculous works are attributed is Apollonius of Tyana, a first-century figure whose exploits were chronicled by his biographer Philostratus in the third century in the *Life of Apollonius*. Apollonius was reported to have resuscitated a young Roman bride who died at the moment of her marriage (*Life* 4.45).

In Jewish sources, there are some reports of individuals who perform marvelous deeds and healings of various diseases and ailments. In the OT, Moses, Elijah, and Elisha are reported to have been the agents or means through whom various extraordinary deeds were accomplished. Two rabbinic figures sometimes compared with Jesus are Honi the circle-drawer and Hanina ben Dosa (first centuries BCE and CE respectively). Hanina is reported to have survived the bite of a poisonous snake (like Paul in Acts 28). In a story remarkably similar to the accounts of the healing of the centurion's son (Matthew 8, Luke 7, John 4), Hanina is also said to have effected a cure at a distance (Babylonian Talmud *Berakoth* 34b). In time of drought, Honi prayed to God for rain, and these prayers were answered (Josephus, *Ant.* 14.2.1 §22; Mishnah *Ta'anit* 3:8).

There are also accounts, in both Jewish and non-Jewish sources, of demon exorcisms. According to Jewish tradition, Solomon was the foremost of Jewish exorcists. Josephus claims that this power had endured to his own day (*Ant.* 8.2.5 §§45-46) and that he himself had witnessed a Jewish exorcist named Eleazar perform an exorcism using Solomon's incantations and drawing the demon out through the nostrils, using a Baaras root (*J.W.* 7.6.3 §§180-85). Jesus seems to have assumed that others carried out exorcisms (Matt 12:27). Tacitus (*Hist.* 4.81), Lucian (*Philopseudes* 16 §§30-31), and Philostratus (*Life of Apollonius* 3.38; 4.20) give accounts of purported exorcisms.

In spite of the variety of accounts in both the pagan and Jewish world about extraordinary events and miraculous healings, there are no extant first-century records of a person who regularly accomplished the deeds that the Gospels report of Jesus or who performed miracles or exorcisms in precisely the way that Jesus did. While miraculous and inexplicable phenomena were not deemed impossible, neither were they simply the common stock of everyday life.

Even so, miracles are not self-interpreting. We note, for example, the variety of responses to Jesus' own miracle-working activity. Some witnesses are said to marvel (Mark 5:20; Luke 8:56); others are afraid (Mark 5:17); some people praise God (Luke 13:17, 18:43); but still others allege that he is in collusion with Satan or that he is mad (Mark 3:21-27 par. Matt 12:22-28; Luke 11:14-22). Some wish to force him to be king (John 6:14-15) or wonder whether he is the prophet or the Messiah (John 7:31, 41-42). In short, the witnesses of Jesus' miracles apparently interpreted them in different ways, placing them in drastically different categories. What categories existed and would have been used by Jesus' contemporaries to make sense of his miracle-working activity?

8.4.3. The Mighty Deeds of Jesus

As noted above, there were first-century Jewish prophets who promised extraordinary feats and signs, mostly acts of deliverance like those carried out by Moses or Joshua (*Ant.* 20.5.1 §97; 20.8.6 §§169-70; *J.W.* 2.13.5 §§261-63), which fits with the OT pattern linking miracles with prophets (Moses, Elijah, Elisha). A striking text from Qumran known as 4Q521 speaks of miraculous deeds, including the raising of the dead, that will accompany the time of the Messiah. While few Jewish texts speak of the hope for a wonder-working Messiah, it may well be that the concept of a miracle-working Messiah had developed by NT times (John 6:15; 7:31; Mark 13:22). It is also possible that miracles startled people into realizing that someone extraordinary stood before them, and they began to wonder if this extraordinary person might be the Messiah. Miracles were not sufficiently common to fail to evoke some wonder about the one who did them.

In the Gospels, the interpretive key to the miracles is less the mystery of Jesus' person than the manifestation of the kingdom of God through them. Although few passages from the Gospels make the connection between miracle and kingdom explicit, Jesus' proclamation of God's salvation comes to particularly graphic expression in his healings and exorcisms. Jesus said that he cast out demons by the Spirit of God (Matt 12:28 par. Luke 11:20) and explained his identity to John the Baptist by referring to prophecies from Isaiah (Matt 11:2-6 par. Luke 7:18-23), and this shows that he regarded his mighty works as manifestations of the presence of the kingdom and indicators of its shape, in contrast to the expectations of others who hoped for "the salvation of Israel" in a form that entailed its political sovereignty. Indeed, his mighty deeds were part of his ministry of the restoration of God's people.

In this regard both those healed and the sorts of diseases from which they are healed provide telling insights into Jesus' ministry. Among those healed are lepers, the lame, the blind, the deaf, those with physical deformities, and those with bodily discharges. While none of these diseases or ailments necessarily implies that one is outside the covenant community, all of them bar access to the temple, because they render one ritually impure or unclean. Jesus himself would have incurred ritual impurity by touching the corpse of a dead person, as he did more than once, and by touching lepers, the woman with the flow of blood, and any Gentile person. Jesus intentionally reached out to those who stood outside the center of Israel, if that center were to be construed along the lines of ritual purity. In this way, Jesus crossed the boundaries of purity and thus manifested the kingdom as God's power and will to restore people to wholeness and to fellowship among and with the people of God.

Jesus further stated that his activity of exorcising demons manifested the presence of the kingdom of God (Matt 12:28; Luke 11:20). His ministry manifested the power of God's Spirit to overcome the demonic forces that ravaged human life and to cleanse the "unclean spirits" that brought not only distress but estrangement from the community. But demon exorcisms exposed Jesus to the charge of sorcery and working against God (Mark 3:22-27), for they raised the possibility that Jesus was in collusion with the forces of evil. He risked such charges, even as he willingly incurred ritual impurity for the sake of releasing the captives (Luke 4:18; cf. Isa 35:5; 61:1). Moreover, his vision of the kingdom did not begin with and focus on the purity of God's people, as did the visions of the Pharisees and the Essenes. His conception of the messianic task envisioned a restoration of God's people along lines quite different from the common picture of the day.

8.5. JESUS AND THE MESSIANIC TASK

Earlier it was suggested that Jesus spoke of himself as a prophet and herald of the kingdom of God. While references to Jesus as "prophet" are found throughout the Gospels and other places in the NT, he is commonly called "Jesus Christ," or "Jesus the Messiah."

8.5.1. Messianic Hopes in the Old Testament

The English word "Messiah" reflects the underlying Hebrew *mashiah*, which simply means "anointed." Where the word appears in the OT, it is usually translated "anointed" in English, referring to the ritual act of anointing by which a king, priest, or other figure was designated or set apart for a particular task. In Greek *mashiah* is rendered as *christos*, from which we get the English word "Christ." Popular opinion to the contrary, there is no actual reference to "the Messiah," by that designation, in the OT. Rather, the word "messiah" occurs as an adjective, most often with reference to the currently reigning king in Israel, but also priests, patriarchs, the people of Israel, Cyrus the Persian king, and even Saul's shield.

The OT contains hopes for a time when Israel's trials, punishments, and exile will be over, the Davidic line will be restored, and Israel will enjoy a sort of golden age. This is not properly speaking a time "beyond history," although its nearly idyllic character would certainly mark a noticeable change in Israel's fortunes in the world. While the focus of this restoration is Israel itself, various epithets are used of the one who might be instrumental in bringing about this era of peace and prosperity. These titles include Prince of Peace (Isa 9:2-7), Branch, or Righteous Branch (Isa 11:1-9; Jer 23:5-6; 33:15), shoot of Jesse (Isa 11:1-9), Davidic prince (Ezek 34:20-24; 37:24-28), ruler in Israel (Mic 5:2-4), leader and commander of the peoples (Isa 55:3-5), and king of Zion (Zech 9:9-10). Such a figure was also referred to as the son of David. As this phrase and all the previous epithets show, the expected figure who would restore Israel was clearly to be a descendant of David, one who would sit on the Davidic throne ruling Israel. That understanding arose from the royal theology that comes to expression in passages such as 2 Samuel 7:12-16, which speaks of the promise of a permanent rule of the house of David.

The exile to Babylon and the destruction of Jerusalem and its temple naturally spelled the end of Davidic rule. But the hope for its restoration came to expression in the prophets, who spoke of a figure who would be that promised son of David, the offspring of Jesse, the prince of David, and so on. "The Messiah" is not used of this figure. Eventually the description of the king as "anointed" led to the use of "messiah" as a title when referring to the hope for a king from the line of David who would come to restore Israel's sovereignty and fortunes. But that development lies beyond the pages of the OT.

8.5.2. Messianic Expectation in Second Temple Judaism

In the extant literature of Second Temple Judaism we find evidence for a variety of hopes for the salvation and restoration of Israel. Among them is the hope for an anointed of the Lord, the Messiah, but that is by no means the only hope expressed there. From the writings of Josephus we also learn of various prophets, revolutionary figures, and would-be kings. Many attracted a following for a period of time, but most also met their deaths at the hands of the Romans. The literary evidence suggests that the picture of first-century Jewish messianic hopes was varied indeed.

One does find, most notably in the *Psalms of Solomon,* which are dated to the first century BCE, the expectation for a Davidic king. This figure is called the anointed one of the Lord and son of David; he is expected to defeat Israel's enemies, gather the dispersed Jews together, and settle the tribes of Israel in the land. Similar hopes for a kinglike figure who will arise to restore Israel and defeat Israel's enemies are found often in the Targumic literature as well as in the Dead Sea Scrolls.

But there were other expectations about what sort of figure might come and what that figure might accomplish on God's behalf. While the Dead Sea Scrolls contain references to a warrior prince, they also include the expectation of multiple messianic figures, including a prophet, as well as the Messiahs of Aaron (a priestly figure) and of Israel or Judah (a royal figure of Davidic descent). In keeping with the sect's priestly leanings, the priestly Messiah figures more prominently and receives preeminence.

The prophetic figure expected at Qumran may have reflected the first-century expectation that God would some day raise up "a prophet like Moses," the figure referred to in Deut 18:15-18. This hope was further developed in the book of Malachi along the lines of the "return" of the eschatological prophet, Elijah, who would presage the Day of the Lord, the day of Judgment (Mal 4:5-6). The expectation of Elijah's return is reflected in various ways in the Gospels. Speculation about Jesus as "the Prophet" can be found in the Gospel of John: "When they heard these words, some of the people said, 'This is really the Prophet'" (John 7:40). Finally, one should add to this mix the evidence noted earlier from Josephus, regarding various short-lived prophetic figures who promised redemption to Israel.

On the whole, these hopes for the future share in common a resolute focus on the deliverance of Israel as a people, often including the expectation of the return of Israel's national sovereignty. They share in common as well a focus on the centrality of the Torah and the necessity of obedience to it, the importance of the temple, and expectation of the fulfillment of the promise to David (2 Sam 7:12-16). The very variety of hopes and expectations for deliverance underscores the need for Jesus to interpret his mission and ministry to his disciples and to the crowds.

8.5.3. Jesus: Prophet, Messiah, Son of Man

The category most readily available to Jesus' contemporaries by which to interpret his ministry and work was that of "prophet." Jesus was known as a prophet in his lifetime (Mark 6:15 par.; 8:28 par.; 14:65 par.; Luke 24:19; John 6:14; 7:40-42). In fact, he spoke of himself as a prophet (Mark 6:4 par.; Luke 13:33) and used language reflecting a self-understanding as one who exercised a prophetic vocation

(Matt 10:40; 15:24; Mark 9:37; Luke 4:43). He compared himself to John the Baptist and to Jonah. The content of his proclamation, including the warning of judgment, the call to repentance, and the delineation of conduct acceptable to God, have their nearest parallels in the prophets of the OT. He performed various symbolic actions, including the triumphal entry and the cleansing of the temple, which reflected the actions of the sign-prophets of the OT.

Various passages do reflect the belief that Jesus is not simply one among the prophets. In an otherwise enigmatic passage, Jesus asserts that "all the law and prophets were until John," implying apparently that what follows John cannot be grouped under that rubric (Luke 16:16). Similarly, although he compares himself with Jonah, he also speaks of something "greater than Jonah" (Matt 12:41; Luke 11:32). When in prison, John the Baptist sends messengers to Jesus to inquire whether he is "the one who is to come," a reference perhaps to the expectation of Elijah, the one who would come as the final prophetic messenger before the "great and terrible day of the Lord." As noted earlier, the expectation of a "prophet like Moses," found in the Gospel of John, was current and thought perhaps to be an apt description of Jesus' role.

The Gospels do not reject the designation of Jesus as a prophet, since a prophet was by definition someone who spoke for God, someone empowered and commissioned to speak the word of God and to announce the will of God to the people. Even Jesus' opponents seem to have understood what was at stake in their debates with him regarding the interpretation of the law and its application to Israel's practices and conduct. What was at issue was fundamentally God's will for Israel, which could be known by faithful study of the Torah, through the requirements of the temple and the cult, or through charismatically endowed messengers. Jesus clearly fit the picture of such messengers, claiming to know and speak the will of God, even when that will contradicted the teachers of the day or criticized the priests in the temple.

It is a popular Christian belief that the Messiah was somehow "better" than a prophet, whereas in reality the expectation was that the Messiah was to be different from a prophet. The Messiah was to be a king, not a proclaimer of God's will, judgment, and redemption. "Messiah" conjured up images of a promised king in a restored kingdom, with a new Davidic king seated on a throne and ruling a political kingdom. But just as Jesus reinterpreted the nature of the manifestation of God's kingdom with respect to Israel, so too he interpreted his own role in keeping with that reshaped kingdom. Not surprisingly, then, in the Gospels Jesus does not interpret his mission in the royal terms documented in several Jewish writings of the first century. One passage that stands out as something of an exception, however, is the "triumphal entry" of Jesus into Jerusalem, where Zech 9:9, with its prophecy of a coming king, is cited to explain Jesus' action. But once again Jesus subverts the messianic expectation of victory and conquest by choosing to enter the city on a donkey, in humility, without troops, and without force. His kingly rule did not make its way through violence, force, or military victory.

Soon after Jesus' entry into Jerusalem, he performed a prophetic and symbolic act in the temple. While this particular action is often called "the temple cleansing," that term is something of a misnomer. Jesus did not aim to "purify" the temple so much as to foreshadow and predict its destruction. Elsewhere he speaks overtly of the coming destruction of the temple, even as his prophetic forebears had done. With the action of overturning the tables of those who changed currency and sold sacrificial animals, Jesus lodges his own protest against the present temple. In such an action he is not alone among first-century Jews. The community at Qumran was disaffected with the present temple and expected a new temple and a restored priesthood to replace the current system in Jerusalem. Indeed, there was rather widespread dissatisfaction with the Hasmonean dynasty, which had assumed control of the temple following the Maccabean revolt, since they could not legitimately trace their line through Zadok. Josephus spoke of corruption in the temple hierarchy. While the temple had been rebuilt following the Babylonian exile and gloriously refurbished by Herod the Great, even at the time of Jesus Jewish literature testifies to the hope for a new temple. Clearly, the Second Temple was not the perfect or final temple. Some texts even connect the messiah with the rebuilding of the temple, since Solomon, the son of David, had built the first temple. Jesus' triumphal entry, coupled with the prediction of the destruction of the temple and the action in the temple courtyard, signaled his warning of God's coming judgment, as well as his own messianic vocation.

Jesus' triumphal entry and symbolic action in the temple enact the messianic vocation to which he believed himself called. To speak of Jesus' messianic "vocation" rather than his messianic "claim" fairly represents both first-century Jewish expectations of a would-be "Messiah" and Jesus' own understanding of his messianic task. Jesus' contemporaries were not waiting for someone to come and announce to them that he was the Messiah. Rather, the evidence suggests that they were expecting a kingly figure, the Messiah, to come and deliver Israel from its enemies, and to restore its sovereignty, peace, justice, and prosperity. This was not a claim to be made but a script to be performed, a program to be enacted. According to the Gospels, Jesus carries out this task in proclaiming God's sovereign rule, or kingdom, and the judgment and salvation effected through it. As the shepherd of Israel foreshadowed in the prophets, he sought the lost and outcast, embodying the promise of the kingdom in table fellowhip and through deeds of healing and exorcism. The triumphal entry and cleansing of the temple are further testimonies to Jesus' messianic task. But that task would be carried out not with show of arms to vanquish Israel's foes nor through the rebuilding of a more glorious temple that would underscore Israel's newly restored position of power. Rather, it is precisely in the refusal to claim power for himself and his people, Israel, that Jesus charts the course of his messiahship.

Following Jesus' resurrection, the early church readily used the title "Messiah" of him because it believed that he had been vindicated and installed in his kingly office and was ruling with authority at God's right hand. In using this term, Christians did not believe that Jesus had "become" the Messiah, but rather that he had assumed the role for which he had been anointed by the Spirit at his baptism and which he had anticipated during his earthly life as a crown prince awaits ascension to the throne.

The Gospels show that Jesus speaks most often of himself as "Son of man," a designation derived from Daniel 7. The underlying Hebrew *(ben adam)* or Aramaic *(bar nasha)* is an idiom meaning "human being" or "mortal" and is used as such not only in Daniel 7, but in Psalm 8 and throughout Ezekiel. What is peculiar of "Son of man" in the Gospels is that it is translated literally, rather than as an idiom. An equivalent idiomatic rendering would have been *anthrōpos,* the Greek word for human being. Some scholars have argued, in fact, that this is the sense in which Jesus originally used the term. However, this interpretation cannot explain all the Gospel passages in which "Son of man" appears, for in some passages it cannot simply be an idiom for "human being." Therefore, others have sought elsewhere for the background of Jesus' use of the term. In the apocalyptic document known as *1 Enoch,* "Son of man" was used as a messianic designation, and other Jewish documents at least suggest that identification. Still, it is telling that when Jesus asks his disciples, "Who do they say that I am?" typical prophetic categories are evoked, and the disciples call him "Messiah," but no one ventures that he is "the Son of man." Not even Jesus' disciples ever come to know or confess this in the Gospels (but cf. John 9:35). This makes it unlikely that Son of man was a well-known messianic designation at his time.

As pointed out above, Daniel 7 refers to "one like a son of man," who apparently represents the people of the saints of the Most High, the faithful of Israel, who receive dominion from God. Yet just as the various beasts of Daniel 7 can refer alternately to a kingdom (such as Persia or Greece), as well as to their ruler or king, so too "son of man" may refer both to the people of Israel and their ruler. Some have therefore suggested a "corporate" interpretation of "Son of man," which Jesus used to designate himself in company with the faithful who gathered around him. They were to share his destiny, and he theirs. While this understanding of Jesus' mission and destiny has something to commend it, it is difficult to believe that in every instance where Jesus used the phrase he intended to convey this full-orbed meaning, or that his hearers would have understood it in this way.

We are left, then, with something of an enigma. It is hard to know how Jesus would have been understood by his own contemporaries if he consistently spoke of himself and his vocation as "the Son of man," and yet that is precisely the case in the Gospels. Even the suggestion that the early church or individual Evangelists have significantly shaped the use of the term does not explain why they chose this term. In fact, curiously enough, while the Gospels present Jesus as repeatedly referring to himself as "Son of man," and only seldom as "Messiah," the situation in the documents of the NT outside the Gospels is exactly reversed. It is assumed that Jesus is the Messiah, but only a few passages outside the Gospels refer to Jesus as "Son of man" (Acts 7:56; Heb 2:6; Rev 1:13; 14:14).

If we turn to the Gospels themselves, we find that the Son of man is often spoken of as God's agent in judgment (Luke 12:8). Such a role would fit well with the substance of Jesus' proclamation of God's coming judgment of Israel. Similarly, it is the claim to be seated at God's right hand in a position of honor and judgment that raises the charge of blasphemy at Jesus' trial (Mark 14:62). But the most memorable sayings of the Gospels present the Son of man not as a powerful judge, but as one who expects to suffer and die. But even this tension may be inherent in Daniel 7, which promises vindication to the son of man, but only after a period of tribulation and oppression.

In fact, the contrast between the "suffering Son of man" of the Gospels and the reigning Messiah of Acts and the epistles may illumine Jesus' choice of the term "Son of man." The early church's preference for "Messiah" follows upon Jesus' resurrection, his vindication by God, and his installation into messianic office. But "Son of man," drawn from Daniel, allows for that period of tribulation and suffering, and even for a time of hiddenness, before the "son of man" receives "dominion, glory, and kingdom" that "will never pass away" (Dan 7:14). Whereas at the time of Jesus, "Messiah" pointed to a visible Davidic kingdom and a ruling king of Israel, "Son of man" was an available biblical image without a hold on the popular imagination that also spoke of dominion, glory, and kingship. The early church quit using Jesus' term once it believed that Jesus' own tribulation was over and that his rule had been vindicated by God. "Messiah" summed up the church's confession that Jesus of Nazareth was the Messiah and had now assumed his rightful throne. Jesus himself had assumed and lived out this messianic vocation in anticipation of God's vindication of him.

8.5.4. Summary

This overview of the terminology used for and by Jesus in the Gospels demonstrates that while all four Gospels clearly regard Jesus as the Messiah, he himself seldom used this term. Moreover, no Gospel contains a passage in which Jesus explains to his disciples why he himself does not simply publicly announce himself to be the Messiah. Any explanation for this silence is a hypothesis that seeks to account for the data in the Gospels. Jesus' own message and actions point to a messianic vocation but one that reshapes the expectations of the messianic role. There is yet one piece of the Gospel tradition to be considered that comprises a singularly important piece of data for illuminating Jesus' mission, and that is the fact of his death on a Roman cross.

8.6. THE DEATH OF JESUS

Within the world of antiquity, how one died was often regarded as one of the best windows into the character of his or her life. This is especially true from the standpoint of the Gospels, which devote significant segments of their narratives to the final weeks of Jesus' life. Two issues quickly become intertwined here: first, the course of historical events leading to Jesus' execution on a Roman cross; second, the meaning associated with the death of Jesus, including the meaning he himself associated with his own death.

Of course, to suggest that Jesus might have interpreted his own death is not to imply that he sought his death. We have no evidence that he embraced the role of masochist or martyr, or that he set out to be rejected and killed. At the same time, it is unthinkable that at some point in his ministry he did not reflect on the possibility of his death. Given the resistance he continued to attract, given the escalation of hostility against him and his message, and given his predilection toward identifying himself with Israel's prophets, he could hardly expect anything other than violent death. Anticipating this, he began to fill his impending death with significance. He viewed his mission as announcing and embodying God's decisive act of salvation and restoration for Israel. This anticipated restoration would bring both judgment on Israel itself, as well as the salvation of Israel, or at least the salva-

---

Jewish Tradition regarding Jesus' Death

The Jewish Talmud contains this account of the death of Jesus:

> On the eve of Passover they hanged Jesus the Nazarene. And a herald went out before him for forty days, saying: "He is going to be stoned, because he practiced sorcery and enticed and led Israel astray. Anyone who knows anything in his favor, let him come and plead in his behalf." But, not having found anything in his favor, they hanged him on the eve of Passover. (*b. Sanh.* 43a)

tion of the restored people of Israel. In the Gospels, Jesus speaks of his death in prophetic terms as a death for others and as an act that established a covenant and so gathered together God's people.

8.6.1. Jesus the Rejected Prophet

In the book of Acts, Stephen is reported as accusing the Jews of persecuting their own prophets (Acts 7:51-53). Paul echoes this charge when he says that the Jews "killed both the Lord Jesus and the prophets" (1 Thess 2:15-16). Israel's rejection of its prophets is thematic in the OT and ancient Jewish writings (1 Kgs 19:10, 14; 2 Kgs 17:13; Jer 7:25-26; 26:5-11). These are accusations the prophets make against their own people, as do Stephen and Paul.

Jesus was evidently not surprised when he, like the prophets of old, encountered resistance and was rejected by his people (Luke 11:49-51 par. Matt 23:34-36; Luke 7:31-35 par. Matt 11:16-19). He spoke of his own death as the fate of a prophet (Luke 13:33) and wept over Jerusalem's rejection of him and previous prophets (Luke 13:34 par. Matt 23:37-39). The parable of the wicked tenants and the vineyard implicitly compares his fate to that of the rejected servants of the vineyard's owner. Since in the OT the vineyard is a prominent symbol for Israel (Isaiah 5), in this parable Jesus foreshadows his rejection by his contemporaries. Even as Israel has rejected its prophets, God's messengers to Israel for judgment and salvation, so now it has rejected God's final envoy. Therefore, Israel's judgment has come, for it has not heeded Jesus' call to repent and enter the kingdom of God. Jesus' death is thus the consequence of his faithful and obedient accomplishment of his prophetic vocation.

But a number of passages in the Gospels also attest to the fact that Jesus expected his own vindication (Mark 8:31; 9:31; 10:32-33; 14:25). Had he not, his expectation of his death would have been tantamount to an expectation of the complete failure of his mission. Again, the model for such expectation can be traced to the OT and particularly to passages that expect and hope for God's deliverance of the righteous who suffer at the hands of the wicked. Sometimes deliverance from trouble, suffering, and persecution is expected in this life (Ps 34:17-19; Wis 2:12-20 and 5:1-7; Daniel 3 and 6). In Jewish apocalyptic texts, vindication is expected in the form of resurrection (Dan 11:29-35; 12:1-3; *1 Enoch* 102-4; *2 Bar* 48:48-50; 52:60-67), an expectation found in the Gospels as well (Mark 8:34–9:1, 31-32; 10:33-34 par.). More specifically, this expectation comes to expression in various sayings in which Jesus predicts the suffering and vindication of the "Son of man." As noted earlier, the Danielic portrait of the "son of man" has inherent within it both the tribulations and vindication of that mysterious figure, which may have made it particularly well suited to Jesus' understanding of his own mission.

8.6.2. "A Ransom for Many"

One of the few passages that explicitly speaks of Jesus' dying for others is Mark 10:45: "The Son of man came not to be served, but to serve, and to give his life a ransom for many." To "ransom" someone means to pay for their release. A prisoner of war may be ransomed from the enemy, and a slave may be ransomed out of slavery, even as God "ransomed" Israel from its captivity in Egypt. Interpreted in this way, Jesus' death becomes part of a larger "new exodus," in which God once again ransoms and restores his people.

According to the Synoptic Gospels, at the Last Supper Jesus spoke of a covenant established through his death. The bread and cup that he distributed to his disciples represent his body and his blood. Paul repeats the traditions about the Lord's Supper, actually providing for us the earliest written account of the words of Jesus at his least meal with his disciples (1 Cor 11:23-26). There are obviously verbal echoes of Exodus' account of a ceremony in which the blood of a sacrificed animal was thrown on the altar as a sign of God's covenant with the people. This blood is called "the blood of the covenant" (Exod 24:7-8; 34:6-10), and Moses' action represents God both making a covenant with Israel and constituting a people of the covenant. The same phrase, "the blood of the covenant," also appears in Zech 9:9-11, a passage already used by Jesus to interpret his kingly entry into Jerusalem. So, too, Jesus' death renews the covenant of God with the people of God by calling together a covenant people who will live together in

An inscription found in the theater at Caesarea Maritima: "Pontius Pilatus, Prefect of Judea, has presented the Tiberieum to the Caesareans" *(Phoenix Data Systems, Neal and Joel Bierling)*

community according to the will of God as taught and interpreted by Jesus, the Messiah.

The Gospel of John interprets Jesus' death as instrumental in the constitution and reconstitution of the people of God. Jesus is "the good shepherd, who lays down his life for the sheep," precisely in order to keep them from being "scattered" by the wolves (10:11-18) so that they may dwell together as one flock, in one fold. In an ironic prophecy, the high priest, Caiaphas, urges the Sanhedrin to sacrifice Jesus in order to spare the Jewish nation from possible Roman retaliation. These words, according to the Gospel, were a prophetic word that Jesus should die "to gather together the children of God scattered abroad" (John 11:52). Similarly, Jesus compares his death to a grain of wheat that falls into the earth and dies in order to "bear much fruit" (12:24). Finally, he announces that when he is "lifted up" on the cross, he will draw all people to himself (12:32). Although the Fourth Gospel does not include the tradition of Jesus' words at the Last Supper, it presents Jesus' death in a similar way: it is that which seals or completes the work of the restoration and gathering together of God's people. This presentation of Jesus' death finds echoes in the Synoptic tradition ("How often I would have gathered you under my wings!") and stands in continuity with Jesus' proclamation about the kingdom of God as God's act of deliverance for his people.

In sum, the few passages in the Gospels that give us Jesus' own interpretation of his death uniformly point to (1) the corporate effects of his death ("a new covenant"; one for many; gathering together) and (2) its eschatological context. It anticipates the kingdom of God as it calls to mind the promises of the prophets. In short, Jesus died as he lived: anticipating, proclaiming, enacting, and mediating the kingdom of God. He died for the same thing that he lived for: the restoration of the people of God.

8.6.3. The Crucifixion of Jesus

While Jesus' interpretation of his death poses a particular set of problems, his crucifixion at the hands of the Romans itself raises another set of questions. To put the issue most sharply, crucifixion was a sentence meted out by the Romans only for certain crimes, especially rebellion against Rome. But the Gospels do not portray Jesus fomenting rebellion against Caesar or his local representatives in Palestine. In fact, Jesus' vision of the kingdom and of his messianic task nowhere explicitly entails the exclusion of Gentiles or the abolition of Roman rule of Israel. The verdict that Jesus was guilty of sedition seems peculiarly ill-suited to the words, deeds, and tenor of his career. When seen in this light, Jesus' death is the result of a tragic miscarriage of justice: tried on false or trumped up charges and crucified for all the wrong reasons, Jesus was misunderstood on a colossal scale.

School of
Giotto,
Crucifixion
(Alinari/Art
Resource, NY)

But that Jesus was crucified by the Romans remains one of the surest pieces of information that we have about him. Crucifixion was not simply the standard form of execution in the day. Josephus records a large number of crucifixions outside Jerusalem under Roman procurators, all for the same crime: resisting or rebelling against Roman occupation. Since crucifixion was the usual means of executing non-Roman citizens who sought to overthrow Roman rule, any particular crucifixion served not only as a grim reminder of Rome's superior strength but also of the futile hopes of those who sought to resist it. The public humiliation of the naked victim, who was tied or nailed to a stake or tree, was obviously intended not just as punishment of the offender but as a deterrent to other would-be revolutionaries. Indeed, the two crucified on either side of Jesus are called *lēstai,* a word that means something more like "rebel" than "thief." The charge on Jesus' cross read "King of the Jews," apparently meaning that Jesus had claimed to be the messianic deliverer of the Israel, which would put him at odds with the Roman provincial government.

From either the Jewish or the Roman point of view or both, Jesus was a threat to the stability of society. According to Luke's version of the trial scene, Jesus was

Paul Gauguin, *The Yellow Christ* *(Albright-Knox Art Gallery, Buffalo, New York)*

indicted before Pilate as one who perverted the nation, forbade paying tribute to Caesar, and asserted his kingship over Israel (23:1-5). From a Jewish perspective, Jesus is thus portrayed as a false prophet — who, through his teaching, signs, and wonders, sought to divert Israel from the path of God's will. In other ways, too, whether in his stance with regard to the Sabbath, his interpretation of the Scriptures, or his action in the temple, Jesus presented a threat to the interpretations of God's purpose sanctioned by the Jewish authorities in Jerusalem. His words at his trial concerning the "Son of man . . . seated at the right hand of God" could also be construed as a blasphemous claim deserving of death. From a Roman perspective, the indictments brought against Jesus suggested that he had a subversive agenda against the empire. And they came at a time when Roman authorities took a dim view indeed of any whose words and deeds might incite rebellion. The problem was easily dealt with, for Rome had dealt summarily with more than one threat to peace and order in the province of Judea in the first century. Crucifixion ended the threat; no action was even taken against Jesus' followers or disciples. That his followers were not pursued suggests, however, that Jesus was not viewed as a general who had raised an army of resistance but as a figure capable of attracting a following and stirring up unrest.

From the Jewish side, much the same thing could be said. Jesus had not simply raised questions about how one ought to interpret the law, understand the will of God, construe the people of Israel, or picture the "kingdom of God," although any of these could have provoked intense debate and open hostility. In the end, he and his opponents were not simply engaged in theological debates so intense that the Pharisees hated him for it and the chief priests sought his death. In providing an alternative vision of how God's rule would be manifested, of how to read the law, of how to understand and be the people of God, Jesus assumed the role of a prophet claiming to speak for God and by God's authority. The rejection of this claim wrote his death sentence.

8.7. THE RESURRECTION OF JESUS

According to the witness of the NT, the crucifixion was not the end of the story of Jesus of Nazareth. Following his crucifixion, he appeared to his followers, who in turn proclaimed him risen from the dead. The apostle Paul thought the resurrection so much the foundation of faith that he wrote, "if Christ has not been raised, then our preaching is in vain and your faith is in vain" (1 Cor 15:14). Yet throughout the ages myriads of theories have been advanced to explain "what really happened." Some are fanciful and even offensive. But in one way or another they struggle to deal with a nearly inexplicable event.

The Gospels themselves contain two kinds of narratives pertinent to understanding Jesus' resurrection. First, there are the accounts of the visits to the tomb, which is found to be empty; second, there are the accounts of the appearances of the risen Jesus to various groups of his followers. These two kinds of narratives differ in their value in our attempts to understand what happened after Jesus' death.

All four Gospels report that early on Sunday morning some women made their way to the tomb where Jesus had been buried. Upon arriving at the tomb, they found that the stone that had been placed over its entrance was rolled away from the mouth of the tomb. Although the names of the women who paid this visit vary from Gospel to Gospel, all four Gospels agree that it was women who first found the tomb empty and that among their company was Mary Magdalene. Instead of finding the body of Jesus, they were confronted by "a young man" or "an angel" or two angels. These angelic visitants told the women that the tomb was empty not because someone had taken Jesus' body but because God had raised him from the dead.

It is clear that the Gospels do not think that the empty tomb "proved" that Jesus was risen. In the Gospel of John, Mary found the tomb empty and asked the as yet unrecognized Jesus, whom she presumed to be the gardener, where he had put Jesus' body. Peter and the Beloved Disciple raced to the tomb and were troubled by the absence of Jesus' body. And before Jesus' appearance to the eleven, they were hiding "for fear of the Jews" (John 20:19). In short, the disciples' behavior on learning that the tomb was empty suggests not celebration and hope but dismay and puzzlement.

Dismay turned to joy only when the risen Jesus appeared to the disciples. It is impossible to determine the exact "nature" of Jesus' resurrection body. According to Luke, Jesus eats fish and bread. In John, Jesus, after passing through "closed [i.e., locked] doors," invites Thomas to touch his hands and then is shown preparing breakfast for the disciples at the Sea of Galilee. The young man in Mark promises the disciples that Jesus has journeyed to Galilee ahead of them. In short, Jesus' actions are much the same as those before his death. The Gospel writers do not conceive of his appearances to the disciples as those of a phantom but as the presence of the risen Jesus among the disciples.

And yet this was not a return to business as usual. Jesus appeared only to his own disciples or followers. There are no public sermons, healings, or confrontations with Jewish leaders — all which would no doubt have made a remarkable impression! Instead, he appears only to his own disciples and seems to appear and disappear from their presence as he wills, and eventually the appearances cease altogether. The disciples seem unable to predict or expect his presence with him. They do not always recognize him. Although Luke states that Jesus was "with them" for forty days, he does not record what was said during all that time. Jesus does not simply resume his previous role. In short, there is both continuity and discontinuity in the nature of Jesus' presence with the disciples before and after his death. However one explains "what happened" in the resurrection, the disciples confessed that the one who had lived and ministered among them and had been crucified by the Romans was now alive and that they were witnesses to this fact.

What Christian faith confesses, however, is not that Jesus "came back to life," a popular but misconceived way of understanding what happened. Jesus was not resuscitated but resurrected. The confession of the NT is that God raised him up to new life and that, having been raised to such life, Jesus will never die. He partakes of eternal life; he has experienced the resurrection that the faithful still await.

It was not unusual for first-century Jews to expect and hope for God's resurrection of the faithful. But this event was understood as a promise for the future and for all the faithful of Israel, not as a reality that could happen to one individual before that general resurrection. So when early Christians proclaimed that God had raised Jesus, they meant that the events that would lead to the final resurrection of the dead had already begun. The "end of the ages" had come, and Jesus' resurrection was a foretaste and guarantee of the future resurrection to life.

Here is where interpretations of what happened to Jesus divide most sharply. It would be possible through the methods of historical inquiry to establish that the tomb had indeed been found empty on the Sunday morning following Jesus' crucifixion. But that event would still demand explanation. And the interpretation found in the NT — that the tomb was empty because God had raised Jesus — cannot be verified by historical analysis. Although one may say that the Christian interpretation fits with the empirical data and, more importantly, arises from the proclamation of Jesus' first followers, nevertheless there have always been other interpretations. Some say that Jesus' followers stole his body, others that they went to the wrong tomb, still others that he "swooned" and was revived and continued to lead a somewhat hidden life until his death. It has also been asserted that the disciples were duplicitous and deliberately invented the resurrection, or that they were victims of mass hallucination. These theories are of course no more capable of being proved than the interpretation offered by Peter, "God has made him both Lord and Christ, this Jesus whom you crucified" (Acts 2:36).

This is in fact the form and substance of the earliest proclamations of Jesus' resurrection, which imply that God vindicated Jesus' life, ministry, and person by raising him to new life. God's vindication of Jesus takes the form of "exalting" him, of raising him to life, and installing him as "Lord and Messiah." Jesus did not enter into the glory of messianic rule during his life as a teacher in Galilee and Judea, nor did he fully accomplish his aims during his lifetime. Without the resurrection, there would have been no story to tell, for Jesus would indeed have died as another deceived messianic pretender. But because of the resurrection, generations of the faithful have confessed that God's intention is to bring salvation through Jesus, an intention that was fulfilled through Jesus' death and resurrection. The resurrection is the central focus of Christian faith and represents part of its irreducible core.

FOR FURTHER READING

Bruce Chilton and Craig Evans, eds., *Studying the Historical Jesus: Evaluations of the State of Current Research* (Leiden: Brill, 1994)

Joel B. Green, Scot McKnight, and I. Howard Marshall, *Dictionary of Jesus and the Gospels* (Downers Grove: InterVarsity, 1991)

Luke T. Johnson, *The Real Jesus: The Misguided Quest for the Historical Jesus and the Truth of the Traditional Gospels* (San Francisco: HarperSanFrancisco, 1996)

Leander E. Keck, *Who Is Jesus? History in Perfect Tense* (Columbia: University of South Carolina, 2000)

Mark Allan Powell, *Jesus as a Figure in History: How Modern Historians View the Man from Galilee* (Louisville: Westminster John Knox, 1998)

John J. Rousseau and Rami Arav, *Jesus and His World: An Archaeological and Cultural Dictionary* (Minneapolis: Fortress, 1995)

E. P. Sanders, *The Historical Figure of Jesus* (London: Penguin Press, 1993)

W. Barnes Tatum, *In Quest of Jesus* (rev. ed., Nashville: Abingdon, 1999)

N. T. Wright, *Jesus and the Victory of God* (Minneapolis: Fortress, 1996)

9. The Acts of the Apostles

9.1. ACTS AND THE NEW TESTAMENT CANON

The book of Acts is unique in the NT on several counts, and its importance is largely linked to that singularity. Most obviously, Acts is distinctive because it represents the only historical narrative of events involving Jesus' followers after the resurrection and first appearances of Jesus. Among the Evangelists, Luke alone has related for us a series of accounts that takes its point of departure from the end of Jesus' ministry. Thus, he alone indicates in such a profound way the continuity between the story of Jesus and the story of the early church.

In chapter 6 we have seen that the Gospel of Luke and the Acts of the Apostles are characterized by unity at several levels, including authorship, theology, and narrative development. The most glaring sign of disunity between these two is their canonical location. Already in the second century, Luke's Gospel came to circulate with the Gospels of Matthew, Mark, and John, together forming the four-fold Gospel canon. The Gospel of Luke, it was thought, could be read best in concert with other narratives of the life and ministry of Jesus rather than in conjunction with its original companion volume. Luke's story of Jesus was thus sundered from his account of the early church, which then found its home in relation to the NT letters, especially those written by Paul. Finally located between the Gospels and the collections of letters in the NT, Acts serves three immediate functions in the biblical canon. First, it provides a bridge from Jesus to the church, showing how the movement initiated by and surrounding Jesus in Palestine developed into communities of believers spread throughout the Roman Empire. This "bridge" is more than a structural convenience that draws together the two collections, Gospels and Letters, however. Second, the placement of Acts in the canon fosters a

The Position of Acts in the New Testament Canon

Although including the Acts of the Apostles in the canon constituted no great problem in the early centuries of the church, the question where to locate the book apparently attracted different responses. In the end, Acts played the crucial role of linking the collection of Gospels and collection of Pauline epistles. The following lists of NT books illustrate the mobility of Acts.

MURATORIAN FRAGMENT (2nd century)	SINAITICUS (4th century)	VATICANUS (4th century)
[Matthew?]	Matthew	Matthew
[Mark?]	Mark	Mark
Luke	Luke	Luke
John	John	John
Acts	Romans	Acts
Thirteen Pauline Epistles	1 Corinthians	James
Jude	2 Corinthians	1 Peter
1-2 John	Galatians	2 Peter
Wisdom of Solomon	Ephesians	1 John
The Apocalypse of John	Philippians	2 John
The Apocalypse of Peter	Colossians	3 John
	1 Thessalonians	Jude
	2 Thessalonians	Romans
	Hebrews	1 Corinthians
	1 Timothy	2 Corinthians
	2 Timothy	Galatians
	Titus	Ephesians
	Philemon	Philippians
	Acts	Colossians
	James	1 Thessalonians
	1 Peter	2 Thessalonians
	2 Peter	Hebrews
	1 John	[the list is incomplete due to the condition of the codex]
	2 John	
	3 John	
	Jude	
	Revelation	
	Letter of Barnabas	
	Shepherd of Hermas	

certain theological perspective from which to read the rest of the NT, for it countenances the spread of the good news to the Gentiles throughout the world and sanctions the work of particular witnesses, including Peter, James, and especially Paul. Third, the chronology of the narrative in Acts provides an outline on which to hang people, places, and events mentioned explicitly and presupposed in the NT letters. Without Luke's historical narrative, we would be hard-pressed to understand the chronology and progression of the Pauline mission, for example, and we would appreciate less fully the role of Peter the apostle and James the brother of Jesus in the earliest days of the Christian movement.

9.2. THE BOOK OF ACTS AS "HISTORY"

The traditional role of Acts in filling in the details of early Christian history raises immediately a series of questions for students of Acts. The most important has to do with the historical veracity or trustworthiness of Acts. Can the narrative of Acts bear the weight of historical reconstructions we might want to place on it? Can we trust it to tell us what actually happened, both in matters of detail and in its grand portrayal of the progress of the early church?

Pessimistic responses to questions of this nature have led many interpreters in the past century to reject the identification of Luke's work with the ancient practice of historiography or history writing. Some prefer to call Acts an example of the ancient novel, designed above all for entertainment, or to think of it primarily in biographical terms. This way of thinking about the nature of Luke's second volume is problematic on various grounds. For example, in his second-century treatise on *How to Write History,* Lucian advised historians to give their audiences "what would interest and instruct them" — indicating thereby that even historiography need not be lacking in aesthetic qualities. What is more, we would be wrong to imagine that failure to do a good job as a historian would require that one be classified as something other than a historian. If we were to find, for example, that Acts is a poor example of historiography on grounds of historical trustworthiness, this would not be sufficient ground to require that we read it according to the rules of some other genre. Choice of genre and quality of performance are separate issues.

Having said this, though, the question remains: How does Acts fare with regard to historical veracity? How one asks this question is important, since the rules of historical writing have changed in the centuries since Luke's day and continue to change today. Our reference earlier to "what actually happened" is actually a misnomer since it sets a standard for historiography that can never be met, not by Acts nor by any other historical narrative. Since the nineteenth century, many of us in the West have been taught to expect from historians a kind of investigative work concerned with "just the facts." The truth is, none of us could write (or be expected to read) "what actually happened," since such a report would require an all-knowing perspective and would be so full of unnecessary and unwanted details as to be impossibly unwieldy. Historians are not interested in "what really happened," but in what they and their communities deem to be significant among the many events that might have been recorded and in the relationships among the events that are recounted.

We recognize today that every statement in a historical work has both a documentary and an interpretive force. This means that the older bias against the historian who acts also as a theologian has little to support it. Thus, the central problem on which the debate on "Luke the historian" has typically turned has had much less to do with the nature of Acts than with modern problematic conceptions of the historian's enterprise. The view of the last two centuries, that historical inquiry is interested above all in establishing *that* certain events took place and in objectively reporting those "facts," has been eclipsed by a conception of the historiographical project in which Luke would have actually found himself more at home. The primary question is not how the past can be accurately captured or what methods will allow the recovery of "what actually happened," for it is increasingly acknowledged that the historical narration of events is always tied to interpretive commitments. Historiography imposes significance on the past both by its choice of events to record and to order and by its inherent efforts to postulate for those events an end and/or origin. Events are woven by historians into chains of causation, with the result that our interest in reading should fall less on *validation* and more on *signification*. The primary issue becomes how the past is represented.

This does not preclude our asking whether Luke has faithfully represented this or that event, but it does suggest that our primary interest in Luke's narrative should lie elsewhere. This is because the most important aspect of Luke's enterprise lies outside the realm of verification and proof. This most important aspect is his claim to provide a divine perspective on the events he records, his claim that what has happened in the early Christian mission has been empowered by the Holy Spirit and guided by God and thus gives expression to the ancient redemptive purpose of God. The events he recounts have been strung together in the net of divine causation, so that Luke's claim to "faithfulness" must be measured first and foremost not on the grounds of historical veracity but on the capacity of his narrative to represent God's viewpoint on these events.

This is not to suggest or even allow that Acts lacks faithfulness to historical events in the mid-first century, nor is it to urge that Acts should be sheltered from historical inquiry. It is rather to refocus the aim of such inquiry. First, typically, the contribution of the historian comes in two activities — the selection of events to recount and the ordering of those events in a coherent narrative. This means that, on matters of detail and with regard to individual episodes, we can expect Luke's activity to have focused on visiting sites and collecting and checking reports. This is inherent to the ancient historian's task. Second, in relation to Luke's historicism, "historical veracity" cannot bypass the question of divine purpose, and "what really happened" cannot be understood apart from God's perspective. To neglect the divine point of view in a historical narrative like Acts is to consider less than the full historical truth.

Undoubtedly, the history of the earliest Christian movement might have been told differently by different historians with different interests. Other histories might have been formulated — focusing less on Jerusalem and Rome, more on Antioch or Galilee or Philippi, for example. Why does Peter disappear in the second half of Acts? What stories might have been told about him had Luke not focused the spotlight so narrowly on Paul and the Pauline mission? Alternatively, by using only the accounts Luke has given us, other narrators might have constructed a narrative of an altogether different sort, designed to give a comparatively novel perspective on the unfolding of events following Jesus' death and resurrection. Indeed, we can be sure that the Jewish leadership in Jerusalem did share a different interpretation of the events. And Luke himself must have written his narrative as he has in order to shape his readers' views of the significance of "the events that have been fulfilled among us" (Luke 1:1). In the first century there must have existed many diverse and competing ways of construing the progress of the early Christian movement — some that endowed it with no importance at all, others that emphasized more the roles of women like Mary Magdalene and Priscilla, and so on. What must be of particular interest to us, then, is that the picture provided by Acts coheres generally with the NT witness as a whole. Acts supports such overall NT emphases as the identification of Jesus of Nazareth with the exalted Lord, the continuity between the message of Jesus and that of the early church, and the portrait of the early church as a missionary movement concerned with how the gospel took root and flourished in increasingly Gentile and urban arenas.

This view of the historiographical task is less interested in whether other ways of telling the story might have been imagined, for this should go without saying; of greater interest is how history has been represented by Luke in this, his second volume.

9.3. THE NARRATIVE PROGRESSION OF THE MISSION IN ACTS

Perhaps the single most important clue for how history has been represented by Luke in his second volume comes in its opening chapter in Jesus' words to his followers, "You will receive power when the Holy Spirit comes upon you, and you will be my witnesses in Jerusalem, in all Judea and Samaria, and to the end of the

Preparations (1:1-26)
The witness of the disciples in Jerusalem (2:1-6:7)
The expansion of the mission beyond Jerusalem (6:8-15:35)
Paul's mission (15:36-20:38)
Paul imprisoned and on trial (21:1-28:31)

earth" (Acts 1:8). Coming in response to the query of his disciples, these words of Jesus substitute a missionary program for their speculation about the timing and substance of end-time events. Just as God knows the "times and seasons" of the fulfillment of his purpose, so he anoints these followers with the Spirit so that they might operate as agents on his behalf. In a statement that will prove to be programmatic for the rest of Luke's narrative, Jesus thus sets the future of Israel within the now more widely defined plan of God.

Jesus' references to a mission in Jerusalem, Judea (i.e., "the land of the Jews"; cf., e.g., Luke 4:44; Acts 10:37), and Samaria represent significant progress in this direction, and portend the development of the mission in Acts 2–8. They also give a centrifugal shape to the mission that is quite remarkable. Although the idea of a universal mission is not unprecedented in Israel's history, analogous end-time scenarios typically showed the nations coming *to* Israel, *to* Jerusalem. Jesus' missionary instructions thus fly in the face of the generally acknowledged holiness of the temple and its status as the location of God's presence. The boundaries to be crossed by this mission are deeply rooted in Israel's self-identity, so that the mission mandated for Jesus' followers calls for a transformation of conventional ideas about "the way God made the world," "the way the world is." But in "evangelizing the poor" (Luke 4:16-30) — that is, in proclaiming good news to those of low social status (women, Samaritans, toll collectors, and the like) — Jesus had already set in motion this world-transforming, revolutionary mission.

Beyond Samaria, the Spirit-endowed mission was to continue to "the end of the earth." Where is "the end"? Ancient geographers spoke of places like Ethiopia and Spain as "the end of the earth," but these make little sense of the Lukan narrative. The first key for understanding this phrase in Acts is our recollection that space is never measured in purely geographical terms but is always imbued with symbolic power. Geography is not a naively given container, but reflects and configures peoples' social world. "New York" or "San Francisco" or "South Africa" — these are more than places on a map. Their social significance extends far beyond their location, so many degrees latitude and longitude. They, like "Jerusalem" and "Samaria," bring to mind powerful social forces — viewed positively by some, negatively by others.

The second key comes in Acts 13:47, where the phrase "the end of the earth" is again found, but with the sense more transparent: "everywhere," "among all peoples," "across all boundaries." Luke thus encourages an identification of "the end of the earth" with a mission across all boundaries and inclusive of all peoples, Jewish and Gentile. In only a very limited sense, then, might one take 1:8 as a diagram of Acts. Much more significant is the way it identifies God's aim within the narrative.

Acts 1:8, then, is not an outline of Acts, but neither is it a prophecy of what is to come. Rather, it is a missionary portfolio, a job description and evaluation instrument for Jesus' followers who are to work as they are empowered by the Holy Spirit. As Jesus' words in Acts 1:8 clarify God's purpose, they also provide a measure by which to ascertain who in the narrative is faithfully serving the will of God. Those who obey the missionary agenda provided here are shown to be operating under the guidance and power of the Spirit and to be following God's plan; they are authentic witnesses.

If we paint with a large brush, we can portray the advancement of the narrative of Acts in five major sections:

9.3.1. Preparations (1:1-26)

The brevity of this section may mask the pivotal role it plays as the hinge between the Gospel of Luke and the book of Acts. In tying together these two volumes the opening of Acts provides a sense of continuity between the story of Jesus and the story of the early church, verifying that all is progressing according to the purpose of God. It is easy to come away from our reading of this section with the impression that Luke is trying, at least in part, to address the problem of coherence in God's salvific design. Just as the ministry of Jesus was firmly rooted in the story of God's salvation in Israel's Scriptures by the opening of the Gospel of Luke (Luke 1:5–2:52), so these opening verses of Acts firmly root the story of the early church in the story of Jesus.

According to the opening verses of Acts, Jesus' ministry is unquestionably foundational to the unfolding narrative of Acts. This is particularly true with respect to Jesus' preparation of his disciples through continued instruction; the continuing role of the Spirit — who anointed Jesus, through whom Jesus carried on his ministry, and who will now empower Jesus' followers in their capacity as his witnesses; the continuing principal role of the imperial rule of God with its alternative vision of the world and challenge to the social order; together with the continuing division of Israel (see Luke 2:34-35), and the mission that crosses all boundaries.

Along with thus rooting the beginning of Acts in the Gospel's account of Jesus' ministry and the ongoing story of God's redemptive purpose, the opening of Acts also begins to show the disciples in a more active role than in the Gospel and portends their ongoing orientation toward God and his purpose. This latter point is signified by the references to their continual prayer and to Peter's appeal to the Scriptures in the matter of Judas's replacement. Replacing Judas to bring the number of apostles to twelve is itself significant in suggesting the centrality of the restoration of Israel, the Twelve Tribes, in Lukan thought. Of course, the amount of space devoted to the story of Judas also serves as a warning that even "insiders" among the people of God are susceptible to stumbling in their commitment.

Other motifs are signaled here at the outset. Acts is introduced as a preeminently *theocentric* narrative, as evidenced by the emphasis on the Father and his eschatological purpose, the centrality of the work of the Spirit in the ministry of Jesus and the prospective mission of the disciples, the presence of heavenly messengers at Jesus' ascension, and the echoes of Scripture (bearing witness to God's design) in this section. A pivotal role will be played by *the Holy Spirit,* introduced as the muscle of the church's mission. The ascension signifies the *elevated status of Jesus,* whose ministry and message is thus vindicated by God, and it serves as a guarantee of Jesus' return. And finally, this opening section of Acts underscores the importance of *service as witnesses* and the *universal character of the prospective mission,* together with the related, *problematic place of Israel as a people in God's redemptive plan.*

9.3.2. The Witness of the Disciples in Jerusalem (2:1–6:7)

The missionary mandate given by Jesus in Acts 1:8 called for the disciples to engage in a worldwide mission. This mission was to have its beginnings in Jerusalem, however, and Luke devotes the first major section of Acts to developing the nature of the Christian mission and community in Jerusalem. Of course, the use of the word "Christian" in this context is only a convenience, since here and elsewhere in Acts, followers of Jesus are understood and represented very much as one among other diverse groups within Judaism.

This section is initiated with the momentous fulfillment of long-held expectations. John had predicted that Jesus would baptize with the Spirit, Jesus had spoken of the Spirit as the gift of the gracious Father, and, following his resurrection, Jesus had again spoken of the "promise of the Father" (Luke 3:16; 11:13; 24:49; Acts 1:4-5). To these words of anticipation are now added Jewish thinking about Pentecost as the time of the giving of Torah and the prophetic utterances of Joel — all highlighting the importance of the coming of the Spirit at Pentecost.

This is the first of many events in Acts that recount the mighty acts of God and that express a need for interpretation and understanding. Here the question is what this speaking of God's acts in other languages means. As Jesus had prophesied (Luke 22:31-32), Peter immediately emerges as a leader among Jesus' followers, and his speech to those gathered in the temple points first to the fulfillment of Israel's hope for the age of salvation, marked by the coming of the Spirit (Joel 2:28-32). He then weaves an argument primarily focussed on Jesus of Nazareth, proving from the Scriptures that the "promise of the Father," the Holy Spirit, has been allocated by God's co-regent, Jesus, whom God has exalted as Lord and Christ. This is crucial for the remainder of Acts, since it gives the basis of Luke's view that salvation for humanity is rooted primarily, and deeply, in Jesus' resurrection and ascension. In this way, what Joel promised regarding "the Lord" — that "all who call on the name of the Lord will be saved" — can be transferred to Jesus. Subsequently in Acts, then, believers are known as those who heal (3:6, 16; 4:10, 30; 19:13), preach (4:12; 5:28, 40), and are baptized (8:16; 10:48; 19:5) in the name of Jesus, who suffer for Jesus' name (5:41; 9:16; 21:13), and "who call on the name" of Jesus (9:14, 21; 22:16).

Luke has more to say about the character of the community being formed among the baptized; in fact, he devotes two summary statements and two brief exemplary accounts to this task. Both Acts 2:42-47 and 4:32-35 employ images from Greco-Roman literary discussion of ideal friendship and from the LXX about the nature of obedient Israel in order to indicate how the church embodied those ideals. One may be able to hear echoes here of Essene practices and of the nature of life characteristic of "the Golden Age" — when all was held in common. Barnabas (4:36-37) appears as a positive example of behavior characteristic of this community, as he submits to the authority of the apostles and shares his possessions with those in need. Ananias and Sapphira (5:1-11), on the other hand, possess only the appearance of belonging to the community of God's people. Misrepresenting their status as members of this extended family of believers, they act rather as outsiders who lie to the community (and thus to the Spirit). As in the Gospel of Luke, so in Acts, the disposition of one's possessions serves as a barometer of the disposition of one's commitments. In these and other ways, the portrait of the disciples takes on that shape portended by Jesus in his earlier teaching about those who share kinship with one another, like brothers and sisters, who hear and do the word of God (Luke 8:1-21).

This is not the whole story of the embryonic church, however. Woven together with accounts of friendship and koinonia are episodes of hostility and rejection. It is especially here that Luke indicates how Jesus' followers have taken on the character of their leader. Like him, they participate in ministries involving signs and wonders, like him they run afoul of the Jewish leadership in Jerusalem, and like him they respond to opposition with prayer and renewed commitment to the mission to which they have been called. One of Luke's most persistent motifs

---

Community of Goods, Friendship, and the Golden Age

Luke's portrayal of the nature of the early Christian community is often compared to ideals of friendship and human beginnings in the Greco-Roman world. Well-known in antiquity is the proverb "Friends hold all things in common" (e.g., Aristotle *Nicomachean Ethics* 9.8.2 §1168b); in Acts 2:44, "believers" rather than "friends" "hold all things in common." Images of the Golden Age in Greco-Roman literature similarly depict humanity's primeval practice of common ownership. For example, in *Georgics* (1) Virgil writes:

> Before Jupiter's day no tillers subdued the land,
>   even to mark the field or divide it with boundaries was unlawful.
> Humankind made gain for the common store,
>   and earth yielded all, of herself, freely,
>   when none begged her gifts.

In addition, among the Essenes we find evidence of economic community within the land of Palestine itself. Luke's portrait thus finds points of contact with wide-ranging cultural ideals, now actualized within the community of believers.

---

comes again to the surface here: persecution leads to further progress in the mission.

Acts 6:1-7 forms a poignant scene of transition to the next section of Acts, for it prepares for a change of focus from the first apostles to another group of leaders in the early church, some from among the Hellenists. These were Greek-speaking Jews within the community of believers, and the vignette Luke provides shows how their influence within the church came in spite of initial prejudice against them. That their widows were being overlooked in the daily distribution of food signifies much more than a practical problem of too many needy people and too little food. Rather, as persons who had been more open to foreign influence, who participated more fully in things Greek, they were suspect in their loyalties toward the ancient ways of God. The solution at which the church arrives is highly symbolic, for it brings some of these relative "outsiders" into positions of leadership — not simply to the work of "waiting on tables," but into the sort of leadership service for which Jesus was already known (see Luke 22:24-27; cf. Luke 12:37).

9.3.3. The Expansion of the Mission beyond Jerusalem (6:8–15:35)

Jesus directed his followers to engage in mission in Jerusalem, Judea, Samaria, and to the end of the earth (Acts 1:8), but thus far they have failed even to cross the city limits of Jerusalem. No doubt this was due in part to the importance of the mission in Jerusalem itself. Equally important, though, is the necessity of making clear the theological rationale for a more expansive mission. Jesus may have been exalted as Lord and Savior, but the universal implications of this divine act have not yet struck his followers. Nor will Jesus' apostles be the first to recognize how widespread the implications of the gospel are; this innovation will come from those Greek-speaking Jewish followers of Jesus recently recognized as leaders in the community. It is through their lives that we begin to see growing evidence of the impulses toward a gospel oriented toward all peoples, Jews and Gentiles, already present in the ministry of Jesus.

Luke's account of the witness of Stephen (Acts 6:8–8:3) is critical for the way it provides the theological and causal underpinnings for the impending mission beyond the borders of Jerusalem. Stephen is represented as an unassailable witness — he has already been authorized as a leader of the church, he is now presented in tones that are deeply reminiscent of Jesus, he speaks as he is empowered by the Spirit, he interprets the Scriptures of Israel, and he has the countenance of an angel. Yet his witness is, from the standpoint of the Jerusalem elite, highly controversial, so much so that it leads to his death as one who has blasphemed God.

Stephen first provides a selective retelling of Israel's history to set forth the pattern of Israel's rejection of God's instruments — Joseph, Moses, the prophets, even Jesus, and now Stephen himself. On this basis he charges that, failing to understand God's purpose, the Jerusalem leadership has misconstrued the Scriptures and turned the temple into a place of idolatry. Importantly for Luke's view that Jesus and the Christian movement fulfill the program of God *from within the story of Israel's restoration,* even Stephen's critique of Jerusalem's rebellion is cast in terms borrowed from Ezekiel 20. The end result is that Jerusalem is rejected as the center of God's presence and thus as the center of faithful response to God. Stephen's death symbolizes the rejection of the good news by the Jewish leadership in Jerusalem. Ironically, it leads immediately to a persecution that helps to fulfill Jesus' words in Acts 1:8. Now, at last, Jesus' followers depart the confines of the city.

If with Stephen we have the theological movement of the mission beyond Jerusalem, it is with Philip that we have the socio-geographical first steps. Philip, like Stephen, is one of the Hellenists brought into the circle of leadership in the church in Acts 6:1-7, and it is he who pioneers the mission first to the Samaritans and then to a Gentile (8:4-40). The interweaving of accounts on Luke's part is important here. After the episode in Samaria, both Philip and Peter depart for other missionary endeavors, but we temporarily lose sight of Peter. In terms of story time, though, while Philip is engaged in conversation with the Ethiopian eunuch, Peter is participating in a ministry that brings him into contact with a paralytic, a corpse, a tanner, and a Gentile household (9:32–11:18). Luke's readers are prepared for these innovations on Peter's part because we have already followed Philip's interaction with a foreigner who, as a eunuch, would have been denied access to even the Court of the Gentiles in the Jerusalem temple. This stage of Philip's mission remains unknown to the church in Jerusalem, however, since Philip moves on to Caesarea (where we will find him again in 21:8). The Jerusalem Christians do hear of Peter's sharing hospitality with Gentiles, and it is only after he shares with them the mighty acts of God that they are willing to accept his ministry as God's doing.

This conjunction of episodes is important for the way it brings together a number of important Lukan motifs. For example, the eventuality of a universal mission is highlighted by these accounts, as well as by Peter's recognition, finally, that Jesus is "Lord *of all*" (Acts 10:36). But Luke does not portray this expansion as an easy one. At every turn it is necessary to show how such innovations are willed by God. The voice of the Spirit, the presence of angels, the giving of a vision, fresh understandings of Scripture, and so on — these are necessary as the church tries to catch up with the work of God along new lines and among new peoples.

As Luke portrays it, the mission thus far expands mostly in relationship to Judaism. The Gentiles who come to faith and receive the Spirit in these texts have already been related to Judaism. Acts mirrors the gradations generally present in the first-century Mediterranean world. There are those who are Jews by ethnic and religious heritage; then there are proselytes, Gentiles who have embraced Judaism — including the sign of the covenant, circumcision; then there are God-fearers, Gentiles on the periphery of Judaism, who identify with Jews in such practices as prayer to the one God, the giving of alms to the poor, attendance at the synagogue for instruction, and so on. Clearly, the Christian mission as Luke understands it is most successful among God-fearers, persons already familiar with the Scriptures of Israel, who have already embraced the worship of Yahweh, but who remain on the margins of acceptance, who do not really belong to the family of God's people. As the story unfolds, it becomes clear that *whether* there will be a mission to the Gentiles is not the central issue. As the account of Peter and Cornelius suggests, the problem with which Luke is concerned runs deeper. It has to do with the shape of the Christian community, and specifically with whether Jewish and non-Jewish followers of Jesus will be able to participate fully together in fellowship.

Before this issue comes fully to the surface, it is complicated by the work of Paul — whom Luke reintroduces between the accounts of Philip and Peter. Paul was introduced in the scene of the stoning of Stephen (Acts 7:58), so it is not surprising to find him again as the enemy of the church in the opening of Acts 9. Luke devotes an inordinate amount of space to his narrative of Paul's conversion, partially in order to indicate the depth of the change Paul experienced and partially to intimate its nature. His "conversion" is represented above all as a "recommissioning" — to serve no longer in oppositio n to the church but as one who is to carry the name of the Lord Jesus "before the Gentiles and their kings and before the people of Israel" (9:15). Ironically, then, he who has persecuted the church now becomes the one against whom Jewish hostility will be directed.

What follows are alternating accounts of Peter and Paul. This allows Luke to demonstrate Paul's legitimacy, as he carries out a ministry that is similar to that of Peter and, indeed, to that of Jesus. It also allows for a mission that is more and more oriented toward the Gentiles, thus setting the stage for the conference on the question of Gentile believers in Acts 15. And it allows for the spotlight to turn more and more from Peter and the Jerusalem beginnings of the church to Paul and the movement of the Christian mission to "the end of the earth."

9.3.4. The Mission of Paul (15:36–20:38)

By this juncture in the narrative of Luke-Acts the primary threads of God's purpose to bring salvation in all its fullness to all peoples have been laid bare. What is more, the new reality of common fellowship between Jewish and Gentile followers of the Way has been secured through the general affirmation of the ongoing significance of Torah for Jews and the superfluity of circumcision for Gentile con-

The bema in the forum of Roman Corinth (see illustration on pp. 330-31 below), the "tribunal" of Acts 18:12, with the Acrocorinth in the background *(Phoenix Data Systems, Neal and Joel Bierling)*

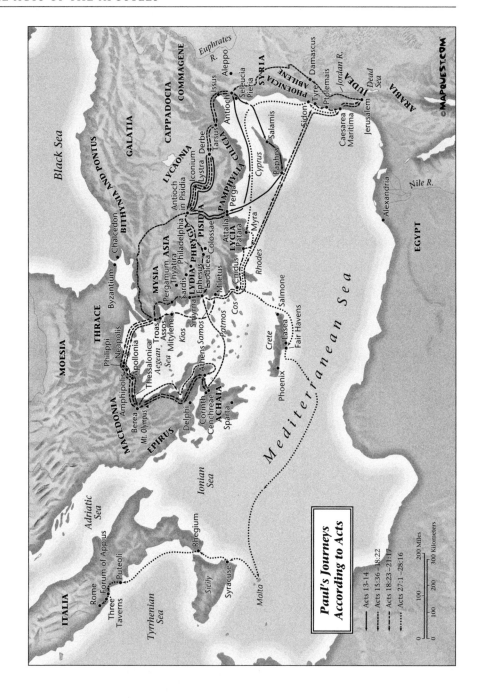

Paul's Journeys According to Acts

Acts 13–14
Acts 15:36–18:22
Acts 18:23–21:17
Acts 27:1–28:16

Greek Philosophical Schools

By the time of Acts, already for some five or six centuries, Greek philosophy had developed along multiple lines, in part due to the lack of system or dogma in Greek religion. According to Acts 17:17-18, Paul encountered representatives of two of these philosophical schools, Epicureans and Stoics, in the marketplace in Athens and entered into debate with them. The Epicurean School, founded by Epicurus (341-270 BCE), regarded the ideal life as one lived in never-ending, undisturbed happiness — free from anxiety, desire, and pain: "We say that pleasure is the beginning and end of living happily" (*Men.* 128). Not surprisingly, although gods exist according to Epicureanism, they are busily living the ideal life of pleasure and take no regard for the world in general or human life in particular. Stoicism, founded by Zeno (335-263 BCE), placed a premium on living in accordance with human nature — that is, in accordance with human reason. This emphasis on rationality, in which both reason and nature were givens, countered any concern with social status and distinctions. This is because the exercise of reason by rational thinkers should lead to convergence in the truth. Happiness for the Stoic is not a matter of affective response but a product of virtue — virtue being understood as the craft of putting things to their correct (i.e., "natural") use.

verts. The story that remains possesses few surprises, then, for the ways of God have been so clearly manifest; what is lacking revolves rather around the question of the shape the mission and Christian community will take as the good news spreads more and more widely.

The final thirteen chapters of Acts center above all on one strand of the developing mission, whose main character is Paul. In Acts 15:36–20:38 he is the pivotal spokesperson for the mission as this is portrayed by Luke. As before, Paul's pattern is to bring the good news first within Jewish contexts, especially synagogues when he can find them. The story Luke recounts, however, is the story of ongoing hostility to the gospel among Jewish leaders and institutions. In one particularly telling account, at Corinth, it is only after departing a hostile synagogue that Paul is able to experience success in his mission among Jews (18:1-8).

This does not mean that Gentiles are necessarily any more receptive to Paul's message. Acts 17 narrates Paul's encounter with Epicureans and Stoics, together with other philosophically minded folk, in Athens. These people completely mis-

The remains of the theater at Miletus, where Paul spoke to the elders of the Ephesian church according to Acts 20

construe his message, assuming at first that he is proclaiming two new gods, "Jesus" and "Resurrection." Allowed to speak in a more formal setting, Paul denounces the idolatry of the city, urging its inhabitants to take advantage of God's gracious provision for their ignorance by turning to him now. Again, though, they fixate on their differences of viewpoint. Hearing in Paul's talk of the resurrection of the dead the idea of the resuscitation of a dead corpse, they dismiss him and his thinking as barbaric.

But in Paul's speeches, as in the book of Acts as a whole, the resurrection cannot be put aside so easily. Luke understands the resurrection and ascension of Jesus as two events that point to the same theological reality — namely, Jesus' vindication by God, Jesus' exalted status as God's co-regent whereby he is able to dispense the gracious benefaction of God. Without the resurrection, there is no Christian message in Acts, and, in these latter chapters, Paul becomes the chief proclaimer and defender of the resurrection as he testifies to its reality and significance.

Throughout this section, wherever he goes, Paul demonstrates in his mission an essential coherence with the portfolio Jesus has given his followers: "You will be my witnesses . . . to the end of the earth" (Acts 1:8). Measured against the canons provided by the risen Lord himself, Paul appears as the consummately faithful witness. Indeed, in his farewell address to the elders among the Ephesian believers, Paul defends his own character and the character of his gospel: he has proclaimed the whole purpose of God, calling on Jew and Gentile alike to respond with faith and repentance, he has been faithful with regard to money (in Acts, a sign of faithfulness of the heart), and he has identified with Jesus in his suffering and single-minded devotion to the divine will (20:17-35).

9.3.5. Paul Imprisoned and on Trial (21:1–28:31)

If Acts 16–20 relate the story of Paul the witness, the final eight chapters tell the story of Paul the accused. Before Jewish and Roman bodies alike, Paul is repeatedly required to speak in his own defense and in defense of the message and movement he has come to represent. What becomes significant in this unfolding narrative is the continuity between Paul the witness and Paul the accused. He uses forensic settings to tell the story of his own encounter with the risen Lord, to argue that the Way he follows is nothing less or more than faithful Judaism, and to insist on the pivotal importance of the resurrection of Jesus.

In these and other ways, Luke maintains his emphasis on the fundamental Jewishness of the Christian movement. Paul participates fully in Jewish rituals, he grounds his message in Israel's Scriptures, and he addresses Jewish audiences as an insider to Judaism.

As the tale of Paul the accused develops, what also becomes clear is Rome's lack of integrity with regard to its prisoner. Roman officials do not use the scales of justice evenly, but seek to win influence with their Jewish audiences by doing them favors. Festus inexplicably tries to have Paul's hearing transferred from the provincial headquarters in Caesarea to the hotbed of anti-Pauline sentiment in Jerusalem. Repeatedly, Roman officials remark about Paul's innocence, yet continue to keep him chained in order to send him to Rome. These and other narrative details like them speak strongly against any notion that Luke is writing his narrative in order to foster good relations between the church and Rome. Instead, Luke shows through Paul's exemplary behavior how Christians ought to face accusations and imprisonment. In the face of opposition, Jewish and Roman, Paul maintains a consistent and faithful witness.

Of course, Luke also takes pains in these final chapters to demonstrate that, however alone Paul may seem, he has hardly fallen from the horizon of God's care. Paul himself is continually aware of the divine necessity that moves events forward toward Rome. And the exciting tale of the attempted winter voyage across the Mediterranean in Acts 27 is interwoven with signs of escalating danger and cause for fear, but also with myriad evidences of God's presence and promises of rescue.

Indeed, the closing lines of Acts have Paul continuing to speak of Jesus and the kingdom with boldness and without hindrance to all who will come, both Gentile and Jew.

Many students of Acts have come to the end of Luke's narrative with surprise and dissatisfaction. Where is any sense of narrative closure? Luke's point may well be that his narrative may have reached its finale, but the story to which he has given witness must continue. Not every event prophesied within the narrative has come to fruition, most notably the complete restoration of God's people and the return of Jesus, promised at his ascension. This is no surprise for Luke, however, who has already indicated, in the opening chapter of Acts, that the present is not to be given over to speculation about God's timing but rather to Spirit-empowered witness to "the end of the earth." It is to such faithfulness that Luke calls believers.

9.4. THE SPEECHES IN ACTS

Among the narrative elements that abound in Acts, the speeches in Acts are especially conspicuous. Many of these are "missionary speeches," delivered to both Jewish and Gentile audiences. These would include such important sermons as those delivered by Peter at Pentecost (2:14-40) and by Paul at Pisidian Antioch (13:16-41) — speeches that play programmatic roles in their narrative contexts. The study of Acts in the past century has been occupied in part with these missionary sermons and especially with the question of how accurately Luke has reproduced early Christian missionary discourse. Other speeches also have important roles in the narrative. These include Stephen's "defense" speech to the Jerusalem council (7:2-53), Paul's farewell address to the Ephesian elders (20:18-35), Paul's forensic addresses before Roman officials (e.g., 24:10-21; 26:2-23), addresses by Peter and James at the Jerusalem Council (15:7-11, 13-21), and so on. Of approximately 1,000 verses in Acts, some 365 are found in major and minor speeches and dialogues in Acts, with direct address responsible for more than half of the book.

9.4.1. The Debate over Sources and Tradition

According to the primary strand of thought about the speeches in Acts in the twentieth century, the chief question to ask of Luke is not how accurately he has transcribed a particular speech but concerning the speech's purpose in the hands of the historiographer. A speech might impart to the reader: (1) insight into the total situation of the narrative, (2) interpretive insight into the historical moment, (3) insight into the character of a speaker, and/or (4) insight into general ideas that might explain a situation. Additionally, a speech might (5) advance the action of the account. With few exceptions, it has usually and simply been assumed that the speeches of Acts were Lukan compositions through and through.

This near-consensus has been based on observations concerning consistency of language and style from speech to speech and between narrative and speech material. In addition, consistency of content from speech to speech, as though they were written from the same outline, has been noticed. But "Lukan artistry" and "Lukan invention" are not the same thing, and today it is increasingly recognized that the question of the historicity of the speech material in Acts has been saddled with an unnecessary dichotomy. The principal question relevant to speeches and speech-making in ancient historiography is not accuracy in its representation of this or that speech. This produces a false either-or choice or a continuum concerned primarily with faithfulness to an alleged source. Instead, ancient writers sought to achieve a twofold balance between artistic and historical appropriateness. They include speeches in their narrative representations of history not to provide a transcript of what was spoken on a given occasion but to document the speech event itself. Historiographers (like Luke) were concerned, therefore, with composing speeches that cohered with their work as a whole in terms of language, style, and content (the literary dimension) and that would not be regarded as anachronistic or out of character with what was known of the person to whom the speech was attributed (the sociohistorical dimension). In other words, literary

On Writing Speeches

For many, Thucydides (*ca.* 460/455–*ca.* 400 BCE) is exemplary among ancient historians. In the lengthy introduction to his *History of the Peloponnesian War* he self-consciously reflects on the inclusion of speeches in his historical writing:

> As regards the various speeches in this book, whether they were made before or during the war, it has been difficult to remember with absolute precision the things that were spoken — both for me concerning what I myself heard and for others who reported them to me. Hence, the different speakers speak as it seems to me they would most probably have spoken (if they had been heard) given the circumstances, while at the same time I have adhered as closely as possible to the general sense of the things actually spoken. (1.22.1)

aspirations do not preclude historical interests, and the presence of Lukan style and theology in the speeches of Acts does not necessarily lead to the inference that these speeches are Lukan in origin. With respect to historical appropriateness, the issue is not narrowly defined in terms of accuracy; instead, the writer would compose a speech in keeping with what could be known of the traditional data available to him.

9.4.2. The Role of the Speeches

What role do the speeches play in Acts? Their significance can be outlined along a number of related lines.

9.4.2.1. A Unified Worldview

The careful reader can discern a pattern in the missionary speeches. For example:

- appeal for hearing, including a connection between the situation and the speech,
- christological message supported with scriptural proof,
- offer of salvation, and (often)
- interruption of the sermon by the audience or by the narrator himself.

Taken as a whole, the speeches in Acts by followers of Jesus evidence a message that is overwhelmingly centered on Christ, but one that also features a medley of recurring motifs, including the centrality of Jesus' exaltation (i.e., his resurrection and/or ascension), together with its salvific effect; repentance and/or forgiveness of sins; the universal offer of salvation; the Holy Spirit; and, frequently through scriptural interpretation, the assurance that the message of this salvation is the manifestation of the divine will. These instances of repetition within the narrative of Acts demonstrate Luke's concern to advance through these speeches a distinct (though not at all points distinctive) view of God's purpose. This perspective is then propagated by each of the major figures who serve as witnesses to redemption in Acts.

9.4.2.2. Performative Utterances

Not all the speeches serve only as "commentary" on the events unfolding in the narrative. As deliberate pauses in the action, they do possess an interpretive function, but they also often have performative roles. That is, they advance the action of the narrative as they provide the logic and impetus for further developments in the realization of the narrative aim of Luke-Acts. The speeches of Stephen and Peter in 7:2-53 and 10:34-43 (and 11:5-17), for example, appear at crucial junctures, pushing the narrative beyond Jerusalem and Judea to Samaria and "the end of the earth" (1:8).

9.4.2.3. Revealed History

Paul's sermon at Pisidian Antioch (Acts 13:16-41) exemplifies a common concern of the speeches to locate historical events in an interpretive web by splicing together in one narrative thread the past, present, and future of God's salvific activity. According to this perspective, the meaning of historical data is not self-evident but must be interpreted, and legitimate interpretation is a product of divine revelation. We cannot expect to know the meaning of historical events or chains of events without their having been collated with the divine purpose. "Meaning" is available with reference to the Scriptures, especially as they witness to the one redemptive purpose of God, which has found its fullest expression in the coming of Jesus. Paul's speech at Pisidian Antioch thus moves deliberately and naturally from divine activity in the OT to the work of John and Jesus and then to the need for present response, thus providing christological interpretations of the Scriptures and of history.

9.4.2.4. Acts as Witness

The sheer quantity of the book of Acts given over to speeches when compared with other examples of ancient historiography, along with the fact that in Acts speeches are typically given by Jesus' witnesses or for or against the witness, suggests another narrative role for the speeches: Luke himself is giving witness, relating "all that God had done with them" (Acts 14:27). Acts thus uses speeches in the spread of God's word.

9.5. THE PURPOSE OF ACTS

Numerous proposals for the purpose of Acts have been defended in recent study, including the following: (1) Acts is a defense of the Christian church to Rome or (2) of Rome to the Christian church or (3) of Paul against those who have sided against Paul's notion that Christianity is the true successor to Judaism; (4) Acts is a work of edification designed to provide an eschatological corrective for a church in crisis; (5) it was written to reassure believers struggling with the reliability of the Christian message — with regard to either its truth and relevance or its firm foundation in the story of God's people; (6) Acts was intended to assist the Christian movement in its attempts to legitimate itself over against Judaism; and (7) Acts was written to encourage among Christians a fundamental allegiance to Jesus calling for a basic social and political stance within the empire.

Because of the narrative unity of Luke-Acts, some of these can be excluded from the outset — namely, those centering on aims particular to Acts or Paul (options 1-3) — since these do not account for the whole of the Lukan narrative. But this does not mean that we should immediately deny that Luke may have had concerns such as these. The Evangelist may have been motivated by multiple aims that might not concern Luke-Acts as a whole. At the same time, as we recognize more and more both the ways in which Luke has portrayed the lordship of Jesus over against that of the Roman emperor and the ways in which the empire has positioned itself against the Christian movement in the latter half of Acts, it becomes increasingly difficult to believe that Luke's primary concern was to encourage from either direction good relations between church and Rome.

We have already seen that the genre of Acts suggests Luke's concern with legitimization and apologetic, and our discussion of the aim of Luke-Acts highlighted the centrality of God's purpose to bring salvation to all (see chapter 6 above). In the conflicted Mediterranean world of the first century, not least the larger Jewish world, it is not difficult to imagine how this understanding of God's purpose and its embodiment in the Christian movement would have been the source of controversy and uncertainty. How could the Christian message, with its emphases on the exaltation of a crucified man and on the inclusion of Gentiles within the historic people of God, attract such heightened opposition from Jewish leadership *and* be a faithful accounting of God's work in the world? Against this backdrop, the purpose of (Luke-)Acts becomes more clear: to strengthen the Christian movement in the face of opposition by (1) confirming Christians in their interpretation and experience of the redemptive purpose of God and by (2) calling them to continued faithfulness and witness in God's salvific project. The purpose of Luke-Acts, then, is primarily ecclesiological, focused on the invitation to participate faithfully as God's people in God's redemptive purpose.

Crucial to this construal of Luke's agenda is his treatment of Judaism. Acts as a whole insists on the continuity between Judaism and Christianity, but it does so in a peculiar way. On the one hand, the use of Scripture, the general portrayal of the Jewish ethos of the Christian movement, and the unrelenting picture of Jesus' followers as persons who saw themselves as kin to the Jewish people all suggest the important degree to which Acts narrates the continuity of the Christian community with the ancient people of God. On the other, it is everywhere evident that Luke is interested in an "interpreted Judaism." That is, Judaism — its institutions, its practices, and so on — are to be embraced fully only when understood faithfully with respect to God's redemptive purpose. But in order to be understood thus, Israel's religion must cohere with the purpose of God as this is articulated by

The Text of Acts

For serious study of the Greek text, Acts presents a special quandary because of the existence of two primary textual types, the Alexandrian and the Western (the latter especially represented by Codex Bezae Cantabrigiensis). The book of Acts in the Western tradition is almost ten percent longer than the Alexandrian, and the character of each of these two textual types is quite distinctive. The essential question is, Whence the Western text? Does the Western text bear witness to an ongoing process of emendation? Can the Western text be traced back to the hand of the Evangelist himself? Or does it display a mixture of more or less original and secondary readings that must be considered on a case-by-case basis?

As early as the late seventeenth century it was suggested that Luke was responsible for two versions of Acts and that this explains the existence of the two major text types. This view has gained new momentum since the onset of redaction criticism in the twentieth century, when it was found that the Western text sometimes displayed Lukan style and theological preferences. In spite of theories of this nature, most scholars contend that the witnesses of the so-called Western tradition do not contain something approximating the original text of Acts and deny that with the Western tradition we have access to a revision, primary or secondary, from the hand of Luke the Evangelist. Most assume that, while the Western text has no claim to originality, it may contain superior readings at some points.

Although today there remains little certainty on the nature of the original text of Acts, then, it remains true that most study of Acts continues to proceed on the basis of the relative superiority of the Alexandrian text type. In some cases, the Western text type is altogether neglected, on the supposition that it represents a deliberate and sustained revision of the book of Acts; in others Western-type readings are considered on a case-by-case basis.

God's own authorized spokespersons. Who speaks for God? First and foremost, God's interpretive agent is his Son, Jesus of Nazareth. In Acts, this role is fulfilled by "witnesses," empowered by the Holy Spirit to continue the witness of Jesus. Luke's presentation suggests, then, the nature of a fundamental struggle between followers of "the Way" and other forms of Judaism. This is a struggle that goes to the very heart of Jewish faith, embracing sometimes competing understandings of

Israel's God and of the meaning of the Scriptures of Israel. It is a struggle of interpretation that is so important and so basic to the identity of God's people that Jesus' followers should not be surprised when they find themselves confronted with opposition. Instead, hostility should be viewed as the arena in which they might renew their fundamental allegiance toward the plan of God manifest in Jesus as they stand firm in their witness among Jews and Gentiles alike.

9.6. THE AUTHORSHIP OF ACTS

As with the NT Gospels, the author of the book of Acts is anonymous. It is generally assumed that the Gospel of Luke and Acts were written by the same person (compare, e.g., Luke 1:1-4 and Acts 1:1-2), and early traditions identify this person as Luke. The oldest Greek manuscript of the Gospel, Papyrus Bodmer XIV, dating from about 200 CE, uses the title "Gospel according to Luke." The Muratorian Canon, from the late second century, also identifies Luke, a physician and companion of Paul, as the Gospel's author — an identification also found in the second-century writings of Irenaeus (*Adv. Haer.* 3.1.1; 3.14.1) and in later writings (e.g., Eusebius, *Hist. Eccl.* 3.4.1-7; 3.24.14-15; 5.8.3; 6.25.6). Until recently, the view that Luke-Acts was authored by a companion of Paul drew additional support from the so-called we-passages in Acts (16:10-17; 20:5–21:18; chs. 27–28). Some now regard these passages as literary creations. At the very least, the author's self-conscious inclusion of himself in the narrative in the latter half of Acts raises the question of authorship for Acts in a way that is not so important for the Gospel of Luke.

Interestingly, however, the "we-passages" do nothing to alter the initial anonymity of the author of Acts. Even when involved in first-person narration, the narrator of Acts identifies himself not as an individual with a name, but as one of a group. He may at times be present as a participant-observer, but his focus is not on his individual identity. Rather, the "we" of his narration contributes to the vividness of his account and invites his audience to read themselves into the narrative. That first-person narration comes in only selected portions of the account underscores that the narrator makes no claim to being a constant companion of Paul and his circle. This speaks against the tradition that Luke and Paul were "inseparable" (Irenaeus, *Adv. Haer.* 3.1.1, 4), but also against those who deny that Luke could have written Acts because the author of Acts could not have been a regular companion of Paul. It also suggests that first-person narration is more than a literary device calculated to enliven the narrative.

The name "Luke" appears three times in the NT — Col 4:14; Phlm 24; and 2 Tim 4:11 — all evidently with reference to the same person, a companion of Paul. This Luke is traditionally identified as the author of the Gospel of Luke and the Acts of the Apostles. The reference in 2 Timothy has little to offer about Luke himself beyond highlighting his faithfulness in comparison with others who are said to have deserted Paul. In Philemon, Luke is identified as a "fellow worker," a term that designates not simply one of Paul's "traveling companions" or "assistants" but a person of comparable stature to Paul himself, a "missionary colleague." Colossians refers to Luke as "beloved physician." This suggests that his knowledge and skills as a healer had won him respect, placing him in the company of those physicians, known in the Hellenistic and Roman periods, who enjoyed high status as students of medicine and philosophy. Because Col 4:10-11 refers to Aristarchus, Mark, and Justus as the only Jews present among Paul's coworkers, it emerges that Luke is a Gentile or at least a non-Jewish Semite. Some who see evidence in Luke-Acts of an author with a notable Jewish background debate this last point. The scriptural intimacy and Jewish interests manifest in Luke-Acts do not require a hypothesis of Jewish authorship, however, but are equally compatible with significant exposure to Judaism by a non-Jew.

Little reason remains, then, not to accept the traditional identification of Luke as the author of Luke-Acts. This would make Luke the most prolific writer in the NT, with some 28% of the NT attributed to him. If Lukan authorship of these NT books is accepted, additional information becomes available from their language and style — for example, that Luke was educated, probably urban, with firsthand exposure to rhetorical training and to Israel's Scriptures, that he wrote from the social location of those who traffic in technical or professional writing, and that he was one of the "people of the Way," a "Christian," either second- or third-generation (see Luke 1:1-4).

FOR FURTHER READING

C. K. Barrett, *The Acts of the Apostles,* 2 vols. (International Critical Commentary; Edinburgh: Clark, 1994/98)

Joseph A. Fitzmyer, *The Acts of the Apostles* (Anchor Bible 31; Garden City: Doubleday, 1998)

Luke Timothy Johnson, *The Acts of the Apostles* (Sacra Pagina 5; Collegeville: Liturgical, 1992)

I. Howard Marshall, and David Peterson, eds., *Witness to the Gospel: The Theology of Acts* (Grand Rapids: Eerdmans, 1998)

Bruce W. Winter, ed., *The Book of Acts in Its First Century Setting,* 5 vols. (Grand Rapids: Eerdmans, 1993-96)

10. *Letters in the New Testament*

Of the twenty-seven books in the New Testament, fully twenty-one appear in letter form, and two additional letters are found embedded within a narrative work (Acts 15:23-29 and 23:26-30). Since the Scriptures of the early church, the OT, contain no letters at all, such a large number of letters would be unusual were it not for the fact that the letter was a very common form of communication in the first-century Mediterranean world. The letters that have been preserved from that time deal with every phase of life — homes, schools, public markets, places of business, religious assemblies, philosophical debates, political forums, and the theater. So pervasive were letters that essays cast in letter form were used for the instruction of students and for other educational or literary purposes, and a favorite form of education was to have students write fictitious letters in the style of some famous orator or intellectual. Letters were therefore indispensable for domestic, cultural, and social life. So it is not at all surprising that the early church's missionaries and congregations, needing to remain in contact with one another, would turn to the letter to do that.

10.1. WRITING MATERIALS AND DELIVERY OF LETTERS

Some of the earliest letters that have been preserved were written on clay tablets with characters formed by pressing the sharp end of a stylus into the clay (cuneiform). Less bulky materials were also used for letters. Some, for example, were written on potsherds, usually on the concave side of pieces of jars (ostraca). Also used were flakes of limestone, pieces of wood, or pieces of parchment, vellum, or coarser leather. Sometimes letters were written on tablets of wood coated with wax, which could then be smoothed over and used again.

A rolled and
sealed papyrus
letter *(State
Museums of
Berlin, Papyrus
Collection)*

By far the most common material for letters, however, was papyrus, used as
early as 3000 BCE. Papyrus (from which our word "paper" is derived) was made
from a reed of the same name that grew abundantly in Egypt, where the "paper"
was manufactured and exported to the whole Mediterranean world. There it
found uses as widespread as our modern uses of paper, from writing material for
philosophical treatises or orders from the king to notes from students to their parents asking for money, or even for wrapping fish.

Papyrus was made by taking the pithy interior of the reed, slicing it longitudi-
nally, laying overlapping strips side by side horizontally ("recto") with another
layer laid vertically ("verso"), and then hammering or pressing it together. A kind
of glue, frequently the muddy water of the Nile, was often applied to make the
reeds stick together. When the finished papyrus was dry, it was polished to make

On the Manufacture of Papyrus

Pliny the Elder was a prominent Roman statesman of the first century, perhaps best known for his multi-volume *Natural History,* which summarized all
contemporary knowledge on nature. The following paragraph describes
how the papyrus reed was used to make paper for writing (Pliny, *Natural History* 13.23.74).

The process of making paper from papyrus is to split it with a needle
into very thin strips made as broad as possible, the best quality being
in the center of the plant, and so on in the order of its splitting up.
The first quality used to be called "hieratic paper" and was in early
times devoted solely to books connected with religion, but in a spirit
of flattery it was given the name of Augustus, just as the second best
was called "Livia paper" after his consort, and thus the name
"hieratic" came down to the third class.

On "Taking a Letter"

Letter writing in Roman antiquity often involved the employment of a secretary (sometimes known as a scribe or amanuensis). The business of correspondence called for other roles as well, including the copyist, the letter carrier, and the one who would read the letter aloud to the addressee(s). In a given instance, the secretary might function in one or more of these additional roles, or in none of them.

In the actual production of letters, the role of secretaries, and thus their potential contribution to the final product, varied widely. In some cases, the secretary essentially controlled some or all of the content of a letter. Accordingly, the secretary, whether named in the correspondence or not, functioned in roles that we might call coauthor or composer. Though the "author" took primary responsibility for the letter, the secretary spoke in the author's voice and represented him or her to the addressee(s) with little or no substantive input from the author. In other cases, the secretary performed at the bidding of the author — serving more as a recorder or perhaps as an editor. As recorders, secretaries might work from their own notes taken from a hearing with the author, they might work with an almost word-for-word dictation, or they might work from the author's own notes or explicit instructions.

the surface smooth. There were a variety of grades of papyrus, depending on size (widths from 15 to 32 cm.), whiteness, and smoothness. Normally twenty sheets of papyrus would be glued into a roll, from which pieces of desired length would then be cut. Writing was done with reed pens, pointed and split like quill pens of a much later time. Ink was kept in a dried cake and was dissolved for writing by being touched with the moistened pen. The best side on which to write was the recto, though if the letter were long enough it could be continued on the verso.

So important was papyrus for the smooth functioning of the Roman world that its sale appears to have been a state monopoly. The Roman author Pliny notes that shortages during the reign of Tiberius upset normal life to the extent that Roman senators were appointed as umpires to supervise the distribution of papyrus (*Natural History* 13.18.89). Because the better grades of papyrus were expensive, sheets of such papyrus were sometimes erased and reused; such a reused piece of papyrus is called a "palimpsest."

For the most part, letters were dictated to a scribe, often a professional who was hired for that purpose. A scribe would be secured if the person wanting to send a letter was illiterate or simply did not want to take the time to write in his or her own hand. Sometimes the scribe would use a wooden tablet coated with wax to take the dictation, then transcribe the letter to a sheet of papyrus. There is evidence that a kind of Latin shorthand was in use by the first century, and there may have been a kind of Greek shorthand as well. The complete letter was then folded in such a way that space was left for the name and place of the person to whom it was addressed. The letter was then tied with string and sealed, often with a mud seal; envelopes were not used.

Delivery of personal letters in NT times was a rather difficult procedure, since postal service for private individuals did not exist as we know it. The first postal service was created by the Persians sometime around the fifth century BCE, with an elaborate network of roads and relay stations for fresh horses. Classical Greece had no comparable service, but one was established in the eastern part of the Mediterranean world by Alexander the Great and his successors. The best system in antiquity was the Roman *cursus publicus,* reserved for military dispatches and official correspondence. It too had an elaborate system of relay stations placed (in Latin, "placed" is *positum,* from which our word "post" is derived) at appropriate intervals. While wealthy individuals and commercial enterprises could hire messengers to carry communications, there was no such service available to the ordinary person. He or she would have to entrust a letter to a friend for delivery, as evidently Paul did when he entrusted to Phoebe the letter he wrote to the Christians in Rome (Rom 16:1-2). Lacking that, one would have to find a traveler going to the destination of the letter to carry it along, obviously not an entirely reliable system.

Because of the fragile nature of papyrus, most of the papyrus letters that have survived to today were written or delivered in Egypt, where the papyrus was preserved from destruction by the dry climate. Indeed, almost all the papyrus letters that we have come from the drier area south of Alexandria and the Nile delta. The earliest period from which a large number of letters have been preserved was the time of Ptolemy II Philadelphos (282-246 BCE). Most such letters are found in Egyptian cemeteries, either buried with the person there entombed, left there to communicate with the dead, discarded there, or put in tombs for safekeeping. Others have even been found used for stuffing the inside of mummified crocodiles.

10.2. DEVELOPMENT AND PURPOSE OF LETTERS

The Greek word meaning "letter" *(epistolē)* derives from a verb meaning "give an oral order," indicating that letters originally served military or diplomatic purposes. It was not long, however, before letters became much more widely used for communication among family members or friends. In fact most of the letters that have been preserved from antiquity deal with matters of household and friendship. Because of the highly stratified society in the Greco-Roman world, many letters deal with client-patron relationships (see chapter 2 above, section 2.3.3), often as a client's means of asking for particular favors from a patron.

Because a letter frequently dealt with matters that, but for distance, would have been conducted face to face, letters were regarded as a substitute for the presence of the person writing and hence as a less satisfactory means of communication. A letter for that reason would often mention a future meeting at which a more satisfactory conversation could be conducted. As a result, ancient stylists compared the letter to half of a spoken conversation and hence argued that the letter should be conversational in tone. A letter was thus not to be overly long or oratorical in tone and was not to contain the technical language of a treatise. Rather, it should, as part of a conversation, communicate the writer's personality and reflect his or her moods (cf. Gal 4:20).

10.3. ARAMAIC LETTERS

Because they were written within a highly stratified society, ancient letters, and even their forms, reflect the relative social status of the writer in relation to the receiver. That is true of Aramaic letters from as early as the fifth or sixth centuries BCE, where forms still evident in letters written centuries later and in other languages are used. So, for example, letters written from an inferior to a superior had one form, while those from superior to inferior had another, and those written between equals yet another. This led to highly stereotyped forms, which allow us even today to determine the relative social positions of the sender and receiver of ancient letters. The order of names at the beginning of a letter was one such indication of social position. When inferiors wrote to superiors, the receiver was named first, then the senders, followed by greetings and invocations to the gods on the addressee's behalf. When a superior addressed an inferior or one wrote to a social equal, the sender was named first, then the receiver; sometimes the invoked divine blessing would also be omitted. Thus, when one wrote to a social superior, the form would be "To A from B, everyday we call on the gods to give you life, prosperity, and health." To an equal or inferior, it would be "A to B, greetings, may the gods bless you richly."

So an Aramaic ostracon from the sixth century BCE begins: "To my lord Mikayah from your servant Gaddul; may you live long and well! I bless you by YHH and Khnum [names of gods]," or, again, an Aramaic papyrus of the same period from Elephantine begins: "To [name illegible] from [name illegible]; may the God of heaven bless my lords richly at all times, and may the God of heaven be merciful to you." Here the addressee is the social superior of the writer. In another sixth-century Elephantine papyrus, the opening reads: "It is . . . the scribe Nakht who addresses the scribe Aau . . . . May Arsaphes [a god] help you and Ptah [another god] . . . gladden you with life. . . ." In this case writer and receiver are social equals. Again, a letter from a Persian official from the fifth century begins: "From Aratahaya to Nakhthor, I send you greetings and best wishes for your good health. . . ." Here the writer is the superior of the receiver. That is also the case with the letter quoted in Daniel 4, where the king's name is given first, then the receivers; the invoked divine blessing is also omitted. Finally, in a letter written between equals, an early form reads: "It is the scribe Meh who greets the scribe Yey Junior: In life, prosperity and health and in the favor of Amon-Re, king of the gods. . . ." Here the opening form: "A to B, greetings" with a following blessing shows writer and receiver to be social equals.

10.4. HELLENISTIC LETTERS

Such stereotypical conventions of letter writings persisted, with some variations, right down to the Greco-Roman period, within which the NT letters were written, much as our conventional "Dear (Name)" and "Sincerely yours" as opening and closing have persisted from earlier times even when the one addressed is not particularly dear to the writer and the writer may be anything but sincere in intention in writing the letter. The Hellenistic letter consisted of three basic parts: letter opening, letter body, and letter closing.

- The opening included identification of sender and receiver, a greeting, and sometimes a health wish and/or a prayer on behalf of the reader.
- The letter body consisted of
  - a body-opening usually giving the intention of the letter and providing a transition to the body-middle,
  - a body-middle where the intention was spelled out, and
  - a body-closing, which usually contained three elements:
    - why the letter was written,
    - how the readers should respond to it and
    - a proposal of further contact by visit or another letter.
- The letter closing included some kind of wish for prosperity for the recipient, and occasionally greetings from third parties.

Not only were the forms stereotyped, but even the language used followed regular patterns.

Because Hellenistic society was as rigidly hierarchical as the Persian and

Egyptian societies of earlier times, the letter opening, as in the Aramaic letters, indicated the social superior by naming that person first. Thus, all petitions to the king and queen of Egypt in the Ptolemaic period (third century BCE onward), and sometimes to other high officials, had the form: "To B (name in dative case) greetings (Greek *chairein*) A (name in nominative case)" meaning "it is to B that A sends greetings." Jewish authors followed the same format, as is indicated by 2 Maccabees, which opens in the form of a letter. It begins with the addressees named first, but then contains two greetings (1:1), one the usual Greek *chairein*, the second the more Jewish wish for peace (Greek *eirēnē*, Hebrew *shalom*). There then follows a thanksgiving (1:11). The body of the letter was usually introduced by the petition itself, or, if addressed to an equal or an inferior, by some such phrase as "I want you to know," "Do not think that," or "I appeal to you." The content was determined by the subject matter of the letter. The closing included the Greek word *eutychei* (sometimes *dieutychei*), meaning something like "good fortune," and used in the sense of "farewell." When the writer was of inferior status, as were the writers of letters of petition to the royal house, no familiar traits such as opening or concluding health wish, prayer of supplication on the recipient's behalf, or greetings from third parties were included.

In more familiar letters, the opening formula was "A (name in nominative case) to B (name in dative case) greetings *(chairein)*" followed by a wish, sometimes in the form of a prayer to the god(s) for the health and prosperity of the recipient. Often attached to this was an assurance of the well-being of the sender. So a letter from the third century BCE begins "Dromon to Zenon greeting. I give thanks to all the gods if you yourself enjoy good health. . . . I myself am also well. . . ." Another from the first century BCE begins "Isadora to her brother Askias greeting and may you at all times enjoy good health, just as I pray. . . ."

The letter closing in familiar letters regularly contained the Greek word *errōso* ("be strong" in the sense of "farewell"), and, if greetings from third parties were conveyed, such greetings were expressed with some form of the Greek verb *aspazesthai* ("greet"), in the imperative if greetings were conveyed to someone ("Give greetings to A"), in the active if the greeting were being delivered by someone ("B greets A").

Depending on the situation, any of the elements could be expanded: the sender could say more by way of self-identification or about his or her situation, and the recipient could be further identified or his or her situation described further. The health wish and/or prayer could also be expanded to conform to the particular circumstances of the receiver. As we shall see below, such expansion is often found in the NT letters, particularly those written by Paul.

10.5. LETTERS IN THE NEW TESTAMENT

The letters contained in the NT do not resemble the common papyri from the lowest levels of Hellenistic culture, nor do they display the marks of those authors who had received formal rhetorical training. Rather, they fall somewhere between those two extremes, and show some additional influence of the Jewish subculture of the period. There was a time when NT scholars classified Hellenistic letters as either letters or epistles, with "letter" designating personal correspondence written in the style of common speech and "epistle" designating more formal correspondence written in a more high-flown literary style. New Testament letters were then put in the former category, as reflecting the more common speech of less educated people. Further analysis has proved that such a differentiation is too broad to account for the many different kinds of correspondence of the period. Current analysis looks at letters in terms of the social status of the writer and receiver and whether the content is of an official or a more familiar nature. In form, NT letters resemble more the familiar than the official letter, although they are longer than most contemporary letters of that type and period, showing the instructional intention of the authors.

A few of the letters in the NT do reflect the form of the typical Hellenistic letter, most specifically the letter between Roman officials embedded in Acts 15:23-29, where both opening and closing forms reflect normal conventions. A second letter in Acts (23:26-30) has a typical Hellenistic opening, but the closing is omitted. The same is true of James, 2 Peter, and Jude. Hebrews, by contrast, has a full epistolary ending but lacks an epistolary opening, and is closest in form in the NT to a treatise produced, partially at least, in the form of an epistle. 1 John, usually included among the "letters" in the NT, has what could be considered a letter-body but neither opening nor closing and so lacks two of the three typical components of the Hellenistic letter.

While the majority of the letters in the NT identify only one sender (Acts 23:26; Rom 1:1; Eph 1:1; 1 Tim 1:1; 2 Tim 1:1; Tit 1:1; Jas 1:1; 1 Pet 1:1; 2 Pet 1:1; 2 John 1; 3 John 1; Jude 1), which is typical of Hellenistic letters, others identify multiple senders (Acts 15:23; 1 Cor 1:1; 2 Cor 1:1; Gal 1:1-2; Phil 1:1; Col 1:1; 1 Thess 1:1; 2 Thess 1:1; Phlm 1), perhaps to identify the content as representing a broader Christian tradition rather than the views of one person. In contrast, only a few letters identify only one person as recipient (Acts 23:26; 1 Tim 1:2; 2 Tim 1:2; Tit 1:1; 3 John 1), while the majority indicate multiple recipients (Acts 15:23; Rom 1:7; 1 Cor 1:2; 2 Cor 1:1; Gal 1:2; Eph 1:1; Phil 1:1; Col 1:2; 1 Thess 1:1; 2 Thess 1:1; Phlm 1-2; Jas 1:1; 1 Pet 1:1-2; 2 Pet 2:2; Jude 1), frequently the members of the Christian community located in the place to which the letter was sent. Typical for NT letters is the expanded form both of the identification of the sender (Rom 1:1-6; 1 Cor 1:1; 2 Cor 1:1; Gal 1:1-2; Eph 1:1; Col 1:1; 1 Tim 1:1; 2 Tim 1:1; Tit 1:1-3;

Phlm 1:1; Jas 1:1; Jude 1:1) and of the recipients (1 Cor 1:2; Eph 1:1; 1 Thess 1:1; 2 Thess 1:1; 1 Tim 1:2; Tit 1:4; Phlm 1:1-2a; 1 Pet 1:1b-2; 2 Pet 1:1b; 2 John 1; Jude 1:1), such expansions composed with specifically Christian vocabulary, which shows the theological framework within which these letters were composed.

It is in the form of the greeting that the difference between the usual Hellenistic letter and the Christian letter begins to be even more apparent. While the normal Hellenistic greeting consists simply in the word *chairein,* the NT letters expand and change the greeting in a number of ways. While two Christian letters (Acts 15:23; Jas 1:1; Acts 23:26 represents itself as secular) do begin with the usual "greetings" (Greek *chairein*), other NT letters, in what may be a play on words, substitute the word "grace" (Greek *charis*) for the common *chairein,* thus immediately differentiating Christian from non-Christian letters. In addition to "grace," some of the letters attributed to Paul (Rom 1:7; 1 Cor 1:3; 2 Cor 1:2; Gal 1:3; Eph 1:2; Phil 1:1; Col 1:2; 1 Thess 1:1; 2 Thess 1:2) and those attributed to Peter (1 Pet 2:1; 2 Pet 1:2) add "peace" (Greek *eirēnē*), thus incorporating both Greek and Jewish greetings. Three letters, including two attributed to Paul (1 Tim 1:2; 2 Tim 1:2; 2 John 3), add a third word, "mercy" (Greek *eleos*) to "grace and peace." Jude also uses three words in the greeting (v. 2), with the characteristic Christian word "love" *(agapē)* in addition to "mercy" and "peace." In all these instances, the expansion on the usual Hellenistic greeting formula embodies typically Christian concepts and immediately shows the different kind of cultural framework within which these letters were written.

The final element of the letter-opening in the Hellenistic letter, the health-wish with its occasional accompanying prayer, is also significantly altered in NT letters. While one NT letter does have a true prayer on behalf of its recipients (3 John 2), others refer to prayer on behalf of the recipients (Rom 1:10; Phil 1:4; Col 1:3; 1 Thess 1:2; Phlm 4). Others substitute a statement of either thanksgiving (Greek *eucharistein*) to God for some characteristic of the recipients (Rom 1:8; 1 Cor 1:4; Phil 1:3; Col 1:3; 1 Thess 1:2; 2 Thess 1:3; 2 Tim 1:3; Phlm 4) or blessing (Greek *eulogētos*), expressing some divine activity related to the situation addressed in the letter (2 Cor 1:3; Eph 1:3; 1 Pet 1:3).

Although the letter-openings of NT letters are thus expanded beyond the normal extent of Hellenistic letters, the form in which the greetings are cast, with the sender named first and then the recipients ("A to B, greetings") shows that they fall in the category of familiar rather than formal letters. Formally, therefore, writer and readers are acknowledged to have the same status, reflecting socially the kind of contact typical between friends or members of the same family rather than the status of suppliants to a superior or the giver of instructions to an inferior. The equality among all Christians, formally expressed by Paul in Gal 3:28 (cf. 1 Cor 12:13; Col 3:11) is thus embodied in the very form of the letters that contain that message.

The letter-body in Hellenistic letters was normally adapted to the situation addressed, and hence Christian letters display no startling distinctiveness by showing that characteristic. The thanksgiving of some NT letters serves as a body-opening in which the intention of the letter or the content to be discussed is given, and the body-closing often refers to a future visit by the author (Rom 15:24; 1 Cor 16:5; 2 Cor 13:1; Phlm 22; 2 John 12; 3 John 13; in Phil 1:26 such a reference occurs earlier in the letter), both characteristics of the body of the Hellenistic letter.

The NT epistolary closings also show the formal characteristics of the Hellenistic letter. Greetings from third parties, also typical of familiar letters, are frequently included, with the characteristic word *aspazesthai* used for that purpose (Rom 16:2-16, 21-23; 1 Cor 16:19; 2 Cor 13:12; Phil 4:21-22; Col 4:18; 1 Thess 5:26; 2 Thess 3:17; 2 Tim 4:9-21; Tit 3:15; Phlm 23-24; Heb 13:24; 1 Pet 5:13; 2 John 13; 3 John 15). While the usual word for "farewell" (Greek *errōsthe*) in the Hellenistic letter appears in only one NT letter (Acts 15:29), two other NT letters contain specifically Christian vocabulary serving the function of the farewell (1 Cor 16:24; Gal 6:24). In most instances, however, a benediction is placed where the farewell would occur in a Hellenistic letter (Rom 16:20; 1 Cor 16:23; 2 Cor 13:13; Gal 6:18; Eph 6:23; Phil 4:23; Col 4:18; 1 Thess 5:23, 28; 2 Thess 3:18; 1 Tim 6:21; 2 Tim 4:22; Tit 3:15; Phlm 25; Heb 13:25; 1 Pet 5:14; 2 John 15; Jude 24-25), showing again the extent to which Christians modified that epistolary form to conform to their own cultural self-understanding. The epistolary closing is adapted in some NT letters in a further way when the identification of the scribe who wrote the letter (as in Rom 16:22), often present in the Hellenistic letter, has in its place words written by the author in his own hand (1 Cor 16:21; Gal 6:11-18; Col 4:18; 2 Thess 3:17), perhaps in a further gesture of familiarity with the readers. A final adaptation of the epistolary closing is the admonition to the Christian recipients to greet one another with a "holy kiss" (Rom 16:16; 1 Cor 16:20; 2 Cor 13:12; 1 Thess 5:14; 1 Pet 5:14), a further indication of the self-understanding of Christians in terms of a family, since kisses were normally bestowed only on family or close friends.

If letters constitute the largest component of the NT, letters claiming Paul as their author constitute the largest component among the letters. Some thirteen letters bear the name of Paul as sender. Although some ancient lists included Hebrews as a fourteenth Pauline letter, it does not so designate itself, and its style and content are different enough from the other letters claiming Paul as author that such inclusion of Hebrews among the Pauline letters has fallen into disuse. The importance of letters in the early Christian movement is indicated by the fact that more letters were written than have been preserved. For example, a letter Paul wrote to the Corinthian Christians (see 1 Cor 5:9-10) and one they wrote to Paul (7:1) have not been preserved, as also Paul's letter to the Laodiceans (Col 4:17). A letter written in Paul's name apparently also circulated early (2 Thess 2:2). Letters also make up the bulk of the opening chapters of the book of Revelation.

The NT letters are placed in the canon after the Gospels and Acts and demonstrate the writings of the apostles whose activities are described in Acts. The letters of Paul are placed first, perhaps because they are by far the most numerous of those accepted into the canon, perhaps because his activity dominates the second half of the narratives contained in Acts. His letters are arranged in descending order of length, with the longest, Romans, first, and the shortest, Philemon, the last.

Following Hebrews, placed where it is because of its early association with Paul but located at the very end of the Pauline collection to designate a certain discomfort with this association, the remaining letters are arranged in the order of the apostolic names listed in Gal. 2:9. Following that order, James is placed first, then the two letters attributed to Peter. The next three letters are associated with John, although they do not bear his name. The first has no epistolary opening at all, while the second and third claim authorship by "the elder," a title early associated with the apostle John. The final letter is Jude, a name included in the lists of apostles given in the Gospels, but omitted from the list in Gal 2:9. Perhaps for that reason it was placed last among the letters.

Through this collection of letters, we gain a lively insight into the minds and hearts of the early Christian communities as they struggled to be faithful to their Lord in the often hostile environment of the first-century Mediterranean word. Careful study of their content will give us a vivid impression of the problems those communities faced, and some of the ways they sought to overcome them. It is upon that study that we embark in the following pages.

FOR FURTHER READING

David E. Aune, *The New Testament in Its Literary Environment* (Library of Early Christianity; Philadelphia: Westminster, 1987), pp. 158-225

William G. Doty, *Letters in Primitive Christianity* (Guides to Biblical Scholarship; Philadelphia: Fortress, 1973)

Stanley K. Stowers, *Letter Writing in Greco-Roman Antiquity* (Library of Early Christianity; Philadelphia: Westminster, 1986)

John L. White, *Light from Ancient Letters* (Philadelphia: Fortress, 1986)

11. Paul and His World

The apostle Paul grew up in, and preached to, a world very different from ours, and it will be helpful to survey some of the aspects of that difference. Unless we are aware of those differences, we are likely to assume that Paul shared our views about the world and then become open to finding something in Paul's writing that the apostle never intended. Reading and understanding ancient documents like the NT require us to pay attention to the presuppositions underlying the writers' views lest we impose our own ideas on the text and then forfeit all chance of learning something from them we have not already known. Ancient documents present a challenge to our way of understanding reality, and the NT is no exception. For that reason, we have to know something about the way Paul's contemporaries viewed the world before we investigate what we can know about Paul's life within that world and about what he intended to say to that world in his letters.

11.1. THE WORLD

While the understanding of the world in which Paul lived was different in many ways from our understanding of the one we inhabit, we will limit ourselves to looking at three aspects that will highlight the differences between the two worlds. Those aspects are attitudes to what is new and what is old, the relationship between religion and politics, and the structure and role of the family.

11.1.1. New and Old

One of the assumptions we bring to our understanding of our world is that what is new tends to be superior to what is old. This expresses itself not only in the desire to be up on the latest fads in speech, clothing, and the like, but also in the language used by those who want to persuade us to act in a certain way, that is, in advertising. For example, phrases such as "new and improved" or "newly discovered formula" reflect our deep-seated conviction that what is new is best and that what is old tends to be outmoded. This outlook assumes that we are cleverer than our ancestors and makes the world as we know it the measure of reality.

This outlook is also often carried into historical study, where the assumption, sometimes declared, sometimes unspoken, is that if something does not or, in our view, cannot, happen now, then it can never have happened. Hence, much of what ancient writers report is considered untrue or impossible, because such things do not happen in our world as we perceive and explain it to ourselves. This makes ourselves and our understanding the measure of historical truth. The present is taken to be superior to the past and hence is used to measure truth from the past.

The world Paul inhabited looked at things quite differently. What was old was considered far superior to what was recent or new. This was based on the view that the world, like a human being, wears out with the passage of time and deteriorates from the better state it once had. So the Roman writer Seneca can say that all believe that people of the past were always superior by nature to those of succeeding generations (*Epistle* 90.44), the Stoic philosopher and orator Dio Chrysostom affirms that there is no doubt that the world, before it was worn out, produced better things (*Discourse* 31.75), and Chrysostom concludes that each succeeding age shows a steady decline and clearly represents less noble features than the preceding periods (*Discourse* 21.1). If, then, the ancients were nobler and more intelligent and closer to the gods, the source of wisdom lies in the past, not the present. The past is the measure of truth, and to prove a thing true one need only prove it was traditionally believed to be true. One thus looked to antiquity for wisdom, an antiquity that, as the orator Quintilian observed, is commended to us by the possession of a certain majesty, almost a sanctity (*Institutio oratoria* 1.6.1). One would not advertise soap in that culture as "new and improved"; one would rather say "unchanged for centuries" or "exactly the same as your great grandmother knew it." What is old is best, and what is new is inferior and looked on with suspicion. The culture had a generally pessimistic outlook, since the future can only be worse than the present. So if Christianity affirmed itself to be a "new religion" it would immediately be met with suspicion if not outright rejection.

11.1.2. Politics and Religion

One does not have to engage in serious conversation very long, particularly about one's religious or political beliefs, to hear that "religion and politics don't mix." The ACLU has devoted virtually all its resources to seeing that such a mixture does not happen in American culture, and the People for the American Way never tire of challenging anything that can look like government sanctioning of some religious belief or practice. American culture simply assumes that the best way for government to function is for it to tolerate or ignore any and all religious beliefs in the conduct of its business.

Again, such a view is almost the polar opposite of the view current in the world of Paul's time. There, one could not imagine a state without its own religion, and any religion not connected with a state or an ethnic group was looked on with great suspicion. The Romans simply assumed that every people had its own god(s) and hence its own religious practices, and Rome did nothing to interfere with the national religious practices of the peoples it conquered and included in its empire, provided the exercise of that religion did not foment rebellion against Rome and its hegemony. The Jewish historian Josephus mentions that Augustus wanted subject nations to continue their own religious customs (*Ant.* 19.5.2) and also reports that the Roman emperor Claudius wrote to Jews (in CE 45) that he wished every nation to maintain the religious practices that are traditional with it (*Ant.* 20.1.2). Romans made no effort to convert conquered peoples to "Roman religion." In fact, the Roman senate once decreed that rules governing the religious conduct of the citizens of Rome could not be applied to people beyond the boundaries of that city, and Emperor Trajan wrote to his friend Pliny (ca. 110) that no foreign city is capable of receiving the kind of consecration conferred by Roman law (Pliny, *Letters* 10.1). The one religion the Romans did suppress on occasion was Druidism, because of its practices of human sacrifice and cannibalism (Pliny, *Natural History* 30.4.13). Nor did Roman custom encourage Romans to participate in foreign religions, although by the middle of the first century CE such restrictions had been eased by Caligula and then Claudius. But even then, it was thought that participation in the rites of a religion other than one's own disgraced and transgressed the god-given dignity of ancestral religion (Plutarch, *On Superstition* 166B).

As a result, nothing in public life was undertaken without first seeking to determine whether the enterprise enjoyed divine favor. Roman priests would observe the flights of birds to see whether they turned to the right *(ad dextram)*, a sign of favor, or to the left *(ad sinistram)*, a sign of disfavor. Or they would consult the entrails of a goat to see whether the shape of the liver indicated favor or disfavor. This kind of religious involvement in public affairs even extended to military campaigns. Pliny tells us that before an enemy's city was attacked, Roman priests, using a prescribed formula, would invoke the local gods, inviting them to abandon the city and go over to the Romans, who would then give them equal or greater worship. In that way, the city would be vulnerable to attack, being stripped of divine protection. Even local celebrations, which included athletic contests, free food, jugglers, magicians, speeches, and parades, would also include sacrifice to the local deities. For the people of Paul's world, any public activity that lacked a religious dimension would have been unthinkable.

The problem that the Christian communities presented to the Romans was not that they represented an "illegal religion." That phrase does not occur in non-Christian Latin literature (nor does "legal religion"), and the Romans were ready to tolerate any religion celebrated by an ethnic group. The problem was that Christians did not constitute a single ethnic group, as did the Jews, for example, nor did they celebrate ancestral rites, presided over by a priesthood, in a temple set apart for such worship. For those reasons, they would not have looked like a religion to Roman authorities in Paul's world. As long as Christians were regarded as a Jewish sect, the Romans had no problem with Christianity, since the Jewish religion was recognizable to the authorities as a religion: its religious customs were observed by one ethnic group that traced its ancestry to Palestine, and it had its temple in Jerusalem, where ancient rites were conducted by a priestly class. Looked at apart from Judaism, however, the Christian communities would have looked more like the kind of groups that proliferated throughout the empire and bore the name *collegium* or *sodalitas.* Such groups shared some common characteristic, such as their trade — wine merchants, for example, or tailors or shipowners — their place of origin, their interest in athletics, theater, or music, their common age or national background, or even the neighborhood they lived in. Again, the problem with the Christians, once they were no longer regarded as a sect of Jews, was that they did not look like any legitimate *collegium,* since not all members of the Christian community had anything in common except their allegiance to Christ. Groups with no common ties among its members, the Romans suspected, were meeting for political purposes (they called such a group a *haetaeria*), and such groups were strictly forbidden. When Christians first encountered persecution, therefore, it was more likely because they looked like an illegal *collegium* than like an "illegal" religion.

What most got Christians into trouble was the fact that, because all public activities included the worship of local gods, Christians could not participate in them and so held aloof from normal social activities. This earned them the accusation that they were afflicted by a "hatred of the human race" (Latin *odium humani generis,* e.g., Tacitus, *Annals* 15.44; Pliny, *Letters* 10.96). Whatever the legal status of Christians was during Paul's lifetime, it was their "standoffishness" that brought them into disrepute with their pagan neighbors throughout the Roman Empire. In all likelihood, such general anti-Christian feelings among local populaces more than imperial edicts motivated the hatred for and persecutions of Christians in general. Christians thus suffered the fate of any group in the empire that isolated itself from society and refused to conform to normal expectations. It was the reaction to such social isolation that tempted Christians, including members of the new groups of converts gathered by Paul in various cities of the empire, to abandon their faith or to compromise it with pagan customs.

11.1.3. Family and Empire

The family as we know it in our world is in a state of transition morally and legally, but generally the word "family" conjures up a unit consisting of a husband and wife and perhaps also children. The changes of the past few decades have tended to equalize the respective functions of husband and wife within the family, so that it is now common for both husband and wife to hold jobs outside the home and to share in care of the children. In our culture, children also enjoy a large measure of equality and even of independence within the family unit; in some instances the schedule of the family tends to revolve around the needs of the children. While the family retains a measure of importance in our culture, it does not represent the structure in terms of which our government is ordered.

Roman Emperors of the First Century			
Augustus	(27 BCE–14 CE)	Vespasian	(69-79)
Tiberius	(14-37)	Titus	(79-81)
Caligula	(37-41)	Domitian	(81-96)
Claudius	(41-54)	Nerva	(96-98)
Nero	(54-68)	Trajan	(98-117)
Galba, Otho, Vitellius	(68-69)		

Such was the case, however, in Paul's world. The basic organization of the Roman world was derived from that of the family, which was highly structured and hierarchical. Family units in the Roman world tended to be quite large, including several generations of adults, along with children, and, in the cases of more affluent families, slaves. Within those families, the basic relationships of husband and wife, parents and children, and master and slaves were highly structured, with each person occupying a set and specified place. Thus, within the hierarchy of the family, the husband stood at the top, then the wife, then the children, and finally the various slaves and attendants. Any family unit that tampered with that structure or that did not observe it scrupulously was liable to social ostracism and even in some cases legal action. Families that did not discipline their slaves, for example, that allowed them to be insolent, or that allowed their children too much freedom would be looked down on by their neighbors, and husbands who did not maintain control over their households would be held in contempt. The orator Chrysostom argued that the very safety of a household depended on the obedience of the slaves, since the disobedience and wickedness of slaves wrecked many households (*Discourse* 38.15). Tacitus argued that because some Germanic tribes had women as rulers they had fallen lower than slaves (*Germany* 45).

These hierarchical relationships were said to be based on "reason," with men having the highest kind of reason, women having reason but in less developed form, children having undeveloped reason, and slaves being devoid of reason altogether. This understanding of familial hierarchy had additional importance because the Romans used it to justify their dominance over all other peoples: because the Romans were superior in "reason," they were able so to triumph over all others. So the orator Cicero could argue that the Romans did not surpass the Spaniards in numbers, the Carthaginians in cunning, or the other residents of Italy in common sense. Rather, they won their empire because of "piety and religion," both characteristics they included under the broader rubric "reason."

This meant that any challenge to the hierarchical structure of the family was a challenge to the right of the Romans to rule the world, since that structure presented the rationale for Roman hegemony. Any group that argued that men and women were equal, for example, that children also had rights over against their parents, or that slaves were the equal of their masters would be open to charges of treason. The philosopher Arius Didymus wrote that seditions in cities occur whenever those with equal rights are compelled to be unequal or when those who are unequal have equality (*Politics* 151.9-12). On that basis, any Roman official who read in Paul's letter to the Galatians that in Christ differences between men and women, Jews and Greeks, and slave and free have been done away with (3:28) would have reason to charge Christians with treason, since such views undermined the very rationale by which Rome justified its domination of the Mediterranean world. Those who accepted the message Paul carried to any who would listen in that world were thus open not only to social isolation because of the accusation that they hated other people, but also to the charge of treason against the Roman Empire, which sat astride that whole world. Having Christ rather than Caesar as Lord was therefore a risky thing in the empire, and the promise it represented and the difficulties it brought will both be apparent in the letters Paul wrote to those communities of Christians scattered in cities around the Mediterranean Sea.

11.2. THE LIFE OF PAUL

As far as the date of Paul's birth is concerned, we have no information at all. He was probably roughly the same age as Jesus, although he could have been ten years younger. His Christian missionary activity took place sometime between 35 and 60 C.E. He does not tell us where he was born, though Acts informs us that he was born in Tarsus. It is clear from Paul's letters that he knew Greek as a native language and that he clearly knew how to deal with non-Jews. Since he apparently came from the Diaspora (Jews living outside Palestine), there is little difficulty with accepting Tarsus as his place of birth. That he was born of Jewish parents is quite certain; Acts makes that point clearly, and Paul himself mentions it several times in different letters. As a good Jew he would have been circumcised a week after his birth, and he confirms that he was (Phil 3:5). That he had two names, one Hebrew (Saul) and one Greek (Paul), is mentioned only in Acts; he never refers to himself as "Saul." Yet his family belonged to the tribe of Benjamin (Phil 3:5), whose chief hero was Saul, and it was apparently the custom for Jewish people in the Diaspora to have two names, one Jewish and one Greek or Roman.

We have no information about Paul's youth, but a tractate in the Jewish Mishnah (*Pirke Aboth* 5.21), admittedly a later text but containing earlier traditions, outlines the normal course of a young man's life as follows: At five years of age, he would begin to learn to read the Scriptures; at ten, he would begin to read the Mishnah; at thirteen, he would take on the responsibility of fulfilling the commands of the Torah. At eighteen he would be old enough to marry. At twenty, a young Jew would be ready to embark on his calling, and he would "assume authority," that is, come of age, when he was thirty.

How much of this was the case with Paul is hard to tell. Whether he ever married, for example, is difficult to determine. There is a later tradition (Eusebius, *Hist. Eccl.* 3.20.1) that Paul addressed his wife in one of his letters (perhaps Phil 4:3), but Acts is silent on the subject. Paul refers at one point (1 Cor 9:5) to his right to be accompanied by "a sister as a wife," which implies he was married, but in the same letter (1 Cor 7:8) he counsels the unmarried and widows to remain as he is, implying that he was not married. It may be that at one point he was accompanied by his wife, but when she died, he did not remarry, but the evidence is quite ambiguous.

That Paul studied with Gamaliel in the course of pursuing his "calling" is affirmed in Acts (22:3), where Paul is reciting his credentials as a Jew, although he does not mention that this study occurred in Jerusalem. Paul himself is silent on that point in his letters, even where he is reciting similar credentials (2 Cor 11:22; Phil 3:5-6) or where he wants to emphasize that he did in fact know Jewish traditions (Gal 2:14). It would have strengthened Paul's point to mention that he studied under Gamaliel in Jerusalem. Yet Paul is addressing Gentiles in those passages,

---

Early Descriptions of Paul

There is no physical description of Paul in the NT, but such descriptions are to be found in later Christian writings. One such description is in a second-century writing called *The Acts of Paul and Thecla* (2.3):

> And he saw Paul coming, a man little of stature, thin-haired upon the head, crooked in the legs, of good state of body, with eyebrows joining and nose somewhat hooked, full of grace; for sometimes he appeared like a man, and sometime he had the face of an angel.

A second, much later description (sixth century) is found in the writings of John of Antioch:

> In person round-shouldered, with a sprinkling of grey on his head and beard, with an aquiline nose, graying eyes, meeting eyebrows, with a mixture of pale and red in his complexion and an ample beard. With a genial expression of countenance, he was sensible, earnest, easily accessible, sweet and inspired with the Holy Spirit.

---

and it is unlikely that the names of famous Jewish rabbis would have meant anything to them. Paul's own testimony about his zealous study of the Jewish law and tradition indicates he did pursue extensive study in those topics, and it could well be that, as Acts suggests, Gamaliel was one with whom Paul studied.

We know that Paul worked with his hands at some trade (1 Cor 4:12; 1 Thess 2:9). Acts tells us that that trade was tentmaking (18:3). Such a trade would have been appropriate for someone who traveled as much as Paul did since it did not require that he carry heavy equipment from place to place. That such a trade meant he worked in leather has been argued, but leather tents were mostly restricted to the military, who had their own tentmakers. More likely he worked with linen, making the kind of tents and awnings that were regularly used in marketplaces, on the beach, over atriums of homes, and wherever else people needed to be protected from the sun.

That Paul was a Roman citizen is attested only in Acts (e.g., 16:37; 22:25-26). Paul never mentions it, and beatings with rods, like those he received (2 Cor 11:25), were not usually inflicted on Roman citizens. Yet, as Acts also makes clear, people were not always careful to ascertain the citizenship of someone they viewed as a troublemaker (Acts 16:22-23, 37-39) before they took action against them. Again, it seems difficult to imagine that such a tradition of Paul's citizenship would arise without any historical basis at all. Thus the information in Acts may very well be accurate.

Paul mentions that he was a Pharisee (Phil 3:5), as does Acts (23:6), and both say that he persecuted the church. Some uncertainty whether that persecution also occurred in and around Jerusalem is raised by Paul's claim that even three years after his conversion he was still unknown by face to the churches in Judea (Gal 1:22). It is difficult to see how he would have been unknown to that degree if he had persecuted those particular Christian communities, although it is possible he directed those persecutions from afar.

That Paul's conversion occurred in the neighborhood of Damascus is mentioned by Acts and confirmed by Paul in Gal 1:17. There are in fact three accounts of Paul's conversion in Acts (9:1-9; 22:6-11; 26:12-26), but they differ in some details (cf. 9:7, where Paul alone sees a light but all present hear, with 22:9, where Paul alone hears but all see a light, or 26:16-18, where Jesus commissions Paul to go to the Gentiles, with 22:14-15 and 9:15, where Ananias informs Paul of his commission). Paul refers to his conversion in Gal 1:15-16 and 1 Cor 15:8 (perhaps also in 2 Cor 12:2-4), but in neither case does he give any details about where he was or what happened in connection with this event, such as being struck blind. He does make clear that this event was on a par with the other appearances of the risen Christ to his disciples (1 Cor 15:3-7) and that it completely turned Paul's life around and reversed his values (Phil 3:7-8). That Paul turned to Christ out of despair or guilt at his inability to fulfill God's law finds little support in his letters. His one statement about his life as a Pharisee claims that as far as doing what was right according to the law, he was in fact blameless (Phil 3:6). One gets the impression both from Acts and from Paul's letters that Christ's appearance to him took him by surprise and turned his life in a direction that he, as the church's zealous persecutor, could hardly have imagined.

It is difficult to know how we are to go about reconstructing the events subsequent to Paul's conversion and the course of his missionary career. Acts records that Paul, struck blind at the time of his conversion, was taken to Damascus where, after being sightless three days, he was visited by a Christian named Ananias, who restored his sight and explained the meaning of his confrontation with the risen Christ. After preaching "many days" in Damascus, a plot against his life made it necessary for him to be lowered over the city wall to escape. He went to Jerusalem, where he met the disciples (Acts 9:17-25). Because of his disputes with "Hellenists," probably Hellenistic Jews, he went to Caesarea and then to Tarsus (9:26-30). Paul, on the other hand, recites a series of events that give a somewhat different picture. Paul insists that immediately after his conversion he conferred with no one, went to Arabia (probably the area to the east of the Jordan River), and then returned to Damascus (Gal 1:15-24). He does report the incident of escaping over the wall of Damascus in a basket and that this escape was necessitated by a plot instigated by King Aretas of Arabia. Evidently Paul had carried on some kind of activity in Damascus, probably Christian proclamation, that got him into trouble with the governing authorities. Paul also states that he did not go to Jerusalem until three years after his conversion, and that at that time he went only for a two-week period during which he met only Peter and James. That Paul supports this statement with an oath is meant to underline its truth. Subsequent to that visit, Paul agrees with Acts when he reports trips to the regions of Syria and Silicia, where, respectively, Damascus and Tarsus were located.

Acts records Paul returning to Jerusalem with Barnabas (ch. 11), going then to Antioch, and beginning his first missionary journey. They return to Jerusalem for a council on how to treat Gentiles who have become Christians (Acts 15), and Paul and others are commissioned to travel to the Gentile churches to tell them of certain food laws they must observe as Christians (Acts 15:22-29). Subsequently, in Antioch, Paul and Barnabas separate as the result of a dispute (15:39-40), and Paul undertakes his second and third missionary journeys without Barnabas. The second missionary journey ends with a visit to Jerusalem (18:22), and the third ends with Paul's final visit there (21:15).

The details we can glean from Paul's letters are difficult to fit into that framework. He insists that his second visit to Jerusalem did not occur until fourteen years had elapsed (Gal 2:1), though it is not clear whether this was fourteen years from the time of his conversion or from the time of the first visit to Jerusalem.

The Reputation of the Pharisees

Throughout his writings, Josephus characterizes the Pharisees as "a body of Jews with the reputation of excelling the rest of their nation in the observances of religion, and as exact exponents of the laws" (*J.W.* 1.110; 2.162). He also points out that they prided themselves on their "adherence to ancestral custom and claiming to observe the laws of which the Deity approves" (*Ant.* 17.41). Paul appeals to their reputation when he recounts his Jewish credentials and shows his particular zeal for the law: "circumcised on the eighth day, a member of the people of Israel, of the tribe of Benjamin, a Hebrew born of Hebrews; as to the law, a Pharisee" (Phil 3:4-5). A similar self-description is found in Acts: "I have belonged to the strictest sect of our religion and lived as a Pharisee" (26:5).

During this visit it was agreed that he would be the evangelizer of the Gentiles and that Peter and the other disciples would have such responsibilities for the Jews (Gal 2:7-9). Paul reports no further visits to Jerusalem, although in Romans he mentions his plans to make a third trip (15:25-28).

In general, the impression one gets from Paul's letters is not so much of three distinct missionary journeys, each ending with a visit to Jerusalem, as it is of a general westward movement, beginning in Syria and Cilicia at the eastern end of the Mediterranean basin (Gal 1:21), and then moving on to Asia Minor (Ephesus, 1 Cor 16:8), Greece (Thessalonica, Philippi, Corinth), and the area lying north of Greece (Illyricum, Rom 15:19). And then Paul proposes, after a visit to Rome, to continue his missionary proclamation in Spain (Rom 15:23-24).

While Paul clearly anticipated possible trouble during his final visit to Jerusalem (e.g., Rom 15:31), we have no report from him in any of his letters of the actual events. While some scholars have proposed that the letter to the Philippian Christians, composed when Paul was a prisoner, was written following his arrest in Jerusalem, there is nothing in the letter to make such a conclusion anything more than speculation. There is an old tradition that Peter and Paul were both martyred under Nero in Rome, perhaps during the persecution of Christians in Rome in 64 C.E., Peter by crucifixion and Paul by beheading (Roman citizens were not crucified).

Clearly enough, Paul the missionary covered a large area, traveling by ship when possible, by foot when necessary, undergoing immense hardships in the course of his journeys. Acts mentions a number of imprisonments and some severe physical abuse in the form of beatings and a stoning, but they are outnumbered in Paul's own catalog (2 Cor 11:23-27), written at what must have been about midway through his career. He enumerates five beatings with a lash, three with rods, and a stoning, some of which left him near death. He mentions three shipwrecks, one of which left him adrift a night and a day at sea, and mentions the kind of hardships any traveler would experience who undertook the kind of journeys that characterized Paul's missionary career.

Both Paul's letters and the accounts of his missionary activity in Acts point to one who traveled tirelessly to announce the good news of God's saving act in Christ. He covered incredible distances under the most trying of circumstances, always pressing on to new areas where the gospel had not been proclaimed while at the same time displaying great pastoral care for the Christian communities he had already founded. It is therefore not surprising that a large portion of our NT is devoted to letters bearing his name.

11.3. PAUL'S INTELLECTUAL WORLD

It is clear that Paul, born and educated a Jew and at home in the secular world of the Mediterranean basin, was exposed to many and varied intellectual currents in the course of his youth and mature life. Although he is remembered as quoting a secular author on only one occasion (Aratus, *Phaenomena* 5, in Acts 17:28) he uses vocabulary associated with the popularized Platonism that characterized much of the intellectual framework of the Greco-Roman world (e.g., the contrast between flesh and spirit in Rom 8:9-13) and reflects the attitude of indifference to worldly relationships often urged by Stoic philosophers (e.g., 1 Cor 7:29-31; 2 Cor 6:10). Yet Paul puts that vocabulary and those attitudes in a framework that is quite different from those of the secular world, so that it is clear that he has not drawn the categories informing and organizing his thought from such sources. And it was in fact hard to speak of the structure of reality or the form of morality without using words that other thinkers had used when discussing similar points. Human vocabulary is finite, and it is not unusual for people with widely differing understandings of reality to use similar vocabulary to make their points. For that reason, similarities in vocabulary or in descriptions of morality do not point to dependence on others who use similar words or thought forms.

Far more often than he cited secular thinkers or used their vocabulary, Paul cited the Jewish Scriptures and reflected Jewish ways of thinking. He was after all steeped in the Scriptures as a result of his training as a Pharisee, and he turns again and again to them to clarify or reinforce a point. In his discussions of law and covenant (Gal 3:17; 2 Cor 3:6) Paul clearly employs vocabulary and concepts familiar to Pharisaic thought, and his concern for entering and remaining in a right relationship with God reflects the very core of the Pharisee's approach to both covenant and law. Yet influenced though he was by those thought patterns, Paul had expressly given up on such an approach to the way humans are to be related in a positive way to a just and merciful God. If he continues to use concepts and vocabulary derived from his Pharisaic background, he does so in a framework quite different from the one in which he would have used them as a Pharisee.

The mode of Jewish thinking closest to Paul's outlook as a Christian apostle, from which he derived the structure of his thought, can best be characterized as apocalyptic. Such thinking was characterized by the notion that the present world and its culture were so unqualifiedly evil that nothing about them could be redeemed. The only way redemption could occur would be by means of a new creation, in which the very structures of reality would be altered and a new reality introduced. Because apocalyptic thinkers thought in terms of history, they tended to call the two shapes of reality the old and the new "age," the Greek word for which has come down into English as "aeon." Thus, the old aeon would come to an end and the new aeon would be inaugurated by God. In order to determine who could participate in the new aeon, the final event of the old aeon would be a universal judgment, during which God would determine would deserved entry into the new aeon. Since many people had died before this judgment, these thinkers argued that in order for justice to prevail and for everyone to be given the same chance, there would be a general resurrection just prior to the final judgment, so that everyone would be placed under the same judgment and thus have an equal chance to enter the new age.

Paul adopted this way of understanding reality because at the time of his conversion he was convinced that God had raised Jesus from the dead. In fact, Jesus' resurrection constitutes the very center of the Christian faith for Paul (cf. 1 Cor 15:14, 17; Rom 10:9). Since the apocalyptic way of looking at reality was the only mode of thinking in the ancient world in which resurrection played a key role, it was inevitable that Paul would adopt it — but also adapt it. He speaks, therefore, of "aeons" (Rom 12:2; 1 Cor 2:6; 2 Cor 4:3; Gal 1:4), but he sees the contrast between the two ages, old and new, in terms of Adam and Christ (e.g., Rom 5:12-17; 1 Cor 15:21-22). Christ, by his death and resurrection, undoes the sin introduced by Adam with his disobedience of God. Christ thus also becomes the one through whom others may share in the resurrection and the new reality (see 1 Cor 15:13-28, 35-55; 1 Thess 4:14-17). Perhaps most importantly, Paul adapted the idea of

Athens: the temple of Olympian Zeus with the Acropolis in the background *(Nicholas Wolterstorff)*

the succession of the old and new ages. The resurrection of Christ, as Paul saw it, signaled the beginning of the new age, yet the general resurrection and the universal judgment had not taken place at that time, as Jewish apocalyptic would have expected with the transition from old to new age. Paul therefore saw that the end of the old and the beginning of the new overlapped, with the new age beginning with Christ's resurrection, but the old age not coming to its conclusion until the return of Christ and the general resurrection.

It is in this time of the overlapping of the ages that we now live, a time in which the redemptive powers of the new age and the sinful and destructive powers of the old age exist and function side by side. The task of the Christian is, therefore, to trust in Christ by confessing him as Lord and doing what he taught people to do and to become part of the Christian community, which is, as it were, a colony of those whose true home is the new age but who now are still forced to live in the midst of the old age (e.g., Phil 4:20). The transformation of reality will mean that the basic structural element will be spirit, not matter; risen Christians will have spiritual bodies that have been delivered from the powers of the old age, namely sin and death (Phil 4:21; 1 Cor 15:42-55). It is in the communities of those who confess Christ as Lord and look to him for their redemption that the new power of the Spirit is already at work. Having entered that community by dying to the old age and to sin by being baptized into Christ, Christians henceforth live within the new reality and are given power to resist the old ways, which lead only to more sin and death (e.g., 2 Cor 5:17; Gal 6:15; Rom 6:5-14). Trusting in Christ and living lives acceptable to God, Christians will be sustained in the final judgment and will enter into the new age with Christ, who by his death and resurrection has opened the way for those born in the age of Adam to participate in the restructured, spiritual reality.

Such is the message Paul announced to the world through which he moved, and it is to those who accepted that message and who determined to live by it that Paul addressed his letters, urging them to continue in their new way of life and to avoid the kind of actions that would deny them the advantages of sharing in the death and resurrection of Christ. We will need to look carefully at the kind of problems Paul faced and the ways he sought to meet them as we examine his letters.

FOR FURTHER READING

F. F. Bruce, *Paul, Apostle of the Heart Set Free* (Grand Rapids: Eerdmans, 1977)

W. D. Davies, *Paul and Rabbinic Judaism* (3rd ed., Philadelphia: Fortress, 1980)

James D. G. Dunn, *The Theology of Paul the Apostle* (Grand Rapids: Eerdmans, 1998)

Gerald F. Hawthorne, et al., eds., *Dictionary of Paul and His Letters* (Downers Grove: InterVarsity, 1993)

W. A. Meeks, *The First Urban Christians: The Social World of the Apostle Paul* (New Haven: Yale, 1983)

N. T. Wright, *The Climax of the Covenant: Christ and the Law in Pauline Theology* (Minneapolis: Fortress, 1992)

12. Paul's Letter to the Christians in Rome

Romans is the longest of the letters of Paul that have been preserved for us, and for that reason also it stands as the first of those letters included in the NT. It is also the most carefully worked-out statement of the way Paul understood the Christian faith.

When he wrote the letter, Paul had never visited Rome, despite his repeated intention to do so (1:11, 13; see also 15:22-23). He was therefore unknown in person to many of the Christians there, though they had surely been informed about him by the many acquaintances there that Paul greets in Romans 16. Yet misunderstandings about Paul's view of the Christian faith were apparently also circulating (e.g., 3:8b), and it would thus be useful for the Romans to have from Paul a firsthand account of the Christian faith he proclaimed to the Gentile world. Perhaps that is also the reason Paul uncharacteristically names no companions or co-senders in this letter; it is evidently intended to be an undiluted account of his own understanding of the gospel.

12.1. THE PURPOSE OF THE LETTER

It is evident that when Paul wrote this letter, a mature Christian community already existed in Rome. Paul acknowledges the fame of their faith "in all the world" (1:8) and expects that they will strengthen his faith as he will strengthen theirs (1:12). The tradition that Paul co-founded the church there (with Peter) can thus not be maintained. As the apostle to the Gentiles, Paul nevertheless feels an obligation to visit the Christians in Rome and to inform them of his understanding of the Christian faith (1:15). He also has in mind as he writes this letter the continuation of his mission to the western half of the Mediterranean world, namely, Spain (15:24). From the language he uses, we may infer, as his readers would have, that he hoped to find support for that mission from the Roman church. We know that Paul received such support from the Christian community in Philippi (Phil 4:14-16), and that may have been the case with some other churches as well. Be that as it may, it is clear that one of the purposes for which Paul wrote this letter was to enlist the help of the Roman Christians for his mission to the western parts of the Roman Empire.

He must suffer one more delay (15:22) before he can come to visit them, however (15:25), a delay to be caused by his projected journey to Jerusalem to complete his promised provision for the poor among the Christians there that he promised to undertake when he met with the disciples in Jerusalem some years previously (Gal 2:10). Paul attached considerable importance to this gift, which he apparently understood in a reciprocal sense — that is, as Jerusalem shared its spiritual wealth — the gospel — with the Gentiles, so in response the Gentiles would share their material wealth with Jerusalem (15:27). That this was more than just a gift for the poor is indicated by Paul's request to his readers that they join him in prayer to God that his gift may be "acceptable to the saints," that is, to the Christians in Jerusalem. But why would there be some question about their accepting a

The Forum
in Rome

gift they had requested (Gal 2:10a)? The likely answer is that because the gift was associated with the legitimation of Paul's mission to the Gentiles by the disciples in Jerusalem (Gal 2:7-9), its acceptance by those same Jerusalem authorities would be further acknowledgment of the validity of Paul's Gentile mission, a validity Paul's dispute with Peter and Barnabas (Gal 2:11-12) and implicitly with the church in Jerusalem headed by James (Gal 2:12) may have called into question. Unless the Gentile mission of Paul were acknowledged by the Jerusalem authorities as legitimate, however, the church would be split into two halves, Jewish and Gentile, and then any mission of Paul to the Gentiles in Spain would only further exacerbate the split in the church as the body of Christ. What was at issue, therefore, in Paul's trip to Jerusalem was nothing less than the unity of the church and hence the legitimacy of the gospel that announced the unity of all people in Jesus Christ (Gal 3:28).

A further danger Paul anticipated with respect to his journey to Jerusalem is evident from his request to his readers that they pray for his deliverance from the "unbelievers in Judea" (15:31a), probably Jews who opposed the Christian faith as Paul himself had. We hear nothing further in the NT about the journey to Spain; Acts makes no reference to it, either as planned or completed, nor is there any additional reference to it in any of Paul's letters. That probably means that Paul was in fact arrested when he went to Jerusalem, and thus his missionary career was brought to an end. Romans may therefore be the last letter we have from the apostle Paul.

An additional purpose for the letter is to present the Roman Christians with a "reminder," apparently of some central points Paul felt it was his mission to emphasize (15:15). It appears from the way he phrases this statement that he does not presume to instruct the Roman Christians in aspects of the faith of which they are ignorant, but rather that he intends to emphasize some points he thinks are central to their faith. That probably also means that Paul has included traditions in his letter that he assumes are known to the Roman Christians since they were generally in circulation among other churches as well. Fragments of such traditions may be contained, for example, in 1:2-4; 3:25-26; or 4:25, as well as in other places. It may also mean that he includes some generalized instruction on problems that his experience has taught him are widespread among Christian churches, such as the problem of diet and the relationship between the weak and the strong (chs. 14–15; more on this below).

Paul's stated reasons for writing this letter therefore include his desire to introduce himself to the Roman Christians in anticipation of his visit there, his desire that they pray for his safe deliverance from his enemies in Jerusalem and the acceptance of his gift by the Jerusalem Christian authorities, his hope for support for his subsequent mission to Spain, and his intention to remind them of some central tenets of the Christian faith that belong to his understanding of the gospel.

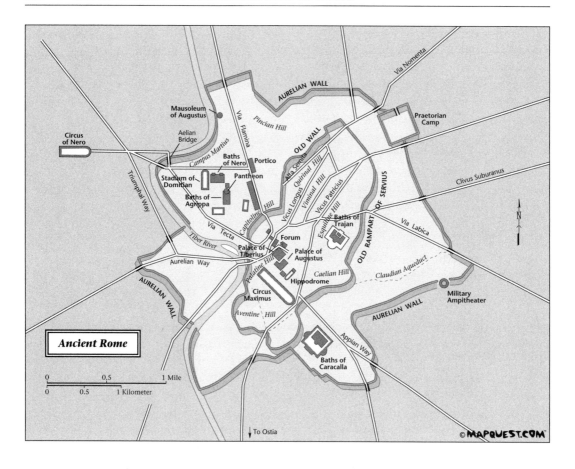

An unstated purpose often espoused by current scholars is Paul's desire to bring reconciliation between feuding factions of Jewish and Gentile Christians in the Roman church. The situation assumed is that the letter was written after Jews (including Jewish Christians), who had been expelled by Emperor Claudius (see Acts 18:2) around 49, had returned to Rome after the emperor's death in 54, only to find that the church in Rome had in the meantime been taken over by Gentile Christians. Those Gentile Christians displayed an attitude of superiority over the returning Jewish Christians, in part at least because the latter belonged to a race that had, by and large, rejected Christ, a rejection by which God had specifically created room for Gentile believers (11:19). The returning Jewish Christians, who probably at least shared in leadership roles in the Roman Christian community prior to their expulsion, for their part questioned the legitimacy of a Christianity that ignored the Jewish law and seemed to think indifference to its food regulations was a proper attitude for the followers of Jesus Christ. It was this situation that threatened to split the Christian community in Rome and that therefore served as the primary occasion for Paul's letter. Paul thus addressed both the ("weak") Jewish and the ("strong") Gentile Christians (chs. 14–15) in an attempt to overcome Gentile arrogance toward the Jewish Christians and to allay Jewish suspicions about the shape of Paul's gospel by discussing the important role Israel played in God's salvific plan, even though the culmination of that plan, Jesus Christ, was more widely accepted by Gentiles than by Jews (3:1-8; chs. 4; 9–11).

Despite the wide popularity of this explanation for the purpose of Paul's letter to the Roman Christians, there are a number of assumptions embodied in it that will not stand careful examination. For example, the assumption that Claudius expelled all the Jews (and therefore Jewish Christians) from Rome is based on three witnesses — Acts 18:2, the Roman second-century-C.E. historian Suetonius, and a fifth-century Christian writer named Orosius. The first two mention only Jews as expelled; Orosius is not sure whether Jewish Christians also were expelled. Orosius is the only one who mentions that the expulsion took place in 49. He cites a passage in the writings of the Jewish historian Josephus as the source of his information, a passage that in fact does not exist.

> In his account of the reign of Emperor Claudius in *Lives of the Caesars* (5.25.4), the Roman author Suetonius records this much discussed event:
>
> "Since the Jews constantly made disturbances at the instigation of Chrestus, he expelled them from Rome."

On the other hand, that all Jews were expelled by Claudius is specifically denied by another Roman historian, Cassius Dio, who says Claudius could not expel them all because of the tumult it would have caused. Rather, he says, Claudius forbade their meeting together, although continuing to permit their traditional way of life. This calls into question the departure of all Jews from the city, as does the fact that such imperial decrees were not always obeyed. For example, several attempts to ban all astrologers from Rome were made, in each case without signal success. That prominent Jewish Christians could be affected, if such a ban were in fact decreed, is likely, as in the case of Priscilla and Aquila, wealthy Jewish Christians who had owned homes in several cities (1 Cor 16:19; Rom 16:5; Acts 18:3), but to assume that every Jew, slave or free, left Rome because of the decree seems unlikely.

Cosmopolitan Rome

Hence, from now on let the reader forever renounce the views of those who make Rome a retreat of barbarians, fugitives and vagabonds, and let him confidently affirm it to be a Greek city, which will be easy when he shows that it is at once the most hospitable and friendly of all cities, and when he bears in mind that the Aborigines were Oenotrians, and these in turn Arcadians, and remembers those who joined with them in their settlement, the Pelasgians who were Argives by descent and came into Italy from Thessaly; and recalls, moreover, the arrival of Evander and of the Arcadians, who settled round the Palatine hill, after the Aborigines had granted the place to them; and also the Peloponnesians, who, coming along with Hercules, settled upon the Saturnian hill; and, last of all, those who left the Troad and were intermixed with the earlier settlers. For one will find no nation that is more ancient or more Greek than these. But the admixtures of the barbarians with the Romans, by which the city forgot many of its ancient institutions, happened at a later time. And it may well seem a cause of wonder to many who reflect on the natural course of events that Rome did not become entirely barbarized after receiving the Opicans, the Marsians, the Samnites, the Tyrrhenians, the Bruttians and many thousands of Umbrians, Ligurians, Iberians and Gauls, besides innumerable other nations, some of whom came from Italy itself and some from other regions and differed from one another both in their language and habits; for their very ways of life, diverse as they were and thrown into turmoil by such dissonance, might have been expected to cause many innovations in the ancient order of the city. For many others by living among barbarians have in a short time forgotten all their Greek heritage, so that they neither speak the Greek language nor observe the customs of the Greeks nor acknowledge the same gods nor have the same equitable laws (by which most of all the spirit of the Greeks differs from that of the barbarians) nor agree with them in anything else whatever that relates to the ordinary intercourse of life. Those Achaeans who are settled near the Euxine sea are a sufficient proof of my contention; for, though originally Eleans, of a nation the most Greek of any, they are now the most savage of all barbarians.

The language spoken by the Romans is neither utterly barbarous nor absolutely Greek, but a mixture, as it were, of both, the greater part of which is Aeolic; and the only disadvantage they have experienced from their intermingling with these various nations is that they do not pronounce all the sounds properly. But all other indications of a Greek origin they preserve beyond any other colonists. For it is not merely recently, since they have enjoyed the full tide of good fortune to instruct them in the amenities of life, that they have begun to live humanely; nor is it merely since they first aimed at the conquest of countries lying beyond the sea, after overthrowing the Carthaginian and Macedonian empires, but rather from the time when they first joined in founding the city, that they have lived like Greeks; and they do not attempt anything more illustrious in the pursuit of virtue now than formerly. (Dionysius of Halicarnassus, *Roman Antiquities* I.89.1–90.1)

Again, the assumption that Paul is addressing both Jewish and Gentile Christians to heal the division between them is nowhere made explicit, or even stated, in the letter. The only people Paul specifically says he is addressing are Gentiles (1:5-6, 13). In 1:14 he says that his obligation to go to Rome concerns both Greeks and barbarians, both categories of Gentiles. Had Paul in fact also been addressing Jews, one would have expected some similarly explicit reference to that fact.

Furthermore, he nowhere gives his desire to heal such a division as a reason for the letter. When divisions were a problem, as in Corinth, Paul addressed the problem directly (1 Cor 1:10). Similarly, when he discusses the church as the body of Christ in 1 Corinthians 12, he again refers to problems of division (12:14-26), something totally absent from a similar discussion in Rom 12:4-11. Nor can one say that in Romans 14–15, with its discussion of weak and strong Christians, the "weak" are necessarily Jews and the "strong" necessarily Gentiles. Paul, himself a Jew, surely belongs to the "strong," as would Priscilla and Aquila, Jews closely associated with Paul. Nor may one assume that all Gentile Christians would automatically eat meat (Rom 14:2), given the association of banquets with Roman cults and the sale in the marketplace of meat sacrificed to pagan gods. A former devotee of a pagan cult or god might well feel it necessary to avoid meat associated with their former life, a problem specifically discussed in 1 Cor 8:4-13, where the "weak" are clearly Gentile Christians. Thus, it is not clear whether Romans 14–15 is intended to address a specific problem in Rome or is a kind of generalized advice, similar to that in 1 Corinthians 8–9, that Paul has included along with similar general advice in Romans 12 and 13.

Finally, Paul's lengthy discussions of the place of Israel in God's plan of salvation owe more to his understanding that the "divine gospel" he was called to preach was rooted in Israel (Rom 1:2-4) than to a supposed desire to convince Gentiles in Rome that they ought not be arrogant toward Jews. Paul's discussions of Israel in Romans in each instance have to do with the substance of his understanding of the gospel; his discussion is thus not simply occasioned by a supposed conflict between Jewish and Gentile Christians in Rome.

That does not mean there were no Jewish Christians in the Roman Christian communities when Paul wrote; the Jewish names among those he greets in ch. 16 demonstrate that there were. Why Paul explicitly addresses only Gentile Christians is due not to any absence, or lesser importance, of Jewish Christians but to Paul's scrupulous abiding by the agreement he reached with the Jerusalem authorities (Gal 2:7-9) that he was to be the apostle to the Gentiles, lest he be accused of violating that apostolic compact.

12.2. WHERE THE LETTER WAS WRITTEN

If Paul does tell us why he wrote the letter, he does not tell us where he was when he composed it. If in speaking of the collection for Jerusalem he mentions the southern half of the Greek Peninsula last (Achaia — Rom 15:26; Macedonia is the northern half of the peninsula) because he is there, then he was very probably writing in Corinth, where Achaia's most important church was. That the woman who carried the letter to Rome, Phoebe, was a deacon in the church at Cenchreae, a harbor town some seven miles east of Corinth (16:1), would seem to add confirmation. Again, if the Gaius who is Paul's host (16:23) is the Gaius whom Paul baptized in Corinth (1 Cor 1:14), then that is yet further evidence Paul is in Corinth. But Gaius was an extremely common name in the Greco-Roman world (for another Gaius, see Acts 20:4). Erastus, mentioned in Rom 16:23 as the city treasurer, may also have been an official in Corinth; an Erastus is mentioned in 2 Tim 4:20 as one who remained in Corinth. An Erastus is identified as a helper of Paul along with Timothy in Acts 19:22. Whether these represent the same person is also difficult to determine; one must wonder if an important city official would have traveled as much as the Erastus of 2 Timothy and Acts apparently did.

Although there can be no certainty in the matter, the most likely point of origin for the letter appears to have been Corinth, where Paul completed the collection and from which he set out for Jerusalem.

12.3. THE LETTER'S AUTHOR AND INTEGRITY

That Paul himself was the author of Romans has never been seriously questioned. Some have questioned whether ch. 16 belonged to the original letter, since it seems strange, they argue, that Paul would have known so many people in a city he had never visited. Yet mobility in the empire in the middle of the first century was great, and many were migrating to Rome during this period. It would also have been important for Paul to name as many people as he could who knew him and could vouch for the authenticity and reliability of his gospel. The extent to which women played key roles in the early church is also evident in this chapter, where, in addition to Phoebe, the deacon who carried the letter to Rome, Paul sends greetings to Prisca (v. 3), Mary (v. 6), Tryphaena, Tryphosa, and Persis (v. 12), the mother of Rufus (v. 13), Julia (v. 15), and the sister of Nereus (v. 15). Depending on the textual tradition (in some early texts the name is given in its masculine form, in others in its feminine form), this list would also include Junia (v. 7). The language used to describe these women indicates that a number of them were active in Christian mission.

In addition to questions about ch. 16, some scholars have from time to time proposed that other passages were added to Romans by copyists, but there is no agreement on such additions. There is a textual problem concerning the location of the benediction in 16:25-27, however. Ancient manuscripts place it at the end of ch. 14, at the end of ch. 15, at the end of ch. 16, at the end of both chs. 14 and 15, or at the end of both chs. 14 and 16, or omit it altogether. Some scholars have concluded that this may indicate that the letter originally ended with ch. 14, or perhaps with ch. 15, but the textual evidence will not allow us to come to any firm conclusions. The thrust of Paul's argument in Romans is not affected by the position of this benediction, so it is a problem we may confess to being unable to resolve without prejudicing our understanding of what Paul has said in the letter.

12.4. THE THEME OF THE LETTER

There is a long tradition, reaching all the way back to the Reformation in the sixteenth century, that the theme of Romans, as of Paul's theology in general, is that people are made righteous before God by faith (or "trust") rather than by works of the law. Because this point is made explicitly in Rom 1:17, that verse has been understood to be the statement of the theme. The remainder of the letter is then the attempt to work out the implications of that theme for Christian faith (chs. 1–8) and practice (chs. 12–15). Yet such an understanding of Romans has had difficulty accounting for the location and content of chs. 9–11, which have consistently, therefore, represented a problem for such an understanding of Romans. Nor is it clear why, after Paul has affirmed that justification by faith has taken place (5:1), he needed to say anything further; he could apparently have turned at that point to showing what justification meant for the way Christians are to live. Such problems indicate that the theme of Romans is probably not to be found in 1:17, important as that verse is for Paul's understanding of God's way of dealing with sinful human beings.

A more appropriate locus for the statement of a theme would be at the beginning of the letter, and in fact that seems to be the case here as well. Surely the content of Paul's ministry, as he himself says at the outset, is the "gospel of God" (1:1), a gospel then defined in 1:2-4. These verses summarize how God has carried out his redemptive plan in the history of the Jews (the prophets, David, vv. 2-3) and in the decisive act of Christ's resurrection (v. 4). This summary leads seamlessly into Paul's declaration of his own call to evangelize the Gentiles (v. 5) as a direct outgrowth of these salvific acts of God. The universality of the gospel's significance, implied by the references to elements of Jewish history and to Paul's call to preach to Gentiles (vv. 2-5), is then in fact made thematic beginning with vv. 14-16, where the universal significance is expressed in terms of two inclusive contrasts: Greek and barbarian (v. 14), Jew and Greek (v. 16). These two passages, 1:2-5 and 1:14-

16, indicate together that the universal availability of divine salvation, understood in terms of its history in God's activity with the Jews, is the theme of the letter.

In 11:32, at the end of the development of his argument in chs. 1–11, Paul again refers to the same theme, declaring explicitly the universality of purpose contained in the divine plan of salvation: God has enclosed *all* people in disobedience, in order to have mercy on *all.* The striking similarity of the statement in Gal 3:22, again in the context of the universal scope of the Christian faith (3:28), indicates that such phrasing may have been a regular part of the way Paul described the universality of the range and application of the gospel. The summary statement in Rom 11:32 leads, then, into Paul's hymnic celebration of how God has acted for human salvation (11:33-36), before he turns in chs. 12–15 to how this understanding of the gospel affects how Christians are to live.

Thus the universal significance of the gospel is announced, an announcement that lies closer to the general content and organization of the letter than the concept of being made right with God through trust. This is not to say that being made right with God through trust in what he has done in Jesus Christ is unimportant for Paul. Such "righteousness through trust" is, however, not the theme of Romans. It is, rather, a statement of the means by which the gospel of God's mercy is made available to Gentiles as well as Jews.

The familiar phrase "justification by faith" can convey some nuances that Paul did not intend. "Justification" in modern English has legal overtones, and justification is often understood as God as judge freeing human sinners from the punishment due their sins. But Paul took this term from the covenant language of Israel, where it describes being in a right covenantal relationship with God. To be made righteous therefore means, for Paul, to leave a rebellious relationship in which one opposes what God wants and to enter into a positive relationship in which one seeks to follow God's will. This is the "new covenant" about which Paul speaks and which was inaugurated by Christ's death and resurrection. One enters that new relationship with God by accepting what God has done for sinners in Christ. Such acceptance is what Paul calls "faith." Again, a better choice of word would be "trust." "Faith" in modern English often means assent to the validity of some intellectual content. But Paul uses that word not to get his readers to assent to the existence of God and Christ, but to place their trust in God and Christ to fulfill what they have promised. In that way, human beings leave their rebellious ways, which have separated them from God, that is, their sin, and now enter a positive relationship through Christ in which they seek to act in accordance with the divine will for human beings as displayed in Christ. For that reason, we use the phrase "righteousness through trust" rather than "justification by faith."

It is, Paul is affirming, no longer a matter of being born into the chosen people, the Jews, but rather of trusting what God has done for all people in Christ. Righteousness by trust is thus the way that God's saving grace is made available to all people. This is shown by the fact that 1:17, with its statement about getting right with God through trust, serves to clarify the announcement in v. 16b that God's saving righteousness is now open to everyone, Jew (first) and Greek — that is, that it is universal in scope. That the history of God's dealing with humanity through his chosen people, the Jews, underlies even that universal expression of God's mercy is shown by its being framed in terms of "righteousness," a concept almost surely borrowed from the covenant language of Israel. It is, furthermore, precisely this announced universal significance of the gospel that makes the discussion in chs. 9–11 essential, and gives poignancy to it. There that universal significance appears violated by the Jews' self-exclusion, rather than by the exclusion of the Gentiles, as was the case before Christ's coming. Thus the means by which God's plan of salvation proceeds, namely, through God's covenant with sinful and rebellious humanity, a point Paul will make in his ensuing discussion, is announced in 1:17, clearly supporting the universal applicability of the gospel, which was announced in 1:14-16. Obviously, getting right with God through trust is an important point for Paul, but it is important as the means by which the universal scope of the gospel is carried out, rather than as the theme of the letter.

12.5. THE CONTENT OF THE LETTER

Paul follows the usual form of the Hellenistic letter, with the kind of adaptations he frequently made. The letter opening (1:1-7) contains the usual elements of the Hellenistic form, but they are lengthened considerably, particularly Paul's self-identification, which includes a summary of the gospel he proclaimed (1:2-6). As usual, he concludes the opening with a wish for divine grace and peace for his readers (1:7). The thanksgiving, again a usual part of a Hellenistic letter, flows into the letter body to such an extent that it is difficult to say exactly where the one ends and the other begins. Scholars usually define the thanksgiving as comprising 1:8-10, with the letter body beginning with 1:11, even though, as its grammar shows, v. 11 is intended to flow as an integral part of the discussion in v. 10.

The letter body comprises 1:11–15:13 and can itself be divided in a number of ways. It is typical to find two main segments of the letter body: the first (1:11–11:36) is a lengthy exposition of various facets of Paul's theme of the universal availability of God's mercy to all people, Jew and Gentile alike. A shorter second section (12:1–15:13) deals with the implications such mercy entails for living together in the Christian community which now includes both Jew and Gentile. We shall find reason, as our discussion proceeds, to divide the first segment into three parts: one dealing with the past (1:11–4:22), one with the present (4:23–8:39), and one with problems related to the future (9:1–11:36). The letter closing, again long by Hellenistic standards (15:14–16:27), is comprised of an account of Paul's travel

Letter opening (1:1-7)
Letter body (1:11–15:13)
    The availability of God's mercy for Jew and Gentile alike
        (1:11–11:36)
      The past (1:11–4:22)
      The present (4:23–8:39)
      The future (9:1–11:36)
    Implications of this mercy for the Christian community of Jews
        and Gentiles (12:1–15:13)
Letter closing (15:14–16:27)
    Paul's travel plans (15:14-33)
    Commendation of Phoebe, greetings, and final exhortation
        (16:1-23)
    Concluding doxology (16:25-27)

plans, closing with a blessing (15:14-33), commendation of Phoebe and greetings to Christians in Rome (16:1-23), which includes a final exhortation (16:17-20) and a concluding doxology (16:25-27).

Paul begins his discussion by announcing that apart from Christ, all of humanity has rebelled against God by turning away from him as the creator of the universe and turning instead to some created entity to which ultimate allegiance is given. Because there was enough evidence in creation itself to warn people away from this act of setting something other than God at the center of their lives (1:19-20), such rebellion against God is culpable (1:21) and brings wrath (1:18, 24-31). Paul understands this substitution of creature for creator as idolatry (1:22-23, 25). It brings in its train the breakdown of human society, including a perversion that extends from the normal relationship between the sexes (1:24-27) to the normal social relationships among individuals (1:28-32). The punishment for such perversion of creation, such idolatry, is the continuation of such perversion; God's punishment is to "give them over" to such activity (1:24, 26, 28). The punishment of sin is to allow sin to continue. People cannot excuse themselves from such activity by condemning others for what they themselves also do (2:1); God judges on the basis of reality, not appearances (2:6, 11). Neither a natural sense of morality in human beings (2:14-15) nor the possession by the Jews of God's covenantal law (2:17-24) can excuse such conduct, since God looks not at outward appearance but at inward reality (2:25-29). That does not mean God has abandoned his covenant with his chosen people, the Jews, even though they have abandoned God through their rejection of Christ (3:1-8), but it does mean that the covenant will not protect them from God's judgment of their rebellious conduct. As a result, Paul concludes, all human beings, Jews and Gentiles, stand in rebellion against God and hence under the power of sin; being a member of the chosen people does not mean such sin will be overlooked (3:9-20).

This is not the final fate of human beings, however, because in Christ, God acted in a decisive way to remain faithful to his sinful creation, but in a way different from the establishment of his covenant with the Jews as his chosen people. To be sure, that covenant, with its law and prophets, pointed to this decisive act of God's faithfulness to his rebellious creation, but members of that covenant are now also included in this new way to be right with God, namely, through trust in

Idolatry and Immorality

The link between idolatry and immorality was current in Jewish literature, as Wisdom of Solomon 14:21-27 demonstrates:

> And this became a hidden trap for humankind,
> because people, in bondage to misfortune or to royal authority,
> bestowed on objects of stone or wood the name that ought not
>   to be shared.
> Then it was not enough for them to err about the knowledge of God,
> but though living in great strife due to ignorance,
> they call such great evils peace.
> For whether they kill children in their initiations, or celebrate
>   secret mysteries,
> or hold frenzied revels with strange customs,
> they no longer keep either their lives or their marriages pure,
> but they either treacherously kill one another, or grieve one another
>   by adultery,
> and all is a raging riot of blood and murder, theft and deceit,
>   corruption, faithlessness, tumult, perjury,
> confusion over what is good, forgetfulness of favors,
> defiling of souls, sexual perversion,
> disorder in marriages, adultery, and debauchery.
> For the worship of idols not to be named
> is the beginning and cause and end of every evil. (NRSV)

Confession of Sin

The following excerpts from one of the Dead Sea Scrolls shows the author's awareness and confession of his own sinfulness, and his need to depend upon God's righteousness for salvation.

As for me,
  my justification is with God.
In His hand are the perfection of my way
  and the uprightness of my heart.
He will wipe out my transgression
  through His righteousness. . . .
From the source of His righteousness
  is my justification. . . .
As for me,
  I belong to wicked mankind,
  to the company of unjust flesh.
My iniquities, rebellions, and sins,
  together with the perversity of my heart,
belong to the company of worms
  and to those who walk in darkness.
For mankind has no way,
  and man is unable to establish his steps
since justification is with God
  and perfection of way is out of His hand.
All things come to pass by His knowledge;
He establishes all things by His design
  and without His will nothing is done.
As for me,
  if I stumble, the mercies of God
  shall be my eternal salvation.

what God has done in Jesus Christ. The cross of Christ, a sacrifice that established the new covenant, must lead to trust in God who in that way put aside human sin (3:21-25). This shows that God, in remaining faithful to his creation ("righteous"), allows his creatures to become faithful to him ("righteous") by trusting in what he has done in Christ (3:26).

What all that means is that confidence in one's relationship to God can now

If I stagger because of the sin of flesh,
     my justification shall be
     by the righteousness of God who endures for ever.
When my distress is unleashed
     He will deliver my soul from the Pit
     and will direct my steps to the way.
He will draw me near by His grace,
     and by His mercy will He bring my justification.
He will judge me in the righteousness of His truth
     and in the greatness of His goodness
     He will pardon all my sins.
Through His righteousness He will cleanse me
     of the uncleanness of man
     and of the sins of the children of men,
that I may confess to God His righteousness,
     and His majesty to the Most High.
Blessed art Thou, my God,
     who openest the heart of Thy servant to knowledge!
Establish all his deeds in righteousness,
and as it pleases Thee to do for the elect of mankind,
     grant that the son of Thy handmaid
     may stand before Thee for ever.
For without Thee no way is perfect,
     and without Thy will nothing is done.
It is Thou who has taught all knowledge
     and all things come to pass by Thy will.
There is no one beside Thee to dispute Thy counsel
     or to understand all Thy holy design,
or to contemplate the depth of Thy mysteries
     and the power of Thy might.

(From 1QS11, Vermes)

only be based on one's trust in Christ, not in one's membership in the chosen people. Membership in the chosen people was to be expressed through "works of the law," works done in obedience to the law. These works included, but were by no means limited to, "works" such as circumcision and the keeping of regulations regarding food and purity that marked Israel off from the nations and so pointed to its unique status. That is to say, Paul here means by the phrase "works of the law" not a general attempt by human beings to earn favor with God through their good conduct. Rather, as 3:28-29 shows, with "works of the law" Paul has in mind the obedience of the Jews to the law. Paul thought only Jews could do "works of the law," since they alone had been given that law by God (so 3:1). Paul will use "works" and "works of the law" in that sense throughout Romans. It is another way of referring to salvation through membership in the chosen people, something Paul insists is not possible (3:30).

God has not changed his mind in asking for trust from his creatures. That was the intent of the law all along (3:30)! This is shown in the story of Abraham, whose trust in God put him into a positive relationship with God long before the law was given (4:1-12). That is also true for the descendants of Abraham, to whom the promise of inheriting the world was given. Because a promise requires trust that it be fulfilled, any confidence based on anything else — including membership in a chosen people to whom God's law was given and so who were obligated to carry out works in obedience to the law — destroys confidence based on trust (4:14-21). The story of Abraham shows, therefore, that from the beginning, God intended that human beings base their relationship with God on trust that he will keep his promises. Thus the true descendants of Abraham are those who share not his gene pool but his trust in God (4:9-13), which allowed him to stand in a positive relationship with God (4:22).

What Paul has described thus far for his readers has all occurred in the past. But its significance is not limited to the past. It also has relevance for the present (4:23-24a, already hinted at in 3:21). At this point in his letter, therefore, Paul turns from a discussion of the past to a discussion of the present. Since Paul's readers are now in a positive relationship with God through their trust in Christ (5:1) as a result of the new opportunity for the forgiveness of sin and a rectified relationship to God offered in Christ (4:24-25), what does that mean for their present life?

Paul turns immediately to the problem of suffering, which was apparently so widespread among Christians that Paul simply assumes its presence. The difference is that for the Christian, suffering can have a positive outcome because it can engender hope, a hope based on what God has done for the Christian in Christ (5:2-5). Paul then explains, as a way of providing implicitly the basis for any Christian hope, what it is that God has done. Such hope, he implies, is based on the fact that before a sinner could do anything to get back into a positive relationship with God, God had already done the decisive thing to that end through the divine act in Christ. God's love was such that he demonstrated his faithfulness to his fallen creatures before they had any chance to respond (5:6-8). As we shall see, this is the basis for Paul's assertion that sinners are saved by grace alone.

If Christ's death has placed the sinner in a new relationship with God (5:9a, 10a), Christ's resurrection gives that sinner hope for a new life in the age to come (5:9b, 10b). It is important to note here that for Paul, salvation belongs to the future. Those who trust in Christ are now set in a positive relationship with God ("made righteous," "reconciled"), but they will not be "saved" until the final judgment (5:9b), at which time they will share Christ's resurrection (5:10b; Paul will have more to say about this in ch. 6). Salvation for Paul is an eschatological concept; that is, it belongs to the end times, when Christ will return and judge all humanity. The Christian can hope for such salvation in the present, but will not experience it until some point in the future, when Christ returns. The upshot of this is that Christians can face such suffering as may come their way with joy because of their present reconciliation with God through Christ.

Paul turns next to the question why such reconciliation (5:11) was necessary. He discusses it in terms of the two figures that represent the two ages that have structured the history of the world, namely, Adam and Christ. While Paul seems to assume that Adam, like Christ, was a discrete individual who lived in the past, of far greater importance for Paul's thought is the representative nature of these two figures. Adam represents one way of pursuing human life, namely, life in rebellion against God, while Christ represents another way of pursuing human life, namely, life in a positive relation to God. In addition, Paul, who knew Hebrew, also knew that in Hebrew "adam" is the generic term for a human being. Whatever Paul may have thought about Adam as an individual, therefore, he also was aware that the author of the story in Genesis intended this figure to represent humankind as a whole.

Adam's Sin

The following quotation from 4 Ezra 7:46-50 (= 2 Esdras 7:116-120) shows an understanding of the effects of Adam's sin that probably dates to the first century:

This is my first and last word: It would have been better if the earth had not produced Adam, or else, when it had produced him, had restrained him from sinning. For what good is it to all that they live in sorrow now and expect punishment after death? O Adam, what have you done? For though it was you who sinned, the fall was not yours alone, but ours also who are your descendants. For what good is it to us, if an eternal age has been promised to us, but we have done deeds that bring death? And what good is it that an everlasting hope has been promised us, but we have miserably failed? Or that safe and healthful habitations have been reserved for us, but we have lived wickedly? *(OTP)*

Paul begins this passage by pointing out that since death is the consequence of sin and is universal, sin must be similarly universal. Sin, in the form of rebellion against God's will, is present when people disobey the law of Moses as surely as it was in Adam's refusal to follow what God had commanded in the Garden of Eden (5:12-14a). Thus, once again (as in 3:9-20), Paul's point is that no one, Jew or Gentile, can claim to be free of rebellion against God. Yet Adam, in setting the pattern for human rebellion, was a reflection of another person who would set a different pattern, namely, Christ (5:14b). Yet Paul wants to make clear that what God did in Christ, namely, act for the reconciliation of sinners, was a far more potent act than Adam's act of rebellion, which represents the way human beings have reacted to God. If it were not, it could not overcome the results of such rebellion (5:15-17). Paul states his conclusion in a reiteration of the contrasting parallelism between the results of Adam's rebellious disobedience and Christ's act of righteous obedience (5:18, 19). The law — and Paul means here the law of Moses, the Torah — served to make painfully evident the extent of human rebellion against God, but such rebellion finally could not overcome God's grace. God's grace is stronger than sin, so that even though sin brought death, God's grace brought a life that overcomes such death (5:20-21).

What conclusion are Paul's readers to draw from the fact that increase in sin simply caused God's grace to increase even more? Should they provoke more grace by creating more sin? Paul's answer is interesting. No, he says, that is not an option, because dead people cannot sin, and as far as sin is concerned, you are dead! Paul can make that statement to his Christian readers because he can assume they have all been baptized, and baptism, he says, links them to Christ's death. But that dead people cannot sin does not help them very much, because dead people cannot do anything else either. Baptism into Christ, however, means sharing not only his death on the cross, but also his risen life. Christians, baptized into Christ's death, therefore now live on the other side of death, sharing in Christ's risen life. But, note carefully, Paul does not say that as Christians have died with Christ, so they have also *risen* with Christ. For Paul resurrection, transformation into spiritual bodies, lies in the future, after God's universal judgment. Therefore, here as elsewhere in this letter, the Christian's resurrection is always spoken of in the future tense. Christians may walk now in newness of life because God raised Christ (6:4), and they are so to regard themselves (6:11), but only in the future will they be raised as Christ was raised (6:5, 6, 7). Since Christians share in that life but do not yet possess it, they are still open to the possibility of falling back into sin; old habits die hard. They must therefore strive not to fall back, because they have been given this new life.

Next question: does this mean that Christians can sin because what controls them now is not law but grace (6:15)? No, because to sin is to be a slave to sin, and that may describe their former state but not their present state. Now they are slaves to God, freed from sin and open to yield their lives to righteousness (6:16-23). Furthermore, because by their baptism they have shared in Christ's death, they are no longer under the law. But how can someone else's death affect my relationship to the law? Paul's example is the married woman: when her husband dies, her relationship to the law has changed. What the law once said to her as a married woman it no longer says because she is a widow. What once would have been adultery — marrying another man — is adultery no longer (7:1-3). Similarly, Christ's death means that Christians can now belong to another, namely, Christ, instead of to sin. Enslaved to sin as they were and now freed by Christ's death, the Christian is now free, as was the widow, to belong to another, namely, Christ. This is important because what the law does is arouse sinful passions (7:5). Now free from the law by Christ's death, however, the law no longer has that effect.

Another question: does that mean that the law is sin (7:7)? No, despite the close link between law and the sinful passions it is capable of raising (7:8-9). It is not the law that is sinful but rather the actions sin can provoke when it takes over the law (7:10-11). The law itself is in fact holy and good (7:12). Does that mean that the good law brought evil consequences, sin and death (7:13)? No, it was sin, which took over the law, that did that. The problem is that the law is not strong enough to resist the power of sin, with the result that sin can take it over and make it serve evil rather than good ends because, while the law is spiritual, the human being is "flesh," that is, enslaved to sin (7:14).

Here we confront a puzzle in trying to understand what Paul is saying. Who is this "I" that he keeps talking about in Romans 7? Some have said it represents Paul as a Christian, and describes the dilemma any Christian undergoes who knows of God's righteous act in Christ and yet is still tempted into sin. Yet Paul's description of the "I" in 7:14 makes that interpretation impossible, since the "I" is "sold under sin," something Paul has been at pains to say is precisely not the state of the Christian (6:6, 7, 11, 14, 17, 18, 20 ["were," not "are," slaves to sin], 22; 7:4, 6), a topic he will resume as soon as he is finished with this discussion (8:1, 2). Given that description of the Christian, whoever else the "I" is in 7:14, it cannot be a Christian.

Perhaps it represents the way Paul the Pharisee felt before he became a Christian. Perhaps it was precisely the despair the "I" felt under the law (7:15-24) that drove Paul when he was under the law to turn to Christ. Yet nowhere does Paul say he was in despair over the law when he was a Pharisee! The only thing he says about himself is that as far as doing right under the law was concerned, he was blameless (Phil 3:6b).

Most likely, the "I" is used here to describe a situation typical of a person under the law, such as Paul before his conversion, but not the inward feelings of such a person, a subjective description as it were, but what such a life looks like from a Christian perspective. It is therefore an objective description of the situation of

"Flesh" and "Body"

"Flesh" and "body" are neutral terms for Paul, and the meaning in any given case must be determined by the context. They can refer to the physical components of human existence, but they can also be used with respect to how one carries on one's life. In ethical contexts, the words tend to portray ways of living.

Thus, "flesh" can be used in a completely neutral way to describe the physical side of life (e.g., Rom 9:3; 1 Cor 15:39), as can "body" (e.g., 1 Cor 5:3; 15:37-38, 44). On the other hand, "flesh" can be used in a negative sense, to indicate life separated from God, and not in accord with the divine will, that is, life in sin (e.g., Rom 7:25; 8:5-8; Gal 6:19), as can "body" (e.g., Rom 1:24; 6:6; 8:13). Further, "flesh" can be used in a positive sense to describe one's physical life in accordance with God's will (e.g., Gal 2:20; 2 Cor 4:11; Rom 1:3), as can "body" (e.g., Rom 8:23; 1 Cor 6:15; 7:34).

Therefore, Paul does not imply that physical life, that is, life in the flesh or in the body, is necessarily evil. It is only when life has its center in something other than God that it is evil and in rebellion against God.

such a person, which is not known to that person until he or she becomes a Christian and can look back and see the dilemma they were in. From such a perspective, the "good" of which Paul speaks is doing God's will, and that means, since the advent of Christ, trusting in Christ rather than in the law for being right with God. But it was the law that led Jesus' contemporaries — including Paul! — to reject Jesus. Thus, seeking to do the good — that is, obeying God's will — they did just the opposite when, because of the law, they opposed Christ. That is the objective dilemma of anyone seeking to be right with God through the law. The very act of taking the law with utmost seriousness led those people, on that basis, to reject God's will expressed in Christ — that is, the "good."

It is not a matter of a moral dilemma. The problem is not the inability to will the good. Paul says explicitly such a person can in fact will to do the good (7:18), that is, will to do what God wants. The problem is that under the law such willing produces the opposite of what the person wants. It is not *willing* the good, that is, accepting God's will, that is the problem, it is *doing* the good, that is, following Christ, and it is just that that the law prevents. And all of that, says Paul, simply proves that the problem with the law when it is under the power of sin is that following it simply leads to more sin. The law is no help in escaping sin; it simply drives a person deeper and deeper into it. That is the objective dilemma of the person who relies solely on the law to point to the way to do God's will. As the fate of Jesus at the hands of those who followed the law showed, a fate Paul the Pharisee actively approved, it led to the utter rejection of Jesus as the expression of God's will.

If Rom 7:13-23 is thus a description of the past, namely, what life under the law looks like from a Christian perspective, the next segment (8:1-39) is a reflection on the present, namely, what life under Christ and freed from the law looks like from a Christian perspective. That life is one in which the enmity between God and human beings is at an end because life is now dominated by the Spirit of Christ rather than characterized by rebellion against God ("flesh") and led astray by the law. To set one's mind on the latter mode of life brings death, but to set the mind on what God has done in Christ brings life (8:6-7).

Because life is the future of those who trust Christ, Paul argues that any suffering devotion to Christ may bring is like nothing compared to that future, a future that will include the restoration not only of individuals but of the whole of creation itself (8:18-25). With the presence of God's Spirit assured (8:26-27), Christians may face the future unafraid, confident that God will not withdraw the love and mercy he has shown, and promised, in Jesus Christ. Nothing, finally, can separate the Christian from the loving care of that God (8:28-39).

That affirmation raises one final problem for Paul, and it concerns precisely the trustworthiness of God's word. God has promised that in Christ nothing can separate us from the divine love, and yet the Jews, God's chosen people, have turned away from God and shut themselves off from God's mercy in Christ. How can Christians be sure it may not also happen to them? If the chosen people have been abandoned, how can Christians, as new "chosen people" (8:28-30), be confident that it could not also happen to them? Did God's word fail, if only some in Israel are among those who have accepted God's gift in Christ (9:1-5)?

That is the problem Paul deals with in the next three chapters (9–11), and he begins by assuring his readers that God's word did not in fact fail (9:6). The reason: God has always dealt with a remnant in Israel (9:6-13), which demonstrates that his dealings with his chosen people were based on mercy, not racial descent or human effort (9:14-16). That same gracious activity is seen in the events of the exodus and in the way God dealt with Pharaoh; the purpose was to show God's power and make known the divine name (9:17-18), so that people would know who is in control of history. In those events, God was acting as the creator, with ultimate power over his creation. Yet how he deals with creation nevertheless makes known his power and demonstrates his mercy (9:19-23), a mercy now continued when God includes Gentiles as well as Jews in his chosen people (9:24-26). To sum up, God historically demonstrated his mercy by dealing with a remnant of Israel, who but for that mercy would also have perished (9:27-29).

In fact, it should now be clear that it was not God's word but Israel that failed. Israel did not see that the way to relate to God was through trust, not racial descent ("law"). That is why they rejected God's mercy in Christ, to whom in fact that law pointed and in whom that very law was fulfilled (9:30–10:4). That means, as Paul argued earlier (3:30), that trust also represented the basis of Israel's law, the reality to which it pointed. Hence one is to live in covenant (righteousness) with the God who gave that law to engender trust, not "works of the law" (race). Because of that fact, Gentiles as well as Jews are included in God's mercy (10:5-13). Such trust is based on hearing the apostolic proclamation of God's gracious acts in Christ (10:14-17). But perhaps Israel could plead that it had not heard that proclamation (10:18) or understood it (10:19). Yet in fact it was not God who abandoned them (10:20) but they who abandoned God (10:21).

That God has not abandoned the Jews, his chosen people (11:1a), is demonstrated by Paul, also a Jew, who has accepted Christ in trust. This simply shows that God has continued his historic practice of working with a remnant of the Jews, the remnant currently being those whom God has set aside as the group who trusts in Christ (11:1b-6; cf. 9:6-13), the remnant Paul earlier identified as those who share not the Jewish genetic pool but the faith of their forefather Abraham (4:11-13). This final remnant of the Jews was created by the fact that the majority of Israel was hardened and so did not accept the renewed relationship with God based on trust in Christ (11:7-10).

That hardening did not have as its purpose the destruction of those hardened, however (11:11). Rather, they, like Pharaoh before them, who was also hardened, were hardened as part of God's merciful plan to include Gentiles as well. In a sense, room had to be created for Gentiles within God's chosen people, and such room was created by hardening, and thus excluding, a part of the Jews.

Gentiles must not think, however, that that shows their natural superiority over the Jews, nor come to the conclusion that God liked them better and so hardened Jews on their behalf (11:11-24). Like an olive tree that has had some branches broken off so that others can be grafted in, those engrafted branches do not naturally belong there, but are there by grace, as it were. So it is with the Gentiles: they have come to share in the promises of Israel (the "root," v. 18) and must respond with gratitude for such kindness.

Yet that is not the end of the story. If God's acts are characterized by such kindness, then it will also finally be shown to the natural branches that were broken off in the first place. In fact, it is part of God's mysterious redemptive plan that part of Israel be hardened until the Gentiles enter into God's promises, but then finally, the remainder of Israel that was hardened will finally also be accepted back in (11:26-27). The mysterious hardening of a part of Israel is thus not permanent; in the end, that part of Israel too will return to Christ and so be saved, since their call as chosen people, despite their temporary opposition to Christ, is irrevocable

(11:25-29). That finally is the answer to the question that prompted this whole discussion (chs. 9–11): Christians may have confidence in the God who called them in Christ because, in the end, such a call is, as the call even to an apparently abandoned Israel shows, in fact irrevocable.

All of this shows that disobedience followed by obedience is the way God has carried out his redemptive plan. All people, both Gentiles and Jews, were disobedient so that God's mercy finally could be shown to all of them (11:30-32). Paul concludes by acknowledging that such a divine plan is impossible for human reason to fathom; it comes from the God who alone controls all things, and therefore the only proper response for the creatures to whom God has shown mercy is to give glory to him (11:33-36).

After concluding the exposition of his Gospel, Paul turns in the final portion of Romans to a discussion of how trust in God and in Jesus Christ finds its expression in the structures of life in a world between the beginning of the new age, inaugurated with Christ's resurrection, and the end of the old age, which will occur with his return in glory. Paul states the theme for this discussion in 12:1-2 and then shows how it works itself out in life with other human beings, both within the Christian confession (12:3-13) and in secular society (12:14–13:10). In the middle of this section, Paul looks at the relationship of the Christian to the secular state (13:1-7). Convinced that anarchy is not a Christian possibility, Paul shows how Christians are to live in terms of the state, following the laws that punish evil and promote good. In so defining the state, Paul makes clear that the God-willed function of the state is to promote the good of its citizens. How Paul would react to a state whose laws sought actively to harm some of its citizens he does not say, but it is clear that these verses are not a call to absolute obedience to anything and everything a state may command its citizens to do. The state Paul describes is defined in 13:3-4, and that is the state he is talking about. Paul concludes this discussion by pointing out that Christians are to hold themselves to a higher standard than that of a debauched society (13:11-14).

Paul concludes this final portion of his letter with the discussion of a concrete example of how Christians, under God's gracious lordship enacted in Christ, are to conduct themselves in regard to differences among Christians (14:1–15:13). Paul uses as his example the difference between the "weak," that is, those who feel it necessary to follow certain dietary restrictions, and the "strong," that is, those who find such restrictions unnecessary (14:2). The point of his long discussion is that neither group should regard their dietary practices as so superior that they are willing to sacrifice fellowship with the other group simply in order to insist on their own way of doing things. Rather, they should be willing to act in such a way as to please others rather than themselves and therefore be willing to welcome one another because, finally, that is the way Christ also acted (15:3, 7). Paul concludes his letter by outlining his travel plans (15:14-33) and

On Repaying Evil for Evil

1QS 10.17-21 (Vermes):

> I will pay no man the reward of evil;
>> I will pursue him with goodness.
> For judgement of all the living is with God
>> and it is He who will render to man his reward.
> I will not envy in a spirit of wickedness,
>> my soul shall not desire the riches of violence.
> I will not grapple with the men of perdition
>> until the Day of Revenge,
> but my wrath shall not turn from the men of falsehood,
>> and I will not rejoice until judgement is made.
> I will bear no rancour
>> against them that turn from transgression,
> but will have no pity
>> on all who depart from the way.
> I will offer no comfort to the smitten
>> until their way becomes perfect.

Plutarch, *Moralia, On Compliancy* 13

For he who said, "A handy arm with knaves is knavery," recommends to us the bad habit of resisting vice by resorting to it; whereas to rid ourselves of brazen and unabashed suitors by being unabashed ourselves, and not, by giving in to shame, to render shameful favors to the shameless, is what is rightly and justly done by men of sense.

Joseph and Aseneth 28:10, 14; 29:3 *(OTP)*

And Aseneth said to them, "I beg you, spare your brothers and do not do them evil for evil, because the Lord protected me against them, and shattered their swords, and they melted on the ground like wax from the presence of fire."

And Aseneth stretched out her right hand and touched Simeon's beard and kissed him and said, "By no means, brother, will you do evil for evil to your neighbor. To the Lord will you give (the right) to punish the insult (done) by them. And they are your brothers and your fathers, Israel's line, and they fled far from your presence. Anyway, grant them pardon."

And Levi ran up to him and grasped his hand and said, "By no means, brother, will you do this deed, because we are men who worship God, and it does not befit a man who worships God to repay evil for evil nor to trample underfoot a fallen (man) nor to oppress his enemy till death."

Genesis Rabbah 38.3 on Gen 11:1

R. Johanan began thus: "Whoso rewardeth evil for good, evil shall not depart from his house." Said R. Johanan: If your neighbor [first] entertained you with lentils and you [subsequently] entertained him with meat, you are still indebted to him; why? Because he showed hospitality to you first. R. Simeon b. Abba said: Not only "Whoso rewardeth evil for good," but even he who rewardeth evil for evil, "Evil shall not depart from his house." R. Alexandri commented on the verse, "Whoso rewardeth evil for good": Now the Torah said: "If thou see the ass of him that hateth thee lying under its burden, thou shalt forbear to pass by him; thou shalt surely release it with him" (Exod 23:5): of such Scripture saith, "Whoso rewardeth evil for good, evil shall not depart," etc.

1 Enoch 95:5 (OTP)

Woe unto you who reward evil to your neighbors!
For you shall be rewarded in accordance with your deeds.

On Attitude toward the Government

Dio Chrysostom, *Discourses* **1.45-46:**

So too among kings, since they, I ween, derive their powers and their stewardship from Zeus, the one who, keeping his eyes upon Zeus, orders and governs his people with justice and equity in accordance with the laws and ordinances of Zeus, enjoys a happy lot and a fortunate end, while he who goes astray and dishonours him who entrusted him with his stewardship or gave him this gift, receives no other reward from his great authority and power than merely this: that he has shown himself to all men of his own time and to posterity to be a wicked and undisciplined man. . . .

Sirach 10:4-5 (NRSV)

The government of the earth is in the hand of the Lord,
    and over it he will raise up the right leader for the time.
Human success is in the hand of the Lord,
    and it is he who confers honor upon the lawgiver.

sending greetings (16:1-16, 21-23), along with a final exhortation (16:17-20) and a benediction (16:25-27).

For whatever reason — that Paul had never visited the church to which he was writing, that he wanted them to understand the gospel he would be carrying to Spain, that he wanted to dispel misunderstandings he knew to be abroad concerning his proclamation of the faith, that he had no questions from his addressees that he needed to answer — unlike virtually all his other letters, the argument in Romans is a sustained one, particularly through the first eleven chapters. It is thus

Hierocles, *On Duties,* "How to conduct oneself toward one's fatherland" 3.39.34-36:

> The person who prefers one finger to the five is stupid. . . . In the same way, that person also is stupid who wishes to save himself more than his fatherland, and in addition acts unlawfully and desires the impossible, while he who honors his fatherland more than himself is dear to the gods and firm in his reasoning. Nevertheless, it has been said that even if one were not numbered with the system but were examined separately, it is fitting that he prefers the preservation of the system rather than his own. For the destruction of the city shows that there is no preservation of the citizen, in the same way that the destruction of the hand involves the destruction of the finger as part of the hand. Let us then sum up, that we should not separate what is publicly profitable from what is privately profitable, but to consider them one and the same. For what is profitable to the fatherland is common to each of its parts, since the whole without its parts is nothing. And what is profitable to the citizen is also fitting to the city, if indeed it is taken to be profitable to the citizen. . . .
>
> Because of this, I say, the person who would conduct himself well toward his fatherland should get rid of every passion and disease of the soul. He should also observe the laws of the fatherland as secondary gods of a kind and be guided by them, and, if someone should attempt to transgress them or introduce innovations we should with all diligence prevent him and in every way possible oppose him. For it is not beneficial to a city if its laws are dishonored and new things are preferred to the old. (from Abraham J. Malherbe, *Moral Exhortation: A Greco-Roman Sourcebook* [Philadelphia: Westminster, 1986], 89-90)

necessary to consider the whole argument step-by-step in the order Paul has presented it, since understanding any part of it depends on understanding its entire sweep. It is not a systematic treatment of all major Christian positions and practices — there is no mention, for example, of the Lord's Supper — but its sustained argument gives us enough of a picture of the form and focus of Paul's proclamation that it can well be used as a kind of intellectual map by which to orient ourselves as we explore the remainder of the Pauline theological landscape. For that reason, it is an appropriate letter to begin the study of the Pauline collection contained in the NT.

FOR FURTHER READING

Paul J. Achtemeier, *Romans* (Interpretation; Louisville: Westminster John Knox, 1985)

C. K. Barrett, *Romans* (2nd ed., London: Black, 1991)

C. E. B. Cranfield, *Romans*, 2 vols. (International Critical Commentary; Edinburgh: Clark, 1975, 1979)

Karl P. Donfried, ed., *The Romans Debate* (2nd ed., Peabody: Hendrickson, 1991)

James D. G. Dunn, *Romans*, 2 vols. (Word Biblical Commentary; Dallas: Word, 1988)

Joseph A. Fitzmyer, *Romans* (Anchor Bible; Garden City: Doubleday, 1993)

Douglas J. Moo, *The Epistle to the Romans* (New International Commentary on the New Testament; Grand Rapids: Eerdmans, 1996)

Stanley K. Stowers, *The Diatribe and Paul's Letter to the Romans* (Chico: Scholars, 1981)

13. Paul and the Christians in Corinth

More than perhaps any other correspondence in the NT, Paul's letters to the Christians in Corinth give us insight into the kinds of problems Paul encountered in proclaiming the gospel of Jesus Christ to a culture that had very different values and practices. Paul visited Corinth a number of times and exchanged a lively correspondence with the Christians there, some of it preserved for us in the NT. The letters we have present a picture of the complex relationship between Paul and the Corinthian Christians. Because it is complex, it is at times difficult to unravel, but we shall consider the evidence we have and sketch out a picture of those relationships. This will give us a chance to look at Paul the apostle in action and at how he confronts theological and ethical problems within the Corinthian Christian community.

13.1. CORINTH AS PAUL KNEW IT

Corinth was situated on a narrow neck of land some four miles wide connecting the Peloponnesus to the south with the Greek mainland to the north. It thus occupied a strategic location for north-south trade routes that had to pass through it either way. It also opened to the Aegean Sea to the east and the Adriatic Sea to the west. The port to the Aegean Sea, Lechaion, lay in the Gulf of Corinth directly to the north of the city and was connected to the city by a road with walls on both sides. The port to the Adriatic Sea, Cenchreae, lay seven miles west of Corinth. It was the site of the home church of Phoebe, who carried Paul's letter to Rome (Rom 16:1). To spare ships the long and sometimes dangerous voyage to the south around the Peloponnesus, a road, the Diolkos, had been constructed to carry

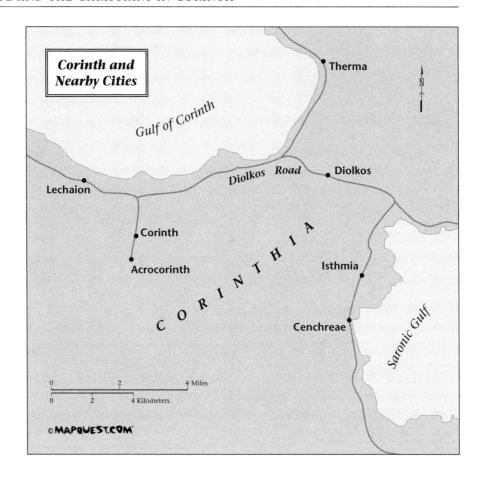

goods overland between the two ports. Thus a ship could be unloaded at one port, its goods carried overland, and then reloaded onto a ship at the other port. Smaller ships were carried across the isthmus on wheeled vehicles; tracks were cut into the Diolkos for that purpose. Because of the inconvenience of unloading and reloading ships at the two ports, there were regular proposals to dig a canal through the isthmus; Julius Caesar proposed to do it (Plutarch, *Caesar* 68.4) as did Gaius Caligula (Suetonius, *Gaius* 21). This was proposed so often that it became a regular point of speculation, along with enlarging the harbor at Ostia or whether there was land to the west beyond the ocean (Quintilian, *Institutiones Oratoria* 3.8.16).

Corinth grew rich from the commerce passing through, and the city was famous for the constant presence of many sailors. Like any town, ancient or modern, where sailors congregated, certain characteristics emerged, among them women of easy virtue. The orator Dio Chrysostom remarked that large numbers of people gathered at Corinth because of the good harbors and the "female companions," (*Discourse* 8.5) and noted that Corinth was known for its elegant and expensive women, leading to the proverb "Not every man can afford the trip to Corinth" (*Discourse* 20.7). The name of Corinth became the base for words coined to refer to various forms of sexual behavior.

Corinth was also noted for a metal compound termed "Corinthian bronze," an amalgam of gold, silver, and copper or bronze. Corinthian bronze was supposedly created by accident, either when Hannibal conquered Illium and burned its treasures (Petronius, *Satyricon* 50) or when a house containing quantities of gold, silver, and especially copper accidentally burned down (Plutarch, *Oracles* 395.2). Collectors drove the price of objects made of Corinthian bronze to great heights, much to the disgust of Seneca (*On Shortness of Life* 12.2; *Helvia on Consolation* 11.3). The Corinthians often put capitals of Corinthian bronze on pillars, giving rise to the "Corinthian" capital (Pliny, *Natural History* 34.7.13), a capital later reproduced in stone.

Finally, like other important ancient Greek cities, Corinth had its games, the "Isthmian Games," which, like the Pythian and the Olympian games, were held at regular intervals and attracted large crowds.

Corinth's site had been occupied for some 4000 years when Paul visited there, particularly the high hill (567 meters) in the southern part of the city, the "Acrocorinth" (Greek for "high Corinth"). Corinth had been conquered and destroyed by the Romans in 146 b.c. and lay in ruins for over a century. It was refounded by Julius Caesar in 44 b.c. as a colony for retired veterans of the Roman legions. This recent new beginning meant that there were no old, landed families residing there and therefore that the newly rich had more upward social mobility than in most other Roman cities. This in turn made this city with a dynamic commercial sector more open to new ideas. Its importance increased until Augustus made it the capital of Achaia (the southern half of the Greek peninsula; the northern half was called Macedonia). It was therefore the residence of a Roman proconsul, who during one of Paul's visits was Gallio (Acts 18:12), the brother of the famous Roman philosopher and literary figure Seneca.

In many ways, the city of Corinth Paul knew was closer to a modern American city than almost any other ancient city. The upward social mobility conferred by large amounts of money, the large athletic spectacles, the love of parties, the problems created by a loosening of sexual limits, the desire to be as inclusive as possible in religious beliefs and practices, the desire to include social customs from secular life into the Christian communities — all of these give to the problems discussed in the Corinthian correspondence an immediacy not always present in ethical discussions contained in the NT letters.

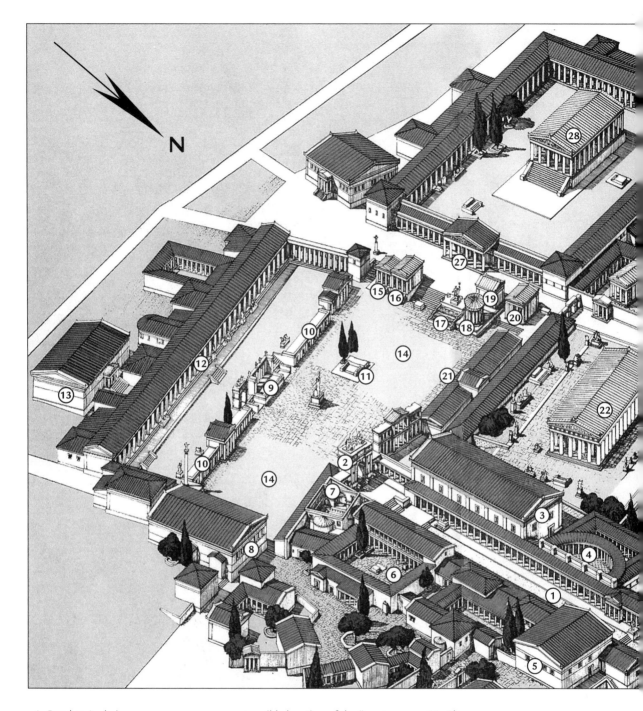

1. Road to Lechaion
2. Monumental Arch
3. Basilica
4. Market
5. Baths
6. Peribolos of Apollo (built in the late first century CE; before that, a possible location of the "meat market" of 1 Cor 10:25)
7. Pirene Fountain
8. Julian Basilica
9. Bema (the "tribunal" of Acts 18:12)
10. Market
11. Altar
12. Stoa
13. Basilica
14. Forum
15. Temple of Venus Victrix
16. Temple of the Cults of Rome, the Emperor, and the Senate

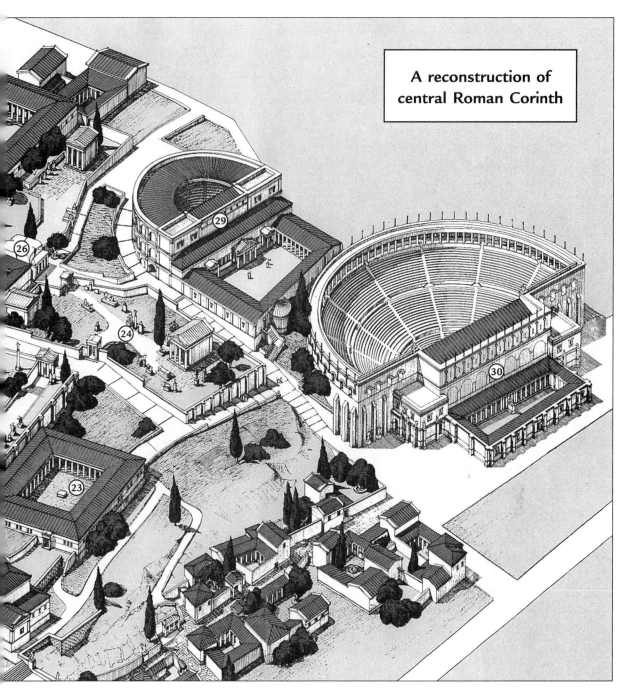

A reconstruction of central Roman Corinth

17. Fountain of Poseidon
18. Monument of Cn. Babbius Philinus
19. Temple
20. Temple of Tyche
21. Market
22. Temple of Apollo (sixth century BCE)
23. Market
24. Shrine of Athena Chalinitis
25. Temple
26. Glauke Fountain
27. Market
28. Temple
29. Odeion (built after Paul's time)
30. Theater

From N. Papahatzis, *Ancient Corinth: The Museums of Corinth, Isthmia and Sicyon* (Athens: Ekdotike Athenon, 1981); for detailed information see http://corinth.sas.upenn.edu.

13.2. THE CORINTHIAN CORRESPONDENCE

Unlike Romans, where the secretary Tertius who took down Paul's dictation adds his own greetings at the end of the letter (16:22), a secretary is not named in either 1 or 2 Corinthians. But Paul's note that he appends a greeting in his own hand at the end of 1 Corinthians (16:21-23) indicates that he followed the usual ancient custom of dictating the letter to another person. It may well be that Paul also wrote the benediction with which 2 Corinthians closes with his own hand, but that remains a matter of speculation. It is likely, from Paul's comments on Timothy (16:10-11), that Timothy carried the letter to Corinth, perhaps accompanied by some others (16:12b). No deliverer is mentioned in 2 Corinthians.

The major literary issue concerning the Corinthian correspondence is the number of letters Paul wrote to the Christians in that city, and how much of that correspondence we still possess. A review of the evidence will show the scope of the problem.

It is clear from 1 Cor 5:9 that our 1 Corinthians is not the first letter Paul wrote to that city. This verse refers to a letter Paul wrote to them prior to the letter we have as 1 Corinthians, a letter that had given them some advice about wrongful association with immoral people that they had misinterpreted. In many ways, the difficulty reflected in that reference to an earlier letter sets the tone for the rest of the correspondence, for the letters we have show such misunderstanding to have been a relatively common occurrence between Paul and the Corinthian Christians.

It is interesting that 2 Corinthians 6:14–7:1 seem to intrude into its present context and concerns precisely that same problem of wrongful association. Signs of textual intrusion are that these verses appear to interrupt their context in 2 Corinthians 6–7, that they make sense in themselves, and, some would argue, that the text of 2 Corinthians 6–7 flows more smoothly when 6:14–7:1 are removed. On that basis, many have argued that we have in these verses in 2 Corinthians a fragment from that first letter to Corinth mentioned in 1 Corinthians 5:9. Be that as it may, 1 Corinthians is the second letter Paul wrote to the Christian communities there.

In addition, Paul mentions in 2 Cor 2:4 a so-called "letter of tears" and refers to it again in 7:8. Its description does not at all sound like our 1 Corinthians. Therefore it is yet another letter Paul wrote, for our purposes a third one.

The letter we know as 2 Corinthians is then a fourth letter. Yet it has a decided break in its tone between chs. 9 and 10. The first part is relatively irenic in tone, whereas chs. 10–13 are quite sharp, laced with sarcasm and irritation. As some scholars have shown, one can identify the content of chs. 10–13, on the basis of Greek rhetorical categories, as a complete unit. Because of the change in tone, many scholars have proposed that these chapters are the harsh letter to which Paul refers in 2:4.

We thus know for sure of four letters. While there are good arguments for the unity of 2 Corinthians, which we will consider later, some things proposed in chs. 1–9 are known to have been completed in chs. 10–13. Thus chs. 10–13 may represent a fifth letter.

Not only did Paul write to the Corinthians; they wrote to him. It is clear from references in 1 Cor 7:1 that Paul had received a letter from Corinth that posed a number of questions for him to answer (see 7:1; 8:1; 12:1; 16:1). It seems likely that the letter was delivered to Paul by Stephanas, Fortunatus, and Achaicus (16:17), with an additional visit by "Chloe's people" (1:11), who then reported additional

---

Paul's Visits to and Correspondence with Corinth

Founding visit

First letter of Paul to Corinth (mentioned in 1 Cor 5:9; perhaps included in 2 Cor 6:14–7:1)

Paul in Ephesus (1 Cor 16:8)

Letter from Corinth (1 Cor 7:1) and report from "Chloe's people" (1 Cor 1:11)

Second Letter of Paul to Corinth (1 Corinthians)

Paul suffers rejection in Asia (2 Cor 1:8-10)

Paul visits Corinth, is rejected, leaves (so-called "painful visit" — 2 Cor 2:1)

Paul sends Titus to Corinth (2 Cor 7:6-7)

Third letter of Paul, the letter of tears/harsh letter (2 Cor 2:4; 7:8); some identify this with 2 Corinthians 10–13

Paul travels to Troas (2 Cor 2:12)

Paul travels to Macedonia (2 Cor 2:13; Philippi? Thessalonica?)

Paul meets Titus in Macedonia (2 Cor 7:6)

Titus reports goodwill toward Paul on the part of the Corinthians (2 Cor 7:7)

Fourth letter of Paul to Corinth (2 Corinthians)

Fifth letter of Paul to Corinth (if 2 Corinthians 10–13 is a separate letter)

information and described some additional problems occurring in the Christian communities in Corinth. The matters reported by Chloe's people are discussed in the first seven chapters.

There was thus a lively correspondence between Paul and the Corinthian Christians. As we have seen, the evidence in the Corinthian correspondence makes clear that we do not possess all the letters Paul wrote (see also Col 4:16, with its reference to a now lost letter to the Laodiceans). One can hope that at some point further letters will be discovered in some hidden place, perhaps somewhere in the Egyptian desert, where so many other ancient manuscripts have been found in recent decades!

When we read the Corinthian correspondence that we have, we find ourselves in the midst of Pauline ethical thinking. And it is clear in such a reading how closely Paul's theological and ethical thinking are related to each other. The material dealt with in this correspondence concerns what can only be described as theological points central to the Christian faith: the relationship between Christ and the sinful world, the meaning and conduct of the Lord's Supper, the import and reality of Christ's resurrection, the relationship between Christians and Jews, and the power and presence of the Holy Spirit, to name but a few. Yet at the same time the letter is immersed in discussions of key ethical questions: marriage and sexual relationships, relationships among Christian and between Christians and non-Christians, the practice of initiating lawsuits, and the use of one's material wealth, among others. It is clear in this correspondence, therefore, that ethics and theology cannot be treated separately. All of Paul's theological points have ethical implications, and all the ethical discussions imply and presume theological foundations. For that reason, to study the Corinthian correspondence is in a profound way to study not only the content of Paul's ethical thinking, but his method of doing ethics as well. The center of both theology and ethics is Christ, crucified but risen, and reigning over all creation. Paul's preaching and writing, his ethics and his theology, are attempts to come to terms with that reality and what it means for life in our world.

13.3. 1 CORINTHIANS

13.3.1. The Origin and Themes of the Letter

1 Corinthians was written while Paul was in Ephesus in the Roman province of Asia (1 Cor 16:8; cf. v. 19a). When it was written can be determined a little more closely than with some other Pauline letters. Because Paul mentions the collection for the "saints" in Jerusalem (1 Cor 16:1), we know that 1 Corinthians, like Romans, which also mentions the collection, must have been written after the

meeting between Paul and some other apostles in Jerusalem (Gal 2:1-10), where it was agreed that Paul should assemble such a collection.

The Collection for Christians in Jerusalem

. . . only they [James, Cephas, and John] wanted us to remember the poor, which very thing I was also glad to do. (Gal 2:10)

Now about the contribution for the saints: as I arranged with the churches of Galatia, so you also are to do. On the first day of every week, let each one of you put something aside, whatever amount seems good, and save it up, lest the whole collection has to be made when I come. But when I do come, I will send whomever you accredit by letter to carry your gifts to Jerusalem. If it seems appropriate that I should go too, they will go with me. (1 Cor 16:1-4)

. . . because our intention is this, that no one find fault with us about this bounteous (gift) which we are administering, because our intention is pure, not only in the sight of the Lord but also in the sight of human beings. (2 Cor 8:20-21)

Now concerning the offering for the saints, it is superfluous for me to write to you, for I know your willingness, concerning which I boast about you to the people of Macedonia [northern Greece], saying that Achaia [southern Greece] has been ready since last year, and your zeal has stirred up the majority of them. . . . Therefore I took it to be necessary to urge my companions to go on to you ahead of me and to arrange in advance for this gift you have already promised to make, in order that it may be ready as a willing gift and not as something snatched from you. (2 Cor 9:1-3, 5)

But now I am going to Jerusalem to give aid to the saints. For Macedonia and Achaia were pleased to make a contribution for the poor among the saints who are at Jerusalem; they were pleased to do it, and they are under obligation to them, for since the Gentiles have shared in their spiritual blessing, they are also under obligation to render service to them with their material blessings. (Rom 15:25-27)

The Delphi Inscription

The following inscription from the first century CE was found at Delphi, Greece. It names Gallio as proconsul, who is also mentioned in Acts 18 in conjunction with Paul's visit to Corinth.

Tiberius Claudius Caesar Augustus Germanicus Pontifex Maximus, in his tribunician power year 12, acclaimed emperor the 26th time, father of the country . . . sends greetings to the city of Delphi. I have long been zealous for the city of Delphi and favorable to it from the beginning, and I have always observed the cult of the Pythian Apollo, but with regard to the present stories, and those quarrels of the citizens of which a report has been made by Lucius Junio Gallio, my friend and proconsul of Achaia . . . will still hold the previous settlement.

How long after that meeting 1 Corinthians was written is difficult to determine, however. Acts 18:12 reports that Gallio was proconsul during Paul's lengthy stay in Corinth (a year and a half according to Acts 18:11). Toward the end of that visit, Paul was set upon by some Jewish opponents and haled before Gallio on charges growing out of Paul's missionary preaching (Paul "persuaded" people to worship God in ways that were contrary to the Jewish law). Because the charges were religious, Gallio refused to intervene. These events are significant for dating the Corinthian correspondence because Gallio's proconsulship can be validated from existing Roman records: it is mentioned in an inscription recording the emperor Claudius's twenty-sixth accolade as "imperator," which occurred in the first half of 52 C.E. This puts Paul in Corinth around the years 52-53. He must have written 1 Corinthians, then, after he had left Corinth and, apparently, gone to Ephesus (so Acts 19:1), therefore no earlier than 53. We do not know how long Paul had been in Ephesus when he wrote, but we may assume it was not long. Hence a date around 53 or 54 is a reasonable conjecture for 1 Corinthians.

The letter follows the customary Hellenistic form, with Paul's usual adaptations. That form includes the letter opening (1:1-3), the prayer (1:4-9), the letter body (1:10–16:4), and the letter closing, with the usual travel plans (16:5-10), greetings from others (16:11-20), and the final salutation (16:21-24).

Although Paul is answering a variety of questions and attempting to adjudicate a number of different problems, two themes predominate. One is the profound difference between the standards of the world and the standards revealed in Jesus Christ. As Paul makes explicit in the first part of this letter, what is reckoned as powerful and wise by the world is proved to be weak and foolish when compared to the divine wisdom revealed in and portrayed by Christ, just as what the world reckons as foolish and weak turns out to be the wisdom and power of God. The reality that demonstrates this fact is the cross of Christ. The cross was the instrument of ultimate degradation in the Greco-Roman world. It was reserved for slaves and non-Roman citizens. Death was slow and extraordinarily painful, with the person ultimately dying for lack of water. After death the body was frequently allowed to remain on the cross, its decay and stench to remind passersby of the futility of attempting to oppose Roman power. It was precisely this instrument on which Christ died, thus proving in the eyes of the world the futility of all Christ's claims and revealing him to be weak and foolish over against Roman power. Yet that death was not defeat but victory, as Christ's resurrection proved, with his death being the means by which God overcame the power of sin and death. Thus the cross proved to be the instrument of God's wisdom and power in dealing with sinful human beings. It is the logic drawn from that reality that informs Paul's descriptions and judgments in the first portion of 1 Corinthians.

The second theme is the lordship of Christ and is derived from the first. That Christians acknowledge Christ's lordship makes it impossible for them to acknowledge any other lordship, religious or political. It therefore makes it impossible for them to participate in the rites of other religions or to follow the customs of secular society in the Greco-Roman world. To do so is to fall back into the realm ruled over by sin and death. In principle, Christ's lordship renders null and void all other lordships, and it is that fundamental fact that led the Corinthians to the conclusion that, since secular customs and society had been negated, their behavior in that society made no difference. Their freedom from that society in Christ, so they reasoned, gave them freedom to do as they wished. Paul is at pains in this letter to make clear that along with that divinely given freedom come responsibilities to obey the will of the God under whose lordship Christians now live. They do not belong to themselves, free to do as they see fit; they belong to Christ, and are therefore under his lordship (7:22-23a). What that means Paul spells out in the second half of the letter.

Finally, it is worth noting that the gospel Paul preached was not unique to Paul, as is indicated by his use of common Christian traditions in this letter. Paul commends the Corinthian Christians for their adherence to the traditions he delivered to them (11:2), and in the course of his discussions he recites two of them — one concerning the institution of the eucharist (11:23-26), the other concerning Christ's death and resurrection (15:3-7). Paul introduces these traditions with the technical Greek words for receiving (paralambanō) and handing on (paradidōmi) traditions. We know that these traditions constituted part of Paul's original proclamation to the Corinthians because in both instances he says that he handed them on earlier.

Paul thus belonged to the total Christian mission, and used traditions known to others as well, just as he was accompanied on his missionary travels by other Christian preachers, in the case of 1 Corinthians, by Sosthenes (1:1). Paul was not a kind of "lone wolf," avoiding all contacts with other Christian preachers. He was rather part of the total apostolic mission to the Greco-Roman world.

Paul's Use of Jewish Traditions

Paul apparently also used earlier Jewish traditions in both his missionary preaching and his writing. One probable example is the strange reference in 1 Cor 10:4 to a supernatural rock that followed the Israelites in the desert, which Paul then identifies as Christ. In the midst of an account of part of Israel's travels in the wilderness, Num 21:16-18a celebrates a well that God gave to the Israelites and concludes in v. 18a: "they went from the wilderness to Mattanah." This last word can mean "gift," and it was so understood in the Aramaic translation of the OT called Targum *Onkelos* ("from the wilderness a gift"). In that targum, the list of places visited by the Israelites is understood to be where that gift from the wilderness — that is, the well — followed Israel. This tradition was then combined with the tradition about the rock Moses struck at Meribah to produce water for the Israelites in the desert, a tradition recorded just previously in the narrative (Num 20:2-13). The final step was to apply another Jewish tradition, known to the Christian author Justin Martyr, namely that "rock" in the OT signified "Messiah." Taken together, we probably have in these traditions the basis for Paul's assertion that a rock, Christ, had followed the Israelites in the desert.

13.3.2. The Content of the Letter

After the letter opening (1:1-3) Paul utters a prayer of thanksgiving to God for the gifts given the Corinthian Christians. The two mentioned, knowledge and spiritual gifts, are also part of the problem in which the Corinthians are involved, namely, their misuse of those gifts. Thus, as so often, Paul summarizes the problems he is addressing at the very outset of the letter.

1 Corinthians

Letter opening (1:1-3)
Prayer (1:4-9)
Letter body (1:10–16:4)
   Responses to the report from Chloe's people (1:10–6:20)
      Factions in the Corinthian church (1:10–4:21)
      Activities arising from a mistaken understanding of
         Christian freedom (5:1–6:20)
   Responses to the Corinthians' letter (7:1–11:1)
      On marriage (ch. 7)
      On food offered to idols (ch. 8; 10:1–11:1)
      Christian freedom and Paul's legitimacy as an apostle (ch. 9)
   Conduct in Christian worship (11:2-34, possibly also responding
      to the letter)
   More responses to the Corinthians' letter (chs. 12–14)
      Gifts of the Spirit, particularly glossolalia (ch. 12)
      Love, the highest gift (ch. 13)
      Glossolalia again, and order in worship (ch. 14)
   The bodily resurrection of Christ (ch. 15)
   The collection for the Christians in Jerusalem (16:1-4)
Letter closing (16:5-24)
   Travel plans (16:5-10)
   Greetings from others (16:11-20)
   Final salutation (16:21-24)

The first problem Paul addresses (1:10–4:21) concerns the report from Chloe's people that the Corinthian Christians have divided themselves into quarreling factions in their apparent attempt to be identified with the most powerful Christian figure. After pointing out that such factional identifications are intolerable because they make Christ a cause of division rather than the one who saved and united them, Paul develops the theme of the contrast between what the world regards as wise and powerful and what Christians know to be wise and powerful through God's act in Christ. This contrast shows that their desire to be identified with powerful figures betrays a lack of understanding of the very heart of the Christian faith. Paul reminds them that the contrast between the values of the Greco-Roman world and the values embodied in the Christian faith was the theme of his preaching among them from the beginning (2:1-5), and it was matched by how he preached: not as a wise man but as one clothed in weakness, so that the Corinthians' confidence should not be placed in the wise Paul but in the crucified Christ. In that way the power of God's Spirit can become manifest.

It is apparent in this discussion that there were those who were criticizing Paul either for his inability as a speaker, for the lack of "wisdom" in his message, or both. Paul points out that his manner of speaking was intended to complement his message (2:1-3) and that in fact he does bring wisdom, but a kind of wisdom not immediately apparent to those who have just accepted the Christian faith, since their definition of wisdom is still attached to their former cultural values (2:6-8; 3:1-3, 18-20). For that reason he is indifferent to the judgment leveled against him and his missionary message (4:3-5) since it comes from people who have vastly overestimated their own importance in and understanding of the Christian faith (4:8-13). They must realize that the disreputable things that happen to Paul in the course of his missionary preaching happen because he embodies the message he proclaims: that weakness and foolishness in the eyes of the world are in fact wisdom and strength in Christ. Paul concludes by noting that he will visit them again in the near future, and that their conduct will determine whether he comes as friend or as one who must chastise his wayward children (4:14-21).

In a second section (5:1–6:20), also responding to the report delivered by Chloe's people (5:1), Paul addresses some activities among the Corinthian Christians that have resulted from a mistaken understanding of the meaning of Christian freedom (6:12). Of the three activities Paul addresses, the first concerns a young man living with his stepmother (5:1-13). Paul does not mention why these two people feel they can flout moral conventions valid even among non-Christians. There is a Jewish tradition, however, that when non-Jews become proselytes and take on the yoke of the Jewish law, they are to be regarded in the same way as newborn babies, and hence any prior relationships are nullified. It is clear enough that Paul also felt that when one becomes a Christian, old things have passed away and all things have become new (2 Cor 5:17; see also 1 Cor 6:9-11), and it is likely that he told the Corinthians this in the course of his gospel proclamation. Perhaps these two people felt that, having become Christians, their old relationships had been severed, so that they were free, as newborn Christians, to assume new relationships as they pleased. Instead of being ashamed to have this practice in their midst, apparently some Corinthian Christians found it a reason for boasting (5:6), perhaps as a radical example of the exercise of their new Christian freedom. Paul will have none of it. People who do such things are to be removed from the Christian community (5:2b, 13b), as Paul reminds them he had told them in an earlier letter (5:9-13).

The second activity Paul addresses is the readiness of Christians to sue one another in Roman courts (6:1-12). Such litigiousness represents defeat for the

Christian community, Paul argues, because it shows that they are unable to base relationships in their community on their new way of life, that they have not adopted the kind of familial love necessary for the new Christian family (6:8).

Paul's summary of his advice in these two matters is summed up in 6:9-11: people who act in a way that severs their relationship with God (i.e., who become unrighteous) will not inherit God's kingdom. Such acts include sexual as well as social perversions, a few of which Paul lists in these verses (for a similar list, see Rom 1:24-32).

In addressing a third activity, Paul quotes a saying — "All things are lawful for me" — that some Corinthian Christians were apparently applying as license to do what they wanted in the physical realm. Perhaps they reasoned that, since God is Spirit, what counts in life is what one does in the spiritual realm, so that one is free to do whatever one wants with the body, since it will be abandoned in the resurrection, when it will be transformed into a spiritual body (see Paul's discussion in ch. 15). Paul concedes that some of the activities thus justified may be lawful, but argues that they are not helpful. Indeed, Christ has taken possession of the Christian soul and body, and as a result one's body also belongs to Christ. Therefore, sexual immorality of any kind is to be avoided, including fornication (6:15) and homoerotic sexual contact (6:9). The presence of God's Spirit within Christians means that they must use the body as a temple of God's holy Spirit, who has now taken possession of them through Christ's death on the cross (6:19-20).

With the conclusion of that discussion, Paul turns his attention to matters raised in the Corinthians' letter to him. It has already become clear that the loose sexual practices of their seaport city have influenced how the Corinthian Christians have lived and have raised questions about how they must now live. Perhaps some felt that absolute sexual abstinence was the only way to react to the kind of immorality they abandoned when they became Christians, just as others seem to have felt that since they were now spiritual, sexual immorality no longer mattered. Paul's basic advice is that if celibacy is not possible for an individual, marriage is perfectly acceptable. What is not acceptable is any kind of sexual contact outside the bonds of the marriage of a man and a woman. One problem underlying this discussion was the tensions that arose when one partner in the marriage became a Christian and the other did not. Paul calls on the authority of a word from Jesus (perhaps the one also remembered in Mark 10:2-9) to argue that, if possible, the couple should stay together, but then Paul adds his own opinion. Ultimately, he says, it depends on the non-Christian partner. If that person wants to separate, the Christian spouse should let it occur, though remaining together is preferable (7:10-16). Saying that a Christian married prior to conversion should remain married leads Paul to reflect on the fact that all Christians should remain in the social status they had when they became Christians (7:17-24).

Paul then turns to advice to those not yet married (7:25-40), where, he admits, he knows no applicable saying of Jesus. He sees nothing against marriage; to be married is certainly not to sin, and those who feel compelled to be married should do so with a clear conscience (7:36, 38). But because Paul thinks the return of Christ is imminent (7:29), he advises that it is better not to take on additional responsibilities in light of that impending crisis. It is clear from this discussion that Paul does not think sexual activity is inherently sinful, but he is strongly convinced that the only appropriate opportunity for acceptable sexual behavior is within the bonds of marriage between husband and wife.

The next point raised in the Corinthians' letter that Paul discusses concerns a Christian's attitude to food offered to idols (ch. 8). Since most of the meat that found its way to the public meat market had in fact been slaughtered at the temple of some Greco-Roman god or goddess, the question of food offered to idols would arise whenever a Christian bought meat. There was an additional problem. Apparently some of the Corinthian Christians, prior to their conversion, had belonged to communities that worshipped one or more of these Greco-Roman deities and in the course of such worship had eaten food in the temple that had been sacrificed there. Consumption of such meat, even by Christians, seemed very much to signal that they had abandoned Christ and reverted to their former idolatrous way of life. Furthermore, it frequently happened that the only available larger rooms for private celebrations such as birthdays, weddings, and the like were in temples (often the basement). Temple authorities added to the income of the temples by renting out these rooms. A Christian might be invited to join old friends for such a celebration, and if food were served, the question would be raised for the Christian whether he or she could eat it and not fall back into idolatry.

Paul's answer is, basically, that Christians whose consciences are clear because they know they have been delivered from the realm of idols by Christ are free to eat any such food. The one limitation arises from the danger that eating such food may tempt Christians with weaker consciences to participate, and then they might feel they have in fact betrayed Christ. Thus, it is consideration for the fate of weaker Christians, not any quality inherent in the food, that is to determine how one acts in this regard. A fellow Christian, Paul says, is more valuable than the exercise of a freedom that may offend, however legitimate that freedom may be.

Interposed into this discussion of how Christians are to conduct themselves with respect to food sacrificed to idols (which is continued in 10:1–11:1) is a discussion of Christian freedom. It is prompted by what seem to be questions about Paul's legitimacy as an apostle, a topic more directly addressed in 2 Corinthians but apparently already present when Paul wrote 1 Corinthians. The issue seems to be his refusal to accept living expenses from the Corinthian Christians while he was carrying on missionary work among them. He defends the right of a Christian proclaimer to such support (9:3-12), but also defends his right to refuse it (9:13-18) so that he may be free to preach the gospel as he sees fit. Paul points out that this is his principle in all his missionary work: he willingly assumes obligations he need not have taken on in order to make his gospel more acceptable (9:19-23). He is apparently unwilling to place himself under any monetary obligation to the Corinthian Christians lest they try to use that obligation to get him to modify his views on what the gospel means for their lives as Christians.

After a brief paragraph exhorting the readers to stay the course of their Christian life as he himself does (9:24-27), Paul returns to the dangers of participation in idolatry. Against some who apparently argued that participation in the Christian eucharist insulated them from any danger involved in participating in idolatry, Paul argues that the Jews also shared such spiritual food and drink at the time of the exodus from Egypt, but that did not insulate them from the evil consequences of abandoning the way of life God had given them (10:1-13). If eating food sacrificed to idols is permissible (10:25-30), participation in cultic meals honoring idols is not (10:14-22). Idols may not be gods, but, Paul says, they do represent demons, and Christians cannot be partners with demons. Christian freedom does not reach that far. But even within the realm where Christian freedom prevails, the good of one's fellow Christian should determine the bounds of one's own freedom. Surely Christians are free to eat what their consciences will allow them; they are not bound by some else's conscience (10:25-30). But such freedom finally is not to be used to seek one's own advantage, that is, to satisfy one's own desires. It is to be used to glorify God (10:31).

Paul turns next to conduct in Christian worship (11:2-34). It is not clear whether this question was raised in the letter from the Corinthians or whether Paul heard of problems in their church by some other means. He is concerned with two problems relating to worship: how participants in worship are to clothe themselves (11:2-16) and how the eucharist is to be celebrated (11:17-34). The first problem concerns primarily who is to have their heads covered in worship. For reasons that remain obscure to us, Paul is adamant that when men utter prayers or "prophecy" (the latter almost certainly meaning preaching or exhortation) their heads are to be uncovered, whereas when women exercise those functions in public worship, their heads are to be covered. Roman men normally covered their heads during some cultic celebrations (Plutarch, *The Roman Questions* 266B.C-D), but had them uncovered during others (e.g., when worshiping Saturn or a god named "Honor"; so Plutarch, *The Roman Questions* 266E-267A), so there is no help from that quarter in understanding the problem Paul is discussing. Long hair on a man was, among other things, the mark of a philosopher, but again there was apparently no stigma attached to long-haired men or short-haired women. Stoics talked much about living in conformity to nature, as Paul argues in this instance (11:14-15), but there is no record that they identified what is "natural" with hair length. We simply do not know the background of Paul's arguments here. But it is important to note that there is no question about women participating in worship through the public utterance of prayers or preaching/admonitions. That point will become important a little later in the letter.

The problem concerning the celebration of the eucharist (11:17-34) is clearly related to Roman custom, however, and it relates to Roman practices at banquets in private homes. Roman houses would not have had a room large enough for all Christians to be in it, so the eucharist was probably observed with people located in several rooms as well as in the atrium. In secular Roman practice, people were seated in various rooms according to their social status, and different foods were served at different times to each room (e.g., Dio Chrysostom, *Discourse* 30.30). Complaints were common (e.g., Juvenal, *Satire* 5.99-104, 146-53, and the text from Martial below). Important guests were served first, and then the others in descending order of importance. It appears that such customs may have been imported into the house churches when the meal and the accompanying eucharist were celebrated in Corinth, even to the point that some people drank too much wine (11:17-22). Paul says that such conduct is not acceptable and reminds the Corinthians of the origin of the Lord's Supper as he had told them earlier (11:23-26). After warning them of the dire consequences of their present eucharistic practices (11:27-32), Paul urges that all eat at the same time; if anyone is unhappy with this arrangement, Paul invites them to eat their fill at home (11:33-34).

The Roman Poet Martial Complains to His Host

You take oysters, I suck a mussel;
you get mushrooms, I take hog funguses;
you tackle turbot [a prized fish], but I brill [a common fish];
a turtle-dove gorges you, before me a magpie that has died
    in its cage.

(*Epigrams* 3.1)

Paul returns to the letter that was sent to him, now responding to questions about spiritual gifts. Pointing out first that the Spirit never prompts anyone to curse Christ and that only by the Spirit's prompting can anyone confess Christ as Lord, Paul then discusses the various kinds of spiritual gifts. Apparently the Corinthian Christians thought there was a hierarchy of spiritual gifts, with some more important than others; speaking in tongues (glossolalia) was regarded as the most important. Paul points out that since all gifts come from the same Spirit, all are of the same value (12:4-11). Furthermore, just as the human body needs all the functions of its parts to perform as a body, so the Christian community, as the body of Christ, needs all the spiritual gifts of its members if it is to function correctly (12:12-26). Paul concludes by pointing out that not all members share all gifts (12:27-30), and then informs his readers that the highest gift of all is love.

1 Corinthians 13 is often called a hymn; it does indeed show exalted language and poetic turns of phrase. Two things are noteworthy about this hymn, in addition to its beauty of phrase and language. The first is that the word for "love" that Paul uses, *agapē* — and here he follows usual Christian custom — was a fairly rare word in the first century. The more common words for love are *erōs*, which is love, often intense, awakened and driven by the value or desirability of the object loved, and *philia,* close in meaning to "friendship," which is a general affection for something pleasing. Christians filled the word *agapē* with the sense of a love that confers value on its object, which may otherwise be quite unlovable. Thus God's love for human beings confers value on human beings otherwise made quite unlovable by sin. That is the love Paul describes in 1 Corinthians 13. The second thing noteworthy about the hymn is that one can virtually substitute "Jesus Christ" for "love" and thus discern the source of Paul's description of love, especially in vv. 1-7. In the remainder of the chapter Paul compares the divine gift of love with gifts the Corinthians apparently valued most highly — prophecy, tongues, and knowledge. Compared to love, these gifts are evanescent and belong to the childhood of the faith. Even compared to faith and hope, Christian love is paramount.

In ch. 14, Paul returns for a lengthier discussion of the gift of tongues. The essential point Paul wants to make is that speaking in tongues without an interpretation of what has been said is of no value to the Christian community. In the absence of an interpretation, a message in tongues can only cause confusion. The desire to avoid the confusion caused by uninterpreted glossolalia leads Paul to discuss more broadly the necessity for order in worship (14:26-33a). And that in turn leads him to a comment on the participation of women in such services (14:33b-36). Here, it appears, Paul is ordering a particularly divisive group, the women, to maintain silence during public worship services. He ends by chiding them that by seeking to dominate the worship services, they act as though they alone had received a word from God.

The problem with such an interpretation is twofold. First, until this moment, Paul has not mentioned any problem concerning women dominating the worship services, so it is strange that such a problem would surface now. Second, and of far more importance, the Greek text will not allow such an interpretation. Greek is an inflected language, which means that the gender of adjectives must agree with the gender of the words modified. In v. 36, the word translated "only ones" is, in the Greek text, masculine! That means Paul has addressed this condemnation not to women, but to men! The Greek makes clear that it is *men* who act as though they alone should be allowed to speak, and it is to them that this rebuke is addressed. It is therefore evident that what Paul does here is what he regularly does in this letter: in 14:33b-35 he quotes what some Corinthian Christians have been saying, and then refutes it (see 6:12-13; 8:4-6; 10:23; 15:35-36; cf. 4:8). Paul is therefore not telling women that they are not to participate fully in worship; he has already assumed that they will do so (11:4-5). He is telling the men who apparently want to restrict women, the men whom he quotes vv. 33b-35, that such an attitude is not to be tolerated since they, the men, did not originate God's word, and that they are therefore not the only ones to whom God's word has come. Hence, they have no right to try to bar women from full participation in public worship. Paul knows that women play an important part in the work of the Christian communities; the women mentioned in Romans 16 confirm that. And here Paul is making sure that the women in Corinth have the opportunity to continue to do so.

Paul then turns to a topic on which in his estimate the validity of the entire Christian faith depends: the bodily resurrection of Christ. It is clear that some Christians in Corinth have denied Christ's resurrection, apparently on the general ground that resurrection from the dead is impossible (15:12). But if Christ has not been raised, Paul asserts, the entire substance of the Christian faith is denied (vv. 13-19). After discussing how resurrection will occur at Christ's return in glory (vv. 20-34), Paul confronts a second problem among the Corinthians: What kind of body is it that is raised, since the physical body rots away in the grave? Paul argues that just as physical bodies are not all the same, so the risen human body will not be the same as the one that died. It will be, he says, a spiritual body rather than a physical body (vv. 35-50). Paul concludes with a recitation of events to occur with the return of Christ, when the riddle of the resurrection will finally be solved and death will be eliminated (vv. 51-57). Knowing that, the Corinthians may confidently continue their work of evangelizing their city (v. 58).

The final topics Paul addresses are the collection for the Christians in Jerusalem and his travel plans. As will become apparent in 2 Corinthians, events had caused these plans to be altered, which got Paul into no little trouble with his opponents among the Christians in Corinth. The final part of ch. 16 (vv. 15-20) attests the lively interchange between people around Paul and the Christians in Corinth: Timothy, Apollos, Stephanas, Fortunatus, and Achaicus all play a part in this interchange. Roman hegemony over the lands surrounding the Mediterranean Sea made travel relatively easy, and that aided the Christians in their endeavors to bring the gospel of Jesus Christ to the whole known world.

The letter concludes with greetings (16:19-20) and some sentences written out by Paul himself (16:21-23). The "holy kiss" (16:20) was a regular practice in early Christian communities (see Rom 16:16; 2 Cor 13:12; 1 Thess 5:26; 1 Pet 5:14) and was intended to demonstrate the close familial ties that bound Christians together.

13.4. 2 CORINTHIANS

13.4.1. The Writing of the Letter

Once more, there is little question that Paul wrote the material contained in our 2 Corinthians. The only real question is whether it was originally a unity or contains portions of a number of letters. Most frequently suggested is that 6:14–7:1 is an intrusion into its present context and originally part of Paul's first letter to Corinth (see 1 Cor 5:9) and that chs. 10–13 are independent from chs. 1–9, primarily because of the change in tone and attitude to the Corinthians, mild in chs. 1–9, harsh in chs. 10–13. Others have proposed that chs. 8 and 9 belong to separate letters since they deal with the same content (the collection for Jerusalem).

There is no manuscript evidence of the material in 2 Corinthians appearing in any other form, of a letter conclusion at the end of chs. 1–9, or of a letter opening in chs. 10–13. Therefore, many prefer to see 2 Corinthians as a unity, written in essentially the form we have it. As we shall see below, chs. 10–13 must have been written after chs. 1–9 and so could not have been part of the harsh letter described in 2:3-4, 9; 7:8, 12, which is also described in a way that would not fit 1 Corinthians. So it is clear the harsh letter was sent after 1 Corinthians and before 2 Corinthians.

Paul was in Macedonia when he wrote 2 Corinthians (2:13; 7:5). He had founded churches in two Macedonian cities that we know of, Thessalonica and Philippi, so he could have been in either city. Given his warm relations with the Christians in Philippi (e.g., Phil 1:5, 7-8; 4:14-16), that is perhaps the more likely city, though we cannot be certain. The date assigned to 2 Corinthians must allow for events that occurred between 1 and 2 Corinthians — Paul's painful visit to Corinth (2:1), the composition and delivery of the harsh letter, the dispatch and return of Titus with news about the reception of the harsh letter (2:13; 7:6, 7), and finally the composition of 2 Corinthians. Some nine to twelve months would allow for these events, so 2 Corinthians must have been written about a year after the composition of 1 Corinthians, perhaps in 55 or 56.

Why Paul wrote this letter is tied up with events between 1 and 2 Corinthians, which we must examine in some detail. In fact, things had gone badly for Paul between the time he concluded 1 Corinthians and wrote the opening chapters of 2 Corinthians. He had suffered reverses in his mission in Asia, that is, Ephesus, and in relation to the Corinthians themselves. He had announced his plans to stay a while longer in Ephesus because he saw good prospects for his mission there (1 Cor 16:8-9), but something had gone terribly wrong (2 Cor 1:8-9a). Acts notes difficulties there with silversmiths and an ensuing uproar before Paul's departure (19:23–20:1), but nothing to account for the language in 2 Corinthians, which describes a deadly peril facing Paul. In addition, Paul had apparently gone directly to

Corinth instead of going first to Macedonia, as he had earlier said he would (1 Cor 16:5). Paul's opponents in Corinth saw this change in plans as evidence of Paul's general unreliability (2 Cor 1:15-17). That visit had also proved disastrous, with someone confronting Paul in a way that caused him great pain (2:1-5). Paul then left Corinth for Troas, where his work was successful (2:12; unfortunately, we have no correspondence to Troas from Paul, so we know nothing about any church he founded there). But after he had left Corinth he had sent a harsh letter (2 Cor 2:4; 7:8), delivered to them by Titus. Even Paul's success in Troas could not comfort him until he found out how the harsh letter had been received and how he stood with the Corinthian Christians (2:13). So, looking for Titus, he went on to Macedonia (2:14). There he learned from Titus that his harsh letter had apparently had the desired effect: the one who had challenged Paul was disciplined by the Corinthian community (2 Cor 2:6), and there had evidently been a reconciliation between Paul and the Corinthian Christians (7:6-13; see also 2:14). It was evidently in Macedonia, after receiving this welcome news, that Paul wrote what we now have as 2 Corinthians if it is a unity, or, if not, at least chs. 1–9.

The main problem to which 2 Corinthians is addressed concerns the validity of Paul's apostolic authority. That question had apparently already cropped up before Paul wrote 1 Corinthians, where he defined his understanding of what an apostle was: one who had seen the risen Christ and had founded a church (1 Cor 9:1-2). Two main issues arise in 2 Corinthians. One is Paul's unreliability as a person, including his boasting about his own qualifications and his apparent disingenuousness about not accepting payment from the Corinthians but seeking a collection for Jerusalem, which some suspected was for Paul himself. The second is that, instead of the kind of triumph one would expect of a messenger of God's power, a power shown in raising Christ from the dead, Paul was continually suffering and being persecuted. That was hardly what a triumphant God would allow to happen to a true apostle, or so the Corinthian opponents of Paul apparently argued. It is the burden of 2 Corinthians to refute these charges, a refutation that also provides the letter with its underlying unity of thought.

13.4.2. The Content of the Letter

In form, 2 Corinthians, as we have it, follows the usual Hellenistic letter structure, as does 1 Corinthians, along with typical Pauline adaptations of that form. The letter opening (1:1-2) is followed by the prayer/blessing (1:3-7) with its usual précis of the letter's contents, the letter body (1:8–13:10), including the announcement of travel plans (12:14; 13:1), and a much shortened letter closing, with a final exhortation (13:11), greetings (13:12), and a final salutation (13:13).

In the first section of the letter body (1:8–2:17), Paul begins his defense by meeting the charges of unreliability. He changed his plans not because of his own whims but because of his relationship with the Corinthians. It was precisely to spare them further pain that he did not pay an immediate second visit to them (1:23). In this first section we catch glimpses of some of the charges leveled by Paul's opponents: Paul vacillates (1:17), his apostolic commission is invalid (1:21-22), and he lords it over the Corinthians' faith (1:24). Yet despite these charges, Paul rejoices that his "harsh" letter has had the desired effect of reestablishing good relations between him and the Christian community in Corinth.

In the second section of the letter body (chs. 3-7), Paul begins by meeting the accusation of self-commendation, which, as the letter makes clear, he is nevertheless forced to do to defend himself against charges that his call to be an apostle is invalid (see 1:12; 4:2; 5:11; 6:4; 10:8; 11:16, 30; 12:1, 5-6). It also appears here that some people from outside Corinth have come with letters of recommendation (from Jerusalem? from other churches?) and have sought to undermine Paul's ministry among the Corinthians (3:1b). His discussion of the superiority of the new covenant in Christ over the old covenant centering in Moses and the law (3:7-18) indicates that these intrusive missionaries may have argued for the continuing validity of the old covenant, like those who opposed Paul in Galatia. Paul argues that Christ is in fact the key not only to the new covenant but also to a proper understanding of the Scriptures of the old covenant.

Paul then introduces a catchphrase that will be the theme for the next chapters, namely, that he is not discouraged, despite failures that he encounters (4:1, 16; 5:6, 8). In fact, such failures are precisely part of God's plan, to show that the power of the gospel comes not from those who proclaim it, but from God himself. If, despite the weakness of those who proclaim the gospel ("earthen vessels," 4:7), God's power still is at work, then it becomes clear what the source of the power is. Just as Jesus' power was manifest only after his suffering on the cross, so the power of God announced by the apostles comes only through the weakness they display. Thus, Paul's weakness is precisely the proof that he is a valid apostle. Therefore, Paul is not discouraged by such evidences of his own weakness, because he knows that God, who raised Jesus from the dead, will also give power to the apostolic message and will ultimately redeem the apostles as well (4:8–5:10). Paul again argues that this does not constitute self-commendation on his part (5:12). Rather, he does what he does because Christ controls him, the Christ whom Paul once viewed from the perspective of "flesh," that is, in opposition to God. Now, however, he views Christ in that way no longer (5:16), since now that he is in Christ, he is a new creature and has been given the task of announcing God's reconciliation of sinful humanity to himself in Christ. It is that announcement that is the task of an apostle (5:17-21). It is therefore precisely the ill treatment Paul suffers as an apostle that confirms the validity of his call: no one, Paul seems to argue, would go through what he went through if the call to proclaim Christ were not legitimate (6:1-13; 7:2-4; the intervening passage, 6:14–7:1, concerns relationships with unbelievers).

Paul returns in 7:5 to the discussion he broke off in 2:13, namely his joy at the happy outcome of the painful confrontation with the Christian community in Corinth and his subsequent harsh letter to them. With this reconciliation now effected between him and them, Paul can turn to his appeal for funds for the relief of the "saints," that is, the Christians in Jerusalem, an appeal that comprises the third section of the letter body (chs. 8–9).

Paul had already urged the Corinthian Christians to begin a systematic collection of money, suggesting they put aside a little each Sunday (1 Cor 16:2). He cites the generosity of the churches in Macedonia (Philippi and Thessalonica) as an example to urge similar generosity on the part of the Corinthians. He also uses the example of the incarnation of Jesus, who became a lowly human being, giving up his heavenly glory (see also Phil 2:6-7), and though rich became poor so that others could be enriched (8:9). After urging completion of the offering (8:10-15) so that there may be equality of resources (v. 14; see the discussion on p. 301 above of the collection's purpose to demonstrate the equality of Gentile Christians with Jewish Christians), Paul tells them he is sending a delegation to precede him to Corinth to pick up their part of the collection (8:16-24).

In ch. 9 Paul discusses the collection again, even though it seems he was finished with it at the end of ch. 8 (so that some scholars have suggested that these two chapters may originally have belonged to two different letters). Paul repeats his intention to send a delegation ahead of himself to collect the gift (9:3-5) and then continues his urging that the Corinthians give generously, assuring them that generosity benefits not only the recipients but also those who give (9:6-15).

The fourth section of the letter body (chs. 10–13) comes as something of a shock, since Paul launches into a vigorous defense of the legitimacy of his apostolic calling, employing sarcasm and using a tone entirely different from that of the first nine chapters. This new tone does not seem appropriate after he has just described his desire that the Corinthians give generously to the collection for the saints, and for that reason many have seen in these final four chapters part of a different letter. However we resolve that issue, it has already been clear in the earlier chapters that Paul's legitimacy as an apostle was being challenged by some people in the Corinthian Christian community. Here he confronts such challenges head-on and meets the criticisms point-by-point.

The first criticism concerned Paul's boldness in his letters over against his humility and meekness when he was present in Corinth (10:1-12). He apparently quotes his opponents (10:10), who contrast the strong language of his letters with his poor oratorical ability and weak bodily presence. What the latter refers to we do not know. We have no description of Paul in the NT other than this, so we do not know if he was deformed in some way or generally of small stature. That he was not a skilled orator he himself admits (11:6).

Coupled with this defense is Paul's answer to the charge that he boasts too much of his apostolic authority (10:9, 13, 15). He points out his right to boast because, unlike those who have come later to a Corinthian Christian community already formed, he was the one who established it in the first place (10:13-14). Thus he at least does not boast about his work while depending on what others have done (10:15-16).

After claiming that these latecomers do not preach a true gospel (11:1-6), Paul turns to another point on which he has been criticized, namely that he has insulted the Corinthians by not accepting payment from them for the apostolic work he has done among them (11:7-15). It is a topic to which he will return. He then returns to his attack on those in Corinth who claim to be superior apostles and disparage Paul (11:12-15). Paul claims that they, in fact, are false apostles. Berating his readers for putting up with the bizarre behavior of these "deceitful workmen" (11:20), he next meets the accusation that he acts like a fool. Fine, Paul says, if fools boast, then let me play the fool and boast (11:16–12:13). Apparently the false apostles have boasted of their status as genuine Israelites; Paul points out they can claim nothing along that line that he cannot claim (11:22). Even their claim to be servants of Christ pales in comparison with what he has undergone as Christ's servant; Paul lists the almost innumerable dangers he has faced and the punishments he has undergone in the course of his apostolic travels and proclamation (11:23-29), even to the point of having to escape from the city of Damascus by being let down in a basket from a window in the city wall, lest he be seized by the governor of the city.

Further, Paul says, if he must boast he will also boast of the abundance of the divine favors shown him, in this instance in the form of divine visions and revelations (12:1-4). To show his modesty, he describes them in the third person, unwilling to boast about himself except in terms of his weakness (12:5), even though any such boast he might make about himself would be true (12:6). To demonstrate his weakness, he tells his readers about a "thorn in the flesh," which he further describes as a "messenger of Satan," given to keep him from becoming too proud of

---

Paul Describes His Life as an Apostle

. . . with many more labors, many more imprisonments, with beatings beyond number, frequently near death. Five times I have received the forty lashes less one from the Jews, three times I have been beaten with rods, once I was stoned, three times I have been shipwrecked, for a night and a day I have been adrift at sea. I have undertaken frequent journeys, have often been in danger from rivers, in danger from robbers, in danger from my own people, in danger from Gentiles, in danger in the city, in danger in the wilderness, in danger at sea, in danger from false brethren, in toil and hardship, with many a sleepless night, in hunger and thirst, frequently near starvation, in cold and without clothing. (2 Cor 11:23-27)

We are looked on as impostors, and yet we are true; as unknown, and yet we are well known; as dying, and behold we live; as punished, and yet not killed; as distressed, yet always rejoicing; as poor, yet enriching many; as having nothing, and yet possessing everything. (2 Cor 6:8b-10)

Right up to the present hour we are both hungry and thirsty, and we are poorly clad and we are buffeted and we are homeless and we labor, working with our own hands. Although we are reviled, we bless; although we are persecuted, we endure; although we are defamed, we continue to encourage. We have become like the refuse of the world, the offscouring of all things right up to the present moment. (1 Cor 4:11-13)

himself as an apostle. Some have speculated that this "thorn" was a bodily ailment, perhaps eye problems (see Gal 4:13-15; Acts 9:9, 18), yet in fact we have no idea what it was. We do not know whether it was physical or spiritual, or permanent or only appeared sporadically. Paul did pray three times to have it eliminated, but to no avail. The Lord's answer to Paul's prayer was that it was necessary so that Paul would remain weak, since only in such weakness could he be strong in Christ. Only when Paul was weak would it be apparent that it was by Christ's strength, not his own, that he accomplished what he did as an apostle (12:7-10).

Paul acknowledges that only a fool would engage in such boasting, yet the Corinthians have forced him to do it by refusing to acknowledge his legitimacy as an apostle equal to the new "super-apostles" who have appeared. He has shown himself in every way to be an apostle, even to the performance of miraculous acts (12:11-12). The only thing he has not done was accept payment from the Corinthians, and he asks sarcastically to be forgiven such wrongful activity (12:13). Yet that raises again the question whether he has been dishonest with them in this matter of refusing payment. Evidently some said that Paul was crafty in refusing payment, intending to raise a much larger collection and then abscond with it (12:14-18).

In the final verses of the letter (12:14–13:10), Paul warns that when he comes to his readers for the third time, he will deal harshly with them if it becomes necessary. It is evident from his language that not all problems have been solved among the Corinthian Christians. The warm and comforting tone of 1:3-7 and 2:14-17 and the assurance that they have proved themselves guiltless (7:11) have now given way to threats that lack of genuine repentance will bring the full apostolic wrath on them (13:2). Paul worries that their faith will prove wanting, and he writes in the hope that he will not have to be severe with them in his use of his authority (13:5-11). Obviously either the situation is different from the one behind chs. 1–9, or Paul is addressing a different group within the Christian community, one whose faithfulness to the Christian way is still in doubt. Paul ends the letter with customary greetings and a benediction (13:12-14).

Despite the differences in tone in this letter, the one element of continuity is Paul's resolute determination to live the kind of life required by the master he serves, namely the Jesus who, though he was crucified in weakness, was nevertheless the expression of God's ultimate power as demonstrated by the resurrection. It is precisely the difference between the expression of God's power in Christ and the way the world defines and perceives power that characterizes Paul's approach to his apostolic task. It is furthermore precisely that approach that has caused problems with the Corinthian Christians and with other "apostles" who sought to portray themselves and the gospel as possessing the kind of power the world knows and expects. This situation is presumed throughout 2 Corinthians and is expressed one last time in 13:4, where the relationship between Christ's death in weakness and resurrection, as the expression of God's power, is again laid out. But the Corinthians must not presume that only Christ's weakness is represented by a true apostle. The power of God displayed in Christ's resurrection is also present in the apostle and his message. For that reason it is dangerous to confuse Christ's weakness with weakness as the world understands it, because in Christ's weakness is also displayed the power of God, which is capable of transforming the world, as Paul explained earlier in 1 Corinthians 15.

Thus both letters share the same basic apostolic premise: the ways of God are unlike the ways of the world, as demonstrated in Christ and now in the apostolic ministry of Paul. Those still wedded to the ways of the world ignore the true power of God in Christ and in the apostolic message at their peril.

FOR FURTHER READING

Gordon D. Fee, *The First Epistle to the Corinthians* (New International Commentary on the New Testament; Grand Rapids: Eerdmans, 1987)

Victor P. Furnish, *II Corinthians* (Anchor Bible; Garden City: Doubleday, 1984)

Dieter Georgi, *The Opponents of Paul in Second Corinthians* (Philadelphia: Fortress, 1986)

Richard B. Hays, *First Corinthians* (Interpretation; Louisville: Westminster John Knox, 1997)

Ralph P. Martin, *2 Corinthians* (Word Biblical Commentary; Waco: Word, 1986)

C. H. Talbert, *Reading Corinthians: A Literary and Theological Commentary on 1 and 2 Corinthians* (New York: Crossroads, 1987)

Gerhard Theissen, *The Social Setting of Pauline Christianity: Essays on Corinth* (Philadelphia: Fortress, 1982)

Anthony C. Thiselton, *The First Epistle to the Corinthians* (New International Greek Testament Commentary; Grand Rapids: Eerdmans, 2000)

14. *The Letter to the Galatians*

No other letter of Paul shows the apostle involved in what he so clearly takes to be a life-and-death struggle for the faith of one of his missionary churches. To be sure, the difficulties confronting him in Corinth threatened his influence in those communities and hence, in his mind, the validity of the gospel they originally received. Yet nowhere does one get the impression that the threat there to the existence of a valid faith in Jesus Christ cut to the very core of the gospel. In this letter to the Christians in Galatia, on the other hand, Paul is clearly fighting for the very soul of the churches there. It appears from the content of the letter that some people have come to the Galatian churches and have announced to them a very different Christian gospel from the one Paul proclaimed. Adherence to the Jewish traditions of law and circumcision was much more important to these "teachers" who had come to Galatia than it was to Paul, to the point that they apparently argued that Paul had not given to the Galatians the whole, true gospel. These "teachers" argued that one could not realize the promises of Christ if one were not a practicing Jew so that one could follow in the footsteps of Abraham, to whom God had originally given the promise of blessing. Thus one had to have both faith in Christ and adherence to the law of Moses, including circumcision, if one were to inherit the promise given to Abraham and realized in Christ.

From this letter it is clear, according to Paul's understanding of the gospel, that if the interpretation of the gospel represented by these "teachers" who sought to undermine Paul's preaching prevailed, the Galatian Christians would have thus succumbed to a perversion of the true gospel of Jesus Christ. This Paul was unwilling to let happen. For that reason, we see Paul at his most combative in this letter to his converts in Galatia.

14.1. THE LETTER

Thematic to Paul's letter to the "churches of Galatia" is Paul's conviction that a right relationship with God is possible only through a trusting relationship to God based on God's act in Christ, not through reliance on one's Jewish heritage demonstrated by undergoing the rite of circumcision and keeping the law.

The point of Paul's discussion of the law and the Jewish heritage here is therefore different from that in Romans. There the point was to insure that the Jewish heritage of the Christian faith not be ignored by non-Jews who became Christian. This is shown in Rom 1:2-5, with its emphasis on the Jewish lineage of Jesus, and continued in such passages as 3:1-8; 3:31–4:22; and chs. 9–11, especially 11:13-32. The point in Galatians, on the other hand, is to insure that the Jewish heritage not be substituted for, or added as a necessary adjunct to, trust in God through Jesus Christ.

Thus, in Galatians, reliance on the Jewish heritage (law and circumcision) and trust in God through Jesus Christ (the gospel) are held to be mutually exclusive. To rely on one is to exclude the other, as Paul makes explicit in 5:2-4. If the need to respect the Jewish history underlying Jesus and the gospel is emphasized in Romans, the danger of placing too much reliance on it is emphasized in Galatians. The problem inherent in relying on "works of the law" for a right relationship with God is not whether a sinful human being can earn a right relationship with God through "good works." Given Paul's view of the power of sin entrenched through human rebellion against God, such a thought would not have crossed his mind. Furthermore, his term is not "good works" but "works of the law," that is, faithful observance of the law of Moses. Such observance characterizes the Jewish heritage, for it was the Jewish people to whom the law was given. To rely on the law therefore implied reliance on one's Jewish heritage, including observance of the law, to the exclusion of total reliance on Christ. For Paul, anything that usurped the place of total and utter reliance on God's grace through Christ for a right relationship with God is in fact impermissible for those who want to accept the apostolic gospel. Such were the implications of Paul's apocalyptic gospel, in which the death and resurrection of Jesus signaled the beginning of the new age. Dissuading the Galatian Christians from believing that it was necessary to add to trust in God through Christ a trust in the Jewish heritage by incorporating themselves into that heritage through circumcision and law is the burden of this epistle.

That Paul regards such an addition to faith in Christ as presenting a singular danger for the Christian gospel is clear from the beginning of the letter, because he does not follow his usual form for the letter opening. In his normal opening he mentions himself and his co-senders and then his addressees, and he wishes grace and peace for them. If any of those elements are amplified — for example, if Paul says more about his apostleship — it is usually in terms of his being chosen by

God (so 1 and 2 Corinthians; cf. Romans). Paul's prayer of thanksgiving for his readers then follows, in keeping with the practice even in secular letters of the time. Finally, Paul regularly includes a prayer for the well-being of the letter's recipients.

The opening of Galatians differs from this normal opening in two significant ways. First, the amplification of Paul's apostleship is negative. Apparently Paul felt that he could not presume, as he did in every other epistle, even where some were questioning his authority (e.g., 1 and 2 Corinthians), that those to whom he was writing would admit his legitimacy as an apostle. With the very first words in Galatians, Paul is involved in defending his apostleship against the accusation that it derived not from God but from some human commission. Thus it is clear from the outset that one of the reasons Paul wrote this epistle was to defend himself against charges that he was not truly an apostle.

Letter opening (1:1-5)
Letter body (1:6–6:17)
  Defense of Paul's gospel (1:6-10)
  Defense of the legitimacy of Paul's apostleship (1:11–2:10)
  Defense of the total sufficiency of trust in Christ as the way
    to obtain God's blessing (2:11-21)
  Defense of the total sufficiency of trust in Christ over against
    reliance on the law (ch. 3)
  The futility of returning to the old (4:1–5:12)
  The proper use of Christian freedom (5:13-26)
  Conduct in the church (6:1-10)
  The meaning of circumcision (6:11-17)
Closing benediction (6:18)

Second, Paul does not include a prayer of thanksgiving in this letter. In every other letter, Paul includes such a prayer, even when his main object is correction (2 Corinthians). In every other Christian community to which Paul wrote, therefore, he could find something in his readers' situation to thank God for. But now he can apparently find no such happy element, or at any rate he did not think it appropriate to express it. This is another indication of how seriously Paul took the problem with which the Galatian Christians confronted him, and it makes clear that a second reason Paul wrote this epistle was to correct a viewpoint that strikes so much at the heart of the gospel that, were it to prevail, the readers would in his view cease to be Christians.

Since the attacks on the legitimacy of Paul's apostleship and of the gospel he preached were so closely related, he begins by defending his gospel (1:6-10), a defense that then immediately shifts (1:11) into a prolonged defense of the legitimacy of his apostleship (1:12–2:10).

Paul begins his defense by declaring that the gospel proclaimed among the Galatians by the invading "teachers" is in fact no gospel at all. Since his gospel was the good news of the sole sufficiency of Christ as God's way of delivering humanity from the burden of sin (so already 1:4), any other version of how humanity is to be so delivered can only be characterized, not as "a *different* gospel," but as a perversion of the gospel, since aside from Paul's message there is no other gospel (1:6-7). Anyone who tries to preach something other than what Paul first preached to them, even if that preacher is Paul himself or even an angel (!), will be accursed, because what they say is a perversion of the gospel (vv. 8-9). To show how serious he is about it and to make sure there is no misunderstanding on the point, Paul repeats the assertion (v. 9).

Paul then raises a question about himself (v. 10) and his motives that gives every indication of being one of the accusations leveled against him by the "Preachers" (we will use this term from v. 8 to identify these opponents) who had come to Galatia and who opposed Paul as apostle and preacher. As in the Corinthian correspondence, Paul quotes a view he opposes, and then corrects it. By noting where he does this, we can to a large extent reconstruct the attacks against Paul. We will do so in the following discussion.

Here, the accusation seems to have been that Paul watered down the true gospel to make it more appealing to his listeners, thus "trying to please humans" rather than God (v. 10). Perhaps Paul's opponents said that he made the gospel easier to accept by ignoring the requirements of the Jewish heritage expressed in the commands of the law, especially circumcision (Paul will return to this later). Included in this may have been the implication that Paul never had been a very good Jew, and hence it was not hard for him to abandon law and circumcision.

Paul's response to this latter accusation is to point to his life prior to his apostolic commission, a time when he was so devoted to his Jewish heritage that he persecuted Christians. Paul had advanced in his knowledge of Judaism and devotion to the "traditions of the fathers" far beyond many of his contemporaries (vv. 13-14). Let there be no claim, therefore, that Paul had lacked zeal for his Jewish traditions, or that he had not valued them highly!

There was a further implication in that accusation, however, and that was the charge that because Paul's gospel reflects his concern that his gospel be pleasing to his listeners, it must be because Paul's gospel has a human rather than a divine source. As he begins to meet that objection, Paul reaffirms (v. 11) what he said at the very outset of the letter (v. 1), namely, that his apostleship was not of human derivation. Paul then recites important events in his life to demonstrate the falsity of such a charge.

He begins with his conversion, which, he notes, involved from the outset his preaching to Gentiles. He thus implies here that his conversion and his commission to go to the Gentiles came at the same time and from the same source. Interestingly, one could infer from the accounts of Paul's conversion in Acts that he received his first instruction in the Christian faith from the Christians in Damascus who took him in after he had met the risen Christ and had been struck blind (Acts 9:8-19), that there he received his commission to go to the Gentiles (Acts 22:10, 14-15), and that subsequently ("after many days," Acts 9:23) he went to the disciples in Jerusalem to learn more about the Jesus he had never seen (Acts 9:26-28).

Paul will have none of that. He insists that he has in fact been commissioned by the risen Lord (vv. 11-12; see 1 Cor 9:1) and that, immediately following that commission, he was not where he could have been instructed about the gospel by any of those who had been called to be apostles before him. Not only did he not go to Jerusalem, he left Palestine altogether for "Arabia" (probably the area to the east of Palestine), and when he returned, it was to Damascus, not Jerusalem (vv. 15-17). In fact, he did not go to Jerusalem until a full three years after he had returned to Damascus, and then he met only two of the disciples, Peter and James. The implication is clear: how could Paul be accused of having gotten his Christianity secondhand? How could he have received his commission from another Christian if he did not meet another Christian until three years or more after he became an apostle? Paul could therefore not have been dependent on the disciples for his initial knowledge of Christ and the Christian way.

It may well be that part of the "Preachers'" claim was that they represented the Christian faith as it was proclaimed by the disciples in Jerusalem. Since, they argued, Paul was dependent on those disciples for his knowledge of the faith and had misunderstood them, it was necessary for the Galatians to listen to the "Preachers" rather than to Paul and his false, misunderstood gospel. That Paul's account here is getting to the heart of the false information circulated about him is indicated by his oath before God that he is telling the truth (1:20). Anything that disagrees with his account is therefore necessarily false.

After he left Jerusalem, Paul says that he went to regions far to the north. As a result, the churches in Judea knew about him only by report, not by sight (1:21-24), having had no opportunity to meet him. Thus not only did he not get his understanding of the faith and his commission from disciples, neither did he get it from any others in Judea who may have been eyewitnesses to Jesus' career. Thus Paul leaves no opening for the "Preachers" to say he got his commission from anyone other than the risen Jesus himself.

Not until fourteen years later was Paul in Judea again. This might mean fourteen years after his return to Damascus (1:17), but fourteen years after his first visit to Jerusalem as a Christian (1:18) is more likely. And still he did not go at the behest of the authorities in Jerusalem; he went up "by revelation" (2:2a), that is, because it was God's will, not the will of the disciples in Jerusalem. Paul's gospel was thus not derived from other people, either in its origin or in the way it affected his life as apostle.

It was therefore only at that advanced point in his career as apostle, during this second visit to Jerusalem, that Paul explained to the Christian authorities there what he was preaching to Gentiles. And it was quite acceptable to them! This is major point for Paul. Not only did he not get his original commission from these authorities, but, when he finally did meet them, they had nothing to add to what he was saying. Equally importantly, they did not even require Titus, a Greek, and hence a Gentile Christian, to take on the yoke of the law through circumcision.

It is at this point that we come to perhaps the major area of disagreement in Galatians between Paul and the "Preachers" who opposed his gospel: they apparently said that his gospel of the sole sufficiency of trust in God's grace in Christ was insufficient. To gain God's full favor, one also had to participate fully in the Jewish heritage, that is, be circumcised and assume the "full yoke of the law." Their argument appears to have been: if Paul had genuine Christianity and understood it correctly, he would also require circumcision and adherence to the law, since that is what the Christian authorities in Jerusalem require. Hence, the "Preachers" insisted that if the Galatians wanted to be fully Christian, they too had to be fully under the Jewish law.

Paul combats their view by reciting his own history with the authorities in Jerusalem. Although "false apostles" insisted that Titus be circumcised, Paul resisted, and the authorities approved his understanding of the Christian faith. With this recitation, the tables are turned. Those who claim Paul is false for not requiring Christians to be fully under the law are themselves now shown to represent a view of Christianity not in accord with that of the Jerusalem authorities (2:1-5).

Paul drives his point home (2:6-10). Not only did those of repute in Jerusalem find no fault with his gospel (they saw nothing to be added to it), they were in fact so impressed by what he had to say that they admitted he had as much right to preach to Gentiles as Peter had to preach to Jews (v. 8). Let Paul's opponents consider that: in mission, the authorities in Jerusalem, whose authority the "Preachers" themselves invoked, put Paul on the same apostolic level as Peter himself.

Paul's meetings with the authorities in Jerusalem, therefore, ended in concord. Far from finding any fault with Paul's gospel, the Jerusalem authorities acknowledged the legitimacy of his proclamation by offering him the right hand of fellowship. So they would oversee the Christian mission to the Jews, while he would continue his mission to the Gentiles. He does concede that they had one request, namely that he have his Gentile Christians help the Christians in Jerusalem ("the poor" was apparently their own self-designation) financially. To that stipulation, Paul says, he readily agreed.

Paul's Opponents in Galatia

A summary of the position of Paul's opponents in Galatia would probably have looked like this:

- Paul is not a real apostle: he was not a follower of the earthly Jesus and so is dependent on others for his knowledge of Jesus and for his commission as an apostle.
- Therefore, he is dependent on the disciples in Jerusalem for his gospel and for his commission as apostle, and so is subordinate to them.
- Paul has misunderstood his secondhand Christianity.
  - He has wrongly jettisoned the Jewish heritage (the law) because he himself was never really a good Jew.
  - Because God gave his promise to Abraham, only the heirs of Abraham will inherit that blessing (see ch. 3). Hence one must be Jew to obtain God's blessing.
  - Therefore, the correct Christian position is not Christ *or* law but Christ *and* law (see ch. 5).

This is the position Paul argues against in his letter to the Galatian churches.

Having recited part of his history to refute charges against the legitimacy of his apostleship and the gospel he proclaims, Paul shifts the focus of the discussion (2:11-21). Still telling of his own history, Paul now turns to a defense of the heart of his gospel, namely the total sufficiency of trust in Christ as the way to obtain God's blessing. Paul understood the attack by the "Preachers" on this point as an attack on the core meaning of God's act in Christ, since for Paul (cf. 5:4), "grace" and "Christ" point to the same reality. But, even more — since Christ is God's grace personified — this attack against the complete sufficiency of Christ is an attack against God himself.

For his defense of the all-sufficiency of grace (i.e., God's promised blessing) through trust in Christ, Paul turns to an account of his confrontation of Peter at

Antioch, which goes to the heart of his dispute with the "Preachers." For a time, Paul says, Peter had admitted that trust in Christ was the sole important point in Christianity. Peter did so by his actions, that is, by eating with Gentiles (2:12a; cf. Acts 10). But then some people came "from James," that is, from the one who was now leading the church in Jerusalem. Paul also identifies them as the "circumcision party," so they evidently said that Gentiles needed to become Jews to obtain God's blessing. Peter then withdrew from table fellowship with Gentiles. Such fellowship was forbidden to Jews by the law, since it would involve eating impure (i.e., non-kosher) food.

By leaving the table, Peter demonstrated the very problem Paul would come to face in Galatia: the belief that one needed to be a Jew (and to prove so by obedi-

---

Separation at Table

The following excerpts from Jewish documents of the first century or earlier reflect contemporary interpretation of the OT commands to be separate from the Gentiles.

From *Jubilees*, a document dating to either the first century BCE or the first century CE:

> And you also, my son, Jacob, remember my words,
> and keep the commandments of Abraham, your father.
> Separate yourself from the gentiles,
> and do not eat with them,
> and do not perform deeds like theirs.
> And do not become associates of theirs.
> Because their deeds are defiled,
> and all of their ways are contaminated, and despicable,
> and abominable.
>
> (22:16, *OTP*)

In the first-century romance called *Joseph and Aseneth*, Joseph's piety is described in terms of his refusal to eat with Gentiles:

> And Joseph entered the house of Pentephres and sat upon the throne. And they washed his feet and set a table before him by itself, because Joseph never ate with the Egyptians, for this was an abomination to him. (7:1, *OTP*)

ence to whole law) to obtain God's blessing given in Christ. Because Paul's argument against Peter in these verses is at the same time his argument against his opponents' charge that he preaches an incomplete gospel by not requiring Gentile converts to Christianity to become Jews, it is not clear where he leaves off quoting what he said to Peter and begins to address the Galatians directly. That is not so important as it might otherwise be, however, since his answer to one is his answer to the others.

He points out that as a result of Peter's abandoning table fellowship with non-Jewish Christians even the trusted Barnabas, who had accompanied Paul on his second visit to Jerusalem, also withdrew from such fellowship. Paul saw the kind of consequences this could have in other Christian churches. It would lead to a split within the Christian community between Jews and Gentiles and to recriminations among fellow Christians, something, Paul points out later, that was already happening in Galatia (5:15).

Paul's argument at this point is compact and complex and needs considerable unpacking if we are to understand it. It is worth the effort, however, since what Paul says will show us not only the key point around which his argument in Galatians revolves, but also some central elements in his understanding of the gospel of Jesus Christ.

Paul's first point against Peter's action is that there is little point in trying to make Gentile Christians act like Jews, as the "people from James" evidently wanted to do, because, says Paul, even Jewish Christians act like Gentiles rather than like Jews. He is not referring here to Peter's earlier table fellowship with Gentile Christians, because that Peter had repudiated. Paul is referring to something far closer to the heart of the matter (2:15-16).

He points out that even those who were born Jews and are thus not "Gentile sinners," as Jews liked to call them — even such Jews have realized, when they became Christians, that there is no hope for Jews as Jews of getting right with God. By becoming Christians they acknowledged that their Jewish heritage, including the law, was not sufficient. Paul is thus pointing to the crux of what Christians really are: those who have realized that their only hope for a right relationship with God lies in abandoning trust in their Jewish heritage and seeking that relationship with God through Christ. When Jewish Christians did that, they had, in fact, abandoned the heritage that had marked them as Jews. So Paul is referring here (2:14) to Peter's original decision to follow Christ and his recognition that the law could not put him in a right relationship with God.

Again we must note that when Paul speaks of "works of the law" he is not referring to earning merit in God's eyes with good works. He refers, rather, to works done in obedience to the law. Since the law was given to Israel, to rely on doing the law is tantamount in the end to trusting in one's ethnic identity as a Jew for God's favor, since only the Jews, those who have the law, can observe its tenets. If one does that, Paul argues, one does not trust Christ, who alone can bring one into a right relation to God. The matter at issue here is the source of that right relationship: is it ethnic identity or is it trust in Christ? It cannot be both. Paul's protracted discussion of who constitute the true heirs of Abraham shows that the point is here Jewish heritage, not earning favor with God by following the moral requirements of the law.

Thus, Paul's argument against Peter is this: we Jews who became Christians have by that act admitted that our Jewish heritage was not sufficient for our relationship with God, and hence we abandoned reliance on that heritage, and with it the law. From that point of view, all Christians live like Gentiles, not like Jews, because Christians no longer rely on the law and all it represents, but on Christ to make them right with God.

Thus, those Jews who see true righteousness in Christ, not in the law, must turn fully to Christ and abandon reliance on the law, because that law (2:16) cannot make one right with God. To put it another way, Paul is arguing that to share in the Jewish heritage does not mean to be automatically in a right relationship with God.

If that is the case, then Christians are on the same level as non-Jews in the eyes of the law; they are outside the circle of those who rely on the Jewish ethnic heritage and thus are on a level with the "Gentile sinners" mentioned in 2:15. This is Paul's point in 2:17 — those who seek to be right with God through Christ are, as far as the law is concerned, on a level with Gentile sinners. Thus, in the eyes of Jews, they appear as sinners. Paul's grammatical emphasis, "even *we ourselves* are found as sinners," indicates that he is thinking of the "sinners" in v. 15.

Paul is thus again pointing out that to seek for one's righteousness in Christ means at one and same time to abandon Jewish heritage and law and thus to act as Gentiles, not as Jews (v. 14). That being the case, he asks (2:17): does our equation of ourselves with "Gentile sinners" by seeking righteousness in Christ, not in the law, mean that Christ has become a servant of sin, since it is because of him that Jewish Christians have abandoned the law and thus put themselves on a level with Gentile sinners? Of course not, among other reasons because of the close link between the law and sin (2:16); until one turns to Christ one is mired in that sin. But the further reason Paul gives in 2:18 is just the point he is making both to Peter, who returned to the law, and to the Galatians, who want to do likewise. Paul points out that the only sin for Christians, Jewish or Gentile, as far as the law is concerned, is to return to that law after they have become Christians. Only if I return to my former state, Paul says, namely relying on my ethnic heritage rather than on Christ for my right relationship with God, do I constitute myself a sinner with respect to the law. Yet even then, it is not Christ who brings sin, but I who bring it on myself. Christ is thus not an agent of sin in causing Christians to abandon the law, because the only sin for Christians in relation to the law is to deny the all-sufficiency of Christ and return to that law as the basis for a right relationship with God.

Thus Paul has made his point with Peter: when you became a follower of Christ, you abandoned the law and thus become like a Gentile. But you cannot escape the subsequent burden of being on a level with Gentile "sinners" (*vis-à-vis* the law) by returning to trust in that law, because that very act is to deny Christ and hence to revert to rebellion against God. That is why Paul has asked (2:14): how can you want Gentiles to trust in the Jewish heritage, including the law, when Jews who have become Christians have themselves by that act abandoned that heritage?

Paul drives his point home (2:19-20): reliance on the law is over for the Christian. The Christian has died to the law as surely as Christ has; that is the meaning of baptism. But this was in fact in accord with the very purpose of the law (2:19). For the Christian, the law has served its purpose: it has demonstrated that one cannot escape sin by means of the law. In fact, following the law leads to sin by fostering rebellion against God through the rejection of Christ and the retention of the law. Therefore Paul has argued: just as surely as Christ died to the law, so the Christian has died to the law. But that means further that Christ is now the one who really lives in the Christian. Thus Christ, not the law, is the principle of the Christian's life. The conduct of that life can be determined only by Christ, by whose life the Christian lives (2:20).

Paul then returns (2:21) to what was apparently a further accusation leveled against him, namely, that by abandoning trust in the heritage of the chosen people, Paul had abandoned God's own grace shown to that people (Paul will argue this point more fully beginning at 3:6). On the contrary, Paul asserts, those who want to return to that heritage abandon God's true grace in Christ, because in so doing they claim a grace from their Jewish heritage that in fact can come only through Christ. They rob the death of Christ of its significance, since Christ's death was unnecessary if grace comes not from it but from the Jewish heritage. Hence the alternative: *either* Christ *or* law. The possibility of Christ *and* law, Paul argues, means to deny the significance of Christ.

Paul has now made his central point and has done so in relation to his dispute with Peter but with the Galatian controversy in mind. He next turns directly to the Galatians (3:1) to drive home the point he has made. He will do this in a variety of ways, but always to the same end, namely to show that the Christian cannot both rely on the law (i.e., become Jewish by circumcision and thus appeal to one's heritage as a descendant of Abraham) and remain one who trusts in Christ. One will trust either in Christ or in one's heritage; one cannot trust in both, for that is to deny the critical significance of Christ's death.

Paul wonders how any people who had had Christ presented to them as vividly as the Galatians had, could abandon that Christ. Paul raises a key question

(3:2): did the evidence of God's presence — the Spirit — come from "works of the law" (i.e., from relying on Jewish heritage) or "hearing with faith" (i.e., from trusting in the gospel Paul preached)? The answer is obvious: when Paul was there and the Spirit came, law was nowhere in evidence. Are you so stupid, Paul asks, that, beginning with God's Spirit, which you received by faith, you are going to return to the arena of the law, namely sinful flesh? Are you going to begin at the top and work downward? That would mean your decision to accept Christ is nullified. How does the presence of God (the Spirit) come, by trust or by law? by reliance on one's Jewish heritage or by trust in God's promise in Christ?

Now if, as the "Preachers" have apparently argued, the key to God's promise is who is to inherit it through Abraham, Paul must next examine Abraham to see what kind of promised blessing is under discussion (3:6-9). Abraham, Paul says, was surely right with God, but it was because of his trust in God. Hence the blessing to Abraham comes to those who follow Abraham's trust and thus show themselves to be his heirs. Hence from the beginning the way was open for Gentiles to share in the blessing God gave to Abraham, because Gentiles can also share in Abraham's trust in God.

Indeed (3:10), those who seek to become Abraham's heirs by relying on the law (i.e., their racial heritage) are under the curse that is invoked on anyone who does not live exclusively by the law (i.e., do all it commands). Yet even if one did live exclusively by the law (v. 11), one would still not be right with God, because God himself has said that only those who are right with God through trust will live. The law, on the other hand, does not foster the kind of trust that brings life, but rather condemns those who follow it to continue in a relation to law that leads to a curse. But that curse has been broken by Christ, who in his death has himself become the curse, and in dying has destroyed it (v. 13). Thus following Christ is now the way to emulate Abraham's trust, which put him right with God. The promised blessing of Abraham, God's very presence (the Spirit), comes to Gentiles through trust, not through circumcision/law/Jewish heritage.

Paul then illustrates his point on the primacy of trust over against the Jewish heritage (3:15-18). Playing on the fact that the Greek word *diathēkē* means both "covenant" and "last will and testament," Paul points out that no one tampers with a person's will. Its bequests cannot be set aside by later decisions of the heirs. Now, the covenantal promise, the "bequest," as it were, that was given to Abraham was given to him and to his "offspring." Paul next uses a familiar Jewish method of interpretation. Note, he says, you who take the law so very seriously, that the word is singular: offspring, not offspring*s*. Therefore, it refers to a single heir and no more. And that heir is Christ. So if one is to inherit Abraham's blessing, one will inherit it through Christ or one will not inherit it at all.

Note further, Paul says, that the law came 430 years after God ratified his covenant with Abraham; remember, he implies, that covenants cannot be set aside.

"Christ Became a Curse for Us"

In Galatians 3:13, Paul quotes Deut 21:23: "anyone hung on a tree is under God's curse." The following quotation from the Dead Sea Scrolls (11QTemple 64.7-13) contains another interpretation of that text from about the same time.

If a man slanders his people and delivers his people to a foreign nation and does evil to his people, you shall hang him on a tree and he shall die. On the testimony of two witnesses and on the testimony of three witnesses he shall be put to death and they shall hang him on the tree. If a man is guilty of a capital crime and flees (abroad) to the nations, and curses his people, the children of Israel, you shall hang him also on the tree, and he shall die. But his body shall not stay overnight on the tree. Indeed you shall bury him on the same day. For he who is hanged on the tree is accursed of God and men. You shall not pollute the ground which I give you to inherit. (Vermes)

Thus the law as a sign of the inheritance of Abraham's blessing cannot annul trust in Christ as the sign of that blessing because the law came after the covenant of trust had already been made. God gave the inheritance as a promise; that promise is fulfilled in Christ. Therefore, Christ is the only way to inherit Abraham's blessing. Nowhere, Paul argues, is the law said to be based on promise. Hence the law cannot be the way to inherit Abraham's blessing. So Paul's logic seems to run.

Given all that, why was the law given at all (3:19-20)? — a logical question. The law was "added on" because of human trespass, until the true heir should appear. Paul adds material about angels and mediators that apparently would be clear to his original readers but that remains somewhat opaque for modern interpreters. It is probably intended to contrast the primary, immediate covenant God made with Abraham with the secondary (through angels) mediated (by Moses) covenant that brought the law. The point of the verses seems to be that because of human sin, some agency was needed to identify sin for what it was, however imperfect that agency may have been, until the true fulfillment of the promise, Christ, should appear. That imperfect agency was the law.

The next logical question is: are then law and promise in conflict (3:21-29)? If the law is not related to the righteousness promised through Abraham, does that mean that the law runs counter to God's promised righteousness by offering another way to achieve righteousness? Of course not, Paul says, because there really is no righteousness possible under the law (for further discussion of this point see Rom 9:32–10:4). If God had established a law that could lead to life, then there would have been a righteousness based on "works of the law." But that was not the purpose of the law. The law was not to be an alternative means of achieving righteousness; rather, as the law itself says (3:22), everything was included under sin, including the law, so that the promised righteousness should come only by faith in Christ (cf. Rom 11:32). Rather, the law kept people pointed to the righteousness to come in Christ so that, when it came, people could turn to it. But once the true fulfiller of the promise has come, the law has no further function. Before Christ, there was a true religious distinction between those who had the law (Jews) and those who did not. Since Christ came, all distinctions based on race, social class, and gender have been done away with (v. 28). Those who are in Christ are those who inherit the blessing promised to Abraham; to move away from Christ is thus to move away from, not into, the promise of God to Abraham.

Carrying through the Implications of Galatians 3:28

It is worth noting that while Paul worked out the implications of the Jew-Gentile dichotomy in detail, he did not do so with the other two dichotomies, male-female and slave-free. Yet the thoroughness he displays in regard to the Jew-Gentile dichotomy shows what he intended with the other two: any religious distinction between the members of the dichotomy is voided in Christ. This is a warrant for Paul's followers to carry out Paul's self-announced program: to eliminate all barriers to full religious participation based on race, sex, or social status within the body of Christ.

Paul then turns (ch. 4) to a variety of arguments showing why it is futile to return to the old once one has embraced the new. The examples are drawn (1) from the Galatians' Gentile past (vv. 1-11), (2) from Paul's time with them (vv. 12-20), and (3) from the law (vv. 21-31). (1) For the Galatians to turn to the law will be to lose their deliverance in Christ from slavery to idols and therefore their status as children of God, a status evident when the Spirit present in their community allows them to address God as "Father." (2) For the Galatians to turn to the law means that Paul's work among them will have been in vain and that they will treat him not as the friend he has been but as an enemy. (3) To return to the law will be

Unity in Christ

Paul's statement at Galatians 3:28 that in Christ "there is no longer Jew or Greek, there is no longer slave or free, there is no longer male and female" reverses sentiment found in Greek, Roman, and Jewish writings. The first-century biographer Plutarch wrote twenty-three pairs of parallel "lives" or brief biographies of famous individuals, designed to highlight certain virtues or vices. The following quotation, attributed to Plato, appears in Plutarch's life of *Caius Marius* 46.1:

> Plato, however, when he was now at the point of death, lauded his guardian genius and Fortune because, to begin with, he had been born a man and not an irrational animal; again, because he was a Greek and not a Barbarian; and still again, because his birth had fallen in the times of Socrates.

Diogenes Laertius, an author of the early third century, wrote a compendium of the lives of the philosophers, which varies the similar comment found in Plutarch (*Lives of the Philosophers* 1.33):

> Hermippus in his *Lives* refers to Thales the story which is told by some of Socrates, namely, that he used to say there were three blessings for which he was grateful to Fortune: "First, that I was born a human being and not one of the brutes; next, that I was born a man and not a woman; thirdly, a Greek and not a barbarian."

Finally, the following variation is found in the Babylonian Talmud (*Menahoth* 43b):

> It was taught: R. Judah used to say, A man is bound to say the following three blessings daily: "[Blessed art thou . . .] who hast not made me a heathen," ". . . who hast not made me a woman," and ". . . who hast not made me a brutish man." R. Aha b. Jacob once overheard his son saying "[Blessed art thou . . .] who hast not made me a brutish man," whereupon he said to him, "And this too!" Said the other, "Then what blessing should I say instead?" [He replied,] ". . . who has not made me a slave." And is not that the same as a woman? — A slave is more contemptible.

to enter into enslavement, pictured allegorically by Hagar and her son, rather than to retain freedom in Christ, pictured by Sarah and her son Isaac, the son born by God's promise. Each of these examples is designed to show that by submitting to the demands of the "Preachers" the Galatian Christians have jeopardized their status as recipients of God's grace, which comes only through Christ.

Signs of the Spirit's Presence

Paul affirms that there are two signs that the Spirit of God is present in a Christian community. The first, discussed in 1 Corinthians, is confession of Christ as Lord (12:3). The second sign, of great importance for Paul since he mentions it in two letters (Gal 4:6; Rom 8:15-16), is calling upon God as Father. Paul's word in Rom 8:15, *abba,* the same word used by Jesus in Mark 14:36, was used by Jewish children to address their fathers. It implies both affection and respect: "my dear father." Where those two elements are present — confessing Christ as Lord and calling upon God as Father — it is proof that the Spirit of God is also present. Where one or the other is absent, it is doubtful that Paul would say the Spirit of God was present there.

The sum of Paul's argument is then drawn up (ch. 5). To return to the law is to forfeit the freedom gained in Christ. Christ and law is not a both/and matter; one does not gain additional standing with God by becoming a Jew (i.e., by taking on the law and becoming circumcised), as the "Preachers" have apparently argued. Rather, one forfeits all standing with God through such a procedure. There is no such thing as part law, part Christ; one relies wholly on the one or wholly on the other. To be under law means to be separated from Christ; the opposite is also true. Thus circumcision is of no help. Here Paul has to deny that he requires circumcision (5:11); apparently the opponents have tried to justify their demand with that spurious claim as well.

Christians are free from the normal separation of humanity into conflicting groups (3:28), but this does not mean they are free for undisciplined acts (5:13). The key point about Christian freedom is that it is freedom to serve others, not to indulge oneself. Such self-indulgence Paul outlines in 5:19-21; those who engage in such practices will not inherit God's kingdom. Rather, freedom requires the kind of self-discipline outlined in v. 22.

In fact, to heed the God-given Spirit, which leads to such acts of disciplined love rather than to surrender to sin-tainted flesh, fulfills what the law actually intends. One need not be circumcised to do that, only be true to Christ (5:23b). In fact, only Christians fulfill God's law, because they are not under the curse, whereas the Jews who do not follow Christ cannot fulfill the law, because they are under that curse.

The letter ends with some advice to the Galatian Christians on how to conduct themselves in accordance with their faith (6:1-10) and closes with a paragraph written in Paul's own hand. In the latter, Paul questions the motives of those advocating circumcision: they want to avoid persecution (from Jews in Jerusalem? from strict Jewish Christians?); they want to gain an advantage (for their party?) by requiring something that they themselves do not do, namely keep the law. The central point, however, is Christ crucified, who by renewing creation makes moot any question of circumcision or uncircumcision (v. 15). It is that new creation that is the true Israel (the "Israel of God," v. 16).

So Paul's argument runs in Galatians, which is at its core an argument for the all-sufficiency of the grace promised to Abraham and realized in the crucified and risen Christ. It is a grace that, because of its completeness, makes unnecessary any and all other means of assuring favor from God.

The Letter of Freedom

Galatians is a letter of freedom in a twofold way: it represents not only freedom from, but also freedom for. It speaks of freedom from

- dependence on creation, which is idolatry,
- dependence on law, which is immaturity/sin, and
- dependence on self, which is slavery to "flesh" (i.e., a life without God at its center).

It also speaks of freedom for

- faith/trust, as heirs with Christ,
- blessing, as children of Abraham, and
- life, as those who receive God's Spirit.

14.2. SOME PROBLEMS

The major literary problems surrounding this letter have to do with the recipients, and therefore the time when it was written. Scholars have raised no serious objections to Paul as author; the letter is almost universally accepted as coming from him. Nor is there any real question about the integrity of the text. Apart from the usual kinds of variations caused by hand copying, the text we have is in all essentials the text as it emerged from the mind, and with respect to the final paragraph, from the hand, of the apostle.

What is in dispute is where we are to locate the "churches of Galatia" to whom the letter is addressed. It is apparent that the addressees belong to a Christian community founded by Paul (4:13, 19), who first visited them because of a "bodily ailment" (4:13) evidently affecting his eyes (4:15). Apparently he had been forced to stop there because of this infirmity even though he had not planned to do so. Where then are these churches to be found?

Galatia may refer to two areas, the ethnic Galatian area in central Asia Minor with its chief city Ancyra (modern Ankara), or the Roman province of that name, which included the lands of Lycaonia and Pisidia to the south and the cities of Pisidian Antioch, Iconium, Lystra, and Derbe. The ethnic area was dominated from the third to the first centuries B.C.E. by invading Celtic tribes from Gaul — hence the name "Galatia." These tribes had the reputation of being wild and uncivilized. In 25 B.C.E., under Augustus, ethnic Galatia became a Roman province when King Amyntas of Galatia was killed preserving his territory in the Taurus mountains and his sons were prevented from inheriting his domain. Does the "Galatia" that Paul mentions therefore refer to the more northern ethnic area in central Asia Minor, or to the Roman province, which included lands to the south of the original ethnic enclave?

When Acts refers to the mission of Paul in central Asia Minor (16:6; 18:23), both Galatia and Phrygia are mentioned, thus pointing to the ethnic area, since there was no Roman province of "Phrygia." On that basis, the Galatia mentioned in Paul's letter would refer to the ethnic area in central Asia Minor (the "north Galatian theory"). On the other hand, some scholars have argued that Paul regularly uses names of Roman provinces when he identifies areas in his letters (e.g., Macedonia and Achaia, Rom 15:26), so that his reference to the province of Galatia here would include the cities in the southern portion of the province (the "south Galatian theory"). Much ink has been spilled in this controversy, since there is no definitive evidence one way or the other. It is not clear, for example, that Paul regularly uses the names of Roman provinces when he refers to areas. It seems likely, for example, that he means the areas rather than the provinces when he refers to Judea (2 Cor 1:16) and Syria (Gal 1:21).

Again, it is clear from the letter that the people addressed are Gentiles —

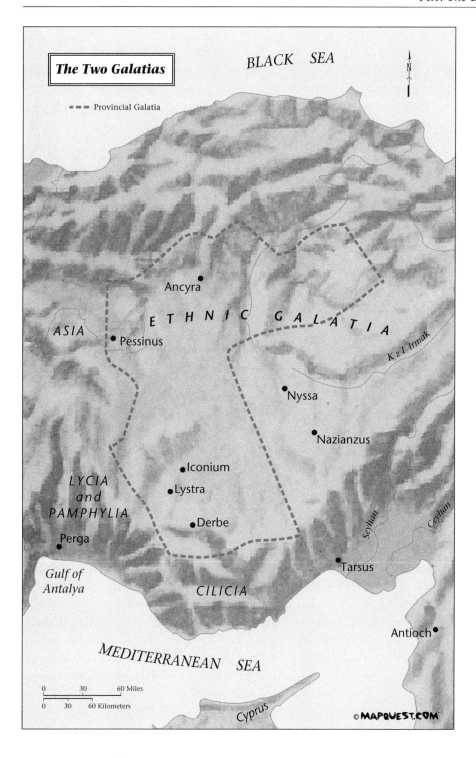

The South Galatian and North Galatian Theories

SOUTH GALATIA	NORTH GALATIA
"Provincial" or "Roman" Galatia	"Ethnic" Galatia
These churches were founded during Paul's first missionary journey, including Pisidian Antioch, Iconium, Lystra, and Derbe (Acts 13:14-15; 14:1; 16:3).	These churches were founded during Paul's second missionary journey (Acts 16:6; 18:23).
Allows for Galatians to be written as early as 48, as the earliest extant Pauline epistle.	Galatians written in the mid-50s, probably after the Corinthian letters, before Romans.
Galatians reports events that precipitated the Apostolic Council (Acts 15).	Galatians was written after the council.

they were idolaters before their conversion to the Christian faith (4:8) and had not been circumcised (5:2; 6:12) — yet according to Acts, Paul dealt with Jews in Pisidia and Lycaonia (Acts 13:14-15; 14:1; 16:3). Furthermore, the communities Paul was addressing were all undergoing the same difficulties, something hard to imagine if the area addressed includes the whole of the province of Galatia. Further, it would be unlikely that Paul would address his readers as "Galatians" (3:1) if they resided only in the southern area of the province, which had belonged to other ethnic groups before they were included in the Roman province of Galatia. All this points to "Galatia" as referring to the ethnic area (the "north Galatian theory").

The decision about the area to which Paul's letter was addressed also has an influence on one's decision about when the letter is to be dated. If Paul is referring to the Roman province, including the southern area, then one may date the letter early if one follows Acts, since Paul had evangelized the southern cities during his first missionary journey. On the other hand, if Paul is referring to ethnic Galatia, it is an area he did not visit until his second missionary journey according to Acts, and hence the letter must be dated somewhat later. Yet we have already seen that Acts is not a complete account of Paul's missionary travels, and many scholars are reluctant to assume chronological exactness with respect to the material in Acts. Finally, and most importantly, the date when Paul wrote the letter and even the people to whom he wrote it are not of any real significance in understanding the problem Paul is addressing and the points he wants to make in this letter to the "churches in Galatia."

This discussion is an indication of the kind of problems that are often associated with the letters of Paul but that finally do not really influence our understanding of the letters. We may learn a good deal from this letter about Paul's understanding of the Christian faith even though we remain uncertain about to whom and when Paul wrote it.

FOR FURTHER READING

Hans Dieter Betz, *Galatians: A Commentary on Paul's Letter to the Churches in Galatia* (Hermeneia; Philadelphia: Fortress, 1979)

F. F. Bruce, *The Epistle to the Galatians* (New International Greek Testament Commentary; Grand Rapids: Eerdmans, 1982)

James D. G. Dunn, *A Commentary on the Epistle to the Galatians* (Peabody: Hendrickson, 1993)

Richard B. Hays, *The Faith of Jesus Christ: An Investigation of the Narrative Substructure of Galatians 3:1-4:11* (Chico: Scholars, 1983)

Richard N. Longenecker, *Galatians* (Word Biblical Commentary; Dallas: Word, 1990)

15. The Letter to the Ephesians

The document we know as Paul's letter to the Ephesian Christians stands at the threshold of a period during which the church began to emerge as a social and intellectual force in the Greco-Roman world. The letter is centered on a theme that both reflects the earlier letters of Paul and points forward to the problems that would confront the church increasingly in the coming decades and centuries, namely, the universal significance of God's act in Christ.

On the one hand, in Christ the division of humanity into Jew and Gentile has been rendered moot, since God has intended Christ to be the way of salvation for all people, Jew and Gentile alike. Ephesians thus shares the theme Paul developed in Romans, although the conflict between Christians of Jewish and Gentile origins that dominates Galatians and is reflected in Romans has begun to fade. There is no reference to that conflict in Ephesians.

On the other hand, the universal significance of God's salvific act in Christ brings the Christian community into confrontation with the worldview of the Greco-Roman world. The universality of the meaning of Christ is expressed not only in its destruction of the barrier between Jew and Gentile but also in its challenge to all attempts to understand the world in terms of a multitude of spiritual powers and divine beings. Ephesians proclaims that Christ is the ultimate ruler of all other powers in the whole of creation and thus is sovereign over all creation, both natural and supernatural. There is therefore no area of culture or religion that God's act in Christ has not affected. Christ is the supreme head of created reality, and all powers that inhabit creation owe him fealty and are subordinated to him. This implication of Christ's universality, already hinted at in Romans, 1 and 2 Corinthians, and Galatians, now emerges as a theme that runs through the letters we are about to consider — Ephesians, Philippians, and Colossians.

15.1. SOME QUESTIONS

The opening words of this letter identify its recipients and the author, but represent a puzzle for a variety of reasons.

First, was it written to the Christians in Ephesus? There are several reason why that does not seem to be the case:

- In the earliest manuscripts we have of this letter, the phrase "in Ephesus" is absent from the letter opening (1:1). This means in all likelihood that the phrase was missing from the original form of the letter. It is highly unlikely that a scribe copying this letter would omit "in Ephesus" from the letter if it were present.
- It is apparent from such statements as those contained in 1:15; 3:2; and 4:21 that the author has no firsthand knowledge of the Christian community being addressed. The author knows them only at second hand. But both Paul (1 Cor 16:8) and Acts (19:1-20) affirm that Paul went to Ephesus. According to Acts, although Paul was not that church's founder, he stayed there some three years evangelizing the area. In 1 Corinthians, Paul notes his opportunity for continuing effective work there. It is unlikely, therefore, that Paul wrote this letter to the Ephesian church, a community he knew.
- There are no references in the letter to any events that occurred during Paul's time in Ephesus, nor are there any greetings to people in Ephesus that Paul knew or from people with Paul who knew people in Ephesus. If Paul had been there three years, such an omission is hard to fathom. The only person mentioned is Tychicus, who carries the letter to Ephesus and will tell the Ephesians more about Paul, a typical procedure in the Hellenistic world.

To whom, then, was the letter originally addressed? Some have suggested it is the letter to the Laodiceans mentioned in Col 4:16, where the Colossians are to exchange letters from Paul with Laodicea, but there is no mention of such an exchange in Ephesians. Marcion, an early collector of Paul's letters, knew of a Letter to the Laodiceans; Tertullian, an early church father, accused Marcion of changing Ephesians into Laodiceans. Yet there is no manuscript evidence that "in Laodicea" ever stood in the letter opening of what we know as the letter to the Ephesian church.

It may be that, like 1 Peter, Ephesians was originally a letter to more than one church, but that, unlike 1 Peter, a designation was not included, so that the churches that received it would know it was a general letter also intended for them. The phrase "in Ephesus" may then be due to an early scribe combining the information that Tychicus delivered the letter (Eph 6:21) with the note in 2 Tim 4:12 that Paul had sent Tychicus to Ephesus. That remains speculative, however. About

all we can say with any degree of confidence is that the letter was not originally addressed to the Christians in Ephesus.

The theater and the road from the harbor in Ephesus *(Phoenix Data Systems, Neal and Joel Bierling)*

The second question is: Did Paul write this letter? If we could be sure that the letter was addressed to Ephesus, we could be equally sure that Paul did not write it, since the letter assumes that Paul did not know the church there, when in fact he did. But there is other evidence that appears puzzling if Paul is the author of this letter in the same way that he is the author of, say, Romans or Galatians.

- Perhaps most importantly, the style of Greek in which Ephesians is written is noticeably different from that of Paul's major letters (Romans, 1 and 2 Corinthians, and Galatians). Ephesians has long, rambling sentences, written in an almost liturgical style, and employs the genitive case far more frequently than the major letters. The first chapter, for example, consists of just two sentences after the letter opening (vv. 3-14 and 15-23); English translations usually break them up into shorter sentences, thus obscuring the difference from the other Pauline letters. To be sure, Paul could also write long sentences and did so in his other letters, but he did not write such sentences so frequently and with the kind of grammatical constructions found in this letter.
- There are enough literary similarities between Ephesians and Colossians that

it appears that the author of Ephesians knew and depended on Colossians, for both many of the ideas and some of the language employed in Ephesians.

- Ephesians also has a number of words that do not appear in the other Pauline letters, and many key phrases that Paul uses do not occur in Ephesians, but this is not so important for determining the identity of the author as are the differences in style and grammatical usage.

None of these arguments will be convincing to those who insist Paul must have written the letter since his name appears on it or otherwise the letter is based on a lie. Yet ancient custom does not support such an assertion. In fact, according to Greco-Roman practice, if one got one's ideas from another, custom demanded that the writing identify the source of those thoughts as the document's author. It was considered dishonest to do otherwise. Given the differences in style and to some extent content, it seems quite likely that a follower of Paul is responsible for the composition of this letter, in which the key themes of Paul's letters, and hence of his thought, are presented, perhaps even, as some scholars have suggested, as a summary of his thought or an introduction to a collection of his letters. Such a person would then have been obliged to identify Paul as the source of the letter by attributing it to him.

None of this means the letter lacks importance for a study of Paul's thought and of the theology of the NT. Twenty centuries of Christians have found Ephesians useful for the life of the church, and its content retains its validity regardless of who set it down. The letter is an excellent summary of Paul's thought about the universal significance of the Christian faith, a point thematic for Paul's letter to the churches in Rome. Whoever wrote Ephesians knew Paul's thought in a most intimate way, whether as a secretary to whom Paul gave general instructions and who then wrote out the letter or as a member of a "Pauline school," that is, a group of people dedicated to following the thought of the apostle to the Gentiles and applying it to new situations as they arose. We may therefore confidently read it to learn more about Paul's message.

Because we do not know to whom the letter was originally written and because there is serious question about its authorship, it is virtually impossible to determine anything more than probabilities about the time or place of its composition. It contains a more fully developed representational christology (meaning that we can determine our future from the career of him whose fate decisively shaped that future, Jesus Christ), a christology hinted at in Colossians and then more fully developed in 1 Peter. The set of rules it contains for the conduct of the Christian households (often designated with the German word *Haustafel*) appears also in Colossians and 1 Peter and was probably made necessary by the increased public notice of Christian conduct. Again, the conflict with the Jerusalem authorities concerning the question of the necessity to become Jewish in order to be

Christian has apparently faded from view. All this suggests that Ephesians was written sometime in the later decades of the first century, perhaps after the fall of Jerusalem in 70 CE. At that point the Christian authorities that had insisted that Christians be circumcised and take on the yoke of the law had lost their base of operations in Jerusalem and hence much of their influence. Thus, their insistence on maintaining Jewish practices was removed as a point of conflict with the Pauline theological perspective.

The letter notes that Paul was in prison (3:1; 4:1; 6:20) when it was composed, thereby providing a point of contact with three other Pauline letters also written from prison, Colossians, Philippians, and Philemon. But because Paul claimed to have suffered many more imprisonments than other apostles (2 Cor 11:23), it is difficult to know at what date one is to assume the letter was written. As we shall see, Colossians and Philemon share a number of names. That is not the case with Ephesians, however, where the only name mentioned in common with Colossians is Tychicus. Ephesians has no names in common with Philippians or Philemon, and hence there has been no attempt to link its imprisonment with those of any of the other "prison epistles." All this means that it is all but impossible to determine where the letter was written.

Apart from the textual uncertainty of the presence of a location to which the letter was addressed ("in Ephesus"), there are no obvious problems with the text. The absence of evidence of additions to the text, or displacements, indicates that the text we have is, allowing for the kind of errors that inevitably creep in when manuscripts are copied by hand, in all likelihood very close to the text as it was originally composed.

15.2. CONTENT

The letter opening (1:1-2) does not include further comments on either sender or receivers and thus resembles the normal Hellenistic letter opening. It does include the usual Pauline grace wish for the readers. The letter also omits Paul's usual thanksgiving prayer for the readers and puts in its place a blessing that introduces the letter body. Although some scholars would identify 1:3-23 as the thanksgiving, the flow of the letter points rather to those verses as belonging to the letter body itself.

The letter body is divided into two parts. The first (1:3–3:21) contains what amounts to a series of meditations on the meaning of Christ both for Christians and for cosmological powers. Unlike the letters of Paul we have examined so far, the readers find themselves, immediately after the letter opening (in 1:3-14), not in some earthly location but in the "heavenly places," the source of the blessings they have received from Christ, whose death has freed them from their sin. In addition

Letter opening (1:1-2)
Letter body (1:3-6:20)
   The meaning of Christ for Christians and for cosmological
         powers (1:3-3:21)
      Christ's universal significance and God's plan to unify all things
            in Christ (1:3-14)
      God's deliverance of sinners through Christ (1:15-2:10)
      The unity of all humanity in the church (2:11-3:19)
      Benediction (3:20-21)
   How the meaning of Christ should affect Christians' behavior
         (4:1-6:20)
      The unity of the church and the diversity of Christ's gifts (4:1-16)
      The need to depart from the former manner of life (4:17-5:20)
      Rules for conduct within the family (5:21-6:9)
      The enemies of Christians (6:10-20)
Letter closing (6:21-24)

to the blessings that God has showered on them through Christ, they have also received God's revelation of his eternal plan, which has as its intention the union of all things, both heavenly and earthly. The proof of this is the presence among Christians of the Holy Spirit, who functions as a guarantee of their inheritance, announced through Christ, until they come into possession of that inheritance.

In this first sentence of the letter body, therefore, the two major themes of this epistle are announced. The first is the universal significance of Christ for the present and future fate of the Christians. The second concerns God's purpose to unify all things in and through that same Christ, so that finally God's plan for the Christians, revealed and enacted in Christ, will be theirs to possess as well. The remainder of the letter will spell out the ramifications of these two points.

The author goes on to an exposition of the significance of Christ (1:15–2:10). The primary point here is that Christ, because of his resurrection and exaltation to God's "right hand" (the place occupied by one specially favored by a ruler), now is far superior to any competing spiritual powers that could threaten his predominance. That predominance is effective not only in the present age but also in the age to come, thus making Christ the supreme head of all creation. And he is also the head of the church, which is described as "his body." Such an understanding of the church, as a body with Christ as its head, is a further development of Paul's idea of the church as the body of Christ, since, though he mentions the head among representative parts of the body (1 Cor 12:16-18), Paul never identifies Christ as the head.

Because Christians are members of the body of which Christ is the head, they are to understand themselves as already with Christ in his exaltation in the heavens. It is by his power that they have been snatched out of their former life, which was under the power of "the prince of the power of the air." "Air" refers here to the region between the earth and the moon, which in Hellenistic cosmology was the abode of evil and wicked spiritual powers. Because of their proximity to the earth, these were the malevolent powers that most influenced the lives of people on earth. Because Christians are now members of Christ's body, they are no longer under the dominion of these malevolent spirits. Like Christ their head, they have already been raised and sit with him in the heavenly places.

This again is a development of what Paul wrote, which was that our sharing in Christ's resurrection will happen only in the future. So certain is the author of Ephesians of the promise of Christ that Christians will one day share in his risen glory that he (or she; given the prominence of women within the early Christian church, we may not rule out authorship by a woman) can write as though it were already the case. Thus, we already share in the reality Christ "represents" by his resurrection and exaltation. There is to be no doubt, however, that Christians' deliverance from the realm ruled by wickedness and evil is pure grace; it is a gift of God and in no way earned or deserved by human beings. The phrase the author uses —

"Mystery"

In modern culture, a "mystery" is something that has not yet been cleared up, as in a mystery story, where something puzzling is eventually figured out. But the word is used differently in Ephesians (1:9; 3:3, 4, 9; 5:32; 6:19). The word "mystery" is derived from the Greek word *mystēs*, which means "initiate." Thus, in the first century, a "mystery" was something no one could figure out; instead a person had to be "initiated into" that knowledge by someone else. The word was used of religious sects whose secret knowledge could only be gained by initiation into the sect; hence they are called "mystery religions." Only the initiate (the *mystēs*) could know the otherwise hidden knowledge (the *mystēria*). That is the sense in which "mystery" is used in the OT book of Daniel, and in Ephesians. It is not something yet to be figured out; it is something that cannot be figured out. What God has revealed in Christ is such a "mystery": if God had not revealed it, it could not be known.

"because it is by grace that you have been saved through faith, and that does not come from you but is the free gift of God" (2:8) — penetrates to the very heart of Paul's theology and demonstrates the extent to which the author of Ephesians knew and understood what the apostle had written.

That Christians should be delivered by Christ is, further, in accord with the eternal plan of God. Thus, Christ's death was not due to an accidental confluence of political, social, and religious forces. His death, like his resurrection and exaltation, was part of God's plan since before the creation of the world. Further, because the church is the body of Christ, the power of the church similarly belongs to that eternal plan. And it is the purpose of the church to make that plan known not only to men and women in the Greco-Roman world and beyond but also to the "principalities and powers in the heavenly places." Thus the church assumes an absolutely central place in God's unfolding and revealing of his eternal plan, a role that is again a further development of Paul's descriptions of the church.

The outcome of Christ's victory over the powers of evil and the deliverance of men and women from those powers is the unity of all humanity in the church (2:11–3:13). This is the second point the author wants to make in this part of the letter body. There is therefore now no longer a distinction between Jew and Gentile; both are united in Christ. Indeed, it is Christ who has broken down the wall that separated Jew from Gentile. This is probably a reference to the wall in the temple in Jerusalem that separated the Court of the Gentiles from the inner parts of the temple accessible only to Jews. This wall Christ has broken through, so that

A Greek inscription from the Jerusalem temple forbidding entry by Gentiles on pain of death *(Israel Department of Antiquities and Museums)*

now both Jews and Gentiles together can come into the presence of God, a presence, as shown by the construction of the temple, once reserved for members of the commonwealth of Israel alone. So the Gentiles to whom this letter appears to be addressed, who once had no part in the covenant of promise God had given to Israel, have now been brought into the inner circle and share access to God.

Thus Christ, by his death, has reconciled former enemies — Jews and Gentiles — and has reconciled them to one another and brought them peace. All now belong to the same family, the church, an institution built on the foundation of apostles and prophets, with Christ the cornerstone. In ancient buildings, the "cornerstone" was a stone with a true 90° corner, used to align the other stones of both foundation and building so that the building would be truly built and thus be able to endure. That is the function Christ is here envisioned as performing. Because of him, the building that stands on the foundation of those who announced his coming both in anticipation (prophets) and in actuality (apostles) is truly built. Thus the church, resting on that foundation, will itself be truly built as the institution envisioned in God's eternal plan.

The author goes on to a wish that his readers may fully comprehend the scope of God's acts through Christ that have made their unity and salvation possible (3:14-19). One is immediately reminded of the lofty language of Rom 8:31-39, though it is obvious that there is no attempt to mirror or paraphrase that language here. This shows again the extent to which the author, if not Paul himself, penetrated the apostle's mind and reflected his spirit. The first part of the letter body is then concluded with a doxology (3:20-21; see Rom 11:36 for a similar end to a major section of a letter).

The second part of the letter body (4:1–6:20) is concerned with how the realities described in the first part impinge on the behavior of Christians as they seek to live lives worthy of the grace God has showered on them in Christ. Perhaps because this was a general letter, and hence its readers would be faced with a variety of external conditions, the exhortations deal almost exclusively with life within the Christian community and with relationships among Christians. The author is of course aware of what goes on outside the Christian communities (4:17-19), and he is also aware of the kind of conflict Christians face with external forces (6:11-12), but the major emphasis is on life within the community. He speaks of non-Christian activity to illustrate what Christians must avoid in their lives with one another (4:25) and of Christians' armor against the forces of evil because that seems necessary so that Christians' prayers within the community and for the community can be effective (6:18-19).

Again following Pauline precedent, our author sets out the theme for the subsequent exhortations in 4:1, as Paul does in Rom 12:1-2. There the theme is that Christians are to become a living sacrifice, here it is living a life worthy of the calling to be a Christian. Since in Christ Christians already share in Christ's heavenly

Christ and the Powers

One of the ways the majesty of the risen Christ is described in Ephesians is by saying that he has been placed above a series of malevolent spiritual powers. Some of these powers are named in 1:21 and 3:10. In the Greco-Roman worldview, the area between the earth and the moon, called the "air," was the abode of evil demonic forces that exercised control over some human affairs. The mention of "the prince of power of the air" in 2:2 shows that this is what is referred to in Ephesians, and the further description in 6:12 shows that the powers are understood to be malevolent toward Christians. Unfortunately, we are unable to tell which of the powers named exercised what specific authority, but their titles point to political authority, reflecting the view that the political forces of the Greco-Roman world were in the hands of demonic forces. Social and political pressure against Christians are thus said to be due to demonic opposition to God. But by the power of the divine armor provided by God (6:14-17), Christians will be able to survive the onslaught.

calling, the plea here is essentially that Christians become in their lives together what they already are in Christ. Again, because in Christ the old walls of separation between races have been broken through, the first point the author makes is that Christians must maintain their unity. In a discussion that again reminds one of 1 Corinthians 12, the author points out that unity does not mean uniformity of gift or function within the church. The Lord the Christians worship is one and the faith they hold is to be held in unity, but within that unity a diversity of spiritual gifts are apportioned to different Christians, so that together, with each contributing his or her gift, all may enjoy the fruits of all the gifts of the Spirit. Doing that will lead to steady growth into the stature of Christ, the head of the body (4:1-16).

This means that Christians may no longer conduct their lives as they did before they became members of the Christian community (4:17–5:20). The author describes a variety of activities, some appropriate for the life of the Christian, some not. That such activities are concerned with life within the Christian community is reinforced when the author explicitly urges his readers not to associate with people outside the Christian community (5:7). The reason is clear: the readers once shared in the dissolute and sinful life now characteristic of those outside the church, and associating with such people will inevitably draw them back into their old way of life (5:7-13). That particular discussion concludes with what appears to be a fragment of an early hymn (5:14). We do not know its source, but the author identifies it as a quotation, and its language and meter indicate that it probably served in a liturgical setting. The passage concludes with exhortations to live a life appropriate for Christians and therefore quite unlike the life of those outside the community (5:15-20).

The theme for the next part of the discussion, the rules for conduct within the family (the *Haustafel*), is given at the outset: "be subordinate to one another out of reverence for Christ" (5:21). By placing his advice to the various kinds of person who constitute a Greco-Roman household under that rubric, the author differentiates what follows very clearly from the kind of advice given in comparable non-Christian household rules. Early Christian authors borrowed the form of such rules, but changed the content dramatically. The purpose of such rules in the non-Christian community was to reinforce the hierarchical structure of the Greco-Roman family (for more on that structure, see pp. 47-48 above) and to quell any attempts to disturb that structure, in which men were preeminent, then women, then children, and finally slaves. Nowhere in those rules would there be found any hint that all were to be subordinate to one another. The word "subordinate" is also important. Often incorrectly translated "subject," the Greek word refers to occupying one's proper place in the order of things. It points not to domination and obedience, but to functioning properly within the good order of the family. And that good order, the author informs his readers at the outset, is determined by the self-sacrificing love of Christ.

The author speaks of the roles of various persons in the household within the framework of that love. Wives are to find their proper relation to their own husbands. Note well, the point here is the proper relation to the husband, not to men as such. Such respect is compared to the respect shown by the church to its Savior Christ. This is not a requirement that a wife do whatever the husband wants and obey whatever he may command, however harmful or perverse it may be. That would be precisely to break the rule that wives find their proper relation to their husbands, because such demands by a husband would already have broken the mutual subordination in Christ characteristic of the Christian family.

Husbands similarly are to exercise their proper relation to their own wives, which is that of Christ to the church, namely willingness to sacrifice oneself for the good of others. Indeed, when a family functions correctly, the husband respects the wife with as much natural spontaneity as he respects his own body, clothing it when cold and feeding it when hungry. Thus, husbands must put the good of their wives before their own good as, the author concludes once more, Christ did for the church (5:32).

Again, the advice to children to obey their parents as their proper role in the order of the family is tempered by the advice to the father, who in the Greco-Roman family was the one chiefly charged with disciplining the children, not to exercise discipline in an arbitrary and heavy-handed manner. Rather, parents are to be mindful again of Christ in the discipline and instruction they give to their children. The idea that children have no rights over against their parents and hence that parents may do what they want with their children, too often the case in the Greco-Roman world, is here decisively countered. Lists of household rules were normally directed only to people subject to others, namely wives, children, and slaves, not to those who held authority, such as husbands, parents, and masters. The mere presence of advice to fathers thus shows the very different milieu in which these Christian household rules were operating.

Slaves are counseled to obey, but with the qualifying note that they are to do so as slaves of Christ as well as of their masters. That automatically limits the kind of obedience a Christian slave could render, for example, to a non-Christian master. As a slave of Christ, for example, the enslaved man or woman could not take part in immoral or blasphemous activities. If such refusal meant they suffered, they had for their example Christ, who also suffered at the hands of an evil world. Such a limit on the slave's behavior in itself broke the absolute power of master over slaves in the Greco-Roman world and was the first step toward realizing the principle Paul had stated, namely that in Christ such distinction between slave and free has no further place (Gal 3:28). This was also therefore a first step toward the abolition of slavery itself.

Such a break with Greco-Roman structures is also evident in the mere inclusion of advice to slave masters. Masters are warned that both they and their slaves have a divine Master over them and stand on the same level in that Master's eyes. Once again, the distinction between slave and master has received its death blow, since both stand equal in the eyes of God.

The author concludes his letter by pointing once more to the kind of enemies Christians face — not merely human opponents, but supernatural enemies who exercise their rule in the world of darkness outside the Christian community (6:10-20). Evidently these powers of darkness do not take kindly to the invasion of their territory by the Christian community, which is under the sway of Christ rather than supernatural powers. Hence they will do all they can to retake control over Christians. Such opposition is real, but Christians have the armor they need to enable them to fight effectively against these supernatural adversaries. The point is that opposition to Christians is not motivated simply by non-Christians' dislike of people who are different. Opposition to Christians has a far deeper and more sinister source; indeed, that source is Satan himself (6:16). Evil is more than just mistakes or human ignorance.

Evil thus represents a power far stronger than anything human beings can overcome on their own. The inability of human attempts to maintain peace in the world and to overcome social evils bears eloquent witness to the validity of that Christian insight. Evil has as its source not human error but a supernatural power intent on the destruction of God's good creation, and the Christian community stands as a bulwark against such destruction. It represents the victorious power, now seen already in Christ, that will one day complete the overthrow of these evil supernatural powers. It is in anticipation of that victory that Christians are now to put on their armor and fight against such evil and wickedness with the only weapons that can prevail against it, the weapons that come from God himself.

The letter concludes with a reference to the person delivering the letter (6:21-22) and a benediction (6:24).

Whether one concludes that the letter was written by the apostle Paul or at a later time by one of his close followers, one cannot deny the power of the Christian witness contained in it and the consummate way in which, without slavishly quoting from the apostle's letters, it represents the heart and core of Paul's proclamation of the gospel of Jesus Christ to Gentiles.

FOR FURTHER READING

Markus Barth, *Ephesians,* 2 vols. (Anchor Bible; New York: Doubleday, 1974)

Ernest Best, *A Critical and Exegetical Commentary on the Epistle to the Ephesians* (International Critical Commentary; Edinburgh: Clark, 1998)

A. T. Lincoln, *Ephesians* (Word Biblical Commentary; Dallas: Word, 1990)

Rudolf Schnackenburg, *The Epistle to the Ephesians* (Edinburgh: Clark, 1991)

16. Paul and the Christians in Philippi

The letter to the Philippians is basically a thank you note to the Christians in Philippi, who have (again) sent Paul a gift of money to support his missionary activity. It is by turns irenic, autobiographical, and polemical. It reveals Paul in all his multidimensional reality, by turns stern teacher, beloved friend, and personal confidant. It gives us perhaps our most intimate glimpse at the apostle to the Gentiles, whose burning conviction that God in Christ has acted to redeem a world rotten with sin drove him relentlessly over long distances to announce that good news to all who would listen.

Few serious scholars have challenged the authorship of this letter; it is almost universally recognized as having been written by Paul to his converts in the Christian community of the city of Philippi. In 356 BCE, when Philip II of Macedonia, the father of Alexander the Great, annexed the area in which the settlement was located, he renamed it after himself — hence Philippi. It was conquered by the Romans some two centuries later (168-67 BCE) and became an important way station on the Via Egnatia, a Roman road connecting northwestern Asia with ports on the Adriatic Sea. In 42 BCE Mark Antony refounded Philippi as a Roman colony and settled veterans of his army there. Augustus refounded it yet once more after the battle of Actium (31 BCE) and settled more of his veterans there. Essentially a Roman outpost, the city was governed by the so-called "Italian law" (Latin *lex Italicum*), which was reserved for the most honored of Roman provincial cities. Although the local language was Greek, Philippi was probably the most latinized of the cities in which Paul established Christian communities. While Paul says nothing of the circumstances surrounding his original visit to Philippi, Acts recounts the difficulties Paul (and Timothy, see Acts 16:3-5) experienced during their proclamation of the gospel there (16:11-39), the first time evangelization had been attempted on European territory.

The forum of Roman Philippi (*Phoenix Data Systems, Neal and Joel Bierling*)

While there seems to have been some sort of conflict within the Philippian church (e.g., 4:2; cf. 1:27; 2:2) and some threat of people from the outside bringing what Paul regarded as a perverted gospel (e.g., 3:2-3), as in Galatia, the main purpose of the letter seems to be to thank the Christians in Philippi for the gift of money they sent to Paul (4:10-19). He also wants to assure the Philippian Christians that Epaphroditus, the courier they sent with the gift, who had fallen ill and then recovered, had in fact represented them faithfully during his time with Paul (2:25-30).

16.1. THE LETTER

Despite the relatively limited content of the letter — it comprises only four chapters — it nevertheless gives us one of our best chances to examine what Paul understood about the significance of the career of Christ (2:6-11) and what he understood his own conversion to be about (3:4-16). All of this is couched in a letter that wants to provide reassurance about a member of the Philippian community who had come to Paul and become ill, and to thank that community for their support for Paul's missionary endeavors. It shows us the extent to which Paul's whole

Letter opening (1:1-2)
Thanksgiving (1:3-11)
Letter body (1:12–4:20)
   Paul's imprisonment has worked to advance the gospel (1:12-18)
   He is confident that he will be released (1:19-26)
   The kind of life the Christians in Philippi are to lead (1:27–2:18)
   Paul's plans to send Timothy and Epaphroditus to Philippi
      (2:19-30)
   General admonition (3:1)
   Argument against those who advocate circumcision for
      Gentile Christians; Paul's example in that regard (3:2-16)
   Paul's characterization of the Judaizers (3:17–4:1)
   The dispute between Euodia and Syntyche (4:2-3)
   General admonitions (4:4-9)
   Paul's thanks for the gift from the Philippians (4:10-20)
Letter closing (4:21-23)

life and thought was wrapped around the task incumbent upon him as an apostle of Jesus Christ.

The letter opening (1:1-2) is one of the briefest in the Pauline corpus. It simply identifies the letter's senders (Paul and Timothy) and recipients and concludes with a typical Pauline salutation. What is unique here is the reference to the "bishops and deacons" at Philippi. Some have suggested that this may be a later addition, since the notion of the bishop as the chief Christian official is not really emphasized until the letters of Ignatius of Antioch, who wrote at the end of the first century or the beginning of the second. Yet the word translated "bishop" simply means "overseer," and the word for "deacon" means "one who serves," so in themselves they need not yet be technical terms for orders of clergy. The organization of the earliest church was apparently quite fluid, and the presence of church leaders called bishops and deacons in one place does not mean the terms were used in all places by this time. Both are also mentioned in 1 Timothy, and the bishop in Titus, but they are absent from the other Pauline letters. Thus it is much more likely that the Philippians had begun to use words to designate the leaders of their Christian community that over time would be adopted more generally by the church, rather than that we have here evidence for an already firm order of church officials.

Paul, as is typical for him, follows the letter opening with a thanksgiving (1:3-11). In Philippians it reflects the support his readers have given him from the time he first arrived in their city and the real affection he feels for them as a result. There is some evidence that the words Paul uses to describe his current status (1:7), namely his "defense" and "confirmation" of the gospel, may be technical legal terms for the part of his trial in which he seeks to rebut the charges against him; because Paul has been imprisoned on account of his gospel (see 1:13), he identifies his testimony in court as testimony on behalf of the gospel. If in fact he is using these words in their legal sense, it may well be that his trial has run its course and that he now awaits the verdict. But he is concentrating here not on his own fate but on the faith of his readers, for whom his prayer is that they prove themselves to be faithful adherents to the Christian faith.

Paul does turn to his own fate as he begins the body of the letter (1:12–4:20). The first point he wants to make (1:12-18) is that his imprisonment, contrary to what one might expect, namely, that it has hindered his proclamation of the gospel, has had just the opposite effect. It has in fact worked to advance the gospel, since it has become clear to those who are responsible for keeping him in prison that the reason for his imprisonment has to do with his being a Christian, not a thief or a murderer or some other sort of social miscreant. That knowledge has apparently lessened the danger he is in, since it has resulted in the Christians where he is imprisoned being even more bold about proclaiming the gospel. To be sure, there are some who seek to take advantage of Paul's inability to move about the area in order to advance a gospel that diverges from Paul's, perhaps even hoping thus to make Paul's imprisonment even more painful. Yet Paul is not upset. The net result, he observes, is that for whatever motive, whether to oppose or support Paul, Christ is being preached, and since that is the major thing, Paul rejoices in it.

Paul assures his readers that he can rejoice in more than that, however. He can also rejoice in his confidence that his trial will have a positive outcome (1:19-26), not least because of the prayers offered on his behalf by the Christians in Philippi. Yet until the verdict is announced, no one knows that outcome. If it is negative, Paul is prepared for that as well, confident that his death will enable him to glorify Christ even as his life has allowed him to do thus far. In fact, Paul does not know whether to hope for acquittal or conviction. The former would mean he could continue his apostolic proclamation, the latter that he could be with Christ apart from the troubles of this life, since the outcome of the trial would apparently be either freedom or execution.

Time in prison was not a usual form of punishment in the Hellenistic world. Normally, a person was imprisoned simply so that the authorities could lay hold of him or her when the time came for the trial. Once the trial concluded, they would be either set free or put to death, though release would sometimes be accompanied by some form of physical punishment, such as beating with wooden poles. In the case of the wealthy and highborn, a third option might be exile to some barren landscape, but ordinarily imprisonment for a specified period of time as punishment was not normally used. Thus Paul can anticipate either freedom or death, and he is confident that since freedom means the opportunity for further apostolic proclamation, he will in fact be released.

Discussion of the outcome of his imprisonment and his possible return visit to Philippi leads Paul to think of his beloved Christians there and the kind of life they are to lead (1:27–2:18). At the heart of this section Paul has included what may be an early confession or hymn centering on the meaning of the career of Christ (2:6-11), a segment of early tradition Paul has adapted to his purposes in this letter.

This confession or hymn is placed in the service of a very practical intention, however, and that is the unity of the Christian community in Philippi, a unity grounded in the willingness of its members to defer to one another (2:3-4). It is further evidence that all of Paul's theology has ethical implications, as all his ethical admonitions are grounded in his theology.

While many scholars have argued that Paul has taken over and even adapted an earlier Christian confession or hymn in 2:6-11, it is not impossible that Paul himself may have written it. Scholars are not in agreement on either the shape of the original tradition or how it is to be divided into strophes as a hymn. There are some words in it that Paul does not use elsewhere, but that cannot be a sure indication that Paul did not write it. His vocabulary was undoubtedly larger than the words contained in his letters. Whether he wrote these verses or is citing them, their point fits well with his theological intention as expressed in his letters, and since he did in fact include it in this epistle, we may have confidence that he found it expressive of the theological point he wanted to make to the Philippians.

Fundamental to this "hymn" is the contrast between what Christ was prior to his incarnation and what he became as a result of it. There has been some confusion on how the unusual Greek word *harpagmon* in v. 6 is to be translated and understood. If it is construed as a participle, it refers to the act of snatching something away, that is, to robbery; if it is construed as a passive verbal noun, it refers to what is snatched away. Yet in either case, it seems odd that Christ would regard equality with God, which he already had according to 2:6a, as either robbery or something he needed to grasp. Neither alternative seems to fit the context. In fact, there is another way to construe the word. It is highly likely that Paul is using an idiom referring to exploitation of something for one's own gain. Hence v. 6 would best be translated "who, although he was in the form of God, did not count that equality something to exploit for his own benefit." Rather, as v. 7 says, Christ emptied himself of that God-likeness and took the form of a vulnerable human being.

A second humiliation followed: not only did Christ give up his God-likeness, he also gave up his human life on the cross in obedience to God (v. 8). Because of that self-denying obedience, God exalted Christ to a higher level than he had before the incarnation and crucifixion by giving Christ God's own name,

"Lord" ("Lord" is used in the Hebrew Bible in place of the personal name of God, *YHWH*, which was never pronounced). As a result Christ has now reassumed his God-likeness, and, having been given God's own sacred name, is now to be publicly worshiped by the whole of creation (vv. 9-11).

Philippians 2:5-11

The notion that somehow Jesus, the man of Galilee, had also shared God's own nature in some mysterious way arose very early in the Christian faith, as Phil 2:5-11 shows. One of the characteristics that Pliny noted when he investigated the beliefs and practices of the Christians in Asia Minor around the year 110 CE was that in addition to pledging to do no wrong, they also sang a "hymn to Christ as to a God" when they assembled (*Letters* 110). That was no problem for Pliny to understand, since the Romans, like the Greeks, knew of many gods. It was a problem for the monotheistic Jewish background out of which Christianity arose, however, and the problem of how there could be one God and yet have Jesus, and later the Holy Spirit, also share that divinity was not worked out until centuries later at the church councils of Nicea (325 CE) and Chalcedon (451 CE). Understanding the reality of a God who is triune and yet one remains at the heart of the Christian faith and distinguishes it from other religions, both monotheistic and polytheistic.

What seems to underlie the emphasis on Christ's obedience in both his incarnation and in his submission to the cross is the contrast with Adam, who, also reflecting God's image, decided to try to achieve divinity in direct disobedience to God's command. On the other hand, Christ, who was already divine, nevertheless in obedience to God sacrificed all for the good of sinful humanity. This reflects elements seen elsewhere in Paul's christological statements (see, e.g., Rom 5:18-19; 2 Cor 8:9).

Having introduced this hymn to Christ with the advice to be willing to put the interests of others ahead of one's own (2:3-4), Paul concludes the hymn by urging obedience to God's will (vv. 12-13). Paul concludes this part of the letter body with further admonitions to peace and unity within the Christian community, conceding that this means that the readers must act in a way quite different from that of their non-Christian contemporaries (2:14-18).

In the next section of the letter body Paul returns to his current situation and his plans to send Timothy (2:19-24) and Epaphroditus (2:25-30) to Philippi. The brief allusion to untrustworthy fellow Christians (2:29) indicates another of the troubles Paul faced in his apostolic ministry. It indicates that when he affirms his personal weakness (as in his letters to Corinth), he means that literally and not just figuratively. He did in fact carry on his mission in what looked more like weakness and defeat than like power and triumph, and, as the troubles at Corinth showed, some fellow Christians derided him for it.

The discussion of Epaphroditus's faithfulness to the task the Philippian Christians had given him (2:25-30) may reflect an impression on the part of some at Philippi that Epaphroditus was lazy or was loafing since he did not return to Philippi sooner. Paul assures them that Epaphroditus's illness was real, nearly fatal (v. 27), and that he had indeed been faithful to their charge that he help Paul, faithful almost to the point of death (v. 30).

Following a general admonition (3:1), Paul turns to an attack on some people who have evidently been urging the Philippians that they must be circumcised and hence become true Jews if they want to be true Christians (3:2-3). After assuring his readers that those who follow Christ are the true circumcision, Paul turns to an account of his own conversion to demonstrate that his denying the validity of circumcision, and hence Jewishness, is not the result of his lack of either (3:4-16). Arguing that he was as Jewish as one could be (vv. 4-6), he relates how at his conversion he renounced it all in order to follow Christ (vv. 7-8). Paul renounced the advantages of membership in the chosen people, along with trust in any sort of righteousness that would come by observing the law or belonging to that people, because a right relationship with God can in fact come only by trusting in God because of what he has done in Christ Jesus (v. 9). Because of what God has done, the "righteousness through the law" now stands in opposition to the "righteousness from God, which depends on faith." This is why Paul follows the way of weakness and self-sacrifice, the way that Christ followed to his death on the cross, so that by sharing in Christ's death, Paul may at some future point share in Christ's resurrection as well (3:10-11), something that at present he has not obtained (vv. 12-13a). Paul sums up his point: forgetting the glories of his Jewish past, he now devotes his total energies to the future, to the time when he will share in Christ's glory (vv. 13b-14), a point he is confident is shared by the mature Christians at Philippi (vv. 15-16).

Paul concludes this discussion (3:17–4:1) with a harsh characterization of the Judaizers, those whom he opposes: their reliance on their Jewish heritage makes them enemies of Christ's cross, since, if they are saved by their Jewish heritage, they do not need the cross (3:18). Their observance of dietary regulations means that they concentrate too much on their stomachs, and their demand for circumcision means that they concentrate too much on their male members ("their

Were the "Judaizers" in Philippi?

It is difficult to determine whether the opponents Paul has in mind in 3:2 are currently present in Philippi, or whether the warning is general in nature, in case people should show up in Philippi with the same kind of message that, for example, the "Preachers" had delivered to the Galatian Christians. The discussion here is short and rather general, with only the third description ("those who mutilate the flesh") openly referring to people who would have shared the views of the Galatian "Preachers." Furthermore, such warnings do not seem to play a role in the remainder of Philippians. As a result, it looks as though this is more a warning of potential danger from outside sources than an attempt to counter the message of people currently active among the Philippian Christians. Paul seems here to want to inoculate his readers against infection with any distorted views of the Christian faith.

shame"). All that means they still function as those concentrating on earthly things (food, physical bodies) rather than heavenly matters (3:19). But in fact Christians must not be so absorbed with matters of this earth and its culture since Christians are like aliens in this world, living apart from their true homeland, where they are citizens. Christians are in fact not at home in the culture and values of this world. Rather, Paul affirms, Christians are citizens of heaven. That is their true homeland, and it is from there that Christ will come to transform reality and redeem sinners (3:20-21). Paul concludes by returning to his opening point: he urges his beloved fellow Christians in Philippi to stand firm (4:1) in the faith they share with him (3:17).

After urging two women who were his helpers in the task of evangelism to give up their dispute with one another and then urging his other fellow workers to help in that reconciliation (4:2-3), Paul provides some general admonitions on the Christian life (4:4-7). Rounding out his discussion by repeating some of the points he made earlier in the letter (4:8; cf. 2:1), Paul then turns to the final topic of the letter body, namely his gratitude to his readers for the gift to him brought by Epaphroditus (4:10-20).

It is evident from this discussion that the Christians in Philippi had underwritten Paul's mission by gifts at other times as well. Paul mentions three other such gifts, one when he left Macedonia and two when he was still in Thessalonica (which, like Philippi, is in Macedonia). So the gift brought by Epaphroditus was the fourth gift of theirs to Paul. Such gifts made it possible for Paul to refuse support from Christian communities, for example Corinth, when in his judgment the community might interpret such support as giving them the right to restrict what he preached. The variations among Paul's various mission churches was evidently such that he would accept support from some but not from others. It may also have been the case that Paul would accept support from a congregation only after he had left the city it was located in, lest again those who supported him might think they could exercise some influence over his ministry among them. However that may be, it is clear that the Christians in Philippi had proved themselves partners with Paul in his apostolic mission, and he was grateful for it, not only for the money but also for the evidence that the gospel had taken root and produced a mature and committed Christian community (4:17). Paul concludes the letter body with a doxology (4:20).

The letter closing (4:21-22) contains Paul's usual greetings, both to his readers and from those around him. While he does not identify his own writing in this instance, it is quite possible that the characteristic benediction with which he closes the letter (v. 23) was written in his own hand.

It is a sign of the extent to which Paul identified himself and his life with the gospel of Jesus Christ that a letter like this one to the Christians in Philippi, essentially a thank you note for a gift intended to underwrite his ministry, would call forth a letter so rich in theological and ethical content. His self-description in 3:7-9, describing his reversal of values on the occasion of his conversion, was patently accurate — he now gave himself totally to the Christ who had turned his life completely around.

16.2. SOME QUESTIONS

The major literary questions about the letter concern when and where it was written and the integrity of the letter as we have it, that is, whether it was originally a unity or consists of parts of two or even three letters combined into the form we now possess.

16.2.1. Place and Time of Composition

In attempting to determine when the letter was written, it is interesting to note that it does not refer to the collection for Jerusalem, as do Romans, 1 and 2 Corinthians, and Galatians. This means that Philippians was written either before Paul had agreed to make the collection (thus making it a very early letter) or after he had delivered the collection to Jerusalem (thus making it a very late letter). Or it could mean that the Philippian Christians had already given (2 Cor 8:2-4) and hence no longer needed to be reminded, in which case the collection's absence from the letter is of no help in determining when during Paul's missionary career the letter was written.

Attempts have made to resolve the problem by determining where Paul was imprisoned when he wrote the letter (1:14, 17). If that could be determined, it might give us a hint as to when he wrote the letter. Although some have argued that the references to imprisonment are symbolic, meant to display Paul's servitude to Christ, most scholars have found here references to genuine physical imprisonment.

To determine where Paul was imprisoned, certain evidence needs to be taken into account:

1. He mentions that it is known throughout "the whole Praetorium" that he is imprisoned for Christ (1:13).
2. He mentions Christians "of Caesar's house" (4:22).
3. He says that a number of people are at work preaching the gospel, albeit from mixed motives (1:15-17).
4. He promises to come to Philippi soon (1:26; 2:24).
5. He sharply attacks what appear to be Judaizers, indicating that they still pose a threat to the gospel to the Gentiles (3:2-3; see also 1:15-17).
6. The letter presumes a number of round-trips between Philippi and Paul's location in prison. Four journeys were completed before the letter was written:
   a. Someone brought the Philippians news of Paul's imprisonment.
   b. They sent Epaphroditus to Paul with a gift.
   c. Someone brought the Philippians news that Epaphroditus had become ill.
   d. Someone told Paul that the Philippians had learned of Epaphroditus's illness and were worried about him.
   In addition, Paul mentions four future journeys:
   e. Epaphroditus will return to Philippi, probably with the letter.
   f. Timothy will bring news to Philippi as soon as Paul knows the outcome of his trial.
   g. Timothy will return to Paul with news of the Christians in Philippi.
   h. Paul will travel to Philippi as soon as he is able.

The three visits relating to Timothy presume the completion of one before another may begin. On the other hand, Timothy will leave when Paul's trial is over, regardless of when Epaphroditus leaves. All this travel assumes a relatively short distance between the site of Paul's imprisonment and Philippi.

Acts mentions two imprisonments that could qualify, one in Caesarea during Paul's trip to Rome and the other in Rome itself. The imprisonment in Rome would account for the presence of the Praetorium and those of "Caesar's house," and in so large a city one could presume many missionaries at work. It appears from Paul's letter to Rome, however, that the threat of the Judaizers had not been felt at its full force there. Further, the travel plans outlined make it difficult to posit Rome as Paul's location, since the distance between Philippi and Rome would require a journey of six or

---

Paul the Prisoner

Some thirty percent of the book of Acts is devoted to scenes in which Paul is under arrest — whether imprisoned or on trial. In cataloging his afflictions, he adds to this picture, noting that his imprisonments far outnumbered those of the false apostles who opposed him (2 Cor 6:4-5; 11:23-29). In several letters attributed to Paul, he describes himself as "in chains" or "in prison" (e.g., Phil 1:7, 13, 14, 17; Col 4:18; Phlm 1, 10, 13; 2 Tim 1:16; 2:9).

In the Roman world, imprisonment was not a legally accepted *punishment* for a crime, but was generally employed as a means to ensure the appearance of the accused at trial. Nevertheless, incarceration might serve as a means of compelling stubborn persons to obey a local magistrate. Confinement was also employed as a form of protection, and, following trial, prisons kept those awaiting sentencing or execution.

Imprisonment might take many forms. Confinement in a state prison was the most severe of these. Less severe was military custody, which might take the form of confinement to a military barracks or camp or even within one's own house or apartment. A person could be ordered into the care of a magistrate, a leading citizen, or even one's own family.

The severity of the confinement, including the added possibility of related scourging and chains, was directly related to one's public status. The higher one's social status, the less severe the measures of confinement. At the same time, imprisonment itself was a form of dishonor, with arrest and incarceration used to silence undesirable persons and those who had been imprisoned suffering the stigma linked to arrest and incarceration. Both Acts and Paul's letters demonstrate the variety of ways in which Paul's chains were challenges and occasions for embodying and broadcasting the gospel. Included among these responses are two found in Philippians and Philemon, where the shame of his bonds becomes for Paul both an opportunity for theological reflection on identifying with the suffering of Christ and a rhetorical device for calling others to embrace humility.

eight weeks. To complete the four journeys outlined in the letter as already completed would require about six months, perhaps longer. Again, the repeated mention of "soon" (2:19, 24) would be unlikely for a journey that at the earliest could be complete only some five or six months hence, allowing time for Timothy to make the round-trip and then for Paul to journey to Philippi. And with Caesarea also the distance is such as to make the journey unlikely, and there is no evidence for members of either the Praetorian guard or Caesar's household in that city.

A more likely imprisonment would be in Ephesus, which, although not mentioned in Acts, is hinted at in Paul's Corinthian correspondence (2 Cor 18-9a; cf. 1 Cor 15:32 for another imprisonment there). Ephesus was near enough to Philippi that the journey by sea could be completed in a matter of weeks, and Paul was imprisoned at Ephesus at the height of the conflict with the Judaizers. We know from inscriptions that there was a Praetorian guard stationed there and members of Caesar's household living there (Latin *qui de caesaris domo*). The travels mentioned in Phil 2:19-24 are in accord with the travel plans outlined in 1 Cor 4:17 and 16:10 (see also Acts 19:22). The journey spoken of in 1 Cor 16:3-4 and Phil 1:26; 2:24 is planned in Acts 19:21 and carried out in Acts 20:1. Origen, a third-century church father, knew a tradition that Philippians was written between the writing of 1 and 2 Corinthians while Paul was in Ephesus.

The traditional site of Paul's imprisonment in Philippi *(Phoenix Data Systems, Neal and Joel Bierling)*

If the foregoing discussion is on target, it would mean Paul wrote to the Philippians during his time in Ephesus, namely sometime in the mid-50s. Such a conclusion, however, must remain tentative, given the tenuousness of the evidence on which it is based.

16.2.2. The Integrity of the Letter

The abrupt change in tone between 3:1 and 2 and the shifting content of the various chapters have prompted a number of scholars to posit that two or perhaps even three different letters were combined to make up what we know as Philippians.

Those who find two letters combined tend to include in one letter 1:1–3:1a and 4:21-23 and assume it was sent after Epaphroditus had recovered from his illness and was about to return home with that letter. The remaining verses, 3:1b–4:20, are then taken to be a note Paul wrote to thank the Philippians when he received the gift of money that Epaphroditus had brought.

Those who find three letters tend to combine 1:1–3:1a with 4:4-7 and 4:21-23 as a general letter urging the Philippian Christians to lead a worthy life and to rejoice in the Lord. A polemical and corrective letter in found in 3:1b–4:3, 8-9, while 4:10-20 comprises the thank you note for the gift Paul received from the Christians in Philippi.

Such speculative reconstructions of the correspondence between Paul and the Christian community in Philippi assume that all ancient letters follow a logical outline and a uniform tone throughout, an assumption that would be incorrect even for modern letters. There is no textual evidence that this letter ever existed in any form but the one we have in the NT, and on that basis it would probably be well to continue to look on it as one letter, existing pretty much as Paul composed it.

How then are we to account for the differences in tone and subject matter? One contributing factor has to do with the technology of ancient letter writing. All ancient writing was done in capital letters with no indication of paragraphs or even sentences. Indeed, there were not even any spaces between words. Documents were written with as many letters across the page as its width would allow, with no regard to where words ended. If the piece of papyrus, for example, was wide enough for sixteen letters, the document would consist of as many sixteen-letter lines as were necessary to convey the material.

So one would have to provide clues about how readers were to understand a letter in some other way than by forming sentences and paragraphs. Clues about the thought structure of a letter would be built into the language of the letter itself. For example, a section of a letter might end with the sentence with which it began

---

Reading

If we still wrote the way people of Paul's day did, Phil 1:12-13 would look like this:

IWANTYOUTOKNOWB
RETHRENTHATWHATH
ASHAPPENEDTOMEHA
SREALLYSERVEDTOADV
ANCETHEGOSPELSOTH
ATITHASBECOMEKNO
WNTHROUGHOUTTHE
WHOLEPRAETORIANGU
ARDANDTOALLTHERET
HATMYIMPRISONMEN
TISFORCHRIST

Add to that the fact that letters were more difficult to make out when written on papyrus than our printed letters are, and it is little wonder that people had a hard time making sense of a piece of writing when they first looked at it. Anyone who could read something straight off at first sight was the object of praise (e.g., Petronius, *Satyricon* 75, which speaks of a young man as "excellent: he can do division and read books at sight").

---

to show that that part of the discussion had been concluded (e.g., Matt 4:23; 9:35). Or one might repeat a statement to show that the discussion was now going on to another topic (e.g., Rom 5:18-19; 2 Cor 5:18-19).

These changes of subject would be emphasized by the voice of the one reading to a group (cf. Col 4:16). Even someone reading to himself or herself would read out loud. When Philip "heard" the Ethiopian reading from Isaiah (Acts 8:30), the Ethiopian was simply following normal practice. And even a person writing vocalized the material as he or she wrote. Even in dictation, the secretary who did the actual writing would vocalize while writing.

It is quite probable that those places in Philippians where Paul changes the subject abruptly, sometimes taking on a very different tone, do not indicate the conflation of different letters. It is much more likely that they were intended as verbal clues to the readers and listeners that Paul was now moving on to another

---

On the Use of a Scribe

If one was using a scribe to write a letter, it was necessary to dictate at a pace that made it possible for the scribe to form the letters on the papyrus. Because the scribe used a split reed pen on the rough surface of the papyrus, it took longer to write than it takes us to write something with a modern pen or pencil on a piece of paper. Thus one had to speak slowly. Seneca, for example, complains of one Vincius that he spoke as slowly as if he were dictating (*Epistula Moralis* 40.10). Such a technique of dictation means that any grammatical confusion in Paul's sentences was not the result of his words pouring out so rapidly that he did not take time to formulate grammatical sentences. Such confusion more likely resulted from the fact that, being forced to dictate slowly, Paul would have forgotten how he began a sentence by the time he concluded it. But in fact there are very few places in Paul where his grammar is jumbled; he apparently knew how to dictate his letters even at the slow pace that dictation required.

---

subject. Thus the short exclamations in 3:2 alert the listeners to a change in subject matter, namely a discussion of what is and is not essential for the Christian faith. Similarly, the repetition in 4:8-9 of the form of the material contained in 2:1 alerts the listeners to the fact that Paul will again change the subject, this time to thanking them for their gift. It is on the basis of ancient letter technology that we can thus argue for the unity of the letter from Paul to the Christians in Philippi.

FOR FURTHER READING

J.-F. Collange, *The Epistle of Saint Paul to the Philippians* (London: Epworth, 1979)

Gordon Fee, *Paul's Letter to the Philippians* (New International Commentary on the New Testament; Grand Rapids: Eerdmans, 1995)

Gerald F. Hawthorne, *Philippians* (Word Biblical Commentary; Waco: Word, 1983)

Ralph P. Martin, *Carmen Christi: Philippians ii. 5-11 in Recent Interpretation and in the Setting of Early Christian Worship* (rev. ed., Grand Rapids: Eerdmans, 1983)

Peter T. O'Brien, *The Epistle to the Philippians* (New International Greek Testament Commentary; Grand Rapids: Eerdmans, 1991)

17. Paul and the Christians at Colossae: Colossians and Philemon

Although only one Pauline letter is specifically addressed to Christians in the city of Colossae, it is evident from the overlap of names with Colossians that Philemon was also written to Christians in that place. For that reason the two letters will be treated together. Because they differ enough in scholarly estimates of authorship and the like, however, Colossians and Philemon still need to be treated as independent letters.

The city of Colossae, along with Laodicea and Hierapolis, was situated in the Lycus River valley some 110 miles east of Ephesus. Although at one time Colossae had been the most important of the three, well known for its industries of wool-working and cloth-dying, by the mid-first century, and so by the time these letters were written, it was the least important of the three. Ancient records indicate it was devastated by an earthquake around 60 CE, and it apparently never recovered as a thriving metropolis.

In addition to the indigenous population of the area, there is evidence to indicate that a considerable number of Jews also lived there. The language in Colossians itself, however, indicates that it was addressed primarily to Gentiles (2:13; this also seems to be indicated by 1:21, 27; and 3:6), in keeping with Paul's mandate from the conference in Jerusalem with Peter, James, and the other disciples (Gal 2:9).

17.1. COLOSSIANS

17.1.1. The Letter

Colossians

Letter opening (1:1-2)
Prayer (1:3-8/12/14)
Letter body (1:9/13/15–4:6)
    A hymn of Christ (1:15-20)
        Christ the image of God and the first-born of creation (1:15-18a)
        Christ the first principle of reality and firstborn from the dead
           (1:18b-20)
    The new relationship with God brought about by Christ's
        reconciliation of all reality (1:21–2:7)
    Theological implications of God's activity in Christ; theological and
        moral problems confronting the Colossian Christians (2:8-23)
    Ethical implications of God's activity in Christ (3:1–4:6)
        Transitional paragraph (3:1-4)
        The church's orientation to the future (3:5-17)
        Household rules (3:18–4:1)
        The need for prayer and appropriate conduct toward outsiders
           (4:2-6)
Letter closing (4:7-18)
    News to be brought by those delivering the letter (4:7-9)
    Greetings (4:10-15)
    Instructions to exchange letters with Laodicea and for Archippus to
        fulfill his ministry (4:16-17)
    Final greeting (4:18)

The letter opening (1:1-2) is brief and indicates that, unlike the situation in Corinth or the Galatian churches, Paul's own authority is not being questioned in Colossae. As here, Paul often mentions Timothy, one of his regular companions on his missionary journeys, as a co-sender of his letters (2 Cor 1:1; Phil 1:1; 1 Thess 1:1; 2 Thess 1:2; Phlm 1). The wish for grace and peace is also typically Pauline.

Also typical is Paul's reference to his prayer on behalf of the readers, although in this instance it is difficult to determine where the prayer ends and the letter body begins. The kind of discussion that normally characterizes the opening of the letter body is underway in 1:13, and hence one might see the letter body beginning with 1:9. Yet that verse and the two or three following it continue the discussion of Paul's prayer on behalf of the Colossian Christians. The form of the letter is typical for Paul — letter opening, prayer, letter body — though difficulties arise when one tries to be precise in determining the limits of each part. Perhaps it would be best simply to note that the content of Paul's prayer leads into the discussion contained in the letter body, without trying to pinpoint too precisely where the one ends and the other begins. Paul could clearly adapt the forms to serve the functions he wished those forms to perform.

Paul leads into his discussion in the letter body by taking up the last phrase in the prayer, namely, the thanks to the Father who has qualified the Colossian Christians to share in the inheritance of those in the light (1:12). The reference to the Christians having been delivered by God from the kingdom of darkness into the kingdom of the Son (v. 13) sets the stage for the remaining discussion in the letter, which concerns itself with both the intellectual and the moral consequences of having been delivered from the "dominion of darkness." Such a radical shift has apparently been difficult for the Colossian Christians to absorb completely, and this letter is an attempt to spell out the consequences of that shift.

The discussion begins with a hymnic explication of who Christ is (1:15-20). It is formed of two parallel strophes (vv. 15-18a and 18b-20). The first strophe delineates Christ as the image of God and the firstborn of all creation, that is, the agent of creation. The second delineates Christ as the first principle of reality and the firstborn from the dead. Some have suggested that because of this kind of parallel structure, this may be an early Christian hymn or confession that Paul quotes to demonstrate to his readers that he and they in fact share the same Christian faith. Whether Paul is quoting exactly an earlier hymn, has adapted it, or even wrote it for this letter, his use of it here clearly shows that he subscribed to its content, so in the end its origin is of less importance than what it says to the Colossians by way of confirming the nature of their faith.

The first strophe is remarkably similar to the kind of description of Christ found in the prologue of the Gospel of John (see especially John 1:1-3). In both instances, the concept seems to reflect Hebrew thinking about a kind of personified Wisdom, who assisted God in the creation of the world (see, e.g., Prov 8:22-30). The first strophe is at pains to point out that there is no order of reality, visible or invisible, natural or supernatural, that was not created through the agency of Christ (Col 1:16). This means that, apart from Christ, the whole of creation would have no coherent center and would fly apart or revert to the chaos from which it emerged (1:17). Christ is thus not only the agent of creation, he is also the agent of the world's preservation.

It is precisely with that head of all creation, namely Christ, that the Colossian

A floor mosaic in the sixth-century-C.E. synagogue at Beit Alpha depicting the sun-god Helios in his chariot surrounded by four women representing the seasons, symbols of the twelve signs of the zodiac, and Hebrew and Aramaic names for the months *(Phoenix Data Systems, Neal and Joel Bierling)*

Christians have to do in the church. The church, in its turn, is nothing less than the body of which Christ is the head (1:18a). The implication, to be spelled out in detail below, is that when one therefore is a member of that body, one has no need to fear or propitiate any other spiritual being, whether angelic, astral, or demonic. Since Christ is head over all of them, to follow Christ is to be delivered from any power such beings might exercise.

The second strophe (1:18b-20) deals with the preeminence Christ has because of his resurrection from the dead. He is thus not only the agent of creation and preservation but also the principal reality in the re-creation of reality at the turn of the ages. As the firstborn of the dead by his resurrection, he is head not only of created but also of re-created, and thus redeemed, humanity. This is possible because in Christ the whole fullness of God is present; to have to do with Christ is therefore to have to do with God himself. If all things cohere in Christ (1:17), then, because of his death on the cross, all things are also reconciled in him (1:20). Thus at the center of created and re-created reality stands the figure of Christ, all powerful because of his unique relationships to God and to all created reality, which owes its present coherence and its future peace to who this Christ is and what he has done.

Paul now makes his first application of the points in the hymn to the Christians in Colossae (1:21–2:7). It is precisely because of what Christ, the very embodiment of God, has done to reconcile all reality on the cross that the Colossians themselves have now been brought into a new reality, a new relationship with

Astrology

Astrology enjoyed great popularity in the Hellenistic world, from the Roman emperor to the lowliest slave. Philosophers debated whether the movement of the stars, particularly the planets, caused fate, or merely reflected the fate that controlled their movements as well. However that was decided, it was agreed one could learn one's future fate if one knew how to read planetary movements correctly. Tied to this was the notion that when the soul descended from the upper realms to be born, each planet exercised an influence on the soul as it passed through the planet's orbital path. Thus, the position of the planets at the time of one's birth was the key to understanding which planets exercised most control over one. Emperors often banned astrologers because they were afraid that, if an astrologer foresaw an emperor's death, some enemy might decide to give fate a helping hand by murdering him.

Christ and therefore with God (1:21-22). To remain in that new reality through continued trust in Christ is of paramount importance for the Colossian Christians, lest they fall back into the evil and darkness of their old way of life (1:23). The remainder of this first segment of the letter body continues with a variety of exhortations to the readers to remain faithful to Christ. Apparently some people would like to persuade the Colossians to abandon their newfound faith (2:4), and so Paul writes to help the readers resist any falling back into the old ways.

The second segment of the letter body (2:8-23) returns to the theological implications of the primacy of Christ in creation and re-creation, with which Paul dealt in the opening hymn. These verses seek to counter the theological and moral problems confronting the Colossian Christians, the so-called "Colossian heresy." Unfortunately, Paul is not as specific about this "heresy" as we would like. He did not, of course, have to spell it out, since obviously the Colossians knew what it was, and he alludes to it only enough to combat it.

From what Paul says, though, it is apparent that those against whom he is writing were arguing that more was needed for one to come to terms with the forces that ruled the world than simple adherence to Christ. The "elemental spirits" of the universe, who were apparently seen as the building blocks of reality, had somehow to be appeased. One way of appeasing them was circumcision (2:11) and submission to certain legal demands, including food laws and celebration of various festivals (2:16; see also 2:20-21). In addition, it was apparently necessary to

Gnosticism

Philosophy's desire to know the true nature of reality found an expression in the Greco-Roman world during the second century in Gnosticism. The name given in modern times to this ancient religious-philosophical movement comes from the Greek word *gnōsis,* which means "knowledge" or "knowing."

Gnosticism held that reality was split into two spheres, the spiritual, which was good, and the material, which was evil. The spiritual was presided over by a panoply of deities, with proportionately less divinity from the highest deity to the lowest. Creation of the world was considered a cosmic accident caused by a lesser deity, who in some texts is identified with the creator God of the OT. Humans were originally spiritual beings, or at least those capable of salvation were. But creation trapped them in physical bodies.

Only possession of knowledge of the nature of reality and of human existence can, the Gnostics held, free a person from slavery to the material in order to emphasize the better part of his or her nature, the spiritual part. This secret knowledge came, many Gnostics believed, from a revealer figure sent by the highest deity. The Gnostics taught this secret knowledge to their followers and thus enabled them to return to the heavenly realm from which they had originally come. Salvation thus had to do not with forgiveness of sin but with removal of ignorance.

For Gnostics influenced by the Christian confession of Jesus as Christ, the Gnostic view of the human body as either unreal or evil carried over into christology. One result was Docetism: Christ seemed to be a real human being, but his flesh was rather like a disguise that he wore, and his humanity was a charade of human existence. He did not truly suffer pain, nor did he really die. Another species of Gnostic christology held that the union of the two natures of Jesus was merely temporary. The heavenly Christ came upon the earthly Jesus at his baptism in the form of a dove and left him at the crucifixion, as Jesus' cry "My God, my God, why have you forsaken me?" makes clear. Thus it was not the divine Savior who died on the cross, but a human being from whom the divine Christ had departed.

The Gnostic systems of thought appeared early in the second century CE as attempts to integrate knowledge from many different philosophies and religions, including Christianity, and thus to solve the philosophical quest for the nature of all reality. Because Gnosticism thus sought to bring together a vast array of ideas that were already circulating in the first century, many of the elements of these systems are mentioned already in some writings of the NT. Yet the full-blown Gnostic systems did not emerge until after the NT documents had been written, so one cannot speak of direct Gnostic influence on the NT.

Gnosticism continued to flourish into the church's fourth century. Church leaders including Tertullian, Justin Martyr, and Irenaeus regarded it as a heresy, that is, as a perversion of Christian belief. The early church historian Eusebius listed a number of Gnostic groups and blamed the church's disunity on them:

> Therefore, they called the Church a virgin, for it was not yet corrupted by vain discourses. But Thebuthis, because he was not made bishop, began to corrupt it. He also was sprung from the seven sects among the people, like Simon, from whom came the Simonians, and Cleobius, from whom came the Cleobians, and Dositheus, from whom came the Dositheans, and Gorthaeus, from whom came the Goratheni, and Masbotheus, from whom came the Masbothaeans. From them sprang the Menandrianists, and Marcionists, and Carpocratians, and Valentinians, and Basilidians, and Saturnilians. Each introduced privately and separately his own peculiar opinion. From them came false Christs, false prophets, false apostles, who divided the unity of the Church by corrupt doctrines uttered against God and against his Christ. (*Hist. Eccl.* 4.22)

Until the middle of the twentieth century most of our knowledge of Gnosticism came from the church's anti-Gnostic writings.

But the discovery of about fifty documents near Nag Hammadi in Egypt in 1945 — apparently the library of a community of Gnostics — changed that. Here for the first time were materials that allow us to study Gnosticism on its own terms. And though the community that possessed this library was apparently influenced by Christianity, their library also included non-Christian Gnostic documents, suggesting that the origins and character of Gnosticism cannot be described simply in terms of "Christian heresy."

practice self-abasement (2:18, 23) and to offer worship to angelic powers (2:18), perhaps lest one in the first instance call attention to oneself and, in the second, arouse the wrath of these supernatural beings. Some of this might remind one of the problems Paul had with the Judaizers in Galatia and Philippi, yet the worship of angels played no part in Jewish ritual and the legal demands seem tied to subordination to the elemental forces of the universe (2:20-21) rather than submission to the law of Moses. It may be that the Colossians confronted a religious amalgam made up of parts of Judaism and parts drawn from the worldview that permeated the Hellenistic world, with its fear of malevolent astral powers that would wreak havoc on the unwary.

Some have suggested that the Colossians confronted what was later known as Gnosticism, which emphasized salvation through knowledge of the nature of reality and of the way the human person fits into that reality. Yet the earliest Gnostic systems of which we have knowledge did not flourish until the first third of the second century and even then did not contain all the elements mentioned in Colossians, such as the need to be circumcised. Some have proposed a kind of Jewish Gnosticism, but we know of no such phenomenon.

Whatever the origin of this "heresy," it is clear that it argued that one needed to do more than just trust in Christ if one was to survive in a world dominated by powerful supernatural forces. One needed somehow to propitiate those forces. Against this, Paul argues for the total sufficiency of Christ. By sharing in Christ's death and resurrection in baptism, Christians are taken out of the realm in which the elemental spirits exercise dominion (2:20). Thus Christ has, through baptism, provided Christians with all the protection circumcision could provide (2:11-12). Indeed, by his death and resurrection, he has defeated all other supernatural powers as surely as a Roman emperor has defeated the enemies he brings back to Rome and parades through the streets before their execution (that is the figure called forth by the language of 2:15). The Colossians are free to ignore this "heresy," with its calls for further acts needed to protect a person from the depredations of evil supernatural powers, because Christ, working in the full and embodied power of almighty God, has in fact become ruler over all other powers that exercise any kind of rule in any portion of reality (2:9). Relation to Christ is quite literally relation to Almighty God, and hence any need to worry about any other spiritual powers, malevolent or otherwise, is rendered irrelevant.

In a transitional paragraph (3:1-4) Paul moves from the theological implications of God's activity in Christ to the ethical implications of that activity. Participation in Christ's death and resurrection means that the Christian is delivered from any concern about earthly realities, that is, about anything existing in the created sphere, which includes all supernatural as well as natural forces. Christians are free to concentrate on the heavenly realm, that is, the future, rather than on the created realm, which belongs ultimately only to the past.

Therefore, Christians are now free to cast off all remaining earthly elements of their lives that bind them to that past (3:5). What that means Paul spells out in the next segment of the letter body (3:5–4:5). The first half of this segment (3:5-17) emphasizes the kind of behavior that must now characterize the Christian community, which has as its primary orientation the future and the new reality God has introduced that leads to that future. Such activity must be different from that followed by the Colossian readers before they became Christians. Their former activity is still bound to the old age, which is doomed to be destroyed when God's new reality comes, and therefore must now be avoided (3:5-11). The word the RSV translates as "nature" and the NRSV as "self" ("old nature/self" in 3:9, "new nature/self" in 3:10) is the Greek word meaning "human being." What is described is the "old" and "new humanity," the point being that as persons develop within the structure of the Christian faith, they have the opportunity, now that sin's hold has been broken, to become new human beings, with a human nature renewed now in the true image of their Creator. The image of God, lost to Adam in his rebellion against God (the "fall"), can now be recovered and restored because of the new reality God has introduced into the world with the death and resurrection of Christ. That is why the church is so central for Paul's theology: it is the new community that can begin to reshape a humanity previously warped and corrupted by sinful rebellion against God.

Paul describes the activity of that new community in 3:12-17. Two general guidelines for conduct are enunciated and explicated. One is that all things are to be done out of love (3:14). One ought not confuse "love" here with emotional states. Christian love, as made concrete in Christ, is action for the good of another, regardless of how one may feel emotionally toward that person. That is why Jesus could tell his followers, "Love your enemies." God's love for sinful humanity was not emotional warmth so much as action for the benefit of human beings, namely, the sending of his own Son to die for sins.

The second guideline Paul enunciates here is the need to do everything one does in the name of Jesus Christ, by whose self-sacrificing love the new reality has been brought into being. This guideline suggests that if one cannot perform an act in the name of Jesus, one ought not to do it. This is simply the other side of the principle that Christians are to do everything out of love. To speak or act in the name of Jesus means one can also give thanks to God by those words or deeds. What therefore cannot be done in thankfulness to God ought also to be avoided.

In practical terms this means that all distinctions carried over from the old way of life are now rendered obsolete in the community shaped by the new reality. Race and social status had importance in the social order dominated by rebellion against God, but in the new social order dominated by Christ's self-sacrificing love such distinctions have no place (3:11). The new humanity, with its restored image of its Creator, makes no invidious distinctions with respect to birth or social status. In Christ, all people stand on the same footing before God: forgiven sinners living in harmony with one another.

While there are no distinctions in status, there are distinctions in function, and it is to those that Paul turns in the final portion of the letter body (3:18–4:6). In brief compass Paul outlines the proper stance of the various members of the Hellenistic household (3:18–4:1). In each case, as in Ephesians but here in shorter form, the emphasis is that actions be undertaken and performed within the over-arching need to remain faithful to God. And, again as in Ephesians, all are reminded of their responsibilities, not only those who in the Hellenistic world were assumed to be subordinate (wives, children, and slaves) but also those who were accorded dominance by the customs and civil codes of the times (husbands, parents, and masters).

Wives are to function within the ordering of the family ("be subordinate") in a way that is appropriate to their participation in the new community of faith ("as is fitting in the Lord"). Husbands are to fit into the family order by loving their wives, with all that means in a Christian context regarding self-sacrifice for the good of others. Children are to obey their parents within the structure of the Christian family, as parents are to require such obedience in a way that does no harm to the children. Slaves especially are to carry out their duties within the structures of the new reality brought by Christ; three times Paul emphasizes that their service to their eternal Lord provides the structure for their useful obedience to their earthly masters. Those masters must also remember that they have their own Master in heaven, who provides the model for treatment of all people, slave or free. Paul concludes with some admonitions appropriate for all members of the Christian household, emphasizing the need for constant prayer as well as for appropriate conduct toward those outside the Christian community (4:2-6).

The letter closing (4:7-18) contains some fairly lengthy greetings to the readers from persons who are with Paul. Tychicus, named first, is apparently the one who is to deliver this letter. It was customary in the Greco-Roman world for the bearer of a letter to expand on its contents and answer any questions the recipients might have about the letter or the situation of the sender (so 4:9b). Onesimus is to accompany Tychicus; he was a member of the Christian community in Colossae. His return may be linked to events recorded in Paul's letter to Philemon.

Paul next mentions three Jewish Christians who share in the mission to the Gentiles that has been entrusted to Paul. The phrase Paul uses to describe them (literally, "from the circumcision") is also used in Gal 2:12 of the group that caused the separation between Jewish and Gentile Christians at Antioch. That now some members of that group accompany Paul in his own missionary travels may be indicated by that language, but use of the same phrase may also simply be fortuitous. Aristarchus is evidently imprisoned with Paul. Mark was a cousin of Paul's onetime companion Barnabas. Mark (also called John or John Mark) had evidently deserted Paul and Barnabas during a missionary journey, and as a result of Barnabas's wish to take Mark on another journey, Barnabas and Paul had a falling out (Acts 15:36-39; cf. Acts 13:13). From then on Paul and Barnabas conducted separate missions. Evidently there had been a reconciliation between Mark and Paul, as evidenced by his presence with Paul when this letter was composed, and Paul can now instruct the Colossian Christians to receive Mark if his journeys take him to Colossae. The third of these Jewish fellow missionaries is Jesus, surnamed Justus. All three obviously are in sympathy with Paul's mission, since Paul identifies them as a comfort to him (4:11).

Epaphras, like Onesimus, was also a member of the Christian community at Colossae and was evidently the one in Paul's missionary party who had evangelized Colossae, and perhaps Laodicea and Hierapolis as well (4:13). The "beloved physician" Luke and Demas, also with Paul at this time, also send greetings. Whether this Luke is also the author of the Gospel that bears that name is by no means certain, since names were attached to the Gospels only many years after they were written. The same would be true of any connection between the Mark mentioned earlier and the Gospel bearing that name.

Those to be greeted include a Nympha who evidently owns a house large enough to accommodate a congregation that meets there. From the language it appears that her house is located in Laodicea and that Paul knows her personally. In that case, while Paul had never visited Colossae, he may in fact have been to Laodicea. Be that as it may, he evidently had also written a letter to the Christians there, and he instructs the Colossian Christians to exchange letters with the community at Laodicea. Unfortunately, that letter to Laodicea has been lost. What ministry Archippus was to fulfill was obviously known to him, but we cannot determine what it was from the scanty information contained in this letter. The mention of Archippus as one of the receivers of Paul's letter to Philemon, however, may give some hint, as we shall see when we turn to that letter. Paul closes this letter with a greeting written in his own hand, as he also did in Galatians (6:11), 1 Corinthians (16:11), and 2 Thessalonians (3:17). He also writes such a phrase in Philemon (v. 9), but for another purpose.

Paul does not refer to an impending visit to his readers, as he did in his letter to the Philippian Christians. This is strange, since Paul does tell Philemon, who apparently lived at Colossae, that he will in fact come to visit him (Phlm 22). But omission of any mention of a visit is appropriate if Paul was not the author of Colossians. The purpose of the letter was evidently to encourage the faith of the Colossian Christians and to emphasize to them the cosmic significance of Christ, thus obviating any need to embellish their faith with additional rituals or elements of belief. That purpose could be accomplished without reference to an impending visit by Paul.

17.1.2. Some Questions

That Paul is the author of the letter has been challenged on both linguistic and doctrinal grounds. The author of the letter was unknown to the Colossians in person (1:4, 6-7; 2:1) as also to the Christians in Laodicea (2:1). Evidently some of Paul's followers had established Christian communities in those places; the prominence of the reference to Epaphras in relation to the Christians at Colossae indicates he was probably the one who evangelized Colossae (1:7), if not also Laodicea and Hierapolis (4:13). In any case, the three communities were evidently closely associated, as their mention in the letter (Laodicea in 2:1, Hierapolis in 4:13) and the advice to the Colossians to exchange letters with the Christians in Laodicea (4:16) indicate.

The author was in prison when the letter was written (4:3, 18; in that light 1:24 may also refer to imprisonment), but there is nothing to indicate where the imprisonment took place. There is also nothing to indicate a lively interchange between the imprisoned author and the recipients of the letter, as there is in Philippians, so the imprisonment could have been in Rome. But again, Paul's references to the many imprisonments he underwent (2 Cor 11:23; cf. 2 Cor 6:5) caution us against assuming that this imprisonment is one of the two (Rome and Caesarea) mentioned in Acts. The nearness of Colossae to Ephesus, which served as headquarters for Paul's missionary activity for a time, and where Paul apparently was also imprisoned, may make it the best candidate for where Colossians was written, as with Philippians. Alternatively, if, as we shall see, it may be best to date this letter late in Paul's ministry, Rome may also come into consideration. The close relationship of this letter to the one addressed to Philemon, which concerns Onesimus, a runaway slave, may, then, indicate that Rome was where Onesimus went to elude detection and capture. Yet Onesimus may also have sought out Paul to mediate his dispute with his master, and then Ephesus would be equally possible as Onesimus's destination, if he knew Paul were imprisoned there. Once again, certainty is elusive.

Arguments against Paul as author focus on language and style on the one hand, and doctrinal content on the other. While a number of words found in Colossians are not found elsewhere in the generally acknowledged letters of Paul (Romans, 1 and 2 Corinthians, Galatians, Philippians, 1 Thessalonians, and Philemon), that is also the case with, say, Philippians and cannot be used alone as a reliable indication of authorship. Vocabulary is to a large extent determined by the problems addressed in a letter, so that each letter of Paul has a large store of words not found in the others. While there are some longer sentences in this letter, they are no longer than one finds in Romans, for example, and they are by no means as characteristic of Colossians as they are of Ephesians. There is some redundancy in the use of adjectives, but not to an extent great enough to disprove Pauline authorship. In style and vocabulary, therefore, the letter could fit the parameters of Paul's writing style.

The problem in doctrinal content centers primarily in one area, namely the understanding of the time of the Christians' resurrection in relation to Christ's. In the two other places Paul has discussed this topic (Romans 6, 1 Corinthians 15), he has been very careful to separate the two. The Christian shares in Christ's death through baptism, but not yet in the same way in Christ's resurrection; sharing in Christ's resurrection is always reserved for the future. The compound verb "crucified with" occurs in the undisputed letters (Rom 6:6; Gal 2:20), as does the compound verb "buried with" (Rom 6:4), but the compound verb "raised with" does not. But in Colossians the author combines these compound verbs and affirms that in baptism the Christian has been both "buried with" and "raised with" Christ (2:12). And the author uses "raised with" a second time as well (3:1). The question is whether Paul, who so carefully avoided ever referring to the Christian's resurrection with Christ in the past tense, could here suddenly, and repeatedly, do just that.

Some scholars have argued that this combination of the sharing of death and resurrection with Christ at the time of baptism may represent a further development in Paul's own thought. Yet Romans, where the distinction is carefully preserved, is surely one of the last letters we have from Paul. And in any case, any argument concerning later developments in Paul's thought could only be made with confidence if we knew the chronological progression of Paul's letters, which we do not.

Yet being raised "with Christ" is qualified in a very Pauline way in this letter. In the first instance (2:12) it is clear that the Christians' being raised with Christ occurs through their faith, their trust, that God has in fact raised Christ from the dead. The second reference (3:1) is immediately qualified by the statement that the Christians' (risen) life is still at this point hidden with Christ in God (3:3), to be revealed only with Christ's return (3:4). Both qualifications lie at the heart of Paul's theology and point to him as the author.

The date of the letter will also have a bearing on the decision as to its author. Ancient records indicate, as we noted above, that Colossae was devastated by an earthquake around 60 or 61, after which it never fully recovered. There is clearly no reference to such devastation in the letter, and one would wonder whether someone writing in Paul's name would, after the earthquake, address a letter to the decimated community. It would perhaps be easier to imagine the letter as written before the earthquake, and thus during Paul's lifetime, than as written after both the earthquake and Paul's death. That a Christian community could have survived in Colossae after the devastation is of course quite possible; unfortunately the area of Colossae has not been the subject of archaeological investigation, so that there is no help from that direction.

In the end, the question is one of content. On the one hand, if one decides that Paul could in fact in this instance have violated his practice of avoiding reference to a current sharing in Christ's resurrection, one will be inclined to accept Paul as author. On the other hand, if one decides that avoiding any reference to present participation in Christ's resurrection was too central to Paul's thought to violate, then one will find here an author steeped in Pauline theology and writing in Paul's name to a congregation that Paul did not found. Both Paul, in Romans, and a follower of his writing in his name, in Ephesians, show that a Pauline letter could be addressed to a congregation that Paul did not found.

When Colossians was written will depend in large measure on one's decision concerning authorship. The traditional dating of Pauline authorship is in the mid-60s. If Paul is not the author, one will need to date the letter subsequent to the apostle's death. As one scholar has put it, if it is from Paul, it must be dated as late as possible in the apostle's career; if it was written after Paul's death, it must be dated as soon thereafter as possible. A date sometime in the 60s therefore seems most likely.

The occasion for writing seems to be a response to news Paul has received about the Christian community in Colossae (1:4), perhaps from Epaphras (1:7b), who was evidently instrumental in the founding of a community of faith in that city (1:7a). The letter was probably intended to strengthen both the faith and the conduct of the Christians there, as Paul says is also the content of his prayers for them (1:9-11). Part of the occasion also lies in what appears to be a temptation on the part of some Christians at Colossae to take seriously a claim that one must also worship angelic beings and submit to rigorous ascetic practices if one is to get on well in a world dominated by such supernatural powers. Whether this is a form of Christian faith to which has been subjoined some elements from Hellenistic popular religion regarding supernatural powers or an alternative way of finding one's way in the world is not clear. In either case, Paul's defense is a restatement of the primacy of Christ over all elements of the created world, natural and supernatural.

It has been argued that Philippians was not a single unified letter from the beginning. Ephesians contains textual evidence that it was not originally intended for readers in Ephesus. And 1 Corinthians, it has been argued, contains at least one passage that was inserted after the letter was written. But no such arguments have been made with regard to Colossians. From all appearances the text we have is essentially the text as it emerged from the mind of its author, apart from the usual changes introduced, for the most part unintentionally, as a result of repeated hand copying.

17.2. PHILEMON

17.2.1. In Relation to Colossians

Although we have been following the canonical order of the letters attributed to Paul, the close relationship between Colossians and Philemon makes it appropriate to discuss them together. That close relationship is indicated in a number of ways. First, the same co-sender, Timothy, is named in both letters. This is not of decisive significance, since Timothy is also named as co-sender of other letters, but it is one small indication at least of the relationship of these two letters.

More important is the appearance of a number of other names in both letters. Most important in this connection is Epaphras (Col 1:7; Phlm 23), evidently a founder of the Colossian church and, according to the letter to Philemon, a fellow prisoner with Paul, a point omitted in Colossians. Also important is Archippus, who is charged with a specific duty in Colossians (4:17) and identified as a fellow soldier of Paul and one of the recipients of the letter to Philemon (v. 2). Onesimus, whose running away is the subject of Philemon, is also mentioned in Colossians (4:9). Other names common to the two letters are Mark, Aristarchus, Demas, and Luke (Phlm 24; Col 4:10, 14). Such a congruence of names of companions of Paul at the time both letters were written indicates that they were composed at roughly the same time and place, and the identification of Epaphras (Col 4:12) and Onesimus (Col 4:9) as coming from Colossae indicates that both letters were written to the same destination.

17.2.2. The Letter

No serious question has been raised against Paul as author of Philemon, and no suggestions have been made about materials added to the letter as Paul wrote it. The integrity of the text is little disputed, with the only changes being those encountered due to multiple copying of material by hand. A well-known alternative reading in v. 9 would substitute "ambassador" for "old man." There is no textual evidence for such a substitution, however. It is a speculation based on Eph 6:20 and should not be included in a translation of Philemon. That Paul was "old" is of little help in determining the date of the epistle, since such an epithet could in the first century easily apply to anyone fifty years or older.

The purpose of the letter was to plead for mercy on behalf of the slave Onesimus, who had in some way alienated his master Philemon and then run away. Under normal practices in the Greco-Roman world, Onesimus could look forward to very harsh punishment should he be returned to his master. Paul's letter seeks to persuade Philemon not to proceed in such fashion.

Philemon

Letter opening (vv. 1-3)
Prayer (vv. 4-7)
Letter body (vv. 8-22)
    Paul's appeal to Philemon on behalf of Onesimus (vv. 8-21)
    Paul's plan to visit (v. 22)
Letter closing (vv. 23-25)

The letter opening follows the usual Pauline format, with sender and recipients named, a benediction, and an opening thanksgiving prayer (vv. 1-7). The relationship among the three recipients is not entirely clear. It may well be that Apphia, the second named, is Philemon's wife, but their relationship to Archippus, whom Paul identifies as his "fellow soldier," is hard to determine. Archippus may belong to the household of Philemon in some way or be related to Philemon. Since he is the last named and since the "your" that identifies the house where the church meets is singular, it could refer to Archippus's house. On the other hand, since Philemon is named first, it is also quite possible that it refers to his house. The several references to "you" and "your" in the remainder of the letter are also uniformly singular, and since the letter concerns Philemon's relationship to the slave Onesimus, it is likely that in all those instances the reference is to Philemon.

The letter body (vv. 8-22) deals with Paul's appeal to Philemon to deal gently with Onesimus, who is returning at the time the letter is being delivered (v. 12). Paul begins his appeal (vv. 8-14) by pointing out that, given his authority in Christ, he has the right to order Philemon to take the appropriate action, but that Christian love constrains him rather to appeal to Philemon to do the right thing. Paul identifies himself as "father" and Onesimus as his "child," evidently referring to Onesimus's conversion to faith in Christ while he was with Paul. Thus Paul would have been happy to have Onesimus (the name means "useful," hence the play on that name in v. 11) stay with him to help him while he was in prison. There were few official provisions for the care of prisoners awaiting trial. Food was meager, when it was provided at all, and no provision was made for clothing, bedding, or any other necessities. What amenities, including sufficient food, the prisoner obtained had to be provided by friends on the outside. It was therefore highly useful to have someone whose responsibility it was to look after a prisoner during the period of incarceration. Such a person Paul would happily have had in Onesimus

(v. 13), but he wants Philemon's return of Onesimus to him to be voluntary rather than compelled (v. 14).

Because Onesimus is now a member of the Christian community, Paul tells Philemon that it is now incumbent on him to welcome Onesimus back not so much as a slave but as a brother in Christ. The reference to receiving Onesimus as a brother "both in the flesh and in the Lord" (v. 16) may indicate Paul's desire that Onesimus be freed, so that he can be Philemon's brother both within the Christian community ("in the Lord") and in secular society ("in the flesh").

Paul's offer to make good on any debt owed by Onesimus to Philemon, an offer guaranteed in Paul's own handwriting (v. 19), has led to the theory that Onesimus, in addition to running away, had robbed his master to finance his escape. Fleeing to Rome to escape detection, it is argued, he came into contact with Paul, who converted him to Christianity and persuaded him to return to his owner. There is another possibility, however. Slaves were often given highly responsible tasks by their master, including managing property and finances for the household. It may well be that Onesimus, holding such responsibilities, was accused of mismanagement by Philemon. Knowing that Paul was imprisoned in Ephesus, Onesimus may well have sought him out as a trusted third party to adjudicate the dispute, knowing of the close relationship between Paul and Philemon. Converted by Paul, Onesimus then returned with Paul's verdict: Onesimus was to be received, not only without punishment but with joy, as a returning member of the family rather than as a mistrusted slave.

It is evident from the tone of the letter that because of the obligation Philemon owes to Paul — Paul may indeed have been the one to lead Philemon into the Christian faith (v. 19b) — Paul could have attempted to compel the result he wanted. Paul chose instead to appeal to Philemon's Christian impulses and so have him do voluntarily what Paul desired, which may well have included not only welcoming Onesimus as a brother, but returning him to Paul to aid him during his imprisonment.

Paul concludes the letter body (vv. 21-22) with a final confident assertion that Philemon will do the right thing. Although Paul concludes by proposing a future visit to Philemon, there is no indication here, as in Philippians, that the outcome of his trial is near or that he expects to be able to make his visit soon. The letter closing is again formed in a fashion typical for Paul (vv. 23-24): following greetings to the letters' recipients, he concludes with a benediction.

17.2.3. Christians and Slavery

A question frequently raised with regard to this letter concerns the apparent willingness of the early Christians to go along with the institution of slavery, rather than attempting to abolish it within the Roman Empire. Such a question totally misunderstands the political structures of the empire and the utter lack of political or economic power in the hands of the early Christian community that might have allowed them to lead the empire toward abolition. Slavery was intricately woven into the fabric of Roman society, and there was no democratic way of introducing legislation to eliminate it. To encourage a slave revolt would have led to bloody extermination of those revolting, as had happened with the slave revolt led by Spartacus a century earlier, and, in all likelihood, the end of the Christian communities that had fostered or supported the revolt.

Within the Christian communities, there is clear evidence that such social distinctions as slave and free, along with racial and sexual distinctions, were regarded as irrelevant in God's sight. Paul's reference to the slave Onesimus as the brother of his owner indicates such a disregard of social convention within the Christian community. Christians would at times purchase the freedom of their own members who were slaves. And there is evidence that Christians would on occasion also sell themselves into slavery, and use the proceeds to feed the hungry (*1 Clem.* 55.2). Given the political structure of the empire, these were apparently the only ways Christians could give vent to their dislike of the institution of slavery.

Regarding slaves as brothers and sisters to those who were free within the Christian communities provided the groundwork, however, for the eventual elimination of slavery, despite the misguided attempts of some to find justification for slavery in the biblical texts. That slavery is finally impossible within a Christian context is indicated by Paul's declaration of equality in Gal 3:28.

In Ephesus, the Gate of Mazeus and Mithridates, two former slaves of Emperor Augustus who, according to the inscription, built the gate as an expression of gratitude (Phoenix Data Systems, Neal and Joel Bierling)

Slavery in the Roman Empire

The status of slaves was quite different in the Roman Empire than it was, say, in the antebellum South in the United States. The large number of slaves in the empire reflected the frequent Roman practice of enslaving rather than slaughtering conquered peoples. It was also a source of revenue for the government, since a 4% sales tax was levied on every purchase of a slave (Tacitus, *Annales* 13.21). Slavery was not tied to race in the Greco-Roman world.

Education of slaves was encouraged, since it enhanced their value to their owners. Nero's personal physician was a slave, as was Epictetus, one of the most famous Stoic philosophers of the first century. Slaves even had the right to demand to be sold to another master if their present master was too harsh (Plutarch, *Superstition* 166D).

Conditions for slaves who worked the mines or plied the oars on ships of war were of course appalling, and the mortality rate was high for those punished with such assignments. The lot of those who worked on the great farms of wealthy owners was less onerous, and the lot of those who worked within households was often quite tolerable. Some were given great responsibility within those households (see Matt 24:45-51; Luke 16:1-13; translations soften these parables by translating "servant" instead of the more accurate "slave"). Most urban and domestic slaves could look forward to freedom by the time they turned thirty, at which time they frequently were awarded Roman citizenship.

Many slaves were paid wages (some even owned their own slaves!), and many purchased their freedom from their owners. Large numbers of people sold themselves into slavery to better their economic position, and people often moved in and out of slavery as their economic condition changed.

FOR FURTHER READING

Markus Barth and Helmut Blanke, *The Letter to Philemon* (Eerdmans Critical Commentary; Grand Rapids: Eerdmans, 2000)

James D. G. Dunn, *The Epistles to the Colossians and to Philemon* (New International Greek Testament Commentary; Grand Rapids: Eerdmans, 1996)

F. O. Francis and W. A. Meeks, eds., *Conflict at Colossae* (2nd ed., Missoula: Scholars, 1975)

Eduard Lohse, *Colossians and Philemon* (Hermeneia; Philadelphia: Fortress, 1971)

Peter T. O'Brien, *Colossians, Philemon* (Word Biblical Commentary; Waco: Word, 1982)

Norman R. Peterson, *Rediscovering Paul: Philemon and the Sociology of Paul's Narrative World* (Philadelphia: Fortress, 1985)

18. Paul's Letters to the Thessalonian Christians

It is evident from 1 and 2 Thessalonians, as it is from Philippians, that the Macedonian Christians were particularly dear to the apostle's heart. He clearly had great success in evangelizing that area, his converts there remained faithful to his teachings, and as a result he was encouraged by them and longed to spend time with them. Considering the treatment he received in Corinth and the questions raised about his gospel in Galatia, it is small wonder that Paul found comfort in the churches in Macedonia.

The city of Thessalonica was located in the Roman province of Macedonia (northern Greece) about 100 miles to the west of Philippi. It was founded about 316 BCE by Cassander, a general of Alexander the Great and a son-in-law of Philip II of Macedonia. Named to honor Philip's daughter Thessalonikeia, who was Cassander's wife, it became the capital city of Macedonia when that area became a Roman province in 146 BCE. It served as the port at the head of the Thermaic Gulf of the Aegean Sea and a main station on the Via Egnatia, an important Roman road connecting the Balkans to Asia Minor. As both administrative center and center for travel and transport, Thessalonica had become an important and prosperous city by the time Paul preached there. Its importance for the churches established by Paul is attested by the many NT references to the Christians there (Acts 17:1-13; 20:4; 27:2; Phil 4:16; 2 Tim 4:10 in addition to 1 and 2 Thessalonians). Despite a generally hostile reception in Macedonia at both Philippi (1 Thess 2:2; Acts 16:22-24) and Thessalonica (1 Thess 3:15-16; Acts 17:5-7), Christian communities took firm root there and continued to support Paul in his missionary enterprise.

18.1. 1 THESSALONIANS

There has been little question that this letter was in fact written by the apostle Paul. Its intended readers were Christians drawn for the most part from among the Gentiles in Thessalonica (1:9; 2:14-16; 4:5). It is apparent that Paul (and apparently Timothy) remained in Thessalonica for a considerable period of time during their initial visit. Paul twice received aid from Philippi during this time (Phil 2:15-16) and settled down to practice his trade so as not to be a burden to his newly-formed church (1 Thess 2:9). Paul's missionary method was apparently to stay for longer periods in places he evangelized, probably announcing Christ to people who came to his rented shop in the forum of a given city rather than standing in a corner of the marketplace for a public oration. He was criticized for being an ineffective public speaker (2 Cor 10:10), and anyway, given the sensitivity of the Roman authorities to any new collegia that were formed, an attempt to form a new Christian community in so public a manner would call unwanted attention to it. Again, even if such preaching were undertaken in the marketplace, its effectiveness would be relatively limited; after a time people would tend to ignore someone who had the same message week after week. It is therefore more likely that Paul carried on his mission on the basis of contacts made in his shop. In that way his gospel gradually spread as he encouraged customers whom he converted to tell their friends about Christ as well.

Some sort of opposition had apparently broken out against the Christians in Thessalonica (2:14b) about which Paul had forewarned them while he was there (3:4). Although Paul has harsh words to say about the Jews who opposed his proclamation of Christ (2:15-16; see Acts 17:5-7), the wording of 2:14 makes it clear that just as Christian Jews in Judea had suffered persecution from their fellow Jews who were not Christians, so the Thessalonian Christians were suffering at the hands of their non-Christian compatriots. Paul, unable to return in person to speak with them (2:17-18), had sent Timothy to encourage them to remain faithful to Christ in the face of their persecution. Timothy's return with good news about how the Thessalonian Christians were remaining faithful to Christ in the face of opposition prompted Paul to write this letter.

18.1.1. The Letter

The letter opening is shorter than that of most Pauline letters, containing almost no qualifications of sender or receiver, nor does Paul identify himself as an "apostle." Perhaps he felt that he was well enough accepted by the readers that he did not need to state it. Two others are identified as senders, Silvanus (or Silas) and Timothy, who may well have accompanied Paul when he founded the church in

---

1 Thessalonians

Letter opening (1:1)
Thanksgiving (1:2-3)*
Letter body (1:6–5:22)
    Paul's preaching of the gospel in Thessalonica and the addressees'
        response to it (1:6–3:13)
    Counsel concerning conduct and eschatology (4:1–5:22)
Benediction and request for prayer (5:23-25)
Letter closing (5:26-28)

*The border between the thanksgiving and the letter body is not definite.

Thessalonica. The salutation is also shorter than the usual form, with the usual "from God our Father and the Lord Jesus Christ" absent.

It is difficult to isolate with any precision the opening prayer of this letter. In content, the opening prayer seems to consist of 1:2-3. Yet the sentence containing those verses continues to the end of v. 5, even though Paul begins to address his readers directly in 1:4. Again, prayer language is found as far away as 2:13, indicating a prayerful attitude that extends far beyond the opening two verses. It is probable, therefore, that we should consider 1:2-3 to be the formal prayer, with 1:3-4 then forming the transition to the body opening, which in its first few sentences continues to be cast in the form of a prayer of thanksgiving.

It is also the case that, typically for Paul, the prayer expresses at least some of the substance he intends to discuss. In this instance, he mentions the Thessalonians' faith, love, and hope (1:3), which he will then discuss at more length in the letter body: faith (1:2-10), love (2:17–3:10), and hope (1:9-12; 3:13; 4:13–5:11, 23). These concepts are important for Paul in other letters as well. Love, for example, figures very prominently in 1 Corinthians 13, and faith becomes thematic in Romans and Galatians. Here the main emphasis appears to be on hope, appropriate in light of the persecution and suffering the readers are presently undergoing.

The letter body is divided into two halves. The first half (1:6–3:13) concerns Paul's original visit to them and their reaction to the gospel then and at the present time. The second half (4:1–5:22) consists of advice from Paul to the Christians in Thessalonica, concerning both their conduct and their beliefs. The letter concludes with a benediction and a request for prayer on Paul's behalf (5:23-25) and a letter closing (5:26-28).

In the first segment of the first half of the letter body Paul rehearses the events occurring when he first went to Thessalonica (1:6–2:16). This segment is itself divided into three parts: 1:6-10; 2:1-12; and 2:13-16. The first part of the discussion concerns the fame of his readers' faith, which has spread well beyond Macedonia and even the other Greek province of Achaia, which helps Paul in evangelizing those areas (1:6-10).

In the second part (2:1-12), Paul recalls to his readers his own conduct during his time among them. He reminds them that he had come to them after suffering shameful treatment in Philippi, and he was apparently opposed in his apostolic proclamation in Thessalonica as well (2:1-2; cf. Acts 17:5-9). This did not hinder him from proclaiming his apostolic message, since that message has divine, not human, origin (2:3-6a). Despite the authority conferred on Paul by that God-given message, he did not exploit his authority among the Thessalonians, but treated them as gently as a nurse treats the children under her care (2:6b-8).

Pursuing such gentleness, he earned his own keep by toiling at his trade so that he would not be a burden to those whom he was evangelizing (2:9). Changing the metaphor, Paul says he acted like a father to his children, guiding them into the kind of life appropriate for them to lead in light of the God who had called them to be subjects of his kingdom (2:10-12).

In the third part (2:13-16) Paul reminds them of their reception of his apostolic proclamation, not merely as Paul's words but as what it really was, namely God's own word at work among them (2:13). As a result, they recapitulated in their life as a Christian community the kind of experiences undergone by the original Christian communities in Judea, namely, suffering at the hands of their compatriots for their acceptance of the apostolic message (2:14). Obviously Paul has a very negative view of those Jews who oppose the mission to the Gentiles as they had opposed the establishment of Christian communities in Judea, and indeed as they had opposed Jesus himself and the prophets before him (2:15-16). Paul here reflects a negative assessment of Israel's history in light of its continued opposition to God's word as spoken through the prophets. This negative tradition concerning Israel's history is as old as Ezekiel, and it was then taken up in some strands of Christian tradition. Stephen's speech at the time of his stoning (Acts 7:1-53) reflects this tradition, and his concluding words sound very much like the phrases of Paul (1 Thess 2:15): "Which of the prophets did not your fathers persecute? And they killed those who announced beforehand the coming of the Righteous One, whom you have now betrayed and murdered" (Acts 7:52, RSV). Paul apparently knew this tradition, and here connects the opposition to the Gentile mission to that same tradition.

In the next segment of the first half of the letter body (2:17–3:13), Paul turns to an account of events that led up to and flow from the visit of Timothy to them. Paul wanted very much to visit them again but was unable to because "Satan hindered us" (2:18). How Satan accomplished that, or what events Paul attributed to the initiative of Satan, he does not say. He could send Timothy (3:2) when apparently he could not return himself, which may point to some sort of opposition in Thessalonica to Paul's presence there. The recollection in Acts that Paul had been driven out by some general civic unrest (Acts 17:8-9) may reflect the reality to which Paul alludes here. However we may want to resolve that problem, it is clear enough that as a last resort Paul sent Timothy to visit them and encourage them in the midst of their "afflictions" (3:2-3) — probably social persecution coming from both Jews and Gentiles.

Archaeological evidence has indicated that a number of religious cults were active in Thessalonica at this time, cults devoted to such deities as Isis, Osiris, Serapis, and Cabirus, along with Jewish synagogues. Because those who became Christian had to abandon their former religious practices, adherents of any of those cults would be incensed when former participants now refused further participation. Given the drive to conformity in the Greco-Roman world, any such nonconformity to general practices would be met with hostility. It is probably from such sources that the opposition to the Christians made itself felt in Thessalonica. Paul had warned them earlier that such persecution would be their lot, and it had in fact now occurred (3:4). He wanted to know if they were holding firm in face of such opposition (3:5), which he also attributes, indirectly at least, to Satan (3:5, there called the "tempter").

Paul's relief at Timothy's positive report (3:6-10) is what prompted this letter, and Paul pours out his relief and gratitude that the Thessalonian Christians have remained firm and have not weakened or given in to the pressures opposing them. He concludes with a benediction (3:11-13) that, as in some other letters (see Rom 11:36; Phil 4:7), separates the didactic from the hortatory portions of the letter body.

The second half of the letter body (4:1–5:22), as we noted above, contains advice from Paul concerning both the conduct and the beliefs of the Thessalonian Christians. He begins with advice on maintaining sexual conduct acceptable to the God who called them from the darkness of their former lives into the light of his kingdom (4:1-8). Sexual promiscuity was as much a characteristic of the Greco-Roman world as it is of the modern world, and Paul warns that such conduct goes against what God wills for his people. To give in to the promiscuity of the age, Paul says, is to disregard not human but divine instruction, and for that reason such promiscuous activity will not go unpunished. God claims the whole of a person, body as well as soul, and a person's conduct must reflect those claims even in that person's sexual activity.

As far as mutual love is concerned (4:9-12), Paul is confident that he does not need to issue any particular advice, since he knows, evidently from Timothy's report, that in this aspect of their Christian lives they are above reproach. His advice

"Who Killed . . . the Prophets"
(1 Thessalonians 2:15)

The negative statements in 1 Thess 2:15-16 regarding the Jews of Judea have led some scholars to question whether Paul could have written these verses. A number of other first-century Jewish sources show that prophetic critique of Jews who did not listen to their own prophets was a regular occurrence.

In *Jubilees* 1:12, these words are attributed to God:

And I shall send to them witnesses so that I might witness to them, but they will not hear. And they will even kill the witnesses. And they will persecute those who search out the Law, and they will neglect everything and begin to do evil in my sight. *(OTP)*

Josephus records numerous incidents in which unjust kings silenced the prophets (*Ant.* 9.166-69, 9.263-66). *Ant.* 10.38-39 relates the misdeeds of Manasseh and the people who followed his evil example:

For, setting out with a contempt for God, [Manasseh] killed all the righteous men among the Hebrews, nor did he spare even the prophets, some of whom he slaughtered daily, so that Jerusalem ran with blood. Thereupon God, being wrathful at these things, sent prophets to the king and the people, and through these threatened them with the same calamities which had befallen their Israelite brothers when they outraged Him. They were not, however, persuaded by these words, from which they might so have profited as not to experience any misfortune, but had to learn from deeds the truth of what the prophets said.

to "live quietly, mind your own affairs, and work with your hands" (4:11) is probably framed in light of the danger represented by hostile forces arrayed against the Christians, often in the form of severe social pressure to conform to the idolatrous customs of their non-Christian neighbors. Minding their own affairs does not mean that they are not to proclaim Christ to their fellow citizens, but it does mean they are not to become busybodies, constantly carping at non-Christians about

In the *Lives of the Prophets,* the deaths of many of Israel's most famous prophets at the hands of their own people are recorded (all from *OTP*):

Isaiah, from Jerusalem, died under Manasseh by being sawn in two, and was buried underneath the Oak of Rogel, near the place where the path crosses the aqueduct whose water Hezekiah shut off by blocking its source (1:1).

Jeremiah was from Anathoth, and he died in Taphnai of Egypt, having been stoned by his people (2:1).

Ezekiel. This man was from the land of Arira, of the priests, and he died in the land of the Chaldeans during the captivity, after having prophesied many things to those in Judea. The ruler of the people Israel killed him there as he was being reproved by him concerning the worship of idols (3:1-2).

Micah the Morathite was of the tribe of Ephraim. Having done many things to Ahab, he was killed by Joram his son at a cliff, because he rebuked him for the impieties of his fathers (6:1-2).

Amos was from Tekoa. And when Amaziah had tortured him sorely, at last his son also killed him with a club by striking him on the temple. And while he was still breathing he went to his own district, and after some days he died and was buried there (7:1-3).

Zechariah was from Jerusalem, son of Jehoiada the priest, and Joash the king of Judah killed him near the altar, and the house of David poured out his blood in front of the *Ailam;* and the priests took him and buried him with his father (23:1).

their unacceptable behavior and pointing to themselves as models of correct living. That they are to work for their own living points to a problem in some areas of the Christian church, where the conviction that the end of the age was imminent led some people to the conclusion that they no longer had to provide for their future, since Christ would arrive at any time in the immediate future. Paul is convinced Christ will in fact return soon, but because the exact time cannot be known, Christians must continue to provide for themselves lest they become a burden on others.

In the next segment (4:13-18) Paul deals with what seems to have been a problem for the Christians in Thessalonica, namely the fate of those who did not remain alive until the return of Christ. Whether they were unsettled because of a faulty understanding of the resurrection, or by some sort of tradition that held only those who were alive when the Messiah came would benefit from his appearance, we do not know. The death and resurrection of Christ are keys to Paul's exposition here, as it is in his theology generally. The Christian will recapitulate Jesus' fate — his persecution, his death, and in the future, when Jesus returns, his resurrection. What is interesting here is that Paul tells the Thessalonians that he is relying on a teaching of Jesus for his information about the order of events at Jesus' return (4:15-17). As in some other cases, we have here a record of a saying of Jesus that is not preserved in the Gospels, indicating that such sayings circulated individually prior to the writing of our Gospels, and that not all such sayings were included in them (for another such saying, see Acts 20:35). We can only wonder about how many other sayings of Jesus Paul knew and had in mind as he carried out his apostolic proclamation and admonition, sayings of which we have no

Meeting in Homes and Businesses

Many of the larger cities in the Mediterranean world would rent stalls in the marketplaces to itinerant workers. People with similar trades tended to rent stalls close to one another, so that people looking for that produce or service could readily find the location. It is likely that Paul carried on his profession — Acts 18:3 tells us it was tent-making — from such a rented stall. From such a location, he could speak to people who came in as he worked, as well as to his fellow craftsmen and craftswomen when no customers were about. It is apparent that he met Aquila and his wife Prisca in this way, since Aquila was a tentmaker as well (Acts 18:1). This meeting also provided Paul a place to stay, perhaps also a common feature of Paul's missionary activity. Paul could then also hold worship services in the home of the person with whom he stayed. In the second century, an opponent of the Christian movement named Celsus complained that Christians carried out their activity not in some great public manner, but privately in homes and places of business, an interesting confirmation that this method of evangelizing had continued to be effective.

other record. It is clear that even if Paul did not have access to the Gospels, which had not yet been written, he was not bereft of traditions about the words and deeds of Jesus.

Paul assures his readers that the dead have not been abandoned by God, since at the time of Jesus' return, they too will be raised to new life and will join those still alive in unending fellowship with Jesus in the new age. Being caught up in clouds and meeting Jesus "in the air" communicated far more to the original readers than we are likely to see there. Clouds were a regular accompaniment of the divine presence in both OT and Christian tradition (e.g., Exod 19:9; Mark 9:7). So their presence here guarantees God's presence at this event. In the Greco-Roman worldview the "air" was the region between the earth and the moon that was inhabited by evil spirits, who fomented evil and harm on earth and sought to hinder the souls of the dead from ascending to the moon, where their evil deeds could be purged by the winds so the souls could return eventually to the eighth heaven. Thus, the point here is not that in some rapturous event, gravity will be overcome and Christians will fly among the clouds. Rather, Paul reports a tradition that speaks of God's presence with the newly resurrected to protect them from the harmful spirits inhabiting the region of the air, so that nothing can then separate them from the divine presence. So complete is the transformation of reality when Jesus returns that even the abode of evil closest to the human sphere has been purged of its ability to harm those now joined with Christ.

One cannot discern the exact timetable of these events, however much one might covet such information. Paul tells his readers (5:1-11) that such information is unavailable, as they well know. Rather than trying to discern which events are the harbingers of such a transformation of reality, Christians are better employed in being ready for Jesus' return at any time, since it will come without warning, like the thief who does not announce his break-in prior to its occurrence (5:2), an analogy that also finds a place in a saying of Jesus (Matt 24:43-44). Using the figures of night as a time for inattention, sleep, and drunkenness, and day as a time of activity, alertness, and sobriety, Paul urges his readers to be children of the day rather than of the night (5:5-8a). Changing the figure, Paul urges his readers to put on the armor appropriate for the battle Christians must fight against the forces of evil pressing in on them. He repeats here the three characteristics of Christian life mentioned at the outset of the letter (1:3): faith, love, and hope (5:8). With that armor, Christians will not despair when evil presses in on them. Rather, they will be confident in the salvation won for them by Jesus Christ, and will in that confidence encourage one another (5:9-11).

Paul concludes with some advice on how his readers are to conduct themselves within the community of faith (5:12-22). It is difficult to determine whether Paul's first admonition (5:12) was prompted by a tendency toward resistance to advice from church leaders that led to some dissension within the Christian com-

Hostility toward Christians

The very nature of the Christians' commitment to Jesus as Lord, a fundamental early confession (see 1 Cor 12:3b), put them at odds with their surrounding culture politically, socially, and religiously. The normal commitment required in the Roman world was to Caesar as Lord, and using "Lord" in that sense with any other person would immediately make one suspect of treason. The Christian commitment to Jesus as Lord meant one could take part in no other religious observances, and this also was counter to the customs of that time. Religions that were not based on racial descent, such as the various mystery cults, did not place exclusive demands on their devotees. People were free to participate in as many cults as they wished. That Christians could not do so made their neighbors suspicious and opened Christians to accusations of hatred for other people and their customs. Add to that the strong pressure in the Greco-Roman world toward social and religious conformity, and it becomes clear why Christians could not look to non-Christians for any form of support. For that reason, the letters of Paul as well as the other letters in the NT stress the need for Christians to support one another and to stand united in the faith, lest the hostile forces arrayed against them break their resolve to continue to live the Christian life.

munity in Thessalonica. The Greek word used of the work of those who labored among the Christians there *(kopiaō)* normally implied the work of proclamation; the Greek word used to designate the second group *(proistēmi)* was usually used for the work of organizational leaders within the Christian communities. This implies therefore some kind of division of labor within the community and indicates that the rudiments of church organization were instituted already during the time of Paul's missionary career.

The remaining admonitions are general in nature and all point to the need for mutual support among the Thessalonian Christians. Because of hostile pressure from those outside the Christian fellowship, a Christian community like the one addressed here was thrown back on its own resources to maintain its stability and morale.

Thus Paul admonishes the readers to do for one another what he himself is trying to do with this letter. His final admonition not to quench the Spirit but to test everything a prophet says is echoed in 1 John 4:1 and apparently was a commonplace of early Christian advice. The point is that while many may claim that what they say has been inspired in them by the Holy Spirit, that alone does not give validity to what is said. Rather, what is said needs to be tested against the norm of what God has already said in his acts with the people of Israel in the OT and more especially through God's word given in Jesus Christ crucified and risen. Finally, the utterance of the apostles themselves provides the key test, and that is why Paul wrote his letters and why they were eventually collected and put into what became the canon of the NT. The need for such testing continues to the present, and the apostolic witness contained in Scripture functions now, as it did when Paul wrote to the Thessalonians, as the norm against which utterances or deeds that claim the inspiration of the Holy Spirit must be validated.

The letter body concludes with a benediction (5:23-24) and a request from Paul that his readers pray for him. The request for intercessory prayer occupies the place usually filled with greetings from people with Paul; apparently in this case Paul, for whatever reason, did not think such greetings appropriate.

The letter closing contains two admonitions. The first urges that the readers greet one another with a holy kiss, the sign that all Christians were members of the body of Christ and hence all members of the family brought into being by Christ's resurrection. The second charges the unnamed recipients of this letter, perhaps the church overseers mentioned earlier (5:12), to make sure that the letter is read in the presence of all the members of the community. The only time they would all be assembled would be for worship, and hence reading this letter would be done in that context. Since it was Jewish practice to read portions of the Torah and the prophets during services in the synagogue, such a context for reading the apostolic letters would be the first step toward regarding them as Scripture. Whether Christian literature was appropriate for reading in worship became at a later time one of the primary tests for determining if such a writing would command the authority that later led it to be included in the NT canon. Paul closes the letter with a salutation of grace that reflects the salutation with which he began the letter (1:1).

This letter gives us an interesting insight into the kinds of problems faced by the earliest Christian communities that sought to live out their Christian lives in the midst of a hostile society. However different from our modern situation the social and political conditions may have been that faced the original readers of this letter, the familiarity of the problems addressed shows the enduring value of the apostolic witness for the correct understanding and conduct of the Christian faith and life.

18.1.2. Some Questions

Where Paul was when he wrote 1 Thessalonians is not clear. He does tell his readers that he was in Athens when he sent Timothy on his mission to Thessalonica, but there is no indication that he was still there when he wrote the letter. According to Acts Paul went to Corinth after he left Athens (18:1), but Acts does not mention Timothy's trip, so that information is not as much help as it might be. Paul may have written the letter from Corinth, but in the absence of evidence all we can do is guess as to his location.

Many scholars accept without question that the letter was written early in Paul's career, and it is often asserted that 1 Thessalonians is the earliest-written document in the NT. When reasons for this conclusion are given, they tend to be the following:

- Paul evangelized Thessalonica early in his second missionary journey, and hence the letter must be early. Yet Paul had gone to Philippi before he went to Thessalonica and his letter to Philippi is never regarded as early. In fact, the date of a letter has no relation to when a church was founded; it may be soon thereafter or be delayed for years.
- There is no formal church organization, which some scholars think indicates a very early date. Yet in fact 1 Thess 5:12-13 does indicate there is already an organization in place.
- 1 Thess 4:13-18 shows that Paul's eschatological hope remains vivid, whereas later in his life he saw it would not come as soon as he first thought. But it is equally vivid in 1 Corinthians 15, and even when he writes to the Romans it remains in place (13:11).
- There is no reference to the collection for the saints in Jerusalem. But as we have seen in the case of Philippians, that may in itself say nothing about when the letter was written, whether before the collection was proposed or after it was delivered, or whether for other reasons it is simply not discussed.
- Paul makes repeated references to the founding visit, indicating that it was recent. But Paul also refers to his founding visit to Philippi, and that does not mean that that letter is also early.
- Paul mentions that he has been bereft of the addressees "for a short time" (2:17), indicating that he has only recently been in Thessalonica. Yet he also says that he has been hindered again and again from coming to see them (2:18), so we do not know how long the separation has been.

There are also a number of indications that the letter was written at a much later time. In addition to the reasons already given, the following points are relevant:

- Paul tells the Thessalonians that the fame of their faith has spread well beyond Macedonia, so that people tell him about the faith of the Thessalonians before he can mention it (1:7-9). That seems to presume sufficient passage of time for such news to be spread.

- Paul's defense of his apostolic practices echoes charges leveled against him in Galatia, namely, that he shaped his gospel to please people, not God (1 Thess 2:4; cf. Gal 1:10), and in Corinth, namely, that he sought by devious means to enrich himself from his preaching (1 Thess 2:5-6; cf. 2 Cor 11:7; 12:16). And in fact these letters to the Galatian and the Corinthian Christians were written later in Paul's career than the presumed early date of 1 Thessalonians.
- Much of the letter reminds his readers of what Paul has told them during his original visit, but if it was written shortly after he left, why would he need to do that? The likelihood is that they would have remembered it, especially since he commends them for their faith.
- Enough people have died to raise the question of what happens to them when Christ comes (4:13-17), and there is no indication that they were martyred as a result of the opposition to the Christians in Thessalonica. That question therefore presumes a longer rather than a shorter period since they became Christians, long enough for enough people to have died of natural causes to raise such a problem.

Such evidence does not prove that this letter was written later on in Paul's career, any more than the evidence cited previously proves that it was his earliest letter. In light of the inconclusiveness of the evidence, it would perhaps be best not to assert as though unquestioned that 1 Thessalonians is the earliest of Paul's letters. We simply do not have enough evidence to make such an unqualified assertion.

18.2. 2 THESSALONIANS

2 Thessalonians is at least the second letter that Paul wrote to the Thessalonian church (2 Thess 3:15), in addition to yet another letter that claimed falsely to be to be from him (2:2). Since the two letters Paul wrote to the Christians in Thessalonica, as well as the apparent false letter, all include discussion of events accompanying the return of Christ, it is apparent that that event excited the interest of these Christians. It may well be that some Christian group especially concerned about Christ's return made its ideas and perhaps even its presence felt in Thessalonica.

18.2.1. The Letter

Aside from two sections (1:5-12; 2:1-12), the content of this letter is similar to that of 1 Thessalonians. The letter follows the typical format of a Pauline letter, with the letter opening (1:1-2) closer in form to the other letters of Paul (Rom 1:7b;

---

2 Thessalonians

Letter opening (1:1-2)
Thanksgiving and prayer (1:3-12)*
Letter body (2:1–3:16)
    An answer to eschatological confusion (2:1-17)
    Problems that have arisen from eschatological confusion (3:1-16)
Letter closing (3:17-18)

*The thanksgiving/prayer section contains in 1:4-10 an unusually long preview of the content of the letter body.

---

1 Cor 1:2-3; 2 Cor 1:2; Phil 1:2; in slightly altered form in Gal 1:3) than 1 Thess 1:1. This means either that Paul is the author of this second letter to the Christians in Thessalonica and uses here his usual form, or, if in fact Paul was not the author, that whoever wrote it knew from other letters the usual Pauline form. If the author did know other Pauline letters, it is strange that he (or she) is so dependent on 1 Thessalonians.

The letter opening also contains, typically for Paul, an opening prayer (1:3-12). As in 1 Thessalonians, the prayer here (1:3, 11-12) is combined with content that belongs more properly in the letter body (1:4-10). Paul often includes in an epistolary prayer some indication of the content of the ensuing letter, but rarely to the extent that he does in both Thessalonian letters. The opening portion of this letter reflects what was apparently a growing persecution of his readers, and Paul seeks to comfort them and give them courage to withstand by reciting the dreadful consequences those who persecute Christians will receive at Christ's return. Paul refers often enough to the coming wrath of God, but rarely in such explicit detail. The return of Jesus will mean affliction for those who afflict the Christians, and their destruction and exclusion from the presence of God. The language and concepts here are closer to what one finds in the Johannine Apocalypse than to material found elsewhere in the Pauline letters, but it does show how extensive such views in fact were within the early Christian movement.

The letter body itself (2:1–3:16) is divided into two parts (2:1-17; 3:1-16), each of which closes with a benediction (2:16-17; 3:16). The first half of the letter body is instructional in nature; the second half (3:1-16) is more hortatory in character. We shall look at each in turn.

Continuing with the topic of the return of Christ (2:1-12), Paul next discusses a problem that has arisen among his readers. From some source — Paul is not sure whether through some Spirit-inspired prophecy or a letter forged in his name (2:2b) — the rumor has spread that Christ has already returned. Some Christians are apparently concerned about how they should assemble to greet Christ when he shows up in Thessalonica. Paul has already spoken of the course of events to occur when Christ returns (1 Thess 4:16-17), but even in the absence of such events, some of his readers, at least, are apparently worrying that the event may have occurred without their knowing it. In response, Paul indicates some of the reasons that it cannot have happened yet, namely, because some events that must precede Christ's return have themselves not yet happened.

It is difficult to fathom the exact meaning of Paul's description of these events, because he is reminding his readers of things he has already told them (2:5). As a result, he does not need to go into great detail identifying whom or what he means by such things as the "lawless human being," also called the "son of perdition" (2:3), who will apparently oppose all religious functions (2:4) and, by seating himself in the temple in Jerusalem, will declare himself to be God. Some have thought this may be a reference to Emperor Caligula's attempt in 39-41 CE to set up a statue of himself in the Jerusalem temple (cf. Mark 13:14), but Paul is speaking here of events that have not yet occurred and has in mind the final enemy of God rather than some human usurper. For that reason some have seen here a reference to the heavenly temple and a war in heaven against God, which resulted in persecution of Christians on earth (as in Rev 13:7-17), but Paul's identification of this opponent as a "human being" (Greek *anthrōpos*) would tend to rule out such an idea.

Since this "lawless person" must appear before Christ returns, the Thessalonians need not yet worry whether in fact Christ's return has already taken place. Paul grants that the "mystery of lawlessness" is already at work; witness the persecution of Christians. But some force is at present restraining the "lawless person" from appearing before the proper time. Although the term "Antichrist" is not used here, it is probably such a figure that Paul has in mind. The identity of "the one who restrains" (or "that which restrains") is also known to the Thessalonian Christians (2:6), so that we are not told who or what that is. Finally, however, this "lawless one" will be revealed once the restraining one is set aside, and then the full satanic force of the lawless one will be revealed in a final cataclysm of evil. At that point, Jesus will return and destroy this Antichrist with the "breath of his mouth." Thus it is evident that the Antichrist is no match for Christ, who will kill him merely by blowing on him. As a result, the readers need not fear for their ultimate destiny; it is in the hands of the One who at the appropriate time will have no problem in eliminating all threat of evil from the world.

These final events will be accompanied by what appear to be miraculous events (2:9), and many will be deceived. That many were already opposing the Christian communities may explain why, even though Paul had told them these events, some Christians in Thessalonica thought their suffering indicated that the lawless one was already exercising final power. Paul is reminding his readers of what they already know, which deprives us of the explanation we would need in order to know exactly what events he is describing. Any attempt to penetrate that veil must be based on speculation. We simply do not know what Paul is referring to. The intention of the passage is not so much to provide a timetable as to warn the readers that, although the return of Christ is imminent, certain events must first occur. In this it shares the intention of the "little apocalypse" in Mark 13 (e.g., vv. 7, 24-27).

The final section of the first half of the letter body (2:13-15) assures the readers that they belong among those who will not be deceived, because they have heard and accepted the truth at the time of their conversion. Their task in the present, therefore, is to hold fast to the truth they have already heard from Paul, whether when he was present or in his letters. The benediction that concludes the first half of the letter body (2:16-17) prays that the divine comfort and hope based on God's grace will continue to sustain the readers in the midst of the persecution they are undergoing.

The second half of the letter body (3:1-16) concerns itself with some problems that have arisen as a result of the confusion about the precise time of Christ's return. After an opening paragraph (3:1-5) in which Paul asks for prayer that he may be delivered from those who oppose him and in which he assures his readers that God will continue to lead and comfort them, Paul turns to the problem of idleness among some of the Christians in Thessalonica. He touched very briefly on this problem in his first letter to this community (1 Thess 5:14), but it has apparently grown in the meantime into a significant problem. Evidently, on the supposition that Christ either had already returned or would in the immediate future, some of the Thessalonian Christians decided that it was not worth working any more, since the whole world would soon end. Such persons were proving to be a burden on the other Christians, both in their ideas and in their imposition on the earnings of others for their food. Paul reminds the readers both of what he said in his visit to them (3:6b) and of his own example: He earned his own keep while preaching to them the gospel of Jesus Christ (3:7-8). He did this not because he had no right to be supported by his converts, but precisely to give them this example. He repeats what he has told them before: Those who do not work have no right to eat the food of those who do (3:10). Furthermore, such people who refuse to work have too much time on their hands and so become busybodies. To all such Paul solemnly commands, by the authority of Jesus Christ, that they work to support themselves.

Paul's final word (3:14-15) is a warning to the readers to have nothing to do with those who continue in their misguided paths despite what Paul has written. The idea is not to punish or reject such people. It is, rather, to make them ashamed of their misguided conduct (3:14b). So one should act toward them as toward a wayward member of the family rather than as toward an outsider and enemy. Paul closes the second half of the letter body as he did the first half, with a benediction (3:16).

In the letter closing (3:17-18) Paul, switching the personal reference from "we" to "I," gives his readers a means of differentiating his authentic letters from those that are not from him, namely, a sample of his handwriting. The inclusion after that statement of the final wish for grace (3:18) may indicate that Paul regularly wrote the concluding wish in his own hand (cf. 1 Cor 16:23; Gal 6:18) even where he does not specifically call attention to it (see 2 Cor 13:14; Phil 4:23; 1 Thess 5:28; Phlm 25). That phrase would then serve the function of authenticating Paul's letters, much as a signature does in a modern letter; since the name of the person sending an ancient letter was given first, there was no reason for a signature at the end.

18.2.2. Some Questions

2 Thessalonians is in some ways so very much like 1 Thessalonians but in other ways so very different that scholars have raised questions about its authorship. Why would Paul have written two letters to the same community, repeating some points almost verbatim and giving what looks like very different advice on others? Some of the major objections to authorship by Paul are the following:

1. The style and vocabulary are somewhat different from those of 1 Thessalonians. The warmth Paul apparently felt for the Christians in Thessalonica expressed in the first letter is gone in the second, and in its place there is a formality of tone not usually used when writing to close friends. There are also a number of words used here that do not appear in other Pauline letters, but that is also the case in most of Paul's letters. Taken in themselves, differences in style and vocabulary are rarely sufficient to rule out Paul as author.
2. That the same persons are identified as senders (Paul, Silvanus, and Timothy) as in 1 Thessalonians indicates that this letter was written a short time after the sending of the first. In that event, the close literary relationship between the two letters and the repetition of content are somewhat strange.
3. The signs that will precede Christ's second coming named in 2 Thess 2:1-12 are nowhere else mentioned by Paul, and the fact that such observable events seem to contradict Paul's claim in the first letter that there would be no such signs (1 Thess 5:2) may point to someone other than Paul as author. Yet both ideas — observable events preceding the coming of the Messiah and the suddenness of the events — are held in apocalyptic Judaism, which influenced

Paul and other early Christians in these matters. Paul is apparently reminding his readers of what he told them when he was with them (2:5). Also to be noted are the different situations addressed. In the first letter the problem is potential despair over the long delay in Christ's return; in the second letter the problem is anxiety about the fact that Christ may already have returned. The two problems require different solutions.

4. Certain characteristics of 2 Thessalonians seem to point away from Paul as author, such as:

   a. The thanksgiving that opens the letter (1:3-12) becomes didactic in character, abandoning its role as prayer. Yet we noted the same problem in 1 Thessalonians, with the difficulty of determining where the prayer ended and the letter body began.

   b. The letter closing (3:17-18) no longer points to intimacy but to validation of the letter. Yet the need to validate the letter is not surprising if, as Paul suspects, a letter is circulating in his name that he did not write (2:12).

   c. 2 Thess 1:1-2a repeats 1 Thess 1:1, which makes it appear that the author of the second letter is dependent on the literary form of the first, unlikely if Paul is the author of both. Yet the letter opening is a Pauline stereotype, and in fact the salutation in the second letter (1:2) is more in accord with normal Pauline practice than the salutation in the first letter (1:1).

   d. The use of the word "tradition," unusual in Paul, and the emphasis on following tradition (2:15; 3:6) are characteristics of a time after the death of Paul, when apostolic tradition began to be structured as a series of doctrines. Yet Paul also reports traditions he taught his readers in other, uncontested letters (1 Cor 11:23; 15:3), and he can refer to the standard of doctrine to which Christians have been committed (Rom 6:17).

   e. The discussion in 2 Thess 3:6-12 shows a literary dependence on 1 Thess 2:9 and 5:14a. Yet the material in the second letter appears to reflect a problem that has worsened since the writing of the first, and the phrase "worked night and day that we might not burden any of you" is the kind of stereotyped phrase Paul would use again and again in defending this practice, a defense also found in the Corinthians correspondence.

   f. If the "man of lawlessness" refers to the myth that Nero, arch-enemy of the Christians, would come back to life, then the letter must have been written after Nero's suicide in 68 CE and hence is not from Paul. Yet the identification of Nero *redivivus* with the man of lawlessness is itself pure speculation.

   g. The mention of forged letters (2:2; cf. 3:17) points to a later period when such forgeries began to appear. Yet this is a problem only if 1 Thessalonians is Paul's first letter. In fact, these references add confirmation to the idea that 1 Thessalonians was written later, rather than earlier, in Paul's career, when Paul was better known as a letter writer.

On the whole, the question of authorship remains open, with evidence pointing in both directions, as was also the case with Colossians. While no certainty is achievable, it does seem on the whole that a good case can be made for Paul as the author of this second letter to the Christian community in Thessalonica.

If this second letter to the Thessalonians was in fact written by Paul, then the readers will very likely be the same group of Gentile Christians to whom the first letter was addressed. Some have suggested that the similarities and differences between the two letters can be explained if the first letter were written to Gentile Christians and the second to Jewish Christians, perhaps even to Jewish Christians who lived in another city (e.g., Beroea, Acts 17:10-12), but there is no evidence to sustain such speculation. It is highly likely that Paul is writing to the same readers to whom the first letter was addressed, responding to a changed situation there.

When and from where the letter was written will be largely determined by the identity of the author. If it was written by Paul, then it was written close enough in time to the first letter that Timothy and Silvanus are still with Paul. The existence of a forged letter bearing Paul's name (2 Thess 2:2) and the need to validate 2 Thessalonians as a genuine Pauline letter (3:17) would indicate a time when Paul was recognized as an authoritative apostle, more likely a time later in his career than earlier. In fact, as we have seen, these points also indicate that 1 Thessalonians was written at a time later than many scholars have posited. Some have argued that the reference to the Jerusalem temple (2 Thess 2:4) indicates that the letter comes from before the destruction of the temple in 70 CE. Yet Paul was apparently executed prior to the temple's destruction, so such a reference could have come at any time during his apostolic career, and a forger could have included that reference to make the letter seem to have been written earlier than in fact it was. Thus the reference to the temple adds nothing to our determination of a date. If, on the other hand, 2 Thessalonians was not written by Paul, then we have no idea when it was written. Those who question Pauline authorship tend to date it in the 80s of the first century.

The same holds true for the letter's place of origin. If it was written by Paul, the likelihood is that it was written from the same place as 1 Thessalonians, perhaps Athens or Corinth. Some have suggested that Paul's need to be delivered from evil opponents (2 Thess 3:2) could point to Corinth (cf. 2 Corinthians 10–13) or even Ephesus (2 Cor 1:8-10). On the other hand, if Paul did not write it, we have no idea of its place of origin. There are no hints in the letter itself on that point, and any proposed solution will be purely speculative.

Some have suggested that 2 Thess 2:1-12, because of its supposedly un-Pauline character, has been inserted into a letter by Paul. But there is no textual evidence to support this suggestion, so that it has not found widespread agreement. Aside from transcriptional errors arising from hand copying, there appear to be no real challenges to the integrity of the text as we now have it.

FOR FURTHER READING

F. F. Bruce, *1 and 2 Thessalonians* (Word Biblical Commentary; Waco: Word, 1982)

Karl P. Donfried and Johannes Beutler, eds., *The Thessalonians Debate* (Grand Rapids: Eerdmans, 2000)

Robert Jewett, *The Thessalonian Correspondence: Pauline Rhetoric and Millenarian Piety* (Philadelphia: Fortress, 1986)

Abraham J. Malherbe, *The Letters to the Thessalonians* (Anchor Bible; New York: Doubleday, 2000)

Earl J. Richard, *First and Second Thessalonians* (Sacra Pagina; Collegeville: Liturgical, 1995)

C. A. Wanamaker, *1 and 2 Thessalonians* (New International Greek Testament Commentary; Grand Rapids: Eerdmans, 1990)

19. 1 and 2 Timothy and Titus

Addressed to two of Paul's coworkers, and concerned with sound teaching and good church leadership for those Christian communities under the care of Timothy and Titus, these letters have been called "Pastoral Epistles" since early in the eighteenth century. Although they are not so much personal letters as general epistles that deal with problems related to the structure and function of church ministry and doctrine, they remain letters, and that means that they were addressed to specific problems at specific times and specific places. They are thus not to be understood as some kind of timeless manuals on how to run a church, any more than, say, Ephesians or 1 Peter, which are also both general letters. Like any other letters, they are addressed to particular problems at a particular time and place, and we must attempt to be as clear about those contexts as we can.

The letters are addressed to Timothy and Titus, two Christian workers known from the other letters of Paul and, in the case of Timothy, from Acts.

Timothy is identified as the son of Eunice (2 Tim 1:5; his grandmother's name was Lois), a Jewish mother, and an unnamed Gentile father (Acts 16:1). He is described as a coworker (2 Cor 1:19) and companion (Acts 17:14-15; 18:5; 19:22; 20:4) of Paul. Paul himself identified Timothy as "brother" (Col 1:1; Phlm 1) and sent him on a variety of missions (1 Cor 4:17; 16:10; Phil 2:19, 23; 1 Thess 3:2, 6). A further indication of Timothy's importance to the Pauline mission is his appearance as co-sender of several of Paul's letters (1 Thess 1:1; 2 Thess 1:1; 2 Cor 1:1; Phil 1:1). Small wonder that the apostle paid tribute to him for his service and faithfulness (Phil 2:19-23; cf. 1 Thess 3:2). When these two letters were written to him, Timothy was envisioned as still a young man (1 Tim 4:12; 2 Tim 2:22), which by ancient reckoning would allow him to be up into his thirties.

Titus is unknown to the author of Acts. Paul identifies him as a person of

Greek origin (Gal 2:3). His importance to Paul is clear from Paul's acknowledgment of him as partner and coworker (2 Cor 8:23) and his attendance, at Paul's behest, at the missionary conference in Jerusalem (Gal 2:1). Titus played an important role as an envoy of Paul to the Christians in Corinth, delivering a letter to them (2 Cor 2:4, 13; 7:6, 8) and mediating in the dispute between the apostle and the churches there (2 Cor 7:13-15). He was also active in promoting the offering for the poor in Jerusalem (2 Cor 8:16-18; cf. 9:5) to which Paul had agreed at the missionary conference (Gal 2:10). There is no reference to his age anywhere in the NT.

Since there is no decisive evidence concerning the chronological order of the three letters, we will consider them in their canonical order.

19.1. 1 TIMOTHY

This letter is unlike the undisputed Pauline letters in that there is no thanksgiving at the beginning of the letter, the letter body shows no orderly development of themes or ideas, and there is no letter closing except for a final brief blessing. In these respects it is virtually identical in form to Titus.

The letter opening (1:1-2) identifies Paul rather extensively as an apostle, but in language different from that of other Pauline letters except the Pastorals. The blessing also differs in subtle ways in both form and content from the usual Pauline blessing (e.g., Phil 1:2). As already noted, there is no thanksgiving.

---

1 Timothy

Letter opening (1:1-2)
Letter body (1:3–6:19)
   True and false teaching (1:3-20; 3:14–4:10; 6:3-5)
   Conduct within the Christian fellowship (2:1-15; 4:11–5:2;
      5:22b-23; 6:11-14)
   Church order (3:1-13; 5:3-20)
     Bishops (3:1-7)
     Deacons (3:8-13)
     Widows (5:3-16)
     Elders (5:17-20)
Final exhortation (6:20-21a)
Concluding benediction (6:22b)

The letter body discusses three general themes, although in no organized or systematic way. We will consider each in turn.

19.1.1. True and False Teaching

The importance of this theme is indicated by where it occurs in the body of the letter. The first treatment (1:3-20) outlines a problem with people who are speculating about "myths and genealogies" (1:3-4), perhaps referring to some sort of Gnostic speculation about the various emanations of the divine godhead that produce a variety of divine beings, and their interrelationships to one another in the divine pantheon. The second problem, perhaps related to the first in that it also promotes deviation from the rule of love (1:5), concerns persons who are teaching "the law" of Moses but do not understand it (1:6-7). Apparently these people seek to apply the law to righteous people, whereas, the author declares, it is really meant to apply to the unrighteous and godless, a point which is clear in sound Christian doctrine (1:8-11). The author then turns to the kind of life Paul led before and after his conversion (1:12-14), pointing out that the intention of the mission of Jesus Christ, to save sinners, also proves true in Paul's case, since, despite his former rejection of Christ, he was also the recipient of Christ's mercy (1:15-17). The witness to this grace is the charge Paul has laid on Timothy, which Timothy is to perform by holding firm to the faith with a good conscience. Two persons who do not represent sound teaching are Hymenaeus and Alexander, who are also mentioned in 2 Timothy, Hymenaeus as one who proclaims that the resurrection of believers has already occurred (2 Tim 2:17-18), Alexander, identified as a coppersmith, as one who did great personal harm to Paul (2 Tim 4:14).

This topic is resumed in 3:14–4:10, where further tenets of the false teaching are identified, namely, the demand for ascetic practices in the matter of sex and food. In such false teaching, sex is forbidden even in marriage and abstention from certain foods is urged. Again, this seems to be a mixture of Jewish beliefs, in the distinction of pure and impure foods, and a Gnostic disdain for the material aspect of reality so as to concentrate fully on the spiritual dimension. Against this, the author argues that God made all things good, and neither sex in marriage nor food labeled "impure" is to be rejected if it is received with thanksgiving to God. Such ascetic practices are identified as "godless and silly myths," and Timothy is urged to have nothing to do with them and to teach Christians to avoid such practices as well. This passage contains a fragment of an early confession (3:16) announcing that Christ himself appeared in flesh, and hence, apparently, life in the flesh is not to be disdained. The confession follows a regular grammatical structure, and alternates between statements about the material (flesh, nations, world) and the spiritual (Spirit, angels, glory), thus pointing to the importance of both aspects of reality for Christians.

The final short passage devoted to true and false teaching (6:3-5) condemns in highly negative terms those who propagate false doctrines.

19.1.2. Conduct within the Christian Fellowship

While there is some overlap between this theme and the previous one, the emphasis here (4:11–5:2; 5:22b-23; 6:11-14) is on the appropriate conduct of believers rather than on description of those who teach inappropriate beliefs and actions. Woven into this material is advice on Timothy's behavior within the fellowship of the Christian community.

Introducing the comments on Christian conduct is a general exhortation to live as good citizens of the civil state (2:1-2), indicating the author's conviction that decent lives led by Christians will not arouse the wrath of the Roman state or of their neighbors. There may have been a tendency among Christians to feel that now that they had a new lord (2:3-7) they were free from civic restraint on their activity. That was not a valid conclusion, however, as is here pointed out.

Bone hair-pins from ca. 100 CE; the one in the center has some gold decoration (Richard Cleave)

The comments about the appropriate dress and adornment of Christian women — gold, pearls, costly attire (2:9) — may be directed to wealthy women who had few pressing duties (and so had the leisure to go from house to house, 5:6, 13) and were targeted by deceiving false teachers (2:13-14), who may indeed have sought their money (6:5). If so, 2:9-12 is directed against such women rather than women in general. Some wealthy Christians apparently thought the admiration awarded them in secular society should be given them also in church and also represented a temptation to poorer church members to court the wealthy among them (in addition to 6:5-10, 17-19, see Jas 2:2-7). The counsel that women bear children (2:15; 5:14) was probably written to counter the asceticism of the false teachers who disdained the physical aspects of marriage

Modesty

That a woman should dress modestly was commonly accepted in antiquity. The following maxim from the *Sentences* of Sextus, 235, expresses this view: "Let moderation be the normal attire of a believing wife." Philo correlates a prostitute's lack of chastity and modesty:

> For the harlot is profane in body and soul, even if she has discarded her trade and assumed a decent and chaste demeanour, and he is forbidden even to approach her, since her old way of living was unholy. Let such a one indeed retain in other respects her civic rights as she has been at pains to purge herself from her defilements, for repentance from wrongdoing is praiseworthy. Nor let anyone else be prevented from taking her in marriage, but let her not come near to the priest. (*De Specialibus Legibus* 1.102)

> Again, the commonwealth of Moses' institution does not admit a harlot, that stranger to decency and modesty and temperance and the other virtues. She infects the souls both of men and women with licentiousness. She casts shame upon the undying beauty of the mind and prefers in honour the short-lived comeliness of the body. She flings herself at the disposal of chance comers, and sells her bloom like some ware to be purchased in the market. In her every word and deed she aims at capturing the young, while she incites her lovers each against the other by offering the vile prize of herself to the highest bidder. A pest, a scourge, a plague-spot to the public, let her be stoned to death — she who has corrupted the graces bestowed by nature, instead of making them, as she should, the ornament of noble conduct. (*De Specialibus Legibus* 3.51)

In a letter to his wife, Plutarch commends her modest attire:

> Your plainness of attire and sober style of living has without exception amazed every philosopher who has shared our society and intimacy, neither is there any townsman of ours to whom at religious ceremonies, sacrifices, and the theatre you do not offer another spectacle — your own simplicity. (*Moralia: Consolation to His Wife,* 609C)

(4:3). The pressure to conform to social norms underlies the advice to slaves not to neglect their duties because of the brotherhood of slave and master within the Christian community: disdain for such norms would bring potentially lethal discredit on the nascent church.

The advice to Timothy assumes his youth and deals with how to function without giving offense to either his contemporaries or those older (4:11–5:2). The advice to consume some wine for the sake of Timothy's health and digestion (5:23) reflects common wisdom of the time. The general advice on his conduct as a Christian leader (6:11-14) reflects not so much advice to Timothy personally, although it is also that, as the ideal activity of the Christian leader in the latter part of the first century.

19.1.3. Church Order (or Structure)

Four groups of persons who apparently played special roles in the Christian community are described: bishops, deacons, widows, and elders. Bishops must display virtues appropriate not only for leadership in the Christian community (3:1-6) but also for maintaining the good reputation of Christians with nonbelievers (3:7). They must be men of decency and have maintained good relations within their own families, and so have been married once (v. 2) and able to manage their own children (vv. 4-5). That they are not to be recent converts (v. 6) indicates the need to be clear about the meaning of the Christian faith in their own lives before they assume responsibility for others. References to money in regard both to bishops and to deacons (3:3, 8) may indicate they received a stipend for the performance of their duties (cf. 5:17-18).

Deacons are described in similar terms (3:8-13). The reference to women in this discussion (3:11) gives no indication that the author is referring to the wives of male deacons. The presence of women as deacons is attested by Rom 16:1, and this lends credence to the supposition that the words against women in leadership positions earlier in the letter (2:11-12) may well be restricted to the women described there.

Much of the description of widows is drawn simply from the need in the ancient world, in the absence of any official institutions for care of the aged, for families to care for their own members (5:3-8, 16). The three conditions laid down for enrollment of widows, however, points to a more specific role for them within the early Christian community. Such a widow must have demonstrated good character during her time in the Christian community (v. 10) and be at least sixty years of age and married only once (v. 9). The advice that younger widows remarry (v. 14) reflects the problems such young women could pose for the church (vv. 11-15) and the apparent condition for enrolled widows that they vow not to remarry

(v. 11b). The letter of Ignatius, a church leader in Antioch in the late first century, to the Christians in Smyrna refers to "the virgins who are called widows" (13:1). This may indicate a further development in this category of church order.

Little is said about elders other than that they should be worthy of the stipend paid them for the performance of their duties (5:17-18). That they were apparently more open to charges against them (vv. 19-20) than the other three offices mentioned may indicate that, in addition to their duties of preaching and teaching (v. 17), they were responsible for the finances of the community, although this must remain conjectural. The reference to laying on of hands (v. 22a) may refer to the way in which elders, or perhaps all church leaders, were commissioned, although in the context that is difficult to determine.

The letter concludes with a final exhortation (6:20-21a) and a concluding benediction (6:22b). The letter closing is much shorter than those of the usual Pauline letter, with the absence here of any greetings or personal remarks. On the whole, the letter gives the impression of a kind of pastoral letter to all who sought advice on the role of members and officers of the Christian community as it sought to make its way in the Greco-Roman world of the late first century.

19.2. 2 TIMOTHY

This letter bears the closest resemblance of the three Pastoral letters to the undisputed letters of Paul, even with respect to its structure. All the elements of the genuine Pauline letters are present. Some have suggested that this letter may have been intended to serve as Paul's farewell testament (for a similar last testament, see Acts 20:17-36), a regular literary form in the ancient world with respect to important people. Yet such statements normally do not take the form of personal letters, and we would probably be better served to treat it as a letter rather than as having some ulterior purpose.

The letter opening (1:1-2) is cast in familiar Pauline style, with a somewhat extended identification of Paul as apostle and the usual opening blessing. As is the case in some of the other letters, it is difficult to determine where the thanksgiving ends and the letter body begins. Perhaps one should regard the thanksgiving proper as contained in 1:3-4, with the transition to the body beginning with 1:5-7, since grammatically those verses belong to the opening sentence. Paul's gratitude for the faith that has been manifested by Timothy's mother (and grandmother!) points to Timothy as a second- or even third-generation Christian.

The letter body (1:8–4:18) alternates between reports of Paul's life and his present situation, and advice to Timothy about his ministry. Beginning with an exhortation to Timothy to be bold in his proclamation of the gospel, that is, of what God has done in Christ (1:8-10), Paul then recounts his own call (1:11-12),

---

2 Timothy

Letter opening (1:1-2)
Thanksgiving (1:3-4)
Transition to the letter body (1:5-7)
Letter body (1:8–4:18)
    Exhortations regarding ministry (1:8-10, 13-14; 2:1-7, 14-17a,
        19-26; 3:14–4:5)
    Paul's call, gospel, and sufferings (1:11-12, 15-18; 2:8-13;
        3:10-13; 4:6-8)
    Troublemakers in the church (2:17b-18; 3:1-9; 4:14-15)
    Request that Timothy come to Paul and news about others (4:9-13,
        20-21a)
Greetings (4:19, 21b)
Closing benediction (4:22)

---

something that seems somewhat out of place if the letter is indeed to be a personal communication to one of his coworkers. In fact, it indicates that the letter is intended for a wider audience, one that may not be so familiar with Paul's career. The body continues with further exhortations to Timothy with respect to his own ministry (1:13-14) and concludes with an account of Paul's current state of affairs, including his betrayal in Asia (1:15) and the kindness of one Onesiphorus (1:16-18), who had aided Paul in both Rome and Ephesus and who is included among those who send greetings at the end of the letter (4:19).

Returning to exhortations to Timothy (2:1-7), Paul recites a series of examples from secular life that have application to Timothy's missionary activity and then gives another summary of the content of his own gospel and the current suffering he is undergoing (2:8-13). Included in these verses is what appears to be a fragment of an earlier Christian hymn or confession (2:11-13) that emphasizes both the connection of the Christian to Christ's fate and the necessity for the Christians not to deny Christ, something apparently required of Christians when pressed by unbelieving neighbors or when questioned by legal authorities. Even in this last case, however, Christ's ultimate faithfulness to sinful humanity is affirmed (see Rom 3:3), in contrast to any supposed danger of Christ denying those who deny him (see Mark 8:38).

Further exhortations to Timothy (2:14-19) include a warning against two men, Hymenaeus and Philetus, who have apparently unsettled the church with their teaching that the resurrection is already past. These same two men were mentioned in 1 Tim 1:20 with no indication there of the content of their teaching, but with the news that Paul had delivered them to Satan (probably meaning that he cast them out of the Christian fellowship). Given the way the two men are discussed, it appears that this reference in 2 Timothy might have preceded the one in 1 Timothy, a possible indication of the chronological order of the letters.

After a discussion of the many kinds of vessels needed in a large household (2:20-21), evidently to indicate that the church as the household of God needs people for menial as well as great tasks, Paul again advises Timothy on how he is to comport himself within the Christian community (2:22-26), perhaps reflecting the way a vessel, once purified, can be of noble use for the head of the household (2:21).

A list of vices (3:1-5) introduces the next segment of the letter body. Then Paul discusses the problems caused by people characterized by these vices, which

Vice Lists

Lists of vices were stock features of ancient moralists and are found in various places in the NT as well. The following list shows the vices and corresponding virtues prized in the Greco-Roman world:

> Similarly, of vices some are primary, others subordinate: e.g. folly, cowardice, injustice, profligacy are accounted primary; but incontinence, stupidity, ill-advisedness subordinate. Further, they hold that the vices are forms of ignorance of those things whereof the corresponding virtues are the knowledge. (Diogenes Laertius, *Lives of Eminent Philosophers: Zeno* 7.93)

From the Dead Sea Scrolls comes a list that has stronger resonance with biblical themes:

> But the ways of the spirit of falsehood are these: greed, and slackness in the search for righteousness, wickedness and lies, haughtiness and pride, falseness and deceit, cruelty and abundant evil, ill-temper and much folly and brazen insolence, abominable deeds (committed) in a spirit of lust, the ways of lewdness in the service of uncleanness, a blaspheming tongue, blindness of eye and dullness of ear, stiffness of neck and heaviness of heart, so that man walks in all the ways of darkness and guile. (1QS 4.9-11, Vermes)

Jannes and Jambres

Jannes and Jambres (2 Tim 3:8-9) are the legendary names given to the magicians of Pharaoh's court who opposed Moses. They are named, for example, in the Dead Sea Scrolls: "For in ancient times, Moses and Aaron arose by the hand of the Prince of Lights and Belial in his cunning raised up Jannes and his brother when Israel was first delivered" (CD 5.17-19). The names were also known outside Jewish and Christian circles but seem originally to have come from these sources. Pliny, for example, in his *Natural History* (30.2.11), writes, "There is yet another branch of magic, derived from Moses, Jannes, Lotapes, and the Jews, but living many thousand years after Zoroaster." In Targum *Pseudo-Jonathan,* commenting on Exod 1:15, Jannes and Jambres interpret a dream of Pharaoh's, predicting the birth of a son through whom Egypt will be destroyed. Because of the dream and its interpretation, Pharaoh orders the midwives to kill all male Hebrew babies. The same Targum names Jannes and Jambres as the sons of Balaam at Num 22:22.

include misleading some of the women in the Christian community (3:6-7). Paul compares such person to Jannes and Jambres, two men who according to Jewish tradition were among the magicians of Pharaoh that opposed Moses (Exod 7:11, 22); the opposition of people characterized by the vices included in the preceding list will have no more success in thwarting God's purposes than did Pharaoh's magicians (3:8-9).

Returning once more to his own career, Paul points out that despite the inevitability of persecution for one who lives an appropriate Christian life (3:10-13), Timothy must continue to lead just such a life, as he has from childhood, when he began to be instructed by the sacred Scriptures. In this context, "sacred Scriptures" can only refer to what we know as the OT, since when this letter was written there were as yet no "Christian Scriptures," that is, a NT. Paul assures Timothy that such Scriptures are valuable because God has inspired them to be useful for religious purposes: teaching, reproof, correction, and training in righteousness, so that those desiring to do God's will may be equipped for their task (3:16-17). This passage says nothing about the NT, or about Scripture being infallible in all matters including natural science and geography. The Scriptures (the OT) are highly valuable in showing people how to live as God wants them to live; that is the burden of these often misused verses.

A Prophet's Inspiration

The following passage from *4 Ezra* describes one version of the inspiration of a prophet and the writings produced under inspiration:

> He answered me and said, "Go and gather the people, and tell them not to seek you for forty days. But prepare for yourself many writing tablets, and take with you Sarea, Dabria, Selemia, Ethanus, and Asiel — these five, because they are trained to write rapidly; and you shall come here, and I will light in your heart the lamp of understanding, which shall not be put out until what you are about to write is finished. And when you have finished, some things you shall make public, and some you shall deliver in secret to the wise; tomorrow at this hour you shall begin to write."
>
> So I took the five men, as he commanded me, and we proceeded to the field, and remained there. And on the next day, behold, a voice called me, saying, "Ezra, open your mouth and drink what I give you to drink." Then I opened my mouth, and behold, a full cup was offered to me; it was full of something like water, but its color was like fire. And I took it and drank; and when I had drunk it, my heart poured forth understanding, and wisdom increased in my breast, for my spirit retained its memory; and my mouth was opened, and was no longer closed. And the Most High gave understanding to the five men, and by turns they wrote what was dictated, in characters which they did not know. They sat forty days, and wrote during the daytime, and ate their bread at night. As for me, I spoke in the daytime and was not silent at night. So during the forty days ninety-four books were written. And when the forty days were ended, the Most High spoke to me, saying, "Make public the twenty-four books that you wrote first and let the worthy and the unworthy read them; but keep the seventy that were written last, in order to give them to the wise among your people. For in them is the spring of understanding, the fountain of wisdom, and the river of knowledge." And I did so. (4 Ezra [= 2 Esdras] 14:23-26, 37-48)

The final segment directed to Timothy (4:1-5) is cast in the form of an exhortation appropriate to anyone who seeks to undertake the work of Christian proclamation. Again, Timothy is prototypical, an example of the kind of person the Christian evangelist ought to be.

Paul concludes the letter body with a recitation of his current circumstances, which have brought him to the verge of martyrdom (4:6-8). After a recitation of the way various people have acted in relation to him (4:10-15; this is introduced with the plea in v. 10 that Timothy come to Paul soon), Paul reports on his trial. No one has testified in his behalf — perhaps a covert reference to the resemblance of Paul's fate to that of Jesus, who was also deserted by his followers at the time of his trial. Nevertheless, Paul was evidently able to present an effective enough defense to be spared condemnation. Yet it is difficult to know whether his rescue from the lion's mouth is to be taken literally as a description of the consequences of a guilty verdict, or metaphorically as deliverance from some other unthinkable fate. In light of Paul's earlier anticipation of martyrdom (4:6-8), his final assurance that God will rescue him from every evil (4:18) may be intended to mean that God will protect him from denying his faith and so ensure his final participation in God's kingdom. If that is so, deliverance from "the lion's mouth" by being given strength to proclaim the gospel rather than deny it may refer metaphorically to deliverance from the power of Satan (for a similar comparison, see 1 Pet 5:8). Paul concludes the letter body with an ascription of praise.

The letter closing contains the familiar Pauline greetings to those with the letter's recipient and from those with Paul. That Timothy is to greet Prisca and Aquila, who are mentioned in both Acts (18:2, 18, 26) and Paul's undisputed letters (Rom 16:3; 1 Cor 16:19), does not aid us in determining Timothy's location, since this Christian couple is reported to have lived at various times in Ephesus, Rome, and Corinth. Erastus, similarly known from both Acts 19:22 and Rom 16:23, is described as remaining in his civic position in Corinth. Trophimus, originally from Asia (Acts 20:4), perhaps Ephesus, accompanied Paul on his final trip to Jerusalem (Acts 21:29) and was the cause of an uproar there. It is uncertain when the illness that caused him to remain in Miletus occurred. Of the remaining names, Onesiphorus, mentioned earlier in the letter (1:16), is otherwise unknown, as are Eubulus, Pudens, Linus, and Claudia. That these last four, along with all the "brethren" (i.e., fellow Christians), send greetings indicates that Paul is no longer deserted by all. The letter concludes with two forms of the familiar Pauline grace wish.

Despite the personal details scattered throughout the letter, the advice contained in it also makes it helpful as a general exhortation to those who look to Paul for guidance so that they might remain faithful to the gospel, whatever difficulties might present themselves. The letter has been used in that way for almost two millennia within the Christian community.

19.3. TITUS

The letter opening of the letter to Titus (1:1-4) is, like that of 1 Timothy, different from the normal letter openings of the undisputed Pauline letters. The introduction of Paul as author is longer than in any other Pauline letter except Romans. Perhaps, as in Romans, this description of Paul's gospel and his apostleship were intended to remind those who read it of the true nature of Paul and of his gospel. Early Christian letters were by and large intended to be read to the assembled Christian community, as is shown by the remarks in 1 Thess 5:27 and Col 4:16, and the author may have had such an occasion in mind when he provided this lengthy introduction. The benediction (1:4b), similar to that found in the undisputed Pauline letters, is nevertheless slightly different, referring to Christ Jesus as "Savior," which is unusual for Paul (Phil 3:20; cf. Eph 5:23); Christ's more normal title in such a place is "Lord." As in 1 Timothy, the normal Pauline thanksgiving is also omitted.

Titus

Letter opening (1:1-4)
Letter body (1:5–3:14)
   Church order (1:5-9)
   False teaching (1:10-16)
   Community relations and belief (2:1–3:11)
   Instructions concerning some fellow Christians (3:12-14)
Letter closing (3:15)

The letter body (1:5–3:14) treats three general topics: church order (1:5-9), false teaching (1:10-16), and community relations and belief (2:1–3:11). The letter body closes with some personal instructions to Titus about some fellow Christians (3:12-14).

The language with which the title "bishop" is introduced (1:7) makes it seem likely that the author uses that title along with "elder" (1:5) to describe the same church leader, unlike 1 Timothy, where the two titles clearly represent two different orders of church leaders. By the time Titus was written, it was common to have such leaders in every Christian community (1:5), who by their lives and teaching were good examples to the other Christians. In this instance, there is strong emphasis on the teaching duties of the elder/bishop (1:9), indicating that such leaders were a first line of defense against those who sought to disrupt the Christian communities.

In a somewhat perfunctory manner, the author describes those against whose false teaching the church leaders are to protect their fellow Christians (1:10-16). As in 1 Timothy, there are statements that could indicate influence from both Judaism (1:14a) and a kind of Gnosticism (1:16a) on the false teachers, although the content of their position is not spelled out in any detail. The reference to their lack of appropriate acts may be a reference to the kind of asceticism against which 1 Tim 2:15; 4:3; and 5:14 warn. But that remains speculative. These short characterizations were useful as reminders to people who were already familiar with the longer descriptions in 1 Timothy.

Under the rubric of the sound doctrine that Titus (presumably along with the elders/bishops) is to teach, the largest portion of the letter body is given over to a list of appropriate activities for various types of people (2:2-6). While not cast in the traditional form of a household code, it functions here in much the same way, giving specific advice to younger and older men, younger and older women, and slaves. In the midst of the "code" is advice to Titus to conduct himself in such a way as to give the lie to those who accuse Christians of evil activity (a similar point is made in 1 Pet 3:15-16). It is likely that such a desire to deprive opponents of evidence for their accusations underlies the advice given to the various groups addressed here.

After a short passage outlining the content of the faith (2:11-14), the letter body continues with general exhortations (2:15–3:2) that appear to call on Paul's own past (3:3-7), described here in terms that are probably shaped to reflect the past of the readers themselves (v. 3), as illustration. The concluding remark — "the saying is sure" (3:8) — indicates that the author is quoting from Christian tradition.

The final exhortations (3:8-11) cast further light on the kind of problem the author anticipates occurring in the Christian community, namely factious disputes triggered by the views of what in 1 Timothy are called "false teachers" (3:9). Discipline against those engaged in such disputes involves isolating them from other Christians (3:10-11).

The letter body closes with some personal notes on Paul's condition at the time of writing (3:12-13). Of those named, Artemas and Zenas are mentioned only here; Tychicus is mentioned in the later Pauline letters (Eph 6:21; Col 4:7; 2 Tim 4:12; cf. Acts 20:4); Apollos was a Christian famous for his eloquence (Acts 18:24) who had worked as a missionary in Corinth with Paul (1 Cor 16:12; cf. 1:12; 3:4-6, 22; 4:6).

The letter closing is brief (3:15), containing a general statement about greetings from those with Paul and to those with Titus. It concludes with a typically Pauline grace wish.

Like 1 and 2 Timothy, this letter, despite being written to ancient readers in the Greco-Roman world, has proved, as have the other NT letters written under similar circumstances, to be useful over the centuries to churches plagued with the same kind of problems addressed here in the earliest period of the Christian church.

19.4. SOME QUESTIONS

One of the more vexing problems with these letters has to do with their authorship. Yet however we decide the issue, it is simply not true, as one scholar has argued, that our judgment of their value depends on whether the person who wrote them was Paul or a disciple of Paul. These letters have been treasured by the worldwide Christian community for almost 2000 years and have proved of value regardless of their author. One does not value the Gospels by who may or may not have written them or regard the author of Hebrews, whoever it may have been, determinative of what value Hebrews has for us. The same is true of these letters. They have proved of value to the Christian church whoever the author may have been.

Those who argue for an author other than the apostle Paul usually cite the following evidence and arguments.

1. The language and style of the Pastorals are quite different from those of the acknowledged Pauline letters. There is a higher proportion of words per sentence appearing nowhere else in the Pauline letters than in any other letter attributed to Paul, and a large number of those words are more characteristic of writings of the early second century than of the other Pauline epistles. Some words that do appear in the undisputed letters of Paul are used in these letters with a different intention: faith, for example, tends more often to refer not to trust but to the body of Christian doctrine (e.g., 1 Tim 1:19; 3:19; 4:1; 2 Tim 3:8; 4:7; Titus 1:13). Truth now also has the same meaning, namely, Christian teaching (e.g., 1 Tim 3:15; 4:3; 2 Tim 2:15; 3:8; Tit 1:14). "Savior" is also used frequently for both Christ and God in the Pastorals; it is used of Christ only once in the undisputed Pauline letters (Phil 3:20; once also in Eph 5:23) and never of God. Most telling of all, some nineteen particles, conjunctions, and adverbs that characterize the undisputed Pauline letters are absent from the Pastorals; an author tends to use such words automatically, and their absence betrays an author other than Paul.

2. The historical situation presumed in the letters is difficult to fit into what we know of Paul. 1 Timothy presumes that Timothy stayed in Ephesus when Paul left (1:3), but there is no indication in Acts or the other Pauline letters that Timothy remained in Ephesus after Paul left. Furthermore, so close a companion of Paul would hardly need such detailed instruction on doctrine and practice as is given in 1 Timothy.

Titus presumes that Paul was in Crete and then left Titus there to continue the work. There is, however, no other indication that Paul ever conducted a mission in Crete or was ever at Nicopolis. The only mention of Crete in connection to Paul is that, as a prisoner, he sailed near there but was driven off by a storm before anchorage for the winter could be achieved (Acts 27).

Similarly, 2 Timothy presumes travels of Paul with and without Timothy that have no other record either in Acts or the Pauline letters.

For such travels to have taken place, one would have to locate them at a time not covered by either Acts or the other Pauline letters. Such a period is possible after Paul's Roman imprisonment, with which Acts concludes. Such a solution has great difficulties, however, among them:

a. The end of Acts gives no information about Paul's release or execution, but Acts 20:25 and 38 clearly imply that Paul never returned to the churches in the East.

b. Similarly, Paul's planned trip to Spain (Rom 15:24), if it occurred, would have taken place after Paul was released from imprisonment in Rome. Such a journey is implied in *1 Clement* 5:7, which says that Paul went to "the limits of the West," that is, to Spain, though Ignatius (*Romans* 2) uses the same word, "West," to refer to Rome. Further, there is no evidence outside Titus for Paul's further mission to Crete.

c. 2 Tim 4:6-8 implies that Paul's martyrdom is at hand, but that makes the request that Timothy come before winter and bring Paul's cloak and a certain manuscript (4:13, 21) somewhat enigmatic, since Paul would not have that much time left to him were he facing execution. Some have suggested that 2 Timothy may incorporate genuine Pauline fragments, but there is no textual evidence to support that idea.

In short, for the Pastorals to have been written by Paul, Paul must have returned to the eastern Mediterranean after his Roman imprisonment and initiated a mission to Crete. Of this journey back from Rome there is no other evidence.

3. The views of the false teachers who are opposed are characterized by a combination of Judaism (abstinence from certain foods: 1 Tim 4:3; 5:23; Tit 1:15) and Gnosticism (opposition to marriage: 1 Tim 2:15; 4:3; 5:14; speculation in genealogies and "false myths": 1 Tim 1:4; cf. Tit 3:9; and affirmation that the resurrection was already past: 2 Tim 2:18). Such teachings do not, however, reflect the full-blown Gnostic systems of the second century and hence cannot be used to argue for that late a date. But, in opposing the false teachings, the author of the Pastorals does not confront them with the gospel of Christ, as Paul does in some of his other letters. Rather, the false teachers are simply denounced and their views contrasted with traditional Christian teachings, from which they have fallen away and to which they should return (e.g., 1 Tim 4:1; 6:20; 2 Tim 1:4; 2:2; Tit 3:10-11).

4. Church leaders — bishops, elders, deacons, widows — occupy a central

place in the letters. While Paul does mention bishops and deacons once (Phil 1:1), he is not concerned with their character or duties. Paul nowhere mentions elders as church leaders, though Acts, written later, assumes the presence of elders in every church (14:23); nor does Paul mention widows. The attempt to regularize the official leadership of the church and to clarify the functions of the leaders also characterizes the *Didache* and the letters of Ignatius (see also *1 Clem.* 44:2), all of which originated late in the first century. That would seem also to point to a later date for the Pastorals.

Although 2 Timothy is closest in style and content to Paul's other letters, the similarity of language and style among the three Pastorals indicates that the same author wrote all three. To account for the differences in style and content by use of a different secretary is to remove Paul from major responsibility not only for these letters but also for his other letters as well. Such a solution also ignores the fact that Romans, written out by Tertius (Rom 16:22), betrays the same style as the other undisputed letters of Paul. It appears, therefore, that the transcriber (a more accurate word than "secretary") of a Pauline letter did not exercise that much influence on style or content.

Perhaps the author of the Pastorals was a student of Paul or a member of his circle, one who therefore had known Timothy and Titus, who had traditions about travels of Paul not mentioned in his letters or in Acts (hence the personal touches in 2 Timothy), and who wished to use them in such a way that the towering stature of Paul as the Apostle to the Gentiles would give added authority to this application of Paul's theology to problems that arose some years after his death. Perhaps the author addressed the letters to two trusted companions of Paul to illustrate for the readers the kind of advice the two would have received from the apostle about their conduct as missionaries in the Greco-Roman world of the first century. In that way, Paul's thought could be applied to the kind of problems that were emerging as the church was maturing and gaining ever larger footholds in the ancient world.

However one may wish to explain authorship and addressees, however, any such explanation remains speculative. While many deem it unlikely that the apostle wrote these three letters, certainty in this matter is simply not available.

Why the letters were written is clear from their content. False teachings have arisen, and there is a need for sound doctrine, pious life, and solid church order. The advice to church leaders indicates that perhaps some of them have been affected by the false teachers denounced in these letters. The advice to such leaders is more prominent in 1 Timothy and Titus than in 2 Timothy, which appears intended to serve as a literary testament of the apostle on his way to his death (2 Tim 4:6-8). The larger motive for the composition of these letters in Paul's name is given in 2 Tim 2:2: the need to pass on the Pauline traditions. In addition, there was the need to apply those traditions to the new problems arising in the latter part of the first century.

When they were written is difficult to determine with any precision. The best guess is probably the last third of the first century, after the death of Paul. It is also difficult to determine their sequence; their current order is predicated on length, and hence the numerations "1" and "2" Timothy refer to length rather than chronological order. It may well be that 2 Timothy was written first, perhaps by someone who knew the details of Paul's last days (2 Tim 4:9-17), and that subsequently 1 Timothy and Titus were written, perhaps by someone else in imitation of the style and content of 2 Timothy.

As to place of origin, 2 Tim 1:15, 18 implies that the letter was written from Ephesus, while 1:17 could be interpreted to mean that Paul was writing from Rome. Tit 3:12 could mean Paul was already in Nicopolis and writing from there. 1 Timothy gives no indication of its place of origin. Some have suggested that the similarity of language and teachings to the *Philippians* of Polycarp, an early second-century bishop in Smyrna, may indicate Asia Minor as the point of origin, but we cannot know with any certainty.

The textual evidence of the letters shows no obvious insertions or dislocations that would compromise their textual integrity. There are some hymnic fragments in the letters (e.g., 1 Tim 3:16, perhaps 6:15-16). Some have suggested that the personal notes in 2 Timothy represent fragments of genuine letters of Paul incorporated into this letter. In either case, the textual evidence indicates that these traditions and fragments were included in the letters from the time of their origin.

FOR FURTHER READING

Martin Dibelius and Hans Conzelmann, *The Pastoral Epistles* (Hermeneia; Philadelphia: Fortress, 1972)

Luke T. Johnson, *Letters to Paul's Delegates: 1 Timothy, 2 Timothy, Titus* (The New Testament in Context; Valley Forge: Trinity Press International, 1996)

J. N. D. Kelly, *The Pastoral Epistles* (London: Black, 1963)

George Knight, *The Pastoral Epistles* (New International Greek Testament Commentary; Grand Rapids: Eerdmans, 1992)

I. Howard Marshall, *A Critical and Exegetical Commentary on the Pastoral Epistles* (International Critical Commentary; Edinburgh: Clark, 1999)

William D. Mounce, *Pastoral Epistles* (Word Biblical Commentary; Nashville: Nelson, 2000)

Jerome D. Quinn, *Titus* (Anchor Bible; New York: Doubleday, 1990)

Jerome D. Quinn and William C. Wacker, *The First and Second Letters to Timothy* (Eerdmans Critical Commentary; Grand Rapids: Eerdmans, 2000)

Frances Young, *The Theology of the Pastoral Letters* (Cambridge: Cambridge University Press, 1994)

20. Hebrews

Few documents of the NT appear, at first glance, to be as removed from the world of the modern reader as the Epistle to the Hebrews. Written in an elegantly polished Greek, it makes puns on Greek terms and names, advances an extensive argument about the nature of the sacrifice of Jesus Christ based on an allegorical reading of the fixtures and furniture of the OT tabernacle, and argues for the superior priesthood of Jesus by comparing him to the mysterious figure Melchizedek, who makes but a cameo appearance in the OT. If these exegetical techniques and theological arguments could once be used persuasively to encourage Christians to persevere in their commitment, they could scarcely serve that purpose for most Christian readers today. Most contemporary readers of Hebrews neither speak nor read Greek, nor do they care for rather esoteric OT details, such as what stood behind the second curtain of the tabernacle (9:3-4) or the significance of Abraham's tithe paid to Melchizedek (7:1-6). But if the rhetorical flourishes and literary style of Hebrews do not generate an empathetic response, its fundamental description of Christian believers as a pilgrim people with a sure guide in Jesus Christ and a definite goal in the heavenly city, in need of faith for the journey they undertake, rings true in every generation where discouragement and distractions threaten such faithfulness.

20.1. THE ORIGINS OF "THE EPISTLE TO THE HEBREWS"

20.1.1. The Genre of the Work

Not only does Hebrews pose peculiar challenges to the modern reader due to its literary style and theological approach, but few questions regarding its origins can

Preface: "God has spoken to us through a Son" (1:1-4)
The superiority of Jesus the Son (1:5–4:13)
    Jesus the Son is superior to angels (1:5–2:18)
    Jesus the Son is superior to Moses (3:1-19)
    Jesus the Son is superior to Joshua (4:1-13)
The superiority of Jesus as High Priest (4:14–7:28)
The superiority of Jesus' ministry (8:1–10:18)
    Jesus inaugurates a better covenant (8:1-13)
    in a heavenly tabernacle (9:1-10)
    offering a better sacrifice (9:11–10:10)
    as a superior high priest (10:11-18)
The necessity of faithfulness (10:19–13:19)
    Exhortations to faithfulness and perseverance (10:19-39)
    Examples of faithfulness from the OT people of God (11:1-39)
    Jesus, the pioneer and perfecter of faith, calls his people
        to follow (12:1-13)
    Warnings against turning away from Jesus (12:14-29)
    Exhortations to faithful living (13:1-19)

be settled with any degree of confidence. Throughout this volume, we have pointed to the genre of a work as an important aid in understanding and interpreting it, but it is not easy to assign a specific genre to Hebrews. It has been called epistle, sermon, and treatise. While Hebrews finds its place among the epistles of the NT canon, it nowhere uses that designation. In fact, it lacks the stereotypical features of Hellenistic letters, including an opening with the identification of sender and receiver, a greeting, and the oft-included wish or prayer for health. It does close with a greeting and benediction, not unlike those of the Pauline letters. And typical of the letters of the NT, the author demonstrates some familiarity with the readers and their situation and wishes to address them specifically with a word of consolation and warning. Thus, while lacking those visible markers that characterize most ancient letters, Hebrews does manifest certain features suggesting that it belongs in that category. By the end of the second century, the document was regularly known as the epistle "To the Hebrews," as the church fathers Tertullian and Clement of Alexandria and the papyrus manuscript 𝔭46 all testify.

Yet other classifications have been suggested as well. The author himself refers to his work as a "word of exhortation" (13:22), which may well designate it as a sermon or homiletic discourse. In Acts, for example, the synagogue officials urge

Paul and his companions to deliver a "word of exhortation" to the people (Acts 13:15), at which point Paul begins a homily that includes a lengthy recitation of God's dealings with Israel, up to and including the sending of Jesus, that is sprinkled with quotations from the OT, and that concludes with an exhortation to respond to this "message of salvation" with faith. Hebrews also mingles all these elements together. Like sermons and homilies found elsewhere in the NT and other sources of the day, Hebrews presents scriptural texts for exposition and as the basis for exhortation and encouragement to the people of God.

Whether properly construed as a letter or as a homily, Hebrews is primarily an exhortation to perseverance in Christian commitment. All its intricate theological and exegetical arguments stand in the service of this admonition to faithful commitment to Christ. The author uses his literary, rhetorical, and theological skills and gifts to hold before his readers a picture of their past, present, and future, the gift of salvation they have been given in Christ, and the hope that is before them, all in order to encourage them to persist in their Christian discipleship. Precisely because of its predominantly pastoral function, it is unlikely that Hebrews should be construed as a theological treatise pure and simple. So long as we keep in mind the pastoral function of Hebrews, it matters little whether we in the end designate it as homily or letter.

20.1.2. The Author of Hebrews

Modern scholars have had a field day offering suggestions regarding the author of Hebrews. It comes to us anonymously, and there are few autobiographical hints or personal references to help us determine who might have written it. The writer places himself outside the circle of the apostles, locating himself in the generation of those who received the message of salvation from those who heard Jesus (2:3). In other words, he was neither an eyewitness of the ministry of Jesus nor one of the first generation of believers.

Because he refers to Timothy (13:23), who is probably to be identified as the Timothy known to us from the Pauline mission, many have sought to place the author within the Pauline circle. Thus suggestions for authorship from early church authors have included Paul, Barnabas, Luke, and Clement of Rome. Later, Apollos, Silvanus/Silas, Priscilla and Aquila, Jude, Epaphras, Timothy, and the deacon Philip were added to the list. Even Mary, the mother of Jesus, has been suggested. Obviously many, if not most, of these suggestions are pure speculation. They do, however, manifest the desire to connect the author with someone who was part of the apostolic circle or with a figure of authority, so as to lend the document a stamp of apostolic approval — an attestation, we might note, that Hebrews itself apparently did not feel compelled to supply. The final

Did Paul Write Hebrews?

Christians who grew up reading the King James Version of the Bible find Hebrews designated there as "The Epistle of Paul to the Hebrews." In one early manuscript, $\mathfrak{P}46$, Hebrews is placed after Romans, indicating that it was accepted as a Pauline epistle. Acceptance of Hebrews as Pauline occurred earlier in the Christian East than the West, where finally in the fifth century the authority of Augustine and Jerome, as well as the designation of Hebrews as Pauline in the Vulgate, carried the day. But there have always been doubts that the designation of the anonymous author of the epistle as Paul was correct. Many early church fathers, including Origen and Clement of Alexandria, record their skepticism. Its inclusion in the canon may have been secured by its attribution to Paul. But the fact that such an attribution cannot be supported cannot remove it from its place in the Christian canon of Scripture.

There are good reasons to doubt Pauline authorship:

- The letter does not claim to be from Paul, a silence not in keeping with Paul's practice.
- The letter lacks typical features of Pauline letters, including any autobiographical or personal references that would help to assign the letter to Paul.
- The letter's literary style and vocabulary are markedly different from the Pauline letters, including the "disputed" Pauline letters.
- Paul typically introduces OT quotations with "It is written," whereas Hebrews never appeals to Scripture as something *written*.
- There are considerable differences in theological emphasis, such as Hebrews' interpretation of Jesus' death along priestly lines, the use of distinctive epithets for Jesus, and the different nuance assigned to "faith," as evidenced in the different use made of Hab 2:4, "The just shall live by faith."
- Paul typically places himself among the apostles, whereas the author of Hebrews speaks of himself as removed from that circle (2:3).

Thus to Origen's statement regarding authorship, "God only knows who wrote it," we may add "Paul did not."

verdict on authorship was issued by Origen when he wrote, "God only knows who wrote it."

But from the document itself we may deduce some features of the author's profile. The author is clearly well-educated, for not only does he write polished Greek but he has had the benefit of an education that included training in rhetoric and at least some Greek philosophy, as well as in techniques of exegesis of the Scriptures. Almost certainly he was of Jewish descent. At some point he came to faith in Jesus as the Messiah, apparently through the testimony of eyewitnesses to Jesus' ministry. The reference to Timothy suggests some affiliation with the Pauline mission. And the mere fact that our author addresses this book to a Christian congregation indicates that he is a person in a position of some authority in the church. He issues commands and warnings without pulling his punches, expecting or at least hoping for a positive response. Yet when he urges his readers to submit to their leaders (13:17), it is more difficult to tell whether he includes himself among the leaders. But at the least he hopes that his counsel for his readers to heed their leaders will be followed.

One of the issues that scholars have thought might be settled, or at least addressed, by solving the problem of the authorship of the letter is the question of its setting in ancient Christianity. Does the intricate argument from OT details tell us about the author of Hebrews, its audience, or both? How diverse was the theology of the early Christian movement? What were the primary influences on it? Some scholars who have placed the author or his audience or both in Palestine have tried to establish affinities with the radically eschatological and dualistic conceptual world attested to us in the Dead Sea Scrolls. Taking nearly the opposite position, other scholars have pointed out similarities to figures of Diaspora Judaism, such as Philo of Alexandria, who were strongly influenced by Hellenistic philosophy. But while Hebrews evidences an eschatological framework, it does not fit the apocalyptic mood or model of the scrolls. And while there are similarities with the Greek-speaking Judaism of Philo, with his allegorizing readings of the OT, still the eschatological tone of Hebrews and its lack of consistent philosophically colored readings of the OT show its great distance from Philo. Hebrews testifies not only to the diversity of early Christianity but also to the difficulty in pinpointing a single sort of Judaism that accounts for all the features and theology of Hebrews apart from its messianism.

Although knowing who wrote Hebrews would not immediately solve all these other problems, they are the sorts of issues that are implicated in the question of authorship and audience. Without further external information we cannot settle these issues decisively. Nevertheless, through an analysis of the contents of Hebrews itself, we may venture some suggestions about the relationship of the author and his audience.

20.1.3. The Audience of Hebrews

It is generally assumed that Hebrews is addressed to Christians whose situation is known to the author, at least in its broad outlines. Whereas Paul typically recalls the circumstances that led to the founding of a particular congregation, we have no reason to assume that this author is the founder of the congregation to which he writes. Almost assuredly he is not. What his particular relationship to this congregation might be remains unclear, but he knows enough about their situation, either firsthand or indirectly, to be concerned for their well-being and to assume that he may address them as a pastor.

The situation of the readers of Hebrews can be reconstructed to some extent from comments the author makes in passing. At some point in their past, soon after becoming Christians, they experienced persecution or harassment. The author speaks of "earlier days," when his readers endured "a hard struggle with sufferings, sometimes publicly exposed to abuse and persecution" (10:32-33). They had not yet, however, experienced martyrdom (12:4). But the mere mention of martyrdom may suggest that the author fears that it is approaching. In the early days after coming to faith, these Christians had demonstrated the strength of their convictions through joyful service to fellow Christians in need, and even endured the loss of property and possessions with equanimity (6:10; 10:34). Now, however, the author speaks of their growth as Christians as stunted (5:11–6:1) and worries that they are in danger of falling back to former ways and perhaps falling away from the Christian faith altogether, perhaps particularly if the threat of martyrdom materializes.

Beyond such information that can be gleaned from the book itself, little can be determined with precision regarding the readers and their social location. That they were Jewish Christians was the assumption of those who first called this document "To the Hebrews." It is argued that such a designation best fits the whole character of the argument of Hebrews, with the central place given to the OT, the appeals to Jewish ritual and culture, sacrifice, the tabernacle, the wilderness wanderings of Israel, and the covenant with Abraham. The argument for the superiority of Jesus and the new covenant he inaugurates over the old covenant would surely make its greatest impact on those who claimed to be the people of that first covenant. The argument that God is concerned not with angels but with the "descendants of Abraham" (2:16) would have the greatest appeal to a Jewish readership.

On the other hand, it can be countered that Paul, when addressing the Gentiles at Galatia and Corinth, introduces complicated OT arguments in support of his case, that part of early Christian catechism was instruction in basics of the OT, and that more than one work in the NT argues that "descent from Abraham" is now properly assigned to those who are related to him through their faith and

Entrance hall of a third- and fourth-century synagogue in Sardis (*J. Finegan*)

obedience to God, not through physical descent (Matt 3:9; Luke 3:8; John 8:37-40; Romans 4; Galatians 4). But whatever merits these counterarguments may have, it is difficult not to see Hebrews as directed toward Jewish Christians, to whom the exhortations and arguments from the exposition of so many OT passages, especially those regarding the wandering Israelites looking for the Promised Land, would have a particularly strong appeal.

Where these Christians lived is also disputed. Palestine, Ephesus, the Lycus Valley, Corinth, and Rome have all been suggested. The greeting in 13:24, "Those from Italy greet you," has made Rome a plausible candidate for the location of the readers. This would square with the fact that our earliest extant reference to Hebrews is found in *1 Clement.* Moreover, some have suggested that the author's description of what the readers have endured in the past can easily be made to fit with certain known facts about Rome. For example, some wish to correlate the statement that in the earlier days these Christians had experienced the plunder of their goods (10:34) with Claudius's decree expelling the Jews (including Christian Jews) from Rome in 49 CE. The prospect of martyrdom and the need for faith and perseverance would be raised by Nero's persecutions in 64-65. But if these historical situations were in view, why is our author so reticent to mention them more specifically? His words regarding the situation of his readers seem much more vague and unspecified. Although that situation can perhaps be correlated with certain events in Rome, this remains at best a guess.

20.1.4. The Date of the Letter

The hypothesis just mentioned, regarding the possible Roman destination of Hebrews, poses the question of the date of the epistle, for if it were indeed addressed to Christians in Rome prior to Nero's persecution, then a date somewhere in the early 60s is demanded. Almost as speculative is the argument regarding the dating of Hebrews with respect to the destruction of the temple and the fall of Jerusalem in the year 70. The references in Hebrews to the sacrifices and the work of the High Priest are in the present tense, which has suggested to many that the temple was still standing and that the sacrifices were still being offered when the author wrote. Those who take this position often argue that had the temple been destroyed, that would have been the linchpin in the author's argument regarding the superiority and enduring nature of the new covenant and the sacrifice that sealed it once for all. Hence, his silence on this matter suggests that the temple is standing and therefore that Hebrews should be dated prior to 70 CE.

Not surprisingly, there are counterarguments. Most notably, the author seems little concerned with the temple and its sacrifices but argues with respect to the tabernacle, precisely because it fit his comparison of the people of the new covenant with the people of the old covenant who wandered in the wilderness. The tabernacle, described in Exodus 25–27, was an elaborate tent constructed of curtains and screens of skins and woven fabrics hung from or over a wooden framework. Thus it could be disassembled and moved. The ark of the covenant was kept behind a curtain (see Heb 6:19; 9:13; 10:20), and there was an altar on which sacrifices were offered (see Heb 7:13; 9:4; 13:10).

The tabernacle symbolized the dwelling of God with his people (Exod 25:8), a function the temple served once the Israelites had settled in the Promised Land. The wilderness generation wandered without coming to its goal, but the generation of the author of Hebrews knows its destination for certain and has a sure guide to lead them there. The wilderness generation had an earthly tabernacle, but Jesus grants entry to a superior tabernacle. This argument would hold whether the temple were standing or had been destroyed. It is often pointed out that Josephus writes of the activities and sacrifices in the temple entirely in the present tense, even though it is clear that Jerusalem had been destroyed two decades earlier.

This overview of the issues of authorship, audience, and date has turned up little more than a host of educated guesses. Little wonder that scholars have sometimes likened Hebrews to Melchizedek himself — "without father, without mother, without genealogy." No doubt the paucity of specific historical references has lent some support to designating Hebrews as neither a letter or sermon but a "treatise," a rather general tractate intended for no specific audience and written on no specific occasion. Such a designation might serve, but not at the expense of turning the pastoral admonitions of Hebrews into abstract arguments or theology divorced from their pastoral function. Moreover, even if author and audience cannot be ascertained with certainty, it is clear that the author writes to warn his readers against not only losing heart, but losing faith. The occasion for the letter is the author's perception that his readers are in danger of either slipping away from their Christian commitment unawares or openly rejecting it. It matters little to him whether it is a Gentile or Jewish past that they slip back into. Either would be abandonment of what God has done for them in Christ. In order to avert such a catastrophe, our author writes this "word of exhortation," the basic literary and substantive structure of which is provided by numerous appeals to the OT Scriptures, which were, for the author of Hebrews, the lively and active word of the living God.

20.2. USE OF THE OLD TESTAMENT

The use of the OT in Hebrews is rich and varied. There are specific and numerous citations of the OT, countless allusions and passing references to OT persons and events, and arguments and admonitions based on expositions of various passages or on explanations of the significance of certain events. A number of the passages that are quoted figure in important ways elsewhere in the NT, as can be seen in the table on page 474. These texts are expounded under the conviction that they speak of realities and promises that have been brought to fullest expression through the work of God in Christ. The texts of the OT are thus read through an eschatological lens. The opening words of Hebrews make this apparent, when the author writes that "Long ago God spoke to our ancestors in many and various ways by the prophets, but in *these last days* he has spoken to us by a Son." It is through the conviction that in Christ the world has entered the era of "these last days" that the author of Hebrews reads and interprets the Scriptures.

Having said that, we must hasten to add that Hebrews does not conceive of Scripture as primarily about a distant past that can only with difficulty be appropriated to the present. Rather, the author assumes that the activity of God as revealed through the OT has direct relevance to readers of every generation. Scripture is not a revelation about the past but a present and living testimony to the work of God, and often the direct speech of God. It has immediate applicability to its readers, although there is both continuity and discontinuity between the periods before and after the coming of Christ. The discontinuity is signaled by the es-

Old Testament Passage	Used In	And Also Significant In
Psalm 2: "You are my son, today I have begotten you."	Heb 1:5; 5:5	Mark 1:11; Matt 3:17; Luke 3:22; Acts 13:33; 2 Pet 1:17
Psalm 110: "The LORD says to my lord, 'Sit at my right hand until I make your enemies your footstool.'"	Heb 1:13. Psalm 110 also provides references to Melchizedek, which the author links with the narrative of Genesis 14	Mark 12:36; Matt 22:44; Acts 2:34
2 Sam 7:14 contains the promise that God will be a father to the descendants of David.	Heb 1:5	
Jeremiah 31: the promise of a new covenant	Heb 8:10; 9:15, 20; 10:16	Luke 22:20; 1 Cor 11:25; 2 Cor 3:6
Hab 2:4: "the righteous shall live by faith"	Heb 10:38	Rom 1:17; Gal 3:11

chatological act of God in Christ. Nevertheless, Hebrews assumes and is predicated on the continuing validity of the OT witness.

Hebrews contains one of the most famous NT descriptions of "the word of God," describing it as "living and active, sharper than any two-edged sword, piercing until it divides soul from spirit" (Heb 4:12). To be sure, in context it is difficult to tell whether Hebrews refers here to the spoken or written word of God, but precisely in that ambiguity we find one of Hebrews' key presuppositions. God speaks through the Scriptures. Hebrews never cites the OT with reference to the author of a particular OT book, nor does it ever introduce its quotations with the formula "it is written." Scripture is not what human authors wrote; it is what God speaks. Twenty-three quotations of about three dozen in all are said to be spoken by God; four are assigned to Christ (2:12, 13; 10:5-7), and four to the Holy Spirit (3:7; 9:8; 10:15-17). One quotation is even introduced with the almost comic note "Somewhere one has testified" (2:6). That rhetorical device probably does not mean that the author has forgotten the source of the quotation but that it is the testimony itself rather than the human witness that counts.

Earlier we commented on the polished Greek and literary facility demonstrated by our author. That his native tongue was Greek is scarcely to be doubted, and it is therefore little wonder that he quotes the OT in its Greek form. For example, in quoting Ps 8:5, he writes that God has made "the son of man" "a little lower than the angels" (Heb 2:7). This is the reading of the Septuagint, which translates Hebrew *elohim* as "angels," an interpretation also found elsewhere in the Septuagint and in the Dead Sea Scrolls. But *elohim* can also be rendered simply as "God," and this translation is found in most English versions of Ps 8:5 based on the Hebrew text. Similarly, at Heb 10:5, the author quotes Ps 40:6, where the Septuagint (40:7) includes the phrase "a body you have prepared for me," which Hebrews takes as a reference to the incarnation of Christ. Unlike the Septuagint, the Hebrew reads "you have given me an open ear." Sometimes the quotations in Hebrews appear to be altered from both the Septuagint and the Hebrew text, probably in keeping with theological explanations of the author himself, or possibly reflecting variant readings of the OT that were known to the author but have not survived in any manuscripts.

Greek Versions of the Old Testament

The Septuagint (abbreviated LXX) is often also called "the Greek Old Testament." The *Letter of Aristeas* reproduces a legend concerning the origin of the LXX, namely, that seventy-two learned elders, six from each of the twelve tribes of Israel, were secluded for seventy-two days and produced a translation so highly praised by the Alexandrian Jewish community that a curse should fall on anyone who changed one word of it. Study of the Septuagint today suggests that it was the work of multiple translators not all in Alexandria and working over an extended period of time. The LXX originated among Jews as a translation for those whose primary language was Greek, but as it became increasingly appropriated by Christians in the first and second centuries, Jews adopted other translations, including those done by Aquila, Symmachus, and Theodotion.

The NT authors often quote the LXX, which sometimes accounts for differences between their OT quotations and the Hebrew OT. The LXX also differs from the Hebrew OT in the contents, number, and order of the books it includes (see the lists on p. 46). Before the achievement of a somewhat "fixed" text in about the second century CE, transmission of the Septuagint text was marked by some fluidity, which is reflected in differences between NT quotations of the Greek OT and the present LXX.

In explaining the OT, the author uses some techniques of interpretation that are rather foreign to modern ways of interpreting the Bible. For example, elaboration of the text, amounting to emendation, can be used as an explanatory technique. Haggai 2:6 reads, "For thus says the LORD of hosts: Once again, in a little while, I will shake the heavens and the earth and the sea and the dry land," but Heb 12:26 changes it to read: "At that time his voice shook the earth; but now he has promised, 'Yet once more I will shake not only the earth but also the heaven.'" By omitting "sea and the dry land," changing the order of earth and heaven, and inserting "not only . . . but also," the author emphasizes the final "shaking" of heaven.

Hebrews shows a common rabbinic exegetical technique of linking together texts on the basis of shared words to form a "catena" (or "chain") of prooftexts, such as collections of texts that have in common the words "son" and "angel" (Heb 1:5-12). Texts from Ps 95:7-11 and Gen 2:2 are brought together because they speak of "rest" (Heb 4:3-4). The author of Hebrews also pays close attention to the literal use of OT words. For example, because Psalm 95 uses the word "today" in speaking to those who would read or pray it, the author of Hebrews assumes that it is directly applicable to readers of his own day.

Citations and explanations of texts of Scripture provide not only much of the density of the texture of Hebrews, but a series of texts also serves to provide its overall structure, both literarily and theologically. Through the regular citation, explanation, and illustration of six central texts (see the table on p. 477), the author makes his appeal to his readers to consider the salvation that God has provided in Christ, and to hold fast to their commitment to him. Thus, as we shall see, not only do the citations of scriptural texts provide the structural framework of the discourse, but they also contain in a nutshell a summary of its arguments and admonitions. In these arguments and admonitions, there is a regular alternation between explanations of the significance and superiority of the ministry of Jesus, the Son of God, and the corresponding expectations of those who would be his disciples. This intricate and close correspondence of Hebrews' understanding of Jesus and its understanding of discipleship is in fact one of the hallmarks of the book. So we will proceed to examine more closely the correspondence between christology and discipleship under the three key christological titles in Hebrews: Jesus as Son, as the "Pioneer" of faith, and as High Priest.

20.3. "IN THESE LAST DAYS, HE HAS SPOKEN TO US THROUGH A SON"

Hebrews opens with a polished preface, what was called an *exordium* at the time. It is a single sentence in Greek, divided in modern translations into four verses, that

The Old Testament in Hebrews

Old Testament Quotation	Cited in Hebrews	Main Point of the Citation	Exhortation to the Readers
Catena: Ps 2:7; 2 Sam 7:14; Pss 97:7; 104:4; 45:6-7; 102:25-27; 110:1; 8:4-6; Isa 8:17-18	1:5–2:18	As Son, Jesus is superior to all other mediator figures, including prophets, angels, and Moses.	Therefore, "how can we escape if we neglect so great a salvation?" (2:3).
Ps 95:7-11	3:7-11 (3:15; 4:3, 7)	Moses and Joshua led the Israelites in the wilderness, but did not give them the "sabbath rest" of Psalm 95, which is now available for God's people who persevere in their journey.	Therefore, "let us make every effort to enter that rest" (4:11) by persevering in commitment to Jesus.
Psalms 2 and 110	5:5-6; 7:17, 21	As Son, Jesus exercises a superior priesthood, offers a better sacrifice, and seals a better covenant.	Therefore, "let us hold fast our confession" (4:14) and "with confidence draw near to the throne of grace" (4:16).
Jer 31:31-34	8:8-12 and 10:16-17	Through Jesus' life, death, and resurrection, God has established the promised new covenant.	Therefore, "let us approach with a true heart in full assurance" (10:22); "let us hold fast to the confession" (10:23).
Hab 2:3-4	10:37-38	Those who hold fast to Jesus will receive what God has promised, even though they cannot now see it.	Therefore, "let us run with perseverance the race that is set before us, looking to Jesus" (12:1-2).
Prov 3:11-12	12:5-6	Trials are not evidence that God has abandoned his people.	Therefore, "lift your drooping hands and strengthen your weak knees" (12:12), and "let us give thanks" (12:28).

encapsulates many of the themes to be developed in the book. Because of its literary beauty and theological density, it is worth quoting here in full:

> Long ago God spoke to our ancestors in many and various ways by the prophets, but in these last days he has spoken to us by a Son, whom he appointed heir of all things, through whom he also created the worlds. He is the reflection of God's glory and the exact imprint of God's very being, and he sustains all things by his powerful word. When he had made purification for sins, he sat down at the right hand of the Majesty on high, having become as much superior to angels as the name he has inherited is more excellent than theirs. (NRSV)

The eschatological perspective of Hebrews is underscored by the contrast between *long ago* and *these last days,* literally "at the end of these days," a phrase reminiscent of other NT designations such as "the last hour" (1 John 2:18), "the end of the ages" (1 Pet 1:20), and "the ends of the ages" (1 Cor 10:11). The conviction that the eschatological hour has struck underlies the argument of Hebrews for the superiority of the Son, who is contrasted with the prophets, through whom God did indeed speak "long ago." Not only is the Son the medium of God's speaking, but he is also the agent through whom God "created the worlds." Here Hebrews presents a motif common in the NT and developed from the wisdom speculation of the OT and texts of Second Temple Judaism that it was through the agency of the Son, God's personified and embodied wisdom, that the world was created (e.g., John 1:1; 1 Cor 8:16; Col 1:16). This affirmation signals the Son's preexistence and, through his participation in both the creation and the sustenance of life, his very divine identity with God. He is, in fact, "the reflection of God's glory and the exact imprint of God's very being," a description that reflects the Hellenistic Jewish book of Wisdom, where wisdom is described as "a breath of the power of God and a pure emanation of the glory of the Almighty . . . a reflection of eternal light, a spotless mirror of the working of God, and an image of his goodness" (Wis 7:25-26). But even more, through this Son "purification for sins" was made. Because of his faithfulness, he is now exalted to the position of greatest honor, designated by the phrase "the right hand of God." Here, in a nutshell, is the christology of Hebrews: the preexistent Son of God is the agent of God's creation and revelation, as well as the one through whom the world is held together; in his human life he made purification for sins; and now he assumes a position of honor and authority. God gives life in all its forms through him; therefore, he is the "heir of all things." As the "heir," Jesus is the one who receives God's promises on behalf of and for human beings.

As Son, Jesus stands in contrast to the prophets (1:1-4), to angels (1:5-14), and to Moses (3:2). All these figures were agents of God's revelation to human beings, and Hebrews accepts the validity and importance of God's speaking through them, while stressing the surpassing greatness of the revelation through the Son. A puzzling feature for some of the book of Hebrews is its lengthy comparison of the Son with angels, designed to demonstrate the superiority of the Son.

The Son has a more excellent name (1:4) than do angels. That name is not specified, although it may be simply the designation "Son" that the author has in view (1:5). In any case, it is not simply the superiority of the name itself, but the superior dignity and worth of the one for whom the name stands that the author has in view. The author argues that the angels are ministering servants (1:7, 14) rather than those who are to be served, whereas the Son is to be worshiped by angels (1:6) and is in fact the agent of God's rule (1:8, 14). The Son, moreover, is eternal (1:8; 10-12). What has generated the author's insistence on the superiority of the Son to angels?

One theory is that the Christians to whom this word of exhortation was addressed were actually tempted to exalt angels above their status, and perhaps even to worship them. In the book of Revelation, for example, the seer John twice falls at the interpreting angel's feet and is cautioned to worship God alone (19:10; 22:9). In Colossians, Paul alludes cryptically to "the worship of angels." Such NT references, along with this data from Hebrews, have led some interpreters to suggest that the worship of angels was not unknown in early Judaism and Christianity. This might suggest that the Christians referred to in Hebrews were in danger of compromising their devotion to the "living God" with worship of other beings. But others have suggested that what Jews and Christians sought was participation in the angelic worship of God in heaven, such as is depicted in Revelation 4–5. Hence, the caution against "worship of angels" is a warning against seeking certain sorts of ecstatic religious experiences too zealously for their own sake.

A final suggestion, perhaps more probable in light of the development of traditions about angels and heavenly figures in the first century, including archangels, the Son of man, and various other heavenly beings, is that it was easy to think of Jesus as an angel, perhaps the chief of all angels. In fact, Melchizedek, to whom Jesus is later compared in this book, is thought by some scholars to be equated with the archangel Michael in texts from the Dead Sea Scrolls (especially 11Q Melchizedek). There are traditions of first-century Judaism that developed the statements in Exod 23:21 regarding the angel of the presence. God warns the people of Israel to listen to his angel: "Give heed to him and hearken to his voice, do not rebel against him, for he will not pardon your transgression; for my name is in him." One speculative apocalyptic text, *3 Enoch* 12:15, speaks of the angel Metatron as "the lesser YHWH," applying the statement of Exodus 23 regarding God's name quite literally, but retaining some contrast with God with the comparative term "lesser." The stress in Hebrews on the excellence of the name of the Son Jesus may have in view a contrast with the angel thought to bear the name of God. Philo speaks of the Logos as an angel. Justin Martyr, a second-century Christian author, calls Jesus an angel and speaks of the OT appearances of the "angel of the Lord" as the appearances of the Logos of God. But the author of Hebrews categorically denies the identification of Jesus as an angel. Jesus is no angel; he is the Son whom the angels serve.

Such is the rich and speculative world of Judaism and early Christianity that may lie behind Hebrews' desire to set the Son above the angels. But the author adduces yet one more function of angels: they were the mediators of the covenant of Sinai, the law. The belief that the law was given through angels appears also in Gal 3:19. That law, according to the author of Hebrews, was valid, and disobedience to it was punished (2:2). But Jesus proclaims a greater salvation, and that message of salvation through the Son is what the author heard from the followers of Jesus and

Angels and the Law

The idea that the law of Moses was given by God through angels comes to expression in both Gal 3:19 and Heb 2:2, and is found also in many Jewish documents of the first century. Philo, the first-century Jewish apologist of Alexandria, Egypt, writes that God must speak through mediators to human beings, who would be incapable of receiving his words otherwise.

These are called "demons" [i.e., "spirits" or "deities" who are not necessarily evil or satanic] by the other philosophers, but the sacred record is wont to call them "angels" or messengers, employing an apter title, for they both convey the biddings of the Father to His children and report the children's need to their Father. In accordance with this they are represented by the lawgiver as ascending and descending: not that God, who is already present in all directions, needs informants, but that it was a boon to us in our sad case to avail ourselves of the services of "words" acting on our behalf as mediators, so great is our awe and shuddering dread of the universal Monarch and the exceeding might of His sovereignty. It was our attainment of a conception of this that once made us address to one of those mediators the entreaty: "Speak thou to us, and let not God speak to us, lest haply we die" (Ex. xx.19). For should He, without employing ministers, hold out to us with His own hand, I do not say chastisements, but even benefits unmixed and exceeding great, we are incapable of receiving them. (*De Somniis* 1.141-43)

what he now reminds his readers of. The law given through angels was valid, but the message of salvation given through the Son is of surpassing value and worth. Therefore, "how shall we escape if we neglect such a great salvation?" (2:3), the author admonishes his readers. God's supreme act of salvation has been accomplished "in these last days" through his Son, not through any angel.

But this Son, through whom the world was made, who is worshiped by angels, and who bears a name more excellent than that of any angel, became "a little lower than the angels" for a period of time, "in order that he might taste death for everyone." Hebrews shares the incarnational christology of other authors of the NT, laying particular emphasis on the real but temporary subjection of the Son to the angels, which enabled him to suffer and die for humankind. The course of his

---

The *Testament of Dan* 6.2 speaks of angels who intercede and mediate for Israel: "Draw near to God and to the angel who intercedes for you, because he is the mediator between God and men for the peace of Israel" *(OTP)*.

According to the Midrash on the Psalms, the angels interceded for the life of Israel so that God might give the Torah to the living:

A bounteous rain (Ps 68:10). When the ministering angels saw that the breath of life had flown out of the children of Israel, they asked the Holy One, blessed be He: "To whom wilt Thou give the Torah, to the dead or to the quick?" At once the Holy One, blessed be He, waved out rains of life over the children of Israel so that they should receive the Torah without abounding spirit.

An early Christian author attributes this mediatorial function to Michael:

And the great and glorious angel is Michael, who has power over this people and governs them; for this is he who put the law into the hearts of those who believe. Therefore he looks after those to whom he gave it to see if they have really kept it. (*Shepherd of Hermas, Similitudes* 8.3.3)

life also distinguishes the Son from the angels, for in his full participation in human life he also becomes like those on whose behalf he suffered and died. In this stress on Jesus' identification with human beings we find one of Hebrews' most characteristic emphases: Jesus is both like and yet also unlike the children of God, whose humanity he shares. Both his likeness and his difference enable him to become the one who brings "many children to glory," as the "pioneer of their salvation" (2:10).

20.4. JESUS, THE PIONEER AND PERFECTER OF FAITH

Hebrews uses a number of distinctive terms to speak of Jesus' saving work as opening a path to God or of Jesus serving as a guide who charts the way for others to follow. The first such term, *archēgos* (2:10; 12:2), is variously rendered in modern English translations as "pioneer" (RSV, NRSV), "author" (NIV), or "captain" (KJV; these versions use "author," "leader," or "prince" for the same word in Acts 3:15; 5:31). Jesus' role as "pioneer of faith" has two aspects: First, Jesus is like his brothers and sisters (2:11-12), sharing "flesh and blood," (2:14) — "like his brothers and sisters in every respect" (2:17). Not only does Hebrews assume and stress the true humanity of Jesus, but it is one of the few NT books that make his humanity theologically important. Jesus' role as "pioneer" is exercised from within the humanity he shares with his brothers and sisters. He is not ashamed to stand with "the descendants of Abraham," to call them "brothers and sisters," and to represent them before God on their behalf.

But, second, as pioneer of faith, Jesus has gone on ahead of his brothers and sisters to glory (2:10) by dying to destroy the power of death and so bring freedom to all who were enslaved to death (2:14-15). The implication is clear: Jesus has blazed a trail that his brothers and sisters are to follow. Because he has endured suffering, died, and been exalted to a position of honor, the pathway is open for others to follow to life in glory with God. In other words, Jesus has done what his brothers and sisters could not do for themselves. Although he has exercised this role from within the common humanity shared with them, the very fact that his life and death liberate his brothers and sisters from the power of death and bring them to God characterizes the unique role that his life and death have. As we shall see, this aspect of Jesus' life and work are particularly summarized under the title "high priest."

Other terms in Hebrews also stress Jesus' role as inaugurating God's great salvation. He is the "source of salvation" (*aitios*, 5:9). Using athletic imagery, Hebrews speaks of Jesus as a "forerunner" (*prodromos*, 6:20) who has entered into the true inner sanctuary ahead of his brothers and sisters and on their behalf. Finally, Jesus is pictured as "the great Shepherd of the sheep" (13:20; cf. 1 Pet 2:25; John

10:1-18). The combined point of these images is to underscore not only the distinctive role of Jesus in bringing God's eschatological salvation, but also his role of bringing human beings to God. Thus while Hebrews stresses the final climactic act of salvation, which God effects through the Son, this act does not simply end God's work but rather opens up a path to the future. The "last hour" thus initiates a whole new era, and into this era Jesus serves as leader, pioneer, forerunner, and shepherd. Those who would be his disciples are therefore depicted not only as the beneficiaries of what he has done but also as pilgrims who must follow attentively and intentionally the path he has charted.

In his description of the pilgrim people of God, the author of Hebrews compares and contrasts Jesus' disciples to the children of Israel who wandered in the wilderness. They, too, had a guide, but Hebrews draws on biblical texts to portray them as rebellious (3:16), unbelieving (3:12, 19), disobedient (4:6, 11), and hard of heart (3:13, 15; 4:10). Therefore, they did not attain the goals they sought. They were unable to enter the Promised Land and cease from their wanderings. In other words, they did not attain rest (3:11; 4:3). Because Jesus' disciples have such a superior leader, the stakes are higher, and those who would follow him must be careful not to duplicate the disobedience and sins of the wilderness generation but to persist in the pilgrimage to enter God's promised rest.

20.5. THE PILGRIM PEOPLE OF GOD

The description of God's people as a "pilgrim people of God" aptly suits both the Israelites who, following Moses and then Joshua, wandered in the wilderness until they reached the Promised Land, as well as Christians who, following Jesus, have as their goal and hope a heavenly country prepared for them by God (11:15). The generation of Israelites that left Egypt and followed Moses was not permitted to enter the Promised Land. A subsequent generation under the leadership of Joshua was permitted to go in, but Hebrews takes its point of departure from the generation that failed to attain what it sought because of its disobedience. Specifically, our author turns to the Psalms to discover an account of their disobedience and God's judgment as a warning to his own readers.

The argument from Psalm 95, the second of the six primary texts that form the literary and theological framework of Hebrews, draws primarily from the portion of the psalm that recounts God's judgment on the disobedience of the people. But our author makes much of one word in the Psalm. It addresses its readers with the admonition, "Today if you hear his voice, do not harden your hearts as in the rebellion" (Heb 3:15, 4:7). Since our author assumes that the Psalm was written by David and, hence, written long after the actual wilderness wanderings (4:6-7, 8), he concludes that the "rest" of which God speaks still remained when Psalm 95 was composed. In other words, it was still "today" when the psalm was written, and it is still "today" for his Christian readers (3:13-15). Those who will enter God's rest are those who remain faithful to Jesus their leader and so become "partners of Christ, if only we hold our first confidence firm to the end" (3:6, 14).

Neither Moses nor Joshua is denigrated, but Jesus is nevertheless shown to be superior to both. Moses, indeed, is called "faithful in all God's house" (3:2; cf. Num 12:7); but his role was that of servant (3:5), whereas Christ is the son of the house. The contrast between a servant or slave in the house and the one who is the son and heir is also found in John 8:34-36 and Galatians 4. In Heb 4:8, Jesus is contrasted with Joshua, whose name in Greek would also be *Iēsous,* or Jesus. Joshua was unable to give the Israelites rest (4:8) but those who have believed in Jesus have entered that rest (4:1-3) and now must maintain their confidence. Although the author uses numerous exhortations to "hold fast" and "stand firm," the picture of discipleship that he paints is anything but static. The life of the disciple is portrayed not as standing still and holding tight but as adventuresome journeying with Jesus, the "trailblazer of faith."

And indeed faith is the appropriate and necessary commitment for the pilgrim people of God. Hab 2:4 is the key passage in this regard, and the key chapter in Hebrews is ch. 11, the catalog of heroes of the faith. Paul cites Hab 2:4 twice (Rom 1:17; Gal 3:11) to establish that God's righteousness is received through trust or faith, not through obedience to the law. But the author of Hebrews cites it for a different reason. His version of Hab 2:3-4 — "In a very little while, the one who is coming will come and will not delay; but my righteous one will live by faith. My soul takes no pleasure in anyone who shrinks back" — is somewhat closer to the Septuagint than to the Hebrew text. What he is most interested in is the contrast between "living by faith" and "shrinking back," which suggests that in Hebrews the Greek word *pistis* is best understood as "faithfulness." Hebrews has in view a solid and firm commitment that induces one to press on rather than to "shrink back," in order to attain those things and that world that are not yet seen (11:1-3).

From the citation of Habbakuk, the author then turns to a long list of examples of faith. Beginning with Abel, the second son of Adam, the survey includes many worthies such as Noah, Abraham, Isaac, Moses, Gideon, David, Samuel, and others who in faith looked forward to receiving what was promised to them. But — and this is one of the chief reasons for which they are all mentioned — they all died before receiving what had been promised to them, namely, the heavenly country that God has prepared for them. In other words, they lived in faith, not receiving the promises, which God has yet to fulfill. Therefore, Hebrews exhorts its readers, who are "surrounded by so great a cloud of witnesses," to "run with perseverance the race that is set before us, looking to Jesus the pioneer and perfecter of our faith" (12:1). Through this exhortation the author points to both continuity and discontinuity between the Israelites and disciples of Jesus. Like faithful women and men in Israel's past, Christians are to "run the race" before them with perseverance. The great difference, however, is that Jesus is both the pioneer and *perfecter* of faith. That is, he can and will bring the wandering saints of God to their goal or destiny.

This idea of perfection must not be misunderstood. The verbal form is used nine times, three times of the Son who is made perfect or is perfected (2:10; 5:9; 7:28), three times of the law, which cannot make perfect (7:19, 9:9, 11), and three times of the saints of God who are made perfect (10:14; 11:40; 12:23). So the idea is primarily of a process, of being made complete, whole, fit, or adequate to a task or for a particular end. It is clear that moral perfection is not in view since Christ, who is said to be without sin, can also be spoken of as being made perfect through suffering (2:10, 5:9) to serve as High Priest for those who are likewise suffering. Similarly, Hebrews does not say that the law is imperfect, but that it cannot make perfect: it could not bring all the saints of old to their promised rest, to the better country, to the heavenly city which they sought (11:10; 13:14). It cannot make those under it complete or whole. The gifts and sacrifices offered up in accordance with the injunctions of the law cannot "perfect the conscience" (9:9). But through Christ, the great High Priest, a sacrifice is offered that can so purify and hence perfect the conscience (9:11-14). This argument regarding the superior high priesthood of Christ is distinct to Hebrews and baffling to modern readers, for whom the rituals of sacrifice, the details of the tabernacle, and the furnishing of the altar carry little emotional appeal or theological persuasiveness. Yet in spite of the initial strangeness of the argument, it contains one of the clearest and strongest statements in the NT of Jesus' humanity as essential for winning salvation for humankind.

20.6. "SUCH A GREAT HIGH PRIEST"

The first reference to Jesus as "high priest" occurs at Heb 2:17, and the image subsequently occupies much of the book's christology. How the term came to be applied to Jesus has been the source of some speculation. Hebrews obviously knows the problem of speaking of Jesus as a priest since he did not come from the priestly line, the tribe of Levi (7:14). Therefore, he refers to Jesus' priesthood as belonging to the "order of Melchizedek." Nevertheless, precisely because the OT says so little about Melchizedek's exercise of his priestly office, most of the features of Jesus' priesthood are drawn from the functions of the High Priest as one who intercedes on behalf of the people for forgiveness of sins before God, and particularly so on the annual Day of Atonement.

Two adjectives, found in conjunction with the first reference to Jesus as High Priest, characterize his work in this regard: he is merciful and faithful. Indeed, as

Melchizedek

The mysterious figure of Melchizedek appears in Genesis 14 as a "priest of God Most High" who blessed Abraham.

> After [Abraham's] return from the defeat of Chedorlaomer and the kings who were with him, the king of Sodom went out to meet him at the Valley of Shaveh (that is, the King's Valley). And King Melchizedek of Salem brought out bread and wine; he was priest of God Most High. He blessed him and said,
>
> > "Blessed be Abram by God Most High,
> >   maker of heaven and earth;
> > and blessed be God Most High,
> >   who has delivered your enemies into your hand!"
>
> And Abram gave him one tenth of everything. (Gen 14:17-20, NRSV)

First-century Jewish sources show that the author of Hebrews was not the first to speculate on the significance of this priestly figure. Philo saw Melchizedek as ultimately a symbol of the one guided by "right principle."

> Melchizedek, too, has God made both king of peace, for that is the meaning of "Salem," and His own priest. He has not fashioned beforehand any deed of his, but produces him to begin with as such a king, peaceable and worthy of His own priesthood. For he is entitled "the righteous king," and a "king" is a thing at enmity with a despot, the one being the author of laws, the other of lawlessness. So mind, the despot, decrees for both soul and body right and hurtful decrees working grievous woes, conduct, I mean, such as wickedness prompts, and free indulgence of the passions. But the king in the first

we have already seen, faithfulness is to be the hallmark of the pilgrim people of God, and in this regard Jesus both serves as an example of faithful obedience to God and may also be trusted to exercise his office of priest faithfully. He can be trusted. He is faithful over God's house. That is, he has faithfully exercised the rule entrusted to him (3:6). Indeed, he has been tested and found faithful (2:18; 4:15;

place resorts to persuasion rather than decrees, and in the next place issues directions such as to enable a vessel, the living being I mean, to make life's voyage successfully, piloted by the good pilot, who is right principle. Let the despot's title therefore be ruler of war, the king's prince of peace, of Salem, and let him offer to the soul food full of joy and gladness; for he brings bread and wine. (*Legum Allegoriae* 3.79-80)

The Dead Sea Scrolls yielded a text now called 11QMelchizedek, which presents Melchizedek as the agent of the liberation promised in the Jubilee year of Leviticus. He is identified both with the figure of *elohim*, understood as a judge, in Psalm 82, and with the proclaimer of Isa 52:7.

. . . And concerning that which He said, In [this] year of Jubilee [each of you shall return to his property; and likewise, And this is the manner of release:] every creditor shall release that which he has lent [to his neighbour. He shall not exact it of his neighbour and his brother], for God's release [has been proclaimed]. [And it will be proclaimed at] the end of days concerning the captives as [he said, To proclaim liberty to the captives. Its interpretation is that he] will assign them to the Sons of Heaven and to the inheritance of Melchizedek; f[or He will cast] their [lot] amid the po[rtions of Melchize]dek, who will return them there and will proclaim to them liberty, forgiving them [the wrongdoings] of all their iniquities. . . . This is the moment of the Year of Grace for Melchizedek. [And h]e will, by his strength, judge the holy ones of God, executing judgement as it is written concerning him in the Songs of David, who said, ELOHIM has taken his place in the divine council; in the midst of the gods he holds judgment. . . . This is the day of [Peace/Salvation] concerning which [God] spoke [through Isa]iah the prophet, who said, [How] beautiful upon the mountains are the feet of the messenger who proclaims peace, who brings good news, who proclaims salvation, who says to Zion: our ELOHIM reigns. (Vermes, 500-501)

5:8-10), so that one of the noteworthy descriptions of him is that he "in every respect has been tested as we are, yet without sin" (4:15). In other words, he has passed the test. He does not need to offer sacrifice for his own sins (7:26-27; 9:6), as does the High Priest of the Levitical system, since he is without sin. In this regard, as High Priest Jesus is not like his brothers and sisters.

Yet in exercising his high-priestly office he demonstrates also that he is merciful, a theme that is reiterated in other ways throughout Hebrews. He has suffered and so can help those who are tested (2:18). He is able to sympathize with human weakness (4:15). From him one may receive mercy and grace in time of need (4:16). He suffered (5:8) and endured hostility (13:3). He lived the life that his brothers and sisters lived. His suffering and experience of human weakness makes him a High Priest who can sympathize with humankind and intercede faithfully on their behalf. Thus his likeness to human beings is also particularly stressed as a feature that makes him a merciful and "perfect" High Priest.

The extensive description of Jesus' priesthood according to the "order of Melchizedek" (ch. 7) is based on Psalm 110, the third of the six OT texts listed above as key texts for Hebrews. It is argued from the psalm that this priesthood is superior to that of the Levitical order because, since Abraham paid tithes to Melchizedek, all Abraham's descendants, including the Levitical priests, did so as well, because, and this is closer to the real point, the Levitical priesthood could not bring people to perfection (7:11), and because the priesthood of Melchizedek is indestructible (7:16), exercised forever (7:17, 21), and held permanently (7:24). Therefore, Jesus is able "for all time" to make intercession on behalf of the saints. He offered one sacrifice for all time, accomplishing his work "once for all" (Greek *hapax*, 9:26, 28; 10:10, 14). His sacrifice is superior because it does not have to be offered repeatedly. Therefore, his is a better priesthood.

The description of Jesus' work as "better" or some aspect of his ministry as "better" or as inaugurating that which is "better" is found in Hebrews thirteen times. The description of Jesus' work and ministry as "better" belongs within the eschatological framework of Hebrews. Because it is the "last days," the time of God's climactic fulfillment of promised salvation, that salvation and all that comes with it are necessarily better. The fifth key OT text is drawn from Jeremiah 31 and speaks of God renewing his covenant with his people and underlies the argument that what God has given in Christ is "better" than all that has been given before.

As we saw earlier, the Son is better than angels (1:4). Christians have a better hope (7:19), a better covenant (7:22), better promises (8:6), and better sacrifices (9:23) because of Christ's superior priesthood. Likewise, they are heading for a better possession, a better country, that is, a heavenly destination rather than an earthly country (10:34; 11:16). What Christians have is better than what came before, but what they do not see is better than what they already have. Christ is the better High Priest, because he is sinless (4:15) and eternal (7:3, 16, 23-25) and belongs to a priesthood of a better order and offers a superior sacrifice (7:27; 9:13) to seal a superior covenant (8:6-13) in a superior sanctuary (9:11).

The contrast between that superior sanctuary and the earthly tabernacle made with human hands (9:1, 24) takes up a good part of chs. 8–9. Christ did not enter into an earthly tabernacle but into heaven itself (9:24). The earthly taberna-

cle is the rather elaborate tent that the Israelites were commanded to make (Exodus 25–27) as a symbol of the dwelling or presence of God among them. Hebrews makes the point that that tabernacle was a copy of the true heavenly sanctuary (8:5). This at once validates the reality of God's presence with the Israelites, as depicted by the Mosaic tabernacle, but it also shows that the tabernacle did not represent the fullness of God's presence. For the heavenly tabernacle is neither made with hands, nor does it belong to this age (9:9, 11, 24); in fact, it is not a tent at all. Through Jesus' ministry, believers may enter the heavenly sanctuary, Mount Zion, the heavenly city, and so into the fullness of God's presence (12:22).

To be sure, these arguments regarding the superiority of Christ, his sacrifices, the heavenly tabernacle, his priesthood, and so on are statements of the author's deepest convictions about Christ and are not susceptible of proof in the ordinary sense. But through these arguments the author lays bare his strongest convictions regarding God's salvation in Christ. God cannot do more than he has done through Jesus his Son. Therefore, Christians are not to lose heart in the midst of their trials and tribulations, but are to persevere on their journey, "looking to Jesus, the pioneer and perfecter of faith."

Relief depiction of the Tabernacle and the Ark of the Covenant from the third- and fourth-century synagogue at Capernaum *(Israel Department of Antiquities and Museums)*

FOR FURTHER READING

Harold W. Attridge, *A Commentary on the Epistle to the Hebrews* (Hermeneia; Philadelphia: Fortress, 1989)

F. F. Bruce, *The Epistle to the Hebrews* (revised ed., New International Commentary on the New Testament; Grand Rapids: Eerdmans, 1990)

George W. Buchanan, *To the Hebrews* (Anchor Bible; Garden City: Doubleday, 1972)

David A. DeSilva, *Perseverance in Gratitude: A Socio-Rhetorical Commentary on the Epistle "to the Hebrews"* (Grand Rapids: Eerdmans, 2000)

Paul Ellingworth, *Commentary on Hebrews* (New International Greek Testament Commentary; Grand Rapids: Eerdmans, 1993)

William L. Lane, *Hebrews,* 2 vols. (Word Biblical Commentary; Dallas: Word, 1991)

Barnabas Lindars, *The Theology of the Letter to the Hebrews* (Cambridge: Cambridge University Press, 1991)

21. James

While often cherished for its "practical wisdom," the NT book known as James has never been able to shake off the judgment of Protestant Reformer Martin Luther that, in comparison to books such as Romans and Galatians, the Gospel of John, and 1 Peter, James was "really an epistle of straw." Those documents were to be prized as the "true kernel and marrow of all the books," because they would "show you Christ" and "teach you all that is necessary and salvatory for you to know." By comparison, James had "nothing of the nature of the gospel about it."

That Luther's harsh evaluation of James as a book bereft of the gospel and of Christ still lingers on in modern interpretations can easily be documented. Interpreters persist in labeling James a Jewish book with but a thin Christian veneer, the most indistinctly Christian document in the NT. Even the assessment of James as a book of practical wisdom reflects Luther's judgment of its shortcomings, inasmuch as it implies that James lacks any genuine theological insight or foundation, though it can be pressed into service a book with "practical" guidelines for everyday life. This view clearly privileges theological argument over practical counsel, "hearing the word" over "doing the word." Ironically, this is precisely the separation that James itself decries. But the tenacity of his witness has never completely silenced his critics.

Questions of one sort or another about James can be traced back farther than the Reformation. The Muratorian Canon, a list of books accepted as canonical that is typically dated to Rome in the middle of the second century (see pp. 600-601 below), does not list James as part of the canon. Writing in the early fourth century, the church historian Eusebius still refers to James as one of the "disputed" books, although he himself deems it apostolic and orthodox and states that it is recognized or accepted by many. The late fourth-century Latin church father and

Greetings (1:1)
The place of suffering and trials in the Christian life
    (1:2-4, 12-16; 5:10-11)
The gift of divine wisdom (1:5-8, 17-18; 3:13-18)
Warnings to the rich and comfort for the poor (1:9-11; 4:13-16; 5:1-6)
Putting faith into practice (1:19-27; 2:14-26)
Impartiality and love of neighbor (2:1-13; 4:11-12)
Use and abuse of the tongue (3:1-12)
Patience, prayer, and endurance (5:7-11, 13-20)

translator of the Vulgate, Jerome, asserted that James had been accepted into the church "little by little."

Who was James? And what sort of letter did he produce such that it could be judged, on the one hand, to merit a place in the canon and, on the other, to be an epistle full of straw?

21.1. "JAMES, A SERVANT OF GOD"

In the prescript of the letter, the author identifies himself simply as "James, a servant of God and of the Lord Jesus Christ." But just this self-designation raises the question of James's identity, for, according to tradition, this is the James called by Paul "the brother of the Lord" (Gal 1:19), who appears elsewhere in the NT as the leader of the early church in Jerusalem. Yet the author of this epistle never acknowledges his fraternal relationship to Jesus, his apostolic commission or role, or his authority with respect to the churches to whom he writes. Since referring to any of these relationships or roles would likely have strengthened the authority of his epistle, the absence of any such reference does raise questions about his identity.

And yet his reticence may actually give us a clue to his identity. The terseness of his self-identification as "James" suggests that he could simply call himself "James" and expect immediate recognition of his identity. Few candidates known to us seem to be viable contenders for this honor other than James, the brother of Jesus. Of course, our roster of possible candidates is limited to the pages of the NT. That there were other important figures named "James" that we do not know cannot be ruled out. But James's acceptance into the canon "little by little" likely assumes the early church's identification of James as "the brother of the Lord."

The Brothers of Jesus

The NT mentions Jesus' brothers in various places:

> On the sabbath he began to teach in the synagogue, and many who heard him were astounded. They said, "Where did this man get all this? What is this wisdom that has been given to him? What deeds of power are being done by his hands! Is not this the carpenter, the son of Mary and brother of James and Joses and Judas and Simon, and are not his sisters here with us?" (Mark 6:2-3, NRSV)

> Then his mother and his brothers came; and standing outside, they sent to him and called him. A crowd was sitting around him; and they said to him, "Your mother and your brothers and sisters are outside, asking for you." And he replied, "Who are my mother and my brothers?" And looking at those who sat around him, he said, "Here are my mother and my brothers!" (Mark 3:31-34, NRSV)

> So his brothers said to him, "Leave here and go to Judea so that your disciples also may see the works you are doing; for no one who wants to be widely known acts in secret. If you do these things, show yourself to the world." (For not even his brothers believed in him.) (John 7:3-5, NRSV)

There are scholars who argue that although the letter is attributed to this James, it was actually written by another, later, figure in the church, a disciple or admirer of James who sought to make his teaching or witness available to later generations. Others have suggested that an otherwise unknown editor has taken material from James and reworked it into its present form — a suggestion already put forward by Jerome. Such arguments typically rest on the alleged difficulty of attributing James's literary polish, grammatical style, rhetorical flourishes, and affinities with Greco-Roman moralists to a Galilean from a family of artisans whose native tongue was Aramaic. As we shall see, very similar arguments are raised against Petrine authorship of 1 Peter. However, Peter's reference to an amanuensis, Sylvanus (1 Pet 1:1; 5:12), has often been taken to alleviate some of the problems in attributing that letter to Peter. James does not explicitly mention use of an amanuensis or refer to any coauthors, as Paul does. Yet this silence does not rule out the possibility that the author had such help, or even that someone unknown to us gathered and shaped material originally from James into its present form, aiming to make James's voice available to subsequent generations. Too little is known of James to allow us to dismiss out of hand the possibility that he stands behind this epistle in some significant fashion.

Jerome on James

The church father Jerome reports these traditions about James:

> James, who is called the brother of the Lord, surnamed the Just, the son of Joseph by another wife, as some think, but, as appears to me, the son of Mary sister of the mother of our Lord of whom John makes mention in his book, after our Lord's passion at once ordained bishop by the apostles of Jerusalem, wrote a single epistle, which is reckoned among the seven Catholic Epistles and even this is claimed by some to have been published by some one else under his name, and gradually, as time went on, to have gained authority. (*De Viris Illustribus* 2)

What we do know of James comes primarily from references in the Pauline letters and Acts. In 1 Cor 15:5-7, Paul singles James out as the witness of a resurrection appearance of the risen Jesus. James figures most prominently in Galatians, where in recounting the story of his conversation Paul speaks of going up to Jerusalem, meeting with James and Peter (Gal 1:18-19), and receiving the right hand of fellowship from them and from John, as they sent him to the Gentiles (Gal 2:9). Later, Paul relates that "certain men came from James" to Antioch (Gal 2:12). Paul does not spell out their exact relationship to James or the exact reason for their visit. But their appearance caused Peter to withdraw from eating together with Gentiles. Peter clearly respected James's authority, and his withdrawal from table fellowship with Gentiles indicates that he assumed that James held a more conservative stance with respect to the ritual requirements of the law. According to Acts, James was a leader of the early Jerusalem church (Acts 12:17; 15:13) who at the Jerusalem conference (Acts 15) laid out the basic requirements to which Gentiles ought to be held and who later appealed to Paul to demonstrate to the Jews in Jerusalem his faithful observance of the law (21:18-25). In these reports from Paul and in Acts, scholars have found evidence of James's conservative Jewish Christian stance toward the law.

In this regard it is striking that Josephus, the first-century Jewish historian and apologist, recounts that Ananus, a Sadducean high priest, had James the brother of Jesus, and others, accused as breakers of the law and stoned to death, leading the citizens of Jerusalem to complain to King Agrippa (*Ant.* 20.200). Remarkably, Josephus's report speaks of James as a *lawbreaker* — exactly the charge that, according to Acts, James urged Paul to show to be false! Josephus's account does not square particularly well with the time-honored assumptions of NT scholars that James was a "conservative Jewish Christian" with respect to the law who had sharp conflicts with Paul, the champion of the radical law-free gospel for Gentile Christians. How does the data of the letter of James bear on this reconstruction?

Josephus on James

In his *Jewish Antiquities* (20.199-201), Josephus, the first-century Jewish historian, writes of the death of James:

> The younger Ananus, who, as we have said, had been appointed to the high priesthood, was rash in his temper and unusually daring. He followed the school of the Sadducees, who are indeed more heartless than any of the other Jews, as I have already explained, when they sit in judgment. Possessed of such a character, Ananus thought that he had a favorable opportunity because Festus was dead and Albinus was still on the way. And so he convened the judges of the Sanhedrin and brought before them a man named James, the brother of Jesus who was called the Christ, and certain others. He accused them of having transgressed the law and delivered them up to be stoned. Those of the inhabitants of the city who were considered the most fair-minded and who were strict in observance of the law were offended at this.

21.2. JAMES AND JEWISH CHRISTIANITY

"Jewish Christianity" is an equivocal term, capable of application to more than one part of the early Christian movement. In its broadest sense, "Jewish Christianity" refers to any of the forms of Christian faith held by Jews who came to acknowledge Jesus as the Christ, the Messiah. In this sense of the term, all the earliest adherents of the Jesus movement were "Jewish Christians." The disciples of Jesus, including Peter and John, Jesus' brothers, including James and Jude, and Paul, the "apostle to the Gentiles," were all Jewish Christians. But Paul's churches consisted mainly of Gentiles who had come to Christian faith and so could be distinguished from Jewish Christian congregations not only because they were shaped by the Pauline gospel, but also because by heritage and birth their adherents came from among the Gentiles of the Mediterranean world. Finally, with reference to the early centuries of the church, "Jewish Christianity" refers to Christian movements of the second and third century, such as the Ebionites, whose continued adherence to various facets of the law, including circumcision and purity regulations, put them outside the mainstream orthodox and increasingly Gentile church.

The estimation and role of the law figure prominently in defining "Jewish Christianity." But from certain perspectives, James might have been viewed with suspicion for failing to champion the distinctive practices — circumcision, food laws, and Sabbath observance. He thus could have been accused of sacrificing just those observances given to Israel by God that marked and assured its continued distinctive identity. To be sure, James does evidence a high and positive view of the law when he speaks of "the perfect law, the law of liberty" (1:25) and warns against transgressing and ignoring the law (2:9-11; 4:11). Yet while James speaks of "keeping the law," he never insists on observance of precisely those aspects of the law that created conflict in the early church, including circumcision, purity and dietary regulations, and Sabbath-keeping.

Instead, in the epistle of James we find the epitome of the law in the command to love one's neighbor, as in Jesus' interpretation and proclamation of the law. James's designation of the "royal law" *(nomos basilikos)* echoes Jesus' proclamation of the kingdom *(basileia)* with the double love command at its center. Like Jesus and the prophets before him, James thus radicalized the application of the law by crystallizing its thrust in terms of love and honor of one's neighbor. Clearly this way of formulating the heart of the law moved inexorably toward a redefinition of the very term "Israel." For if Israel were no longer to be distinguished by those traditional markers of circumcision, Sabbath-keeping, and food laws, which were the notable signs of its faithful observance of the law, how would it be defined? James's answer to this implicit question is that "Israel" is to be defined by its faithfulness to the law interpreted in terms of the command to love one's neighbor, in obedience to the Lord, Jesus, in whom are gathered "the twelve tribes in the Dispersion."

21.3. "TO THE TWELVE TRIBES IN THE DISPERSION"

The recipients of the letter are designated as "the twelve tribes in the Dispersion." At first glance, this seems to refer to Jews living outside the Promised Land. The phrase "the twelve tribes" continued to be used as a metaphor for Israel as the people of God, long after twelve distinctly identifiable tribes were more of a memory and ideal than a visible reality (*2 Bar* 77:2; 78:4; *Pss. Sol.* 17:26-28; Josephus, *Ant.* 1.221; Matt 19:28 par. Luke 22:29-30; Rev 7:5-8; 21:12). However, the hopes lingered that the dispersed people would be gathered from out of the Dispersion. In some Jewish writings such restoration is thought of as part of the work of a future king from the line of David, while in other documents such hopes focused on God's activity without any particular human intermediary.

The use of this typical designation for Israel in a letter written by someone who acknowledges Jesus as Messiah and Lord raises the question of the identity of the epistle's addressees. In particular, two interrelated questions arise: (1) Does the designation of the readers as "the twelve tribes" indicate that they were Jewish Christians, or should it be taken figuratively as referring to all Christians as the "true" Israel or people of God? (2) Should the reference to them being "scattered among the nations" be taken literally as a geographical "exile," or metaphorically, signifying that their true home is their heavenly home and their dwelling on earth a kind of "exile" or sojourn in an alien land? Although these are the options typically suggested, they are not mutually exclusive. If the readers are understood to be Jewish Christians, as is typically the case, that does not settle the question whether they were "dispersed" or distant from their native land, from their true heavenly home, or from both. On the other hand, neither does the use of "Jewish" terminology settle the question of the identity of the readers, since the NT elsewhere gives ample evidence of the redefinition of the people of the Messiah, both Jew and Gentile, as bearing the marks and responsibilities of the "Israel of God." Striking parallels exist between James's designation of his readers and 1 Peter's ("to the exiles of the Dispersion," 1:1), and that epistle goes on to apply language used of Israel in the OT ("a royal priesthood, a holy nation, God's own people," 2:9-10; cf. Exod 19:6; Hos 1:8-10) to a Christian community that clearly included Gentiles.

So although the letter's address alone does not settle the question of its readers' identity, when taken with other evidence, it strongly suggests that its readers included Jewish Christians, even if perhaps they were not all Jewish. To be sure, they are *messianists,* as the identification of Jesus as "Lord and Christ" has already made clear, and so they are an "Israel" whose hopes have been fulfilled in the coming of the Messiah. The use of "the twelve tribes" as a self-designation by an avowedly messianic sect would clearly indicate that the group believed that the restoration of Israel had begun.

The other evidence for the identification of James's readers as Jewish Christians consists of the indirect testimony of the letter itself. Its affinities with Jewish wisdom literature, respect for the law, resolutely theocentric ethic, and use of phrases such as "synagogue" for the congregation (2:2) are at least compatible with the theory of a Jewish Christian readership. Moreover, the sorts of issues with which James deals differ markedly from the substance of many a Pauline letter. Paul dealt mainly with Gentiles, or with congregations with a significant proportion of Gentiles, who not only had to be taught the Christian faith but also socialized into the convictions and morality that had long been part of the fabric of Israel's corporate life. Hence, Paul deals in his letters with issues of sexual morality, idolatry, relationship to pagans and to social customs of the Hellenistic world, the relationship of the law to the Spirit and Christian behavior, and even the nature of the resurrection. James, on the other hand, reflects few of these concerns. His voice sounds much more like the prophets of the OT, who warned Israel against lip-service to Yahweh, cheating the poor, defrauding widows and orphans, and trusting in one's own success and riches. The "Jewishness" of James turns out on closer inspection not to distinguish the document from that which is distinctly Christian, but to align it with the prophets of the OT and the teaching of Jesus. Given the portrayal of James in the NT, the contents of the letter, and the address to the readers, it seems best to conclude that James was writing to a group of Jewish Christian readers.

Beyond that general identification, it is difficult to determine more specifically the social location or situation within the congregation's life that provided the occasion for this epistle. While most ancient Greek manuscripts designate this document "the epistle of James," some add the adjective "catholic," meaning "general" or "universal," to qualify "epistle." This small addition arose from the letter's lack of specific reference to persons, places, incidents, or relationships that might serve to identify its readers. And if the letter in some way represents both the teaching of James and the work of a later collector or editor, it would be quite difficult to give a precise picture of the readers of the final edition of this material.

Still, the letter does seem to be written with specific readers with a particular set of problems or concerns in mind. On the one hand, the injunctions of the letter have in view some who are rich and powerful, warning them against their continued self-indulgence, favoritism, and neglect of the poor. On the other hand, some of the readers are poor, oppressed by those with power and privilege, and in need of encouragement and exhortation to persevere in the face of adversity. Both groups are admonished to preserve peace and love in their communal life, although the warnings against the rich have an entirely different tenor than the exhortations to the poor. James can be both prophet, warning of the coming doom of those who fail in their obligations to their humbler brothers and sisters, as well as pastor, encouraging those who are struggling and suffering. One detects James's pastoral stance in his frequent references to his readers as "brothers and sisters" and "my beloved." He exhorts his readers as fellow sojourners out of his sense of communal responsibility and commitment. As "the twelve tribes of the Dispersion," Christian sojourners on a pilgrimage home, they are encouraged and exhorted to persevere on that journey together.

21.4. THE GENRE OF JAMES

As already mentioned, ancient manuscripts of James entitle it an "epistle." The opening verses of James, with their terse greeting typical of Hellenistic letters, seem to confirm that description. Yet beyond that prescript, James has few features testifying to its epistolary character. It lacks any sort of formal closing and signature (but cf. 1 John), any personal greetings, the names of any members of the congregation(s) addressed, or references to specific present situations or past events. It betrays no evidence of the nature or duration of the relationship between James and his readers. In other words, James is hardly a personal letter of the sort known to us from other specimens in the NT or the Hellenistic world. In other respects, James differs from the apostolic epistles of Paul, with their assertions of apostolic authority and intricate theological arguments for his understanding of the gospel and its implications. James does not elevate his status or authority, a lacuna that some Greek manuscripts sought helpfully to rectify by introducing the term "apostle" or even "the holy apostle" following "James." Outside the letter's opening, James never asserts his apostolic authority, refers to his past or present labors, or cites personal circumstances to motivate his readers. Perhaps this is to say no more than James is not Paul!

In terms of its form, James's most striking affinities are not with the Pauline letters but with moral instruction and wisdom literature of both the Jewish and Greco-Roman world. Greco-Roman moral treatises intended to instruct one toward the goals of virtue, conceived of in terms of a well-ordered life marked by virtues such as control of one's emotions, speech, and conduct. The virtuous life could even be framed in "theological" terms by relating the life of the virtuous person to God. For example, the philosopher Plato urges "moderate conduct" since it is "dear to God" and bears out the maxim that "like is dear to like" (*Laws*, 716D-E). Numerous other points of overlap between James and the Greco-Roman moralists can be adduced. Testing proves the virtue of the "wise" *(sophos)* person (Jas 1:2), who can be called a "friend of God," a term associated in the OT with Moses and in Jewish thought with Abraham (Exod 33:11; 2 Chron 20:7; Jas 2:23). The life of the virtuous person is marked by self-control, especially of one's speech (1:19; 3:1-12) and passion and desire (4:1). Congruity between the principles to which one holds and one's concrete conduct is expected. Images such as reining in one's tongue or passions as one controls a horse, guiding a ship with a small rudder, and the mirror as a metaphor for moral self-reflection (1:23-24) are features of James seen in Hellenistic treatises as well. These themes and metaphors are of particular interest because they serve in both James and Hellenistic moral treatises to sketch the portrait of a truly "wise" person as the self-disciplined person.

But there are significant differences as well, which lead us to consideration of the wisdom literature such as one finds in the books of Proverbs in the OT and Sirach and Wisdom in the Apocrypha. James shares a number of similar themes with this wisdom literature, including the importance of single-minded devotion to God, the role of testing and discipline and their relationship to wisdom, the power as well as the pernicious effects of speech, the connection between anger and communal strife, the lure and ultimate emptiness of wealth, and the sharp contrast between righteousness and wickedness, which are closely associated with wisdom and foolishness. And while self-discipline plays an important role here, more important still is the communal dimension of life. Self-discipline is not an end in itself, but serves to foster the love and peace that ought to characterize the congregations of those who profess obedience to the one true God. As can be seen from the examples in the table on page 501, it cannot be doubted that James was familiar with the wisdom writings of the OT.

But James also manifests points of contact with ancient Jewish and Christian tradition known as "the two ways." One ancient Christian document of the early second century begins, "There are two ways, one of life and one of death, and there is a great difference between the two ways" (*Didache* 1:1). There the "way of life" is defined as following the commandments to love God and neighbor, and the way of death is the way of wickedness, cursing, murder, adultery, lust, fornication, theft, idolatry, witchcraft, robbery, false witness, and "a double heart." While there are differences between the vices denounced in the *Didache* and in James, both share the tendency of the "two ways" tradition to depict these two ways of living as starkly opposed to each other, with no middle ground. One path leads to God, one path leads away from God, and a person inevitably walks one path or the other. The effort to straddle the line is criticized by both James and the *Didache* as "double" thinking, which cannot be done any more than one can walk in two directions at once. This "two ways" traditions grows out of the biblical wisdom tradition, which paints the opposition between "wisdom" and "foolishness" in sharply contrasting colors and correlates them with "righteousness" and "wickedness." The hortatory tone of James, with its numerous admonitions, its warnings to the disobedient, and its description of consequences and promise of rewards, allows it to fit easily into the "two ways" tradition.

James's wide-ranging contacts with numerous moral traditions of early Jewish and Christian literature and its apparent familiarity with the themes and concerns of the Greco-Roman moralists tell us as much about the world from which the document emerged as they do about the specific sources that may have influenced James. James's similarities with the literature of the Hellenistic moralists point to the extent

James and Wisdom

Jas 1:5: "If any of you is lacking in wisdom, ask God, who gives to all generously and ungrudgingly, and it will be given you."	Prov 2:6-7: "For the LORD gives wisdom; from his mouth come knowledge and understanding; he stores up sound wisdom for the upright."
Jas 1:7: ". . . for the doubter, being *double-minded* and unstable in every way, must not expect to receive anything from the Lord."	Sirach 1:28: "Do not disobey the fear of the Lord; do not approach him with a *divided mind.*"
Jas 1:10-11: "The rich will disappear like a flower in the field. For the sun rises with its scorching heat and withers the field; its flower falls, and its beauty perishes. It is the same way with the rich; in the midst of a busy life, they will wither away."	Prov 11:28: "Those who trust in their riches will wither, but the righteous will flourish like green leaves."
Jas 3:2: "Anyone who makes no mistakes in speaking is perfect, able to keep the whole body in check with a bridle."	Prov 10:19: "When words are many, transgression is not lacking, but the prudent are restrained in speech."
Jas 3:6: "And the tongue is a fire. The tongue is placed among our members as a world of iniquity; it stains the whole body, sets on fire the cycle of nature, and is itself set on fire by hell."	Prov: 16:27: "Scoundrels concoct evil, and their speech is like a scorching fire."
Jas 4:1: "Those conflicts and disputes among you, where do they come from? Do they not come from your cravings that are at war within you?"	Prov 29:22: "One given to anger stirs up strife, and the hothead causes much transgression."
Jas 1:19-20: "You must understand this, my beloved: let everyone be quick to listen, slow to speak, slow to anger; for your anger does not produce God's righteousness."	Prov 14:17: "One who is quick-tempered acts foolishly, and the schemer is hated." Prov 14:29: "Whoever is slow to anger has great understanding, but one who has a hasty temper exalts folly." Prov 15:18: "Those who are hot-tempered stir up strife, but those who are slow to anger calm contention."
Jas 1:27: "Religion that is pure and undefiled before God, the Father, is this: to care for orphans and widows in their distress, and to keep oneself unstained by the world."	Prov 14:31: "Those who oppress the poor insult their Maker, but those who are kind to the needy honor him."
Jas 2:1: "My brothers and sisters, do you with your acts of favoritism really believe in our glorious Lord Jesus Christ?"	Prov 18:5: "It is not right to be partial to the guilty, or to subvert the innocent in judgment."

to which Hellenism and Judaism had already interacted prior to the first century, even in Palestine, as well as to the fact that the themes dealt with by James and others are the common stuff of everyday life. Themes such as communal interaction, power, money, speech, testing, and suffering weave their way through James as they do through the prophets, the wisdom literature, and the Hellenistic moralists. James draws together those instructions particularly relevant to those "in the Dispersion."

But the one source and influence that we have thus far left out of consideration may well be the most significant for James: the traditions of Jesus' teaching. In particular, James demonstrates striking points of contact with the traditions common to Matthew and Luke from the hypothetical source called Q. James exhibits the same emphasis on eschatology and the coming judgment, the wisdom themes of trust in God, integrity in lifestyle, and circumspect behavior, and the prophetic critique of all injustice, oppression, and abusive use of wealth and status. These are all also features of Jesus' teaching.

21.5. JAMES AND JESUS

As we noted above in our discussion of Jesus' teaching (ch. 8), Jesus emphasized that the moral requirements of the law — justice, mercy, and faith — were the heart of God's will for Israel and were to be the norms governing its life as a people of God. Jesus spoke of the entire law as summarized in two commands: love of God and love of neighbor. The greatest commandment in the law called for wholehearted devotion to God: "You shall love the LORD your God with all your heart, and with all your soul, and with all your might" (Deut 6:5), which Jesus not only quoted (Matt 22:36) but also paraphrased in assertions such as, "No one can serve two masters. . . . You cannot serve God and mammon" (Matt 6:24). James sounds the notes of this call to a single-minded, unswerving commitment to God in his warnings against "double-mindedness" (1:7; 4:8) and that "friendship with the world is enmity with God" (4:4). The second commandment, love of neighbor, shapes James's numerous moral commandments, including the exhortations to guard one's tongue, control anger, lessen strife, foster peace, and be impartial; to take care of widows, orphans, and the poor and oppressed; to pray for those in need; and to strive to make one's religious profession live through particular expressions of love in word and deed.

Just as we tabulated some of the comparisons between James and wisdom literature, so too we can graphically set out some of the parallels between James and the teachings of Jesus as found in the Synoptic Gospels. Some of the contacts suggest direct dependence on or use of traditions of Jesus' teaching, while others show that James reflects the same spirit as that found in the Synoptic traditions (see the table on pp. 504-5).

James follows Jesus in locating the heart of the law in the twin commands to love God and neighbor (cf. Gal 5:14). James also emphasizes — as did Jesus — the singular importance of congruity between profession of one's faith in God and expression of love for one's neighbor, with an emphasis on the expression of that love in the merciful, charitable, and humble stance one takes with respect to others. In fact it can easily be argued that the links between the ethic of James and the teaching of Jesus are as strong as, if not stronger than, those between any other document of the NT and the traditions of Jesus. But precisely because James echoes various traditions so clearly and because the letter lacks any specific description of the occasion for which it was written, it is difficult to pinpoint the specific situations that James wished to address.

In general it is clear that the epistle of James represents the application of Jesus' messianic interpretation of the law and of life before God. More specifically, these injunctions, clustered as they are around actions toward one's neighbor and particularly around relationships between rich and poor, suggest that James was indeed dealing with a congregation, or perhaps several congregations, marked by factionalism and partiality, with the rich neglecting the poor and so failing to love God and neighbor. These difficult trials may have tempted the poor to lose hope. But both groups may have been subject to anger, misuse of the tongue, envy, doubt and wavering, and an ultimate failure to trust in God. The imperatives of the book of James show how "friendship with God" is to be lived out in a number of specific cases and how both rich and poor can be tempted to abandon their "friendship with God" in favor of "friendship with the world."

21.6. DOERS OF THE WORD

The injunction to be "doers of the word, and not merely hearers" (1:22) is programmatic for the content and outline of James. This is scarcely remarkable given James's impressive contacts with the OT prophets, Proverbs and wisdom literature, and the teaching of Jesus, all of which insist on the integral connection between conduct and commitment, behavior and believing, doing and hearing. But James does not urge simply a general "doing," as though he were simply encouraging his readers to do something or to do more than they were currently doing. He is not interested in "works" for their own sake, but rather urges his readers to act on their professed belief in God ("hearing the word") by living a life that exhibits trust in God in a consistently gracious, giving, hospitable, and merciful way of life ("doing the word"), particularly in relationship to the poor and humble, such as widows and orphans (1:27). Without such care for the lowly, without love, one's faith is dead.

Thus while both rich and poor are addressed throughout the letter, and many

James and Jesus

Jas 1:6: "But ask in faith, never doubting."	Matt 21:21: "If you have faith and do not doubt."
Jas 1:12: "Blessed is anyone who endures temptation. Such a one has stood the test and will receive the crown of life."	Matt 10:22: "But the one who endures to the end will be saved."
Jas 2:14-16: "What good is it, my brothers and sisters, if you say you have faith but do not have works? Can faith save you? If a brother or sister is naked and lacks daily food, and one of you says to them, 'Go in peace; keep warm and eat your fill,' and yet you do not supply their bodily needs, what is the good of that?"	Matt 7:21-23: "Not everyone who says to me, 'Lord, Lord,' will enter the kingdom of heaven, but only the one who does the will of my Father in heaven. On that day many will say to me, 'Lord, Lord, did we not prophesy in your name, and cast out demons in your name, and do many deeds of power in your name?' Then I will declare to them, 'I never knew you; go away from me, you evildoers.'"
Jas 1:22: "But be doers of the word, and not merely hearers who deceive themselves."	Luke 6:49: "But the one who hears and does not act is like a man who built a house on the ground without a foundation." Luke 11:28: "But he said, 'Blessed rather are those who hear the word of God and obey it!'" (cf. Luke 8:15).
Jas 3:10-12: "From the same mouth come blessing and cursing. My brothers and sisters, this ought not to be so. Does a spring pour forth from the same opening both fresh and brackish water? Can a fig tree, my brothers and sisters, yield olives, or a grapevine figs? No more can salt water yield fresh."	Matt 7:16: "You will know them by their fruits. Are grapes gathered from thorns, or figs from thistles?" (cf. Matt 12:34-37)
Jas 2:5: "Has not God chosen the poor in the world to be rich in faith and to be heirs of the kingdom that he has promised to those who love him?"	Luke 6:20: "Blessed are you who are poor, for yours is the kingdom of God."

of its injunctions could be applied quite generally, it is clearly the rich who come in for the harshest criticisms. So, for example, when James urges and warns his readers not to show partiality, the conduct one is to avoid is demonstrated by the contrast between how a rich person and a poor person are welcomed in the syna-

Jas 2:13: "For judgment will be without mercy to anyone who has shown no mercy; mercy triumphs over judgment."	Matt 5:7: "Blessed are the merciful, for they will receive mercy."
Jas 4:8: "Draw near to God, and he will draw near to you. Cleanse your hands, you sinners, and purify your hearts, you double-minded."	Matt 5:8: "Blessed are the pure in heart, for they will see God."
Jas 3:18: "And a harvest of righteousness is sown in peace for those who make peace."	Matt 5:9: "Blessed are the peacemakers, for they will be called children of God."
Jas 4:6, 10: "But he gives all the more grace; therefore it says, 'God opposes the proud, but gives grace to the humble.' . . . Humble yourselves before the Lord, and he will exalt you."	Matt 23:12: "All who exalt themselves will be humbled, and all who humble themselves will be exalted."
Jas 5:2-3: "Your riches have rotted, and your clothes are moth-eaten. Your gold and silver have rusted, and their rust will be evidence against you, and it will eat your flesh like fire. You have laid up treasure for the last days."	Matt 6:19-21: "Do not store up for yourselves treasures on earth, where moth and rust consume and where thieves break in and steal; but store up for yourselves treasures in heaven, where neither moth nor rust consumes and where thieves do not break in and steal. For where your treasure is, there your heart will be also."
Jas 5:12: "Above all, my beloved, do not swear, either by heaven or by earth or by any other oath, but let your 'Yes' be yes and your 'No' be no, so that you may not fall under condemnation."	Matt 5:34-37: "But I say to you, Do not swear at all, either by heaven, for it is the throne of God, or by the earth, for it is his footstool, or by Jerusalem, for it is the city of the great King. And do not swear by your head, for you cannot make one hair white or black. Let your word be 'Yes, Yes' or 'No, No'; anything more than this comes from evil."

gogue. For anyone to honor the rich at the expense of the poor is to dishonor the God who has "chosen those who are poor in the world to be rich in faith and heirs of the kingdom" (2:5). What James condemns is the partiality demonstrated toward the rich. But in subsequent passages he makes it clear that the rich, who revel in their possessions, honor, and status in this life, will soon find their position and those of the poor reversed (5:1-6). Their future destiny of misery, a life without any wealth, wearing nothing but rags for clothes, surely mirrors the plight of those whom they neglect in the present life.

What it means to be a "doer of the word" is to live as God commands and to act as God acts. The character and activity of God are central to the theological vision of James, and form the basis for the shape of the faithful life of discipleship enjoined within it. Divine sovereignty, a basic tenet of Jewish and Christian convictions about God, serves as the explicit and implicit warrant for many of James's arguments and commands. There is one God (2:19; 4:12), who, as the source of all goodness, is untainted by evil (1:13, 17, 20) and gives generously to all who ask (1:5, 7, 17; 3:15, 17; 4:6). God is a righteous and impartial judge (2:12-13; 4:12; 5:7-9), whose will is effected in the world (4:15; 5:11). God responds to the prayers of the oppressed (5:4), rewards the humble and faithful (1:12; 2:5), but judges the proud and fickle. Indeed, God has chosen the poor (2:5; 4:5) and opposes those who oppress them, inasmuch as the poor, like all human beings, are made in the likeness of God (3:9).

The theme of the "likeness of God" marks James's injunctions in two ways. First, those who desire to live in friendship with God must respond to God in appropriate ways. God's sovereignty calls for the response of humility, trust, obedience, and prayer. In light of God's future judgment, James urges people to perseverance, faithfulness, and purity of heart. God generously gives wisdom, and not only are people enjoined to ask God for it, but are then to live out of the rich supply of that gift. By humble reception of the gift of wisdom from God, they manifest their responsiveness to the Giver. But a second way in which the theme of the "likeness of God" comes out in James is in the call to imitate God. God is merciful, generous, and impartial, taking the side of the poor and oppressed. Just as God has chosen to exalt the poor, so those who desire to be "friends of God" are to eschew favoritism toward the rich and powerful and serve the poor. Commitment to a generous and merciful God who espouses the cause of the poor and humble thus prescribes a way of life marked by the same qualities and behavior: faith must be put into practice.

A conspicuous feature of James's vision of the life of faithful discipleship is the emphasis on speech as indicative of inner character and integrity. Of the nearly sixty imperatives in James, just over half deal with conversation and speaking, and the basic guideline is laid out early on: "Let everyone be quick to listen, slow to speak, slow to anger" (1:19). People should "bridle their tongues" (1:26; cf. 3:2-3), otherwise their "religion is worthless." These are strong words. Control of one's tongue was a virtue prized by various Greco-Roman moralists as well as by the wisdom teachers of Israel. While James esteems the one who can control his or her tongue, he admits that consistent mastery of one's words is nearly an impossibility.

"No one can tame the tongue — a restless evil, full of deadly poison" (3:8). Yet he does not limit his horizons simply to control of speech. For it is human speech, above all else, that gives insight into the human condition: "With [the tongue] we bless the Lord and Father, and with it we curse those who are made in the likeness of God" (3:9). The failure to put faith into practice, against which James speaks so vehemently, reveals itself nowhere more clearly than in the human propensity to profess faith in God while dishonoring those made in the likeness of God. James does more than decry the inability to control one's tongue. He also points forcefully toward the positive use of speech in its role in instructing (3:1-2), blessing others, and manifesting the traits of wisdom, gentleness, peacefulness, impartiality, humility, and integrity. His ethic of Christian discipleship aims not at heroic conduct but at disciplines of conduct for the long haul of everyday life.

The realism of James's moral vision also displays itself in his injunctions to endurance, patience, and maturity. Life brings trials, and they are the means by which a mature faith is developed. Christians should therefore respond to the trials of life with joy. In this thinking James is not alone, for similar trains of thought can be found elsewhere in the Old and New Testaments and in the apocryphal wisdom books (1 Pet 1:6-7; Rom 5:3-4; Hebrews 12; as well as Prov 27:21; Sir 2:1-6; Wis 3:4-6). Job, the paradigmatic sufferer in the OT, is adduced as an example not only of patience, but of endurance in testing (5:11). That James opens his epistle with the theme of perseverance in testing suggests the particularly difficult situations of oppression and suffering that occasioned his writing. Some of his addressees were oppressed and suffering and, due to their position or status in life, had little or no power to change their circumstances or deal with their oppressors as equals. James encourages them to "persevere," in part because in all likelihood they have few other options. James thus reflects traditional injunctions of Jewish and Christian literature to persevere, but the pointed references to the rich who oppress the poor (2:1; 5:4-6) give a glimpse of at least some of the situations in which these injunctions found an audience in need of reassurance and encouragement.

Indeed, James's harshest invective is directed towards the rich who oppress the poor. He minces no words in warning them of their coming doom:

> The rich will disappear like a flower in the field. For the sun rises with its scorching heat and withers the field; its flower falls, and its beauty perishes. It is the same way with the rich: in the midst of a busy life, they will wither away. (1:10-11)

> Listen! The wages of the laborers who mowed your fields, which you kept back by fraud, cry out, and the cries of the harvesters have reached the ears of the Lord of hosts. You have lived on the earth in luxury and in pleasure; you have fattened your hearts in a day of slaughter. (5:4-5)

These descriptions of the rich echo the prophetic characterizations and denunciations of the abuse of the poor by the rich, such as one finds in Isa 3:11-15; 5:8-10; 9:18–10:4; Amos 2:6-7; 5:11-12; 6:4-6; 8:5-6; Micah 2:1-5, and in other parts of the OT that make provisions for the needs of the poor (Exod 22:21-7; Lev 25:35-55; Deut 10:16-19; 15:7-11). Observations about the temporary nature of riches echo proverbs of the wisdom tradition that warn against trusting in one's wealth (Job 15:30; Prov 2:8; Sir 14:11-19). And of course it is difficult to miss the parallels to the traditions of Jesus' teaching, in which warnings against riches, self-sufficiency, partiality, and oppression of the poor are often coupled together (Matt 6:19-21; Luke 12:13-21). While James's warnings to the rich have ample precedent, therefore, in the OT and teachings of Jesus, the extent to which the theme is highlighted in James suggests that the relationships of the rich and poor and the power and peril of wealth were not just traditional themes but also reflections of concrete problems with which James had to deal. And since the rich are addressed directly, they seem to be part of the assembly of Christians to whom the letter is written. But while the poor are referred to as "brothers and sisters," the rich are never called by that designation, indicative of James's warnings that they are not living out the faith they profess. He warns his readers against the lure of riches, the temptation to be partial to the rich, and the neglect of the poor among them, for such behavior is not fitting for those who desire friendship with the very God who has "chosen the poor." James's criticism of the norms of a culture that values wealth and possessions as the marks of achievement, status, and worth provides another example of the way in which he warns that "friendship with the world is enmity with God."

James sets his instructions and warnings in an eschatological framework, speaking of rewards and punishment due at the coming judgment. Not only does he warn the rich against the coming judgment at the "last days" (5:1-6), but he also encourages the faithful to persevere through temptation so that they may receive "the crown of life" (1:2-4, 12). He speaks of the poor as "heirs of the kingdom" (2:5), reflecting Jewish eschatological language of "inheriting" the kingdom or the land. Judgment also figures prominently in the important section on mercy, faith, and works (2:12-13) and is one of the prerogatives that belong to God and ought not be usurped by human beings (4:11-12). Finally, the "coming of the Lord" (5:7) provides the warrant for patience and perseverance (5:7-11), as well as for repentance and mourning (5:1). Ultimately, James's warnings of judgment and promise of reward derive from his vision of the demand and character of God, who works justice and gives mercy to the humble and lowly. Those who hear the word of this God are also to do it.

21.7. HEARING AND DOING, FAITH AND WORKS

We come, then, to a discussion of the passage to which the entirety of James's epistle is sometimes unfortunately reduced, the discussion of faith and works in 2:14-26. James begins his discussion with the query, "What good is it, my brothers and sisters, if you say you have faith but do not have works?" This rhetorical question makes perfect sense in light of his earlier directive that people are to be "doers of the word, and not merely hearers," another formulation in which James joins together love of God and neighbor. Jesus' warnings that only the one who "does the will of my Father in heaven" will enter the kingdom strikes the same note. James's exposition of the relationship of faith and works is one way in which he casts his argument about hearing and doing.

But his treatment of faith and works (2:14-26) uses language and imagery that seems directly related to, and in some way dependent upon, Paul's discussion of the same issues:

Gal 2:16: "Yet we know that a person is justified not by the works of the law but through faith in Jesus Christ."

Rom 4:2: "For if Abraham was justified by works, he has something to boast about, but not before God."

Jas 2:21: "Was not our ancestor Abraham justified by works when he offered his son Isaac on the altar?"

Along with the juxtaposition of "faith" and "works," particularly striking is James's use of the key text Gen 15:6 — the only OT text to link "faith" and "righteousness" — to bolster his point that Abraham's "faith was active along with his works, and faith was brought to completion by his works" (2:22). Gen 15:6 is also crucial to Paul's argument in Galatians (3:2-7) and Romans (4:3-22, especially vv. 3-8) that Abraham and his true descendants are justified by faith, not works of the law.

The apparently vexing problem of the differences between James and Paul can be alleviated to some extent by noting that they are talking about different problems and using the same vocabulary (faith, works) to make rather different points. Paul's concern is with the relationship between "works of *the law*" and "faith in Christ," whereas James's reference to "works" lacks the crucial interpretative phrase "of the law." For Paul the pressing theological point has to do with how the coming of the Messiah, Jesus, affects the role and function of the Mosaic law, particularly for Gentile believers. In that regard, "Christ" and "law" stand in tension with each other.

But for James the issue is quite different. James is arguing for the inseparability of religious convictions ("faith") and concrete behavior ("works") *within* the context of the messianic community. James is not arguing for "justification by works" against the Pauline gospel of "justification by faith." Rather, he is concerned with the relationship of "faith," construed as one's basic commitments and beliefs, and "works," conceived of as tangible deeds of love and mercy. Thus he writes:

Erasmus's Paraphrase

The great Renaissance scholar, and one of Martin Luther's adversaries in debate, Erasmus of Rotterdam, produced a number of paraphrases of the NT. The following excerpt comes from his paraphrase of the book of James:

But what is faith without love? Love moreover is a living thing; it does not go on holiday; it is not idle; it expresses itself in kind acts wherever it is present. If these acts are lacking, my brothers, I ask you, will the empty word "faith" save a person? Faith which does not work through love is unproductive; no, it is faith in name only. An example here will make clear what I mean. If someone says blandly to a brother or a sister who lacks clothing or daily food, "Depart in peace, keep warm, and remember to eat well," and after saying this, gives him or her none of the things the body needs, will his fine talk be of any use to the ones in need? They will be no less cold and hungry for all his fine talk, which is of no help to their need. He gives them only verbal support, but does nothing in actual fact. A profession of faith will certainly be equally useless if it consists only of words and does nothing except remain inactive as though dead. It should no more be called faith than a human corpse merits the name of human being. Love is to faith what the soul is to the body. Take away love and the word faith is like something dead and inert. It will do you no more good before God to confess in words an idle faith than fine speech benefits a neighbor in need when he must be helped with action. People think they are being mocked when you say to them, "Keep warm and well fed," and give them neither food nor clothing. Just so the person who offers no tangible proofs of his faith but repeats every day, "I believe in God, I believe in God," seems to be mocking God. A person who gives lip-service to love possesses a fruitless charity. In the same way a person whose belief is only a matter of words possesses a faith that serves no purpose.

Those who look into the perfect law, the law of liberty, and persevere, being not hearers who forget but doers who act — they will be blessed in their doing. (1:25)

The law enjoins doing, acting; but it is the perfect law of liberty, the "royal law," which is fulfilled in loving one's neighbor:

You do well if you really fulfill the royal law according to the scripture, "You shall love your neighbor as yourself." (2:8)

Here there are striking points of contact with Paul, who in Galatians writes:

For you were called to freedom, brothers and sisters; only do not use your freedom as an opportunity for self-indulgence, but through love become slaves to one another. For the whole law is summed up in a single commandment, "You shall love your neighbor as yourself." (5:13-14)

For both Paul and James, Christian freedom gives the opportunity not to do whatever one wants, but to love one's brothers and sisters. Thus when James writes, "be doers of the word and not merely hearers who deceive themselves" (1:22), he makes the same point that Paul makes in Rom 2:13, "For it is not the hearers of the law who are righteous in God's sight, but the doers of the law who will be justified."

But James is fighting on a different front. He is concerned to correct those who argue that only "faith," taken as orthodox belief, really matters. To prove the point, he cites the basic tenet of Judaism, that God is one, taken from the familiar *Shema:* "Hear, O Israel: The Lord is our God, the Lord alone. You shall love the Lord your God with all your heart, and with all your soul, and with all your might" (Deut 6:4-5). James comments that it is good to believe these words: "You believe that God is one; you do well" (2:19). But to emphasize the folly of leaving it there, he adds: "Even the demons believe — and shudder." The demons recognize the existence of the one God. The question that naturally follows is what one does in response to such belief. According to James, the demons merely shudder. Those who truly believe in the one God will respond neither by "shuddering," nor by merely "hearing," but by "doing" what that one God commands in "the royal law according to the Scriptures, 'You shall love your neighbor as yourself.'"

21.8. JAMES WITHIN THE CANON

At the outset of this chapter, we noted Luther's harsh condemnation of James: "it does not show you Christ" and has "nothing of the gospel about it," he wrote. Luther was referring in part to James's lack of explicit Christian themes such as the significance of the death and resurrection of Christ and the gift and work of the Holy Spirit. But in its canonization and subsequent use of James, the Christian community has found an important guide for its corporate life together. Unflinching in its insistence that faith and works, hearing and doing, commitment and conduct, belong together, James offers the reader no easy path of discipleship and gives the lie to every profession of Christian faith that does not see love of neighbor as an indispensable expression of love of God.

James is not a book *about* Christ and the cross. But it is a book that sounds much like Jesus and often speaks in tones uncannily reminiscent of Jesus' own teaching. It urges its readers to the same single-minded devotion to God and uncompromising commitment to the neighbor. It promotes justice, mercy, integrity, humility, faithfulness, and perseverance; it attacks injustice, pride, dishonesty, and self-sufficiency; it promises the good gifts and wisdom of God to all who ask in humility and faith. In all these respects, it echoes the very voice of Jesus and his call to the kingdom of God and thus does indeed "show Christ."

FOR FURTHER READING

Richard Bauckham, *James: Wisdom of James, Disciple of Jesus the Sage* (New Testament Readings; New York: Routledge, 1999)

Andrew Chester and Ralph P. Martin, *The Theology of the Letters of James, Peter, and Jude* (Cambridge: Cambridge University Press, 1994)

Peter Davids, *The Epistle of James* (New International Greek Testament Commentary; Grand Rapids, Eerdmans, 1982)

Patrick Hartin, *A Spirituality of Perfection: Faith in Action in the Letter of James* (Collegeville: Liturgical, 1999)

Luke Timothy Johnson, *The Letter of James* (Anchor Bible; Garden City: Doubleday, 1995)

Robert W. Wall, *Community of the Wise: The Letter of James* (The New Testament in Context; Valley Forge: Trinity Press International, 1997)

22. 1 and 2 Peter, Jude

22.1. "CATHOLIC" EPISTLES?

These three letters are typically numbered among the NT "catholic letters." This implies that they lack the specificity of address of, say, Paul's letters to the Corinthians or Thessalonians; they are "catholic" ("general, universal") in this sense. This designation and their location in the NT also speak to their function within the canon. They appear in the second of two collections of letters, the first comprising the correspondence attributed to Paul and the second the series of NT documents from Hebrews through Jude. As *letters* these materials are recognized as attempts to address needs that arose in communities struggling to embody within their common lives the message of the gospel. The presence of *two letter collections* reminds us that even earliest Christianity was not univocal in its understanding of the gospel. The diversity of concerns addressed and modes of addressing those concerns within and between these two sets of letters points to the self-correcting and mutually informing conception of Christian discipleship. Study of 1-2 Peter and Jude, among the catholic letters, then, should serve to assist the church in avoiding the reductionism of its understanding of the Christian message to the Pauline apostolate. For understanding the NT and earliest Christianity, Paul's is an important voice but not the only one.

At the same time, it must be noticed that inclusion of these three letters among the "catholic" collection represents a distortion of their historical address. Jude, for example, is a genuine letter, developed for and sent to a real audience in the context of a particular set of circumstances. The salutation of 1 Peter specifies an implied readership that is not universal (even in the ancient sense of "addressed to the whole Roman world") but rather located in five geographic areas of Asia

Jude 17-18	2 Pet 3:1-3
But you, beloved, should remember the predictions of the apostles of our Lord Jesus Christ — that they said to you, "In the final time there will be scoffers who will indulge their own ungodly lusts."	Beloved . . . you should remember the predictions of the holy prophets and the commandments of the Lord and Savior through your apostles. First, you must understand this, that in the final days scoffers will come, scoffing, indulging their own lusts. . . .

Minor (i.e., modern Turkey). 2 Peter probably shared a similar address (3:1: "Beloved, this is now the second letter I am writing to you . . ."). These facts do not render the category "catholic" altogether specious but require that it be nuanced somewhat in order to allow our reading of these letters within their own sociohistorical contingencies and not as context-less documents.

These letters are often treated together, the first two for reasons more apparent than the third. As their titles indicate, 1 and 2 Peter are both attributed to the apostle Peter, and this has led to their being examined side-by-side in order to ascertain a possible "Petrine" gospel. The prospect of their being used in this way has been complicated by persistent questions regarding the authorship of both. Less obvious at a superficial level but more consequential is the correlation of 2 Peter and Jude. To close readers of these two letters, some sort of literary relationship is evident — particularly with reference to Jude 4-13, 17-18 and 2 Pet 2:1-18; 3:1-3.

Among the possible explanations for this correspondence, the two that have attracted the most support are Jude's dependence on 2 Peter and 2 Peter's dependence on Jude. How one adjudicates between these choices is dependent on how one settles issues of authorship and dating and on the opinion one forms concerning the soundness and style of these letters. What this level of accord between the two does not require is that we assume that both letters arose from and/or were designed to address comparable circumstances or that they must share a singular theological perspective. As in other instances of intertextuality, the appearance of a prior (or sub-) text in a fresh co-text invites reflection on how that subtext functions in its new setting; the presence of both lingering similarities and striking dissimilarities is not only conceivable but almost guaranteed. In the end, this requires that each of these documents be read first on its own terms, against its own sociocultural horizons, and within its own world of meaning. Irrespective of any literary relationship between 2 Peter and Jude, moreover, given its canonical title and attribution to the apostle Peter, 2 Peter invites theological reflection in relation to 1 Peter.

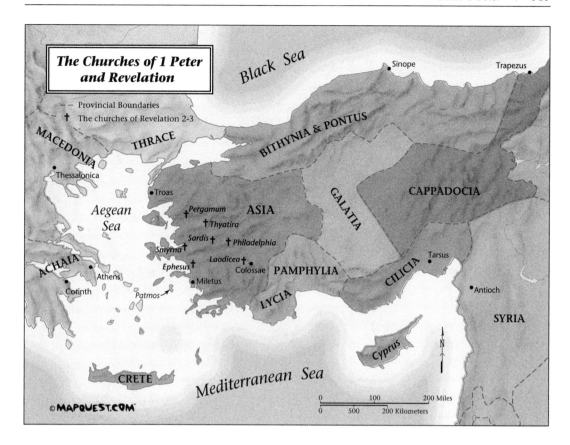

22.2. 1 PETER

According to the author's own description, 1 Peter is "a brief letter" written to encourage and instruct *(parakaleō)* its recipients and to testify concerning the grace of God (5:12). Who are these recipients, and what is their situation? The question of the provenance of 1 Peter is intimately tied to the issue of authorship.

The document itself is cast in the form of a letter, complete with identification of the author ("Peter, an apostle of Jesus Christ") and addressees ("to the exiles of the dispersion, 1:1) in its introduction, and the expected greeting (from "Babylon," i.e., Rome) in its conclusion (5:12-14). Its lack of greater specificity in its address marks it as a circular letter (cf. Acts 15:23-29; Col 4:16). This is a form otherwise known in OT and Second Temple Jewish literature, where it was used to address the people of God in particular locales — "the Jews in Egypt" (2 Macc 1:1–2:18) or the Jewish exiles in Babylon (e.g., Jer 9:4-23; *2 Baruch* 78–86; cf. Jas 1:1).

A relief representation
of Peter crucified
upside-down
(W. S. LaSor)

Of course, in the case of 1 Peter, the "diaspora letter" has its origin *in* Babylon
rather than its having been sent *to* the Babylonian exiles, but in other respects we
find analogous perspectives when comparing this document with the relevant
portion of *2 Baruch*. This is true not least in their perspective on suffering as a mi-
nority under foreign rule, leading to the possibility that the author of 1 Peter was
consciously influenced by the form of a circular diaspora letter recognized among
the Jewish people.

A Letter from Baruch

The *Syriac Apocalypse of Baruch,* also known as *2 Baruch,* is a Jewish document dating roughly from the early 2nd century CE. Although the author speaks of the destruction of Jerusalem in 587 BCE, the occasion of this writing is the aftermath of the Roman destruction of Jerusalem and the temple in 70 CE. In fact, the importance of the book lies in its portrayal of Jewish faithfulness in the absence of the temple. Chs. 78–86 constitute a letter to the nine and a half tribes in which the Jews of the diaspora are encouraged to obey and trust God. The following excerpt, which conveys a sense of the struggle of the dispersion, is the introduction to the letter.

And the whole people answered and they said to me:
Everything which we can remember of the good things which the Mighty One has done to us we shall remember, and that which we do not remember he knows in his grace. But do this for us, your people: Write also to our brothers in Babylon a letter of doctrine and a roll of hope so that you might strengthen them also before you go away from us. For the shepherds of Israel have perished, and the lamps which give light are extinguished, and the fountains from which we used to drink have withheld their streams. Now we have been left in darkness and in thick forest and in the aridness of the desert. (77:11-14, *OTP*)

22.2.1. The Addressees

What might this entail concerning this author's audience? Less than one might think. This is because the content of 1 Peter seems to vacillate with reference to the ethnic identity of its implied readership.

The form of the letter, together with the opening phrase "exiles of the dispersion" (1:1), suggests an audience of Jewish Christians in Asia Minor. This possibility is supported by the significant and abundant use of the OT throughout the letter and especially by the repeated identification of its readers as Israel and the silence with regard to the tensions arising from having Gentiles and Jews together in the churches. What is more, persons outside the community are called "Gentiles" (2:12; 4:3). Given the attribution of this letter to Peter, it is also of interest that, according to Paul, Peter's mission was to the Jews (Gal 2:7).

On the other hand, repeated references to the pagan character of their background suggest strongly that the majority of the addressees were in fact Gentiles (1:14, 18; 2:10, 25; 4:3-4). The comment that prior to their conversion they had neither faith nor hope in God (1:21) likewise urges their identification as Gentiles. What of evidence to the contrary? With respect to the importance of the OT to this letter, it must not be forgotten that the OT was *the* Bible of earliest Christianity, so that we would be amiss to suppose that even Gentile converts would not know its content well. Peter himself is known to have had a ministry in the Gentile world (see Acts 10:1–11:18; 1 Cor 1:12). Most importantly, 1 Peter employs as a central motif the identification of Israel and the church, with the result that normal usage of such terms as "Jewish" or "Gentile" cannot be assumed. The new people of God envisioned in this letter is none other than the people of Israel — so this document's "Jewishness" insinuates less a description of the ethnic origins of its implied audience than a clarification of its readers' status before God.

This means that Peter's "exiles" and "aliens" are foreigners in an important but metaphorical sense. They are not "Jews" living among "Gentiles" in the expected sense of these terms, as though the author were concerned with their ethnic or political status. Attempts to find in Peter's descriptive terms a reference to his readers' economic status founders similarly on a problem of category. Whether a person was "rich" or "poor," as we have come to understand these terms in the last two centuries in the West, was of relatively little consequence in Roman antiquity. Having little income did not of necessity deprive one of family and friends, just as having great wealth did not of necessity guarantee that one might exercise elevated power and privilege in society. One's social status was a product of numerous intersecting considerations, relative income or access to the means of production only one of them (see chapter 2). In fact, there is no basis within the letter itself for suggesting that Peter's audience occupied any rung on the ladder of economic measurement other than would have been characteristic of first-century Christians as a whole; hence, one might expect his readers to represent the broad spectrum of people living in Asia Minor, other than those of the ruling elite.

If not in a political, ethnic, or economic sense, how should we think of 1 Peter's "exiles" and "aliens"? On this, the letter is actually quite straightforward. These are people whose commitment to the lordship of Jesus Christ have led to transformed attitudes and behaviors that place them on the margins of respectable society. They have become the victims of social ostracism, their allegiance to Christ having won for them slander, animosity, reproach, scorn, vilification, and contempt. In the larger world, status was achieved by conformity to dispositions that had become so conventional that they were largely unspoken, taken for granted; noncompliance and other forms of social distinctiveness were regarded negatively. Rich or poor in economic terms, born into a good family or bad — these and other factors paled into insignificance for the readers of 1 Peter, whose reformed allegiances and transfigured practices distinguished them from Roman society. Previously, they had participated in the mainstream of Greco-Roman society, but now their lack of acculturation to prevailing social values marked them as social misfits to be held in contempt. 1 Peter was written to address Christians in such general circumstances as these — not so much to resolve the enigma of the suffering of God's people as to articulate how best to relate to a society set against those allegiances, attitudes, and actions that are consistent with God's agenda.

22.2.2. Author and Setting

By whom was this letter written? In spite of the clear identification of the author as "Peter, an apostle of Jesus Christ" (1:1), doubts about Petrine authorship continue to linger. This is primarily because the letter's author evidences relatively superior facility in Greek (relative, that is, to other forms of NT Greek), employs the OT in its Greek version rather than in Hebrew, and manifests some training in the canons of Greco-Roman rhetoric. In short, it is doubted whether Peter the Galilean fisherman would have been capable of authoring such a document. Such considerations are easily laid to rest, however, by the implication of 1:1 and 5:12 that Peter commissioned this letter, not actually writing it — a task that would have been undertaken, then, by Sylvanus, "a faithful brother." Again, then, we are presented with the difficulties resident in our quite modern notions of "authorship," notions that do not typically allow for the continuum of influence and participation by individuals and communities in the Old and New Testaments. Assuming that the figure of Peter stands immediately behind the writing of this document, this would require that the letter originated prior to his martyrdom (*ca.* 64-65 CE).

Scholars seeking to locate more precisely the historical situation about which Peter is concerned in this letter have sometimes pointed to the period of the persecution of Christians under Nero in the 60s. This would make sense of references to malice, imprisonment, the "fiery ordeal," and the general feeling of apprehension that characterizes the document as a whole (see 4:4, 12, 16). Such specificity actually introduces more problems than it solves, however, since it would require Peter to have addressed a situation in which he himself, and not his audience in Asia Minor, was embroiled. The Neronian persecution, after all, was localized in the vicinity of the city of Rome, but 1 Peter implies that it is the Christian population of Asia Minor that is caught up in marginality and scorn. In fact, specificity at this level is unnecessary, since nowhere does Peter imply that the persecution being experienced by his readers carried with it the legitimacy of Roman decree. Christians in the first-century Mediterranean world would have attracted widespread but localized ill will for their failure to participate in the religious celebrations that permeated Roman culture — some in honor of the goddess of Rome herself, *Roma,* others in honor of the emperor and his divine attributes, and so on. Failing to associate themselves with these religiocultural activities, Christians would have invited social ostracism and other forms of harassment. Indeed, their behaviors would have been perceived by the general populace as antisocial, perhaps even bordering on the unlawful; failing to participate in these activities, they would have been charged with bringing on the city or town the disfavor of the gods. Official Roman policy need not have dictated action against Christians for followers of Jesus as Lord to be subjected to mob action on account of their association with the name of Christ.

If it is impossible to associate the historical situation of 1 Peter with official persecution under Nero, the same may be said of other official actions against Christians under the emperors Domitian (81-96) and Trajan (97-117). Like the situation under Nero, so in these later cases we are not to imagine a formally mandated, empire-wide persecution of Christians.

The presence of unofficial harassment instigated by the populace in areas throughout the empire is easier to imagine, even if it is also more difficult to use as a means of dating 1 Peter. It is of interest, though, that the book of Revelation, written in the mid-90s, takes a much less generous view of the Roman government than does 1 Peter. Peter is under the impression that the government is both capable of and committed to fulfilling its divine mandate "to punish those who do wrong and honor those who do right" (2:13). John's social analysis has led him to a quite different conclusion. He views the empire as a blasphemous power that has set itself over against the will of God and thus against the people of God. Since the audiences of 1 Peter and Revelation overlap significantly (see Revelation 2–3), it would appear that John wrote at a time when relations with the Roman world had further deteriorated. This again would support an earlier rather than later dating of 1 Peter.

Nevertheless, the message of 1 Peter would not be unduly altered were we to locate its origins later in the first century. Its use of "Babylon" as a byname for Rome may point to such a later occasion, since this appellation gained currency only in the last three decades of the first century. Of course, dating the letter during this period would rule out the possibility of Peter's direct involvement in its content, in which case one might posit another leader associated with the apostle within the Christian communities of Rome. Early or late, the same social setting is plausible — social ostracism as a form of persecution instigated by popular sentiment.

With regard to the authorship of 1 Peter, a further issue that has troubled some is its apparent lack of a distinctive Petrine theology. More than one modern reader of 1 Peter has quipped that, apart from the direct attestation of the document to Peter, one could have imagined that the letter was penned by Paul. Affinities with James and with other NT documents are also easy to document. Such thinking begs the important question, What do we know of Peter's theology, apart from the correspondence that has come to us in his name? The ancient tradition that relates the origins of the Gospel of Mark to the apostle Peter, even when taken at face value, does not suggest that we have direct access through the Second Gospel to Peter's understanding of the faith (see above, chapter 6). Nor do the speeches attributed to Peter in Acts give us such access, since they have been shaped by their appropriation within the Lukan narrative. Hence, we lack unimpeachable canons against which to measure how "Petrine" 1 Peter actually is.

22.2.3. The Letter's Place in Early Christianity

What is evident is the remarkable degree to which the thought of 1 Peter belongs within the mainstream of early Christian thought as this is represented in the NT. Several common strands are woven together.

(1) At several points, 1 Peter appears to reflect traditions about Jesus underlying the Gospels. Perhaps as many as a score of such parallels between 1 Peter and the Gospel tradition have been identified. This congruence not only points to the familiarity of the author of 1 Peter with Jesus material, but also raises the question how that material has been deployed in this letter to "exiles in the dispersion." Three comments are apropos. First, it is clear that Peter views the present experi-

Some Jesus Traditions in 1 Peter	
1 Pet 3:9: "Do not repay evil for evil or abuse for abuse; rather, repay with a blessing."	Luke 6:28: "Bless those who curse you."
1 Pet 3:14: "But even if you do suffer for doing what is right, you are blessed."	Luke 6:10: "Blessed are you when people hate you, and when they exclude you, revile you, and defame you on account of the Son of man."
	Matt 5:10: "Blessed are those who are persecuted for righteousness' sake. . . ."
1 Pet 2:12: "Conduct yourselves honorably among the Gentiles, so that, though they malign you as though you were evildoers, they may see your honorable deeds and glorify God when he comes to judge."	Matt 5:16: "Let your light shine before people in order that they might see your good works and glorify your heavenly Father."

1 Peter, Romans, and James

1 Pet 1:14: "Like obedient children, do not be conformed to the desires that you formerly had in ignorance."	Rom 12:2: "Do not be conformed to this world. . . ."
1 Pet 4:10-11: "Like good stewards of the manifold grace of God, serve one another with whatever gift each of you has received. Whoever speaks must do so as one speaking the very words of God; whoever serves must do so with the strength that God supplies. . . ."	Rom 12:6-7: "We have gifts that differ according to the grace given to us: prophesy, in proportion to faith; service in serving. . . ."
1 Pet 1:6-7: "In this you rejoice, even if now for a little while you have had to suffer various trials, so that the genuineness of your faith . . . may be found to result in praise and glory and honor when Jesus Christ is revealed."	Rom 5:3-5: "We also boast in our sufferings, knowing that suffering produces endurance, endurance produces character, character produces hope, and hope does not disappoint us, because God's love has been poured into our hearts through the Holy Spirit that has been given to us."
	Jas 1:2-3: "Consider it all joy when you face all kinds of trials, knowing that the testing of your faith produces endurance; and let endurance have its full effect, so that you may be mature and complete, lacking in nothing."

ence of Christians in the Roman provinces of Asia Minor in relation to Jesus' prediction of the certainty, perhaps even inevitability, of suffering for those who follow in his footsteps. Since Jesus anticipated such situations, they should neither come as a surprise to his followers nor be taken as evidence that his followers have brought suffering on themselves by stepping outside the will of God. As Peter writes, "Beloved, do not be surprised at the fiery ordeal that is taking place among you, as though something strange were happening to you" (4:12). Instead, Peter advises, drawing on the pattern of Jesus' own career, present suffering is the context for faithful perseverance and the harbinger of restoration and glory (4:13; 5:10). Third, in this new historical context, Peter has translated Jesus' command,

"Love your enemies, do good to those who hate you" (e.g., Luke 6:27), into a commission for Christian behavior in this oppressive social setting.

(2) The congruity between 1 Peter and other NT texts is also plentiful and pervasive, more than enough to indicate the conformity of this letter to the trajectory of Christian tradition and interpretation otherwise present in the NT. But Peter is doing more than mimicking early tradition. In the same regard one may also point to the use of presumed liturgical traditions in 1 Peter, such as, for example, the hymnic or confessional material in 1:18-21; 2:21-25; 3:18-22. All this is to say that 1 Peter participates in the process of drawing on and reformulating the developing tradition of the church as it seeks to instruct and encourage Christians in Asia Minor. Peter appears to have his own access to elements of the tradition also picked up by Matthew and Luke, Paul and James, and others, and, like them, he embeds those materials within his own constructive thought as he addresses the needs of his audience. In this way, he indicates the immediate relevance of the gospel to the conditions of his readers.

Other Parallels in 1 Peter

1 Pet 2:6-8	Rom 9:32-33
1 Pet 2:13-17	Rom 13:1-7
1 Pet 3:8-9	Rom 12:16-17
1 Pet 1:3	Eph 1:3
1 Pet 1:10-12	Eph 3:5
1 Pet 1:14	Eph 2:2-3
1 Pet 2:4-6	Eph 2:20-22
1 Pet 3:22	Eph 1:20-22
1 Pet 1:23–2:2	Jas 1:10-11, 18-22
1 Pet 4:8	Jas 5:20
1 Pet 5:5-9	Jas 4:6-10
1 Pet 1:1; 2:11	Heb 11:13
1 Pet 1:2	Heb 12:24
1 Pet 2:25	Heb 13:20
1 Pet 3:9	Heb 12:17
1 Pet 3:18	Heb 9:28
1 Pet 3:18	Heb 9:28
1 Pet 4:6	Hebrews 11
1 Pet 4:14	Heb 13:13

(3) First Peter teems with citations and allusions from the OT, especially the Psalms, Proverbs, and Isaiah; in fact, the OT is the source of virtually all the metaphors used in the letter. The immediate effect of the use of Israel's Scriptures in 1 Peter is to root fundamentally both the message of this letter and, just as importantly, the identity of its readers in scriptural authority. Also worth noting is how the author of 1 Peter employs Scripture in ways comparable to those of other NT writers. For example, one can compare the drawing together of OT texts in 1 Pet 2:4-10 with a similar exegetical argument in Rom 9:25-33. This demonstrates again how seeped in Christian tradition 1 Peter is, including the selection and interpretation of OT texts.

(4) Finally, we may turn attention to the use of "household duty codes." Such codes (sometimes known by their German name *Haustafeln*) were known throughout the Greco-Roman world, including the world of Hellenistic Judaism (e.g., Josephus, *Ap.* 1.190-210; Philo, *De Decalogo* 165-67) and the literature of the NT (Eph 5:21–6:9; Col 3:18–4:1; 1 Pet 2:13–3:12). Typically characterized by a mutuality of relationships within the household — husbands/wives, slaves/masters, etc. — these codes embodied basic socioeconomic values in Roman culture. That is, they articulated in concrete terms lines of authority and submission and the duties of obligation categories of people such as men, women, children, and slaves (see pp. 387-88 above). Because they were based on the fundamental understanding of the human community assumed and propagated by the Roman Empire, any attempt to subvert their categories would be viewed as a threat to the glue of the empire itself.

22.2.4. The Household Code's Place in the Letter

According to the NT evidence, Christian communities did not merely absorb Roman household codes into their common life, but "baptized" them, adapting them to the demands of the Christians' faith commitments. Christian innovations included the introduction of a call to *mutual submission* as an interpretive heading for the household code (Eph 5:21), the introduction of the phrase *"in Christ"* as part of formulating a new set of norms by which to live, and the *adaptation* of the household code to particular social scenes. As such, the use of household duty codes functioned as rhetorical devices for communicating particular responses in particular social settings and not as pieces of legislation for Christian existence in all times and places. Apparently, the struggle with community identity among believers led to adaptations of normal social institutions as the numerically rather insignificant Christians explored means for coexistence with wider society.

In 1 Peter the household duty material appears immediately after a major shift in the structure of the letter, marked by the address "Beloved, I urge you . . ."

Philo on the Fifth Commandment

The Alexandrian Jew Philo (first century CE) devotes his treatise *De Decalogo* to an introduction and exposition of the Ten Commandments. His discussion of the fifth commandment, "Honor your father and mother," echoes the concerns of the household duty code.

> In the fifth commandment on honouring parents we have a suggestion of many necessary laws drawn up to deal with the relations of old to young, rulers to subjects, benefactors to benefited, slaves to masters. For parents belong to the superior class of the above-mentioned pairs, that which comprises seniors, rulers, benefactors and masters, while children occupy the lower position with juniors, subjects, receivers of benefits, slaves. And there are many other instructions given, to the young on courtesy to the old, to the old on taking care of the young, to subjects on obeying their rulers, to rulers on promoting the welfare of their subjects, to recipients of benefits on requiting them with gratitude, to those who have given of their own initiative on not seeking to get repayment as though it were a debt, to servants on rendering an affectionate loyalty to their masters, to masters on showing the gentleness and kindness by which inequality is equalized. (31 §§165-67, LCL)

in 2:11 (cf. 4:12). Peter has thus turned from an elaborate theological description of his readers' Christian identity to the behaviors that appropriately follow from their identity. The behavioral distinctives that he begins to enumerate in 2:13 are concrete ways in which his audience is to relate to a social situation in which they have the role of "aliens and exiles." It has been argued that Peter has adopted the form of the household duty code in order to encourage these Christian believers to adapt themselves more fully to Roman society, so that he would be urging them, for the sake of their own survival, to give up some of their distinctives and to embrace more fully practices deemed honorable in the ancient Mediterranean. But such a reading would require that we view this section of the letter as being in unbending tension with the rest of the letter. What is crucial elsewhere is that one do what is honorable in the sight of the Lord; repeatedly, too, Peter warns his readers to expect nothing less than hostility and slander. More likely, then, the household code has the opposite force. It is designed to warn against compromise with Roman social values even though failure to do so will invite further suffering. This interpretation is borne out by two considerations.

First, the household duty code as it is represented by 1 Peter lacks the formal parallelism expected in materials of this sort. True, husbands are mentioned alongside wives, but the amount of material devoted to wives is far out of proportion to the instruction directed to husbands, and slaves have no counterpart in the list.

Second, at the center of 2:13–3:12 is a section extolling the example of Christ, so that the whole can be understood in terms of an inverted parallelism:

> 2:13-17: Instruction for everyone
>   2:18-19: Instruction for slaves
>   2:20-25: The example of Christ
>   3:1-7: Instruction for wives and husbands
> 3:8-12: Instruction for everyone

The pivot point of Peter's instruction is thus the example of Christ, who suffered unjustly and did not reciprocate with abuse, but rather entrusted himself to the God who judges justly. By emphasizing slaves and wives and correlating their recommended behavior with that of Christ, Peter paints his audience as persons without power and privilege in society. They should expect to be treated like those who are powerless in household relationships, knowing, however, that their appropriate conduct will have a redemptive effect akin to that of Jesus. His death had the effect of restoring those who have gone astray; analogously, maintenance of Christian behavior in the midst of unjust suffering might bring to faith those who presently abuse them (see 2:12; 3:1).

---

1 Peter

Letter opening (1:1-2)
Letter body (1:3–5:11)
  The chosen people, God's household (1:3–2:10)
  Engagement in the household of Rome (2:11–4:11)
  Partners in suffering and glory (4:12–5:11)
Letter closing (5:12-14)

22.2.5. The Letter's Themes

The overall structure of 1 Peter is similar to what one finds in the Pauline letters, particularly as this is shaped by the canons of Greco-Roman rhetoric. 1:1-2 serves as the introduction of the letter, denoting author and audience. 1:3–5:11 constitutes the main body of the letter, and 5:12-14 serves as the letter's closing. The body of this letter is notoriously difficult to outline, since Peter has provided little in the way of structural markers by which to follow the development of his argument. The address "beloved" appears twice, in 2:11 and 4:12, and this has served to divide the body of the letter into three parts: 1:3–2:10; 2:11–4:11; and 4:12–5:11.

The first part of the letter body has as its focus the identity of God's people, and this is developed primarily in terms borrowed from the Scriptures of Israel. God's people should not interpret their suffering as a contradiction of their status before God. Suffering serves rather as proof of their identification with Jesus. Though resident as aliens in this historical time and place, their share in God's salvation brings with it a living hope and the promise of a new home. As the people of God they are already living new forms of existence oriented toward the values and practices of the new reality of God's redemptive work. Yet they live in a world very much shaped by old realities; hostility and conflict is therefore almost inevitable. From this concern with the identity of God's people, 1 Peter moves in its second and third major sections to outline how Christians might comport themselves in these circumstances and place their present trying experiences in proper perspective.

Together with the book of Revelation, 1 Peter is unrivaled among NT documents for its concern with questions of Christian identity, constitution, and behavior in a hostile world. Although their answers differ, the two books are similar in their fundamental orientation to Christ and in their deep-rootedness in Israel's Scriptures. For 1 Peter, Christian communities, like Israel in the OT narratives, must struggle with how to maintain a peculiar identity as God's people in the midst of contrary cultural forces of all kinds. This is accomplished by identifying with Christ, both in his suffering and in the promise of restoration and justice. By maintaining their allegiance to the living God, they have a living hope certified by the resurrection of Jesus to life. Their inheritance is nothing less than eschatological salvation — imperishable, uncorrupted, unfading.

22.3. 2 PETER

One of the more pressing issues underlying any interpretation of 2 Peter is recognition of the sort of document it is. "Genre," we may recall, is not a package into which one pours content. Instead, decisions about genre associate a literary product with others like it, raising expectations regarding the substance of the document as well as the experience of reading it. "Content" and "form" are not easily separated.

These factors are of special interest in the case of 2 Peter since it represents the fusion of two genres: letter and testament. It actually refers to itself as a letter (3:1), and it takes the form expected of a letter. It opens with a letter opening (1:1-2), with identification of the author ("Simeon Peter") and the audience ("those who have received a faith . . .") and the customary greeting ("grace and peace"). From there it proceeds to assert its theme (1:3-11) and occasion (1:12-15) and then goes on to the remainder of the body of the letter. There is no formal letter closing, but this is not without analogy even in Christian letter-writing (see James). Although the designation of the letter's implied audience may seem rather general or vague, this impression is immediately modified by the actual content of the letter, in which the author addresses a specific occasion, and by 3:1, which reminds the audience of a first letter (presumably 1 Peter) and thus urges the view that the first recipients of 1 and 2 Peter overlapped significantly.

If 2 Peter is a letter, however, it is also manifestly a representative of the "testamentary literature" known in Hellenistic, OT, Second Temple Jewish, and early Christian writing. For example, in the OT we have the addresses attributed to Jacob (Genesis 48–49) and Moses (Deuteronomy 31–34), and in the NT the use of this form is evident in Luke 22; John 13–17; and Acts 20:17-38. Often taking the form of a farewell discourse, the testament gave opportunity for a great leader to recapitulate his teaching and to instruct his progeny or people, often in association with revelations concerning the future. Because such instruction is associated with the final days or hours of a respected figure, these words carry special gravity and focus. The anticipated pattern is replicated in 2 Peter with reference to (1) the précis of Peter's teaching in 1:3-11, (2) the recognition of Peter's approaching death and concomitant wish that his message be remembered after his death (1:12-15), and (3) predictions of the rise of false teachers (2:1-3; 3:1-4), against which his teaching is to serve as an antidote.

In the case of 2 Peter, the combination of these two genres has produced an effect that deserves brief exploration. By their nature, letters have the capacity to allow one person or group to communicate with another across geographical distance. Testamentary literature, on the other hand, has as its aim communication with those who are temporally distant. A "testamentary letter," then, has the capacity to allow an honored figure to speak across time and space — even, as it were, from the grave. Indeed, this seems actually to have been the case with 2 Peter, for here the prophetic voice of Peter is employed to show that circumstances contemporary with the writing of the letter were anticipated long ago by the apostle. And thus the apostolic message was brought directly to bear on a later situation.

The genre of 2 Peter itself thus points to its authorship in the name of, rather than by, the apostle Peter. Of course, the author of 2 Peter is explicit in tying his letter to the apostle — both by introducing Peter's name in the introduction to the letter and by referring to the previous letter, 1 Peter, in 3:1. Why has the author done so? In all likelihood this was an attempt to inscribe the message of 2 Peter into the authority of the apostle and to bring the weight of the leadership of the church at Rome and thus of its greatest leader into the fight against false teachers. As one of Peter's associates in Rome, the author has worked to continue Peter's influence after his death. The procedure adopted by the otherwise unknown author of 2 Peter would have been akin to the practice of those who passed on the words of OT prophets — who spoke their prophecies rather than writing them — and in doing so allowed their influence to be felt in new and changing situations.

What little evidence we have for dating 2 Peter corroborates this perspective on the document. First, in 3:4 we read of the passing of "the ancestors" — undoubtedly a reference to the first generation of Christians, that generation which, it was supposed, was to have seen the second coming of the Lord. When was this generation gone? It is hard to imagine that the "scoffers" could have spoken of "the ancestors" as gone before the 80s of the first century. This date comports well with the second piece of evidence — namely, the reference to Paul's letters as "Scripture" (3:15-16) — a comment that assumes some sort of collection of Paul's letters ("*all* his letters") and at least the beginnings of a tradition of interpreting them as in some way authoritative for the church. Such a scenario is difficult to date before the closing decades of the first century. Given Peter's martyrdom in Rome in 64 or 65, this data requires that 2 Peter be attributed to the circle of Peter's associates rather than to Peter himself.

For some, Peter's associates writing in Peter's name entails an act of subterfuge. Three observations militate against such a conclusion. First, the genre of 2 Peter itself promises something other than straightforward authorship. As a "testament," 2 Peter would have been recognized immediately by persons in the Hellenistic world as a literary fiction with respect to its attribution to Peter. This is the nature of the literary form chosen for this communiqué.

Second, writing in the name of another was widely practiced in Hellenistic Judaism without necessarily raising issues of honesty and deception. Earlier, of course, the speaking prophets' words were committed to print by other persons, and these are included in the Scriptures of Israel. Later documents circulating in the name of Enoch or Solomon or the Twelve Patriarchs did not raise problems of authorship, in spite of the fact that they could not have been written by those to whom they were attributed. Even Paul knows of a letter written in his name (2 Thess 2:1-2), and it is interesting that the objection he raises is to the content of the letter and not, per se, to the fact that someone had written in his name. Contemporary western sensibilities concerning plagiarism are not easily applied to societies distant from our own — whether geographic or temporal.

Third, 2 Peter gives the impression that its author saw himself (or themselves) as doing nothing more than reformulating the message of the apostle for a new day, and doing so in a way that was faithful to Peter's own influence and contribution to the faith. And, in including 2 Peter in its Scripture, the church recognized the fundamental coherence of the letter's message with the apostolic proclamation — a point that cannot be made of many other early documents that carry the name of this apostle.

The immediate occasion of the letter is the emergence of a perceived heresy, with the result that the polemical tone of 2 Peter is especially pronounced. The false teachers against which the message of this testamentary letter is aimed looked with skepticism on the eschatological teaching of the church and argued against any notion of judgment or other intervention by God in the world to bring justice and abolish evil. Instead, the world would continue along its present course undisturbed — a viewpoint much at home among some Hellenistic philosophical circles, such as the Epicureans. Contrary ideas propagated by the apostles were, the false teachers said, invented by the apostles themselves, who were intent on using the heavy hand of fear of judgment to control behavior in the believing community. Even OT texts mined for their eschatological content are said by the false teachers to have been erroneous. But these teachers, having renounced eschatological expectation and the related notion of divine judgment, also loosened ethical mores: "They have left the straight road and have gone astray" (2:15).

Against this perspective, 2 Peter launches a virtual phalanx of rebuttals:

- It defends the eschatological message of the apostles by recalling the apostles' eyewitness testimony to the transfiguration of Jesus, at which time Jesus was appointed by God to a future role of eschatological rule and judgment (1:16-18).
- It grounds the apostolic message in the Scriptures, argues for the divine inspiration of the Scriptures, and insists that their meaning is not to be renegotiated according to the whims of every person (1:19-21).
- It underscores the certainty of judgment (2:3-10) and warns the opponents that divine judgment will envelop them, too, on account of their false teaching and influence (2:1-3).
- It insists that the fate of the world has always been and continues to be in the hands of God (3:5-7).
- And, employing traditional Jewish thought, it observes that the perception of delay with regard to Jesus' return is due to a misunderstanding of the nature of time, is a failure to appreciate that the Lord allows further opportunity for repentance, and is not a sign that the apostolic message is wrong (3:8-10).

Intermingled with the development of his argument, the author has placed material of a more testamentary nature. This allows him to highlight the faithfulness of the apostle Peter, who is thus seen earlier to have predicted the rise of false teachers such as those 2 Peter is written to combat. Peter's prophecies are even now being fulfilled, allowing the author to interpret the presence of these false teachers as a part of revealed history and thus to undermine their influence.

2 Peter testifies to the inseparable connection between theology and morality — or, in this case, between eschatology and ethics. On the one hand, the author can draw an unmistakable line from denial of eschatological judgment to entanglement in worldly defilements. On the other, he can affirm the eschatological vision of divine intervention, then ask, "What sort of people ought you to be?" For him, the apostolic message regarding the end times has as its immediate corollary lives of holiness, godliness, peace, and purity (3:11-14).

---

2 Peter

Letter opening (1:1-2)
Letter body (1:3–3:18)
   Summary of Peter's teaching (1:3-11)
   Peter's "Testament" (1:12-15)
   The authenticity of the apostolic message and refutation
     of false teachers (1:16–3:10)
   Exhortation to life lived in knowledge of the coming eschaton
     (3:11-18a)
Closing doxology (3:18b)

Jude

Letter opening (vv. 1-2)
Letter body (vv. 3-23)
   Reason for writing: the emergence of false teachers (vv. 3-4)
   Refutation of the false teachers' future judgment (vv. 5-16)
   The prophecy of the apostles (vv. 17-19)
   Exhortations in view of coming judgment (vv. 20-23)
Closing doxology (vv. 24-25)

22.4. JUDE

In spite of its inclusion among the so-called "general" or "catholic" letters, Jude, too, is a genuine piece of correspondence. It has the generic features of a letter — the introduction naming the sender as "Jude, a servant of Jesus Christ and brother of James" and receivers as "those who are called and loved in God the Father and kept for Jesus Christ" and providing initial greetings (vv. 1-2), followed by statements of focus and occasion (vv. 3-4) and the main body of the letter (vv. 5-23). A rich doxology closes the document (vv. 24-25). One might have expected more by way of information about Jude's implied audience, but the content of the letter intimates that its message is not concerned with heresy in general. Rather, it is oriented toward particular exigencies as well as, then, a localized audience.

Nevertheless, apart from the formal ingredients expected of a letter, Jude shares a mode of construction perhaps more reminiscent of a sermon or address than of a letter. The interchange of Scripture and interpretation leading to an appeal to the audience suggests very much the self-conscious adoption of a sermonic manner of communicating. In this case, the letter-like form of the document allows, first, a sermonic message to be delivered to an audience geographically removed from the author, the letter functioning as a virtual stand-in for the author. Second, the letter-like form highlights both the occasional nature of this literary product and also its pastoral focus.

That focus is actually two-edged. This sermonic letter contains a relatively lengthy section of polemics against false teachers and thus undergirds the primary aim of its message, which is to appeal to Christian believers "to contend for the faith" (v. 3). What can be said about these false teachers? This group is made up of itinerant charismatics who have infiltrated the church or churches to which Jude addresses his letter. They have substituted the authority of their own charismatic experiences — visions, revelations, and other ecstatic phenomena — for the authority of Scripture (i.e., the law) and the ethical teachings of Christ. This has led them to reject all moral authority so as to indulge in behaviors that contravene traditional Jewish morality; what is more, they teach others to do the same, so that the church is in danger of losing its distinctive identity through increased openness to the pagan practices of the larger society.

It may be that these false teachers have taken some of their initial cues from the apostle Paul, whose gospel emphasized freedom. Paul, of course, also recognized and countered the problems of using freedom as an occasion for indulging sinful appetites. His letters show that he had to help his churches understand his message of freedom within the context of the responsibility of walking in the Spirit, and that very fact is evidence enough of the possibility that teachers such as these would fail to hear or embrace such balance. The first aim of Jude's letter, then, is to expose these false teachers and their teaching as heretical.

By way of countering these false teachers, Jude engages in a lengthy section of scriptural interpretation (vv. 5-23). The pattern is well known: a reference to a biblical account is followed by its exposition, always with an eye to the contemporary circumstances of Jude's audience. By this means, these false teachers are branded as nothing more than the latest in a long line of ungodly characters whose fate and judgment have already been determined. They are numbered among sinners of all ages who have been condemned in Scripture for their libertine attitudes and instruction. They should be understood in particular as those of the last days who, it was predicted, would pursue their own desires and whose judgment in the end time has been foretold.

The nature of Jude's polemic, together with his use of the Hebrew version of the Scriptures, suggests this letter's provenance in a Palestinian Christianity at home with apocalyptic forms of interpretation. There is no reason, then, not to credit Judas, the brother of Jesus (and thus of James "the Just"), with this letter.

As polemical as this large section of the letter may be, the primary concern of Jude is pastoral. His readers are to stand firm in the faith of the apostles. This is "the faith once delivered to the saints" (v. 3), the content of which is not so much spelled out as assumed. By falling into immoral ways and rejecting any more authority, he writes, the false teachers have actually "denied our only Master and Lord, Jesus Christ" (v. 4). It is not to be so with Jude's readers, however (vv. 20-23). (1) They are to take as the church's substructure this "most holy faith"; building on the foundation of apostolic witness, they will not find themselves on the slippery slope of taking their own experiences as infallible or sufficient guides for faithful living. (2) They are to practice prayer as this is inspired by the Holy Spirit; in this way, Jude does not reject charismatic experience out of hand, but insists that the spiritual experiences claimed by the false teachers are inauthentic. (3) Jude's readers must keep themselves in the love of God. In this co-text, such an admonition is undoubtedly linked to ethical responsibility. (4) They are to set their hope on the coming of the Lord, which will usher in eternal life for those who remain faithful. (5) Finally, Jude advises his readers on how they are to relate to these false teachers and to those who have begun to follow them. The hope of restoration to sound faithfulness is left open, and Jude's readers are to practice love toward the false teachers and their followers. Nevertheless, one must not forget that false teachers and their instruction are like a contagion that must be avoided.

The letter as a whole is framed with references to the keeping power of God:

To those who are called, who are beloved in God the Father and kept safe for Jesus Christ. . . . (v. 1)

Now to him who is able to keep you from falling, . . . to the only God our Savior. . . . (vv. 24-25)

Jude is clear in his perception that his readers must "contend for the faith" by resisting the teaching of these intruders and by engaging in faithful obedience. He is perhaps even more clear in his confidence that the power necessary to bring his readers to eschatological salvation resides in and will be exercised by "the only God, our Savior," to whom all praise is given.

FOR FURTHER READING

Paul J. Achtemeier, *1 Peter* (Hermeneia; Minneapolis: Fortress, 1996)

Richard J. Bauckham, *Jude, 2 Peter* (Word Biblical Commentary; Waco: Word, 1983)

Andrew Chester and Ralph P. Martin, *The Theology of the Letters of James, Peter, and Jude* (Cambridge: Cambridge University Press, 1994)

Peter H. Davids, *1 Peter* (New International Commentary on the New Testament; Grand Rapids: Eerdmans, 1990)

Leonhard Goppelt, *A Commentary on 1 Peter* (Grand Rapids: Eerdmans, 1993)

Jonathan Knight, *2 Peter and Jude* (New Testament Guides; Sheffield: Sheffield Academic, 1995)

J. Ramsay Michaels, *1 Peter* (Word Biblical Commentary; Waco: Word, 1988)

Jerome H. Neyrey, *2 Peter, Jude* (Anchor Bible; New York: Doubleday, 1993)

23. 1, 2, and 3 John

23.1. THE SETTING OF THE EPISTLES OF JOHN

In its struggle to define itself over against the religious and philosophical movements of the ancient world, the emerging Christian movement was no stranger to conflict and controversy. As we have seen in the case of the Pauline churches, conflicts often arose within the Christian community regarding the appropriate beliefs and practices of those who called themselves followers of Jesus Christ. The epistles of John are the literary testimony to, and deposit of, such a disagreement, apparently so intense that it led ultimately to the rupture of the community. Indeed, the rupture may well have been inevitable, since the issues at stake lay at the very heart and soul of the Christian faith. Among the debated issues were the identity of Jesus Christ, the significance of his death, the nature of salvation, and the shape of Christian discipleship. As we shall see, the exact shape of the problems that these three short epistles seek to address resists anything more than a tentative reconstruction. Nevertheless, the internal evidence of the epistles themselves, coupled with data drawn from some other ancient writings, allows us to offer some more specific hypotheses concerning the conflicts and problems within the Johannine community that these epistles seek to address.

In 1 John the author remains anonymous, whereas in 2 and 3 John the author identifies himself as "the Elder," and the recipients are named as "the elect lady and her children" (2 John) and Gaius (3 John). A perusal of the three epistles suggests that 1 and 2 John were written to address the same issues, whereas 3 John, although likely written at about the same time and by the same author, was written to deal with a different problem. The stylistic data suggests that the three letters could well have been authored by the same person. The following scenario offers a plausible explanation for how the letters are related: 1 John is a pastoral treatise, written to and circulated among a number of churches. 2 John was a cover letter sent with it to a specific but unnamed church. 3 John was sent, along with the other two, specifically to Gaius, who was probably a leader in the church that had received the other two letters. For the sake of convenience, the author is often called "the Elder," even though this designation is not used in 1 John, and it is not certain that all three epistles were written by the same author.

The letters provide evidence of a community consisting of a network of smaller congregations that sprang from the same source and belonged more or less loosely together, much as one speaks of the "Pauline mission churches." In this case, scholars speak of "the Johannine community" because the primary literary deposit of their beliefs and struggles comes from the so-called Johannine literature of the NT. Traditionally, this category has included the Gospel of John, the three epistles of John, and the book of Revelation. But whereas the Gospel and letters share similar themes, theological concerns, and a common idiom, Revelation is different enough both literarily and theologically that it is difficult to assign it with certainty to the circle of churches whose Christian faith was expressed in and nurtured by the Gospel and epistles of John.

The letters were probably written after the Gospel to deal with problems that had arisen in the church. According to later church tradition, the author of all four documents was the apostle John; hence, his name was assigned to the Gospel and the letters, which come to us anonymously. Today we use that traditional designation when we speak of "the Johannine community" and "the Johannine literature." But a better understanding of these letters and the situation that they addressed can be gleaned from studying these documents on their own terms rather than from speculation about their unnamed author or authors, who remain largely unknown to us in any case.

23.2. THE CONFLICT: DATA FROM THE EPISTLES

Both 1 and 2 John repeatedly emphasize the importance of adhering to that which "you have heard from the beginning," including particularly the commandment to love each other (1 John 1:1; 2:7, 24; 3:11; 2 John 5-6). Each epistle refers to "deceivers who have gone out into the world," characterizing them as "liars," "antichrists" and "false prophets," who speak by the power of the "spirit of error" (1 John 2:18-22, 26; 4:1-6; 2 John 7). Of great concern to the author is that his readers persist in holding onto and living out the truth that they have been taught (1 John 1:6; 2:4, 8, 21, 26-27; 3:18-19; 4:6; 5:20; 2 John 1-4). Clearly, the author views the teaching and practice of these false prophets as a threat to the proper understanding of truth and to the well-being of his readers. What, then, is the scope and content of the teaching against which our author issues such stern warnings?

A host of statements in the epistles can be pieced together in an effort to characterize the teaching of the false prophets. The author warns his readers against claiming to be without sin (1 John 1:8–2:2); he chastises those who claim to know God, but disobey God's commandments (1:6-7; 2:4-6; 5:2-3), or who claim to love God, but do not love their brothers and sisters (2:7-11; 3:10-18, 23; 4:7-11, 20-21); he cautions against loving the world and warns against its power and allure (1 John 2:15-17; 4:4-6; 5:19). These admonitions focus on the way of life of those who claim to be Christians, suggesting that the author and his community are at odds with these false prophets about the shape of the life of discipleship. Do Christian believers continue to sin? Must they keep the commandments of God? What should be their relationship to "the world"?

Alongside statements that point to the conflict over the nature of the Christian life, there are a series of statements that indicate an equally serious disagreement about the person of Jesus Christ. These statements include the following: "Who is the liar but the one who denies that Jesus is the Christ?" (1 John 2:22; 5:1); "this is the antichrist, the one who denies the Father and the Son" (2:22); "every spirit that confesses that Jesus Christ has come in the flesh is from God" (4:2; 2 John 7); "every spirit that does not confess Jesus is not from God" (1 John 4:3); "God abides in those who confess that Jesus is the Son of God, and they abide in God" (4:15; 5:5, 10, 13); "This is the one who came by water and blood, Jesus Christ, not with the water only but with the water and the blood" (5:6). Together these statements yield a list of what the author urges his readers to confess and believe: Jesus is "the Messiah"; he has "come in the flesh"; he is the Son of God; he "came by water and blood." In simplest terms, they are to "confess Jesus."

But what is the relationship of all these statements to each other? And what were the false prophets saying or teaching? Not only is recognition of Jesus as the Christ, the Messiah, foundational to understanding the nature of his mission, but early in the church's life it formed the heart of confession of Jesus. Indeed, it is hard to imagine "Christians" who did not acknowledge that Jesus is "the Christ." Hence, the more specific affirmations that Jesus had come "in the flesh" and that he came "by water and blood" likely point to the author's concrete concerns with respect to the teachers whom he wished to discredit. The precise contours of their false teaching are lost to us and can only be reconstructed by trying to puzzle out why the author of the epistles makes these various affirmations. But it is clear that the essence of the dispute centers not on whether Jesus is the Messiah, but rather on the proper way to construe what that means, as interpretative clauses such as "Jesus Christ *come in the flesh*" demonstrate. This particular confession gets close to the heart of what the author confesses and his opponents deny, for he stresses quite emphatically the reality of Jesus' existence: "what we have seen with our eyes, what we have looked at and touched with our hands, concerning the word of life . . . we have seen it and testify to it . . . we declare to you what we have seen and heard . . ." (1 John 1:1-3).

There are other affirmations about the person, life, and death of Jesus that help shed light on the false teaching by adding another aspect to our understanding of it. In a number of places, the author puts special stress on the forgiveness of sins that comes through Jesus. His death "cleanses us from all sin" (1 John 1:7); he is the "atoning sacrifice for our sins, and not for ours only but also for the sins of the whole world" (2:2); he appeared to take away sin (3:5) and to "destroy the works of the devil" (3:8). This work was accomplished ultimately through his death, a fact that seems to require both renewed emphasis and interpretation for the readers. The author reminds his readers that Jesus "laid down his life for us" (3:16) and that he came "not with water only, but with the water and the blood" (5:6). "Blood" is a shorthand term for Jesus' death, and the reality and significance of Jesus' death seem to be among the disputed items as well.

From this data taken from the epistles it is not a simple step to a full-scale characterization of the author's opponents and their beliefs. But we get significant assistance from other literature of the time that helps us locate this false teaching on the map of beliefs in the ancient world. In particular, the writings of the church fathers Ignatius, from the early second century, and Irenaeus, from the late second century, give us evidence of heresies that bear some striking similarities to those apparently being combated in 1 and 2 John. A look at selections from their writings will serve to shed some light on the issues in the Johannine community.

23.3. HISTORICAL PARALLELS AND
THE SHAPE OF THE FALSE TEACHING

The false teaching combated by the author of 1 John with emphatic statements like "By this you know the Spirit of God: every spirit that confesses that Jesus Christ has come in the flesh is from God" (1 John 4:2; 2 John 7) seems to be related to the Docetism that Ignatius argued against in the early second century. But the beliefs of those who had left the Johannine community, often called "the secessionists," do not seem as fully developed as the Docetism of Ignatius's letters or of the Gnostic systems attacked by later church fathers (see "Gnosticism" on pp. 412-13 above). The letters of Ignatius and of John show that varying views of the nature of Jesus' human existence already competed for ascendancy in the first century of the church's life, views that would later be taken up into fully developed Gnostic thought. These theories tended to minimize, if not utterly deny, the reality of Jesus' flesh and humanity. By denying the reality of the incarnation of Jesus, they struck at the very heart of the confession, found in the Gospel of John, that "the Word be-

Ignatius on Docetism

Ignatius was a bishop of the church of Antioch in Syria in the early second century who was martyred in Rome *ca.* 110. During his journey from Antioch to Rome under Roman guard, he wrote letters to churches primarily in the region of Asia Minor, including some mentioned in the NT — those in Ephesus, Philadelphia, Smyrna, and Rome — and also to the churches in Magnesia and Tralles. And he wrote a letter to Polycarp, bishop of Smyrna in the first half of the second century.

In several of these letters Ignatius wrote vehemently against a heresy now called "Docetism." The term comes from the Greek word *dokein*, which means "to seem": those Ignatius wrote against held that Christ only *seemed* to have a genuine body of flesh and to suffer and die. Ignatius wrote that they refused to confess Jesus as *sarkophoros*, literally "flesh-bearer" (*Smyrneans* 5.2). He insisted in response that Jesus' birth, suffering, and resurrection were real historical events (*Magnesians* 11) and that Jesus' death and resurrection occurred "in the flesh" (*Smyrneans* 1.2; 3.1). Furthermore,

[Jesus] suffered all these things for us that we might attain salvation, and he truly suffered even as also truly raised himself, not as some unbelievers say, that he only seemed to suffer. . . . (*Smyrneans* 2)

There is one Physician, who is both flesh and spirit, born and yet not born, who is God in man, true life in death, both of Mary and of God, first suffering and then not suffering, Jesus Christ our Lord. (*Ephesians* 7.2)

But if, as some affirm who are without God — that is, unbelievers — he only seemed to suffer (but it is they who only seem to be!), why am I a prisoner, and why do I even long to fight with the beasts? In that case I am dying in vain. (*Trallians* 10)

Since the epistles of John are generally dated to the end of the first century and often located in the region of Asia Minor and, more specifically, in Ephesus, it is easy to imagine that the Docetism that Ignatius opposed was related in some way to the false teaching combated by the author of 1 John.

came flesh and lived among us" (John 1:14). 1 and 2 John reaffirm this fundamental conviction with the assertion, "he came in the flesh."

This leads us to two questions about the struggles in the Johannine church that led to its division. First, how could some members of a community that knew of the incarnation of the Word as recorded in the Fourth Gospel have been led to beliefs about Jesus and his incarnation that seem tantamount to an outright denial of that incarnation? Second, what was the relationship between this denial of Jesus' incarnation and the views of Christian discipleship held by the dissidents?

It is striking that at least one Gnostic document contains the claim that the Gnostic believers "have never sinned" *(Second Treatise of the Great Seth),* a claim rejected by the author of 1 John (1:8–2:2). In another Gnostic treatise, *The Gospel of Mary,* the risen Jesus tells Peter that sin is not a moral failing but a problem arising from the mixing of the spiritual and material realms. Again, 1 John stresses that sin and righteousness are manifested in morality, in concrete conduct. It may be that those who left the Johannine community valued the heavenly and spiritual realm and despised physical matter in such a way that it led them to lay all their emphasis on the heavenly Christ rather than the human Jesus and on their own "spiritual" status as the children of God rather than their day-to-day actions. They had attained their heavenly and spiritual status already in this life and did not need to wait for it. They were, in fact, no longer subject to the evils of this world; as those born of God, they were righteous like Jesus (2:1-2; 3:2) and God, whose children they were (3:1-3). They had been "born from above" by the power of "water and the Spirit" and belonged no longer to this world but to the world above. Just as Jesus came down from heaven, so they had been taken up to the heavenly realms. Taken to its extreme end, such a view evacuates the future of any promise of transformation, since that transformation has occurred now and decisively in this life. The perfection promised for the future belongs to the children of God now, leading them to claim "we have no sin."

Incarnation and ethics were thus inextricably linked together. If one disregards the significance of Jesus' incarnation, life, and death, it follows rather naturally that one will disregard the significance of all human life. The affirmations that Jesus "came in the flesh" testify to the significance of human life, whether it be Jesus' life or that of his followers.

The differences in views regarding Jesus, his incarnation, and ultimately the whole basis of the Christian life led to irreconcilable differences between two factions in the Johannine community, and some left the community. The author of the epistles interprets their departure as evidence that they were committed to a fundamentally different understanding of the Christian faith: "They went out from us, but they did not belong to us; for if they had belonged to us, they would have remained with us. But by going out they made it plain that none of them belongs to us" (1 John 2:19; 2 John 7). They had not remained faithful to the under-

"We Have Not Sinned"

The Gnostic document called *The Second Treatise of the Great Seth* contains a litany of persons and acts deemed sinful by the Gnostics, interspersed with the refrain "We have not sinned." The "Hebdomad" in the text below is an emanation or divine being in Gnostic cosmology.

For Adam was a laughingstock, since he was made a counterfeit type of man by the Hebdomad, as if he had become stronger than I and my brothers. We are innocent with respect to him, since we have not sinned. And Abraham and Isaac and Jacob were a laughingstock, since they, the counterfeit fathers, were given a name by the Hebdomad, as if he had become stronger than I and my brothers. We are innocent with respect to him, since we have not sinned. David was a laughingstock in that his son was named the Son of Man, having been influenced by the Hebdomad, as if he had become stronger than I and the fellow members of my race. But we are innocent with respect to him; we have not sinned. Solomon was a laughingstock, since he thought that he was Christ, having become vain through the Hebdomad, as if he had become stronger than I and my brothers. But we are innocent with respect to him. I have not sinned. The prophets were laughingstocks, since they have come forth as imitations of the true prophets. They came into being as counterfeits through the Hebdomad, as if he had become stronger than I and my brothers. But we are innocent with respect to him, since we have not sinned. (Nag Hammadi codices VII.62.27–63.26; translation from James M. Robinson, ed., *The Nag Hammadi Library* [revised ed.; San Francisco: Harper and Row, 1988])

standing of the faith that had been handed down to them "from the beginning" (1 John 1:1; 2:7, 24; 3:11; 2 John 1:5-6) but had gone "beyond it" (2 John 9). Their departure also showed their failure to obey God's command to believe in Jesus and the basic command that Jesus himself had given them, that they love their brothers and sisters (1 John 3:23), even though they claimed to be without sin.

1 and 2 John aim to reassert and reaffirm, in light of threats from the false teachers and the disruption caused by the split within the church, the teaching that the author and his community had received "from the beginning." While the little

epistle of 2 John alludes to the problem, 1 John constitutes the Elder's arguments for his understanding of the faith over against that of his opponents. 3 John treats a problem that has been created by this situation. Most likely these epistles would not have been read by those who had already left the church. They were intended primarily for those who had remained with the community. 1 John in particular has the dual function of exposing falsehood but also encouraging and reassuring the readers of the genuineness of their faith, and exhorting them to faithfulness and perseverance in it. No doubt the split within the community had caused many to question their own standing as God's children, to wonder whether they had failed to come to a full experience and understanding of their Christian existence. The Elder thus not only wishes to proclaim once more the truth as he himself has heard it, but to call to mind the richness of the experience of love, fellowship, forgiveness, and joy that has marked their life of faith.

23.4. 1 JOHN

Although we refer to 1 John as a letter or epistle, it actually bears none of the marks of ancient correspondence. It does not name its recipients, it begins with no greeting or wish for health, and it contains no closing. It has been variously labeled a circular epistle, a tract, a sermon, a treatise, or a pastoral manual, and some have even suggested that it is a compilation of sermons or parts of sermons or letters. If 1 John were a composite document, that might explain the difficulty readers have had in tracing the development of thought and argument and in detecting a transparent structure. The epistle seems to begin almost in the middle of a thought without a proper introduction, it frequently returns to and repeats previous themes, it does not always manifest transitions between sections, and it ends abruptly with the cryptic exhortation, "Little children, keep yourselves from idols." Unlike other NT authors, such as Luke, Paul, or the author of Hebrews, the Elder is given neither to rhetorical flourish, intricate exegetical arguments, nor literary device and style. In his straightforward and unadorned manner, he summarizes his central pastoral concerns for the well-being of his flock, for their understanding of the significance of Jesus' life and death on their behalf, and for their life together in Christian fellowship and love, which together yield the fruit of joy.

The theological and pastoral themes that provide the epistle's center of gravity are hallmarks of the Johannine tradition, particularly as given expression in John 14–17, the "Farewell Discourses." There Jesus gives his final instructions to his disciples, exhorting them to love each other (John 13:34-35; 14:21-24; 15:13-17; 1 John 3:11-18; 4:7-12, 16-21; 5:1-3), to heed the teaching of the Holy Spirit (John 14:25-26; 15:26-27; 16:13-15; 1 John 2:26-27; 4:1-7, 13), to dwell in unity with God and each other through the work of Jesus Christ (John 14:20, 23; 15:1-

---

1 John

The testimony of eyewitnesses to the Word of Life (1:1-4)
The fundamental contours of the Christian life (1:5-2:27)
  Forgiveness of sin (1:5-2:2)
  Faithfulness and obedience to God's commands (2:3-14)
  Not loving the world (2:15-17)
  Avoidance of false prophets and reliance on the Holy Spirit
    (2:18-27)
The family of God (2:28-3:24)
  The privileges of God's children (2:28-3:3)
  The call to righteousness (3:4-10)
  Warnings against a divided family (3:11-17)
  Living together in love and faith (3:18-24)
The fundamental commands: to believe and to love (4:1-5:12)
  The Spirit testifies to the incarnation of Jesus (4:1-6)
  The people of God are characterized by their love for each other
    (4:7-12)
  The call to obedience: abide in faith and love (4:13-5:5)
  The testimony to Jesus, the incarnate Son of God (5:6-12)
Closing exhortations (5:13-21)

11; 17:21-23; 1 John 1:3), to be on their guard against the pressures and hatred of the world (John 15:18-23; 16:31-33; 17:11; 1 John 2:15-17; 5:4-5, 19), and to live in the joy and peace given to them by Jesus (John 14:1, 27; 15:11; 16:20-24; 20:19-21; 1 John 1:4; 3:19-22). The epistle applies these themes to the problems now facing the Johannine community.

1 John was likely written, then, after the Gospel of John to deal with problems that had arisen in the community sometime later. Of course, the two documents can be difficult to compare, since the Gospel presents a narrative of some of the words and deeds of Jesus, whereas the epistle contains the exhortations and admonitions of an early Christian teacher and pastor. Even so, important differences may be detected. The Gospel aims to encourage faith in Jesus as the Messiah, the Son of God (John 20:31). Jesus is presented in the symbols of Judaism (temple, law, Moses, prophet, Passover) as the fulfillment of God's promises to the people of Israel. But these symbols scarcely appear in 1 John, which lacks OT citations, references to Jewish feasts or customs, and arguments regarding Jesus'

messianic role. As we have suggested, those who fell within the dissident faction so stressed the divine aspect of Jesus' person that they neglected his human life and death. This is almost, ironically, the opposite of the problem in the Gospel itself, where the well-known earthly origins of Jesus present a stumbling block to the claims made for and by him: "Can anything good come out of Nazareth?" (1:46) and "How can he now say, 'I have come down from heaven'?" (6:42). The ordinariness of his human life mocks claims for his exalted status. But in the epistles, not only the significance but also the reality of that human life disappear into Docetic conceptions of Jesus. Put differently, whereas the Gospel declares that Jesus is the *Messiah, the Son of God,* 1 John insists that the Messiah, the Son of God, is *Jesus.*

23.4.1. Witness to the Truth

Evidence of both the problem plaguing the author's community and his response to that problem surfaces in the very first sentence of the letter, where the Elder bears testimony to the historical reality and significance of the events surrounding Jesus' life. In the first four verses, the Elder speaks of "what we have heard, what we have seen with our eyes, what we have looked upon and touched with our hands concerning the word of life" and asserts, "we have seen it and testify to it," and "we declare to you what we have seen and heard" (cf. 4:14). The "we" in this series of statements is, of course, the author and those who support him in one way or another. This group emphasizes its continuity with eyewitness testimony to and about Jesus' life and mission. But nowhere does the Elder call attention to himself, speak of himself as an "apostle" or as one of "the Twelve," or tell us his name. What he does stress is a specific task, that of "testifying" and "declaring." Thus he calls attention to the reality and truth to which he bears witness. He functions in the role of a witness, a role honored by the Johannine community and variously assigned in the Fourth Gospel to the Baptist (John 1:6-8, 15, 32-34; 3:26; 5:33), the Samaritan woman (4:39), the Scriptures (5:39), the Spirit (15:26), the Father (5:37; 8:18), Jesus (3:11) and Jesus' works (5:36; 10:25). But in the Gospel, these witnesses testify to Jesus as the Messiah, the one sent by God; in 1 John, the author and his fellow Christians bear testimony to the historical reality of the events of Jesus' life and death, well aware that others see those events differently and, hence, do not listen to them (4:6; cf. John 3:11). Because of the competing interpretations of the traditions about Jesus, the author exhorts his readers to "test the spirits" by the confession that "Jesus Christ has come in the flesh" (4:2), declaring that the Spirit and God (5:7-12) together confirm the author's testimony to the life and death of Jesus.

Thus the active verbs — have heard, have seen, testify, declare — characterize the role of the witness in the court of law. In ancient Jewish courts, judges passed the verdicts based on the evidence borne by the witnesses who appeared before them. Here the author is the witness and the readers are the judges who will either credit or discredit the testimony offered. Thus the Elder's authority lies in his role and function as a witness, which in turn depends on the reality of that which he has seen and heard and the truth to which he bears witness. Not only does he offer his testimony to what he has seen and heard, but he wishes to offer a persuasive interpretation of that reality, an interpretation that, he argues, has been consistent *from the beginning.*

23.4.2. The Significance of Jesus' Life and Death

Specifically, the core of the author's witness has to do with the reality of Jesus' life and the meaning of his death. While the author affirms the reality, even the palpability of the events of the life of Jesus, the epistle does not actually mention any of the specific deeds or activities of Jesus except his death. For example, none of the signs is recounted or adduced as evidence for Jesus' identity, nor are the signs even mentioned. Except for the command to love one another, the words of Jesus play no significant part in the epistle. These absences do not suggest that the Elder was uninterested in these aspects of Jesus' life, but rather that the focal point of concern was the very fact of Jesus' life and the meaning of his death.

That the meaning of Jesus' life and death belong together is illustrated already in the Gospel of John. Beginning with the resounding affirmation "The Word became flesh and dwelt among us," the Gospel goes on to speak of Jesus' flesh in terms of his sacrificial death: "And the bread that I will give for the life of the world is my flesh" (John 6:51-58). Here, too, Jesus insists that "Unless you eat the flesh of the Son of man and drink his blood, you have no life in you." These very graphic statements speak of Jesus' life-giving death in terms of his giving of his "flesh" *(sarx)* and "blood." This emphasis on the need for Jesus' death is picked up in 1 John, for apparently that very need had been disputed. For, as noted earlier, where there is no sin there is no need of atonement, and apparently certain members of the Johannine community had begun to claim that as children of God, they no longer sinned. The author of 1 John argued that they might as well deny their need for Jesus' death. And to do so would be to flout the witness of the Spirit and of God. Obviously these views cannot exist as two expressions of truth, and eventually those who held them could no longer coexist in the community. Those who were not in agreement with the author left. Thereby they violated, according to the Elder, the two most fundamental commandments: they neither believed in the name of God's son Jesus Christ nor loved one another (3:23). They ceased believing when they abandoned the truths about Jesus held and declared by the Elder

Dualism

The following text from the Dead Sea Scrolls, with its sharp "dualism" between two "spirits," no longer made it necessary to brand the dualism found in 1 John (and the Gospel of John) as "Greek" rather than "Jewish," once it had been discovered and published. The contrast between light and darkness and righteousness and falsehood, the image of "walking" in the ways of truth and light, and the contrast between the two spirits are found also in 1 John.

> He has created man to govern the world, and has appointed for him two spirits in which to walk until the time of His visitation: the spirits of truth and falsehood. All the children of righteousness are ruled by the Prince of Light and walk in the ways of light, but all the children of falsehood are ruled by the Angel of Darkness and walk in the ways of darkness.
>
> The Angel of Darkness leads all the children of righteousness astray; and until his end, all their sin, iniquities, wickedness, and all their unlawful deeds are caused by his dominion in accordance with the mysteries of God.
>
> But the God of Israel and His Angel of Truth will succor all the sons of light. For it is He who created the spirits of Light and Darkness and founded every action upon them and established every deed [upon] their [ways]. (1QS 3:17-25, Vermes)

and his supporters "from the beginning," and they failed to love each other by their failure to maintain the unity of relationship within the family of God.

24.4.3. The Family of God

And, indeed, the language for believers is strikingly familial. Believers are "children of God" (*tekna tou theou*, 3:1), "born of God"; they confess God as "Father" (3:1); they are "brothers and sisters" to each other, and some even seem to have the designation "fathers" (2:13, 14); they inherit through Jesus, the Son of God (*huios tou theou*, 1:3; 2:22-25; cf. John 8:34-35). The Elder repeatedly addresses his flock as "little children" (*teknia*, 2:1, 12, 28; 3:7), and "beloved" (*agapētoi*, 2:7; 3:2, 21;

4:1, 7, 11; cf. 3 John 1, 2, 5, 11). The poignant scene at the cross in the Gospel of John, in which Jesus entrusts his mother and the "disciple whom he loved" to each other, establishes the new family that would be born, as Jesus warned, out of divisions within existing families. The Johannine community had already experienced such painful division as the Christian movement became ever more distinct from its Jewish roots, and now experienced it again as the community itself split over different understandings of the Christian faith. Whereas the familial imagery had once referred to the family created by Jesus' call, as over against the natural family of Judaism, now the imagery was pressed into the service of designating those who remained faithful to that message that had been passed down from the beginning of the family's existence.

But the family imagery may also provide useful evidence regarding the internal structure and organization of the Johannine community. Although the author refers to himself as "the Elder" in 2 and 3 John, there are no other traces in the epistle of offices or functions in the church, such as one finds hints of in Acts and the Pauline correspondence. A high premium is placed on the role of the Spirit, whose primary function is construed in terms of teaching and inspiring prophets to teach the truth. Undoubtedly those members of the community who had left it also claimed to be inspired by the Spirit. They may well have claimed that their understanding of the faith and teaching was the direct leading of the Spirit into deeper insights into Jesus and the meaning of his life and death. But, as the author of 1 John warns, the claim to have the Spirit does not automatically imply that one speaks by the power of that Spirit: "Beloved, do not believe every spirit, but test the spirits to see whether they are from God; for many false prophets have gone out into the world" (4:1). He then goes on to give one of two primary tests by which one can "know the Spirit of God: every spirit that confesses that Jesus Christ has come in the flesh is from God, and every spirit that does not confess Jesus is not from God" (4:2-3). While the community acknowledged itself to be guided by the teaching and inspiration of the Spirit, which, according to Johannine tradition, "blows where it chooses" (John 3:8), nevertheless the work of the Spirit was understood to be circumscribed by the testimony of those who had witnessed, and now bore testimony to, the reality of Jesus' life and death. The Spirit would not lead prophets into confessions and teaching that took the original testimony in such a fundamentally different direction.

23.5. 2 JOHN

The shortest of the NT writings, 2 John seems somewhat redundant after the lengthier and more developed first epistle. The contribution of 2 John to our understanding of early Christianity and the Christian faith lies not so much in its theological assertions, which are consistently more terse than those of 1 John, but in the framework it provides for reading 1 John. If in 1 John we see the problem from the vantage point of the church from which the false prophets "went out," in 2 John we see the problem with the eyes of the church in which they may then have showed up to preach and teach. The purpose of 2 John is to deal with the problem of itinerant teachers whose heresies had been enumerated and condemned in 1 John (v. 7). How does the church treat those who had gone out teaching in ways contrary to the truth (vv. 7, 10, 11)?

Unlike 1 John, this letter opens in traditional form with the designation of the author ("the elder") and the recipients ("the elect lady and her children"). And yet the identifications offered are unusual, for where one would typically expect personal names, here we have title and metaphor. Suffice it to say that the original readers knew full well who the Elder was, and the title suggests both a specific function within the church (Jas 5:14; 1 Pet 5:1; 1 Tim 5:17; Tit 1:5) and a position of authority. "The elect lady and her children" is likely a personification of a local church and its members; we would say "the church and its members," even as Paul tells the church at Corinth, "You are the body of Christ and individually members of it" (1 Cor 12:27). Regularly in the Scriptures, the people of God are compared to

The baptistry of the restored third-century house church in Dura-Europos, on the Euphrates River
(Yale University Art Gallery)

Early Christian "House Churches"

According to the NT, the earliest Christian believers gathered for fellowship and worship in private homes (Acts 2:46; 5:42; 12:12). This was not a novel practice, but followed the pattern of contemporary Judaism. Archaeological excavations show that the "synagogues" of first-century Judaism were at first rooms in private residences. Later both Jews and Christians began to renovate private residences for the exclusive use of gathering together, so that the earliest buildings set aside strictly for worship and fellowship were originally private homes. Some archaeologists have suggested that a building at Capernaum that was renovated to serve as a gathering place for Christians was originally the home of Peter. The practice of using private homes continued until the growth of the Christian movement caused Christians to search for larger gathering places in public buildings, and until Emperor Constantine, in the early fourth century, recognized Christianity and extended freedom of worship to Christians. Constantine also generously sponsored building of structures dedicated exclusively to worship, particularly in Palestine, Rome, and Constantinople.

a woman, the bride of Yahweh or Christ or God's children (Isa 54:1, 13; Jer 6:21; 31:21; Lam 4:2-3; John 3:29; 2 Cor 11:2; Gal 4:25-26; Eph 5:23; Revelation 18–19). Again the image is familial. Even as John and 1 John speak of believers as "children of God" (e.g., John 1:13; 1 John 3:1-3) and "brothers and sisters" of each other, so here, too, the church is conceived of as a mother and her children. The elder writes to a specific house church some distance away to warn against the activities and teaching of a rival missionary group who have left the larger community.

In his greeting to the congregation, the Elder uses two words that become thematic throughout the epistle: love (vv. 1, 3, 5-6) and truth (vv. 1-4). According to the Elder, those who have left the church have failed to show love for their brothers and sisters, presumably by leaving the church. Hence, love and unity are closely related, even as they are in John 14–17, in Jesus' discourses about the importance of loving one another and living in unity with each other and with God. Truth includes those matters of confession and practice that ought to characterize the Christian believer. Thus the author speaks not only of "knowing the truth" (v. 1) but also of "walking in the truth" (v. 4). The truth that they are to know has at its heart "the coming of Jesus Christ in the flesh" (vv. 7-9; cf. 1 John 4:1-2). The traveling prophets, those who are "deceivers" and "antichrists" (v. 7), have shown by their false teaching about Christ, their misconstrual of the status of the Christian, and their departure from the Johannine community their failure both to "know" the truth and to "walk" in it.

The Elder's admonitions about these false teachers are stern and unyielding: "Do not receive into the house or welcome anyone who comes to you and does not bring this teaching" (v. 10). In fact the attitude manifested here has led scholars to paint a picture of a beleaguered and ingrown community that has turned increasingly inward upon itself. But the Elder's command does not intend to promote hostility toward and separation from the world. Rather, the context of the epistle makes it clear that the house in question is the house church (v. 10). In other words, the Elder commands the church not to sanction false teaching by allowing the false teachers opportunity to speak. The church members are to test the spirits of the prophets (1 John 4:1-7) and, having tested them, to stand firmly for the truth.

---

2 John

Letter opening (vv. 1-3)
Letter body (vv. 4-11)
    Mutual love among Christians (vv. 4-6)
    The danger of false teachers (vv. 7-11)
Letter closing (vv. 12-13)

3 John

Letter opening (v. 1)
Prayer and thanksgiving (vv. 2-4)
Letter body (vv. 3-12)
    Affirmation of Gaius's hospitality for itinerant preachers (vv. 4-6)
    Plans concerning Diotrephes, who opposes such hospitality
        (vv. 7-10)
    Exhortation not to imitate Diotrephes (v. 11)
    Endorsement of Demetrius (v. 12)
Letter closing (vv. 13-15)

23.6. 3 JOHN

3 John is also a genuine letter, but unlike 1 and 2 John it is a personal letter addressed to Gaius. The letter itself has three main purposes: the author commends Gaius and his practice of welcoming traveling prophets (vv. 5-8), criticizes the behavior of Diotrephes, who refuses to follow the practice of Gaius (vv. 9-10), and commends one of these prophets, Demetrius (v. 12). 3 John may well have been a letter of commendation for Demetrius to be carried by Demetrius himself (cf. Rom 16:1-2; 2 Cor 3:1-3).

To understand these commendations and condemnations, we need to place them in the context of Johannine church life. Because the larger community consisted of a number of smaller congregations scattered over an area wide enough to prohibit easy contact with the Elder, communication through letters and messengers such as Demetrius was crucial to maintaining contact and strengthening fellow believers. Apparently the Elder had sent out emissaries before, just as he was now sending Demetrius. But the rupture in the community over matters of belief and practice, resulting in the secession of some individuals, had complicated matters. Not only were there emissaries of the Elder, but those who had seceded from the community likely also maintained contacts in various congregations. They would have neither cut off all fellowship nor abandoned their own commitments to preaching and teaching their understanding of the faith. It might not have been easy to distinguish truth from error or the faithful from heretical teachers, especially since both sides may have used traditional confessional formulas, albeit with different interpretations.

The Elder commends Gaius for "walking in the truth" (vv. 3-4) and, specifically within this letter, for welcoming the "brothers" (v. 5), sending them on their way "in a manner worthy of God" (v. 6), supporting them (vv. 7-8), and being their "coworkers in the truth" (v. 8). These "brothers" were probably itinerant teachers and emissaries of the Elder. The hospitality given them amounted to more than provision of room and board, as welcome as that would have been. The Elder is commending Gaius's hospitality because it ensures the propagation of the truth.

On the other hand, the Elder condemns the attitude and activities of Diotrephes, whose offenses consist of refusing to acknowledge the Elder's authority (v. 9), spreading false charges about the Elder (v. 10), and refusing to welcome those sent out, apparently by the Elder (v. 10). Moreover, although the Elder alludes to an earlier letter that he has written "to the church" (v. 9), perhaps to try to address some of the problems that figure in 1 and 2 John, that letter has been ignored, and Diotrephes, who, according to the Elder, "likes to put himself first" (v. 9), seems responsible. While it is tempting to think of Diotrephes as one of the heretical teachers who has left the community, the Elder never criticizes Diotrephes with respect to his

Discerning the Prophets

Itinerant teachers and preachers were not uncommon in the early Christian movement. These quotations from the *Didache,* which is from the second century, show the difficulty and necessity of discerning the true prophet from the false prophet:

> Let every apostle who comes to you be received as the Lord, but let him not stay more than one day, or if need be a second as well; but if he stay three days, he is a false prophet. (11:4-5)

> Not everyone who speaks in a spirit is a prophet, unless he has the behavior of the Lord. From his behavior, then, the false prophet and the true prophet shall be known. (11:8)

> Let everyone who comes in the name of the Lord be received. . . . If he who comes is a traveler, help him as much as you can, but he shall not remain with you more than two days, or, if need be, three. (12:1-2)

faith or teaching. It seems unlikely that these would have gone unmentioned had the Elder known of any heretical inclinations held by Diotrephes. That Diotrephes has set himself against the Elder seems clear; why he has done so, whether out of personal spite or deeply held convictions, remains unclear. But he must have been a person of some influence in the church in order to prevent the Elder's letter from getting a proper hearing, to refuse a welcome to those itinerant teachers, to prevent others from doing so, and even to go so far as to "expel them from the church" (v. 10). While the Elder proposes a visit to deal with the problem, he encourages Gaius to persist in his course and resist Diotrephes' pressure. Demetrius can be expected to assist Gaius if Gaius will welcome the Elder's emissary and adhere to the truth that he proclaims.

FOR FURTHER READING

Raymond E. Brown, *The Epistles of John* (Anchor Bible; Garden City: Doubleday, 1982)

Rudolf Bultmann, *The Johannine Epistles* (Hermeneia; Philadelphia: Fortress, 1973)

Judith Lieu, *The Second and Third Epistles of John: History and Background* (Edinburgh: Clark, 1986)

————, *The Theology of the Johannine Epistles* (Cambridge: Cambridge University Press, 1991)

I. Howard Marshall, *The Epistles of John* (New International Commentary on the New Testament; Grand Rapids: Eerdmans, 1978)

Stephen S. Smalley, *1, 2, 3 John* (Word Biblical Commentary; Waco: Word, 1984)

Rudolf Schnackenburg, *The Johannine Epistles* (New York: Crossroad, 1992)

Georg Strecker, *The Johannine Letters* (Hermeneia; Minneapolis: Fortress, 1996)

Marianne Meye Thompson, *1, 2, 3, John* (Downers Grove: InterVarsity, 1992)

24. Revelation

Perhaps no NT document simultaneously engages the imagination of its readers and frustrates their understanding as much as Revelation, the last book in the canon. In its pages one encounters vivid descriptions of fantastic creatures, including heavenly beings who are "full of eyes in front and behind, each with six wings"; a red dragon with seven heads, ten horns, and seven crowns; a beast rising from the sea who is part leopard, part bear, and part lion; and white, red, black, and pale green horses whose riders bring slaughter, destruction, famine, and pestilence to the earth. No shades of gray and brown dull these scenes, which are splashed with vivid colors — red, white, black, green, purple, blue, and gold. Cities, buildings, and thrones are made of precious jewels and metals, including sapphires, amethysts, emeralds, pearls, gold, and bronze. Everything seems to be counted and numbered: 144,000 people are "sealed out of every tribe of the people of Israel"; "thousands of thousands" sing to the Lamb; four living creatures circle the heavenly throne; four angels stand at the four corners of the earth; seven angels blow seven trumpets and pour out seven bowls of wrath; "the number of the beast is 666"; the heavenly city has twelve gates, is guarded by twelve angels, and is built on twelve foundations. And finally, the scenes of the book are marked by a constant din: unceasing singing, including choruses of praise, laments, and dirges, blowing of trumpets, crashes of thunders, loud cries, and constant prayers. No book is quite so intense, vivid, full of material to engage the senses — and enigmatic to its readers. Its mysterious puzzles have opened the floodgates for all sorts of imaginative and fanciful interpretations, some that stretch the imagination far beyond anything found in the book itself. As G. K. Chesterton once wrote, "Though St. John the Evangelist saw many strange monsters in his vision, he saw no creature so wild as one of his own commentators."[1]

But the exotic features of the book of Revelation are less responsible for outlandish interpretations of it than are the mistaken expectations so often brought to it by its modern readers. Because commentators past and present have assumed that their own experience and contemporary events of their world will unlock its secrets, Revelation has been interpreted in light of everything from the Reformation to Hitler, atomic weapons, and the European Union. Ironically, however, the more commentators have sought to make the book relevant by applying its prophecies to their own times, places, and situations, the more they have missed the paths that lead to genuine understanding and appreciation of the power of this mysterious book. Attention to its historical context, social and religious milieu, and literary genre sheds considerable light on its form, content, and function and so clears the way for us to hear the warning of the risen Jesus: "Let anyone who has an ear listen to what the Spirit is saying to the churches" (2:7, 11, 17, 29; 3:6, 13, 22).

24.1. THE GENRE OF REVELATION

Revelation has characteristics of three genres: letter, prophecy, and apocalypse. As we will see, it has both structural traits and substantive similarities with each of them. But despite these similarities, it is not a perfect specimen of any of them. Its uniqueness lies not only in its combination of these genres but also in the adaptation of each to serve the author's purposes.

24.1.1. Revelation as Circular Letter

Like other letters in the NT, Revelation has a prescript naming its author and addressees, an opening greeting (1:4-6), and a postscript (22:21). But the similarities go beyond structural markers. Of all the NT documents, the letters can most transparently be shaped by the particular needs or concrete situations of their intended readers and can address them most specifically. That Revelation is a letter suggests that it deals with concerns or problems arising from the readers' historical circumstances, that the author is fully aware of those circumstances, and that he addresses himself to them with prophetic wisdom and pastoral counsel. The recipients of this circular letter are "the seven churches that are in Asia" (1:4), and John incorporates into his letter a specific message to each of these churches (chs. 2–3).

---

1. *Orthodoxy* (New York: Dodd, Mead, 1947), 29.

Some of these churches (Ephesus, Laodicea) are referred to elsewhere in the NT, and others (Smyrna, Philadelphia) are known to us from the writings of early church authors such as Ignatius. Revelation was likely intended also for other Christian congregations in Asia Minor, of whom these seven were representative. John may have deliberately cast his book in the form of a letter in order to place it within the early Christian tradition of letter-writing. It follows that Revelation is to be read with the same sorts of historical and contextual sensitivities and questions that guide our reading of the letters of Paul, John, and Peter. Revelation was written first to address the concerns and needs of its first-century readers.

The island of
Patmos
*(Nicholas
Wolterstorff)*

24.1.2. Revelation as Christian Prophecy

The author of Revelation also refers to his writing as a *prophecy,* thus placing it within the prophetic tradition of the Old and New Testaments (1:3; 22:6-7, 18-19). At the outset of the Revelation, we read this benediction: "Blessed is the one who reads the words of the prophecy, and blessed are those who hear and who keep what is written in it; for the time is near" (1:3). Two points are of significance here. First, the command to "read" and the reference to "hearers" indicate that the context in which the book was to be read was the gathering of Christians for worship, where the Scriptures and letters from apostles or their delegates were read and where prophecies were uttered (cf. 1 Corinthians 12–14; 1 John 4:1-7). Second, the author of the Revelation warns that the words of the book are to be *kept*. While it is a book that discloses and prophesies, it is above all a book that, like the writings and words of all the prophets, intends to admonish, correct, and encourage its readers. It calls for repentance, obedience, faithfulness, and perseverance. This is not a code needing to be cracked; it is proclamation that needs to be heard and obeyed.

24.1.3. Revelation as Apocalypse

The book of Revelation also belongs to a genre of ancient Jewish and Jewish Christian literature designated by modern scholars as *apocalyptic literature*. The Greek word *apokalypsis*, meaning disclosure or revelation, is found in the opening words of Revelation: "The *revelation* of Jesus Christ" (1:1) and provides the basis of both names of the book: either the English translation of *apokalypsis*, the Revelation, or a transliteration of the Greek word, the Apocalypse.

The modern term *apocalyptic* is applied by modern scholars to a number of literary works dating from about 200 BCE to 200 CE. These works have in common a similar worldview, known as *apocalypticism*, which generally views the world in a radically dualistic framework that is often embodied in the conflict between God and his angels, on the one hand, and the devil and demons on the other. Because apocalypticism assumes conflict of cosmic dimensions, it also hopes for imminent divine intervention to deliver the faithful. Such divine intervention, it is typically predicted, will produce a drastic change in the situation of the world and inaugurate the resurrection of the dead and the final judgment, which will determine the destinies of all persons. In spite, then, of the suffering and ills of the present life, apocalypticism expects that God will vindicate his faithful saints, punish the disobedient and apostate, and triumph over all powers of evil. Although elements of apocalypticism can also be found in the teachings of Jesus, Paul, and other figures of the NT, none of them left behind a written *apocalypse*.

An *apocalypse* is a literary work, typically a prose narrative in the first person, in which the narrator records a series of revelations received through either visions or journeys to heaven or both. These experiences disclose transcendent realities to the "seer." The secrets that are made known typically take the form either of a historical narrative leading to the present and foreshadowing God's assured future salvation, or of heavenly mysteries currently unavailable to human beings. Apocalypses tend also to use symbolism of numbers, animals, and other figures that must be interpreted for the seer. The seer is guided by a heavenly escort, usually an angel, who serves as interpreter of the visions and experiences.

Revelation shares many of these features with Jewish writings such as *2 Baruch*, 4 Ezra, and *1 Enoch* and with early Christian writings such as the *Shepherd of Hermas*. Yet even though apocalypses have certain features in common, it should not be supposed that a simple template existed for the writing of an apocalypse. Not all apocalypses have all the traits generally deemed common to "apocalyptic literature." Revelation, in fact, manifests features that are both shared by and different from other apocalypses.

24.1.3.1. Pseudonymity

A striking instance of one of the distinctive features of Revelation is the author's presentation of himself simply as "John." As noted above, the human "seer" of the apocalypses typically writes in the first person. But in Jewish apocalypses the author always writes under a pseudonym, presenting himself as a worthy ancient fig-

---

Early Christian Apocalypses

In addition to the Revelation, there are other Christian apocalypses. The following three come from the first and second centuries.

- *The Ascension of Isaiah:* The first part of this book (chs. 1–5) narrates Isaiah's confrontation with false prophets, leading to his martyrdom; the second part (chs. 6–11) describes Isaiah's ascent to heaven, and his vision of the descent of "the Beloved" (Jesus) from the seventh heaven to earth and his return to the seventh heaven.
- *The Shepherd of Hermas:* This first person narrative was written by Hermas, a Christian living in Rome in the first half of the second century. The book gets its name from the angelic interpreter who appears to Hermas as a shepherd. Along with other angelic beings, the Shepherd mediates to Hermas revelations and visions of transcendent realities. Additionally, the book has a strong ethical focus, and a portion of the book consists of twelve sets of commandments (the "Mandates"). It treats the problem of Christians who have lapsed following their baptism, and believes that a second repentance is possible.
- *The Apocalypse of Peter:* Written in the second century under the name of Peter, this apocalypse describes a journey through hell and heaven, and the torments and blessings to be experienced in each of these realms. This work subsequently influenced Dante's *Divine Comedy*.

ure such as Adam, Abraham, Moses, Enoch, or Ezra. Christians also adopted the strategy of pseudonymous writing, and Christian apocalypses appeared under the names of ancient prophets, such as Isaiah, and of the apostles, including Peter, Thomas, and Paul. The purpose of pseudonymous writing seems to have been twofold. First, it allowed otherwise unknown authors to claim the authority of a revered religious figure for their work and so to gain a hearing for it. Second, writing under the name of a figure from the distant past allowed the actual author to write of contemporary events under the guise of predictive prophecy, since from the vantage point of the fictitious author those events lay far in the future. Pseudonymity appears to have been primarily a literary technique, and not one meant to deliberately deceive its readers.

Revelation, however, is not pseudonymous. The author names himself as "John," and the authority of his writing depends to some extent on the relationship he has with the recipients of the document. His self-portrait — "I, John, your brother who share with you in Jesus the persecution, the kingdom, and the patient endurance" (1:9) — points to his knowledge of their situations and his affiliation with them in their trials. Moreover, in keeping with the early Christian movement, John demonstrates a lively sense of his own prophetic commission and authority (1:1, 4, 9-11, 19; 10:8-11; 22:9). It may well be that this strong prophetic consciousness supplied John with the motivation to write under his own name rather than the name of an ancient figure.

24.1.3.2. Symbolism

Surely the most noticeable aspect of the Revelation, which it shares to some extent with other apocalyptic literature, is its vivid symbolic imagery. Colors, numbers, animals of all sorts, artifacts such as lampstands and buildings, and plants and trees all carry symbolic connotations. But it is crucial to see that not all the imagery and symbols function in exactly the same way. The symbolism of Revelation varies. Sometimes it is explained by the author; sometimes stock figures and imagery of biblical and apocalyptic literature are employed; sometimes the details are there merely to heighten the drama and sensory impact of the work.

A common but erroneous reading of Revelation flattens all the imagery into code that must be deciphered by lining up the "symbol" in the book with an event, person, or reality in history, whether past, present, or future. Once deciphered, the imagery itself becomes dispensable. To be sure, some of the imagery refers to historical realities in the first-century author's and readers' world. For example, the author pictures a woman seated simultaneously on "many waters" and on a "scarlet beast that was full of blasphemous names, and it had seven heads and ten horns." On her forehead is the name "Babylon" (17:1-6). Each item in this picture represents ancient Rome in some way. Rome was known in all the world for its command of the seas (the "many waters"), "blasphemous names" refers to the deification and worship of emperors, and Rome was identified in various ancient Jewish and Christian sources by the name of the ancient enemy of the people of God, Babylon. Finally, the interpreting angel tells the seer that "the seven heads are seven mountains" (17:9), and the seven hills on which Rome was built were well known. The author of Revelation intends for the reader to identify the woman seated on the beast with Rome; he does not conceal Rome in cryptic code but describes it with symbols that quickly point to Rome. The symbols do not conceal; they reveal. The images of Rome as a beast, a harlot, and the fallen city of Babylon reveal something of the fluidity of the imagery of Revelation, which, like a kaleidoscope, can be constantly varied to give its readers ever new views. And the cumulative force of these symbols also guide the reader's understanding of the symbolism, even though Rome is not explicitly named.

At other places, the angel interprets the symbol for the seer, who in turn gives the reader that interpretation in written form. An opening vision of one "like a Son of man" amid seven gold lampstands holding seven stars in his hand (1:13-16) is immediately interpreted: "The seven stars are the angels of the seven churches, and the seven lampstands are the seven churches" (1:20). Later, four horses are described and then interpreted as conquest, slaughter, famine, and death (ch. 6). The great red dragon of ch. 12 is explicitly called "that ancient serpent, who is called the devil and Satan, the deceiver of the whole world."

But other symbolism in Revelation is more general in nature. Colors often have symbolic value. White conveys righteousness or purity, gold represents great value, red indicates blood and hence destruction and death, and purple is the color of royalty. That God and the Lamb are pictured as seated or standing on thrones signifies sovereignty and dominion, particularly in the political realm. The depiction of all the creatures who continually sing, pray, and prostrate themselves around the throne presents God and the Lamb as worthy of worship. The court of heaven (4:2) is also pictured as a synagogue in which a scroll is read (ch. 5), a temple with an altar on which incense is offered (8:3), and a law court from which the Accuser is thrown out (12:10). Just as one reality can be pictured by a number of images and symbols, so too any one symbol can carry rich and multiple meanings.

The numbers in Revelation are also highly symbolic. As a number associated with heavenly or divine realities, seven plays an important role in the book: there are seven angels, seven spirits, and three sets of seven judgments (trumpets, seals, and bowls) and the Lamb has seven eyes. Duration of time is often measured in increments of seven, including 3½, or in increments of ten (e.g., ten days or one thousand years). Four is the number of the corners of the earth, and the heavenly city is built "four square." According to ch. 7, the number of those sealed is 144,000, derived by multiplying $12 \times 12 \times 1000$, which indicates the great number

(a countless crowd according to v. 9) of the people of God. The formulaic and re-
petitive use of numbers underscores their symbolic function.

Some of the imagery in Revelation serves primarily to add to the detail and
vividness of the descriptions. The seer's attempts to put into words his vision of
God on the heavenly throne yields this description: "And the one seated there
looks like jasper and carnelian, and around the throne is a rainbow that looks like
an emerald . . . and in front of the throne there is something like a sea of glass, like
crystal" (4:3, 6). Only a stunning lack of imagination would miss the evocative appeal of such imagery. Similarly, the description of judgment and catastrophe contained in the sixth seal draws on imagery from OT prophets (Isa 13:10; 50:3; Joel
2:10): "the sun became black as sackcloth, the full moon became like blood, and
the stars of the sky fell to the earth as the fig tree drops its winter fruit" (6:12). Such
vivid language intends to warn of the dire consequences of judgment, not to predict the literal collapse of the physical world. A mighty angel is pictured as "coming down from heaven, wrapped in a cloud, with a rainbow over his head; his face
was like the sun, and his legs like pillars of fire" (10:1). This evocative description
portrays the power and glory of God's designated messenger in a medley of OT
imagery. A tremendous earthquake (16:17-21) portends the fall of Babylon. But so
do the images of Babylon as a harlot who is stripped, devoured, and burned by the
beast (17:16) and of Babylon as a city that is besieged, sacked, and leveled by an invading army (ch. 18). These various descriptions of the destruction of Babylon offer the reader insight into the nature of Rome and its great power, while at the
same time foreseeing its complete judgment and punishment.

Unquestionably, however, the most common interpretive error in reading
the symbolism of Revelation is to confuse the symbols of the book with its message. The symbols are not the message; they carry and embody the message. John
was not projecting and predicting a time when one by one these symbols would
"come to life" and be realized in historical events. He was not predicting such a
time because he wrote to awaken and shape the moral and religious imagination
of Christians of his own day. The symbolism is meant to stimulate these Christians
to see the world as it truly is, not to veil it from their sight until some future generation should discover what twenty centuries of readers had missed all along. But it
is equally a mistake to read the symbolism, as some have done, as "timeless" representations of the eternal struggle between good and evil. Again, John wrote a prophetic word to address the lives of Christians of his own time and place. To trans-
mute John's descriptions of the difficulties of their existence into vague "timeless
symbols" would devalue their own suffering and struggles, and render too remote
the real threat posed by the deceitful allure and power of Rome.

Put differently, the visions and heavenly journeys described in Revelation
have as their main content not so much the heavenly world or the future. Rather,
the main content of those visions consists of the world of the Roman Empire and

the book of Revelation explains its origins to a large degree but does not completely account for the ways in which apocalyptic literature and convictions could be adapted by various other groups. Moreover, the view that apocalyptic literature intends to offer its readers comfort and assurance does not exhaust what Revelation is up to, as some of the edicts of chs. 2–3 amply attest. In these chapters, laxness, self-sufficiency, syncretism, and materialism are named as threats to the faithfulness of the churches. The problem was not that these Christians were being persecuted for their faith by the government or ostracized by their neighbors, but that they had made too cozy a peace with the prevailing cultural and political ethos. That is the crisis in which they found themselves, although they did not see it. They did not need comfort, but rather to be jolted, to have their eyes opened.

The visions of Revelation depict in graphic and fantastic ways the reasons not only that endurance was needed, but also that the dulled sensitivities of Christians needed to be sharpened: the world in which first-century Christians lived was not always what it seemed, and there were real threats, both subtle and obvious, to holding steadfastly to faith in God. Revelation functions rather like a political cartoon, exaggerating certain features of its subject and drawing in bold, stark strokes to make its point. Like many political cartoons, it protests what it sees and is open to being misunderstood, disbelieved, or ignored. Its power to persuade lies, to some extent, in the eye of the beholder, who chooses whether to allow the picture to become the prism through which the world is viewed. And just as political cartoons are often unintelligible to subsequent generations that lack knowledge of the context in which those cartoons arose, so too the book of Revelation often seems merely like an enormous and perplexing puzzle to subsequent generations of readers. Not surprisingly, knowledge of the first-century historical context serves to further illumine Revelation.

24.2. THE HISTORICAL CONTEXT OF THE BOOK OF REVELATION

24.2.1. Roman Military Might

The NT was written, and all the events and persons found within it took place, within the far-flung borders of the Roman Empire. There were undeniable benefits for those who lived under the so-called *pax Romana*, the "Roman peace," which to a large extent united the Mediterranean world economically, politically, and culturally and brought a relative measure of peace and stability to its inhabitants. Yet in spite of the positive contributions of Roman rule to the ancient world and even to the spread of the early Christian movement, the NT authors often manifest a wary attitude toward Roman political dominion.

The author of Revelation is more than wary. His book contains the most sustained critique of Roman power in the NT. As the dominant military power of its time, Rome resembled a grotesque and formidable beast, seeking to devour and kill (ch. 13). Military victories brought wealth, power, and influence to Rome, which was able through its military might to assert political and economic dominance. Rome is also portrayed as a harlot, trying to seduce and corrupt the inhabitants of the "great city that rules over the kings of the earth" (17:18). The images of Rome as a beast and a woman are brought together in ch. 17, where the woman is pictured riding on the back of the beast. In other words, the corrupting influence of Rome has gained its power and made its way on the back of its military conquests.

But in spite of its military might and reasonable tolerance of the diversity within its borders, Rome was not always able to control its subjects and keep chaos at bay. Although certain periods of the first century were rather stable politically, the middle portion was marked by considerable turmoil, particularly during the catastrophic reigns of Gaius "Caligula" (37-41 CE) and Nero (54-68). As we shall see, the actions of these emperors bear on the interpretation of some of the more widely disputed symbolism of the book of Revelation.

24.2.2. Roman Economic Power

Rome's "dominion over the kings of the earth" (17:18) naturally extended to the economic realm. Rome needed its provinces to supply food for its population and taxes to support its various projects of constructing buildings, roads, and fleets of ships for trade and travel and for its armies. It also imported, along with the basic necessities, vast quantities of luxury goods. Rome's obsessive appetite for luxury goods is one of the causes of her condemnation: "The merchants of the earth have grown rich from the power of her luxury" (18:3). Rome's imports included gold, silver, bronze, precious stones, pearls, fine linen, purple cloth, silk, exotic wood, ivory, marble, spices, wine, cattle, sheep, horses, and slaves (18:11-13). By listing slaves, "human lives," last in the list of imports, John graphically and ironically points out the extent of Rome's depravity. While "human lives" ought to be valued above all, they are valued least by Rome, whose trade places them on the same level as gold, silk, and cattle.

24.2.3. Roman Emperors and the Imperial Cult

One of the ways in which the corrupting influence of Rome was demonstrated most vividly was through its propagation of the state-sanctioned cults of the deities of the empire and its tolerance of the cult of the emperor. The phenomenon of

Bust of Emperor
Vespasian *(Ewing
Galloway, N.Y.)*

emperor veneration or, more precisely, of paying homage or giving divine honors
to the emperor or his "guardian spirit," began with Augustus and continued into
the second century, thus encompassing the time during which the NT documents
were composed. Even so, the imperial cult was always more popular in the provinces than in Rome. The imperial cult was actively promoted, particularly in Asia
Minor, by the local elites. Generally, when an emperor was considered "divine," it
was because of his alleged apotheosis or "deification" after death, the evidence of
which was the ascent of his soul to the heavens. The earliest emperors, including
Augustus, Tiberius, and Claudius, explicitly refused to allow temples and statues to

be built in their honor and rejected other forms of honor that would signify their deification while they were alive. But the populace of the provinces often had no such scruples, and there is evidence of temples and statues being constructed in honor of the emperors and acts of venerating them or their guardian spirits even while they were living.

The tradition that only dead emperors were deified was ignored by Caligula, the emperor after Tiberius. Dressing in the garb of the deities, Caligula gladly welcomed and even demanded divine honors, such as the construction of temples to him. Such a course was bound to lead to conflict with the monotheistic Jewish and Christian faiths. When some Greeks in Alexandria tried to set up images of Caligula in the synagogues, the famous Jewish writer and apologist Philo wrote a long treatise and led a delegation of Jews to Caligula to complain about the impossibility of worshiping the emperor. Caligula also tried to have a large image of himself set up in the Jerusalem temple, but the order was never carried out. Although Caligula's demands never rose to the level of demanding veneration by all his subjects on penalty of death, his actions recalled the desecration of the temple

The Problem of the Christians

A letter from a early second-century Roman governor to Emperor Trajan regarding those accused of being Christians:

I have hesitated a great deal on the question whether there should be any distinction of ages; whether the weak should have the same treatment as the more robust; whether those who recant should be pardoned, or whether a man who has ever been a Christian should gain nothing by ceasing to be such; whether the name itself, even if innocent of crime, should be punished, or only the crimes attaching to that name. . . . I ask them if they are Christians. If they admit it I repeat the question a second and third time, threatening capital punishment; if they persist I sentence them to death. For I do not doubt that, whatever kind of crime it may be to which they have confessed, their pertinacity and inflexible obstinacy should certainly be punished. There were others who displayed a like madness and whom I reserved to be sent to Rome, since they were Roman citizens. . . . All who denied that they were or had been Christians I considered should be discharged, because they called upon the gods at my dictation and did reverence, with incense and wine, to your image which I had or-by Antiochus Epiphanes, referred to cryptically in Daniel as "the abomination that desolates" (9:27; 11:31; 12:11).

Nero's infamy as a persecutor of Christians is attested by the Roman historian Tacitus (*Annals* 15.38, 44). When fires swept through Rome, destroying much of the city, in 64-65 CE, it was rumored that Nero himself had set them. Tacitus comments that Nero needed a scapegoat and found it in the "notoriously depraved Christians," whom he had tortured, crucified, burned alive, and thrown to wild beasts. Because Christians refused to honor the gods of the Roman state, they were deemed "antisocial" and "atheistic" — and Nero used these "crimes" to rationalize the torture and deaths of those who were willing to acknowledge their faith. According to tradition, it was under Nero's persecution that both Peter and Paul were martyred. However, Nero's persecution was localized, confined to Rome itself, and was not linked to Christian refusal to worship him. And yet, from about 65 on, Nero appeared on coins styled as Apollo, with the crown of the deified emperor and the title "divine" (*divus*), a provocative action to Christian and Jewish sensibilities.

Nero committed suicide in AD 68 when he learned that the Roman senate had

dered to be brought forward for this purpose, together with the statues of the deities; and especially because they cursed Christ, a thing which, it is said, genuine Christians cannot be induced to do. . . . The matter seemed to me to justify my consulting you, especially on account of the number of those imperilled; for many persons of all ages and classes and of both sexes are being put in peril by accusation, and this will go on. The contagion of this superstition has spread not only in the cities, but in the villages and rural districts as well. . . .

Trajan responds:

You have taken the right line, my dear Pliny, in examining the cases of those denounced to you as Christians, for no hard and fast rule can be laid down, of universal application. They are not to be sought out; if they are informed against, and the charge is proved, they are to be punished, with this reservation — that if any one denies that he is a Christian, and actually proves it, that is by worshipping our gods, he shall be pardoned as a result of his recantation, however suspect he may have been with regard to the past. . . . (Pliny the Younger, *Ep.* 10.96-97, translation from Henry Bettenson, *Documents of the Christian Church* [2d ed., New York: Oxford University Press, 1963])

Philostratus on Nero

In traversing more of the earth than any man yet has visited, I have seen hosts of Arabian and Indian wild beasts; but as to this wild beast, which the many call a tyrant, I know not either how many heads he has, nor whether he has crooked talons and jagged teeth. In any case, though this monster is said to be a social beast and to inhabit the heart of cities, yet he is so much wilder and fiercer in his disposition than animals of the mountain and forest, that whereas you can sometimes tame and alter the character of lions and leopards by flattering them, this one is only roused to greater cruelty than before by those who stroke him, so that he rends and devours all alike. And again there is no animal of which you can say that it ever devours its own mother, but Nero is gorged with such quarry. (Philostratus, *Life of Apollonius of Tyana* 4.38)

declared him a "public enemy." But apparently rumors arose that he had not died, had come back to life, or had actually escaped to the east, perhaps to the Parthians, and would return. These rumors became embodied in the myth of his return, which has come to be known as *Nero redivivus* ("Nero returning"). In fact, several imposters claiming to be Nero appeared in the course of the first century trying to capitalize on that expectation, and some garnered the support of the Parthian kings.

One of the most enigmatic of Revelation's puzzles — the meaning of the number 666 — can be worked out with reference to Nero. John is using *gematria*, a technique in which each letter of the alphabet is assigned a numerical equivalent. The sum of the numerical values of the Greek word "beast" *(thērion)* is 666; hence, "the number of the beast . . . is 666" (13:18). But 666 is also "the number of its name" and "the number of a person" (Rev 13:17-18; 15:2). When Nero Caesar is written in Hebrew characters, their sum is 666, so that he is that person. Other descriptions of the beast recall the legends of Nero's mysterious death and expected return. According to 13:3, "One of its heads seemed to have received a death blow, but its mortal wound had been healed," a cryptic statement referring to the expectation that Nero would return and the empire would continue to exert its power and influence. Similarly, in 17:8 the beast is described as "the one who was, and is not, and is about to ascend." This designation not only alludes to the myth of Nero's death and return, but does so in a parody of the description of the eternal God as "the One who is and who was and who is to come" (1:4, 8; 4:8; 11:17; 16:5) and of the risen Christ as the one who "was dead" and is "alive forever and ever"

(1:18). The beast with "seven heads" with "blasphemous names" on its heads evokes the coins issued by Roman emperors, including Nero, with their names and images and the title *divus* (divine) stamped upon them. John has refracted the portrait of the "beast" through the description and legends regarding Nero.

Modern ideas about the separation of "church" and "state" can mislead us

Ancient Examples of Gematria

- On a graffito from Pompeii (first century): "I love her whose number is 545."
- Suetonius (*Nero*, 39) reports that the following verse circulated during Nero's reign: "A new calculation: Nero killed his own mother." The numerical value of Nero (1005) is the same as that of "killed his own mother." Popular rumors held that Nero was responsible for the murder of his mother, Agrippina.
- *Sibylline Oracles* 1:325-28 contains the following cryptic reference to Jesus: "I will state explicitly the entire number for you. For eight units, and equal number of tens in addition to these, and eight hundreds will reveal the name." The number 888 corresponds to the letters in the Greek word *Iēsous*: I = 10 + ē = 8 + s = 200 + o = 70 + u = 400 + s = 200.
- The fifth book of the *Sibylline Oracles* begins with a long list of emperors of Rome from Julius Caesar to Hadrian by alluding only to the numbers corresponding to their initials. For example, "One who has 50 as an initial will be commander." This reference to Nero continues: "a terrible snake, breathing out grievous war, who one day will lay hands on his own family and slay them, and throw everything into confusion. . . . Then he will return declaring himself equal to God."
- Rabbinic tradition (*Talmud Yerushalmi* 5a; *Lamentations Rabbah* 1:1b, §51) asserts that the name of the Messiah would be Menahem ("comforter") because the Hebrew consonants of the name have the same numerical value (138) as those of "branch," a title for the Davidic Messiah (Zech 3:8; 6:12).
- If Nero Caesar is written in Hebrew characters as *nron qsr,* the sum of the letters comes to 666: *nun* = 50 + *resh* = 200 + *waw* = 6 + *nun* = 50 + *qoph* = 100 + *samekh* = 60 + *resh* = 200. Some NT manuscripts give the number of the beast as 616, based on an alternate Hebrew spelling of Nero Caesar based on the Latin pronunciation.

about the nature of religion in ancient Rome and its relationship to the political and social realms. Religion was part of the ancient civil order, not something practiced alongside it or in addition to it. John portrays the far-reaching nature of Roman military, social, and economic power, embodied particularly in the person of the emperor, as finding its most sinister form in the imperial cult. But even so, John does not attack the practices associated with the imperial cult as blatant idol worship; the word "idolatry" does not appear in Revelation. This tacit recognition of the civic and political function of the imperial cult again points to the sweeping critique that John offers of the empire. The Roman quest for power by military strength, reflected in economic hegemony and insured by the social and political function of the state cults, was tantamount to blasphemy, to usurping the proper place of God (13:1). In light of the insatiable appetite of Rome for power and a consequent appetite for the necessary allegiance of its subjects, it is unavoidable that Christians will come into conflict with it again and again, even as they had under Nero and would under any sort of Nero *redivivus*.

24.2.4. The Date of the Book

Traditionally the Apocalypse has been assigned to the later years of the reign of the Roman emperor Domitian (81-96). Not only does this date agree with the statements of the earliest witnesses, including Irenaeus, Tertullian, and Eusebius, but it also makes sense of the situation of those addressed in the Apocalypse. Domitian was known as a second Nero, a self-glorifying tyrant, who demanded that he be addressed as "our Lord and God," an inclusive designation that heightened its offense to Christians. Along with Caligula and Nero, Domitian was apparently one of the emperors who accepted and even encouraged divine honors during his lifetime and not merely following his death. Yet there is little evidence that Domitian was responsible for systematic or widespread persecution of Christians because of refusal to worship him or offer sacrifice or incense in his name. We have no corroborating evidence of widespread martyrdom of Christians at this time, but neither is widespread martyrdom presupposed in the book of Revelation. The church of Smyrna, for example, has experienced the death of only one martyr (2:13).

Domitian's reputation no doubt elicited memories of Caligula and Nero, both self-glorifying enemies of the people of God. However, regardless of the reigning emperor, John viewed the Roman Empire itself as the blasphemous beast, the great harlot, and the city doomed for destruction. The actions of certain emperors served to sharpen this portrait. But it did not take a particularly "bad" emperor to evoke John's prophetic apocalypse any more than a "good" emperor would have caused him to revise his portrait of Rome. He wrote about the empire more than about any specific emperor. Given the historical circumstances and

John's literary technique and theological viewpoint, a date for the publication of Revelation under the emperor Domitian commends itself. Not only did Domitian claim the scandalous title "our Lord and God" for himself, but by the end of the first century Christianity was more widespread than it was during the time of Nero.

24.3. THE REVELATION OF JESUS CHRIST

24.3.1. Prologue: Visions of God and Christ (ch. 1)

The opening verses of Revelation actually give us a genealogy of its origin: it was given by God to Jesus Christ, who made it known to John through an angel, who in turn made it known to the servants of God. The Revelation concerns "what must take soon place," with the Greek construction *(dei genesthai)* expressing the conviction that God's purposes, as they are revealed in this book, will be accomplished. The various names and descriptions of God in the first chapter underscore that conviction. The eternal God is the one "who is, who was, and who will be." God is described as the "Alpha and Omega," the first and last letters of the Greek alphabet, that is, as the one who holds not only the beginning and end of all

Prologue: visions of God and Christ (ch. 1)
The risen Christ speaks to his church (chs. 2–3)
Visions of the heavenly throne room (chs. 4–5)
Preliminary visions of judgment and salvation (chs. 6–11)
    The seven seals and the 144,000 (6:1–8:5)
    The seven trumpets (8:6–11:19)
Visions of final judgment (12–19:10)
    The woman, the dragon, and the two beasts (chs. 12–13)
    Visions of judgment and salvation (ch. 14)
    The seven bowls: the completion of God's judgment (chs. 15–16)
    The judgment of Babylon (chs. 17:1–19:10)
God's victory (19:11–22:9)
    The Rider on the White Horse (19:11-21)
    The final defeat of Satan (20:1-10)
    The judgment (20:11-15)
    The new Jerusalem (21:1–22:9)

things but all that lies between as well. God is therefore "the Almighty." Nine of the ten uses of this designation for God in the NT are found in Revelation. As one of the Septuagint's translations of the Hebrew phrase meaning "the Lord of hosts," the term stresses not so much God's power as God's supremacy over all things. Just as God made his name known to Moses before sending him to the Israelites in Egypt, so here too God reveals his name to John as the one who comes with salvation and judgment. In addition to the interpreting angel, the angels of God figure prominently in this book, not only as John's guide on his heavenly journey, but as agents of God's judgment and salvation.

The opening chapter also presents a vision of the risen Christ as "the faithful witness, the firstborn of the dead, and the ruler of the kings of the earth." These descriptive phrases refer respectively to Jesus' earthly life, resurrection, and present sovereignty, and each aspect becomes paradigmatic in some way for believers. Throughout Revelation Jesus will be held up as a model of faithful witness to God that the people of God are to emulate (cf. 1 Tim 6:13). Those who are faithful until the end can expect to be raised to life and reign with God and the Lamb. They can be assured that although the "kings of the earth" seem overwhelmingly powerful, as the "firstborn of the dead," Jesus indeed is "King of kings and Lord of lords" (19:16).

Christ appears to John as "one like a son of man," a clear allusion to Daniel 7. But the subsequent description of him as having hair as white as snow, eyes of fire, feet of bronze, and a voice like many waters combines elements of both the "Ancient of Days" and the "son of man" from Daniel. Here the risen Jesus is also described as "the First and the Last," a title that appears again in 2:8 and 22:13, but is used elsewhere in the Revelation (1:8; 21:6-8) and in the OT for God. The implications are clear: the supremacy and sovereignty ascribed to the eternal God can also be assigned to the one who "was dead . . . and is alive forever and ever." Reducing this vision of Jesus to prose runs the risk of diluting its awe-inspiring majesty, which the reader can sense to some extent by identifying with John's response: upon seeing the risen Jesus, John is stricken with terror, "and fell at his feet as though dead" (1:17). This powerful and majestic figure then begins to issue proclamations to his churches, and commissions John to write them down.

John is introduced as one who has been banished to the island of Patmos, a punishment that was not necessarily unduly harsh and could even be voluntarily chosen. If Domitian's successor followed usual custom, John might well have been granted amnesty on Domitian's death. While "in the spirit," John received a vision of the risen Christ and a commission to speak specifically of what he had seen. By now it should be clear that in recording the visions that he sees, John deliberately crafts his narratives with images and language redolent of the OT, allusions to his social, political, and religious milieu, and theological motifs drawn from apocalyptic literature.

24.3.2. The Risen Christ Speaks to His Church (chs. 2–3)

In chs. 2–3, the risen Jesus speaks to the seven churches of Asia Minor in the form of imperial edicts. By thus casting Jesus' words, John underscores once more Jesus' supremacy, especially with respect to competing sovereigns. In these edicts, which address the same issues in straightforward prose as the rest of the book does in apocalyptic language and imagery, John writes to sharpen his readers' abilities to discern the perils posed to their faith by the syncretistic religious milieu and the social pressure to accommodate their ways of life to the dominant norms of their culture. Thus they are warned against association with the cults of pagan deities (2:6, 14-15, 20, 24) including the Roman gods and the imperial cult, as well as against materialism (3:17), waning faith (3:2-3), and failures to love God and neighbor (2:4-5).

John perceives the life of Christian discipleship as a spiritual struggle with ultimate consequences. In this struggle, some "conquer" and others fail. Seven times in chs. 2–3 Christians are exhorted to "conquer" (2:7, 11, 17, 26; 3:5, 12, 21), which is also paraphrased by admonitions to "endure" (2:2-3, 19; 13:10; 14:12) and to

Ruins of a second-century temple at Ephesus *(Nicholas Wolterstorff)*

The remains of the temple of Artemis in Sardis *(Phoenix Data Systems, Neal and Joel Bierling)*

"keep," which has multiple objects, including "what is written in this book" (1:3; 22:7, 9), "my works" (2:10), "my word" (3:8), and "the commandments" (12:17; 14:12). The depiction of the life of the church in martial imagery in chs. 2–3, where it is clearly metaphorical, suggests the metaphorical nature of the rest of the imagery of warfare and conquest in the book. Although the struggle that John describes is real, it is not military but has to do with faith and obedience. What the risen Jesus promises in the edicts of chs. 2–3 to those who "conquer" are the blessings of salvation.

Each of these gifts of salvation listed in chs. 2–3 is mentioned again a number of times in the visions of the final creation of the new heaven and the new earth in chs. 19–22. Those who are barred from the holy city are the cowardly, faithless, polluted, murderers, fornicators, sorcerers, idolaters, and liars (21:6-8) — precisely the sins against which Christians are warned in chs. 2–3 and which the rest of the world is accused of throughout the book (9:20-21; 21:7; 22:15). Those who are found guilty of them experience the second death rather than the blessings of eschatological salvation. The words of the risen Jesus in chs. 2–3 warn believers of the need for vigilance and faithfulness.

24.3.3. Visions of the Heavenly Throne Room (chs. 4–5)

The last of the seven edicts ends with the statement "To the one who conquers I will give a place with me on my throne, just as I myself conquered and sat down with my Father on his throne" (3:21). This verse serves as a pivot between chs. 2–3 and the visions of the heavenly throne room in chs. 4–5 and also gives the reason Jesus shares God's throne: he has "conquered." In his faithfulness he becomes a model for Christians. Just as the vision of the risen Jesus in ch. 1 introduces the edicts to the churches in chs. 2–3, so the visions of the heavenly throne room (chs. 4–5) introduce the visions of salvation and judgment that comprise most of the second part of the book. These are contained in the scroll sealed with seven seals (5:1), which only "the Lion of the tribe of Judah, the Root of David," the Lamb who was slaughtered and now lives, is worthy to open. This scene indicates that God's purposes in history, contained in the scroll, will be carried out through the agency of the risen Christ. Already presented in chs. 2–3 as Lord of the church, he now appears with God sovereign in all the world and so calls the world to repentance, obedience, and faith.

Not only are chs. 4–5 pivotal in the structure of the book, they dramatize the following foundational theological convictions of the Revelation:

- God is the transcendent, holy God, on whom all things in heaven and on earth depend, because he is the Creator (4:11) who also makes all things new. The world is not under the control of human or demonic powers, but is ruled by God. As sovereign, God steers the course of history toward his final victory over evil.
- That final victory is a matter of hope and expectation, but not only so: The decisive victory has already been won through the death and resurrection of Jesus, the Lamb who was slain yet lives and shares with God in ruling the universe.
- Worship, obedience, and honor are the only appropriate responses to God and to the Lamb.

The prophet John is taken up to heaven not so much to see heaven itself, but to see the entire universe from the standpoint of heaven, from the perspective of God's sovereignty. This vision also lays the groundwork for understanding the transitory and sinister nature of the throne of the beast described in later scenes (13:2; 16:10). While the beast's throne or sovereignty appears to be powerful and permanent, it cannot last, because it is but a weak and even demonic mockery of God's eternal rule. Chs. 4–5 thus serve as both the structural and theological heart of the book.

24.3.4. Judgment and Salvation Inaugurated:
Preliminary Visions of Judgment and Salvation (chs. 6–11)

After the visions of the heavenly thrones, the seven seals of the scroll begin to be opened. These seals contain alternating visions of judgment and salvation, which portend the certainty of God's judgment and the promise of God's salvation with a variety of images in kaleidoscopic fashion. The narrative serves not to unfold a predetermined timetable of events, but to warn of the certainty of judgment and to assure the faithful that nothing can separate them from God's sovereign purposes for their salvation.

24.3.4.1. The Seven Seals and the Sealing of the 144,000 (6:1–8:5)

The first four seals, the famous "four horsemen of the apocalypse," represent conquest or invasion, blood and warfare, famine, and death. Through these means God effects judgment on the earth. In the midst of such afflictions, the faithful experience persecution and are subject to martyrdom for the witness that they bore to the word of God (the fifth seal; 6:9-11). Understandably they cry to God for justice and vindication, but are told they must "rest a little longer" since the day of judgment has not yet come. The sixth seal then pictures, in typical apocalyptic imagery of earthquake, blackening sun, blood-red moon, falling stars, and disappearing land, sea, and sky, the judgment of "the kings of the earth and the magnates and the generals and the rich and the powerful" (6:15). In very brief compass, but in intense and horrific imagery, these seals present God's judgments on "the inhabitants of the earth" and hold out the promise of God's justice for those who are followers of the Lamb.

This promise is explicated more fully in the vision of the sealing of the 144,000, symbolic of their protection and future salvation (ch. 7), and the opening of the seventh seal, which brings a great silence during which the prayers of the saints are brought before God and the request for vindication is answered. The 144,000, later described as "first fruits for God and the Lamb" (14:4), are culled out of the twelve tribes of Israel, the ancient people of God, thus fulfilling certain eschatological hopes for the regathering of the twelve tribes of Israel. They are joined by a "great multitude that no one could count, from every nation, from all tribes and peoples and languages" (7:9), symbolizing the universal nature of the people of God drawn together in Christ. They have "the seal of the living God" (7:2) on their foreheads, later described as the name of God (9:4; 14:1; 22:4), of which the infamous "mark of the beast," the name of the emperor, will be an obvious parody (13:16-18; 14:9-11; 20:4). These are the faithful worshipers of God who have not compromised their discipleship by veneration of the emperor or complicity with the empire's standards and norms. Not surprisingly, the 144,000

Albrecht Dürer,
*The Four Horsemen
of the Apocalypse
(National Gallery
of Art, Washington,
D.C.—Rosenwald
Collection)*

are depicted as standing "before the throne of God," worshiping him "day and night" (7:15). This is a vision of the salvation of the faithful, showing the continuity between their lives on earth and their future destiny. Here, as there, they are presented primarily as worshipers of the living God.

24.3.4.2. *The Seven Trumpets (8:6–11:19)*

The seven seals are followed by seven trumpets and two visions, which together re-capitulate the seven seals by again presenting alternating visions of judgment and salvation. The judgments effected by the six trumpets, while destructive and hor-rendous, are limited and partial, lasting for set periods of time and affecting some of the earth and its inhabitants. The first four trumpets particularly describe events affecting the cosmos in ways reminiscent of the plagues of Egypt, thus suggesting that these plagues are part of the judgment that begins the new exodus, the redemption of God's people from every tribe and nation. The depiction of the forces unleashed by the fifth trumpet borrows the description of the plague of locusts from the prophet Joel (2:4, 10) and from the plagues of Egypt, to describe a marauding, demonic host, led by an "angel" named Abaddon and Apollyon, names that mean death and destruction. The sixth trumpet unleashes four angels, two hundred million troops of cavalry, horses the color of fire, with smoke and fire coming from their mouths and tails that sting like serpents.

This stream of plague and destruction is not an end in itself. Just as the plagues of Egypt were directed against the Egyptians and designed to encourage Pharaoh to release the Israelites, so these plagues are directed only against those people "who do not have the seal of God on their foreheads" (9:4) to bring about their repentance and turn them from worshiping demons and idols to worship of the true God (9:20-21). Strange as it may seem, the purpose of these judgments is ultimately to bring people to know and worship God. That the plagues do not touch those who have God's seal, those who have the name of the Lamb and his Father on their foreheads (14:1), means that they are not subject to God's punishment. They are redeemed by God through the death and resurrection of Christ.

Even though there is a temporary delay of the final judgment (10:1-4), it will surely come (10:6-7; cf. 6:11-17). That judgment is depicted in the seventh trumpet with the acclamation of the eternal rule of God and his Messiah. Again, this series of seven ends with a scene of the worship of God, the ultimate goal not only of the book of Revelation, but also of God's purposes for the world.

24.3.5. Judgment and Salvation Consummated: Visions of Final Salvation and Judgment (chs. 12–22)

By now it should be clear that the "revelation of Jesus Christ" promised in the opening verse of the book is not a static description of Jesus and his life and ministry. Instead, from the beginning of the book, that revelation has led to warnings about judgment, descriptions of conflict, prophecies of martyrdom, and the revealing of numerous enemies of the faithful, enemies who disobey God and persecute his witnesses. The revelation of Christ has created crisis and conflict in the world. For as God's supreme disclosure of his purposes of salvation for the world, the revelation of Christ, by calling for and demanding faith, obedience, and worship, brings judgment to those who do not respond and salvation to those who do. This is an important vantage point from which to interpret the thrust of the book. For although the author of Revelation writes out of and in genuine times of crisis in his environment, his ultimate theological point is that God's purposes in Christ inevitably come into, and indeed create, conflict with the purposes and designs of earthly powers and authorities who pursue their own power and goals without proper acknowledgment of the sovereignty of God. With ch. 12, the conflict intensifies, coming to its climax in the description of the conflict between a dragon and a woman and her newborn child.

It is not too much to claim that the book of Revelation is about true and false worship and that John wishes to force the choice between worship of the "beast" and worship of God and the Lamb. All of John's visions stand in the service of this fundamental proclamation: "Fear God and give him glory, for the hour of his judgment has come; and worship him who made heaven and earth, the sea and the springs of water" (14:7). In chs. 12–14, this choice and the inevitable conflict are graphically and symbolically portrayed in some of Revelation's best-known imagery. Culminating in a grand vision of the worship of God and the Lamb and the acclamation of their sovereignty, the visions of chs. 12–22 overlap to some extent with those of chs. 6–11. There are again alternating visions of judgment and salvation. But this time the narrative moves to its conclusion with the creation of the new heaven and the new earth, the redemption of all things, and the final victory of God and the Lamb.

24.3.5.1. The Woman, the Dragon, and the Two Beasts (12:1–13:18)

In these chapters we find a vivid description of the conflict between the messianic people on the one hand and the Roman Empire and the imperial priesthood on the other. There are five main characters:

- A pregnant woman "clothed with the sun" and wearing a "crown of twelve stars" (12:1-2) represents Israel about to give birth to her son, the Messiah.
- The woman's son, described in the language of Psalm 2 as destined to rule all nations with a rod of iron, is the Messiah, Jesus.
- A great red dragon with seven heads, seven crowns, and ten horns, identified as "that ancient serpent . . . the devil and Satan, the deceiver of the whole world," is defeated by the heavenly hosts. Thrown down to the earth, it pursues the woman and child. But the child is snatched to safety, and the woman is provided a place of refuge from the dragon's onslaught.
- A beast rising out of the sea, with ten crowns and blasphemous names on its heads, one of which "seemed to have received a death blow, but its mortal wound had been healed." As noted above, this description makes use of the Nero *redivivus* legend to depict not only the reigning emperor but, through him, the Roman Empire. The assertion that it received its power and authority from the dragon indicates the ultimately demonic character of Rome's oppressive and self-aggrandizing power.
- A beast that comes from the earth and tries to make people venerate the first

beast represents those who participate in the cult of the emperor, particularly in the eastern part of the empire where the seven churches of chs. 2–3 were located. "The mark of the beast" (13:17-18) is given to those who fall prey to the strictures of those who insist on veneration of the emperor as a condition for civil peace.

24.3.5.2. Visions of Judgment and Salvation (14:1-20)

A quick succession of scenes constitutes ch. 14. In contrast to those who admired and worshiped the beast (13:3-4), ch. 14 opens with another vision of the 144,000 who have been redeemed and are here described as worshiping God with a new song. Angelic heralds repeat the summons to worship God (14:6-7) and warn of the consequences for worshiping the beast (14:9-11). The Son of man, announcing that the time for the consummation of all things has come, calls for the harvest, an image for judgment but also often of salvation (14:14-20).

24.3.5.3. The Seven Bowls: The Completion of God's Judgment (15:1–16:21)

The final judgment is described in the imagery of seven bowls of wrath poured out on the earth by seven angels (chs. 15–16). Again, interspersed with the account of these plagues are vignettes of the faithful worshiping God rather than the beast (15:2-4), singing "the song of Moses, the servant of God, and the song of the Lamb," as they are gathered beside "the sea of glass." Their hymns of praise recall the song of victory that Moses and the Israelites sang after their deliverance from Pharaoh and his troops at the Red Sea (Exodus 15). So now those who have conquered the dragon and the beasts by their faithfulness praise God for this new exodus and the redeeming Lamb of God.

The judgments of the bowls are poured out on the earth, but, in spite of the crescendo of destruction, the people of the earth do not repent (16:9, 11). In a parody of the drying up of the Red Sea, which allowed the children of Israel to escape their pursuers, the sixth angel pours out his bowl on the river Euphrates so that it dries up, allowing "the kings of the east," Rome's own vassal kings, to cross over, apparently to launch an assault on the great city, which leads to its destruction (cf. 17:15-18). The kings of earth gather at "Harmagedon," a play on the name Megiddo, the site of several battles in the OT. While much has been made of the prediction of "Armageddon," no battle bearing this name is actually described in the book of Revelation, and there is no further mention of it beyond this one cryptic reference to a place where the kings of the earth assemble.

24.3.5.4. The Judgment of Babylon (chs. 17:1–19:10)

The judgment of Babylon, already foreshadowed in 14:8, is not so much described as assumed and announced in the visions and laments of chs. 17–18. John first sees "Babylon" depicted as a great whore, guilty of impurity, fornication, of leading many others astray, and of being "drunk with the blood of the saints and the blood of the witnesses to Jesus" (17:6). Since sexual impurity is a biblical symbol for idolatry or forsaking God's ways and commandments, the point is clearly that Babylon has been a tyrannical force not only in oppressing and ultimately killing those who withstood its power, but also of fostering worship of false gods. Particularly in view here are those who bore faithful witness to Jesus and lost their lives for it. The woman is seated on the seven-headed beast (ch. 13), whose ten horns indicate great power. After all, this woman is "the great city that rules over the kings of the earth" (17:18).

Although this beast that "rules over the kings of the earth," makes war on the Lamb, the Lamb conquers, since he is "Lord of lords and King of kings, and those with him are called and chosen and faithful." While the imagery here is military, depicting the Lamb as the victor in a war, two telling items point to its symbolic character: First, the victory of the Lamb has already been portrayed in ch. 5 as occurring through his death and resurrection. Second, the designation of those who accompany the Lamb makes it clear how their victory has been achieved: they are called, chosen, and faithful. Nothing is said of military prowess or armed victories. Rather, they are those who have borne faithful witness to Jesus.

The fall of Babylon is lamented on earth by the kings and merchants of the earth who profited from its power and wealth, but celebrated by the faithful with songs of praise to God for his just judgments and vindication of his saints (19:2). Once again, the vantage point from heaven differs radically from that of those on earth. The laments of the kings and merchants in ch. 18 make it clear that Babylon's sin lay not only in its persecution of God's saints but also in its obsessive and abusive appetite for luxury and its self-assurance that nothing could ever destroy it. Repeatedly the heavenly chorus sings, "In one hour your judgment has come" (18:10; 17, 19), indicating God's ultimate sovereignty as well as the temporal and fleeting nature of all of Rome's power, glory, and wealth.

24.3.6. The Victory of God (19:11–22:9)

Now, at last, attention shifts from the scenes of judgment, death, and destruction to four vignettes that together dramatize God's great victory and final redemption of the world.

24.3.6.1. *The Rider on the White Horse (19:11-21)*

Jesus appears, not as a slain Lamb, but as a victorious rider on a white horse. Although he is said to "make war," and is accompanied by the armies of heaven and equipped with a sharp sword, he is the only one who fights. This scene underscores his sovereignty: while the beast wore ten crowns, this rider wears "many diadems"; while the beast ruled "the kings of earth," this rider bears the name "King of kings and Lord of lords" and is further described as Faithful, True, and the Word of God. He executes judgment in righteousness (19:11), a judgment described in rather gruesome detail (19:17-21), as the birds of the air are called to gorge themselves with the flesh of all those who had followed the now defeated beast. In a grim reversal, those who had feasted in luxury now find themselves as the food of birds. The two beasts, however, are thrown into the lake of fire.

24.3.6.2. *The Final Defeat of Satan (20:1-10)*

The beasts, tools of the great deceiver Satan, have been destroyed, but Satan's final destruction is pictured in a separate scene. Here Satan's character as a deceiver, "that ancient serpent," the one who "deceived the nations" (20:3, 8, 10) through the beasts and the false prophet, is emphasized. This adversary of faith has nevertheless been resisted by those who gave their lives "for their testimony to Jesus and for the word of God," and refused to worship the beast or receive his mark. They were not deceived by the promises held out by the empire or the demands to honor the emperor as the one who bestows peace and salvation. Their lives on earth were given over to God, and though on earth they met with death, they are raised to life, "blessed and holy," and join Christ in his reign. Satan, however, finds his ultimate place not on a throne, but alongside the beast and the false prophet in the lake of fire. This is his final end; but in fact every scene in the book that portrays him in conflict with the Lamb ends in his being either defeated or thwarted in some way, thus showing the futility of his attempts to vanquish the Lamb or his followers.

24.3.6.3. *The Judgment*

In a terse presentation of final judgment, all the dead are judged according to their deeds, and all those whose names are not written in the "book of life" are also thrown into the lake of fire, as are also Death itself and Hades. This is the end of evil. The "book of life," a feature of other apocalyptic writings (Dan 7:10; *1 En* 90:20; 4 Ezra 6:20), has been referred to several times previously. It contains the names of those who belong to the lamb of God, who have persevered, and borne faithful witness, and have not worshiped the beast (3:5; 13:8; 17:8; 20:12, 15; 21:27).

24.3.6.4. The New Jerusalem (21:1–22:9)

In the grand climactic vision, John sees a new heaven, a new earth, and the holy city of God. There is a stunning contrast between the description of Babylon the great harlot and Jerusalem the bride of God. Babylon is a sinister parody of the holy city. While there are detailed and elaborate descriptions of the holy city and

The Two Cities	
BABYLON	**CITY OF GOD**
Invitation: "Come, I will show you" (17:1)	Invitation: "Come, I will show you" (21:9)
"The great harlot" (17:1)	"The Bride, the wife of the Lamb" (21:9)
"Seated upon many waters" (17:1)	"Coming down out of heaven from God" (21:10)
Arrayed in purple and scarlet, with gold, jewels, and pearls (17:4; 18:16-17)	Has the glory of God; its radiance is like a most rare jewel, like a jasper, clear as crystal (21:11)
A "name" on her forehead (17:5)	God's name on the foreheads of the servants of God and the Lamb (22:4)
The mother of abominations (17:5)	Nothing "unclean," no abominations shall enter (21:27; 22:3a)
Their names are not written in the book of life (17:8)	The names of those who enter are written in the Lamb's book of life (21:27)
The kings of the earth shall destroy the harlot (17:15-18)	The kings of the earth shall bring their glory into the city (21:24)
Babylon, a "dwelling place of demons" (18:2)	The New Jerusalem, the dwelling of God (21:3, 22)
Moving toward doom (18:1-3, 9-19)	Destined for eternal glory (21:10–22:5)
"Worship God" (19:10)	"Worship God" (22:9)

of its size and construction and the various precious jewels and metals of which it is made, it is holy and valuable because in it God himself dwells with his people (21:1-4). The city needs no temple, for God and the Lamb are the temple; it needs neither sun nor moon, for the glory of God and the Lamb are its light and lamp; it needs no locked gates, for only what is righteous and pure enters into it; it knows neither death nor suffering, but is characterized by abundance and fertility, watered by the river of the water of life, producing fruit from the tree of life. But above all else, in the holy city the purposes of God are perfectly accomplished as "his servants will worship him; they will see his face, and his name will be on their foreheads" (22:4).

24.3.7. Epilogue and Postscript (22:10-21)

Little remains to be said. Final warnings are issued; final benedictions spoken. The Revelation ends with a fervent prayer for Jesus' return and the promise of his grace for all his saints. Straining toward the future with expectation, the saints on earth are nevertheless promised, for the present, the grace of the Lord Jesus Christ, which encompasses their lives from beginning to end.

24.4. SUMMARY

For many twentieth-century readers of the Apocalypse, it has been hard to imagine what positive purposes can be served by its unrelenting scenes of destruction and death, which so often seem to breed fear and revulsion rather than repentance, awe, and worship of God. But the visions of Revelation have as their dual aim the "revealing" of Jesus Christ and the consequent "revealing" of the nature of the powerful political, social, and economic forces that both subtly and openly lead people from the living God to serve false gods of their own making. These two "revelations" belong together, for the revelation of Jesus Christ is also a revelation of his sovereignty over all "the kings of the earth," and few earthly kings are eager to share their power. Hence the revelation of Christ inevitably brings with it the unmasking of any authority that does not acknowledge his sovereignty. The various ever-changing scenes of John's apocalypse serve to sharpen the eyes of its readers regarding the self-deifying state and to dispel all simplistic notions about the state's desire to be a servant of God or to use its power for the purposes of God.

John's Apocalypse intends to engage and shape the theological imagination of its readers by giving them a view of the world from the vantage point of heaven. With divinely guided insight, its readers are to see the glories of ancient Rome in a new light: not as the magnificent and benevolent empire bringing peace and prosperity to the world, but as a great harlot, a deceiver of nations, a beast that attacks and devours, a desolate city, the haunt of foul beasts. This is not the Rome that the world sees, but it is how God sees the city as it pursues its self-aggrandizing and self-deifying course. To be sure, some will object that things are not so bad as John makes them out to be and protest with respect to the unquestionably good things that Rome brought to the world. But apocalypticism paints its scenes not in subtle shades but in bold images, on a canvas larger than life, not simply as a ploy to get attention, but as a way of waking up its readers to realities to which they are likely to become hardened over time. In fact, precisely because human sensibilities are so easily lulled into complacency, John's Apocalypse blares its message of God's sovereignty and the call to faithfulness, obedience, and worship.

FOR FURTHER READING

David E. Aune, *Revelation,* 3 vols. (Word Biblical Commentary; Dallas: Word, 1997/98)

Richard J. Bauckham, *The Climax of Prophecy: Studies on the Book of Revelation* (Edinburgh: Clark, 1993)

————, *The Theology of the Book of Revelation* (Cambridge: Cambridge University Press, 1993)

G. K. Beale, *The Book of Revelation* (New International Greek Testament Commentary; Grand Rapids: Eerdmans, 1999)

George B. Caird, *A Commentary on the Revelation of St. John the Divine* (Harper's New Testament Commentaries; New York: Harper and Row, 1966)

R. H. Charles, *A Critical and Exegetical Commentary on the Revelation of St. John,* 2 vols. (International Critical Commentary; Edinburgh: Clark, 1920)

Gerhard Krodel, *Revelation* (Augsburg Commentary on the New Testament; Minneapolis: Augsburg, 1989)

Frederick J. Murphy, *Fallen Is Babylon: The Revelation to John* (The New Testament in Context; Valley Forge: Trinity Press International, 1998)

Leonard L. Thompson, *The Book of Revelation: Apocalypse and Empire* (New York: Oxford University Press, 1990)

25. The Formation of the New Testament Canon

To speak of the NT "canon" is to refer to the collection of writings regarded by the Christian community to be of unique and normative significance for its life and thought. Those writings thus represent the standard or norm of belief and practice for the Christian community. Such a canon is simply an expression of the authority acknowledged by, and functioning within, that community.

In the following pages we will investigate the way in which certain authoritative writings were singled out as adequate to perform this canonical function, review the various changes that occurred in that collection of normative literature, and identify the criteria that were applied in that rather lengthy and complex process of selection.

The formation of the canon represented the working out of forces that were already present in the primitive Christian community and that would have made some form of canon virtually inevitable. Certain external pressures on that community, however, also contributed to the content and shape of the final canon, and we must examine them as well. As we shall see, the process of forming and finally "closing" the canon was simply an outgrowth of the process by which traditions produced by, and preserved within, the Christian community were collected, reworked, and combined into the books themselves that finally comprised the canon. In that sense the canon is the end of the process begun when first Israel and then the primitive Christian community sought to preserve for future generations accounts of events that were foundational for their respective communities. It is the traditions that grew out of such a desire to preserve the memory of foundational events — the exodus of Israel from Egypt, the captivity in Babylon, the resurrection of Jesus — that were finally written, organized, and preserved in the canon.

25.1. INTERNAL FORCES AFFECTING THE SHAPE OF THE CANON

25.1.1. The Shape of the Church's Commission

The very nature of the early Christian community displays certain characteristics that from the outset played a part in shaping the final canonical collection of literature. The early community understood itself to be commissioned by its risen Lord to spread the good news of the imminent incursion of God's rule into the world. Jesus himself had sent out his followers to announce such news (Mark 3:14 and parallels for the twelve; Luke 10:1-12 for the seventy), as indeed he had announced he would when he called his first followers (see Mark 1:16-20 and par.; the phrase "fishers of men" implies such missionary activity). The Gospel of Matthew closes with the risen Christ commissioning his closest followers to undertake a worldwide mission of witness to what he had said and who he was.

If such a worldwide mission was to be undertaken, it would require missionary activity by more than simply the twelve closest followers of Jesus. Others would have to be, and were, involved in such missionary outreach, as the book of Acts makes clear. The danger that arose when that wider missionary proclamation was undertaken was that the information about Jesus that made up the content of that early preaching would be diluted or distorted. Preachers would undertake the missionary task who were not reliably acquainted with the traditions about Jesus (an example of that can be found in Acts 18:24-26) and who would then have to be corrected by people better acquainted with those traditions. Yet even such reliable people would be in too short supply as the community began to grow and spread ever more widely. Some more reliable method needed to be found to preserve the integrity of the Christian proclamation throughout the missionary movement.

Two types of literature grew up to meet such needs. One consisted of reliable accounts of the career and teachings of Jesus. They were drawn up for a variety of purposes: they could be used as handbooks by preachers; they could be used for missionary purposes such as the conversion of those who read those accounts; they could also be used to correct false impressions and false practices within the communities to which they were addressed. Such collections of traditions about Jesus were eventually refined into the Gospels as we know them in the NT.

A second type of literature produced to exercise oversight over the faith of mission communities was the pastoral letter, designed to meet and correct problems that arose when no reliable missionary could be present (Galatians is such a letter). In that way, the authority of the apostle could be exercised over a wider geographic area and with a larger time frame than the physical presence of the missionary made possible.

The Christian community's understanding of its mandate as one of proclaiming the good news about Jesus and about what his career meant for the relationship between God and the human race carried within itself, therefore, the twofold structure of the faith that came to be expressed in the division of the NT canon into Gospels (Lord) and epistles (the witness of followers). While this distinction within the canon was not in fact carried through for more than a century after the Christian community was formed, the very nature of the Christian faith is reflected in it and perhaps made such a shape inevitable for its canon.

25.1.2. The Use of the Jewish Scriptures

Another factor that influenced the primitive community in its writing and collection of literature that was eventually to become canonical is found in the fact that the Christian community understood itself as an outgrowth, indeed as the fulfillment, of Judaism. Jesus was understood to be the fulfillment of both the law (Pentateuch) and the prophets (see Matt 5:17), and the writings of the Jewish community, interpreted in light of the Christian faith, continued to be used well into the second century as primary sources for the missionary activity of the primitive community. Indeed, in virtually every NT reference to Scripture, the material quoted comes from those writings taken over from the Jewish community, that is, from what Christians call the "Old Testament."

It was this appropriation of the authoritative writings of the Jewish community that represented a further impetus toward the formation of a Christian canon. It demonstrated the value of written documents for the life of a community of faith and in that way hastened the production of specifically Christian literature. The use of the Jewish writings as "Scripture" also opened the way to regarding specifically Christian literature in a similar way. The reference in 2 Pet 3:15-16 to the letters of the apostle Paul as "Scripture" shows that this process had begun at an early stage in the development of a body of Christian literature.

It would be incorrect to speak of the influence of a Jewish "canon" at the time the Christian community began, if by "canon" we mean a collection of books that is complete and closed and on which there is universal agreement. An attempt to define such a collection of Jewish writings did not occur until the end of the first century (at Yavneh, about 90 CE), perhaps in response to the appropriation by the Christian community of the Jewish Scriptures, but even then it is probably incorrect to speak of any kind of closed Jewish canon. Nevertheless, the presence in the Jewish community of a collection of authoritative writings exerted a significant influence in the direction of the formation of a similar body of authoritative literature indigenous to the Christian faith.

25.1.3. The Passing of Time

A third factor at work in the Christian community was simply the passage of time. The primitive community had within it persons who had known the earthly Jesus and/or had seen him after he rose from the dead. In that situation, although the production of literature for internal use was important, the community was still small enough that an authoritative person (e.g., an apostle) could be called on to resolve disputes within individual congregations. If an apostle could not be there in person, he could at least send a letter answering questions that arose (as in 1 Corinthians).

As time passed, however, and the community grew larger, such an appeal became more difficult. Even more, as the years passed, the first generation, the apostles and others who had known Jesus personally, began to die out. It thus became apparent near the end of the first century that the community faced a future in which it would be impossible to appeal to a member of that generation to resolve problems that arose.

If an apostle could no longer be called upon to resolve disputes, the only recourse was to comb the writings of the apostles for hints about how problems were to be resolved. That in its turn meant that certain writings now had to carry the importance that the eyewitnesses themselves had carried. Instead of receiving solutions to problems directly from the apostles themselves, the community now had to resolve such problems by interpreting the apostolic traditions. In other words, instead of the apostles bearing authority, that authority now had to be vested in the apostolic traditions.

But where was true apostolic tradition to be found? After all, anyone could claim apostolic authority for a position, and it could no longer be verified by direct appeal to that apostle. And where was the valid interpretation of apostolic tradition to be found? After all, anyone could claim validity for his or her opinion, and it could no longer be verified by asking the apostle directly. A writer of the early fourth century, Eusebius, attests the crisis that the death of the first generation precipitated: "But when the holy group of the Apostles and the generation of those to whom it had been granted to hear with their own ears the divine wisdom had reached the ends of their respective lives, the federation of godless error took its beginning through the deceit of false teachers who, noting that none of the Apostles still remained, barefacedly tried the counter-proclamation of 'knowledge falsely so-called' against the proclamation of the truth" (*Hist. Eccl.* 3.22.8).

25.2. EXTERNAL FORCES AFFECTING THE SHAPE OF THE CANON

The Christian community was not given the luxury of working out its canon at leisure. External pressures hastened and shaped the process of canon formation and invested what otherwise might have been a leisurely process with life-and-death urgency.

25.2.1. Marcion's Canon

The earliest of those external forces was exerted by a man named Marcion. The son of a wealthy shipbuilder, Marcion came to Rome from Sinope in Pontus (in present-day Turkey), became a member of the church there, and supported it generously. About the year 144, however, it became evident that his understanding of the Christian faith was radically different from that of the Roman Christian community, and Marcion withdrew to form his own church. Believing all of material creation to be evil, the work of a vengeful god who was ignorant of the higher God of love, Marcion held that the redemption Christ brought sprang from the desire of the higher God to redeem those who accepted Christ from the evils of this world.

Since the vengeful god was the one to whom the Jewish Scriptures point, in Marcion's view, Christ did not come to fulfill, but to abolish the law and the prophets. For Marcion, the Jewish Scriptures had only negative significance; it was from such a religion that Christ had come to redeem humanity.

Because Marcion could therefore not call on the OT writings as an authoritative body of literature, as did the Christian community at that time, he substituted for those writings the letters of the apostle Paul, in whom Marcion found opposition to the Jewish law, and the Gospel of Luke, which he found to be "Pauline" in its theology. In order to conform those documents more closely to his point of view, Marcion apparently purged from Paul's letters passages that spoke in a positive way about the Jewish faith, its law, and its prophets and similarly excised from Luke material that showed OT influence, including the first two chapters of the Gospel.

Marcion seems to have been the first, therefore, to form a specifically Christian collection of authoritative literature. Yet he had appropriated that literature to support religious views that the Christians in Rome and elsewhere felt compelled to reject. The Christian community thus faced a problem: could they afford, in rejecting Marcion and his views, also to reject the literature he claimed to support such views, namely Paul's letters and the Gospel of Luke? If not, how could that literature be reclaimed? Marcion thus forced the Christian community to hasten the process of deciding what literature was indispensable and what was not.

Instead of rejecting the literature Marcion had appropriated, the community retained both the letters of Paul and the Gospel of Luke, thus confirming in their literature a structure (Gospel, Apostle) which, as we have seen, was inherent in the Christian faith (Lord, followers). The community further affirmed that there were also other Gospels of equal authority to that of Luke and other epistles of equal authority to those of Paul. From other early Christian writings it is obvious that by the time Marcion appeared in Rome, all the literature contained in our present NT had been written, along with a good deal of other Christian literature. The Christian community therefore did not create what came to be regarded as canonical literature to combat Marcion. Rather, it simply reaffirmed that its basis of authority was broader than one Gospel and one apostle, and it reaffirmed the authority of the writings of the Jewish community of faith as well (i.e., the OT).

25.2.2. The Montanists

A second external factor that played a significant role in the way the Christian community understood its own canonical literature was the movement centering around Montanus. Montanus appeared in Phrygia (also in present-day Turkey) about the middle of the second century and announced that, with his appearance, the final stage of Christian revelation, the time of the Paraclete (the Holy Spirit; see John 14:16, 26; 15:26) was at hand. He affirmed that the end of the ages was therefore imminent and that the New Jerusalem (see Rev 21:2) was at hand. He also called for a more rigorous ethical life and forbade all attempts to escape the persecutions being visited on the Christian communities. Accompanied by two "prophetesses" (Maximilla and Priscilla), Montanus traveled widely, announcing the new age of the Spirit and the end of the world. In many ways, Montanus and his followers appeared to be a renewal of the apocalyptic fervor of the earlier Christian communities.

Because Montanus claimed powers promised in a writing that was widely accepted as authoritative (the Gospel of John), and seemed to renew the early fervor of the Christian movement, he represented a significant alternative to the other Christian communities. How was his influence to be countered? The Christian community could not deny that the Holy Spirit had been promised to them, but they could, and did, deny Montanus's claim that that Spirit spoke as authoritatively through him as it had through the apostles of Christ. But to do that, the Christian community had to affirm that the apostolic period was normative for the understanding of any further communications from the Spirit. Since the followers of Montanus also produced a body of literature, the Christian communities who opposed him had to affirm that only those writings that drew on apostolic traditions were authoritative and were therefore the norm for the faith of the community.

25.2.3. Other Non-Orthodox Movements

The second and third centuries saw other movements that understood themselves as representing truer expressions of the Christian faith than that represented by the more "orthodox" communities, and each of them appears to have produced its own body of literature. The most prominent among these are the Gnostic movements, which in one form or another announced a secret knowledge that would deliver the Gnostic initiate from the evil realm of matter to the superior realm of the spirit. Several "gospels" were produced by these movements (e.g., the Gospels of Truth, of Philip, and of Thomas), each purporting to contain the secret and thus true teachings of Jesus. Although they produced no new apostolic epistles, they did appropriate Paul, through allegorical interpretation, as a witness to their beliefs.

It was in the context of such varied claims to the truth of the Christian faith that the "orthodox" communities argued about which writings could be regarded as authoritative and hence as properly belonging to a canon that alone would provide the norm by which true Christian faith was to be measured. We must now look at the actual process of sifting books as it proceeded in the first three centuries after the birth of Christ, and then examine the criteria by which some books were chosen and others rejected.

25.3. THE GROWTH OF THE NEW TESTAMENT CANON

We would have quite a false understanding of the process of canon formation if we were to imagine that it was limited simply to deciding whether or not the twenty-seven books now included in the NT canon belonged there. It would be false on two counts. First, the total of twenty-seven books was only agreed upon late in the process of canon formation; earlier writers tended to limit the number to twenty or twenty-two. Thus, we must not imagine a process in which, as it were, all twenty-seven books were lying on a table in a conference room with church authorities discussing them one by one to determine whether to include them. As we shall see, such a "conference" never took place.

Second, such an understanding is false because it does not take into account the large amount of literature circulating in the Christian community by the second century. The canonical process was one that had as a major component the determination of which writings from that mass of literature produced in the first century should even be considered as candidates for authoritative status. Nor did the flow of literature cease with the close of the first century. Gospels and epistles continued to be produced until well into the second century, so the Christian communities had to be engaged in a continuing process of deciding which books

Minuscule 2^e, a twelfth-century Greek manuscript, here showing Matthew 16:1-11 with marginal notes added by Erasmus of Rotterdam in the sixteenth century

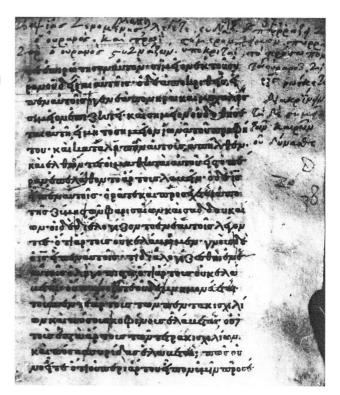

were to be held as canonical, that is, as normative for faith and practice, and which were not. Gospels such as those of Truth, of Philip, and the like, produced by the Gnostic movements, were never serious candidates for canonical recognition, but other Gospels, such as the *Gospel of the Hebrews* and the *Gospel of Peter,* were known from early times and were quoted by some early Christian writers. In addition to a larger number of Gospels, there were many epistles, again of early origin and quoted by early Christian writers, such as the *Epistle of Barnabas* and the correspondence between Jesus and Abgar, about which decisions had to be made. There was still other literature, such as the Teaching of the Twelve Disciples (= the *Didache*), the *Shepherd of Hermas,* a variety of Acts of individual apostles (Thomas, Matthew, Peter, Paul and Thecla, and others), as well as numerous apocalyptic writings besides the Revelation of John (apocalypses of Peter, Paul, Thomas, and of Stephen). All these and more were circulating, and some communities found one or more of them useful for instruction or for reading in their worship services. That meant that those writings also had claims to authoritative status that had to be weighed and evaluated.

Alongside such written material, oral traditions about Jesus continued to circulate, some similar to, but some also quite different from, the traditions contained in the four Gospels we have in the NT. An early second-century Christian, Papias, is reported to have said that he preferred oral to written sources of information about Jesus: "For I did not suppose that information from books would help me so much as the word of a living and surviving voice" (reported in Eusebius, *Hist. Eccl.* 3.39.4). Justin Martyr, writing later in the second century, knew and included in his writings a number of such sayings of Jesus that are not in our four Gospels, showing how persistently such sayings survived. Justin evidently thought they had equal authority to the words of Jesus in the written Gospels. But if writings could be produced in the names of various apostles, it would be even easier to produce unwritten sayings of Jesus. Apart from a written source, how could the authenticity of

The beginning of the Gospel of John in Erasmus's 1516 Greek-Latin edition of the New Testament

such sayings be validated? The Christian community had to decide what to do about the authority of these oral sources as well.

Given the mass of literature that was circulating and even being produced on into the second century and beyond, it is surprising how quickly agreement was reached on a core of writings acknowledged to be authoritative. From quotations of sayings of Jesus in what are called the writings of the Apostolic Fathers (Christians from the generation after that of the apostles) who wrote in the later first and early second centuries, it is evident that our four canonical Gospels not only nearly exhausted the reliable traditions about sayings of Jesus, but also that all four were already widely known in many Christian communities. A consensus had therefore emerged by the end of the first century that the Gospels of Matthew, Mark, Luke, and John were significant sources of information about, and authoritative expressions of, the Christian faith. The question to be decided was thus whether one or more other Gospels (such as the Gospels of Peter or of the Hebrews) ought to be added to those four.

An early consensus seems also to have arisen concerning the letters of Paul as authoritative documents of the Christian faith. In late first-century and early second-century Christian writings, there is no unanimity on how many letters Paul had written. Some thought Paul had written Hebrews, others did not. Marcion knew a letter of Paul to the Laodiceans (see Col 4:16), which others doubted Paul had written. Most of the letters of Paul present in our NT, however, were already known and widely regarded as authoritative by the first decades of the second century. Letters from the three "pillars" of the Jerusalem community — Peter, James (Jesus' brother, not the James who was the brother of John), and John, so identified by Paul in Gal 2:9 — were also known and highly regarded, although there was no unanimity on how many from each author ought to be accorded authority.

In addition to these Gospels and letters, other literature was highly regarded such as the Acts of the Apostles, the *Shepherd of Hermas,* the Revelation of John, the *Revelation of Peter,* the *Gospel of Peter,* and the *Epistle of Barnabas.*

25.4. THE PROCESS OF CANONICAL SELECTION

The recognition that some form of written authority was necessary in order to maintain the purity of the faith was one thing; agreeing on what those written authorities ought to be was another. We have already seen that the Scripture of the Christian community from the outset was the OT, in most cases in its Greek translation (the "Septuagint"). Paul quoted from many of its books in his letters, Jesus is remembered to have used it as authoritative, and the Gospel writers also made use of it in their interpretations of Jesus' mission, understanding him to have fulfilled the promises about the Messiah contained in the Jewish Scriptures.

In the second century, Justin reported that our four Gospels were held to be of equal value with the Jewish Scriptures. Another writer of about the same time, Irenaeus, a bishop of Lyon in France, not only knew of our four Gospels but also held in high regard the letters of Paul, 1 Peter, and 1 John. In addition, he named as "Scripture" the *Shepherd of Hermas* and the Wisdom of Solomon and saw no reason to question the authoritative nature of the Revelation of John. It is clear, therefore, that by the last quarter of the second century a collection of specifically Christian writings was beginning to emerge as authoritative and to be used alongside the Jewish Scriptures.

While all four Gospels were generally acknowledged at this time, there was still some doubt about the Gospel of John, perhaps because of the use made of it by Montanus and some Gnostics. Even as late as the early third century, a bishop of Rome, Hippolytus, felt it necessary to defend the validity of that Gospel against attacks on it by a certain Gaius.

A good summary of early views about which books were considered authoritative is found in a list called the "Canon Muratorianus," named after Muratori, a librarian in Milan who discovered and published the list in 1740. It seems to come from some time in the later second or early third century and appears to have been translated from Greek (our only text is in Latin). Although the beginning is lost, it includes as authoritative the Gospels of Luke and John (the lost beginning very likely names Matthew and Mark), the Acts of the Apostles, thirteen letters of Paul (Hebrews is omitted), Jude, 1 and 2 John, the Wisdom of Solomon, the Revelation of John and the *Revelation of Peter,* although it is conceded that this last one is not universally recognized. The list rejects letters of Paul to the Laodiceans and to the Alexandrians that were apparently also circulating, along with the Gnostic Gospels and the writings of Marcion and Montanus. The *Shepherd of Hermas* is also mentioned as useful but not to be read publicly in the churches. We do not know how widely the views contained in the Canon Muratorianus were held, but the list does show that what we know as the canon had not yet emerged, since some of our NT books are missing (Hebrews, 3 John, James), and some others not in our NT were still present (Wisdom of Solomon).

With the appearance of Origen (185-251) the collection of Scripture we know as the "New Testament" (Origen used that designation for Christian Scriptures) began to emerge, although still in somewhat shortened form. He acknowledged as Scripture (and probably by now as "canonical" as well) the four Gospels and Acts, fourteen letters of Paul (including Hebrews, even though Origen did not think Paul wrote it), 1 Peter, 1 John, and the Revelation of John. Absent are 2 and 3 John (Origen knew them but doubted their genuineness), 2 Peter (also known but doubted), James, and Jude. It is noteworthy that Origen introduced three categories of Christian writings: in addition to those surely to be regarded as authoritative and those surely not to be so regarded, Origen included a third category,

Canon Muratori

. . . .
at which however he was present and so he has set it down.

The third Gospel book, that according to Luke.
This physician Luke after Christ's ascension (resurrection?),
since Paul had taken him with him as an expert in the way
    (of the teaching),
composed it in his own name
according to (his) thinking. Yet neither did he himself see
the Lord in the flesh; and therefore, as he was able to ascertain it,
    so he begins
to tell the story from the birth of John.
The fourth of the Gospels, that of John, (one) of the disciples.
When his fellow-disciples and bishops urged him,
he said: Fast with me from today for three days, and what
will be revealed to each one
let us relate to one another. In the same night it was
revealed to Andrew, one of the apostles, that,
whilst all were to go over (it), John in his own name
should write everything down. And therefore, though various
rudiments (or: tendencies?) are taught in the several
Gospel books, yet that matters
nothing for the faith of believers, since by the one and guiding
    (original?) Spirit
everything is declared in all: concerning the birth,
concerning the passion, concerning the resurrection,
concerning the intercourse with his disciples
and concerning his two comings,
the first despised in lowliness, which has come to pass,
the second glorious in kingly power,
which is yet to come. What
wonder then if John, being thus always true to himself,
adduces particular points in his epistles also,
where he says of himself: What we have seen with our eyes
and have heard with our ears and
our hands have handled, that have we written to you.
For so he confesses (himself) not merely an eye and ear witness,
but also a writer of all the marvels of the Lord in
order. But the acts of all apostles
are written in one book. For the "most excellent Theophilus" Luke
summarises the several things that in his own presence
have come to pass, as also by the omission of the passion of Peter
he makes quite clear, and equally by (the omission) of the
    journey of Paul, who from
the city (of Rome) proceeded to Spain. The epistles, however,
of Paul themselves make clear to those who wish to know it

which there are (i.e. from Paul), from what place and for
     what cause they were written.
First of all to the Corinthians (to whom) he forbids the heresy
of schism, then to the Galatians (to whom he forbids) circumcision,
and then to the Romans, (to whom) he explains that Christ
is the rule of the scriptures and moreover their principle,
he has written at considerable length. We must deal with these
severally, since the blessed
apostle Paul himself, following the rule of his predecessor
John, writes by name only to seven
churches in the following order: to the Corinthians
the first (epistle), to the Ephesians the second, to the Philippians
the third, to the Colossians the fourth, to the Galatians the
fifth, to the Thessalonians the sixth, to the Romans
the seventh. Although he wrote to the Corinthians and to the
Thessalonians once more for their reproof,
it is yet clearly recognisable that over the whole earth one church
is spread. For John also in the
Revelation writes indeed to seven churches,
yet speaks to all. But to Philemon one,
and to Titus one, and to Timothy two, (written) out of goodwill
and love, are yet held sacred to the glory of the catholic Church
for the ordering of ecclesiastical
discipline. There is current also (an epistle) to
the Laodiceans, another to the Alexandrians, forged in Paul's
name for the sect of Marcion, and several others,
which cannot be received in the catholic Church;
for it will not do to mix gall with honey.
Further an epistle of Jude and two with the title
     (or: two of the above mentioned)
John are accepted in the catholic Church, and the Wisdom
written by friends of Solomon in his honour.
Also of the revelations we accept only those of John and
Peter, which (latter) some of our
people do not want to have read in the Church. But Hermas
wrote the Shepherd quite lately in our time in the city
of Rome, when on the throne of
the church of the city of Rome the bishop Pius, his brother,
was seated. And therefore it ought indeed to be read, but
it cannot be read publicly in the Church to the other people
     either among
the prophets, whose number is settled, or among
the apostles to the end of time.
But we accept nothing whatever
from Arsinous or Valentinus and Miltiades(?), who have also
composed a new psalm book for Marcion,
together with Basilides of Asia Minor,
the founder of the Cataphrygians.

(translation from Schneemelcher, pp. 34-36)

those about which opinions differed. The third category is most interesting for our purposes, since the books in our NT that Origen omitted from the first category he included in the third category, along with the *Shepherd of Hermas.*

Eusebius, our source for much of our knowledge of the first three centuries of the Christian community, still retained this threefold classification. Eusebius reckoned as genuine the four Gospels, Acts, fourteen letters of Paul, 1 John, and 1 Peter. Disputed books included James, Jude, 2 Peter, and 2 and 3 John. Interestingly enough, he included the Revelation of John in both the recognized and disputed categories, indicating the division of opinion that persisted about that book. By his time, the *Shepherd of Hermas,* the *Epistle of Barnabas,* the *Apocalypse of Peter,* and the Wisdom of Solomon had all disappeared from serious contention as canonical Christian Scripture. It is clear from this that the canonical process was more a paring down of a larger list than the expansion of a narrower list, and that acceptance on one list did not mean acceptance by a later generation.

It was not until the year 367 that a list of Christian Scriptures as we know

The Canon according to Athanasius

It being my intention to mention these matters, I shall, for the commendation of my venture, follow the example of the evangelist Luke and say: Since some have taken in hand to set in order for themselves the so-called apocrypha and to mingle them with the God-inspired scripture, concerning which we have attained to a sure persuasion, according to what the original eyewitnesses and ministers of the word have delivered unto our fathers, I also, having been urged by true brethren and having investigated the matter from the beginning, have decided to set forth in order the writings that have been put in the canon, that have been handed down and confirmed as divine, in order that every one who has been led astray may condemn his seducers and that every one who has remained stainless may rejoice, being again reminded of that.

[After listing the contents of the OT canon, Athanasius goes on to the NT.]

Continuing, I must without hesitation mention the scriptures of the New Testament; they are the following: the four Gospels according to Matthew, Mark, Luke and John, after them the Acts of the Apostles and the seven so-called catholic epistles of the apostles — namely, one of James, two of Peter, then three of John and after these one of Jude. In addition there are four-

them in the NT finally appeared. In his thirty-ninth festal letter, published in 367, Athanasius, then bishop of Alexandria, listed our twenty-seven books as the "springs of salvation" and as included in "the canon." The books from Origen's and Eusebius's "disputed" lists were not included, and those in the "rejected" category were also specifically rejected: Wisdom of Solomon, *Shepherd of Hermas,* Sirach, the Teaching of the Apostles *(Didache),* and some others. They can be used with profit as "reading matter" but not as canonical, that is, as the rule of Christian doctrine and action. Athanasius makes it clear enough that the idea of a Christian canon has now fully emerged, even though it is still not universally recognized and will not be by Christians from Syria until early in the seventh century.

It is worth noting that the process of selecting authoritative books grew out of the life of the Christian community, as that community used those books and found some more valuable than others, rather than being determined by some assembly of church officials. In a sense, the canon developed with the community. It

---

teen epistles of the apostle Paul written in the following order: the first to the Romans, then two to the Corinthians and then after these the one to the Galatians, following it the one to the Ephesians, thereafter the one to the Philippians and the one to the Colossians and two to the Thessalonians and the epistle to the Hebrews and then immediately two to Timothy, one to Titus and lastly the one to Philemon. Yet further the Revelation of John. . . .

But for the sake of greater accuracy I add, being constrained to write, that there are also other books besides these, which have not indeed been put in the canon, but have been appointed by the Fathers as reading-matter for those who have just come forward and wish to be instructed in the doctrine of piety: the Wisdom of Solomon, the Wisdom of Sirach, Esther, Judith, Tobias, the so-called Teaching of the Apostles [the *Didache*] and the Shepherd [of Hermas]. And although, beloved, the former are in the canon and the latter serve as reading-matter, yet mention is nowhere made of the apocrypha; rather they are a fabrication of the heretics, who write them down when it pleases them and generously assign to them an early date of composition in order that they may be able to draw upon them as supposedly ancient writings and have in them occasion to deceive the guileless.

(Thirty-ninth Festal Letter, 367 CE;
translation from Schneemelcher, pp. 49-50)

therefore grew up out of the community, from the grassroots, as it were, rather than having been imposed from above by some authoritative person or council.

25.5. CRITERIA OF CANON SELECTION

Because the canon represents a collective decision reached by the Christian community at large over a period of centuries, we will not find a document in which the criteria for canonicity are given in detail. We will have to determine what those criteria were from hints given by second- and third-century authors when they discuss which writings they thought were authoritative for the Christian community, and which were not. We need also to keep in mind that even after a given criterion was accepted, problems could arise when someone attempted to apply that criterion. If authorship by an apostle, for example, were a criterion for regarding a writing as authoritative, the decision still needed to be made about whether or not an apostle wrote a certain book. The Revelation of John was attributed to Jesus' disciple John but also to the Gnostic Cerinthus. James was attributed variously to James the brother of Jesus or James the son of Zebedee, the brother of John. Whether or not Paul wrote Hebrews was also, as we have seen, open to debate.

Some hints about the criteria by which a group of canonical writings was selected from the many writings circulating in various Christian communities in the second through the fourth centuries have appeared in our discussion of the various categories into which Christian writings were placed. Some authors, for example, implied that their reason for attributing authority to a given writing was that it was highly valued by a number of Christian communities. Other authors mentioned the fact that some writing was cited in another, early writing as a reason to take the book seriously. We have already mentioned the criterion of apostolic authorship. Similar to it is the criterion of apostolic tradition: does the writing in question represent the kind of Christian teaching associated with the apostles? We need now to look at each of these criteria to see how it was applied and which of them seemed to be more important.

25.5.1. Use of a Writing by the Community

As we have seen, public reading of Christian writings, as well as portions of the OT, was a regular part of the primitive community's worship. Justin Martyr mentions readings from the apostolic memoirs and from the prophets. Dionysius, a bishop of Corinth in the second century, wrote to Soter, bishop of Rome: "Today we observed the holy day of the Lord and read out your letter, which we shall continue to read from time to time for our admonition, as we do that which was formerly sent to us through Clement" (quoted in Eusebius, *Hist. Eccl.* 4.23.11). That was not a unique occurrence. Eusebius, writing of the same epistle sent by Clement to the churches in Corinth near the end of the first century (we know it as *1 Clement*), remarked that "We have ascertained that this letter was publicly read in the common assembly in many churches, both in the days of old and in our own time" (3.16.1).

That such public reading of Christian literature goes back to the earliest times of the Christian community we know from some of the literature produced at that time. In the NT letter to the community at Colossae, the author, writing in the name of Paul, exhorts the recipients to read the letter publicly and then to exchange it for a letter written to the community at Laodicea (Col 4:16). There is every likelihood that the other letters of Paul were intended similarly to be read publicly to the community, most likely in a setting either of worship or of instruction.

It is clear from this that the practice of reading Christian literature aloud in contexts of worship and catechetical instruction caused certain Christian communities to value what they found useful for such purposes. The public reading of material therefore elevated that material, as it were, to candidacy for inclusion in the canon. But it seems to have functioned in a negative rather than a positive way to this extent: unless a writing was used publicly in worship by some community, it could not be taken seriously as a normative statement of the faith, but such public use alone was not enough to confer normative (or canonical) status on such a writing.

25.5.2. Quotation in Ancient Authorities

Quotation in ancient (i.e., early Christian) writings was important, because it was a part of the intellectual environment of the Hellenistic world to revere what was ancient and to question what was new. In that kind of cultural and intellectual milieu, to prove a thing ancient and traditional is very close to proving it true, and thus writings that contain truth must be of an early origin. Finding Christian literature that was quoted in the very early years of the primitive Christian community would thus be desirable, if not absolutely necessary, in order for that literature to be taken seriously as a possibly normative expression of the faith.

Important as such quotation in early authorities might have been, however, such mention by itself was again not sufficient to guarantee inclusion, finally, in the Christian canon. As in the case of public use, quotation by ancient authorities lent authority to a given writing, enabling it to be used by the community, and placing it in candidacy, as it were, for canonical inclusion. But by itself, such attestation was once again not the major consideration.

25.5.3. Apostolic Origin

The major consideration for final inclusion in the canon emerges with some clarity from precisely those writings of the second through the fourth centuries which we have been considering. It was whether or not the writing could sustain for itself a claim to apostolic origin. Yet how that "apostolic origin" was understood and how it was demonstrated present a more complex picture than we might at first suspect.

The most obvious way to demonstrate apostolic origin for a writing would be to claim that it was written by an apostle. For that reason, there was a good deal of discussion in the early Christian community about whether or not a given writing could legitimately claim to have been written by an apostle. The Gospels of Matthew and John, for example, were accepted as having been written by the two apostles who bore those names, and Mark and Luke were held to reflect the preaching of Peter and Paul respectively. Those who rejected the Revelation of John did so, with some regularity, by denying that its author could have been the same person as the apostle who wrote the Gospel of John, thus effectively denying to the Revelation apostolic authorship.

Yet the picture is complicated by the fact that some accepted the Revelation of John who also remained unconvinced that the apostle John had written it. Dionysius, a bishop of Alexandria in the mid-third century, in discussing the authorship of the Revelation of John, wrote: "That [the author] then, was certainly named John and that the book is by one John, I will not gainsay. . . . But I should not readily agree that he was the apostle, the son of Zebedee, the brother of James, whose are the Gospel entitled According to John and the Catholic Epistles" (quoted in *Hist. Eccl.* 7.24.7). In a similar disregard for authorship, Eusebius quotes Origen, who accepted Hebrews as normative, as saying about its author: "But who write the epistle, in truth God knows," the implication being that Origen himself certainly did not (6.25.14).

That same Dionysius carried out what even by modern standards must be called a sophisticated analysis of the language, style, and content of the Johannine literature and came to conclusions virtually similar to those currently held by many modern scholars, namely that Revelation and 2 and 3 John were written by an author other than that of the Gospel and 1 John (reported in *Hist. Eccl.* 7.25.19-27).

It is therefore somewhat simplistic to argue that, since those who collected the canon did so on the basis of beliefs about the apostolic authorship of the NT books we can no longer share, the modern Christian need no longer take seriously their decisions about the canon. In fact, apostolic authorship, while valued, was not the sole, or even always the major, factor in determining the apostolic origin of the material.

25.5.4. The Rule of Faith

It was not authorship but content that was the determining factor. The reason is clear enough: most later forgeries were also written in the names of the apostles, thus rendering such apostolic identification invalid as a primary consideration. Eusebius, discussing the various forgeries that bear apostolic names, points specifically to the fact that in such forgeries "the type of phraseology differs from apostolic style, and the opinion and tendency of their contents is widely dissonant from true orthodoxy" (3.25.6-7). Similarly, Serapion, bishop of Antioch in the late second century, was asked by some members of his community if the *Gospel of Peter* could be used as authoritative for the Christian community. He answered in the affirmative on the basis of its reputed authorship. When, however, he read the "Gospel," he withdrew his approval, since the content was not such as to uphold its claim to apostolic origin (see *Hist. Eccl.* 6.12.2-6). Clearly enough, it was the content of a given writing, not the person who may or may not have written it, that in the final analysis determined whether it would be included in the canon.

What all of that demonstrates is that before the limits of the canon of authoritative writings were determined, a criterion was already in operation that enabled those early Christians to differentiate writings to be accorded normative status from those that were not, regardless of a writing's claims about authorship. That criterion came to bear the name *regula fidei* or "rule of faith." Perplexing as it may seem, however, during a major portion of the period of canon formation, that rule of faith had received no fixed formulation. Such fixed formulations were to begin only with the confession adopted at the Council of Nicea in 325.[1] Nor was there a major expression of that rule of faith apart from the writings that eventually were included in the canon. Therefore, if the community selected the books to be included in the canon, those books themselves contained the criterion the community applied in their selection. It was, to be sure, as circular a process as it appears, but that is how, as nearly as we can determine, the canon was formed. Certain writings grew out of the common faith of the Christian community and were judged by the community, over many decades and through intimate use, to be clear and hence authoritative expressions of that common faith.

The process of canonical selection was therefore virtually identical to the process by which, for example, those traditions of the sayings and acts of Jesus were selected that were finally included in the four Gospels. The Gospels do not under-

---

1. The so-called "Apostles' Creed," though it contains phrases from the earliest period of the Christian faith, did not receive its present formulation until sometime in the sixth or seventh century. Its origin is unknown, and it never was accepted as authoritative by the Eastern Orthodox churches. It therefore could have played no role in defining the content of the "rule of faith" during the period of canonical formation.

stand themselves to be exhaustive records of everything known about what Jesus said and did. John 20:30 and 21:25 make that abundantly clear, as do the frequent summaries of Jesus' activity contained in the Synoptic Gospels. It was the experience of the community that, so it appears, led to some traditions being included in the Gospels and others omitted. In the same way, it was the common experience of the community with a wide variety of early Christian literature that it studied, proclaimed, and read in its worship that finally, over the course of two or three centuries, led that community to decide which individual writings from that literature represented the normative expression of that rule of faith, the *regula fidei.*

There were, in summary, a number of factors that led the early community to take seriously as normative for its faith and practice a wide variety of Christian writings. The use of such writings in the public worship of the community, their attestation in other early writings, and the claim to authorship by an apostle all caused such literature to be taken seriously by the community as an expression of its common faith. But in the final analysis, only those books became normative, and hence were included in the canon, that in the judgment of the community contained the purest form of the rule of faith. That judgment was based on content, as we have seen from our survey of a number of authors from the period during which the process of canonical selection was underway.

One can say, therefore, that the formation of the canon was coterminous with the life of the Christian community during its first three centuries of existence. It is not the case that some synod or council of bishops decided which books should be normative and thereafter required for Christians to accept. Rather, the books that finally were included in the canon were included because over the centuries Christians had come to use them in their worship and instruction and to revere them for the power they displayed in engendering, enriching, and correcting Christian faith. The canon thus represents the collective experience and understanding of the Christian community during the formative centuries of its existence.

FOR FURTHER READING

F. F. Bruce, *The Canon of Scripture* (Downers Grove: InterVarsity, 1988)

Harry Y. Gamble, *The New Testament Canon: Its Making and Meaning* (Philadelphia: Fortress, 1985)

Bruce M. Metzger, *The Canon of the New Testament: Its Origin, Development, and Significance* (Oxford: Clarendon, 1987)

Wilhelm Schneemelcher, *New Testament Apocrypha,* translation ed. R. McL. Wilson, I: *Gospels and Related Writings* (revised ed., Louisville: Westminster/John Knox, 1991), pp. 10-50

B. F. Westcott, *The Canon of the New Testament* (sixth ed., New York: Macmillan, 1889)

Index of Names and Subjects